STEWART STYLE 1513-15

Essays on the Court of James V

Edited by

JANET HADLEY WILLIAMS

TUCKWELL PRESS

First published in 1996 by
Tuckwell Press Ltd
The Mill House
Phantassie
East Linton
East Lothian EH40 3DG
Scotland

Copyright © The Editor and Contributors severally, 1996
All rights reserved

ISBN 1 898410 82 8

British Library Cataloguing-in-Publication Data
A Catalogue record for this book
is available on request from the
British Library

Printed and bound by
The Cromwell Press
Broughton Gifford
Melksham, Wiltshire

CONTENTS

Illustrations	vii
Contributors	ix
Acknowledgements	x
Abbreviations and Short Titles	xi
Introduction	xiv

1. Florens Wilson: A Distant Prospect — 1
   DOMINIC BAKER-SMITH

2. John Asloan and his Manuscript: An Edinburgh notary and scribe in the days of James III, IV and V (c. 1470-c. 1530) — 15
   CATHERINE VAN BUUREN

3. The Correspondence of Gavin Douglas — 52
   PRISCILLA BAWCUTT

4. The King in his House: Three Architectural Artefacts belonging to the Reign of James V — 62
   HELENA M. SHIRE

5. Exchequer, Council and Session, 1513-1542 — 97
   ATHOL L. MURRAY

6. Music for 'Goddis Glore and the Kingis' — 118
   HELENA M. SHIRE

7. *Greysteil* — 142
   JOHN PURSER

8. *Trip and goe, hey*: 'A truly Scottish song' — 153
   KENNETH ELLIOTT

9. William Stewart and the Court Poetry of the Reign of James V — 179
   A. A. MACDONALD

10. David Lyndsay and the Making of King James V — 201
    JANET HADLEY WILLIAMS

CONTENTS

11. The Final Folios of Adam Abell's 'Roit or Quheill of Tyme': 227
An Observantine Friar's reflections on the
1520s and 30s
ALASDAIR M. STEWART

12. The Scots-Gaelic Scribes of Late Medieval Perthshire: 254
An overview of the orthography and contents of
the Book of the Dean of Lismore
DONALD E. MEEK

13. Iconography and Literature in the Service of Diplomacy: 273
The Franco-Scottish Alliance, James V and Scotland's
two French Queens, Madeleine of France and
Marie de Guise
DANA BENTLEY-CRANCH and
ROSALIND K. MARSHALL

14. Outward Signs of Majesty, 1535-1540 289
CHARLES J. BURNETT, ROSS HERALD OF ARMS

Index 303

ILLUSTRATIONS

GREYSTEIL
    (p. 143)

1. Musical edition and reconstruction of the epic song, *Greysteil*.

TRIP AND GOE, HEY: 'A TRULY SCOTTISH SONG'
    (pp. 163-174)

1. Musical edition and reconstruction of the medley, *Trip and goe, hey*.

ICONOGRAPHY AND LITERATURE IN THE SERVICE OF DIPLOMACY
    (between pp. 288 and 289)

1. Jean Clouet, *Madeleine as a child.*
        Musée Condé, Château of Chantilly.
        (Photo Giraudon.)
2. Corneille de Lyon, *Portrait of a Gentleman reputed to be King James V of Scots*
        Polesden Lacey, The McEwan Collection.
        (The National Trust.)
3. Corneille de Lyon, *Madeleine aged 16.*
        Château of Blois.
        (Courtesy of the Director of the Château et Musée de Blois.)
4. *Madeleine* in Francis I's *Book of Hours.*
        Bibliothèque Nationale, ms N.A. Latines 82, fol. 100^r.
        (Photo Bibliothèque Nationale de France, Paris.)
5. *Madeleine* in G. Roville, *Promptuarii Iconum*, II, 243.
        British Library 7755C20
        (By permission of the British Library.)
6. Woodcut illustrating the wedding-ceremony of James V and Madeleine, in
        Jean Leblond, *Nuptiaulx Virelayz*, Paris, 1537 [Old Style].
        B.L. 11475.a.58.
        (By permission of the British Library.)
7. Corneille de Lyon, *Mary of Guise.*
        (Scottish National Portrait Gallery)

ILLUSTRATIONS

OUTWARD SIGNS OF MAJESTY, 1535-1540
(between pp. 302 and 303)

1. The Arms of James V surrounded by the Garter of England,
   Statutes of the Order of the Garter, 1535.
   NLS MS 7143, fol. 11.
   (Courtesy of the Trustees of the National Library of Scotland.)
2. The Royal Arms of Scotland surrounded by a collar of thistles,
   Cartulary of Cambuskenneth Abbey, c. 1535.
   NLS Adv. MS 34.1.2., fol. 1.
   (Courtesy of the Trustees of the National Library of Scotland.)
3. Gold and Billon coins of James V.
   (Courtesy of the Trustees of the National Museums of Scotland.)
4. The Arms of Madeleine impaled with those of James V, c. 1537.
   Pierpont Morgan Library MS 527, title-page.
   (Courtesy of the Pierpont Morgan Library.)
5. The Crown of Scotland, 1540.
   (Courtesy of Historic Scotland.)
6. The Royal Arms of Scotland, as adopted by James V, in John Bellenden,
   Hystory and croniklis of Scotland, Edinburgh, c. 1536-37.
   NLS H.33.b.7, title-page.
   (Courtesy of the Trustees of the National Library of Scotland.)
7. Carved stone panel, Abbey Strand, Palace of Holyroodhouse, c. 1540.
   (Courtesy of Historic Scotland.)
8. Carved stone panel from the Bishop's Castle, Glasgow, c. 1540.
   (Courtesy of Historic Scotland.)
9. Heraldic Font, Newbattle Abbey, c. 1540.
   (Courtesy of Society of Antiquaries of Scotland.)
10. The Arms of the two Queens of James V, in Sir David Lyndsay's Armorial,
    c. 1538-42.
    NLS Adv. MS 31.4.3, fol. 22.
    (Courtesy of the Trustees of the National Library of Scotland.)

❖

CONTRIBUTORS

DOMINIC BAKER-SMITH is Professor of English Literature, University of Amsterdam.

PRISCILLA BAWCUTT is an Honorary Fellow in the Department of English Language and Literature, University of Liverpool.

DANA BENTLEY-CRANCH is a freelance writer and art historian.

CHARLES BURNETT is Ross Herald of Arms and Curator of Fine Art at the Scottish United Services Museum, Edinburgh.

CATHERINE VAN BUUREN is an editor and retired member of the English Department, University of Leiden.

KENNETH ELLIOT is an Honorary Senior Research Fellow in the Department of Music, University of Glasgow.

JANET HADLEY WILLIAMS is a Visiting Fellow in the Department of English, The Australian National University.

ALASDAIR MACDONALD is Professor of Mediaeval English Language and Literature, University of Groningen.

ROSALIND MARSHALL is a writer, historian and Assistant Keeper, Scottish National Portrait Gallery.

DONALD MEEK is Professor of Celtic, University of Aberdeen.

ATHOL MURRAY is an administrative historian and Keeper of the Records of Scotland 1985-1990.

JOHN PURSER is a poet, playwright, composer, radio broadcaster and lecturer based in Glasgow and Skye.

HELENA SHIRE (d. 1991) was Senior Research Fellow in Arts, Carnegie Trust for the Universities of Scotland (1961-63) and Foundation Fellow of Robinson College, Cambridge.

ALASDAIR STEWART is lecturer in the Departments of German, and Politics and International Relations, University of Aberdeen.

❖

ACKNOWLEDGEMENTS

This book has been a collective rather than an individual effort, and it is a great pleasure to be able to record appreciation of the many involved in it. First to be mentioned is Dr Helena Shire, whose excellent idea it was. Secondly, as editor I'm glad to be able to thank the contributors for agreeing to write, and with such expertise and enthusiasm; it has been a privilege to work with them.

Thirdly, warm thanks are given to those who provided critical comment on the various articles. Prof. J. Aitken, Dr H. MacQueen, Prof. D. Mennie and Dr D. Sellar were among them; others are mentioned within the contribution concerned. Expert assistance and support were also given generously by Mr P. Campbell (School of Music, Australian National University and PC Publishing, Canberra), Dr D. Delmar Evans, Dr Alisoun Gardner-Medwin, the late Miss E. Mennie, and Dr M.H.B. Sanderson.

Formal thanks, fourthly, are given here to the libraries and archives worldwide that have provided excellent service and allowed quotations or reproductions to be made from their material. All of the exceptionally able librarians, some known only by the quality of their detective work, others as lasting friends, could never be thanked adequately. I would like to mention in particular those in Petherick Reading Room at the National Library of Australia, who gave invaluable help during the editing process.

There are very many friends, family, and colleagues who have given encouragement and shared their knowledge; among them are Dr J.H. Alexander, Mrs M. Anderson-Smith, Mrs C. Bromwich, Mrs and Mrs A. Bolton, Mrs Margaret Dent, Dr D. Eichberger, Dr W.K. Emond, Mrs D. Garden, Mrs R. Greentree, Mr and Mrs. J. Hadley, Dr M. Kelley, Mr F. Langman, Ld J. Lewis, Dr E. Lyle, Dr M. Mackay, Mr and Mrs J.D. McClure, Dr and Mrs A. Rastawicki, Mr and Mrs W. Warden, Dr T. Weir, and Mrs B. Williams. My husband, Dr Ian Williams, has played an important part: his skill and patience solved many production challenges; his support to me was vital. My appreciation is heartfelt.

❖

Abbreviations and Short Titles

Asloan MS	The Asloan Manuscript, NLS MS 16500.
Asloan MS	*The Asloan Manuscript*, ed. W.A. Craigie, 2 vols, STS, Edinburgh and London, 1923-25.
ADCP	*Acts of the Lords of Council in Public Affairs 1501-1554: Selections from Acta Dominorum Concilii Introductory to the Register of the Privy Council of Scotland*, ed. R.K. Hannay, Edinburgh, 1932
APS	*The Acts of the Parliaments of Scotland, 1509-1603*, ed. T. Thomson and C. Innes, 12 vols, Edinburgh, 1814-75.
Bann. MS	The Bannatyne Manuscript, NLS, Adv. MS 1.1.6.
Bann. MS (facsimile)	*The Bannatyne Manuscript*, facsimile edn, D. Fox and W. Ringler, London, 1980.
Bann. MS	*The Bannatyne Manuscript*, ed. W. Tod Ritchie, 4 vols, STS, Edinburgh and London, 1928-34.
B.L.	British Library.
CSP Scot.	*Calendar of State Papers Relating to Scotland and Mary Queen of Scots, 1547-1603*, ed. J. Bain et al., 13 vols, London, 1898-1969.
DNB	*Dictionary of National Biography*, ed. L. Stephen and S. Lee, London, 1885-1900.
DOST	*A Dictionary of the Older Scottish Tongue from the Twelfth Century to the End of the Seventeenth*, ed. W.A. Craigie et al., London, Chicago and Aberdeen, 1931-.
EETS	Early English Text Society.

ER	*The Exchequer Rolls of Scotland*, ed. J. Stuart et al. Edinburgh, 1878-1908.
James V Letters	*The Letters of James V*, collected and calendared R.K. Hannay, ed. D. Hay, Edinburgh, 1954.
L&P Henry VIII	*Letters and Papers, Foreign and Domestic, of the Reign of Henry VIII, 1509-1547*, ed. J.S. Brewer et al., 21 vols in 35, London, 1862-1932.
MB XV	*Music of Scotland 1500-1700*, ed. K. Elliott, song texts ed. H. M. Shire, Musica Britiannica XV, 1957; 3rd rev. edn, London, 1975.
M. Folio MS	The Maitland Folio Manuscript, Cambridge, Pepysian Library, 2553.
M. Folio MS	*The Maitland Folio Manuscript*, ed. W.A. Craigie, 2 vols, STS, Edinburgh and London, 1919-27.
NLS	National Library of Scotland.
PSAS	*Proceedings of the Society of Antiquaries of Scotland.*
RMS	*Registrum Magni Sigilli Regum Scotorum: Register of the Great Seal of Scotland*, ed. J.M. Thomson et al., Edinburgh, 1882-1914.
RPC	*Register of the Privy Council of Scotland*, ed. J.H. Burton et al., 14 vols, Edinburgh, 1877-98.
RSS	*Registrum Secreti Sigilli Regum Scotorum: Register of the Privy Seal of Scotland, 1488-1567*, vol. I, ed. M. Livingstone, Edinburgh 1908.
SHR	*Scottish Historical Review.*
SHS	Scottish History Society.
SRS	Scottish Record Society.
State Papers, Henry VIII	*State Papers, King Henry the Eighth*, 11 vols, London, 1830-52.

STC	*A Short-Title Catalogue of Books Printed in England, Scotland and Ireland 1475-1640*, comp. A.W. Pollard and G.R. Redgrave, London, 1926; 2nd edn, ed. W.A. Jackson, F.S. Ferguson and K.F. Pantzer, London, 1976-86.
STS	Scottish Text Society.
TA	*Accounts of the Lord High Treasurer of Scotland*, ed. T. Dickson and Sir J. Balfour Paul, 11 vols, Edinburgh, 1877-1916.
Wing	*Short-Title Catalogue of Books Printed in England, Scotland, Ireland and Wales, and British America and of English Books printed in other countries 1641-1700*, comp. D.G. Wing, 3 vols, 1945; rev. edn, New York, 1972-88.
Works Accounts I	*Accounts of the Masters of Works for building and repairing of Royal Palaces and Castles, 1529-1615*, vol. I, ed. H.M. Paton, Edinburgh, 1957.

INTRODUCTION

> All the things that light up this period for me
> are seldom found within the covers of the same book.

The period mentioned above was the reign of James V of Scots; the comment Helena Shire's. It was one of many in a dialogue over several years about the need for an enquiry into the complex and fascinating topic of this last Stewart reign before the Reformation. Of particular interest was the 'style King James V'. Could it be perceived in the artefacts of the period? Of these, what were retained from the previous reign and earlier? What were created during the reign itself? Research was well begun when Dr Shire died in 1991, and it is in tribute to her that these studies now appear. Her own lively and learned mind informs two of the following contributions.

Responding to the riches of a period somewhat neglected, the fourteen specialist articles within these covers present fresh insights into the music, the poetry and prose in Scots, Gaelic and Latin, the architectural achievements, manuscript compilation, civil and judicial administration, the iconography, and heraldry of James V's reign. These subjects are discussed in awareness that the era had particular and often fruitful tensions. Having lost in the long minority after Flodden the progressive momentum of the James IV era, James V's court belonged in time to the Renaissance, but was rooted in the continuation of the old ways of the Middle Ages. The reign witnessed both the acceptance and the questioning of the old values, and sometimes a memorable merging of the old with the new.

To the questioning there was an open-mindedness, and also a restraint that was permitted to last only for the brief period of the reign. The quandaries of the scholar open to the new non-dogmatic modes are revealed in Professor Dominic Baker-Smith's study of the Scots-European humanist, Florens Wilson. A literary miscellany compiled during James V's minority by the notary, John Asloan, is imbued, on the other hand, with an assured conservatism. Dr Catherine van Buuren finds that this large collection was forward-looking in the freedom with which its devotional, moralizing and entertaining works were gathered, and in its implied awareness and assessment of a growing reading public. Yet she observes that the manuscript belonged firmly to the Catholic Middle Ages, offering no hint of the religious controversy that was beginning to have an impact in Scotland, and which would affect to the degree of editorial censorship the literary manuscript compiled by George Bannatyne during the next reign. There was also

INTRODUCTION

moral certainty in the contemporary chronicle of James V's reign compiled first in Latin and then in Scots by Adam Abell, an Observantine friar writing at Jedburgh. All the same, Dr Alasdair Stewart stresses that the chronicle was not simply source-derivative, but individualized by Abell's specific interest in the work of the Franciscan order. Abell, Dr Stewart perceives, was acutely aware that events at this time within Scotland had an international dimension: the impact of Henry VIII's policies, experienced first hand as those who were persecuted crossed the border for shelter, was set down alongside the record of the Ottoman Turkish conflict in Europe and anecdotal reporting of the New World then being evangelized. Where the differing ways of thinking attempted to accommodate or recognize each other, however, the results could be works of outstanding accomplishment. In the musical sphere, there were sophisticated compositions associated with the court, such as the part-song *Trip and goe, hey* reconstructed here by Dr Kenneth Elliot. These compositions preserved though they transformed traditional patternings. In the domain of royal architectural façade and interior they were splendidly embodied. Dr Helena Shire notes the importance, within a European as well as a Scots frame, of the intelligent interrelation of Christian, classical and probably pagan motifs on the king's palace at Stirling.

James V, for the first half of his reign king yet 'no king', was himself a symbol of the period's struggle for equilibrium. Supporters of a range of views surrounded him, at the one extreme advocating continuation of the traditional alliance with France and enmity with England, at the other seeing merit in rebuilding the peace with England while maintaining ties with France. Dissension on such a fundamental issue meant stable government was set to one side as faction leaders rose and fell and with them their prominent supporters. Among the latter was Gavin Douglas, distinguished poet, bishop, one-time government administrator, but also uncle of Archibald, earl of Angus, to whose fluctuating fortunes Gavin became linked. Mrs Priscilla Bawcutt's analysis of his surviving correspondence illuminates the cost Douglas paid, personally and professionally, but also tells us much about the uncertainties of the era in which he lived. Dr Athol Murray documents the administrative impact of these uncertainties. Want of stability set back the tentative improvements made under James IV to the execution of civil justice and the introduction of better training for the judiciary. Ultimately, however, it forced some positive changes. Dr Murray discusses the effect of the judicial reforms of 1532, and points out that a separate privy council emerged soon after the end of James V's reign.

Though there was unpredictability beyond the inner household, within it an effort was made to give the young king some sense of stability. Dr John Purser, through the example of *Greysteil*, and Dr Helena Shire, from the details of a fragmentary official record, consider the ceremonial and recreational activities of the court musicians who had been retained, in reduced numbers, from the previous reign. The fostering also of the king's own musical interest is examined by Dr Shire, who notes that this had important results after the minority ended. The king sought then to restore the Chapel Royal, but it is revealing of the particular difficulties of his reign that James saw in the renewal both a monument to his father and a barricade against Lutheran encroachment.

Part-time poets and translators among the household servants, some of whom, like the musicians, had begun court service during the previous reign, offered their new monarch works in styles and on themes that reflected the literary flowering under James IV. They addressed the youthful king in ballats of careful advice and moralizing praise. And later, when certain other interests of the king emerged, there were works also of courtly love and satiric 'remeid' of love. These are discussed by Professor Alasdair MacDonald, who observes that though these poets had the ease, if not always the skill, of the earlier writers such as William Dunbar, there was some loss of confidence beneath the surface. Of the servitor-poets, only perhaps David Lyndsay, the trusted familiar of the king's boyhood, had the knowledge that a more dramatic presentation was most likely to hold the king's interest when counsel was offered. My own study considers how Lyndsay sought thus to help the young monarch understand his role and his *regnum*, and to present a recognizably 'James V' royal image. Nonetheless, Lyndsay himself pointed out the importance of the works of others to this process, especially those of Gavin Douglas and John Bellenden (of whom a full-length critical study is eagerly awaited). Bellenden's modernizing Scots prose translation of Boece's *Scotorum Historiae* gave a traditional, king-centred message new impetus. From a more entertaining perspective, that revealed an appreciation of Henryson's earlier achievement, Lyndsay's royal parrot reinforced it (*Papyngo*, 322-24):[1]

> Sen first kyng Fergus bure ane Dyadame,
> Thov art the last king, of fyue score and fyue,
> And all ar dede, and none bot thov on lyue....

James's increasing interest in his office is evident. Ross Herald, Charles Burnett, rightly emphasizes the importance the adult king gave to his heraldic representation. On his outer gateway at Linlithgow palace the Scottish king displayed the orders of chivalry bestowed upon him by other kings—the Garter of England, the Golden Fleece of Burgundy and the St Michael of France—but he placed his own, the Thistle, amongst them. His instruments of office—the sceptre for justice, the sword for authority, the crown, closed for *imperium*, bejewelled in expression of divine wisdom in rule—were redesigned as James reasserted and enhanced the value of the monarchy to Scotland. Informed notions of sovereignty became, too, a significant factor in the negotiations for the king's marriage. Tracing their intricacies, Drs Dana Bentley-Cranch and Rosalind Marshall find that while James V preferred to the last minute a marriage to the Scottish noblewoman Margaret Erskine, he sought international éclat from his

---

[1] *The Works of Sir David Lindsay of the Mount*, ed. D. Hamer, 4 vols, STS (Edinburgh and London, 1931-36), I, 65.

choice of queen, as well as remedy for the realm's pressing financial needs. The results, the illustrious French marriages, reaffirmed Scotland's involvement in the European balance of power and, with that, James V's support for the old religion. Later, at the height of his reign, James V's unprecedented circumnavigation of the kingdom affirmed his authority at the realm's outer reaches, notwithstanding the disparities of race, culture or political organization that were to be found there.[2] The way in which the Celtic 'half' of James's kingdom reacted in turn to its encounters with the king from the south, and in particular to his display of *imperium* in the 1540 voyage, is less well known. Such evidence as can be found is surprising, suggestive once more of both the tensions within and the preconceptions without the kingdom.[3] Yet during the period of James V's reign these cultures did communicate, producing some outstanding artefacts. One was the Scots-Gaelic manuscript now known by the name of one of its scribes, the Dean of Lismore. Professor Donald Meek points out that its several compilers looked to the rich cultural resources of the classical Gaelic world, employed an orthography based on that of Middle Scots, and responded at the same time to the humanistic principles of contemporary European scholarship.

These essays indicate the diversity and depth of current research into the James V era. They also look forward to further studies: yet to be examined, for example, is the Latin verse of the period—for which an author free to collaborate here could not be found. The intriguing and contradictory character of James V himself, revealed from many crucial viewpoints in these essays, demands a book-length scholarly biography. The fourteen studies here thus have begun an investigation, in the hope of inspiring future research, by asking the question: was the particular 'style' of this period, formed in the attempts to come to terms with the old world and the new, so closely identified with James V that on his death it 'alluterlye' ceased to be?

Janet Hadley Williams
Canberra

---

[2] This royal journey had further consequences, the draughting of the earliest chart of the Scottish coastline; see further, *Alexander Lindsay A Rutter of the Scottish Seas Circa 1540*, ed. A.B. Taylor, I.H. Adams and G. Fortune, Maritime Monographs and Reports No. 44 (London, 1980) and M. Destombes, 'La Plus Ancienne Carte Régionale de L'Ecosse (1559)', *Gazette des Beaux-Arts*, Ser. 6, 78 (1971), 305-6.

[3] At the meeting of the king with the Earl of Atholl, for example, the provision of magnificent temporary accommodation in the midst, seemingly, of 'bot wode and wildernes', gave a severe jolt to James V's travelling companion. A cultivated papal visitor, he had till then, it was reported, believed that this northerly region was the 'erse of the warld'. See R. Lindesay of Pitscottie, *The Historie and Cronicles of Scotland*, ed. Æ. J.G. Mackay, 3 vols, STS (Edinburgh and London, 1899-1911), I, 335-38, but on the usefulness and difficulties of Pitscottie's work as a source: G.G. Wilson, 'History and the Common Reader? Robert Lindsay of Pitscottie's *Cronicles*', *Forum for Modern Language Studies*, 29.2 (1993), 97-110. For further references to James V's reception in the northern parts of his kingdom: W. Douglas Simpson, 'A Chronicle History of Dunvegan Castle', *Transactions of the Gaelic Society of Inverness*, 37 (1934-36), 370-97 (377).

1

FLORENS WILSON: A DISTANT PROSPECT

Dominic Baker-Smith

Whatever the form under which he was baptized, Florens Wilson's adoption of the Latinized name Volusenus placed him clearly within the ranks of an international humanism. We may convert it back as Wilson, but his evident Latin preference has a significance not only for the deracinated character of his own career but equally for the harsh dilemmas that hung over its later years. We can be thankful, nevertheless, for an unusual sense of place which frequently surfaces in his writings and lends an unexpected immediacy, whether it be the location of a *locus amoenus* on the slope of Fourvières or a recollection of lumbermen jumping logs on the river Tay.[1] Memorable among these is the recall, at a critical juncture in the *De Animi Tranquillitate*, of a walk taken some twenty years before on the river bank at Elgin in the company of John Ogilvie when the conversation, prompted by the opening lines of Horace's first satire, turns on the restless cravings of the human spirit.[2] This flashback from the Rhône to the Lossie frames a cultural moment of some interest. In typically humanistic style Wilson tends to insert references to recent encounters with friends or potential patrons in his writings, and he had probably revisited Ogilvie in 1535, some eight years before the *De Animi Tranquillitate* appeared from the press of Sebastian Gryphius in Lyons. Certainly Wilson sent Ogilvie a copy of the 1533 edition of Erasmus's *Apothegmata* and the evidence supports a visit to Scotland around this time. Thus, the covering letter to Ogilvie included greetings to Hector Boece, who was to die in 1536.[3] The accounts of that walk by the Lossie may contain an element of rhetorical elaboration but the specific details suggest a germ of historical fact: Wilson places it after he had studied philosophy for four years—which sounds like an elevated description of the university arts course—and before he had crossed into France. This Horatian discussion can be placed, therefore, at the conclusion of his studies at the new

---

[1]Fouvières is the site for the debate in the *De Animi Tranquillitate* (Lyons: S. Gryphius, 1543), while Tayside timber floating is described in the *Scholia in Scipionis Somnium* (London: Robert Redman, [1534?]; the latter is reproduced in W. Linnard, 'Timber Floating: An Early Record on the Tay', *Scottish Studies*, 25 (1981), 77-79.
[2]*De Animi Tranquillitate* (hereafter *D.A.T.*) ed. cit., p. 140. The episode may echo an earlier Horatian discussion on a river bank near Paris between Erasmus and Volusenus's Aberdeen mentor, Hector Boece: see Erasmus's dedication of his *De casa natalitia Jesu* to Boece in *Opus Epistolarum D. Erasmi*, ed. P.S. Allen (hereafter 'Allen'), I, epist. 47.
[3]The volume is now lost, but a description can be found in *Notes and Queries*, 2nd Series, 8 (1859), 203; the covering letter requested the loan of a horse. See also W. Douglas Simpson, 'Tolquhon Castle and its builder', *PSAS*, 72 (1938), 252-55.

King's College in Aberdeen where Boece was the Principal. It is a symbolic episode in the emergence of a native humanism, one which Boece had done his part to foster.

But where does this fit into the sparse records of Wilson's own movements? There is no record of his birth or of his death, only the tradition that he came from Elgin, studied in Aberdeen, and spent much of his time in France where he was apparently still alive in 1551.[4] One hint does survive in the *Bibliotheca Universalis* of the great Swiss naturalist Conrad Gesner: there he records meeting Wilson at Lyons in 1540 and expresses great hopes for his talents, seeing that he is still a young man, 'iuvenile adhuc aetate'—a formula which indicates he was not yet forty. If we allow that by 1526 he is already recorded in a letter from George Lawson to Thomas Cromwell as a tutor in the household of Wolsey's son, Thomas Winter, that suggests at least a man in his early twenties. So a birth-date in 1504 may not be far from the mark, making his entry at King's College, Aberdeen, fall around 1518-19.[5] It seems certain that the highly individual pattern of his career owes much to the special character of Bishop Elphinstone's foundation. Anticipating later founders like John Fisher at Cambridge and Richard Fox at Oxford, Elphinstone recognized the need not only for articulate clergy but also for civil servants in the new humanist stamp. Hence the emphasis given to latinity at King's; while Hector Boece was trained in the Paris schools, his appointment at Aberdeen clearly owes something to his literary and historical interests. Then one of the several innovations made by Elphinstone, whose humanist sympathies are suggested by the manuscript of Valla's *Elegantiae* in his library, was the post of grammarian. Perhaps this was first seen as a remedial device to sharpen up the students' Latin, but under the energetic regime of John Vaus 'humanity' appears to have been an integral part of teaching in the Arts course. How far Greek was on offer is not clear, but Wilson's competence in it, and his interest in Hebrew, may reflect the stimulus provided at Aberdeen. When, years later, Jacopo Sadoleto expressed wonder that Wilson's elegant Latin should issue from such a remote corner of the world he was being tiresomely chauvinistic.

Sympathy with the new philological concerns of humanism was not the only novelty at King's College. In view of Wilson's later involvement in the crisis of what can be briefly defined as evangelical humanism, it is interesting to notice the religious style of Elphinstone's foundation. The bishop must have had some part in the decision in 1509 to appoint Erasmus tutor to the young Archbishop of St Andrews, Alexander Stewart. In any case Hector Boece, who

---

[4] Most accounts kill him off in 1546, but A. Bleton records him in Lyons in 1551, giving the annual St Thomas lecture (*Les Oraisons Doctorales de Saint-Thomas*, Lyons, 1891, p. 41); the reference was spotted by J. Durkan, 'Florens Wilson's Death', *Innes Review*, 3 (1952), 65-66.

[5] Conrad Gesner, *Bibliotheca Universalis* (Zurich: C. Froschoverus, 1548), p. 245; Lawson to Cromwell, *L&P Henry VIII*, IV, pt. iii, App. 84. John Ogilvie was still alive in 1570 (*Fasti Aberdonenses*, pp. 128-29).

was in Aberdeen by 1498, was already a friend of Erasmus. It cannot be said that he brought Erasmian ideas with him: the first important religous work by Erasmus, the *Enchiridion Militis Christiani*, (*The Handbook of the Warfaring Christian*), did not appear until 1504. Rather Boece brought back with him from Paris a cluster of ideas in which recognition of the necessity for a pastoral theology was bound up with the philological interests of humanism. Between them these ideas provoked a return *ad fontes*, to the original cultural sources, whether classical or patriotic. The importance of Boece lay not least in his familiarity with the Parisian scene, and he continued to follow developments there; it was in 1526 that he returned there to take his doctorate in theology. As a result Aberdeen was alert to the emergence of a specifically religious mode of humanism that was expressed not simply in the writings of Erasmus but in the important editions and commentaries of the reform-minded group led by Jacques Lefèvre d'Etaples. Lefèvre's works were advanced for undergraduates no doubt, but the more accessible didactic works of Erasmus were certainly used. In 1528 the college was visited by a Danish merchant, Johannes Bibliopegus, who expressed delighted surprise at discovering disciples of Erasmus, 'in ultimo pene orbis recessu', again this remote corner of the earth.[6] His visit stirred Boece to write to Erasmus, reminding him of their friendship at Montaigu and describing the central role allotted to his writings, in particular the *Paraphrases*, at Aberdeen. Even allowing for some rhetorical hyperbole, it is clear that Erasmus was a vital intellectual presence in the curriculum and his ideas played a decisive role in the formation of the students' own. It must have been a welcome change for Erasmus, at a time when he was under attack on all sides, to receive Boece's valedictory assurance that 'the college of Aberdeen is yours, and devoted to your writings before all others'.[7]

It is important to remember that Erasmus owed his prominence to the way in which he diagnosed certain contemporary problems, most notably the irrelevance of much academic theology to urgent pastoral needs and the negative results of the consequent split between doctrine and devotion. His writings were a rallying point, but it is misleading to treat 'Erasmianism' as if it were the only alternative to conventional theology prior to the Reformation. Wilson's often quoted remark in the *De Animi Tranquillitate* (1543), that Erasmus 'was a man of outstanding natural gifts, of retentive memory and extensive reading, learned in both the classical tongues; if he had given a little more attention to philosophy and been more exact in his use of Latin, nothing from our own time or from earlier ages might be found...to compare with his writings,' is not a bad eulogy, but the reservations are revealing. So far as the Latin is concerned, it is very much what might be expected from a Lyons-based humanist in 1543, while the

---

[6] The phrase is Boece's, so Bibliopegus can be exonerated of chauvinism. Boece's letter and Erasmus's response are printed in *Opus Epistolarum*, ed. Allen, VII, no. 1996; VIII, no. 2283.
[7] 'Vale, et Aberdonen[se] studium generale agnosce tuum, voluminibusque a te editis plus ceterorum mortalium addictum' (Allen, VII, 400). At the trial of Sir John Borthwick in 1540 Erasmus's *Paraphrases* were listed among his 'heretical' books.

philosophical censure, which has its justification, could well reflect attitudes learned in Aberdeen. Wilson was certainly not a scholastic: he is prepared to define philosophy in a substantially moral sense as the art of living, that is, of tranquillity. While, in typically humanist style, he attacks the use of over-subtle disputation in theology, he nevertheless approves the use of dialectic, provided that it is handled with restraint.[8]

If nothing else, this is a useful reminder that general sympathy with Erasmus did not mean an uncritical adoption of his ideas. Both Hector Boece, together with his vice-principal William Hay, combined professional grounding in scholasticism with openness to the new modes. Prominent among these must be counted the Florentine Platonism of Marsilio Ficino, whose *Theologia Platonica* was certainly known to Wilson,[9] and the religious humanism of Lefèvre d'Etaples. The canonist Alexander Galloway, who held the office of rector five times, had a comprehensive list of books which included the *De quadruplici vita* (Lyons, 1507) by Ficino's French disciple Symphorien Champier, Lefèvre's *Commentarii in epistolas Pauli* (Paris, 1517), two works by Carolus Bovillus, a number of patristic works (among them Lefèvre's edition of Paradisus of Heraclides), a complete Cicero (Paris, 1520) and the *Opuscula* of Petrarch. There are grounds for believing that King's College remained faithful to the moderate reform spirit represented by Erasmus and Lefèvre until Catholics were removed from office in 1569. Alexander Anderson, the last Catholic Principal, owned works by Lefèvre and Josse Clichetove as well as Erasmus's *Paraphrases* and his edition of Irenaeus's *Contra Haereses*. If, as Coissac put it, Aberdeen 'fut le boulevard de la Renaissance en Ecosse', it provided its students with an ideal formation for entry into the intellectual ferment of evangelical reform.[10] If we compare Florence Wilson to his English friend Thomas Starkey (c.1498-1538), who left Oxford for Italy at much the same time that Wilson left Scotland, it is not unreasonable to suppose that the Aberdeen graduate was more alert to continental developments. It was the intimate link with French culture that enabled centres like King's College, or the Cistercian house of Kinloss under its enlightened abbot Robert Reid, to provide initiation into humanist reform.

It is not clear exactly where Wilson went after his conversation with Ogilvie on the banks of the Lossie. According to his own words he crossed into France, yet we first hear of him in Lawson's letter when he was part of an English establishment: Lawson requested Cromwell, 'Ask my gossip Bonvice to write to Mr Florens to see that my son George be kept continually at school'. Lawson's 'gossip' was the Luccan merchant Antonio Bonvisi, best known to

---

[8]On Erasmus see *D.A.T.*, p. 344; on dialectic, ibid., p. 12.
[9]*Scholia in Scipionis Somnium* (London: R. Redman, [1534?]), sig. Fii; Boece owned Ficino's *De Triplici Vita*, a health guide for the intellectual.
[10]On the background see J. Durkan, 'Early Humanism and King's College', *Aberdeen University Review*, 163 (1980), 159-79, and in *Humanism in Renaissance Scotland*, ed. J. MacQueen, (Edinburgh, 1990), pp. 132-33; 150-51. J.B. Coissac, *Les Universités d'Ecosse* (Paris, 1915), p. 133.

posterity as an intimate friend of Thomas More; George Lawson the younger was one of the companions of Thomas Winter, then the fifteen year old Dean of Wells, who arrived in Paris in 1526 to advance his studies. His chief tutor was the distinguished humanist Thomas Lupset. It was an advantageous situation for Wilson, one that opened up exciting possibilities for potential patronage, in England, France and even Italy. Gabriel Harvey, a later aspiring humanist-politician who failed to make it, writes in his *Marginalia* of Henry VIII's four 'heroici consiliarii'—Wolsey, More, Cromwell and Gardiner. Wilson was linked with all four, and one can add John Fisher, the bishop of Rochester, for good measure.[11]

Wilson's English contacts were of central importance for his career. Like John Major, he looked to a dynastic union of England with Scotland which would end the tradition of hostility and the *De Animi Tranquillitate* expresses his pain at the 1542 campaign which culminated in Solway Moss. England gave him the opportunity to serve figures of prominence, and it provided him with further contacts abroad. Through Bonvisi, whose generosity he later celebrated in an attractive complimentary poem, Wilson gained access to Luccan circles and this had importance for the development of his religious ideas. Then his involvement on the fringes of Henry VIII's efforts to have his marriage annulled had its benefits in terms of patronage. His first published work, the *Psalmi quintidecimi enarratio* (Paris: Cyaneus, 1531) is dedicated to the Cardinal of Lorraine, to whom he had been introduced by Sir Francis Bryan and Guillaume du Bellay, both of whom played important diplomatic roles in Anglo-French negotiations. Though Wolsey fell from influence in 1529 Wilson remained on close terms with Thomas Cromwell until at least 1536, and the *Scholia in Scipionis Somnium* was dedicated to his son Gregory. Wilson was engaged to purchase books, and he reported to Cromwell on the religious tensions in Paris, notably those stirred up by the Lenten sermons preached in 1531 by Gerard Roussel, chaplain to Marguerite of Navarre and an associate of Lefèvre d'Etaples. It is revealing that Wilson obtained details of the charges against Roussel from Guillaume du Bellay: on both sides of the Channel he was linked to those who favoured moderate reform and saw royal control rather than the Papacy as its most effective agency, at least until a Council could be summoned. In the early 1530s there was an obvious coherence between the advocates of Henry's divorce and the exponents of humanist scholarship; while Wilson was engaged in English affairs he was also at work on Hebrew, studies reflected in his commentaries on Psalms 15 and 50 and in his gift to George Buchanan of Sebastian Münster's *Dictionarium Hebraicum*. The two psalm commentaries, printed in 1531 and 1532 by Cyaneus (who also issued Calvin's humanist edition of Seneca's *De Clementia* in the latter year), were a public declaration of alignment with the newly founded Collège Royal, and it was appropriate that one should be dedicated to a French

---

[11] *Gabriel Harvey's Marginalia*, ed. G.C. Moore Smith, (Stratford-upon-Avon, 1913), p. 122.

patron, Lorraine, and the second to the increasingly influential bishop of Winchester, Stephen Gardiner.

The dedication of *In psalmum 50 enarratio* to Gardiner is a virtual encomium of England, and Thomas More is named as one of its ornaments. Between 1529 and 1536 Wilson held (or at least laid claim to) the living of Speldhurst in Kent. This was in Fisher's diocese of Rochester, and his allusion to Fisher in the *De Animi Tranquillitate* clearly points to personal acquaintance. All this must have made him a thoughtful observer of events during the critical summer of 1535. On June 10, just twelve days before Fisher's execution, Antonio Bonvisi's servant stated to commissioners in the Tower that it was Wilson who had brought news of Fisher's nomination as cardinal from the French ambassador's house. It must have been at this tense period that he walked in Bonvisi's London garden in the company of another Henrician apologist, Thomas Starkey, who advised him to visit Carpentras and consult its distinguished bishop Jacopo Sadoleto. Starkey had met Sadoleto there during a visit with Reginald Pole in 1532, and his suggestion was a response to Wilson's wish for a period of quiet reflection. Maybe this reflects growing unease on Wilson's part with the drift of events in England, but it fitted well with his plans to travel to Rome in the entourage of Jean du Bellay, sent by Francis I in a last-ditch attempt to resolve the crisis over Henry's marriage. Taken sick at Avignon, Wilson presented himself at Sadoleto's door; when he wrote to Starkey in November, 1535 it was as master of the school at Carpentras, a guest at Bonvisi's house during a brief trip to Lyons.[12]

One of the most interesting consequences of this friendship with Starkey is the perspective it offers into the intellectual preoccupations of so-called 'evangelical humanism'. Thanks to the education he had received at Aberdeen, Wilson appears to have been well equipped to participate in the irenical manoeuvres of the 1530s, but even as early as 1536 such moderation was under threat and by the Diet of Regensburg in 1541 it was doomed. Such a prospect was not evident to its adherents as Wilson's later writings can witness. The attitudes characteristic of the movement (although tendency would be a more appropriate word) can be seen as consequences of the application of humanist techniques to religious experience. There is the stress on authentic sources, on a return to a patristic and positive theology relating to pastoral rather than dogmatic concerns, on personal devotion rather than outward ceremony, and underlying all these a religious application of rhetoric, of language as a medium that could touch and excite subjective response. Wilson's criticism of the scholastic theologians, the *recentiores*, is representative:

---

[12]*L&P Henry VIII*, VIII, 856, 43; IX, 867. See also T.F. Mayer, *Thomas Starkey and the Commonweal* (Cambridge, 1989), p. 216.

they may possess both method and subtlety, but the content is meagre and too often they show off their talent in light and foolish issues. When they treat religious matters there are no flames, none of that force of language by which the reader can be stirred to love.[13]

The subjective emphasis can be seen as a product of the rhetorical interests at the heart of humanism, and a natural reaction to the pastoral irrelevance of much academic theology. When Cardinal Pole notoriously advised Vittoria Colonna 'to believe as if her salvation depended upon faith alone, and to act, on the other hand, as if it depended upon good works' he was adopting a style typical of the evangelicals or 'spirituali', one which treats the economy of grace as a matter for subjective response rather than formal affirmation.[14] Justification by faith, although it was taken over by the Reformers, remained an option (an increasingly suspect one) for Catholics until Trent threw it out, and it naturally cohered with the subjective ideals of evangelical humanism. What was edited out was the Lutheran corollary of total depravity. Clearly Pole did not mean by his formula quite the same thing as Luther: it is the rhetorical, or subjective, use of doctrine that makes the evangelicals so ambiguous to us and so confusing to their contemporaries. It was inevitable that they would try to bridge the gap, to salvage those features of the Reformers' theology which lent themselves to subjective exploitation; it was equally inevitable that, as confessional lines were drawn and then hardened by political consideration, the evangelical position would become untenable or devious. Calvin's derisory term, Nicodemite, was all too apt.

1536 marks the last direct contact of Florens Wilson with English affairs: on 20 June he wrote to Cromwell from Paris, mentioning an apology for Henry that he plans to bring with him in a last attempt to secure his benefice. At the same moment Reginald Pole's *De Unitate* reached England; Starkey read it in July. This marks something of a watershed: Cromwell had made use of the evangelicals to win control of the *ecclesia anglicana*, but his interests turned now to more radical alliances. If Wilson ever delivered his apology nothing came of it, and Starkey, his political optimism withered, followed the middle way in religion and dabbled in subversion.[15] The spirit of the evangelicals is well conveyed in Starkey's comment—written in more confident days—on Luther, 'whose jugement I estyme veray lytyl, & yet he & hys dyscypullys be not in al thyngys heretykys, wherfor I wyl not so abhorre theyr heresye that for the hate

---

[13]*D.A.T.*, p. 343 ('Recentioribus, qui sunt innumeri, et methodus quaedam est, et acuminis sane plurimum: sed magna est rerum ieiunitas, et saepissime in ludicris et frivolis ambitiose ostentant ingenium. Siquando illis sacra tractantur, nullae sunt flammae, nullus impetus orationis, quo incendatur ad rerum amorem lector.')

[14]D. Fenlon, *Heresy and Obedience in Tridentine Italy* (Cambridge, 1972), p. 96.

[15]Mayer, *Starkey*, pp. 242, 259-62; his involvement in the Exeter conspiracy is described pp. 271-76.

therof I wyl fly from the truth'.[16] Such a stance of personal discrimination was under growing threat in the late 1530s and it was surely for this reason that Wilson moved south to the comparative freedom of Lyons.

Perhaps Bonvisi gave him help. At any rate some of Wilson's most significant acquaintances there were to be Luccans: the first of his books to appear from the press of Sebastian Gryphius was the *Commentatio Quaedam Theologica* (1539) which he dedicated to Francesco Turretini. This is a remarkable work which, because of its rarity, has been neglected by religious historians: in elegant Latin it presents an inner colloquy between God and the soul which is saturated with scriptural allusion. It is an intriguing spectacle, this Aberdeen graduate based in Lyons producing a representative expression of evangelical devotion.[17] Judging by the reference in the dedication to those friends who had urged its publication, the manuscript must have circulated when the court was at Lyons in 1538 and Gardiner was present as English ambassador: he is listed among the friends, as are his nephew Germain, and Sir John Borthwick, *enseigne* of the Scottish Archers. Within a year Borthwick, who had his own contacts with Cromwell and clearly favoured a national reform of the Scottish Church, would be condemned in Scotland as a heretic and his image burned in his absence. Germain Gardiner, by contrast, lost his life on the scaffold in 1544 as a recalcitrant papist. Also in the list is 'tota familia Bonvisiana'. The fact that these varied friends should applaud the *Commentatio* in 1538, yet follow such different confessional paths, points to the crisis of evangelism.[18]

Lyons provided a congenial haven for Wilson, apparently for the rest of his days. An important trading centre, it had no *parlement* or university to restrict toleration, and the presence of a thriving merchant community, together with banking and legal interests, favoured lay cultural initiatives. The circle of the printer Gryphius matched this mood: not only did he emulate Aldus in printing the classics but, as the main French source of Erasmus, he was also a supporter of religious moderation. Wilson appears to have worked as a proof-reader for him and, like others in the circle, he was employed by the lay-directed Collège de la Trinité where one of his pupils was Sebastian Castellio, a future prophet of religious toleration. The Neo-Latin activity which flourished in Lyons during the late 1530s is characterized by an emphasis on purity of classical style and by a highly eclectic religious language which prizes personal devotion above devotional precision. And the Italian influence was important: through Sadoleto,

---

[16]Thomas Starkey, *A Dialogue between Pole and Lupset*, ed. T.F. Mayer (London, 1989), p. 90. The bulk of this work was written in 1532.

[17]Copies of the Gryphius edition are in the National Library of Scotland and Manchester University Library; the Bibliothèque Nationale has the 1544 edition printed by H. Curio at Basle. See D. Baker-Smith, 'Florens Wilson and the Politics of Irenicism', *Acta Conventus Neo-Latini Torontonensis* (Binghamton, 1991), pp. 189-98.

[18]On Borthwick and the Cromwell connection generally see J. Durkan, 'Scottish "Evangelicals" in the Patronage of Thomas Cromwell', *Records of the Scottish Church History Society*, 21 (1981-83), 127-56.

Gryphius kept in touch with evangelicals there, and it was to him that Sadoleto turned in 1535 to urge the publication of Aonio Paleario's *De immortalitate animorum*.[19] During these years Lyons was the literary homeland of the evangelical movement. If one work could be said to represent that Indian summer it is the *De Animi Tranquillitate*, and it is fitting that the book opens with such a specific evocation of place. This is the hillside of Fourvières, overlooking the city, and the three friends who walk up it to begin their discussion are Wilson himself, Francesco Michele and Demetrio Caravalla. The dialogue over the popular humanist theme of 'tranquillitas animi'—translated by Sir Thomas Wyatt as 'Quyete of Mynde'—is initiated as a reaction to Wilson's distress at two items of news: one is the outbreak of hostilities between Scotland and England, the second the flight of three leading evangelicals to the Reformed sanctuary of Zurich. The first reference is clearly to the campaign, initiated by the English in August, 1542, which led to the Scottish disaster at Solway Moss, and in expressing his anguish at the war between two lands that meant so much to him Wilson reveals his strong feeling for his homeland: 'nothing is dearer than the land of our birth, in Homer's words, "even if one dwells in a rich house far off in a foreign land"'.[20] The flight of Peter Martyr Vermigli, along with Bernardino Ochino and Paolo Lacizi, also occurred in late August, and was a profound shock to those with evangelical sympathies: it appeared to confirm the worst suspicions of their critics. Though Wilson could not know it, both these events were to have a grave effect on religious affairs in Scotland and in Italy, but even so they must have been hard to bear. What gives his book its special focus and urgency is the fact that it is written out of immediate confrontation with these anxieties—and that it is dedicated to Francesco Michele. Michele, referred to as the son of Bonaventura (pp. 98-99), can be identified as that Francesco Michele who, together with Regolo Turretini, father of the Francesco Turretini to whom the *Commentatio Theologica* was dedicated, is listed among the 'godly Church of faithful men' that Vermigli had gathered around him at S. Frediano in Lucca. His presence in Wilson's dialogue is the result of his flight from the witch-hunt that followed Vermigli's escape.[21]

All these give Wilson's handling of his theme an interest and immediacy beyond the realm of the average humanist dialogue. And if most of the talking is done by his *persona*, Florentius, yet the exchanges carry an unusual conviction. The opening section (pp. 6-140) turns over the issues of human suffering and moral autonomy, adopting an eclectic position which favours Aristotle but betrays enthusiasm for Plotinus. At the same time Florentius, echoing Erasmus,

---

[19] On Gryphius see D. Baker-Smith, 'Florens Wilson and his circle', *Neo-Latin and the Vernacular in Renaissance France*, ed. G. Castor and T. Cave, (Oxford, 1984), 83-97; also 'Florens Wilson and the Politics of Irenicism', 189-92.
[20] *D.A.T.*, p. 7. Wilson doesn't slide over the English initiation of hostilities though he flatters Henry.
[21] For Vermigli's circle see P. McNair, *Peter Martyr in Italy* (Oxford, 1967), p. 236; the devastating effect of his flight is described by A.J. Schutte, *Pier Paolo Vergerio: the Making of an Italian Reformer* (Geneva, 1977), p. 161.

can criticize those 'theologi nostri' who try to fuse religion and peripatetic philosophy (p. 86); the implication is fideistic: while moral wisdom can guide us towards the good, human fulfilment depends on the imperceptible operation of grace. This, indeed, is the general argument illustrated in the dream allegory which provides a narrative frame for the greater part of the book. Florentius describes a dream which was supposedly provoked by his conversation with Ogilvie on the banks of the Lossie many years before. The setting is, indeed, an idealized version of the landscape around Elgin, the natural charm heightened by the addition of exotic mediterranean foliage.[22] Here the dreamer discovers a splendid temple, presided over by Democritus and adorned by eight columns marked with inscriptions of moral counsel. These are highly general, indeed commonplace: 'We must not regard things which are extraneous as our own or particular to ourselves' (p. 189); 'It is shameful and vain to seek rest in outward things' (p. 189); 'Prefer to be what you are rather than what you wish, and on this account judge yourself to be blest' (p. 309). As Erasmus remarked in the preface to the 1500 *Adagia*,

> [the sages of the ancient days] took so little pleasure in the talkative ways of the sophist that they reduced the ancient and celebrated secrets of philosophy to a few very brief adages, deliberately adding a dash of obscurity by employing either a metaphor or a conundrum or something of the kind.[23]

Wilson may have left out the spicey dash of obscurity but the intention is clear enough. This is a temple of pagan moral wisdom, the uttermost that human insight can attain. Even so, the dreamer is not satisfied: in an argument that closely parallels the platonism of Ficino he points out that the needs of our nature can only be met in a posthumous existence, a challenge that Democritus cannot meet. At this stage, prompted by grace (a point that Wilson is at some effort to emphasize), the dreamer falls on his knees in prayer and is rewarded with the vision of a second temple, one which surpasses the first in all respects. Here the custodian is St Paul, and none can approach except those drawn by grace. Inscribed over the entrance are the words of Psalm 83 (84), 'Happy those who live in your house', and the two columns which flank it bear the inscriptions, 'Know thyself', 'Know thy God'; finally, on the frieze above, Paul points to the figure of Christ on the cross. Here is the true point of rest for all human yearnings: even as he awakes the dreamer is enthralled with joy (p. 370).

---

[22] D.A.T., pp. 141-42. Wilson's awareness of natural beauty is especially striking, both here and in the initial proposal to walk on Fourvières (p. 6), as well as in *Commentatio Theologica* (1539), pp. 54-55, where the human role is that of priest in the temple of creation.

[23] To Lord Mountjoy (letter 126), *Complete Works of Erasmus* I (Toronto, 1974), 263.

Since ambivalence is the hallmark of the evangelicals, it is not surprising that Wilson has been claimed both as a Calvinist and as a traditionalist.[24] Neither seems wholly appropriate. Since he is well aware of the arts of language, indeed is insistent on their pastoral necessity, it is important to recognize the nuances which are signalled at the climax of his book. Two themes are evident, the sinful state of man and the mercy that God extends to him. It is helpful to slip back here to the commentary on Psalm 50, the expression of David's sorrow for his sin with Bathsheba and the killing of Uriah: it is the vulnerability of God's chosen one that should be a warning to us of our own frailty, but David's despair is countered by his trust in God's mercy. At the same time Wilson carefully steps back from the position of those who do not simply deny the efficacy of human works in the process of justification but even label them as sinful. Clearly he has the Reformers in mind.[25] There are no signs that the position has altered eleven years later. The concluding discussion in the *De Animi Tranquillitate* (pp. 364-92) is between Wilson and Michele, the dedicatee of the book and a refugee from the Inquisition; all the signs are that Wilson is trying to put before his friend a genuine compromise which can reconcile tradition with that vivid personal sense of God's mercy which was the most appealing aspect of Luther's teaching.[26] Tradition means simply those central doctrines which are supported by the consensus of Christian teachers over the centuries; here Wilson matches Starkey who appeals to 'the sentence of the auncyent interpretarys of Chrystys doctryne &...the consent & custume of the Church, usyd from the begynnyng unto thys day'. Such a formulation suited those who looked to a future Council to resolve current disputes.[27] But justification by faith is a knotty issue, as Francesco himself recognizes in the dialogue; it seems necessary to distinguish between those who took it literally, as Luther did, as an expression of the irrelevance of good works, and those who saw it as a necessary devotional emphasis.

The two inscriptions on the Pauline temple are important: 'Know thyself', 'Know thy God'. When Calvin echoes this exact formula in the opening of his 1539 *Institutes* it is in order to execrate human nature; Wilson can sound negative, but in the whole scheme of his work there is no support for the idea of total depravity. The essential thrust is to present the loving initiative of God's redeeming power, against which all concern with human merit fades into

---

[24]For a Calvinist Wilson see J. Kraye, in *The Cambridge History of Renaissance Philosophy*, ed. C.B. Schmitt and Q. Skinner (Cambridge, 1988), pp. 314n., 332; as one whose '[theological] sympathies lay with the old order', A. Broadie, 'Philosophy in Renaissance Scotland', *Humanism in Renaissance Scotland*, ed. MacQueen, p. 89.

[25]*In Psalmum 50 enarratio* (Paris, L. Cyaneus, 1532), pp. 6-7, 27-28; cf. *D.A.T.*, p. 365. For a lucid review of the issues relevant to Wilson's case see R. Rex, *The Theology of John Fisher* (Cambridge, 1991), chapter 7.

[26]Thus even Fisher, a strong opponent, shows some convergence 'which perhaps reflected the response of a pastoral theologian to one of Luther's more attractive doctrines', Rex, ibid., p. 128.

[27]S.J. Herrtage, *Starkey's Life and Letters* (London, 1878; rpt. New York, 1975), p. lii. Cf. Erasmus to Pirckheimer in 1527, 'The church I call the consensus of the whole Christian people' (Allen, VII, 216).

irrelevance. On the dogmatic level Wilson cannot fail to recognize that God is the creator of nature as well as religion; while the Pauline temple has priority, that of natural wisdom has a contribution to make (p. 391). Resemblances between his approach to tranquillity and Calvin's can probably be traced to a common source, the valedictory work of the greatest French humanist of the age, Guillaume Budé, which came out in 1535 as a highly personal reflection on the stark dilemma of the decade, the *De Transitu Hellenismi ad Christianismum*. The title provides its own summary of Wilson's theme, and locked away in Budé's disconcerting Latin are the essential features of the evangelical position. Democritus in particular is marked out for his teaching on *euthymia* or *tranquillitas animi* and due stress is given to the role of self-knowledge, the anchor of moral understanding. Yet the persistent theme of the *De Transitu* is the Pauline one of Christ crucified as the focus of all hope and trust, the ground of authentic tranquillity. Again, Budé has been seen as a crypto-Protestant, but his carefully stated emphasis on the freedom of the will to co-operate with grace distinguishes his position from that of the Reformers, however hostile his remarks on Catholic forms. Men of goodwill on both sides must try to move beyond the audacity and the guilt which are the negative features of both sides.[28]

The position that Wilson urges on Michele in the closing pages is just such a stance of critical fidelity to tradition, insisting on the gratuitousness of salvation and on the necessity of a subjective element in faith, one that extends belief (*fides*) into personal commitment (*fiducia*). A recent study of John Fisher has shown how, in spite of his polemical antipathy to Luther, his emphasis on subjective confidence in the availability of grace led him 'closer to Luther than Catholic orthodoxy was subsequently to allow'.[29] We should not lose sight of that 'subsequently', yet it is significant that Wilson at such a critical juncture in his argument—focussed on the issue of certainty about our acceptibility to God— should cite Fisher as an authority to endorse his optimistic economy of grace. To some extent he may be half-consciously hiding behind Fisher's reputation as an opponent of Luther in order to slip in a controversial emphasis. Yet it is clear that his real priority is to hold out a positive vision, founded on a deeply personal sense of indebtedness to Christ.

At the request of his companions, Florentius concludes the dialogue by singing his Horatian ode on true tranquillity, 'Quid vos, o superi boni', so that discussion both begins and ends with Horace, though in the latter case it is a Christian imitation. In one sense this expresses the sophistication of the evangelical position and its consequent vulnerability. By the time Gryphius printed the *De Animi Tranquillitate* things had already gone too far: the collapse of talks between Catholic and Reformed representatives at Regensburg in 1541

---

[28]*De Transitu* (Paris, R. Stephanus, 1535): Democritus, fol. 106; self-knowledge, fols. 43, 46; Pauline 'staurophoria', fols. 121, 127-28; the will, fols. 11, 46; Church disunity, fols. 20-26. The latter include his hopes for a Council.
[29]Rex, *Theology of John Fisher*, pp. 120-21, 128.

was an ominous signal that the two sides were further apart than moderates like Contarini had realized.[30] Eventually Francesco Michele, like Francesco Turretini, found his way to Geneva (as did Guillaume Budé's widow): moderate positions had decreasing appeal. Virtually the last glimpse we have of Wilson dates from 1546 when he wrote to Sadoleto for advice as he faced the prospect of a return to Scotland. Sadoleto's response is remarkably irenical for a cardinal writing from Rome and avoids all specific mention of doctrine; all it urges is a spirit of loyalty, of submission to the established usages of the Church. He speaks more in sorrow than anger of those who pursue divisive interests without regard to consensus and tradition. Wilson's reply has recently been discovered in the Vatican library and we can now see this brief correspondence as deeply humane, and not without its element of pathos. Wilson is grateful for the fatherly counsel of his benefactor but clearly uneasy about its practical application: support for Rome in England is death (as he had good reason to know), the situation in Scotland overshadowed by English interference is little better. Then, many of his highly placed patrons are themselves involved in heresy, and while he will not join them conditions compel him to be a little more timid in the cause of the Church. His letter conveys the anxiety of a moderate confronted by the social pressures which aggravated religious dissension: no resolution can be hoped for until church leaders live more in accord with the Gospels. Further, he reveals, it has been his wish to consult Sadoleto about controverted issues, 'especially since there are among them (i.e. the Reformers) doctrines which are not wholly displeasing to me'; but this seems too dangerous, too open to misconstruction, and he prefers silence:

> Truly, I promise that to the very end you will never hear that your Florentius has used anything but moderation in all controversy, for so my own temper and upbringing, as well as your advice, have always directed me.[31]

These are striking words in their context, and they are the last we hear from Wilson. They can stand for a generation that was overtaken by events. There were, of course, many issues under discussion, yet it is more probable that the matter he wished to discuss with Sadoleto related to the critical theme of justification, the doctrine which even at that moment was under passionate scrutiny in the Council at Trent. The debate opened on 21 June, 1546, exactly a month before Wilson's letter; by the following January the evangelical position had been unequivocally condemned.[32] It appears that Wilson did not return to Scotland, news from that direction cannot have been encouraging; in 1551 he is

---

[30] See P. Matheson, *Cardinal Contarini at Regensburg* (Oxford, 1972), especially pp. 178-79.

[31] Sadoleto, *Epistolae*, ed. V. Alexander (Rome, 1760), III, 433-35. Wilson's letter is Vatican Library, MS Barberini Lat. 6509, fol. 27; I am most indebted to Dr John Durkan for generously supplying me with a transcript. The letter is dated 21 July, time enough for Wilson to have heard of Cardinal Beaton's murder.

[32] The progress of the debate is plotted in D.B. Fenlon, *Heresy and Obedience in Tridentine Italy*, pp. 137-60.

sighted for the last time, delivering the annual oration at the installation of new magistrates in Lyons. Given the tenor of his message to Sadoleto the silence of his later years is suggestive. But from the vantage point of more than four hundred years it is possible to respect his moderation, his oecumenical instincts, with new sympathy. In spite of his emigré existence and the cosmopolitan diversity of his patrons, Wilson exemplifies in a vivid way the possibilities generated by the arrival of new ideas in Scotland. That final letter to Sadoleto, with its allusion to his own upbringing, owes something to the positive spirit and openness which Boece had promoted in Aberdeen; at the same time it betrays a deep sense of despondency about their survival in an age of confessional polarization.

2

JOHN ASLOAN AND HIS MANUSCRIPT:

AN EDINBURGH NOTARY AND SCRIBE IN THE DAYS OF JAMES III, IV AND V (C. 1470-C. 1530)

Catherine van Buuren

In my 1982 edition of *The Buke of the Sevyne Sagis* from the Asloan Manuscript, I devoted several chapters to the manuscript itself and to the man who executed the volume practically single-handed,[1] but I had already published my findings as to his identity in 1966, in an article in *English Studies*.[2] John Asloan was an Edinburgh notary public whose activities are recorded in and around Edinburgh from February 1494/5 till 3 March 1529/30.[3] More recently, it was found that Asloan's name occurs among those of the witnesses to a deed dated 11 December 1532, and this is the last we hear of him in this capacity.[4]

Beside his notarial work Asloan busied himself with scribal projects: witness the appearance of his handwriting in several extant literary manuscripts, such as the *Scottish Troy Book* fragments, inserted in Lydgate's *Troy Book* in Bodleian Library MS Douce 148, and the First Edinburgh Manuscript of Wyntoun's *Chronicles* (National Library of Scotland MS 19.2.3). At the end of the Douce MS, Asloan states that he wrote and 'mendit' it at the instance of 'ane honourable chaplane Schir Thomas ewyn' in Edinburgh, but there is no such identification in the Wyntoun MS, since it has lost its final leaves and with them a possible colophon.

---

[1] *The Buke of the Sevyne Sagis*, ed. C.C. van Buuren (Leiden, 1982), pp. 5-12 and 21-30. His manuscript (National Library of Scotland Acc. MS 4233, now MS 16500), is published as *The Asloan Manuscript*, ed. W.A. Craigie, 2 vols, STS (Edinburgh, 1923-25). The first volume contains the prose items, beside 'The Buke of the Chess', item 2; the second volume contains only verse, but some of the lost items may have been in prose. All quotations, unless otherwise indicated, are from this edition. Both folio references and page numbers in Craigie are usually given, to enable easy consultation of either Craigie, the various editions of parts of the manuscript, or of the manuscript itself.
[2] 'John Asloan, an Edinburgh Scribe', *English Studies*, 47 (1966), 365-72.
[3] On notaries, see John Durkan's 'The Early Scottish Notary', *The Renaissance and Reformation in Scotland*, ed. I.B. Cowan and D. Shaw (Edinburgh, 1983), pp. 22-40, and J.J. Robertson, 'The development of the law', *Scottish Society in the Fifteenth Century*, ed. J.M. Brown (London, 1977), pp. 136-52. Contemporary evidence on the office of notaries is found in the 'Buke of the Chess', ll. 1418ff, Craigie, I, 127f. (fol. 64).
[4] *Protocol Book of John Foular, 1528-1534*, ed. J. Durkan, SRS, (Edinburgh 1985), p. 150. Priscilla Bawcutt very kindly brought this to my notice.

Sir Thomas Ewen was chaplain at several altars in St Giles' Church, Edinburgh: his name is recorded many times in a number of contemporary sources, such as notarial instruments and protocol books, in which we find repeated evidence that sasine of pieces of land was given to him, dating between May 1509 and December 1529.[5] He must have been a very rich man when in July 1529 he took measures for a chaplaincy to be created for the saying of masses for his soul. He was still alive in June 1532.[6] It is quite possible that he, like other churchmen of his days, collected and owned manuscripts and had them repaired when he found parts missing in them.[7]

Beside the colophon in the Douce MS, proof that Asloan and Ewen knew each other is also found in a number of documents where they appear together, one of which, dated 9 March 1517/18, was even 'done in the chamber of Schir Thos. Ewyn'.[8] As they were in regular contact with each other, it is no wonder that Thomas Ewen engaged Asloan to do scribal work for him. Notaries, for that matter, often busied themselves with the production of manuscripts, on both commercial and non-commercial bases.[9]

Whether, however, Asloan executed his MS for Thomas Ewen cannot be established. Asloan's original table of contents mentions seventy-one items in all,[10] but Asloan's items xxiiij-xlix and lxiiij-lxxj have not come down to us, and as the end of the volume has not survived, we cannot know what a possible colophon might have told us. Therefore there is no evidence that the Asloan MS was written for Sir Thomas Ewen,[11] although recently it has been argued wrongly that this was the case.[12]

For whoever Asloan wrote it, there can be no doubt that he penned the whole volume himself, except for item xix: 'the buke callit the spectakle of lufe', fols. 137-150^b (I, 271-98), which ends with the words: 'Explicit the spektakle of luf per M G. Myll' (for further discussion of which see the section

---

[5]Van Buuren, 'Asloan', 366ff.

[6]Ewen is mentioned again among the witnesses of deeds executed on 14 June 1532 (*Protocol Book of Foular*, ed. Durkan, pp. 132-33).

[7]See D.E.R. Watt, 'Editing Walter Bower's *Scotichronicon*', *Proceedings of the Third International Conference on Scottish Language and Literature (Medieval and Renaissance)*, ed. R.J. Lyall and F. Riddy (Glasgow, 1981), p. 166.

[8]See van Buuren, 'Asloan', 369. The text is: 'Acta erant hec in camera Domini thome ewyn capellano...'. D. McKay, 'Parish Life in Scotland, 1500-1560', *Essays on the Scottish Reformation*, ed. D. McRoberts (Glasgow, 1962), p. 95, states: 'The gift of a chaplainry normally brought with it a chamber, possibly, but not frequently, situated within the church like the priest's cell above the south transept in St Michael's, Linlithgow'.

[9]R.J. Lyall, 'Books and book owners in fifteenth-century Scotland', *Book Production and Publishing in Britain 1375-1475*, ed. J. Griffiths and D. Pearsall (Cambridge, 1989), pp. 239-56 (244ff); Van Buuren. 'Asloan', 370, and *Sevyne Sagis*, ed. van Buuren, p. 27.

[10]Craigie, I, ix, notes this, but argues that the actual number of pieces was 61 [sic], 'as the chapters of the first treatise have been numbered separately, with the exception of the last'.

[11]See van Buuren, 'Asloan', 371.

[12]J. Boffey and J.J. Thomson, 'Anthologies and miscellanies: Production and Choice of Texts', *Book Production*, ed. Griffiths and Pearsall, p. 297, note 100.

below on item 9), and one leaf of 'The Buke of the Chess', fol. 53 (I, 105), which was written by a later hand, presumably because an original leaf was lost. Otherwise we find Asloan's name at the end of nine of the twenty-six surviving items, numbers 1, 2, 4, 10, 11, 40, 41, 46 and 49 (herein given a new numbering, as set out below).

The manuscript has two tables of contents. One, of the items now in the manuscript, is in the hand of Alexander Boswell, one-time owner of the manuscript;[13] the second, in Asloan's hand, lists the seventy-one items originally constituting the volume. The thirty-four lost items are in two groups; twenty-six between 'Of the feignd false ffryar of Tungland', fol. 212^b (II, 94), and 'The Buke of the Howlat', and eight after the third of the 'Ballats of our Lady', fol. 304^b (II, 278). Among these lost items we find a number that have been recorded elsewhere, such as Henryson's 'testament of Cresseid' and six of his *Fables*; pieces by Dunbar, for example, the 'goldin ta(rge)', the 'disputacioun betuix the nychtingale and the merle' (found mentioned again in the second batch of lost items as 'the disputacoun betuix the merle & the nychttingale'), 'Dunbarris Derige of Edinburgh & striuling'. Since these have been edited from other sources we know their contents and quality. There are also lost items, however, which so far have appeared nowhere else and which therefore must keep us guessing.

ASLOAN UNDER JAMES III, IV AND V (1460-1542)

In 1494/5 Asloan was active at Linlithgow as procurator for the Herris family, who were Galloway men.[14] He must have been of age at the time, holding this responsible job, and so we may assume that his birth must have taken place c. 1470. Therefore he lived during the reigns of Jameses III-V, that period of fluctuating fortunes for the country and the monarchy. There were the recurring minorities and their concomitant regencies; there were civil wars under James II and James III, with continual troubles and threats from England, many difficulties in national and international politics, widespread and persisting lawlessness, the complications of the Auld Alliance, and drawn-out negotiations over royal marriages, which occasionally took the shape of shameful chicaneries. Asloan as a burgess of Edinburgh must have been aware of much of this. Moreover, as a notary public he would have been in touch with members of society who mattered, for he would have been involved in numerous transactions dealing with property of various kinds. He would therefore have been aware of the economic trends in the capital.[15]

---

[13]On this see *Sevyne Sagis*, ed. van Buuren, pp. 31-40.
[14]*Sevyne Sagis*, ed. van Buuren, pp. 21-25.
[15]For an overview, see J. Wormald, *Kirk, Court and Community: Scotland 1470-1625* (London, 1981), pp. 3-72, and, for James V's minority, G. Donaldson, *Scotland: James V-James VII* (Edinburgh, 1971), pp. 31-42. For political conditions in more detail, see J. Wormald, 'Taming the Magnates?', *Essays on the the Nobility of Medieval Scotland*, ed. K. Stringer (Edinburgh, 1985), pp. 270-80, and R. Mason, 'Kingship, Tyranny, and the Right to Resist', *SHR*, 66.2, (1987), 125-51. For

He must have been a fairly well-educated man, acquainted with Latin, who had learned to write a legible hand and was conversant with the relevant aspects of the law.[16] Whether, however, Asloan was a clergyman, married or not, is not clear from the records. In the docquet of one of the surviving documents from his hand he states that he is a clerk of the diocese of St Andrews 'sacra apostolica auctoritate notarius' (SRO GD 28, Yester 381).

We know something of what in another field, and in sizeable quantity, Asloan must have written down during the hours that his notarial duties did not claim him.[17] On the other hand, unlike a number of protocol books of other notaries of his time, Asloan's have regrettably not come down to us, nor do we know when he was created notary. In order to qualify as a notary one had to have, beside the intellectual gifts mentioned above, a suitable character for the responsibilities concomitant with the function, a willingness to apply oneself assiduously to the duties implicit in the job, and the ability to carry out accurately and in good faith such business as came one's way, such as testaments, bequests, contracts, decrees, but most often sasines concerning land and property.[18]

THE CONTENTS OF THE ASLOAN MANUSCRIPT

In volume I of his edition of the Asloan Manuscript, Sir William Craigie printed the two tables of contents found at the beginning of the manuscript. The first, headed, 'The Contents', was compiled by Alexander Boswell, later Lord Auchinleck, who also numbered the folios as he found them extant in the volume.[19] The second table is headed 'Heir begynis *(the contentis of the)* buke follow*(and)*'. With the exception of the words in parentheses, which are in Alexander Boswell's hand, the table is in Asloan's own hand, and it enumerates the items the manuscript must have contained originally.

Since this study will describe all the items Asloan intended to hand down to his readers, and is also an attempt to find out why he wished to enter just these in his manuscript, it is important to clarify the system of numbering used for easy reference. Therefore a list of Asloan's sixty original items, with their locations in Craigie's two-volume edition, where possible, follows. It is slightly simplified as to titles, with abbreviations expanded.[20] It should be noted that between items 43 and 44 Asloan had 'Item ane ballat of luf' (liiij), fols. 243-46, which was a displaced part of Item 49 'the maying and disport of chaucer'; in

---

economic conditions, see also M. Lynch, 'Continuity and Change in Urban Society, 1500-1700', *Scottish Society 1500-1800*, ed. R.A. Houston and I.D. Whyte (London, 1989), pp. 85-117 and *The Scottish Medieval Town*, ed. M. Lynch, M. Spearman and G. Stell (Edinburgh, 1988).

[16]For instances of his notarial activities, see van Buuren, 'Asloan', 369-70.
[17]This has been noted fully in *Sevyne Sagis*, ed. van Buuren, 26-30.
[18]See Durkan, 'The Notary', 22-40.
[19]See also *Sevyne Sagis*, ed. van Buuren, pp. 414ff.
[20]For clarity Craigie's use of a form of 'y' for the thorn has been silently emended to 'th'.

Craigie's second volume these folios are placed where they belong: between fols. 298 and 299 (pp. 259-66). Craigie retained the original folio numbering—this numbering, it is to be remembered, being in a later hand than Asloan's, probably that of Alexander Boswell—so it is still possible to ascertain where Asloan had placed this 'ballat'.[21]

Vol. I	1.	John Ireland (fols. 1-40^b)	1
	2.	Buke of the Chess (fols. 41-76^b)	81
	3.	The Cart of the Warld (fols. 77-86)	153
	4.	The Porteous of Nobleness (fols. 86- 92^b)	171
	5.	The Scottis Originale (fols. 93- 98^b)	185
	6.	Part of the Ynglis Cronikle (fols. 99-107^b)	197
	7.	Ane Schort Memoriale for Addicioun (fols. 109-123^b)[22]	215
	8.	The Scottis Cronikle (fols. 124-136^b)	245
	9.	The Spectacle of Luf (fols. 137-150^b)	271
	10.	The Sex Werkdayis and Agis (fols. 151-166^b)	299
Vol. II	11.	The Sevyne Sagis (fols. 167-209^b)	1
	12.	The Iustis &c. (fols. 210-211^b)	89
	13.	The Fen3eit Freir (fols. 211^b-212^b)	92
	14.	The Testament of Cresseid	Lost
	15.	The Disputacioun betuix the nycht. & the merle	Lost
	16.	The Goldin Targe	Lost
	17.	Master Rob. Hendersonnis Dreme on Fut by Forth	Lost
	18.	The Sawis of the angell, &c.	Lost
	19.	The Buke of curtasy and nortur	Lost
	20.	The document of Schir Gilbert Hay	Lost
	21.	The Regiment of Kingis with the buke of phisnomy	Lost
	22.	A ballat of the incarnacioun	Lost
	23.	A ballat of steidfastness	Lost
	24.	A ballat of recompence	Lost
	25.	A ballat of our lady of pete	Lost
	26.	A ballat of disputacoun betuix the body and saull	Lost
	27.	A ballat of the devillis Inquest	Lost
	28.	A ballat of our lady	Lost
	29.	The buke of colkelby	Lost
	30.	The buke of the otter and the ele	Lost
	31.	The flyting betuix kennyde & dunbar	Lost
	32.	Fablis of Esope And first of the paddok and the mouss	Lost
	33.	The preching of the swallow	Lost
	34.	The lyoun and the mouss	Lost
	35.	Chanticlere and the fox	Lost

[21] Ibid., pp. 10-14.
[22] As is clear from Asloan's own index he meant 'The Scottis Cronikle' to precede the 'Schort Memoriale', but when the MS was inlaid and rebound they changed places. They are now items 7 and 8, instead of the original xviij and xvij.

	36.	The tod and the wolf	Lost
	37.	The parliament of bestis (=The trial of the fox)[23]	Lost
	38.	By a palace as I couth pass	Lost
	39.	A ballat of Treuth	Lost
Vol. II	40.	The Buke of the Howlat (fols. 213-228^b)	95
	41.	The talis of the fyve bestis (fols. 229-235^b)	127
	42.	The wplandis mouss & borowstounis (fols. 236-240)	141
	43.	The crying of ane playe (fols. 240-242^b, incomplete)	149
		(43* ane ballat of luf is part of item 49)	
	44.	Orpheus and Euridices (fols. 247-256^b)	155
	45.	The thre prestis of Peblis (fols. 257-262^b)	175
	46.	The contemplacioun of synnaris (fols. 263-290)	187
	47.	The passioun of Jhesu (fols. 290^b-292)	242
	48.	Ane ballat of Our Lady (fols. 292-292^b)	245
	49.	The maying and disport of Chaucer (fols. 293-300^b)	247
	50.	Ane ballat of Our Lady (Ross mary...) (fols. 301-301^b)	271
	51.	Ane ballat of Our Lady (Closter of Crist) (fols. 301^b-303)	272
	52.	Ane ballat of Our Lady (Hale sterne...) (fols. 303-304^b)	275
	53.	The Buke of ralf col3ear	Lost
	54.	The Buke of Schir Gologruss & Schir Gawane	Lost
	55.	The disputacoun betuix the merle & the nychttingale	Lost
	56.	Dunbarris Derige of Edinburgh & Striuling	Lost
	57.	Ane ballat of all officeris	Lost
	58.	Ane ballat of making of	Lost
	59.	Ane ballat of pacience	Lost
	60.	Ane ballat of warldlie plesance	Lost

Of 60 original items   13 + 13 have survived,
                          26 + 8 have been lost.

THE ITEMS OF THE ASLOAN MANUSCRIPT

1. **John Ireland's devotional contribution** (c. 1490), does not have a short title, but it is prefaced by an eleven-item explanation of the subjects. The forty-folio long work is unique and so far not edited. In his long exordium, Asloan twice mentions Ireland as the author.

Craigie (I, v), calls this '[a] long and dull treatise on Penance and Confession, in eleven chapters and extending to 80 pages'. Some of the subjects of this edifying piece of prose are: the sacrament and virtue of penance, the confession sacramental with its condition and profits, of satisfaction sacramental, of alms-deeds and mercy spiritual and corporal, of fasting, of prayer, of charity and of mercy.

---

[23] This link was made by editor Denton Fox, *The Poems of Robert Henryson* (Oxford, 1981), p. 234.

On folio 30^b (I, 60), l. 17ff, the author makes the very interesting statement that he compiled the book:

> for the honour of god and proffet of the peple nocht in paris quhar I haue waikit to study bot in the castell of Edinburgh In the court of our souerane lord. I submit to the correctioun of the haly kirk, the halye sete of rome, the vniuersite of paris, The kirk and vniuersiteis of scotland and all other personis that It pertenis to and has autorite thairof prayand the redar humily...&c. [Punctuation added.]

Some twelve lines later, he ends with 'Amen' and 'finis', but on the following page the author states that he is now going to declare 'the mater and the table of confession...'. At the bottom of fol. 32^b (I, 64) he writes: 'Consider perfytlye thir Rewlis followand', and in the last fourteen pages there follow the table of confession, the five wits, the seven deadly sins, the seven virtues, the ten commandments, the seven deeds of mercy, and the twelve articles of truth. Finally we find, fol. 40^b (I, 80): 'Explicit Per manum Johannis asloan' and again 'Finis'.

The elaborate style of Ireland's *Meroure of Wyssdome*, composed for James IV c. 1490, is not so prevalent in the present piece.[24] Indeed, it employs a style with mostly paratactic structures; the words chosen are for the most part simple and uncomplicated although, in the nature of the case, there is a great quantity of words of Latin derivation. This would suggest that the Asloan treatise is the earlier of the two, and in a recent study Dr Sally Mapstone drew the same conclusion.[25]

The work is set up very methodically and the tone is that of a kind master, concerned to be understood by his pupil(s). The author often speaks in the first person and addresses his pupil/reader as 'thow', 'thou', 'the', with possessive pronoun 'thi'; 'we' and 'ws' are also frequently used.[26] He repeats himself now and then, as a good teacher should do.

Occasionally the author introduces Latin phrases which are usually not elucidated. Did he take it for granted that his reader knew enough Latin? Even so, the work is not addressed to one person, nor to men only, as is evident, for example, on fol. 1^b (I, 2-3), 27ff:

> I haue purposit to treate part of materis of theologye tuichand & concernand the saifte of mennis saulis and womennis, strenthing

---

[24] See R.J. Lyall, 'Vernacular Prose before the Reformation', *The History of Scottish Literature*, I, ed. R.D.S. Jack (Aberdeen, 1988), 163-82 (171-73). Contrast, for example, the complexity of the example Lyall discusses on p. 171. See also J.H. Burns, 'John Ireland and *The Meroure of Wyssdome*', *Innes Review*, 6 (1955), 77-98.

[25] The Advice to Princes Tradition in Scottish Literature, 1450-1500', Diss. Oxford, 1986, Chapter 8.

[26] But cf. Craigie, I, 38 (fol. 19^b), bottom line: 'ȝou in ȝour ressonable commandementis ...ȝou...'; further down the page there is 'ye' and 'yow'.

of thar conscience, Indusyng thaim to trast in god, thair makar and saluatour... [Punctuation added.]

Women are mentioned again on fol. 31^b (I, 62), l. 10, and fol. 33, (I, 65), lines 5 and 22, and not just as instruments of the devil! Yet Ireland must have had educated persons in mind, for his Middle Scots is interlarded richly with Latin phrases, moderately at the beginning, more and more frequently as he goes along, desisting, however, after fol. 32^b (I, 64), except for two 'verses' at the end of the chapter on 'The Vij deidis of mercy', fol. 38 (I, 75), and at the very end, on fol. 40^b (I, 80).[27]

From its subject-matter, direct authorial comment and the stylistic features mentioned above, it seems to me that we can place this piece of didactic prose in the advice-to-princes genre.[28]

In Asloan's numbering Ireland's piece is entered as eleven chapters, so that the 'Buke of the Chess' is his twelfth item.

2. *The Buke of the Chess*, beginning, 'Sone efter the tyme that ald saturnus', is unique, and anonymous. It has 2130 lines in five-stress couplets.[29] It starts in a somewhat miscarried high-style[30] introduction which is soon abandoned, then continues in rather unimaginative plain narrative verse.[31]

This item is derived from the *Ludus Scaccorum*, a moralizing and allegorizing explanation of the medieval form of the game of chess, written in Latin prose c. 1275 by Jacobus de Cessolis, a Dominican of Northern Italy. The original Latin version exists in a great number of manuscripts throughout Europe. 'The Buke of the Chess' is most probably based on the Latin original, though considerably shortened. Sir Alexander Boswell had it printed on his private Auchinleck Press in 1818.[32]

Mapstone discusses this item of Asloan's in her unpublished dissertation, appropriately classifying it as advice-to-princes literature.[33]

---

[27] For aspects of style and wording, see A.J. Aitken's 'Variation and Variety in Written Middle Scots', *Edinburgh Studies in English and Scots*, ed. A.J. Aitken, A. McIntosh and H. Pálsson (London, 1971), pp. 177-209.

[28] For a very lucid treatment of Ireland's *Meroure*, see Mapstone, 'Advice Tradition, 1450-1500', Chapter 8, and her forthcoming work, 'The Wisdom of Princes: Advice to Rulers in Late Medieval Scotland'.

[29] Craigie's number of lines, 2191, is incorrect. It should be 2130.

[30] C.S. Lewis, *English Literature in the Sixteenth Century, excluding Drama* (Oxford, 1954), p. 74-76. More recently A.J. Aitken has written an important article on this subject: 'The Language of Older Scots Poetry', *Scotland and the Lowland Tongue*, ed. J.D. McClure (Aberdeen, 1983), pp. 18-49. Aitken calls this 'courtly verse in the grand manner' (pp. 21-23).

[31] More attention will be given to this in the edition I am at present preparing for the Scottish Text Society.

[32] Sir Alexander Boswell (1775-1822), James Boswell's elder son, set up a private printing press at his country estate, Auchinleck, in Ayrshire, and called it the Auchinleck Press. Here he published a number of works, some in a series called *Frondes Caducæ* of which *The Buke of the Chess* is one. See *Sevyne Sagis*, ed. van Buuren, pp. 34ff.

[33] Advice Tradition, 1450-1500', chapter 5.

3. ***The Cart of the Warld***. Asloan calls it 'the diuisioun of all the warld callit the cart schortly drawyn In Yngliss'. It is about nine folios of prose, a topographical tour of the 'known' world, derived from a number of chapters of Higden's *Polychronicon*, as translated into Middle English in 1387 by Trevisa (Book I, Chapters 5, 6, 7, 11 and 9).[34]

This is a very desultory piece of writing with a great number of geographical names. Many of these seem hard to trace, if they are at all anywhere near fact. The information in such pieces was welcome to the gullible contemporaneous reader.

Craigie says (I, vi): 'Either an inferior text was employed or Asloan was careless, for the errors and omissions are numerous, and not a few passages are misleading or meaningless'. The first of Craigie's suggestions is most likely, for although Asloan in his long manuscript does make mistakes now and then, they are always only minor ones,[35] or an occasional misreading or displacement of a line. He could not be described as careless. None of the rest of the items in his manuscript is as chaotic as this one.[36]

4. ***The Porteous of nobleness***. Heading the text of this item are Asloan's words: 'Heir followis the wertuiss of nobilness and portratouris thairof Callit the Portuuss and matynnis of the samyn'. Of c. 7 folios, and dated c. 1490 by *The Dictionary of the Older Scottish Tongue*, the item is a prose translation, so far not edited, of the French poem, *Le Bréviaire des Nobles* by Alain Chartier (c. 1385-1433).[37] William Beattie knew about this source of 'The Porteous of nobleness' as early as 1948 and told Sir William Craigie about it then, in a letter dated 8 June 1948.

In the Chepman and Myllar print of 20 April 1508 only the last five pages of this piece have come down to us; fortunately Asloan gives the full text, probably copying from the print,[38] but omitting the colophon, which states that the work was translated from French into Scots by one Andrew Cadiou, an Aberdeen notary and burgess,[39] who was possibly identical with 'Andreas

---

[34]Craigie, I, vi.

[35]Sampling from the 'Buke of the Chess', these include: 'his' for 'this' (14), '&' for 'as' (152), 'lawis' for 'landis' (271).

[36]*The Cart of the World* was edited by G.G.J. Weynen, as an unpublished 'doctoraal' essay, Nymegen, 1983.

[37]William Beattie gives a short bibliographical notice of it in 'Some Early Scottish Books', *The Scottish Tradition, Essays in Honour of Ronald Gordon Cant*, ed. G.W.S. Barrow (Edinburgh, 1974), pp. 117f. For texts of Alain Chartier in British libraries see F. Ridley, 'X. Middle Scots Writers', *A Manual of Writing in Middle English 1050-1500*, ed. A.E. Hartung, IV (Connecticut, 1973), 79f., and C. Meale, 'Patrons, Buyers and Owners: Book Production and Social Status', *Book Production*, ed. Griffiths and Pearsall, pp. 201-38 (228).

[38]D. Fox, 'Manuscripts and Prints in Scots Poetry in the Sixteenth Century', *Bards and Makars*, ed. A.J. Aitken, M.P. McDiarmid and D.S. Thomson (Glasgow, 1977), p. 157, holds the view that, though Sir William Craigie has said that 'there is every likelihood that Asloan copied from the print', Asloan does contain a few superior readings.

[39]Lyall, 'Vernacular Prose', *History of Scottish Literature*, ed. Jack, p. 170. The Chepman and Myllar colophon reads: 'Heir endis the porteous of noblenes translatit out of ...anche in scottis be Maister Andrew Cadiou imprentit in the southt gait of Edinburgh be Walter Chepman ... Androw Millar the .xx. day of apile the yhere of god .CCCCC.+viii. yheris', *Chepman and Myllar Prints. A*

Cadoen' of the diocese of Aberdeen, an advocate.[40] It was meant as a handbook of good behaviour for '... euery man that will be maid parfyte'. Such a man is to 'say and reid contynually his matynnis & houris on this porteuss' fol. 86 (I, 171). This exhortation is worded several times on the following page, leading up to the twelve 'wertuiss of nobleness: 'faith', 'lawte or treuth', 'honoure', 'ressoun', 'worthyness', 'luf', 'curtasy', 'deligence', 'clenlyness', 'largess', 'soberness', 'perseuerance'. They have an average length of 27 to 28 lines, and in each, except the eleventh, the end consists of an address of two to five lines headed: 'O noble man', followed by a relevant statement. For example, at the end of the virtue of love, there is: 'O noble man be luf we ar adunit to god and be luf and frendschipe in erd all thing Is conseruit. Tharfor he *th*at has nocht luf & frende has na thing', fol. 90 (I, 179, punctuation added). After elaborating on each of these the author concludes with a five-line stanza rhyming ababb:

> Nobles Report 3our matinnis in this buke
> and wysly luke / 3e be nocht countrefete
> Nor to retrete sen lawte seikis na nuke
> And god forsuke breuely for to trete
> All that falss ar / and nobles contrefeit
>   (fol. 92^b; I, 184)

Le bréviaire des nobles in its time was an important guide to the right behaviour, and it has been recorded how young gentlemen at the time were required daily to memorize passages from it.[41]

The tone of the piece is quietly but slightly insistently didactic, again an item very apt as advice to a young prince or nobleman.

5. **The Scottis originale**. The opening lines (fol. 93; I, 185) note that 'the nacioun of scottis begouth in the tyme of moyses', when the king of Egypt gave his only daughter Scota in marriage to Gathelos, the son of the king of Athens, '... Sa that the opiniones of tham ar nocht trew that sayis or trowis that we come of brute quhilk come of tratouris of troye as Is wele kend and conte/nit in the story of troye maid and compylit be the clerk callit gwydo de columna' (ll. 24ff).[42] This is a prose treatise of about six folios, on the origin of the Scots. An earlier version of it is extant in a Panmure manuscript of c. 1460.[43]

---

facsimile with a bibliographical note, ed. W. Beattie (Edinburgh, 1950), p. 5. Beattie notes (p. x) that Andrew Cadiou graduated with an MA degree from Paris in 1472.

[40]Ibid., p. x. See also an article to which Priscilla Bawcutt drew my attention: H. Booton, 'John and Andrew Cadiou: Aberdeen Notaries of the Fifteenth and Early Sixteenth Centuries', *Northern Scotland*, 9 (1989), 17-20.

[41]For an edition of the French original see *Le bréviaire des nobles*, ed. W.H. Rice, *Romania*, 75 (1954).

[42]Gwydo de columna or Guido delle Colonne is the 13th-century author of the *Historia Destructionis Troiae*. Basing himself on Benoît de Sainte Maure, he gave Western Europe the Troy story.

[43]This is published in the *Bannatyne Club Miscellany*, ed. T. Thomson, III (Edinburgh,1855), 35-42.

On fol. 95 (I, 189), l. 13, after the words 'our souerane lord', Asloan has inserted 'Iames the fyft' which, as Craigie notes (I, vii), 'has nothing corresponding to it in the earlier copy'. On fol. 97^b (I, 194) 'thar awne cronikle callit policornica' is cited as bearing witness that Henry II of England is 'cummyn dovne lyne be lyne fra the devill' (l. 28).

It is a fluent account in simple language. Its viewpoint is very anti-English, especially in its railings against the many English perfidies against the Scots.

6. *Part of the Ynglis Cronikle* is titled 'ane tractact of a Part of the yngliss cronikle schawand of thar kingis Part of thar ewill & cursit governance'. A unique prose item, of nine folios, it is an answer to '—3our falss and fen3eit writ That 3e call ane cronikle'.

The wicked English are addressed, told (fol. 99 [I, 197], l. 15) of their descent from the Trojan traitor Brutus, and the devil, 'as Is schawin in 3our awne policronicone... ', and given various examples of their kings' evil traits and tricks. It is not very exact, missing out on things that are now considered of greater importance or of greater saliency. These, however, may not have been known to the compiler of this 'Cronikle'. The account ends on fol. 107^b (I, 214) with the arrest of Dame Eleanor Cobham, which took place in 1441. The following folio is blank paper, probably not later than Asloan's, but it has no watermark. Therefore we cannot decide what happened to a possible fifty more lines about English kings and their vile treatment of their neighbour, the kingdom of Scotland.

7. *Ane schort memoriale of the scottis corniklis for addicoun*,[44] is the title given to this unique collection of important historical data in simple narrative prose. It fills fifteen folios, and is recounted in two series of entries, dealing with the periods of 1428-60 and 1420-55 respectively, mostly during the reign of James II.

---

[44]This item should have followed the next. For the confusion in the binding here, see *Sevyne Sagis*, ed. van Buuren, p. 11. Asloan's own index indicates what his intention was. See also Craigie's comment (I, vii-viii.); on fol. 121^b (I, 234) there is an entry for 20 April 1449, dealing with the death of one Sir James Auchinleck. The entry appears to be faulty. For the revenge taken on the perpetrator of the deed by the Earl of Douglas see another version in Lindesay of Pitscottie's *The Historie and Cronicles of Scotland*, ed. Æ.J.G. Mackay, I (Edinburgh, 1899), 79. It is possibly this James Auchinleck's land that was given to Thomas Boswell by James IV in 1504; see *Sevyne Sagis*, ed. van Buuren, p. 33, note 9.

On 28 September 1776, James Boswell noted: 'I had read with my father an old Scots chronicle in a manuscript collection which belonged to Lord Kincardine, his grandfather. It was curious reading and improved me in the habit of knowing old writing' (*Boswell in Extremes, 1776-78*, ed. C. McC. Weis and F.A. Pottle (London, 1971), p. 34). It is probable that James and his father had been reading in the Asloan MS. The earliest known owner of the MS is, therefore, Alexander Bruce, the second Earl of Kincardine (d. 1680). (See item 26.)

The name 'Auchinleck Chronicle' was given to this volume of historical writing when it was published by T.G. Stevenson in 1877. The 'Auchinleck *Manuscript*' (my italics; see item 26), had been given to the Advocates' Library in 1744; so this could not have been the manuscript handled by Alexander Boswell and his son in 1776 (see *Sevyne Sagis*, ed. van Buuren, p. 33).

'Ane schort memoriale' contains a great number of short items, very often concerned with murders and other villainous tricks, perpetrated by Scots among themselves, such as treachery and military raids, cases of arson, destruction, perfidy and perjury, often of local interest only.

The leaves are imperfectly bound, and since the source must have been faulty, Asloan's pages are chaotic and there are several gaps. (In Craigie's edition we find the wrongly placed leaves readjusted, in what seems to be the best solution to the puzzle.) Nevertheless, more recent historians have attached much value to this 'Memoriale', quoting it as fact. Christine McGladdery, for instance, in her book, *James II* (Edinburgh, 1990), devotes her Chapter VII to James II and the historians, with Asloan's 'Auchinleck Chronicle' very much in the foreground. Calling it 'a vital source for the reign of James II' (p. 160), she prints the text from the Asloan MS in full in her Appendix 2, with the folios in their numerical sequence, and a somewhat unorthodox, and silently introduced, 'modernization' (?) of the original spelling.

'Ane schort memoriale' is appreciatively discussed in Norman Macdougall's 'The Sources: a reappraisal of the legend', in *Scottish Society in the Fifteenth Century*, ed. J.M. Brown (London, 1977), pp. 10-22.

8. *The Scottis Cronikle*. Asloan's heading calls this prose work 'ane tractat drawin owt of the scottis cronikle begyn/nand in the thrid age of the warld' (fol. 124; I, 245). In straightforward and simple narrative prose, it comprises thirteen leaves, beginning, like the 'Scottis originale', with Gathelos,[45] and ending with 1488, in which year James IV was crowned in June, while the last mention in the same sentence is that of the end of August 1513 when 'he wan norhame/ In the 3ere of God $I^M V^C$ and xiij 3eris with mony diverss strenthis & castellis on the yngliss bordour' (fol. 136^b I, 270). The rest of the page is blank; Flodden, 9 September 1513, is not mentioned. Craigie (I, viii) tells us that this was compiled from Fordun or some similar source, and has no independent value.

The 'Cronikle' is divided into eighty chapters, some of which are no longer than two lines. In the first few pages attention is devoted to ancient history, with Caesar and Claudius mentioned. In chapter 39 (787AD), in which Charlemagne appears, the compiler notes that 'the noble vniuersite of pariss [was] foundit be twa scottis men that was callit Ihon and Clement' (fol. 128; I, 253).

Macbeth is mentioned in chapter 56. The War of Independence is discussed at length in Chapters 67-72, with 'the falss tratour eduard langschankis king of yngland' (fol. 133^b) coming in for his well-earned part of angry invective. The chronicle concludes after eight more chapters on two folios.

9. *The Spektakle of luf* is headed: 'Heir begynnis the lytill buk entitillit and callit the Spektakle of luf Or delectatioun of luf of wemen quhilk Is devydit in viij partis' (fol. 137; I, 271). There is a prologue and eight parts which are

---

[45] We are told that 'he brocht with him the chiar of marbill that he was crovnit In' (fol. 124, ll. 10-11).

neatly set out on the first page, which the composer calls Chapters i to viii. A prose work of fourteen folios, this item is a unique moral treatise in the anti-feminist mirror tradition, like 'The Buke of the Sevyne Sagis', item 11, below.

'The Spektakle opens with the information that the author, 'musing vpone the restles besynes of [*th*]is] translatory warld', 'tuk a lytill buk in latyn' to pass his time. After reading it, he 'thocht the mater gud and proffitable to be had in to our wulgar and matarnall toung' to cause people to 'eschew the delectatioun of the flesche quhilk Is the moder of all vicis' (fol. 137^b; I, 272).

The treatise tells of a good knight who narrates to his son, a young squire, histories and *exempla* about several categories of women whose enjoyment should be avoided. Already in the first tale (chapter ii) the son is so far persuaded that Papa is right that he begs him for stories so that he may 'tak examplis by vtheris' (fol. 140; I, 277, ll. 16-17). Thus it goes on with many *exempla*, most fairly well known, and most of the personal names different from the common spelling or misread and quaintly spelled. In the end, however, the young man is advised 'to cheiss ye a wyf cummyn of a gud houss & lynage...that Is of ȝung age...and thus leif with hir Vnder the haly band of matermoney And happines sall habound to ye...' (fol. 149^b-150; I, 296-97, ll. 21ff).

Among the *exempla* are some in the *Seven Sages of Rome*-tradition. On fol. 145 (I, 287), for example, we find a parallel of the 'defowl[ing]' of the queen (*Sevyne Sagis*, ed. van Buuren, ll. 241-49) and on fols. 146^b-147^b (I, 290-92), the story VIDUA, also known as 'The Matron of Ephesus', easily the most unlikeable tale in the *Seven Sages of Rome* sources. (This happens to be missing from the Asloan 'Buke of the Sevyne Sagis').

As I have noted previously,[46] the 'Spektakle of Luf' is different from the rest of the manuscript; the colophon says: 'Explicit *the* spectacle of luf per M G. Myll' and the handwriting is not Asloan's. The paper on which it is written is the same as that used for the preceding and following items. It is stated again in the text that this little book was 'translatit out of latyn' and that it was done 'at The cyte of Sandris' (which Craigie, I, viii, takes to stand for St Andrews), 'The x. day of Iulij The ȝer of god ane thowsand four hundreth nyntye and twa ȝeris be ane clerk quhilk had bene In to venus court mair than the space of xx ȝeris...' (fol. 150; I, 297, ll. 5-10).

The identity of 'G. Myll' so far has not been discovered and scholars cannot be sure whether he was the translator or just the copyist. The fact that he used the same paper as Asloan makes it probable that he worked in the same 'office' with the notary. It so happens that a 'Gilbert Myll' figures as one of the witnesses in the earliest extant notarial instrument of John Asloan in the capacity of notary, dated 9 March 1517/18 (SRO GD 28 Yester 381). He did this in Sir Thomas Ewen's room; he, too, was a witness. The translator was, as he states himself, in 1492 'ane clerk quhilk had been In to venus court mair than the space of xx ȝeris...'. He would then, if he had started early with his venerian activities—say, at the age of eighteen—have been born c. 1456. If Myll were the

---

[46]*Sevyne Sagis*, pp. 9-10.

translator, it would therefore be as a rather old man that he penned the 'Spectacle of Luf' for the Asloan Manuscript, c. 1515, and appeared as a witness in 1518 and later.

This piece again is a simply-worded narrative, mainly paratactic, pleasantly didactic and very readable. The obvious authorities are quoted, but the reader is not expected to be learned.

10. *The Sex Werkdayis and Agis*. The full heading is: 'Heir begynnis ane extract of the bibill of the sex werkdays according to the sex agis / quhilkis restit in the sevynt And figuris of the ald testament & newe'. An anonymous, unique, prose work of sixteen folios, the 'Sex Werkdayis' is dated 1495 by *DOST*, and the item's most recent editor, L.A.J.R. Houwen, whose edition is noted below, accepts this.

The work is a compendium of biblical and classical literature, packed with the obvious information from the Old and New Testaments, with many historical and geographical data thrown in. Such data are sometimes duplicated, and presented in a rather random, less wholesomely instructional manner (in contrast to other items so far viewed), and interspersed with a number of Latin phrases.

Craigie speaks of it (I, viii-ix) in a somewhat derogatory way. More appreciative is Houwen, in his well organized and meticulously executed edition. This has a readily accessible text, a useful glossary, and extensive textual notes.[47]

11. *The Sevyne Sagis* begins: 'Ane empriour in tymes bygane', and is a unique, anonymous poem in plain narrative style.[48] It fills forty-two leaves, fols. 167-209^b, and opens Volume II of Craigie's STS edition of the Asloan MS. Its 2782 four-stress lines of rhyming couplets contain a version of the frame story of the Seven Sages, at the time widely known throughout Europe (*Liber de Septem Sapientibus* or *Historia Septem Sapientum*).[49] The story's popularity is attested by its existence in more than twenty European languages. Its sources and parallels reached the West from the Middle East.[50] The Asloan version is entirely independent of that in the extant English manuscripts,[51] as also of the later Scottish version of John Rolland of Dalkeith (fl. 1560).[52]

Asloan's text is defective; it lacks two out of the usual fifteen tales in which the seven sages contend in turn with the queen-stepmother for the life of the young prince they have educated. In Asloan there are seven told by the sages, and one, the final tale told by the boy, which reveals the rationale of the whole

---

[47]*The Sex Werkdayis and Agis: an Edition of a Late Medieval Scots Universal History from the Asloan Manuscript* (Groningen, 1990), and see also, L. Houwen, '*The Sex Werkdayis and Agis*: Text and Context', *English Studies*, 69 (1988), 372-85.

[48]Aitken, 'Language of Older Scots Poetry', p. 19.

[49]*Sevyne Sagis*, ed. van Buuren and, by the same author, 'A Middle Scots Version of the Seven Sagis of Rome', *Studies on the Seven Sages of Rome and Other Essays in Medieval Literature*, ed. H. Niedzielski, H.R. Runte and W.L. Hendrickson (Honolulu, Hawaii, 1978), pp. 63-78.

[50]*Sevyne Sagis*, ed. van Buuren, sec. XIV.

[51]*The Seven Sages of Rome' (Southern Version)*, ed. K. Brunner, EETS (London, 1933).

[52]*The Seven Sages of Rome, translatit out of prois in Scottis meter*, ed. G.F. Black, STS (Edinburgh, 1931-32).

structure. The two missing tales were skipped after line 2234, the sixth sage's and the following by the queen, probably VIDUA and ROMA.[53] This was done either by Asloan or by his model.

All the tales, mostly explained allegorically, are meant as warnings for the king/emperor, the father of the prince; those by the sages are against women in general, later against the queen especially; those by the queen herself against sons, sages and credulous men. The work is linked to 'The Spektakle of Luf' in its anti-feminist features.[54]

The 'Buke of the Sevyne Sagis' is, in my view, one of the most entertaining in the whole manuscript, certainly among the extant pieces. After all the serious entries that precede it, the variety of the seven sages' tales is like a reward for the assiduity shown by the reader so far. Possibly this makes unjustifiable assumptions about how the manuscript was read and how compiled. Some later items, moreover, are also light and amusing.

12. ***The Iustis betuix the Tal3eour and the Sowtar*** begins 'nixt at a tornament was tryit', to reveal that it is a version of the middle part of Dunbar's 'Fasternis Evin in Hell'.[55] Versions are also to be found in the Bannatyne MS (fols. 111-112^b; STS edn, II, 295-98) and Maitland Folio MS (pp. 161-65; STS edn, II, 183-87).[56] Asloan's has 108 lines presented in six-line stanzas, rhyming aa4b3cc4b3. In Kinsley's edition, as in the earlier text of Mackay Mackenzie,[57] the poem is printed in twelve-line stanzas.

This is a piece of coarse fun, deriving, as Kinsley notes (pp. 339-40), from the 'parody of chivalric romance...and...the medieval tradition of "brawl" poetry, in which peasant merry-making at a wedding or some other public occasion reaches its climax in licentious and violent farce'.[58] Kinsley's edition of this poem, as with others, is usefully supplemented and corrected by the information in Bawcutt's valuable review article, 'The Text and Interpretation of Dunbar', *Medium Ævum*, 50 (1981), 88-100.

13. ***The Fen3eit Fals Frere of Tungland***. The opening line is: 'As 3ung aurora with hir cristall hale'. The work (fols. 211^b-212^b; II, 92-94), is by Dunbar. In this manuscript it is imperfect, breaking off at line 69 where 'the great lacuna' (Craigie, II, vi), which runs to twenty-six items, begins.

A burlesque, in which alliteration is a notable feature, the poem appears here in eight-line stanzas rhyming aaa4b3ccc4b3. Both Mackay Mackenzie (pp.

---

[53] See *Sevyne Sagis*, ed. van Buuren, Appendix VI, pp. 439-46, where I have shown how the tales figure in the known medieval versions.
[54] P. Bawcutt, *Dunbar the Makar* (Oxford, 1992), p. 296, agrees on this point.
[55] *The Poems of William Dunbar*, ed. J. Kinsley (Oxford, 1979), pp. 154-57. Kinsley gives it the title 'The Turnament'.
[56] Ridley, 'X. Middle Scots Writers', *Manual*, ed. Hartung, IV, 79-80.
[57] *The Poems of William Dunbar* (London, 1932), pp. 123-26.
[58] See also Bawcutt, *Dunbar the Makar* (pp. 288-92 in particular), and her article, 'The Earliest Texts of Dunbar', *Regionalism in Late Medieval Manuscripts and Texts*, ed. F. Riddy (Cambridge, 1991), pp. 183-98.

67-70) and Kinsley (pp. 161-64) give it a different shape from that in Asloan: the opening and closing stanzas have 24 lines, rhyming aaa4b3cccbdddbeeebfffbgggb, with the interspersing six stanzas of 16 lines each, rhyming aaabcccbdddbeeeb. They follow the text as in the Bann. MS (fols. 117-118^b; STS edn, II, 311-15).

We come now to the first group of lost items, twenty-six in number. Since we are trying to find out why Asloan compiled his manuscript, and why he chose the items found in it, the lost pieces must be investigated as well as the extant ones.

14. *The Testament of Cresseid*, by Robert Henryson, is the first of the lost items. Beside it, there are seven more lost pieces by Henryson: six of his *Fables* (items 32-37), and item 17, otherwise non-extant, 'Maister Robert Hendersonnis Dreme on Fut by Forth'. Among the preserved poems further on in the Asloan MS, we find item 42, Henryson's fable, 'The Two Mice', here called 'The wplandis mouss & borowstounis', and item 44, 'Orpheus and Erudices'.

Henryson's works have been edited most expertly by Denton Fox[59] and the reader is directed to this volume for further study of the separate items still extant.

15. *The disputacioun betuix the nychtingale & the merle*, may be identified with a bird debate by Dunbar (Kinsley no. 16, ['The Merle and the Nychtingall'], pp. 60-63), in which the blackbird defends 'a lusty lyfe in luves service [bene]', l. 8 , and the nightingale the love of God: 'All luve is lost bot upone God allone', l. 16. These two lines are refrains for alternate eight-line stanzas, of which there are fifteen. The rhyme scheme is ababbcbc, with five stresses to the line.

It is surprising to find this same poem again later in the manuscript. It is item 55 among the second group of lost items, then given the title 'The Disputacoun betuix the merle & the ny^{t}tingale'. This is not unique, however, for later compilers Maitland and Bannatyne also sometimes present a piece twice.

Though doubly lost here, the poem has fortunately come down to us in both the Bann. MS (fols. 283-284^b STS edn, IV, 87-91) and the M. Folio MS (pp. 165-68; STS edn, I, 188-91). The latter has defects, which are noted by Kinsley, *Poems of Dunbar*, p. 274.

16. *...goldin ta(rge)*. The title of this poem, as with some others, has been affected by damage to the top of the leaf in Asloan's index. The poem is Dunbar's dream vision, of 279 lines in thirty-one nine-line stanzas, rhyming aabaabbab, with five stresses to the line. It has come down in a Chepman and Myllar print,[60] and in the Bann. MS (fols. 345-348^b; STS edn, IV, 252-61) and M. Folio MS (p. 64-81; STS edn, I, 89-97). Recent editions include those of Kinsley (*Poems of Dunbar*, text, pp. 29-38, notes, pp. 245-55), and Bawcutt and

---

[59]*Poems of Henryson*, op. cit.
[60]See *Chepman and Myllar Prints*, ed. Beattie, pp. 89-100.

Riddy (*Longer Scottish Poems I: 1375-1650* (Edinburgh, 1987), text, 205-14, notes, 378-81).

17. ***Maister Robert Hendersonnis Dreme On fut by forth*** is regrettably not recorded elsewhere, though *The Complaynt of Scotland* (c. 1550) mentions it.[61]

18. ***...sawis of the angell / Deid / quhyte dragoun Devill wysmen blak dragoun 3oung man and of the sawlis in hell.*** This title has also been damaged, but the word 'sawis', which Craigie does not print (II, xiv), is nevertheless still legible.

It is possible that this is one of the 'improvised *ludi*' mentioned by A.J. Mill in *Mediaeval Plays in Scotland* (Edinburgh and London, 1927). She concludes her Chapter I on folk plays with the sad remark that 'we have to be content with references to communal ridings, dancing, archery contests and improvised *ludi*' (p. 35).[62] In the present case we might presuppose an early example of a schoolmaster's effort to write a 'play' for his boys, or a choirmaster for his. If Nicholas Udall could do just that with his *Ralph Roister Doister* in ?1553-56,[63] then why should not a Scottish schoolmaster have had a similar inspiration somewhat earlier, and have made a religious play in which about a dozen parts were to be performed, each dragon perhaps giving two boys their tasks?

The fact that in Asloan's table of contents, in spite of the damage to that part of the page, the word 'sawis' ('words') can still be read before 'of the angell', may point to spoken words, especially as this word is found nowhere else in Asloan's titles. Lyall ('Lost Literature', p. 40), concurs: 'This is unlike anything else I know of, in Scotland or elsewhere: was it a dialogue or a short play, presumably on the themes of sin and damnation?'

A.J. Aitken, however, does not agree with this view.[64] He points out that 'saw' could also stand for 'proverb' [*OED*, s.v. *saw* sb. 2, 4; *MED*, s.v. *sau)e*, 4] and believes that this item may have been a collection of proverbs, listed under the headings found in the title. Groping in the dark as we are in any attempt to relate other proverbial material to Asloan's vague title of item 18, it is useful to look at some of the available collections.

First, the M. Folio MS also includes a collection of saws (pp. 139-40, STS edn, I, 159-61), in which, however, there is no reference to any of the subjects mentioned by Asloan. This same collection is found in the Bann. MS,

---

[61] Robert Wedderburn, *The Complaynt of Scotland*, ed. A.M. Stewart, (Edinburgh, 1979), p. 50 (fol. 50^b). R. Lyall ('Lost Literature of Medieval Scotland', *Bryght Lanternis*, ed. J.D. McClure and M.R.G. Spiller, Aberdeen 1989, pp. 33-47), refers to the appearance of the piece in *The Complaynt of Scotland*. Lyall gives the title as 'On fut by forth as I culd found', but the actual spelling in *The Complaynt* is 'fortht'.
[62] H.S. Bennett remarks in *English Books and Readers* (Cambridge, 1969), p. 150: 'As for drama, it will be remembered that the early sixteenth century saw the flourishing of the interlude'.
[63] E.K. Chambers, *The Medieval Stage* (1903; rpt. Oxford, 1967), II, 196 and 202, n. 2.
[64] Private communication, October 1992.

fols. 134ᵇ-135ᵇ (STS edn. III, 8-10). Two other items in the M. Folio (p. 294; STS edn. I, 344), both anonymous, are short rhymes in the proverbial manner. The first begins, 'Ane ȝoung man chiftane witles', but cannot be reckoned as a proverb about a young man, which is what we are looking for. The second begins, 'Tak tyme in tyme, and no tyme defer'. It expresses the wish that the king reign in virtue.

Secondly, *Fergusson's Scottish Proverbs*, (ed. E. Beveridge, STS, Edinburgh, 1924), includes the categories mentioned by Asloan in the title of item 18. There are nineteen proverbs associated with 'devil', three with 'dead' or 'death', one with 'angelis', four with 'wyse man' or 'men' and five with 'dragon'. Fergusson's year of birth is reckoned to be c. 1525;[65] therefore he was a generation or so younger than Asloan, and the proverbs in the collection may for the greater part have been familiar to Asloan.

The James Carmichael Collection of Proverbs in Scots, ed. M.L. Anderson (Edinburgh, 1957), has twenty-four proverbs with 'devill', eighteen with 'dead' or 'death', one with 'young man', eight with 'wyse man' or 'men'.

B.J. Whiting, 'Proverbs and Proverbial Sayings from Scottish Writings before 1600', *Mediæval Studies*, 11 (1949), 123-205, and 13 (1951), 87-164, mentions fifteen proverbs with 'devil/l', six with 'death', seven with 'angel', one with 'soul', two with 'young man', nine with 'wise man', five with 'dragon' (no colour specified).[66]

Items 19, 20 and 21, to judge by their titles, are all works of instruction and advice and may belong together.

19. **The buke of curtasy and nortur**, though no such title is otherwise known in Middle Scots, has parallels in Middle English and Early Modern English. There is, for example, *The Babees Book*, EETS (London, 1868), where several works, with such titles as John Russell's 'Boke of Nurture'[67] and 'The Boke of Curtasye',[68] are found. Whether the lost version in Asloan had any connection with Gilbert Hay (fl. c. 1419-60), the translator from the French of *The Buke of the Law of Armys, The Buke of Knychthede* and *The Buke of the Governance of Princes*, cannot be established. See also under items 57 and 58 below.

20. **The document of Schir Gilbert Hay** must obviously be Hay's work, but which of his three known prose translations, listed above, went by this title is not known.[69] It should be borne in mind that the word 'document' in Hay's

---

[65] See Erskine Beveridge's 'Introduction' to his edition, pp. ix-xi.
[66] For a helpful review article, see C.O. Parsons, 'Scottish Proverb Books', *Studies in Scottish Literature*, 8.3 (1971), 194-205.
[67] This is edited from BL MS Harleian 4011 (c. 1460).
[68] This is edited from BL MS Sloane 1986 (c. 1430-40).
[69] See *Gilbert of the Haye's Prose Manuscript (AD 1456)*, ed. J.H. Stevenson, STS, 2 vols (Edinburgh and London, 1901-14), or, for extracts. G.G. Smith, *Specimens of Middle Scots* (Edinburgh and London, 1902), pp. 78-83 and 84-92. Lyall ('Lost Literature', pp. 40-41), is 'unwilling even to speculate' whether one of Hay's known pieces was the 'document' in Asloan's

vocabulary as elsewhere at the time often meant 'teaching' (see *DOST*, s.v.). Therefore, either his *Buke of the Lawe of Armys* or his *Buke of the Order of Knychthede* or perhaps both, might be considered as this 'document'.

21. ***The Regiment of Kingis with the Buke of phisnomy***. The first part of the title, 'The Regiment of Kingis', is most probably that of another translation from the French by Hay, which is more often called *The Buke of the Governaunce of Princes*. The French model is a version of the *Secreta Secretorum*, an important work in the advice-to-princes tradition, known in several languages throughout Europe.[70]

Regarding the second part of the title, the 'Buke of phisnomy', John Cartwright's observations, in his article 'Sir Gilbert Hay and the *Alexander* tradition', are pertinent: 'Hay also includes at the end of the *Secretum* section, which Aristotle calls a "regiment" (*Buik*, 9359 [9356]), a section of physiognomy, which is often found associated with the *Secretum* but is not included in Hay's prose version'.[71] It would seem that this section *was* included in the version that Asloan copied for his manuscript, if we assume that this was in prose.[72] Among the chapters of *The Buke of the Governance of Princis* (STS edn, vol. II) are 'How princis sud attour all thing tak kepe to thair hele'; 'How and in quhat maner thai suld governe thair hele keping', 'Quhat things fattis or lenys men moost', and 'Quhat kyndis of metis are best for man'. There is ample reason to range such chapters under the heading 'Phisnomy', as is done in Asloan's item 21.

Given that the title of this item combines 'the Regiment of Kingis' with 'the Buke of phisnomy', I believe, furthermore, that the lost Asloan work is unlikely to have been the short poem of 291 lines beginning 'Rycht as [all] stringis ar reulit in a harp', also called 'De Regimine Principum', which is found

---

manuscript or another, lost work. He concedes that it 'might, for example, *just* fit the instructional framework of *The Buke of Knychthede*'.

[70] M.A. Manzalaoui, 'The Secreta Secretorum in English Thought and Literature from the Fourteenth to the Seventeenth Centuries', Diss. Oxford, 2 vols, 1954; same author, 'The *Secreta Secretorum*: the Medieval European version of Kitab Sirr-ul-Asrar', *Bulletin of the Faculty of Arts of the University of Alexandria*, 15 (1961), 83-105; *Secreta Secretorum: Nine English Versions*, ed. M.A. Manzalaoui, EETS (London, 1977). Notably, in the titles or chapter-headings of several of these nine English versions words and phrases such as 'Phisnomy', 'Guyding of the Body', 'bodely hele' occur. Similarly in *Three Prose Versions of the Secreta Secretorum*, ed. R. Steele, EETS (London, 1898), the three pieces each have such chapters as 'Of the kepyng of the body, after the consayl of lechis', 'That Physnomie is a necessary scyence to know the maneris of menn', 'Of that Same science of Physnomye in a shortyr manere'.

[71] *Scottish Language and Literature, Medieval and Renaissance*, ed. D. Strauss and H.W. Drescher (Frankfurt am Main, 1986), pp. 229-38 (234-35); same author's ongoing edition of Hay's *The Buik of King Alexander the Conquerour* STS (Edinburgh, 1986-1990-), and, same author, 'Basilisks, Brahmins and Other Aliens: Encountering the Other in Sir Gilbert Hay's *Alexander*', *Studies in Scottish Literature*, 26 (1991), 334-42 (336-37) on the physiognomy.

[72] See Lyall, 'Vernacular Prose', 167-70. For biographical details of Hay, see *Longer Scottish Poems*, ed. Bawcutt and Riddy, 55; *Haye's Prose Manuscript*, ed. Stevenson, I, xxiii-xxxv, and F. Riddy, 'The Revival of Chivalry in Late Medieval Scotland', *Actes du 2ᵉ Colloque de Langue et Littérature Ecossaises (Moyen Age et Renaissance)*, ed. J.-J. Blanchot and C. Graf (Strasbourg, 1978), pp. 54-62 (57f.). See also *The Prose Works of Sir Gilbert Hay*, III, ed. J.A. Glenn, STS (Edinburgh, 1993).

in the *Liber Pluscardensis* (ed. F.J. Skene, Edinburgh, 1877, I, 392-400). However, since this latter poem is one of the items in the Chepman and Myllar Prints,[73] where it figures between Dunbar's *Golden Targe* and *The Maying and Disport of Chaucer*, it is perhaps wise to be cautious about its possible form in the Asloan MS.

After the lost pieces connected with Hay there are seven items (22-28), also lost, called 'ballats'. *DOST* calls a *ballat* 'a ballad or song, originally one accompanying a dance'. For Asloan, as with his contemporaries it could be inferred, this word appears to have meant simply 'poems'. Bannatyne, we remember, wrote on the first page of his MS, 'Heir begynnis ane ballat buik'.[74]

22. *A ballat of the Incarnacioun*, and
24. *A ballat of recompence*, are unknown. No items of similar title appear elsewhere. The latter may have been a petitionary piece, from a poet to his patron.

25. *A ballat of our lady of pete* and
28. *A ballat of our lady* are evidently examples of Marian hymns, their traditional titles preventing any attempt to differentiate them further.

23. *A ballat of steidfastness* may be compared with Chaucer's short poem, 'Lak of Stedfastnesse', with its subtitle 'Balade'.[75] Chaucer's 'Envoy', addressed to King Richard, places it well within the advice-to-princes genre. It is obvious that this poem of Chaucer's was known in Scotland since it is found in both the Bann. MS (fol. 67; STS edn, II, 164-5) and M. Folio MS (pp. 329-30; STS edn, I, 397-98). There may be similar links in the case of item 39.

26. **Item** *a ballat of disputacoun betuix the body & saull*. The title of this piece in Asloan's listing may have been derived from or be identical to the early thirteenth-century Middle English *Debate of the Body and Soul*, perhaps in a Scotticized form. In Britain it is found in several manuscripts, among which is the so-called 'Auchinleck Manuscript' now in the National Library of Scotland, dated 1330.[76] The poem edited (Laud MS 108) is 488 four-stress lines in eight-

---

[73] See pp. 101-108, and bibliographical note, xii, in *Chepman and Myllar Prints*, ed. Beattie.

[74] Similarly, Priscilla Bawcutt observes that Dunbar '...often refers to his poems as "ballatis". A *ballat* at this time could have almost any form, and deal with any subject. The term appears almost as flexible as *poem*, yet it seems to have possessed certain connotations. A ballat tended to be short, and to retain its original links with singing, dancing and music ('William Dunbar and Gavin Douglas', *History of Scottish Literature, I*, ed. Jack, 73-89, especially 75-76).

[75] *The Works of Geoffrey Chaucer*, ed. F.N. Robinson (1957; rpt. London, 1970), pp. 537 and 852.

[76] See the facsimile edition, *The Auchinleck Manuscript, National Library of Scotland, Advocates MS. 19.2.1*, ed. D.A. Pearsall and I.C. Cunningham (London, 1977). An early edition of the Middle English *Body and Soul* is in *Erlanger Beiträge zur englischen Philologie*, I, 1889, ed. W. Linow. See also O.F. Emerson, *A Middle English Reader* (1905; rpt. New York, 1950), pp. 47-64 and notes, pp. 266-70. The fact that at least seven manuscripts have come down to us testifies to its great value for the readers of its day, in OE and ME, as well as in the rest of Christian Europe. Beside the item in Adv. MS 19.2.1, there are three manuscripts each in the Bodleian Library and the British Library.

line stanzas rhyming abababab. It is a dream vision, starting 'Als I lay in a winteris ny3t'. The poet sees the body of a dead knight lying on a bier, whilst his spirit 'was oute and scholde away'. For more than fourteen stanzas it addresses the body in a speech full of reproaches. The body bemoans its bad life, but the soul says it is too late now, and that it has to go, for 'Hellehoundes here I 3elle' that are coming to fetch it. These devils are described with great gusto, the ten stanzas also detailing the way in which they torture the soul. The soul calls on Jesus for mercy, but the fiends tell him there is no help for him, and haul him off. The poet awakes in great fright, thanks Christ for his mercy, and exhorts other sinners to confess and repent. If Asloan's piece was a Scottish version of this poem, which Kittredge, for example, called 'incomparably the best embodiment of the theme that can be found in any literature', its loss is a great pity.[77]

27. *A ballat of the devillis Inquest* is in all likelihood one of Dunbar's dream-visions. This title is used by Mackenzie in his edition of Dunbar's poems (pp. 76-79 and Appendix B, pp. 238f). Both Mackenzie, and Tom Scott in his *Dunbar, A Critical Exposition of the Poems* (Edinburgh, 1966), pp. 81-84, use this title, following its use in the Bann. and M. Folio MSS. James Kinsley, however, uses the poem's refrain, 'Renunce thy God and cum to me' as title in his 1979 edition (pp. 166ff).

Discussions of the poem are found in J.W. Baxter's *William Dunbar: A Biographical Study* (Edinburgh, 1952), pp. 111-12 and Appendix VI, B, and, more recently, in P. Bawcutt's 'Elrich Fantasyis in Dunbar', *Bryght Lanternis*, ed. McClure and Spiller (pp. 162-78, especially 168ff).

29. **The buke of colkelby**. This poem is very probably the anonymous work, 'Colkelbie Sow', dating from the fifteenth century, which has come down to us in the Bann. MS. This poem is of about 900 lines in a variety of metres, and consists of a Prohemium and three Fitts. The tale is of Colkelbie, a peasant, who sells a sow for three pennies, and of the consequent hilarious adventures around the pennies and the ways in which they are spent.

Popular for the boisterous and bawdy way in which it told its story, it was well-known in its day, for both Dunbar and Douglas, for example, mention it.

The poem in the Bann. MS was recently edited by G.C. Kratzmann in *Colkelbie Sow and The Talis of the Fyve Bestis* (New York and London,

---

[77] See *Manual of the Writings in ME*, III, vii. 18e, and *Index of ME Verse*, no. 351, p. 57. Like the Asloan MS, the Auchinleck MS was in the possession of Alexander Boswell (1706-82) for a time; the latter MS was presented by him to the Advocates Library in 1744, but we do not know whether the s.-c. Auchinleck MS, like the Asloan MS, came to him through his grandfather (see note 42 above and *Sevyne Sagis*, ed. van Buuren p. 37, note 14). About the relationship of James with his father see my 'Requiem for an Angered Father', *Time and Tide: writings offered to Professor A.G.H. Bachrach*, ed. C.C. Barfoot et al. (Leiden, 1980), pp. 127-38. See also the perceptive comments of Gilbert Burnet (1643-1715) in *The History of My Own Times*, 2 vols (London, 1724-34), II, Chapter 1.

1983).[78] C.D. Jeffery discusses the poem's language in *'Colkelbie Sow*: an Anglo-Scots Poem' in *Proceedings of the Third International Conference*, ed. Lyall and Riddy, pp. 207-24. Klaus Bitterling has written 'On Some Literary Traditions of *Colkelbie's Sow*', in *Bryght Lanternis*, ed. McClure and Spiller, pp. 104-17.

30. **The buke of the otter and the ele.** Nothing is known about this piece. R.J. Lyall has remarked that it is 'one of the more tantalising titles of lost items in the Asloan MS', adding that 'it looks like a lost fable, one without Æsopic precedents as far as I can establish and perhaps a genuinely native contribution to the tradition'.[79] My own recent investigations among European fable-collections have not revealed any title like that of this piece: indeed neither otter nor eel are found among the many beasts that do appear in fable-literature.

31. **The flyting betuix Kennyde & Dunbar.** The only work of the flyting genre in Asloan's manuscript, this lost item has come down to us in the Bann. MS (fols. 147-54; STS edn, III, 44-62), the M. Folio MS (pp. 53-63; STS edn. I, 71-88) and in an imperfect Chepman and Myllar print.[80]

The poem is no. 23 of Kinsley's edition of Dunbar (pp. 76-95 and 282-98). Priscilla Bawcutt discusses the flyting in general and the present piece in particular in 'The Art of Flyting'.[81] There is also Dorothy Riach's 'Walter Kennedy's Part in *The Flyting of Dunbar and Kennedie*', *Scottish Language and Literature*, ed. Strauss and Drescher, pp. 369-79, which lists commentators on the poem from 1834 onwards. W. Baxter's *Dunbar* includes comment upon the poem (pp. 62-84).

The subsequent lost items are a group of Henryson's *Fables*. They are listed below in Asloan's ordering, with the Roman numbering in Denton Fox's edition given in parentheses after each title.

32. **Item the fablis of Esope And first of the paddock and the mouss** (XIII);
33. **the preching of the swallow** (VIII);
34. **the lyoun and the mouss** (VII);
35. **of chanteclere and the fox** (III);
36. **of the tod and the wolf** (IV);
37. **the parliament of bestis** (V), that is, 'The trial of the Fox' (see *Poems of Henryson*, ed. Fox, pp. xxxix and 234).

Fox's numbering gives the conventional sequence of these six fables in early prints (see pp. 1ff and lxxvff of Fox's edition). Neither Asloan nor Bannatyne

---

[78] See also F. Riddy's review of Kratzmann's edition in *Scottish Literary Journal*, Supplement 20 (1984), 10-11.
[79] 'Lost Literature', *Bryght Lanternis*, ed. McClure and Spiller, p. 40.
[80] See Beattie's note, p. xiii, in *Chepman and Myllar Prints*.
[81] *Scottish Literary Journal*, 10.2 (1983), 5-24. See also her 'Dunbar: New Light on Some Old Words', *The Nuttis Schell*, ed. C. Macafee and I. Macleod (Aberdeen, 1987), pp. 83-95.

observe this order. They agree in grouping III, IV and V together in that order; all three deal with the best-known tricks of the fox. Fables IX and X, in which the fox and wolf 'collaborate' in dealing with a human being, are found in neither Asloan nor Bannatyne.[82]

38. **Item** *By a palace as I couth pass*. No relationship between this poem and any known piece has so far been established, nor, as yet, is there the possibility of attaching the work to any poet's name.[83]

39. *A ballat of treuth*. Like item 23 this may be linked tentatively with Chaucer; see above. Chaucer's short poem called 'Truth' in F.N. Robinson's edition (*Works*, p. 537), originally had the title 'Balade de bon Conseyl' or some similar designation, as Robinson points out (p. 860), in most manuscripts and early prints. The 'Bon Conseyl' would fit well with the many advice-pieces found in the Asloan MS.

The following thirteen items are extant in the manuscript.
40. *The buke of the howlat*. This item, beginning 'In the myddis of may at morne as I ment', is the long poem of Richard Holland, who closes the work with his own name. Holland flourished about 1450. His fate was bound up with that of the Douglases of Moray. After their defeat by James II in 1455 and the death of Holland's patron, earl Archibald, the family had to go into exile in England, and Holland went with them. He died there, probably in 1482. In the last stanza of 'The Howlat' Holland tells us that he wrote this work for '...ane dow of Dunbar' (Elizabeth Dunbar, countess of Moray), 'Dowit with ane Douglas'.

'The Buke of the Howlat' is a diverting allegorical fable of 1000 alliterative lines in 77 thirteen-line stanzas. These, rhyming ababababc4dddc2, have a wheel and not completely consistent concatenation. The poem is also preserved in the Bann. MS (fols. 302-310^b, STS edn, IV, 128-58). We are told that the author, strolling along on a May morning, comes across an owl lamenting his ugliness. After an appeal to the pope (the peacock), the owl is given a better appearance with the help of a feather from each of the other birds (ll. 880-84). However, he becomes so 'pompos, impertinat and reprovable' (l. 924) that Dame Nature at the request of all the birds has him reduced to his former hideous shape. The moral is pointed in lines 950-87.

---

[82]For further comments and criticism see J. MacQueen, *Robert Henryson: A Study of the Major Narrative Poems* (Oxford, 1967); R.J. Lyall, 'Politics and Poetry in Fifteenth and Sixteenth Century Scotland', *Scottish Literary Journal*, 3.2 (1976), 5-29; D. Gray, *Robert Henryson* (Leiden, 1979); S. McKenna, 'Legends of James III and the Problems of Henryson's Topicality', *Scottish Literary Journal*, 17.1 (1990), 5-20.
[83]Consultation, producing negative findings, has included: *Index of ME Verse*; *A Manual of Writings in ME*; and W.A. Ringler, *Bibliography & Index of English Verse Printed 1476-1558* (London and New York, 1988).

Bawcutt and Riddy include a useful fresh edition of the poem in their *Longer Scottish Poems* (pp. 43-84; notes pp. 323-40). This includes a bibliography of studies on the poem.[84]

41. ***The talis of the fyve bestis***. The poem's first extant line in the Asloan MS is 'And in *th*is fair way persaif I wele a thing'; regrettably this unique text of 422 lines is without its beginning, and has also suffered damage to the outer top-corner of the second folio. The better part of the work is in five-stress couplets. *DOST* dates the poem c. 1500.

The five beasts, each telling a tale in front of a king (l. 61), who in the wolf's part is called '*th*is lyoun' (l. 369), are a horse, a hart, a unicorn, a boar[85] and a wolf. The hart's tale, which has incurred the damage, is in eight-line stanzas rhyming ababbaab in tetrameters.

The tales are told as pieces of advice to king Lion: that of the horse is followed by a *moralitas fabule* of fourteen lines (43-56); that of the hart by an eight-line stanza in pentameters beginning 'now be this tale I wald ȝe wnderstud...' (l. 119), whereas the tale itself is in tetrameter. The unicorn's tale concludes with 'Now be this tale ye ȝe sall wele wnderstand' (l. 269), and the boar's tale[86] with 'Nowe be this tale It may richt wele be sene' (l. 353), followed by fifteen lines of advice. The wolf tells no tale but makes an impudent complaint, and when he has been chased away, the author himself voices the advice attached, 'Now be this wolf schortly be myne awyss...' (ll. 405ff). In this section it is made clear that the four virtuous beasts stand for prudence, justice, magnanimity and 'continence' (self-restraint, chastity), the wolf for the sin of covetousness.

A good deal of attention has been paid to this poem. There is an edition by G.C. Kratzmann, *Colkelbie Sow and The talis of the Fyve Bestes* (New York and London, 1983).[87] The Unicorn's Tale is edited by D. Gray in his *Oxford Book of Late Medieval Verse and Prose* (Oxford, 1985), pp. 156-59 and 452-53.

42. ***The wplandis mouss & borowstovnis***, with the first line, 'Isope myn auctor makis mencioun' and the colophon, 'Heir endis of the twa myss', is

---

[84] An earlier edition appeared in *Scottish Alliterative Poems in Riming Stanzas*, ed. F.J. Amours, 2 vols, STS (Edinburgh and London, 1892-97). A new STS edition is being prepared by M.A. Mackay.

[85] The earlier explanation of MSc. *bair* (l. 281 and after l. 288 in 'The bares taile') as 'bear' is refuted in P. Bawcutt, 'Bear or Boar in *The Tales of the Five Beasts?*', *Scottish Literary Journal*, Supplement 13 (1980), pp. 11-12.

[86] The episode of the life of Alexander the Great used in the boar's tale is also found in the *Ludus Scacchorum*, with a very sketchy mention of it in the Asloan MS's 'Buke of the Chess', ll. 359f.; after l. 360 part of the text is missing.

[87] See also Kratzmann's 'Chaucerian Style in the Unicorn's Tale', *Scottish Literary Journal*, 5.1 (1978), 17-22, and his *Anglo-Scots Literary Relations 1430-1550* (Cambridge, 1980), 94-99, where the Unicorn's Tale is said to be 'a free adaptation of lines 1251-1502 of the twelfth-century Latin ecclesiastical satire the *Speculum stultorum* of Nigel de Longchamps, monk of Canterbury; Mapstone, 'Advice to Princes, pp. 202-43 (and her related forthcoming book); and, by the same author, '*The Talis of the Fyve Bestes* and the Advice to Princes Tradition', *Scottish Language and Literature*, ed. Strauss and Drescher, pp. 239-54.

the only one of Henryson's *Fables* that has survived in the Asloan MS.[88] That it is found here separate from its 'sisters', the lost items 32-37 (see above), may foster the assumption that Asloan entered the several items in his manuscript as they became available to him, or were submitted to him by his possible employer.

43. *The maner of the crying of ane playe*. This item begins, 'Harry harry hobillschowe'. It continues for 165 lines, after which all is missing. The work is also found in the Bannatyne MS (fols. 118^b-119^b; STS edn, II, 315-320), where it is called 'Ane littill Interlud of þe droichis [dwarf's] pairt of þe play'. There is no ascription to Dunbar there, although the question of the item's author remains contested. David Laing, according to Mackay Mackenzie, was the first to attribute it to Dunbar.[89] It was also included in Laing's two-volume edition, *The Poems of William Dunbar* (Edinburgh, 1834). In W.C. Hazlitt's re-arranged and revised edition (an amalgamation of Laing's *Select Remains* with the same editor's *Early Metrical Tales* of 1826), which was called *Early Popular Poetry of Scotland and the Northern Border,* 2 vols (London, 1895), the work was more or less firmly assigned to Blind Harry, the author of *The Wallace* (II, 11). In the STS edition of 1884-93, the poem was again attributed to Dunbar;[90] similarly in J. Schipper's edition (Vienna, 1891-94). Mackay Mackenzie puts it among 'Some Attributions (pp. 170-74)[91] as does Florence Ridley in her chapter on the Middle Scots poets in *A Manual*, ed. Hartung (IV, 1055-56). J. Kinsley in *Poems of Dunbar*, however, ignores the poem entirely. Bawcutt, in *Dunbar the Makar* (pp. 257-58) includes it among other 'anonymous' poems from the Bann. MS.

43*. Item *ane ballat of luf* was misplaced as a separate poem, even in Asloan's own list of contents, but it is properly part of item 49, 'The Maying & disport of chaucer', as Asloan calls it.
See item 49 for further discussion.

44. *The buke of schir orpheus & Eurudices his quene*, which opens, 'The nobilnes and gret magnificence', has come down to us in three witnesses. Besides the Asloan MS, there is a Chepman and Myllar print[92] and the Bann. MS version (fols. 317^b-325; STS edn, IV, 182-201). The three texts, as Craigie notes (II, vii), are printed in full in G. Gregory Smith's edition of Henryson's poems for the STS, 3 vols (Edinburgh, 1906-14), III, 26-87.

---

[88]See *Poems of Henryson*, ed. Fox, pp. 9-19; commentary pp. 201-11 and introduction pp. xli-lxxxii.
[89]*Poems of Dunbar*, p. 228. Mackay Mackenzie himself gives no source, but this attribution is found in Laing's *Select Remains of Ancient Popular Poetry of Scotland* (1822).
[90]*The Poems of William Dunbar*, ed. John Small, with W. Gregor, G.P. McNeill and Æ.J.G. Mackay, 3 vols (Edinburgh and London).
[91]G.F. Jones, in his article, 'William Dunbar's "Steidis"', *Modern Language Notes*, 64 (1954), 479-80, still takes this item to be Dunbar's work.
[92]See *Chepman and Myllar Prints*, ed. Beattie, pp. 149-68.

Speaking of the relationship of these witnesses, Fox (*Poems of Henryson*, p. cxi), concludes that 'A [Asloan] and B [Bannatyne] have, in some small measure, a common source which is not Cm [Chepman and Myllar], and that while A must be based on a text very similar to Cm, it is not copied from Cm'.

In the Asloan version, there are a few small gaps in the *Moralitas*, which Fox notes in his edition (pp. 419, 421, 422). The same fragments are lacking in the Chepman and Myllar print.

Gray, in *Robert Henryson* (pp. 209-240) discusses the great popularity of the story in the Middle Ages, giving many references; MacQueen (*Henryson: A Study*, pp. 24-44) discusses this in less detail.

45. ***The talis of the thre prestis of peblis***. This item, which begins: 'a Kyng thar was sumtyme & eike a quene', is written in pentameter couplets.

There are three witnesses extant:
1. 359 lines preserved in Asloan; the text breaks off at the bottom of fol. 262^b, possibly on account of the incompleteness of Asloan's model;
2. 115 lines found in Scottish Record Office MS RH 13/35, dated 1582-86;[93]
3. complete (1344 lines) in the Robert Charteris print of 1603.

Three priests, John, William and Archebald, foregather in their town of Peebles and have a meal together. They tell each other stories. Master John begins with the tale of the three questions (ll. 63ff). A king asks his burgesses, 'Quhy burgess barnis thryffis nocht to *the* thrid aire'. He asks his nobles, 'Quharfor and quhy and quhat It is *the* caiss sa worthy lordis was in my eldaris days…And now in 3ow I fynd þe hale contrare'. His question to his churchmen is 'quharfor It Is & quhy…'. Asloan stops here (l. 359), at the bottom of a verso.

There is an edition by T.D. Robb, *The Thre Prestis of Peblis*, STS (Edinburgh 1920). This gives a useful introduction to various aspects of the text, dating 'the completed composition some time between 1484 and 1488' (p. xiv).[94] It includes the Asloan fragment of 359 lines as well as the full text of the Charteris print (although for this Robb used the imperfect Oxford copy Douce 527). There is a facsimile reprint of the superior National Library of Scotland copy of the Charteris print, *Thrie Tailes of the Thrie Priestis of Peblis*, (Amsterdam and New York, 1969). Marion Stewart has written on the fragment, SRO MS RH 13/35, about which nothing was previously known.[95]

---

[93]See S. Mapstone, 'The Thre Prestis of Peblis in the Sixteenth Century', *A Day Estivall*, ed. A. Gardner-Medwin and J. Hadley Williams (Aberdeen, 1990), pp. 124-42. See also Mapstone, 'Advice to Princes', pp. 316-55, idem, 'Was there a Court Literature in Fifteenth-Century Scotland?', *Studies in Scottish Literature*, 36 (1991), 410-22, and C. McDonald, 'The Three Prestis of Peblis and The Meroure of Wyssdome: A Possible Relationship', *Studies in Scottish Literature*, 17 (1982), 153-64.

[94]See also C. MacDonald, op. cit., in which a post-1490 date is proposed.

[95]'A Recently-Discovered Manuscript: "ane taill of Sir colling ye kny^t"', *Scottish Studies*, 16.1 (1972), 23-39; '"King Orphius"', *Scottish Studies*, 17.1 (1973), 1-16, and *King Orphius, Sir Colling, The brother's lament, Litel Musgray*, ed. M. Stewart and H.M. Shire (Cambridge, 1973), pp. 18-21.

The question of authorship of the *Thre Prestis* has been addressed most recently by Fox (*Poems of Henryson*, p. xxviii, n. 3). He does not accept the attribution to Henryson of D. MacDonald,[96] citing the weak verbal parallels and 'the lame, padded and heavily-end-stopped couplets' of the *Thre Prestis*.[97]

46. ***The buke of the contemplatioun of synnaris*** is headed: 'Heire ffollowis The contemplacioun of synnaris appliand for euerilk day of the oulk And first for monunday of the blyndand blunder and viciouss wanyte of this warld'. It begins, 'this brevit buke of sobir quantite'.

As presented in the Asloan MS 'The Contemplacioun of synnaris' has 1552 lines in eight-line stanzas rhyming ababbcbc. The metre is not strictly five-stressed in each line. *DOST* dates the poem before 1499.

Craigie (II, viif.) states that one stanza is omitted after line 184, and notes the loss of a leaf after fol. 278, which implies a lacuna of 53 lines. He therefore numbers accordingly, placing the lacuna between ll. 880 and 934.

The author's name is not mentioned by Asloan, but it is found, as Craigie notes (II, vii), in BL MS Arundel 285, dated 1539-55: 'Heir begynnis the contemplacioun of Synnaris compilit be frer William of Touris of the ordour of the frer minouris'. This refers to the Observant Franciscan friar, William of Touris, c. 1455-c. 1505. Craigie adds that Douce records a similar ascription in Royal Society MS 275, at the end of the poem: 'ex compilatione et translatione fratris William of Touris Ordinis Minoris', but Craigie does not state where Douce says this.

There is another manuscript version of this work, MS Harleian 6919, also noted by Craigie. This dates from c. 1550. An early printed edition of the composition was Wynkyn de Worde's, which appeared in 1499. H.S. Bennett, in *English Books and Readers 1475 to 1557* (Cambridge, 1952), p. 42, includes the Prologue to the print, from which it appears that the work was commissioned by Richard Foxe, Bishop of Durham.

A recent major study of the *Contemplacioun of Synnaris* is A.A. MacDonald's 'Catholic Devotion into Protestant Lyric: the Case of the *Contemplacioun of Synnaris*', *Innes Review*, 35.2 (1984), 58-83. This dates the work between 1494 and 1499, and recognizes its considerable significance in the religious literature of late-medieval Scotland and during the Reformation, and its importance in the charting of the life of James IV. MacDonald also gives more detail on the life and career of William of Touris, whose thesis, it is argued, was that the king should remember his responsibilities and that justice for the king's subjects is conditional upon the monarch's fixing his mind on the King of Heaven and on the mercy of Christ. This study also includes an edition of the

---

[96]'Henryson and the *Thre Prestis of Peblis*', *Neophilologus*, 51 (1967), 168-77.

[97]See also the gentler exposition of the poem by R. Fulton, '*The Thre Prestis of Peblis*', *Studies in Scottish Literature*, 11 (1973), 23-46.

Bannatyne fragment.[98] See also item 56 for James IV's interest in the Observant Franciscans.

47. *Ane ballat of the passioun* is headed: 'Heir begynnis the passioun of Ihesu'. It opens 'amang thir freris in a closter' and after ninety-six lines ends 'Quod dunbar'.

The item is also found in the M. Folio MS (pp. 203-207; STS edn, I, 229-34), where it has six additional stanzas after line 96. It also appears in BL MS Arundel 285, fol. 170, with six more stanzas than Asloan's version. It is not clear why Asloan has only twelve stanzas, one of which is first deleted by a line drawn through its initial letters and then repeated in its proper place, or why he has closed in mid-page with 'Quod dunbar'. Craigie implies (II, 282) that some scribal inattention, only partly rectified, could have been involved.

The poem has eight-line tetrameter stanzas, rhyming ababbcbc. The last line in the first stanza, 'And sodanely I slepit syne', gives the work the shape of a dream-vision. All the Asloan stanzas after the first end with 'O mankynd for the luf of the'. The additional stanzas in Arundel 285 have end-lines differing from those in the first part.

Kinsley, who gives the poem the title, 'The Passion of Christ' (*Poems of Dunbar*, no. 3, pp. 7-11), includes eighteen stanzas. He calls it a 'hortatory narrative of the Passion...framed in a Good Friday vision, followed by a simple form of meditation' (p. 230).

The end-lines of the six final stanzas wanting in Asloan are slight variations on 'blissit salvatour Jesu', 'Only for luif of sweit Jesu', and 'Befoir the crose of sweit Jesu'. The last of these describes the author's awakening from the dream, 'With spreit halflingis in effray' (140), and of what follows immediately,

> Than wrayt I all without delay
> Richt heir as I have schawin to ȝow,
> Quhat me befell on Gud Fryday
> Befoir the crose of sweit Jesu.
>   (ll. 141-44).

48. *Ane ballat of our lady* begins: 'O hie empryss and quene celestiale' and ends with line 40, ' In to ȝour Innocens dovne has sent' at the bottom of a page.

It consists of five stanzas in pentameter lines rhyming ababbaba. Craigie (II, ix) notes that:

---

[98] A. A. MacDonald is preparing an edition of the poem for the Scottish Text Society. See also his 'Religious Poetry in Middle Scots', *History of Scottish Literature*, I, ed. Jack, 91-104. J.A.W. Bennett has edited the Arundel 285 text in *Devotional Pieces in Verse and Prose*, STS (Edinburgh and London, 1955). See also D.J. Young, 'A critical edition of *The Contemplacioun of Synnaris*, based on the three MSS and the printed text of 1499, with an introduction, notes and glossary', Diss. (B. Litt.) Oxford, 1955.

[a]nother copy with an additional verse is found in MS Arch. Seld. B. 24, fol. 137^b, and is there attributed to Chaucer. It is possible that Asloan's original ended imperfect, as there is no indication of a missing leaf.

However, W. W. Skeat, in his edition of Chaucer (Oxford, 1894-97, I, 47), denies this poem is Chaucer's. As to a possible missing leaf, there certainly seems to have been a loss where this poem is concerned, for the opposite leaf (between fols. 278 and 279) is clearly missing.[99] This is where we find the lost leaf noted by Craigie (II, 282), in the *Contemplatioun of Synnaris*, after the end of the 'Contemplation of Thursday', at the bottom of fol. 278^b (II, 218).

49. *The Maying and disport of chaucer*, headed 'Heir begynnis the mayng and disport of chauceir' opens 'In maij quhen flora the fresche lusty qwene' and ends, 'Heir endis the mayng and disport of chaucer per m. Io. asloan'.

The item is of 651 five-stress lines in seven-line rhyme royal stanzas with the scheme ababbcc; 93 stanzas with an envoy of two stanzas of eight lines each, rhyming ababbcbc. However, in Norton Smith's edition, from Bodleian MS Fairfax 16, the poem has 95 seven-line stanzas, with an envoy of two eight-line stanzas, one headed 'L'envoye' and the other 'Lenvoye de quare'.[100] Two stanzas (ll. 113-26) are not found in Asloan's version. That they are really missing is clear from the context, for l. 127 (Norton-Smith) refers to 'This erber' which was first mentioned in l. 125, but which is not found in the Asloan MS. It so happens that Asloan's l. 112 is at the bottom of fol. 294^b: this may be the cause of Asloan's skipping two stanzas, if his model had two more, when he turned to the top of a new page of his own manuscript.

The heading given to the poem in the Asloan MS points to an early ascription to Chaucer. This is also found in the Selden MS and the Chepman and Myllar print. Even when later the poem was given its 'proper' title, 'The Complaynt of the Black Knight', it was still thought to be one of Chaucer's works. When it was recognized as Lydgate's the poem still retained its association with 'the Black Knight'. The critic Alain Renoir, for example, uses the title 'Complaint of the Black Knight' in his 1967 study of Lydgate.[101] Editor John Norton-Smith, however, found that the original title was 'A complaynt of a louers lyfe' (p. 161), and consequently gave it this name in his edition. In 1974 William Beattie, correcting his own earlier use of the 'Black Knight' title in the 1950 facsimile edition of the Chepman and Myllar prints, corroborated this: 'The true title is [']The Complaynt of a loueres lyfe['], found

---

[99] I take it that this part of the MS was gathered in sixteens. Watermark VIII (see *Sevyne Sagis*, ed. van Buuren, pp. 16-19), occurs on fols. 263-91, one sixteen of fols. 263-78, and one of x 279-292 x with the first x lost between fols. 278 and 279, where fifty-three lines are missing.

[100] John Lydgate, *Poems*, ed. J. Norton-Smith (Oxford, 1966), pp. 47-66; notes pp. 160-76. See also *The Minor Poems of John Lydgate*, ed. H.N. MacCracken, 2 vols (London, 1911 and 1934).

[101] *The Poetry of John Lydgate* (London).

in De Worde's edition of about 1525 in the British Museum (formerly Chatsworth)'.[102]

The number of extant manuscripts of the poem is moderately high: Norton-Smith records eight (p. 160); Renoir, ten (p. 149, n. 33), and of early prints there are several. Craigie (II, ix) states that 'Asloan's copy agrees very closely with that found in MS. Arch. Seld. B. 24, and with the print by Chepman and Myllar, of 1508, STS's edition, pp. 181-203)'. It is clear in his opinion that all three have a common source, but are otherwise independent of each other. Denton Fox, however, has compared Asloan's text of Lydgate's *Complaynt* with that of Chepman and Myllar and has found that Asloan 'does contain a few superior readings'.[103]

Although this poem is now supposed to be one of Lydgate's early works, dating probably from before 1412, its appearance in the Asloan MS is in accordance with the high regard in which Chaucer was held. Lydgate, it should perhaps be remembered, frankly acknowledged Chaucer as his master: C.F.E. Spurgeon, for example, found the expression 'my master Chaucer' was used twelve times in several works of Lydgate.[104] And we must not forget that plagiarism was not the sin it became later.[105]

At the bottom of fol. 300^b is: 'Heir followis diuerss ballatis of our ladye'.
50. [*Ane ballat of our lady*]. The poem has not been given a title. It begins, 'Ross mary most of wertewe virginale' and ends with the word 'finis'.

This anonymous work, which incorporates a good deal of alliteration, has six stanzas in pentameter lines rhyming ababbcbc, with a last-line refrain: 'O mater Ihesu salue maria'.[106]

This item, as H.N. MacCracken noted in 1909, is also found in NLS Adv. MS 18. 5.14, fol. 1^b, and in the Makculloch MS in the Edinburgh University Library. MacCracken also drew attention to a fourth manuscript, 'in a book probably written in the hand of William Forrest, priest and poet, not earlier than 1581, since this date occurs in the earlier part of the book'.[107] I.C. Cunningham has edited the version in NLS Adv. MS 18.5.14. In his opening survey of all these manuscripts, Cunningham states that Asloan's text is the best, and that in all four the poem is anonymous.[108]

---

[102]Beattie, 'Some Early Scottish Books', *Scottish Tradition*, ed. Barrow, pp. 116-17.

[103]Fox, 'Manuscripts and Prints', *Bards and Makars*, ed. Aitken et al, p. 157.

[104]*Five Hundred Years of Chaucer Criticism* (London, 1914), pp. 15ff.

[105]Renoir, in his first chapter, noted that many critics of Lydgate parroted the work of their predecessors: hence their recurring complaints that Lydgate is 'unbearably long-winded and slow-moving'. To my mind this underlines their unawareness that knowledge of time-context is necessary to balanced evaluation.

[106]See, however, *Poems of Dunbar*, ed. Mackay Mackenzie, where it is included among 'Attributions', no. 87, pp. 175-77 and note on p. 230. See also T. Scott, *Dunbar*, n. 73, pp. 304f., and P. Bawcutt, 'An Index of Early Scottish Verse', *Studies in Scottish Literature*, 26 (1991), 254-70, in which she notes that the poem was 'once erroneously attributed to Dunbar' (p. 261).

[107]See 'New Stanzas by Dunbar', *Modern Language Notes*, 24.4 (1909), 110-11.

[108]'Two Poems on the Virgin (National Library of Scotland, Adv. MS 18.5.14)', *Edinburgh Bibliographical Society Transactions*, 5.5 (1988), 32-40.

51. [*Ane ballat of our lady*]. This follows the word 'finis' after the previous poem and is again untitled. Its first line is 'closter of crist riche Recent flour delyss' and ends, 'Quod kennyde'.

This is a poem of nine stanzas, each of eight five-stressed lines rhyming ababbcbc. The last line of each stanza is in Latin. These lines are:

> Sancta maria Virgo Virginum
> Sancta et Immaculata virginitas
> Quibus te laudibus referam nescio
> Speciosa facta es et suauis
> Dominus tecum gracia plena aue
> Benedicta tu in Mulieribus
> Et benedictus fructus ventris tui
> Cum Ihesu Xristo filio tuo
> O mater dei memento mei yi man

Craigie notes (II, ix) that 'It was printed by Laing in his edition of Dunbar, II, 93-95, and hence by Schipper'.[109]

52. [*Ane ballat of our lady*]. Kinsley uses this title (*Poems of Dunbar*, no. 2, pp. 4-7 and 225-30), but again the poem has no heading, and starts immediately after 'Quod Kennyde'. Its first line is 'hale sterne superne / hale Ineterne' and it ends, 'Quod dunbar'.

No other versions of this have come down to us. It consists of seven twelve-line stanzas of great virtuosity, rhyming a4b3abababcbab. The a-lines have triple internal rhyme with frequent aureation and alliteration. The c-lines are 'Aue maria gracia plena' in each stanza.[110] Bawcutt has discussed these features in valuable detail.[111]

These 'Ballatis of our ladye' are the last pieces preserved in the Asloan MS. The items mentioned after these in Asloan's Table of Contents have been lost. They are:

53. **Item *the buke of ralf col3ear*.** This item has fortunately come down elsewhere in a unique copy of one of Robert Lekpreuik's prints (1572), and a good deal of attention has been devoted to it.

Ralf Col3ear is a comic romance of the Matter of Charlemagne by an anonymous author. It was popular in Asloan's day, witness mention by Dunbar in 'Schir, 3it remember', l. 33.[112] Gavin Douglas also refers to the tale in the

---

[109]Schipper followed *Poems of Dunbar*, ed. Laing, in his *Walter Kennedy* (Vienna, 1901), no. 4, p. 17.
[110]See also *Poems of Dunbar*, ed. Mackay Mackenzie, no. 82, pp. 160-62, notes 226-27 and Scott, *Dunbar*, pp. 303-4.
[111]*Dunbar the Makar*, pp. 354-58.
[112]Dunbar begs the king to reward him for his services, just as 'Rauf Col3ard' and others have been properly rewarded for theirs, Kinsley, no. 42, pp. 124 and 320.

Palice of Honour, l. 1711,[113] and somewhat later it is mentioned in the *Complaynt of Scotland*, of c. 1550, on fol. 50.[114]

The poem is 972 lines in alliterative stanzas of thirteen lines with a wheel, rhyming abababc4dddc2.

There are three modern editions, with useful introductions and listings of other editions and studies: 'The Taill of Rauf Coilyear', *Longer Scottish Poems*, ed. Bawcutt and Riddy, pp. 94-133, notes 345-55; *The Tale of Ralph the Collier*, ed. E. Walsh (New York, 1989), and *Medieval English Romances*, ed. D. Speed, 2 Parts (Sydney, 1989), i, pp. 195-234, 303-16, and 341-42.

54. ***The buke of schir gologruss & schir gawane*** is another long poem, of 1,326 lines, written in alliterative stanzas of thirteen lines. In this it is similar to *The Buke of the Howlat* and *The Awntyrs of Arthure at the Terne Wathelyne*, with rhyme and alliteration; see *Manual*, ed. Hartung, I, 61. It was edited by F.J. Amours in *Scottish Alliterative Poems*, II, where he assigned a date to the poem of c. 1470, and that seems to be a fairly accurate supposition.[115] The *Complaynt of Scotland* mentions it (fol. 50^b). *DOST* dates it a. 1500.

55. **Item** *the disputacoun betuix the merle & the nychttingale*. See item 15 above.

56. **Item** ***Dunbarris Derige of Edinburgh & Striuling***. Though lost in the Asloan MS the poem is found in the Bann. and M. Folio MSS. The title used by Kinsley (*Poems of Dunbar*, no. 22, pp. 72-6 and 280-2), 'The Dregy of Dunbar Maid to King James the fourth being in Striviling', comes from the Bann. MS, though there (fol. 102) the king is called 'James the fyift'. It is a parody of the Office of the Dead, and takes the form of a letter to James IV staying at Stirling; the delights of Edinburgh are compared to the hardships the king is voluntarily undergoing at Stirling, where he regularly retired during Lent, to stay at the house there of the Observant Franciscans,[116] which friary he himself helped to establish.

The poem consists of 111 lines, on the whole of tetrameter couplets. The three responses are in the French *triolet*; for example, the first 'Responsio, Tu autem Domine' is:

    Tak consolatioun   in ȝour pane,
    In tribulatioun   tak consolatioun,

---

[113]*The Shorter Poems of Gavin Douglas*, ed. P. Bawcutt, STS ((Edinburgh and London, 1967), pp. 109 and 205.
[114]Wedderburn, *Complaynt of Scotland*, ed. Stewart.
[115]See E. Walsh, '*Golagros and Gawane*: a Word for Peace', *Bryght Lanternis*, ed. McClure and Spiller, 90-103, and W. Beattie, *Chepman and Myllar Prints*, pp. x-xi and 7-52.
[116]For the Observant Franciscans see R. Nicholson, *Scotland: The Later Middle Ages* (Edinburgh, 1974), p. 560; R.L. Mackie, *King James IV of Scotland* (Edinburgh, 1958), pp. 117, 119, 154, 231; D.E. Easson, *Medieval Religious Houses, Scotland* (London, 1957), pp. 109ff.

>   Out of vexatioun   cum hame agane,
>   Tak consolatioun   in 3our pane.

The last fifteen lines are in Latin.[117]

57. **Item** *ane ballat of all officeris*. It is tempting to assume that this and the following item 58 are both by Dunbar like the two preceding ones. I would then in the first case suggest that Kinsley no. 44 may have been Asloan's piece. This is a complaint, of which the first two lines are: 'Schir, 3e have mony servitouris / And officiaris of dyvers curis'. The poet subsequently enumerates thirty-three 'officers and servants' in the rest of that stanza, and beginning with l. 39 another twenty kinds of people surrounding the king. These, he says, are all rewarded suitably (l. 64), but he himself gets nothing. After this the poet vents his indignation at this injustice with intense venom in the last ten lines.

Another possible source for 'ane ballat of all officeris' might be the third book of *The Boke of Curtasye* (BL Sloane MS 1986, c. 1430-40, ed. F.J. Furnivall, EETS, London, 1868). This book is called 'De officiarijs in curijs dominorum' (pp. 309-27, that is, ll. 351-848). It is in four-stress couplets beginning: 'Now speke we wylle of officers of court, and als of hor mestiers'. However, it seems more in keeping with the other pieces in Asloan's book to assume that these missing pieces were of Scots derivation. Even so, it is important to realize that in Asloan's days there were Scottish manuscripts of Russell's book. In R.J. Lyall's list, 'Fifteenth-Century Scottish Manuscripts: A Further Revised Checklist',[118] two manuscripts of Russell's are noted: 24. BL MS Harleian 4764 (2) dated 1497 and copied out by the notary public, Richard Stirling (Striveling),[119] and 56. NLS MS Adv. 35.6.7, dated c. 1480.

58. **Item** *ane ballat of making of*. This title, given for the item in Asloan's Contents, seems to me incomplete, with possibly the word 'complaint' missing. I would suggest that this poem may have been Kinsley's no. 45. The first two lines of this poem are: 'Complane I wald, wist I quhome till / Or unto quhom darett (= direct) my bill'. These Dunbar poems that are possible sources are each given the title, '[To the King]' by Kinsley, but this is editorial only.

59. *Item ane ballat of pacience*. There is no poem among Dunbar's works, nor anywhere else so far examined, which might fit this title. There is a thematic association with the Bannatyne item on the manuscript's fol. 74:

---

[117]Bawcutt, *Dunbar the Makar*, pp. 198-203, discusses the poem in detail.

[118]Presented at the Fourth International Conference of Scottish Language and Literature (Medieval and Renaissance), Germersheim, 1984, the list is unpublished.

[119]Stirling is mentioned in van Buuren, 'Asloan', 370, and *Sevyne Sagis*, ed. van Buuren, note 2, p. 30.

> Grund the in pacience / blind nocht thy conscience
> Do thy god reuerence / Thankand him ay
> Dress the with diligence / To put away negligence
> Ceiss the with sufficence / This warld will away
> ffinis

Priscilla Bawcutt points out that this short poem is also found in John Maxwell's Commonplace Book as item 19a.[120]

60. **Item** *ane ballat of wardlie plesance*. For a lost poem with a similar title, Dunbar's 'Off lentren in the first mornyng' (Kinsley no. 59, pp. 174-5 and 351), could be put forward. In it, the ten four-line stanzas (with four stresses to the line, rhyming aabb), each end with the line 'All erdly joy returnis in pane'.

Another candidate might be M. Folio MS, p. 292 (STS edn, I, CXV, p. 341):

> This wardlie Ioy is onlie fantasie
> Quhairof no eirthlie wycht can be content
> Quho maist hes wit leist sould in it effy
> quho traists it maist maist sall him repent
> Quhat valis all yis riches and yis rent
> Sen no man knawis quha sall his tresour haif
> Preswme not gevin yat god hes to ye lent
> within schort tyme ye quhilk he thinkis to craif
> Explicit

CONCLUSION

Of the sixty pieces brought together by Asloan, thirteen are unique. Of these, nine are extant. For four we have only the titles, but these are sufficiently distinctive to permit the assumption of their unique character.

Six authors are actually named by Asloan: Ireland, Henryson, Dunbar, Kennedy, Hay and Chaucer, the latter in error for Lydgate. In the cases of six other authors, the names can be deduced from their items, since they are also found elsewhere: Alain Chartier, Lydgate, Holland, William of Touris, Trevisa (translated by Higden), and perhaps Fordun (see item 7).

Nineteen of the extant items have an explicit, nine with Asloan's name, one with that of 'G. Myll'; three state 'Quod dunbar'; one 'Quod kennyde'; one, 'Explicit ye buke of orpheus'; three, 'Heir endis' with the title of the item, and one ends with the word 'finis'. Apparently it was usual to end with some statement: in the Asloan MS only incomplete items lack an explicit. (With the 'Fyve Bestis' it is the beginning that is missing.)

---

[120]'The Commonplace Book of John Maxwell', *A Day Estivall*, ed. Gardner-Medwin and Hadley Williams, pp. 59-68 (63), and note 10.

All the verse modes used in the Asloan MS fit within A.J. Aitken's categorizations in his article, 'The Language of Older Scots Poetry'.

The surviving items are in Scots, except for 'The mayng & disport of chaucer' (49), which is Lydgate's, and 'The Cart of the World' (3), derived from Higden's *Polychronicon*, in Trevisa's Middle English translation; in both the spelling is partly Scotticized.

If Asloan's manuscript had come down to us in its original shape it would have been a hefty tome of more than a thousand pages. What is extant comprises 304 folios. It is my conjecture that there were about 232 folios now lost. For the lost items recorded elsewhere, it is possible simply to add up the number of pages they have filled in their sources, at a rate of about thirty lines per page, in Asloan's manner. For the other lost items a more impressionistic valuation is necessary.

The sequence of the items in the manuscript raises some questions. As I noted in my edition of the *Sevyne Sagis* (p. 12), a number of the pages in the MS are rather dirty. They happen to be for the most part first pages of quires, beginning new items: fols. 1, 17, 76^b, 77, 123^b, 124, 137, 167, 182 and 182^b, 213, 247, 257, 304^b. From this it appears that the part of the John Ireland item beginning with fol. 17 is not separated from the 'Buke of the Chess' by a soiled page. Items 3, 4, 5 and 6 were then written in one go; so were 9 and 10; the second part (from l. 952) of the 'Buke of the Sevyne Sagis' with 12 and 13; the 'Howlat' with 41, 42 and 43; the 'Thre Prestis of Peblis' (45) to the end (item 52, 'Hale sterne superne'). The extant pieces were thus collected in ten lots, by no means equally divided into sixteens.

The sequence of items may also be considered from other points of view. Mapstone, for instance, has argued:

> [i]t would seem that for Asloan there was some general felt distinction between the two sorts of material, and the most obvious would appear to be a separation of instructional or historical pieces, and more imaginative literature. *The Buke of the Chess* may be placed where it is simply because the poem came into Asloan's hand at that point, but he may also have felt it to be more fittingly placed amidst the more serious moral works.[121]

Of this kind of evidence there is more to consider than the placing of the rhyming 'Buke of the Chess' among prose items. The placing of the serious 'Contemplacioun of Synnaris' right after the entertaining 'Thre Prestis'; the separation of the 'Twa Myss' from the other Fables; and the location of the 'Mayng and disport' between two 'ballats' of Our Lady, all in the tenth lot (as outlined above), from fol. 257 to the end (fol. 304^b), also help to persuade me to assume that Asloan, or his exemplar, copied the items as they became available

---

[121] Mapstone, 'Advice Tradition, 1450-1500', p. 249.

to him. The place of 'The Iustis betuix the tal3eor & the sowtar', which is the middle (B) part of Dunbar's ['Fasternis Evin in Hell'] (Kinsley, no. 52, pp. 150ff), ending in mid-page with 'Quod dunbar', again supports the argument that Asloan wrote down each item as it came to him (or had come to his possible model).

When Asloan started to compile his *magnum opus*, say c. 1515, James V was a very young boy in the hands of a capricious mother and a malevolent stepfather. James was therefore not in a position to influence 'his' court. It was not until 1528 at the age of sixteen that he shouldered personally the royal responsibility. Asloan may have taken some time to finish the manuscript, on top of his notarial day's work, but it is highly unlikely that it would take him some fifteen years.[122] So far the last mention of Asloan found in the records is of December 1532, which would mean that although he lived for four years during the personal reign of James V, his manuscript must have been finished long before, and that he must have been between sixty and sixty-five by then. That most of the items in his MS are products of the fifteenth century supports this, although those by Dunbar, or some of them at least, may have been of the early sixteenth century.

Thus, though we may posit that the reign of James V belonged to the Renaissance, we can hardly say that Asloan's MS is a Renaissance miscellany. It belongs clearly to the Catholic Middle Ages. The work shows this in its composition: the majority of the items are advisory, instructive, moralizing or devotional. To break this down further: thirteen are advisory, five informative, six moralizing, together with nine fables and eight devotional works; that is, forty-three items out of sixty and practically all the extant items except possibly some of Dunbar's, are before or c. 1500.

It is true that soon after 1517 Lutheran books began to come into the country and in 1525 parliament legislated against them.[123] There is no evidence, however, that Asloan had anything to do with the movement that led to the Reformation. He was probably no longer alive when it started to matter, and at the time Asloan was at work on his manuscript John Knox was a toddler. For Asloan the issue cannot have had the disturbing quality it evinced later.

The context of the Asloan MS becomes even clearer when it is set beside those other major sixteenth-century miscellanies, the Bannatyne and Maitland MSS. Between these later compilations and Asloan is a caesura constituted by the change in religion. Bannatyne and Maitland, moreover, seem to have admired and collected poems for their value and fame as poetry, whereas Asloan or his client apparently compiled his volume of prose and verse pieces for their sober value as educatory and edifying matter, with the odd tidbit thrown in. In this Asloan was in agreement with the general tendency among the reading public of his day and that of the fifteenth century and earlier, and his items would have interested the greater part of the literate population. Devotional, moralizing and

---

[122]Craigie II, x, says: '...the writing throughout is that of John Asloan, and is very uniform in character from beginning to end.' I agree unreservedly with this view.

[123]*APS*, II, 295, and Donaldson, *Scotland: James V-James VII*, pp. 22f.

advisory literature in the vernacular was still valued when Asloan was collecting his items. Yet the entertaining items he also included point to an increasing freedom of choice for the compiler, and this is no doubt due to what the Renaissance added to civilization. With the expansion of the merchant class, furthermore, the reading public was growing. Denton Fox has noted, for instance, that while earlier works such as the *Bruce* and the *Howlat* were written for a patron, Henryson's *Fables* probably were not.[124] (The allusion to the 'requeist' of a noble lord in Henryson's prologue to the *Fables*, Fox considers to be merely emphasizing the poet's modesty.) Fox adds that Henryson's Latin quotations and legal details suggest a 'reasonably learned and sophisticated audience'. Remarking upon the foundation of the universities of St Andrews, Glasgow and Aberdeen, he comments further, that 'learning did make some headway in Scotland during the fifteenth century...; burgesses did, at least intermittently, prosper; and the very existence of works like *The Thre Prestis of Peblis* and *The Talis of the Fyve Bestis* presupposes a reading public'. Sally Mapstone has pointed out that in the first half of the fifteenth century great works like Wyntoun's *Chronicle* and Bower's *Scotichronicon* were produced for lairds and lower nobility, and has concluded that as a sign of lay literacy at the time 'this sort of material...has regularly been underestimated'.[125]

It would appear, therefore, that Asloan was a man of orthodox tastes. He collected a number of mostly instructive pieces of prose and poetry and wrote these down in his 'office' in the hours in which he had no notarial business to transact. He composed his manuscript from pieces that came into his hands in the sequence indicated by his own Table of Contents, interlarding the serious matter with some fashionable lighter-hearted poems like those of Dunbar. Whether he produced this work for himself or as a commission cannot be established. In the latter case we may take it that his patron would now and then visit him to see how the work was progressing, perhaps bringing in some new items at the same time. He cannot have been dissatisfied with the result.

---

[124] 'Middle Scots Poets and Patrons', *English Court Culture in the Later Middle Ages*, ed. V.J. Scattergood and J.W. Sherborne (London, 1983), pp. 109-27 (116-17). See also M.B. Parkes, 'The Literacy of the Laity', *Literature and Western Civilization: The Medieval World*, ed. D. Daiches and A. Thorlby (London, 1973), pp. 555-77, and G. Olsen, *Literature as Recreation in the Later Middle Ages* (London, 1982).
[125] 'Was there a Court Literature?', 413.

3

THE CORRESPONDENCE OF GAVIN DOUGLAS

Priscilla Bawcutt

Readers of Scottish poetry probably associate Gavin Douglas more closely with James IV than with James V. His translation of the *Aeneid* and the appended Thirteenth book of Maphaeus Vegius was completed not long before Flodden, on 22 July 1513, and he then seems to have resolved to devote himself to 'grave materis' (Prologue 13, 188) and to say farewell to poetry:

> Thus vp my pen and instrumentis full ʒor
> On Virgillis post I fix for evirmor
> ...
> Adew, gallandis, I geif ʒou all gud nycht,
> And God salf euery gentill curtas wight.[1]

But Douglas lived until September 1522, and thus experienced the troubled first decade of James V's reign, when—as one anonymous witness put it—'all the court was rewlit be the erle of Angus, Mr Gawin Dowglas, and the Drummondis, but nocht weill'.[2] What survive from that period of his life are not poems but letters; these writings, although not unknown to scholars, have been somewhat neglected. Yet they are extremely interesting, and for a variety of reasons: personal, socio-historical, literary and linguistic. If read in conjunction with the other letters written to or concerning Douglas, they illuminate both his personality and the murky politics of the time; and as instances of an early Scottish poet's correspondence they have not only literary value but extreme rarity.

The nine letters known to me are preserved in the Cotton Collection at the British Library, and among the State Papers at the Public Record Office.[3] They do not seem to have been utilized in the first biography of Douglas, contained in Thomas Ruddiman's *Virgil's Aeneis Translated into Scottish Verse* (Edinburgh, 1710). Sir Henry Ellis was the first to print four of the letters in his *Original*

---

[1] See the 'Conclusio', in *Virgil's Aeneid Translated into Scottish Verse by Gavin Douglas*, ed. D.F.C. Coldwell, 4 vols, STS (Edinburgh and London, 1957-64), IV, 187.

[2] *A Diurnal of Remarkable Occurrents*, ed. T. Thomson, Bannatyne Club (Edinburgh, 1833), p. 5. I emend 'erlis' to 'erle'. On Douglas's life and the letters' historical context, see P. Bawcutt, *Gavin Douglas: a Critical Study* (Edinburgh, 1976), ch. 1.

[3] On the antiquary Sir Robert Cotton, his interest in Scotland, and the way he obtained material from the official collections of state papers, see K. Sharpe, *Sir Robert Cotton* (Oxford, 1979), chapter 1 and C.G.C. Tite, *The Manuscript Library of Sir Robert Cotton* (London, 1994).

Letters Illustrative of English History (3rd series), I (London, 1846). Brief synopses of all of them were furnished in *The Calendar of Letters and Papers relating to the Reign of Henry VIII*, ed. J.S. Brewer and J. Gairdner, II, parts 1 and 2 (1864), and III, part 2 (London, 1867). But the first scholar to publish copies of all Douglas's letters, together with much other important material relating to his life, was John Small in volume I of his edition of *The Poetical Works of Gavin Douglas* (Edinburgh, 1874). Volume IV of Sir William Fraser's *The Douglas Book* (Edinburgh, 1885) also contains transcripts of these letters. Most recently Peter Beal, in his *Index of English Literary Manuscripts I: 1450-1625* (London, 1980), lists the letters and their locations, but strangely does not inform the reader that transcripts of them are available in Small and Fraser.

Small's edition of Douglas's poems has many deficiencies, but his 'Biographical Introduction' is still extremely valuable, and has by no means been superseded. The reader interested in Douglas's letters will find them here, conveniently collected together, and, for the most part, accurately transcribed. (My later quotations from the letters, although checked with the originals, are therefore given page-references to this work.) But one caveat is necessary. Small attributes to Douglas a 'Memorial', or list of accusations against the Duke of Albany (compiled in 1521), saying that it is 'undoubtedly in his handwriting'; Beal, however, calls it a scribal copy, and Douglas's authorship, although probable, is not undoubted.[4] Small also attributes to Douglas a particular letter (see lxxxix-xc), which seems more likely to have been written by Robert Cockburn, who succeeded Douglas as Bishop of Dunkeld. It is addressed to Cardinal Wolsey, signed 'Dunkeld', and dated 27 February with no indication of the year. It has much in common with Douglas's style and displays his usual hostility to the Duke of Albany; Coldwell thus follows Small in assuming that it is one of Douglas's pleas to Wolsey in 1521.[5] But the hand differs from that of Douglas's other autograph letters, and it also contains the following complaint: 'The said Lord [Albany] takkis plane part with the freir that seykis pensyoun apon my beneficie of Dunkeld, and sais largislie that I sall regret that euir I yeid that gait' (xc). Some letters from James V to the pope, Clement VII, refer to this controversy over Dunkeld; and one, written on behalf of Cockburn and dated 15 September 1524, notes that there was a report

> that the pope had granted some pensions from the fruits, in particular one to James Creichton, a Dominican. There is strong feeling about support from the church of Dunkeld for people who are of no use to the crown or the realm, and particularly in this case, in which the vows of his order incapacitate the pensioner.[6]

---

[4]Small, I, cvi; Beal, p. 3.
[5]Coldwell, I, 16.
[6]*James V Letters*, p. 104.

This would suggest that the writer of this particular letter was Robert Cockburn rather than his predecessor in the see, and that it should be dated 1523 rather than 1521. Such difficulties as to date and attribution are not unusual with letters of this period, and it seems advisable to give a brief check-list of those definitely known to be written by Douglas. He undoubtedly wrote many more that do not survive, yet there may be others in existence, so far unidentified, among the public records in Edinburgh or London, or in family papers. It seems useful therefore to document the present state of our knowledge.

A CHECK-LIST OF THE LETTERS OF GAVIN DOUGLAS

1. To Adam Williamson, 18 January 1515. Perth.
   B.L. MS Cotton Caligula, B II, fol. 374.
   Autograph: 'wyth the hand of' Douglas.
   [Small, I, xxxvi-xxxix; Fraser, IV, 68-70.]

2. To Adam Williamson, 21 January 1515. Perth.
   B.L. MS Cotton Caligula, B II, fol. 373.
   Autograph: 'Wyth my hand in hast'.
   [Small, I, xxxix-xli; Fraser, IV, 70-71.]

3. To Lord Dacre, 21 January 1515. Perth.
   B.L. MS Cotton Caligula, B I, fol. 29.
   Autograph: 'wyth hand of 3our cousyng'.
   [Small, I, xli-xlii; Fraser, IV, 72.]

4. Joint letter from Douglas and Robert Cockburn, Bishop of Ross to Cardinal Wolsey, 27 June 1517. Abbeville, France.
   B.L. MS Cotton Caligula, B VI, fol. 203.
   Hand of amanuensis, signed by Douglas and Cockburn.
   [Small, I, lxxxiv; Fraser, IV, 75, who dates 1518.]

5. To Cardinal Wolsey, 24 December, 1521. Waltham Cross.
   P.R.O. SP 49/1/127.
   Autograph: 'by the hand of' Douglas.
   Facsimile in *Facsimiles of National Manuscripts of Scotland*, ed. J. Robertson et al., part 3 (Southampton, 1867-1871), no. xiv.
   [Ellis, no. cviii; Small, I, xcviii; Fraser, IV, 82.]

6. To Cardinal Wolsey, 31 December 1521. London.
   P.R.O. SP 49/1/128.
   Hand of amanuensis, 'subscriuit' by Douglas.
   [Small, I, xcviii-xcix; Fraser, IV, 82-83.]

7. To Cardinal Wolsey, 1 January 1522. London.
   B.L. MS Cotton Caligula, B VI, fol. 246.
   Hand of amanuensis, 'subscriuit' by Douglas.
   [Ellis, no. cix; Small, I, xcix-c; Fraser, IV, 83-84.]

8. To Cardinal Wolsey, 6 January 1522. London.
   B.L. MS Cotton Caligula, B VI, fol. 506.
   Autograph: 'wyth the hand of' Douglas.
   Facsimile in Beal, *Index*, plate xi.
   [Small, I, ci; Fraser, IV, 84-85.]

9. To Cardinal Wolsey, 31 January 1522. London,
   P.R.O. SP 49/1/130.
   Hand of amanuensis, 'subscriuit' by Douglas.
   [Ellis, no. cxi; Small, I, ciii-vi; Fraser, IV, 85-87.]

ATTRIBUTIONS

- To Cardinal Wolsey, 27 February ?1521 or ?1523. Edinburgh.
  B.L. MS Cotton Caligula, B I, fol. 82.
  [Small, I, lxxxix-xc.]

- 'Memorial' of charges concerning the Duke of Albany. 1521.
  B.L. MS Cotton Caligula, B III, fols. 311-13.
  [Small, I, cvi-cxiii.]

What is the nature of these letters? Douglas is no Keats, and if we wish to know something of his ideas on poetry we must read the Prologues to the *Eneados*—themselves verse-epistles—rather than his extant letters. These, like so many others from this period, are practical and ultilitarian; their object is to give information or to get something done—to extract money, perhaps, or to request some favour. Douglas's letters have been preserved, not because of his high reputation as a poet, but because they contained information about Scottish affairs that was considered useful to the English government. (The same seems to be true of the one surviving letter of Sir David Lyndsay, which is also in the Cotton Collection.)[7] The first three, dated 1515, belong to the period when Douglas was one of several eager contestants for the see of Dunkeld. The fourth is a request for a safe-conduct through England, after Douglas, now a bishop, had participated in a diplomatic mission to renew the old alliance between Scotland and France. By contrast, the last five, all addressed to Cardinal Wolsey between 1521 and 1522, belong to the close of Douglas's life, when he was in

---

[7] See *The Works of Sir David Lindsay*, ed. D. Hamer, 4 vols, STS (Edinburgh and London, 1931-36), IV, 255.

increasingly desperate straits. The Duke of Albany's return to Scotland in 1521 was not welcome to the Douglases: the Earl of Angus fled to the Borders and formed a league with the lords Home and Somerville, while Gavin Douglas, his uncle, was sent to London in an attempt to enlist English support against Albany.

Only a handful of what must have been an extensive correspondence survives. Adam Williamson, his servant and confidant, begins one report to Douglas by stating: 'I haff raseyvyt a lettre from the Quenys Grace and iij other from your lordschipe, with on masse of lettris dyrect to Master Ihon Berry in Flandres...' (xxiii). One is made vividly aware of this 'masse' of letters posting between Scotland and Douglas's agents in London and the papal *curia*, or being despatched to Lord Dacre, warden of the Marches, or to bankers in Florence and Flanders. One is also made aware of the difficulty of getting at the truth about distant events, and distinguishing a fact from rumour. Douglas thus writes somewhat sceptically in January 1515:

> Gyf the kyng of Frans [Louis XII] be ded it is rycht euyll for bayth thir realmys. Bot heyr is arryvyt a Franch schyp the xv day of this moneth instant, quhilk proportis na thyng therof, and therfor I wondyr quha suld haf schawyn my Lordis of Consell thar syk tythyngis. (xl)

The sense of conspiracy and continual plots and counter-plots is very strong. Thus Adam Williamson writes from London: 'thei labour agens you heyr' (xxiv); and Douglas himself says of John Duncanson, a servant of Albany's who had just arrived in London, and whom he regarded as his enemy: 'he fenyeis hym famyliar wyth me, quharby perauentur I sall knaw sum pert mayr of his mynd, albeyt I knaw ellis the fynes [subtlety] of the man, and nayn mayr dowbyll in our realm' (ci). The correspondence gives intriguing glimpses into the working of the patronage system, and illustrates the necessity to lay out fees and bribes in the right places. Douglas thus writes, 'Master Adam, brother...I haf gevyn the mony [money] quhar ye bad me. Lat se quhou ye kan convoy syk a mater for your frend' (xl); and Alexander Turnbull, his agent in Rome, in turn later writes to him, 'had nocht bene the respect of that money, we suld nocht haue gotten our entent in Dunkeld' (lvii). It is clear that once Douglas had obtained his bishopric, both of his agents expected to be rewarded for their services. Williamson thus writes, 'I besek yow, be gud Lord to my sister and to hir husband Ninzeane Inglis. I luk for a prebend of Dunkeld' (lix). What is particularly striking is how again and again these letter-writers complain about the unruly state of Scotland at this time, the intense factionalism, and, above all, the lack of *justice*. Douglas indeed writes (xxxix-xl):

> I assur yow the pepyll of this realm ar sa oppressyt for lak of justyce by thevys, rubry [robbery] and other extortiones that thai wald be glayd to leyf ondyr the gret Turk to haf justyce.

In tone this resembles an anonymous poem in the Bannatyne Manuscript, addressed to the Duke of Albany and presumably written in this period, with the refrain, 'In lak of iustice this realm is schent allace'.[8]

The letters tell us much also about Douglas's personality. They reveal his ambition for high office in the Church, and specifically for promotion to Dunkeld, 'quhilk'—as he informs Williamson—'now is vacand and but pley [unencumbered by litigation], and an rycht gud Byschopry of rent and the thryd Seyt of the realm' (xxxvi). Clearly evident is his long-continued rivalry with Andrew Forman, then Bishop of Moray, whom he terms 'yon euyll myndyt Byschop of Murray' (xxxvi) and 'yon dyssatfull Byschop of Murray' (xli). They also reveal how important to Douglas were the bonds of kinship, and how strong his attachment to his own family: in one letter he requests assistance from Lord Dacre, 'sen our houssys are of the auld allyat and mekyll tendyr acquentans and kyndnes hes beyn betwyx tham of lang tym' (xlii), and in a later one he terms Albany a 'capitale and dedelie inimye to me and all my hous' (xcix). Adam Williamson, Douglas's agent, adroitly appeals to all these emotions, when urging him to a specific course of action:

> Tak good tent to my vorddis...yff yee soo doo yee shall haff in
> Scotland what promocioun that it shall plesse you to haff, and
> Murray shall be a sclayff as he begane...as I haue vryttyn afore,
> your blood is maid for euer. (xxiv)

As an illustration of Douglas's prose style I reproduce the complete text of his last surviving letter, a moving and 'dolorous' epistle, written at a time when he clearly felt isolated, and betrayed by his own party. It is freshly transcribed, and contains a few corrections of Small's readings (see ciii-cvi), such as *ony* for *only* (7), *trew cristen* for *true Christis* (22), and *devitee*, 'duty', for *deuisee* (69). Ths punctuation is my own.

> Plesit 3our Grace, sen I herd the tythingis and wrytingis of
> 3isterday I am and haif bene so dolorous and full of vehement
> ennoye that I dar nocht auentour cum in 3our presence; quhilk
> causis me thus wryte to 3our nobill Grace, beseking the samyn
> of 3oure grete goodnes to haif compacience of me desolatt and
> wofull wyght. Albeyt I grant I haif deseruyt punycioun and am
> vnder the Kingis mercy and 3ouris, not for ony falt or
> demeritt of my avne, but by raison of thair vntreuth that
> causit me labour for the wele of thair prince and thair
> 10 securite quhilk now has wrocht thair avne confusioun and
> perpetuall schayme, and has servit me as 3our Grace may
> considdyr that sollistit the Kingis hyenes and 3our Grace to

---

[8]See *Bann. MS*, II, 197-99 (fol. 78ᵛ).

wrytt and doo for thame so oftyn tymes and so largely in
diuers sortis, als wele to thair support and confort,
quhairof as now I most nedis vnderly 3oure mercy. Albeit I
dowte not bot 3our hye prudence consideris profoundly my part
thairof, and my hole trew mynde all tyme but ony
dissimulance, that in goode fayth am forthir dissauit in this
mater then ony vtheris, by raison quharof I am so full of
sorowe and displesour that I am wery of my avne lyfe, and
promittis to God and 3our noble Grace, as 3our humle seruand
and ane trew cristen preist, that I sall neuir heve or tak
way with the Duke of Albany, the vnworthy Erl of Anguse, nor
na vtheris that assistis to the said Duke, but 3our expres
commaunde and avise; nor neuer sall pass in Scotland but at
3our plesour, so lang as this wikkyt Duke is thairin or has
rewle thairof, and I traist my brother and vther my frendis
will vse my consale. Albeyt 3on 3oung wytles fwyll has runnyn
apoun his avne myscheyf be continewall persuasioun of wylye
subtile men and for lak of good counsale, schewing to him—
I dowte not—mony fen3eit lettres and wounderful terrouris:
that the Lord Hume and vtheris wald pass in and lefe him
allane, and that I wald be takin and haldin heyr, and that
Galter, the Dukis secretar, had appoyntit with the Kingis
Hienes for his distructioun, and the Duke to marye the Qwene.
I dowte not sik thingis and mekle mayr has bene sayd, and
with this the wrytings at 3our Grace causit me send furth of
Hamtoun Courte on Sant Thomas daye com not to him quhill the
xiiii day of Januar, and so he has remanyt confortles in the
menetyme, quhill the tothir subtile folkis had convoyit
thair mater. Wald God I had send ane seruand of my avne with
tha writingis or past myself with thame, in cais I had lyin
vii 3eris eftir in preson, for I fynd absence ane schrew, and
deligence with expeditioun mycht haif done grett goode.
Albeyt of verite thair may be nane raisionable nor honest
excuse that suld caus ony creature brek his lawte or promyt.
And I beseyk God that I may see him really punyst for his
demerittis and promysis brokyn mayd to the Kingis hienes and
me his vncle, and sall be glad to sollist the Kingis hienes
and 3our Grace to this effect at all my powere. Nochteles
I beseke 3our Grace to remembre the welefare and securite of
the Kingis grace of Scotland, my souerane lord and maister,
and to sollist the Kingis hyechnes to that effect, for his
Grace has maid no falt but is aluterly innocent. This is and
was my principall directioun, and caus of my hyddyr cuming,
as 3our grace full wele vnderstandis. Albeit I wald haif
procurit, as I cowth, the weylfayr of my self and frendis

>   besyde, gif thai had not wrocht in the contrar, to thair awne
>   distruccioun and myne sa fer as in thame lyis. And gif I
> 60 durst be so bald as to sollist ȝour Grace and schow quhat
>   wayis war best for the weylfare of the ȝoung Kingis grace, my
>   souerane, I wald be glayd to endeuour myself thairto at the
>   command of ȝour Grace. In cais now I dar not auentour to
>   propone na sik thingis, by raisoun that I am dissauit be my
>   most tendyr frendis in my fyrst interprys, incontrar to all
>   goode lyklyhod or naturall equite. Besekking ȝour Grace of
>   ȝour gracious ansuer and quhat ȝe will command me to doo, and
>   to be my good lorde, and to lat me knaw gif it be ȝour
>   plesour that I awayt apon ȝour seruice and doo my devitee as
> 70 I aucht of dett, and wald be glayd so to doo, for furth of
>   this realme will I not depart so lang as I may remane thairin
>   with the Kingis plesour and ȝouris, quhat penurite and
>   distres so euir I sustene, And ȝour gracious ansuer herupoun
>   in wourde, be message or writing, I humly beseyk, or gif it
>   pleis ȝour Grace I cum myself to ȝour nobill presence
>   thairfor. And God allmychty preserue ȝour Grace eternalye.
>   At the In of Carlile the last day of Januar, subscriuit
>   with the hand of ȝour humble seruitor and dolorus chaplan of
>   Dunkeld, etc.

At this time most formal correspondence—whether with foreign kings or with the papal *curia*—was still conducted either in Latin or in French. Douglas's own petitions to the *curia*, references to which in the Vatican archives have recently been noted, would certainly have been written in Latin.[9] Letters to Scottish or English correspondents were more likely to be written in native Scots. Yet in late medieval Scotland, as R.J. Lyall observes, 'there is no significant corpus of vernacular letters to compare with those produced by the Pastons, Stonors, Celys and other English families';[10] not surprisingly, there has been little attempt to study their style and language.[11] Although only a few letters written in Scots survive from before 1500, there are plenty extant from the mid-sixteenth century onwards, such as those addressed to James V by Cardinal Beaton,[12] or contained in the huge and varied collection, edited for the Scottish History Society by A.I. Dunlop as *The Scottish Correspondence of Mary of Lorraine* (1927). They provide the best parallel to this earlier body of material associated with Douglas, illustrating the range of epistolary styles and

---

[9] See Bawcutt, 'New Light on Gavin Douglas', *The Renaissance in Scotland: Studies in Literature, Religion, History and Culture Offered to John Durkan*, ed. A.A. MacDonald, M. Lynch and I.B. Cowan (Leiden, 1994), pp. 95-106.
[10] See 'Vernacular Prose before the Reformation', *The History of Scottish Literature I: Origins to 1660*, ed. R.D.S. Jack (Aberdeen, 1988), p. 166.
[11] See, however, A. Meurman-Solin, *Variation and Change in Early Scottish Prose: Studies Based on the Helsinki Corpus* (Helsinki, 1993), especially pp. 121-24.
[12] See A. Lang, 'Letters of Cardinal Beaton 1537-1541', *SHR*, 6 (1909), 150-58.

conventions available, as well as showing up Douglas's comparative distinction as a letter writer.

In tone and style there is a striking difference between Douglas's letters to Adam Williamson, which are frank, intimate, and colloquial-sounding, and those addressed to Cardinal Wolsey, which—not surprisingly—are somewhat devious and far more deferential in manner and ceremonious in style. This is apparent even in the choice of epistolary formulae, normal at the beginning and end of letters.[13] When Douglas addresses Williamson, he begins 'Brothyr master Adam, I commend me hartly to yow', and he ends with the brief 'God keyp yow' (xxxix, xli). But when he writes to Wolsey, deference is indicated by greater circumlocution: in one letter, for instance, he salutes him with 'My lord, in all humble and dew maneyr I recommend my lawful seruyce onto your grace', and takes his leave with 'And the blyssyt Lord preserue your grace in lang and eternall prosperite' (xcviii); in another he writes 'And the haly Trinite preserue your grace eternaly' (xcix). David Beaton regularly uses the same valedictory formula, in one letter to James V Scotticizing it to 'And sanct Andro preserue 3oure grace eternally'.[14] This florid and redundant style is marked by the use of 'doublets', or balanced pairs of near-synonyms. The device is very common in *The Eneados*, but it is not peculiar to Douglas, and characterizes much verse and prose written at this time. It was common, for instance, in Caxton, whose prose Douglas despised: 'Hys febil proys beyn mank and mutulate'.[15] In the letter quoted above there are many such pairs, of nouns—'tythingis and wrytingis' (1), 'falt or demeritt' (7-8)—and of adjectives—'desolatt and wofull wyght' (5-6). This latter phrase has a slightly poetic ring, and recalls the way in which Dido's sister, Anna, speaks of herself as a 'dissolate wight' (*Eneados*, IV.xii.66; cf. IX.v.150).

The syntax of Douglas's prose resembles that of his verse. It is characterized by the piling up of dependent clauses—temporal, relative, concessive—and is sometimes difficult to punctuate. An instance in this letter is the repeated use of clauses that start with a vaguely concessive *Albeyt*; I here treat them as separate sentences, in an attempt to clarify the structure and sense. The series of noun clauses (32-35), apparently in apposition to 'terrouris', is also striking. Yet this complicated, Latinate, and not invariably successful syntax is sometimes effectively varied; by the simple and affecting exclamation, 'Wald God I had send ane seruand of my avne with the writingis...in cais I had lyin vii 3eris eftir in preson' (41-43), or by the striking inversion—'furth of this realme will I not depart' (70-71).

---

[13] For valuable discussion, see two articles by N. Davis: 'The *Litera Troili* and English Letters', *Review of English Studies*, n.s. 16 (1965), 233-44; and 'Style and Stereotype in Early English Letters', *Leeds Studies in English*, n.s. 1 (1967), 7-17.
[14] Lang, 'Letters of Beaton', 158.
[15] See *Eneados*, V Prol. 51; cf. also 1 Prol. 138-45.

The spelling of this and other letters is sometimes anglicized, but—as might be expected—there are none of the striking archaisms or southern English forms and words that are so characteristic of Douglas's poetic style. Indeed there are many distinctively Scottish features, such as the use of *at* as a relative pronoun (37), or the *-is* ending of the verb in such expressions as 'I am wery...and *promittis* to God' (20-21), or 'na vtheris that *assistis* to the said Duke' (24). There are several peculiarly Scottish idioms, such as the phrase 'really punyst' (47); this apparently means 'punished in respect of one's property, as by fines or confiscation' (see *DOST, really,* adv. 2, which does not include this particular citation).

This letter, like others, hurls brief pungent insults (reminiscent of the flyting tradition) at those who have offended Douglas; the exasperation with his nephew is clear in '3on 3oung wytles fwyll' (28). Here, as elsewhere, Douglas sometimes uses a proverb to emphasize his point: 'I fynd absence ane schrew' (43) does not seem otherwise recorded in Scots, but is found in English usage (see Whiting, A 17[16]). It is worth noting that Douglas's correspondents, Adam Williamson and Alexander Turnbull, are particularly fond of sprinkling their letters with proverbs and axioms: 'the deid preves the man' (lviii; cf. Whiting, M 57); 'A dum man gettis seldum land' (lix = Whiting M 276); 'Today a frend, tomorn a foo' (xxiv; cf. Whiting, F 635); 'This storm is sa wiolent that it ma nocht lest' (lxxiii = Whiting, S 798). Turnbull attributes one cynical saying to the Italians: 'The Italianis has ane proverbe—*fidelis seruus asinus perpetuus*'. What follows shows that this is a ploy to ingratiate himself with Douglas: 'I waite that I serf na Italiane; I traist sickirlie that I serve ane noble, discret and kind lord, the quhilk was neuir unkind to nane that deseruit kindnes nor reward' (lvii-lviii).

Douglas did not live to see the brief revival and subsequent overthrow of his own 'hous' in the 1520s, nor did he witness the flowering of the arts associated with the personal reign of James V. This correspondence shows him to have been as self-interested as most ambitious churchmen of the time. Yet when he speaks of the young James, then a boy of nine—'I beseke 3our Grace to remember the welefare and securite of the Kingis grace of Scotland, my souerane lord and maister...for his Grace hes maid no falt but is aluterly innocent'—the words have a tenderness and loyalty that sound genuine. No one, on the strength of these letters, is likely to claim that Douglas's prose is as impressive as his poetry; what they do show is that, in either medium, he is a forceful and eloquent writer.

---

[16] References are to B.J. and H.W. Whiting, *Proverbs, Sentences and Proverbial Phrases from English Writings Mainly before 1500* (Cambridge, Mass., 1968).

4

THE KING IN HIS HOUSE:

THREE ARCHITECTURAL ARTEFACTS BELONGING TO THE REIGN OF JAMES V

Helena M. Shire[1]

In earlier days a great foundation or building was created in such a way that in its design it 'belonged' to cosmic order. It might signify its belonging also to worldly order—to the pattern of powers on earth. (The great example of the first is the cruciform church. For affinity to worldly hierarchy the coat of arms above a castle gateway.) This it might do through its shape or form through use of symbol prominently displayed or reticently sited. Such a symbol was often, so to speak, the headdress. For a person in daily life then, the headdress, the covering of the noblest part of the body, was significant of power or rank, status or calling. For a great building such headdress could be the crown or its variant, the tiara of the Holy See, the cross or the weathercock or both together. Certain important foundations of the epoch of King James V profess in one of these ways their allegiance to the greater power structure, terrestrial or cosmic, indicating their place in it as we shall see. In so doing they refer to and define the nature of the *regnum* of the King of Scots, for kingship in itself was an aspect of cosmic order.

Two very fine exemplars companion one another in the small northern burgh of barony, Old Aberdeen.[2] The College founded in 1490 as of 'St Mary in the nativity' by Bishop William Elphinstone (but later coming to be known as the royal college, or the King's College of Aberdeen)[3] wears on its tower a stone crown as of the Emperor of the Holy Roman Empire. At the other end of the little town stands the ancient Cathedral of St Machar, whose two pointed towers, or spires, at its west end are triple-cupped, in design suggesting the triple crown of the Holy See. The two foundations were linked. The Bishop in St Machar's Cathedral was Chancellor of the University. They were, moreover, both Marian

---

[1] The title, notes and references, and small additions to the text requested by Helena Shire, are by Janet Hadley Williams. Dr L. Macfarlane is warmly thanked for his expert advice to both of us.

[2] See L.J. Macfarlane and A. Short, *The Burgh and Cathedral of Old Aberdeen 1489-1989*, Friends of St Machar's Cathedral Occasional Papers No. 12 (Aberdeen, 1989), pp. 3-4, in which the significance of this privilege, granted to Aberdeen in 1489, is discussed in detail.

[3] W. Orem, *A Description of the Chanonry, Cathedral, and King's College of Old Aberdeen, in the years 1724 and 1725* (Aberdeen, 1791), p. 146.

in dedication, Bishop William Elphinstone having a special devotion to the Blessed Virgin.

It is my purpose to look into the nature of three distinguished architectural artefacts in Scotland that belong to the reign of James V and show how their design serves to reflect or celebrate the nature of his kingship, the concept of it entertained by his people, by certain eminent subjects of his concerned in the design and execution of the building, or held by the king himself. They are—the heraldic ceiling above the central nave in St Machar's Cathedral, Old Aberdeen, completed by 1520 when the king was a minor, the exterior of 'The King's House', the new palace he built at Stirling about 1540 and, to a lesser degree, the ceiling within that new palace, which graced the royal presence chamber. To all three could be given the title 'Style King James V' and all are of the highest distinction in themselves, idiosyncratic and individual or unique, unprecedented in Scotland or unparalleled at the time.

I

THE HERALDIC CEILING OF ST MACHAR'S CATHEDRAL, OLD ABERDEEN, C. 1520

The Cathedral of St Machar in Old Aberdeen is an early foundation indeed. The legend goes that in the sixth century Macarius or Machar was sent by St Columba to build a church at a place where a river approaching the sea formed a crook like that of a bishop's staff. He found it here, near the mouth of the River Don.[4]

The building that stands today dates from the later fifteenth century. It is of granite, though the twin towers at the west end are formed of Morayshire freestone in their upper reaches. It stands incomplete, a nave and transepts only. Perhaps indeed the whole cathedral-church as planned never reached completion. In the earlier sixteenth century it extended to a chancel, transept and choir and later a great central tower was added. Certainly the fall of the central tower in the seventeenth century has left a building that is a partial monument only to the imagination, energy and achievement of the founders and the patrons who followed after them.

The nave with its north and south aisles is complete and of most spacious dimensions. The walls of granite and the roof (of timber) were in place by 1500 under Bishop William Elphinstone. The question then arose: in what manner

---

[4]T. Innes, *The Civil and Ecclesiastical History of Scotland AD LXXX-DCCCXVIII*, ed. G. Grub, Spalding Club (Aberdeen, 1853), p. 194.

should the central nave be ceiled? Granite was deemed a stone whose heaviness and density rendered it unsuitable for vaulting, so a flat ceiling was decided on (in contrast to several fine vaulted wooden ceilings of the time)—a flat ceiling of wood. Such is the explanation usually accepted but it is worth noting that this was the very time of transition from vaulting to the flat ceiling elsewhere, in noble secular building on the continent—for instance in Cracow, Poland, in that most prestigious of new royal palaces erected within the precincts of Wawel Castle. (This is not the only link between the Wawel and building in the style King James V.)

The ceiling occupies the whole space over the central nave. It measures 33' by 136'.[5] It is of wood throughout—panelled—the surface of the wood being painted. And throughout its length run three columns of coats of arms, carved, of powers sacred and secular, in Europe and in Scotland at the time. It is unique in its imaginative scope as in its colourful and intricate workmanship.

This masterpiece of ecclesiastical architecture was described and its nature expounded a hundred years ago by the Principal of the university, William Duguid Geddes (later Sir William) and Peter Duguid. A volume of the New Spalding Club is devoted to their study, *The Heraldic Ceiling of the Cathedral Church of St Machar, Old Aberdeen* (Aberdeen, 1888). Their powers of exposition, vast scholarship and sympathetic insights are so remarkable that I do not hesitate to draw on them at every turn—the more so because the work is not easily accessible. There is, however, a pamphlet published by the Friends of St Machar's Cathedral (Occasional Papers No. 2) that gives a clear account with interesting historical details, by David McRoberts (Aberdeen, 1981).

The project of a flat ceiling on a grand scale for an eminent ecclesiastical building offered a challenge and a superb opportunity. How should it be devised so that it should play its part in the design of the cathedral as a whole? A ceiling was a covering above, a canopy, a *celure*. (There may indeed be a connection between the word 'ceiling' and *cælum*, the heavens.) It could not but body forth in some sense the canopy of the heavens. It should then fittingly feature the powers of the heavens whether spiritual orders of cherubim, thrones, dominations or astronomical manifestations of planets or zodiacal signs. Both such modes of celebration, of decoration for beauty or for edification, of the canopy appear in architecture of the time elsewhere.

But the Bishop and his architectural mentors, or his colleagues in chapter decided otherwise. What is celebrated here and displayed in splendid array is the

---

[5]For the latest plan see R.G. Cant, *The Building of St Machar's Cathedral*, Friends of St Machar's Cathedral, Occasional Papers No. 4 (Aberdeen, 1979), p. 2, considered by Dr Macfarlane to be more accurate than Kelly's estimate in *Logan's Collections*, ed. J. Cruikshank, Third Spalding Club (Aberdeen, 1941), p. 141.

powers of Christendom on earth. 'The shields of the earth belong unto God' (Vulgate, Psalm 46.10).

Using the rich language of heraldry the design chosen presents a panoply of the powers of western civilization through their shields and crests. This heraldic ceiling after many vicissitudes was completed under Bishop Gavin Dunbar in 1520-1521 when King James was still a boy. The world order indicated by the display is therefore the world order into which he was to enter in a few years to play his part as young monarch. It has been pointed out that the timing for such a design was particularly happy: in that year or two peace prevailed between the two great powers, the papacy and the Holy Roman Empire. The account of Geddes and Duguid (pp. 15-16) runs thus:

> On the pannelled ceiling at the intersections of the mouldings or cross-bars occur the several series of heraldic shields, which are arranged in three parallel longitudinal rows, sixteen in each row, and all carved in low relief. Each shield has proceeding from it on either side an escrol on a lighter ground than that of the ceiling, bearing in black text with red inital letter the official designation, in Latin, of the dignity represented. The order of dignity advances as you proceed from the west eastward; the extreme west is occupied by the three *local* corporate bodies, two municipal and one academic. The place of honour for the highest *European* dignitaries—a trio with shields having their several devices upon a ground of imperial *gold*—is at the extreme east, where the nave joined on to the cruciform and more sacred portion of the building. Further, the trio at the extreme west is in remarkable symmetry with the trio at the extreme east. In each case, two temporal or secular powers flank at either end of the nave a spiritual or intellectual power, and the place of honour, such as is given to the Pope between Emperor and King, is correspondingly assigned to the University, which stands flanked at the west end by the two municipal corporations.

The whole design is a cosmos, or system beautiful in its order. As with any artefact of this epoch, to read it aright we need to note not only what is included and where, the relation of part to whole and part to part, but also what is absent and why that may be.

As befits an expression in an ecclesiastical context of European Christendom, the central column is of the power of the Church on earth. At its head is the coat of arms of the Pope, Leo X—his personal arms as Giovanni de' Medici—though the 'keys of office' appear behind. After him the highest Christian dignitary of Scotland, the Archbishop of St Andrews, then the Archbishop of Glasgow and thereafter the bishops of King James' kingdom, in a due order and precedence. After them, the Prior of St Andrews as representative of monastic foundations of eminence, and then the University of Aberdeen, founded but recently in the King's father's time, as *Collegium Sanctae Mariae in nativitate.*

ALTAR (East)

NORTH ROW	CENTRE ROW	SOUTH ROW
ᐁ Holy Roman Emperor *Charles V*	ᐁ Pope Leo X *Giovanni de' Medici*	ᐁ King of Scotland *James V*
ᐁ King of France *Francis I*	ᐁ Abp of St Andrews *Andrew Forman*	ᐁ St Margaret of Scotland
ᐁ King of Spain (Leon and Castile) *Charles V*	ᐁ Abp of Glasgow *James Beaton*	ᐁ Duke of Albany *John Stewart*
ᐁ King of England *Henry VIII*	ᐁ Bishop of Dunkeld *Gavin Douglas*	ᐁ Earl of March unheld
ᐁ King of Denmark *Christian II*	ᐁ Bishop of Aberdeen *Gavin Dunbar*	ᐁ Earl of Moray *James Stewart*[6]
ᐁ King of Hungary *Louis II*	ᐁ Bishop of Moray *James Hepburn*	ᐁ Earl of Douglas unheld 1520
ᐁ King of Portugal *Emmanuel*	ᐁ Bishop of Ross *Robert Cockburn*	ᐁ Earl of Angus *Archibald Douglas*
ᐁ King of Aragon *Charles V*	ᐁ Bishop of Brechin *John Hepburn*	ᐁ Earl of Mar unheld 1520
ᐁ King of Cyprus vacant	ᐁ Bishop of Caithness *Andrew Stewart*	ᐁ Earl of Sutherland *Adam Gordon*
ᐁ King of Navarre *Henri II*	ᐁ Bishop of Galloway *David Arnot*	ᐁ Earl of Crawford *David Lindsay*
ᐁ King of Sicily *Charles V*	ᐁ Bishop of Dunblane *James Chisholm*	ᐁ Earl of Huntly *Alexander Gordon*
ᐁ King of Poland *Sigismund I*	ᐁ Bishop of Argyll *David Hamilton*	ᐁ Earl of Argyll *Colin Campbell*
ᐁ King of Bohemia *Louis I*	ᐁ Bishop of Orkney *Edward Stewart*	ᐁ Earl of Errol *William Hay*
ᐁ Duke of Bourbon *Charles of Bourbon*	ᐁ Bishop of the Isles ? vacant	ᐁ Earl Marischal *William Keith*
ᐁ Duke of Gueldres *Charles of Egmond*	ᐁ Prior of St Andrews *John Hepburn*	ᐁ Earl of Bothwell *Patrick Hepburn*
ᐁ Burgh of Old Aberdeen	ᐁ University of Aberdeen	ᐁ Royal Burgh of Aberdeen

---

[6] James Stewart, natural son of James IV, was the current title holder, but the arms depicted are those of Randolph, nephew of Robert the Bruce; see Geddes and Duguid, *Heraldic Ceiling*, pp. 40 and 107.

It is of note that the transition from the Pope to the Archbishop of St Andrews is direct. No intervening power intrudes, though intervention from English Archbishops was frequently offered and pressed. Scotland, then, in terms of the Church, is under the simple jurisdiction of the Holy See. Independence from England is here firmly indicated.

To the north side of this column of spiritual powers runs the corresponding column of secular potentates—here of Europe as a whole. Naturally at its head stands the Holy Roman Emperor, Charles V. The double-headed eagle is there but the arms are those of that high office, not of Charles V personally. (Probably his personal blazon of King as well as Emperor was too elaborate to be easily depicted and convey its message clearly.) Behind him, a column of kings is ordered according to their status and their relations with the kingdom of Scotland. First comes the King of France—then the King of Spain (of Leon and Castile, that is) who was Charles V. (France and Spain rank before England in diplomatic status.) Only after these the King of England, Henry VIII, who suffers the indignity, subtly conveyed in heraldic terms, of blazoning his three leopards only, without the quartering of the French fleur-de-lys which he affected, to indicate his claim on France. The King of Denmark, Christian II, was not only a royal great-grandfather of King James V, he was also the master of a kingdom that had close trade connections with Scotland. Of the farther reaches of Europe into Slavonic lands only Poland and Bohemia appear, as belonging to the world of the Catholic papacy.

After the kings, two dukes, the first of Bourbon and Vendôme, the second of Gueldres, both of whom had had or in the future might form marital ties with a Stewart king. Then the apt tailpiece: the arms of the Burgh of Old Aberdeen. The descent of secular power is traced out and the connection aptly made to the region, honouring the small but ancient Burgh of Barony.

The positioning of the columns on either side of the central one is subtly done, and like so much else in the ordering of this array, thought-provoking. As we look towards the east, this column of secular powers may well be placed on the *left* hand of the central column, on the sinister or not-so-noble hand in heraldic terms. But in ecclesiastical or liturgical bearings, the north takes precedence over the south: the succession of kings in Europe rightly takes precedence over the secular dignitaries of Scotland, the king and his 'peers'. There would be no cause for these to demur, however: the southern column could also be gratified in its dexter or nobler position heraldically considered.

This southern column is headed by the King of Scotland, the young James V. As he was a boy at the time there was no consort in question and a careful avoidance of the Queen Mother, Margaret Tudor, is noticeable. (She had by this time married a Douglas and was contending the regency.) In her stead appears the shield of another Margaret, the Saint of Scotland, wife of Malcolm Canmore.

Then the Duke of Albany, a royal Stewart, acting Regent of Scotland in 1520. Thereafter the earls of Scotland, again in a due order of precedence or preference. And the tally of secular powers is rounded off by the arms of the Royal Burgh of Aberdeen. Even in this brief account something may be gathered of the intricacy of pattern, of comparative judgements that have been made, the eloquence of precedence or of juxtaposition. (On this the study of Geddes and Duguid, pp. 17-69, makes absorbing reading.)

It has been noted that the three-column procession of the powers of Christendom on earth is moving eastwards towards the site of the high altar. Indeed as one stands below with head bent back, observing, they seem to move. (A similar illusion prevails in Blythburgh, where the angels extending from the central bosses of the tie-beam roof, looked at in this way, take wing and seem to fly.)[7] The integration of the heraldic ceiling with the design of the church as a whole may be discerned in farther aspects—though these are lost to us now. On the pulpit was carved a very fine rendering of the instruments of the Passion, in heraldic terms the arms of *Christus armiger*, Christ the knight. (The panel was hacked out by a local reforming vandal and was among the looted treasures lost at sea along with the stolen cathedral bells.)[8] The heraldic and chivalric interest extends in time and place. The *arma Christi* appeared again on the tomb of Bishop Gavin Dunbar who died in 1532 (but these also were hacked out and destroyed).[9]

Beyond the high altar the reredos (erected by Elphinstone or an immediate predecessor), was considered one of the finest pieces of workmanship in Scotland—'and had few equals anywhere'.[10] It was very lofty, reaching almost to the roof. It was surmounted by three great timber crowns. (Reredos and crowns were destroyed, in the 'downtaking' ordered by Mr William Strachan, minister of the Cathedral, and Dr William Guild in December 1642.)[11] (Which crowns they were is not on record. They are unlikely to have been a 'Three Kings' trio. They are very likely, in my opinion, to have been, again, the crowns of Pope, Emperor and King of Scots.) Thus overhead the procession of the three columns of shields

---

[7] See the *Guide*, Holy Trinity, Blythburgh ([Halesworth], 1991), pp. 7-8. (Miss A. Beaufoy, of Ipswich, Suffolk, gave valuable assistance in the verification of Blythburgh's Holy Trinity as the church in question; Professor and Mrs C.A. Mayer, and Dr A. Gardner-Medwin provided additional very helpful information.)

[8] See D. McRoberts, 'Material Destruction Caused by the Scottish Reformation', *Essays on the Scottish Reformation*, ed. D. McRoberts (Glasgow, 1962), pp. 415-62 (p. 444, n. 129); P.J. Shipton, 'Bells Restored to St Machars', *The Restoration of St Machar's Cathedral*, ed. J.H. Alexander et al., Friends of St Machar's Cathedral Occasional Papers No. 14 (Aberdeen, 1991), p. 27.

[9] See Orem, *A Description*, p. 132; Geddes and Duguid, *The Heraldic Ceiling*, Appendix II, p. 147 and McRoberts, 'Material Destruction', p. 456. See also C. Carter, 'The *Arma Christi* in Scotland', *PSAS*, 90 (1956-57), 116-29 (esp. 118 and 119).

[10] K.E. Traill, *The Story of Old Aberdeen* (Aberdeen, 1929), p. 74.

[11] See Orem, *A Description*, pp. 132-33 and J. Spalding, *Memorialls of the Trubles in Scotland and in England 1624-1645*, II (Aberdeen, 1851), 216-17.

attained a fitting climax.¹² The heraldic ceiling itself was beyond the reach of vandals. *Laus deo*. And above the high altar was the beautiful image of Our Lady of Aberdeen, bearing on her arm not only the Christ child crowned but carrying her sceptre and crowned as Queen of Heaven, the figure of succour and of good success. (This wonderful image was sent abroad for safekeeping after 1625, and is found in the church of Finistère in Brussels.)¹³

It should also be held in mind that the interior walls of the cathedral we know were brightly painted and who can tell how elaborate a co-ordination there may not have been between designs on the walls and the *sens* and *matière* of the splendid and significant canopy above.

The theme of 'sovereignty' and of crowns of great splendour must have dominated the eastern aspect of St Machar's Cathedral. Scrutiny of the columns on the heraldic ceiling reveals the importance of headdress. Where it is apposite the headdress of the potentate is indicated in his crest. The Pope has his tiara, the Emperor his notable crown, closed and two tier—as the sign of overall *imperium*, the bishop his mitre. Other kings have the open crown or circlet only—except the King of Scots. Heading his own column, and therefore not figuring in the other column, under, or behind the Emperor, his coat of arms is surmounted by the crown of Scotland. The 'closed crown' of imperium. A certain national independence and a certain claim to *regnum* of a special nature can be read into the general intricate disposition of shields in the array of Christendom. It is expressed also in the nature of the headdress.

For a hundred years in Europe the nature of the crown of individual kings of nations had been a matter of interested debate. King James III of Scots had asserted the nature of his *regnum* by moving from the open circlet of earlier times to the closed crown. It appears on his coinage. The closed crown of *imperium* laid claim in several ways to independence of authority in the king: it indicated that he was not subject to or vassal of any other secular power (though acknowledging in his own way the overall sway of the Emperor). In particular the constant claims by England that in one sense or another Scotland was its vassal continued to anger the northern kingdom. Secondly, his power as king within his own kingdom was absolute. Thirdly, that kingdom of Scotland being composed of regions disparate in language, in cultural background, as in historical development, it was important that the *regnum* should be understood as paramount: his was in a sense rule over an empire of peoples. And lastly the closed crown of imperium could be taken as a reminder that Scotland had never

---

¹²L.J. Macfarlane, in 'The Liturgical Significance of Gavin Dunbar's Ceiling', Friends of St Machar's Cathedral, *Annual Report 1992* (Aberdeen, 1992), pp. 7-9 (9), agrees that Alexander Galloway was inspired by the crowns of the reredos to design the heraldic ceiling so that all the shields were orientated towards the high altar and the reredos, after Psalm 47, vv. 9-10.

¹³Orem, *A Description*, p. 132 and D. McRoberts, 'A Scottish Madonna in Brussels', *Scottish Art Review*, 13.2 (1971), 11-14.

been conquered by the Romans—unlike its neighbouring kingdoms on the continent. Recognition of the sway of the Emperor of the Holy Roman Empire could be regarded therefore as on a different footing. (I wonder if this somewhat extreme vaunt may not be relevant to the heraldic choice of the Emperor's arms on the St Machar ceiling—and the significance of the siting, as we saw. The King of Scots in the array devised is not placed among the followers of the Emperor. And it is the shield of office of Emperor that is presented, not the personal arms of Charles V.)

Although the King was only seven years old when the ceiling was perfected, it preserves and celebrates an image of the world of his time and of his place in it.[14] We do not know for certain who devised the ceiling, but we have some interesting information. We know that two powerful Bishops of Aberdeen, first William Elphinstone and then Gavin Dunbar, had a major hand in the matter. And there is evidence to suggest that two local men were closely connected with its design and creation, James Winter and Alexander Galloway.

The tradition that the craftsman who built St Machar's ceiling was an Angus man, James Winter, is recorded as early as 1791 by W. Orem, in *A Description of The Chanonry, Cathedral and King's College of Old Aberdeen* (p. 61). If this is correct, Winter was highly skilled, for the assembling, carving and colouring of the heraldic and other decoration was a major project. As for the ceiling's designer, the very likely local name is Alexander Galloway's. Galloway was a distinguished canon lawyer, with considerable artistic and administrative talent. He was rector of Kinkell, Official of the diocese, Elphinstone's commissioner of works and eventually, university Rector.[15] He may have been one of the small team that sought local material for the compilation of the Aberdeen Breviary;[16] he was certainly closely involved in or responsible for many architectural projects. Among these were the permanent bridge over the Dee, the Greyfriars' Church, and the beautiful sacrament houses at Auchindour, Kinkell, Kintore, Dyce and King's College Chapel.[17] For the latter College's Rector, Galloway may have designed the Mace of Office; it was certainly his gift.[18]

Yet there was surely an association of several exceptional men behind the achievement of the heraldic ceiling. Besides Galloway, and Bishops Elphinstone and Dunbar themselves, it must be assumed that the Lyon King of the day, Sir

---

[14] L.J. Macfarlane, *William Elphinstone and The Kingdom of Scotland 1431-1514* (Aberdeen, 1985), provides excellent discussion of this world and time. Macfarlane notes (p. 432) that Elphinstone was made a guardian of James V in 1513.
[15] Macfarlane, *William Elphinstone*, p. 220.
[16] Ibid., pp. 242-43.
[17] Ibid., pp. 267-69, 256, 269, and 335. See also Macfarlane, 'Liturgical Significance', p. 8.
[18] See A.J.S. Brook, 'An account of the maces of the Universities of St Andrews, Glasgow, Aberdeen and Edinburgh', *PSAS*, 26 (1892), 440-514.

William Cumming of Inveralochy, advised,[19] though there are no surviving records of it. Hector Boece, first principal of the University of Aberdeen, biographer and historian, lecturer in theology and arts, showed a very close interest in the ceiling. In his *Murthlacensium et Aberdonensium Episcoporum Vitae*, he describes St Machar's bell-towers, and reports as he ends his book, 31 August 1521, that the ceiling was largely completed. It does not seem unlikely that he was 'one of the historical advisers for to the project'.[20] And there were others, such as James Brown, Dean of the Chapter, whose input in the very early days of the St Machar's planning would have been valuable. In Dean Brown's case, we know from his beautifully illuminated Book of Hours of his interests in the 'Scottis use' of the liturgy and in artistic work of the highest quality.[21]

The King, then, in the devising of this cosmos traced in heraldic language, had himself no part. We are fortunate that in this case it is possible to glimpse the 'committee' or council of minds whose enthusiasm and skills went to evolving and perfecting it. It makes it the easier to envisage a posse of minds and skills for the creation of the other two masterpieces to be reviewed, though in them the king himself has patently been concerned and at the heart of the matter.

Did King James V see and approve this picturing of his world and of kingship in the splendid interior of St Machar's Cathedral, its procession of shields overhead, the 'three great timber crowns' surmounting the reredos, the other sacred heraldry in the carving and above the altar the most lovely image of the Queen of Heaven, splendidly crowned and sceptred, her crowned child on her arm?[22] In 1541 King James rode with his Queen Marie and spent a week in Old Aberdeen lodged in King's College.[23] Both were in black for the recent deaths of two young princes. Our Lady of Aberdeen, of succour and of happy outcome, cannot have gone unregarded.

When we come to consider the panache of King James V's own building programme we should bear in mind not only the impact, on a King of a poor country, of Renaissance France with its rising splendours under Francis I, but also of the works that were going forward in Scotland in the reign of his father James IV and in his own boyhood. These were ensembles of richness and imaginative scope, with distinguished design and craftsmanship—especially in carved and coloured wood—coming into being, for example, in St Machar's

---

[19]In 1506, Cumming, who was possibly related to the Aberdeen Medicinar, Mr James Cumming, had granted half of his lands of Audcall and some feu duties from Inveralochy to King's College for the support of a theology student. See Macfarlane, *William Elphinstone*, p. 340 and note, and Orem, *A Description*, p. 157.
[20]See G. G. Simpson and J. A. Stones, 'New Light on the Medieval Ceiling', *The Restoration*, ed. Alexander et al., pp. 21-26 (24).
[21]See D. McRoberts, 'Dean Brown's Book of Hours', *Innes Review*, 19.2 (1968), 144-67.
[22]See further J.S. Richardson, 'Fragments of Altar Retables of Late Medieval Date in Scotland', *PSAS*, 62 (1928), 197-224 (200).
[23]J. Leslie, *The History of Scotland from the Death of King James I in the Year 1436 to the year 1561*, Bannatyne Club (Edinburgh, 1830), II, 246-47.

Cathedral, Old Aberdeen. And these not only presented for the monarch's view an envisioning of *regnum* in Scotland and Europe and sovereignty in the universe, but were available also to the simplest soul wandering in through the cathedral porch.

II

THE KING'S HOUSE AT STIRLING: ITS CARVINGS IN STONE

During the earlier 1530s King James V, bachelor monarch, was persuaded to consider marriage with one or another princess from abroad. Not unnaturally thoughts turned to royal residences, the need to renew the older palaces within and without. Work was done at Holyrood then Linlithgow, while improvement—renewal and extension—was made to the Palace of Falkland. There a wing was created in fine renaissance style: design and decoration should be in the manner of residences for royalty being built on the continent. This wing included an innovatory feature, a series of portrait medallions in stone sited on the outer walls, on the eastern and southern aspects—in a fashion already admired in France.[24] Preparations were also under way for the carving of five large stone images meant for the outside of the Chapel. These were being made by Peter Flemisman doubtless a stone-carver hailing from the Low Countries.[25] These carvings for the exterior walls of a royal building are a foretaste of what was to come.

The initiation of the King's building programme has usually been considered in isolation—in relation to the King only, his sojourn in France, his desire to rival and excel. But it may also helpfully be viewed in relation to the ambitious work that had been going on elsewhere in Scotland and was still proceeding in the ambience of ancient cathedral and new university—especially in the northeast under first, Bishop William Elphinstone, then Bishop Gavin Dunbar. By the same token, the uniqueness in these islands of the renaissance palace of Falkland at its time of building has been acknowledged but not widely recognized.[26] In the case of Stirling, the uniqueness and idiosyncrasy of its scheme of exterior sculpture has not been recognized for what it is. True, scholarly search for models for the fourteen main statues has been undertaken—and with success[27]—but interpretation of the *raison d'être* and the overall

---

[24] See D. Bentley-Cranch, 'An Early Sixteenth-Century French Architectural Source for the Palace of Falkland', *Review of Scottish Culture* [*ROSC*], 2 (1986), pp. 85-95 and J.G. Dunbar, 'Some Sixteenth-Century French Parallels for the Palace of Falkland', *ROSC*, 7 (1991), pp. 3-8.

[25] *Works Accounts*, I, 256.

[26] For an early instance, see M. Girouard, 'Falkland Palace, Fife—I', *Country Life*, 27 August, 1959, pp. 118-21 (121).

[27] See Royal Commission on the Ancient and Historical Monuments of Scotland [RCAHMS], *Stirlingshire: An Inventory of the Ancient Monuments*, 2 vols (Edinburgh 1963), I, 220-23.

THE KING IN HIS HOUSE

significance of the scheme of the sculpture as an artefact has never been attempted.[28] Had either renaissance palace or sculpture-invested exterior been the first in a long lineage the situation might have been different. Cruden points out that the 'Court School' ceased, but strangely enough he does not connect this cessation to the early death, in 1542, of the King himself.[29]

The year 1536 saw the 'wedding journey' of the King and his company of courtiers to France and a leisured stay there of six months, during which he saw a goodly sample of the new building undertaken by Francis I—as well as, we cannot doubt, great masterpieces in ecclesiastical architecture from earlier ages, such as Nôtre Dame in Paris or the cathedral of Chartres. This meant stimulus to his taste and a spur to his ambitions. As early as December 1536 in France he procured for his building programme in Scotland the services of more than one promising young architect.[30] We know the names of some, and dates of employment, but little else about them.[31]

On his return to Scotland with Princess Madeleine de Valois of France as his bride, he proceeded to create and perfect a new royal residence, 'The King's House', within the precincts of Stirling Castle. This new palace is the finest example of renaissance architecture in Scotland, in itself an idiosyncratic masterpiece. The palace (or rather what remains of it today after certain demolitions) is oblong, on a site sloping up from south to north: the south-exposed wall is then the taller by nearly a storey, its foot in the 'Prince's Garden'.[32] The south and north walls form the longer side of the rectangular plan. The western wall was built flush with the precipice edge of Stirling rock and there were apparently no visual features on its expanse, which could be viewed only from very far below. On the east side is the main entrance to the palace where it opens on a fine courtyard square central to the scheme of Stirling Castle as a whole. Today this courtyard is impressively completed by Parliament House and the Chapel Royal—but this last dates only from 1594, when it was built anew for the baptism of Prince Henry Frederick. In King James V's time the Chapel Royal was, one gathers, a less imposing building with a thatched roof.[33]

Safe within the encircling battlements of the ancient stronghold the new palace needed no structural defensive features. Its shape belongs to the new renaissance fashion, a comely framework for apartments spacious, comfortable and elegantly disposed. Its signal to the world was of the standards in 'way of

---

[28] RCAHMS, *Stirlingshire*, I, 220 even goes so far as to say, 'the iconography of the figure sculpture is very varied and does not conform to any one scheme or pattern'.
[29] S. Cruden, *The Scottish Castle*, 3rd edn (1960; rpt. Edinburgh, 1981), pp. 145-46.
[30] Dunbar, 'Some French Parallels', pp. 5-6.
[31] RCAHMS, *Stirlingshire*, I, 184.
[32] Possibly the area below the south wall and Prince's Tower now called the Bowling Green. For several payments in 1531-32 relating to 'the garding' at Stirling, see *Works Accounts*, I, 109-10.
[33] See *Works Accounts*, I, 310 (1583): '...the thak thairof resaveis weit and rane...'.

life' set by the King, the progressive nature of the King's concept of his 'House', his wish to declare himself as belonging to the movement for new-style building and gracious living he had met in royal circles on the continent—indeed through architectural design in that field not only to rival but to excel. This he achieved with the first 'renaissance' palace in these islands. It is not through its shape, however, that the new palace signals its larger affinity, how it belongs—as 'The King's House'—to the greater order of the cosmos. This function has been committed to the figuration with which three of the exterior walls have been invested. This architectural feature is a new phenomenon, unparalleled at the time and, I believe, in these islands unprecedented—except for the earlier aspects of the King's programme, the wall-medallion scheme integrated with the architectural scheme at Falkland, and the recorded sculpture there of the five large images in stone for the Chapel exterior. Unprecedented, we can say, unless we look back to much earlier ecclesiastical building—to Nôtre Dame or Chartres. It is not until a good generation later, in 1575, that an eminent building, the Heidelberger Schloss—also a palace built within an ancient stronghold—shows walls that are similarly invested with statuary integrated into the architectural design of a new building in renaissance style. And it is not until 1604 in Scotland that the planets portrayed each in his or her character, play a part in an architectural scheme out of doors. The pleasance at Edzell Castle, a home of the Lyndsays, has on the walls, surrounding its garden, carvings of the planets in order together with the liberal arts.[34] There Sol is not kingly though he has his Leo in attendance with him. He is beautifully portrayed to render the turn of the year as, sweeping his long cloak, he has turned to go, but looks back towards us over his shoulder.

The 'King's House' at Stirling has been described in technical and conscientious detail with many photographic illustrations in the volume, *Stirlingshire*, by the Royal Commission on the Ancient and Historical Monuments of Scotland.[35] The palace has been appreciated by several architectural historians as a 'first' in Great Britain, as an outstanding achievement in its scheme of almost life-size sculpted renaissance statues on ornamental columns, which occupy recessed bays on the north, south and east façades of the building. These are part of a larger design of sculptured figures that appear, some at a level above (that is on the level of the roof parapet), some below, as heads or head-and-shoulders, on the corbel-ends. Below these again are ranged carved beasts or birds, real or grotesque. There is no other example in Scotland of the time, or later, of such eloquent and elaborate presentation of statuary in a comprehensive scheme on the outer walls of a noble residence or indeed on any building of a public or private nature, secular or ecclesiastical.

---

[34]See further, W. Douglas Simpson, with revisions by R. Fawcett, *Edzell Castle* (1952; rpt. Edinburgh, 1982), pp. 6-12.
[35]Op. cit., I, 41-43; 179-223 and Plates 1 and 53-91.

In the figuration of the stone carvings supported by the building's surface plan and integrated with it, an intention can be discerned. The mien of the building retains only a trace of the defensive / offensive manner of earlier royal sites, when the king's home was a castle or stronghold. This 'King's House' needs no blank lower wall-surface, no firing point or loopholes. It could be planned as 'a renaissance palace in a style that left the gothic behind'. The fourth side, the exposure to the west, was perhaps defensive in its siting on the precipice edge. But for the other three the defensive / offensive office is, I have suggested, subsumed into the choice and disposition of images in stones. Now to demonstrate that. Beyond this defensive / offensive aspect, which clearly declares itself on the south side as we shall see, is a greater consideration—the effecting of an affinity or 'belongingness' of the King's House to the great powers of the cosmos. The King, the King's House, must be defended. By what powers?

The carved figures are sited at more than one level—indeed the style of carving varies from one level to the other, which probably indicates workmanship by different craftsmen. The concept of the human figure varies likewise and indeed the 'worlds' drawn on by the carvers, some of which have been traced, hail from different regions of Europe—as we shall see.

First, for the exposure to the south—on the highest level on the roof's parapet appear certain men-at-arms, each mounted on a short pillar. They are variously dressed and accoutred, each busily making ready to wield or discharge his weapon. There is an arquebusier, a swordsman, and a bowman. The figures are lively devised in their activity. These are types of soldiery that would have constituted the King's guard. They are less than life-size and have been compared in workmanship to the figures on the fountain in the palace of Linlithgow, where the stone-carvers are believed to have come from France.[36]

The exposure is to the south—to the sun, but also towards England, the enemy. The men-at-arms at roof-level are visible from the ground, indeed noticeable from a point outside the encircling Castle walls. The presence of such apotropaic figures on the roof or skyline of a castle is a mode no-one knows how old. (The north of England has several examples extant—for instance, those at Raby Castle or at Alnwick.) The idea was to give the impression from afar of busy, protective activity, but also to ward off attack by a 'presence'. It would seem that similar figures were at this time to be seen on the roof of Falkland Palace if we interpret Slezer's picture aright.[37] (They have long since disappeared.)

Beyond the arquebusier on the parapet wall his foot on his own short column sits patiently a figure that I find as moving as any in the palace

---

[36] RCAHMS, *Stirlingshire*, I, 220.
[37] John Slezer, *Theatrum Scotiae* (London, 1693), plate 12. See also K. Cavers, *A Vision of Scotland* (Edinburgh, 1993), p. 29 (Falkland) and p. 25 (Stirling).

scheme—an old man with a bag over his shoulder, poorly dressed. Is this the 'poor man' of 'the poor man's king'? Is his inclusion gratuitous to the scheme of soldiery or is he eloquently in place—'the poor man pays for all'? He is certainly poverty, patience and resignation personified, here directly depicted not expressed *via* an allegorical abstraction.[38]

On the south face, some way below these roof-top soldiers is sited the series of large figures, human, or quasi-human, male and female, more or less life-size. These are five in number on the south wall. Statuary at this level continues right round the palace to the north-east corner. Clearly it is a major feature of the new King's House. I suggest that these figures constitute a series not only ordered but significant in their sequence and siting.

Counting from the southwest corner the first of these figures is a girl, a young woman, all but naked, throwing a ball. Below her on her pedestal there are ball-flowers. (The long sequence will end with a companion figure to this one.) Next her comes a page or a young man very short in stature, a thickset corpulent squat and smiling figure carrying a shield with the device of a sunburst. Patently his 'service', his loyalty, is solarian. His right arm has completely disappeared so we cannot know if he too was throwing, say, a ball. The fourth bay's figure is a companion to this, who is seen to be throwing a ball, a play-ball or perhaps a 'fireball' such as were thrown in modish fire-work entertainments. He is equally stocky and corpulent and his shield bears a lion-mask. This is again a principal solarian symbol: Leo is the zodiac sign for the planet Sol and the lion-mask and sun-burst are associated with him as King Sol in presentations of the planets—indeed these two appear as attributes of kingship in general. The balls, be they flower-balls or fireballs, are—to judge by the thrower's gesture—being thrown *at* someone not *to* another person and the gesture is offensive or perhaps defensive but in the spirit of happy play—perhaps as in the seasonal ball-game of spring celebration. Below the first-named, the girl, the male figure on the corbel-head wears a quasi-classical costume—a toga tied on one bare shoulder. Such a costume in the representation of the time signified a power from classical antiquity, a king or hero. This could be Pluto and the girl above him a Proserpina. Between the two page-attendants and so at a central point of the south-face statuary is a larger figure, seated—a devil, depicted in a manner accepted in the sixteenth century. He may have been winged.[39] He certainly has claws for hands and feet, a human mask on his belly and another on his huge tail, which curls forward under his seat, between his legs. In his left hand he holds a ball or ball-and-sceptre. His right hand is idle and rests on his thigh. His look is grim but the expression on the human mask is merry. The authority of this seated figure is declared in the two shield-bearing attendants on either side testifying to solarian power.

---

[38]This figure been variously interpreted. See RCAHMS, *Stirlingshire*, I, 220-21.
[39]See RCAHMS, *Stirlingshire*, I, plate 69B.

The south-facing aspect of the King's House, then, belongs to the sun and to the noble planet Sol (himself a king among the planets), to whom belongs kingship and the protection of kings. The children of Sol are short in stature. In calling they number kings, judges, soldiers, players of noble instruments such as lyre or harp—but also in matters of religion, hypocrites and servants of anti-Christ. The sun, as planet Sol, was half-beneficent, half-malevolent, but was tempered for good by association with Jupiter or Venus.

The south aspect of the palace, we recall, looked to England, where danger lay. The defensive / offensive mien of the stone images 'guarding' the palace on its south wall centres in this figure of the devil, seated as it were in judgment. Why the devil, here? It was not unknown for fearsome carved masks of beast, monster or fiend to be placed on the outside wall of a castle, witness Caerlaverock, where a devil- or beast-mask once looked fiercely upon the enemies of the Maxwells, who were the castle's masters.[40] What is the devil doing on a palace wall, in figuration given over to Sol? Is he there to express the malignant aspect of Sol's influence? Clearly he can serve to alarm or threaten, to ward off hostile approach. An understanding that at the heart of the sun is evil, in the midday sun lies violent danger, is ancient, deep-rooted and widespread.[41] Men knew 'sun-stroke' and feared it. The sun in the Old Testament is by no means always beneficent and unfrightening. There is, moreover, biblical authority for the devil in this solarian context. In the Vulgate's Psalm 90, the protective psalm, the terrors and dangers against which protection is sought include 'the demon of the meridian', the devil of the noontide sun:

5. Scuto circumdabit te veritas eius—non timebis a timore nocturno
6. A sagitta volante in die a negotio perambulante in tenebris ab incursu *et daemonio meridiano*.

He has disappeared from the later post-Reformation version, but the sixteenth century in England knew 'the devil at noontide'. And French idiom to this day speaks of 'le démon de midi': he is instigator of the sudden and violent stroke of evil impulse that can destroy a man in middle age, his happiness and his family, his sanctity even—as in Shakespeare's *A Winter's Tale*. In this royal palace wall-of-the-sun, of the planet Sol, the devil has a place, if only to threaten a foe.

At the same level, the south-east corner of the palace has St Michael, a figure standing spearing a dragon-beast below him. His head and upper torso are missing so one cannot check his identity by the device on his headgear. A very similar figure, however, known to be St Michael and less devastated by

---

[40] See C. Tabraham, *Scottish Castles and Fortifications* (Edinburgh, 1986), p. 27.
[41] For literary examples: *The Tain*, trans. T. Kinsella (London, 1969), p. 194, or 'Eger and Grine' [sic], in *The Percy Folio of Old English Ballads and Romances* (London, 1905-10), I, 205-46, ll. 889-94. This edition uses the 1867-68 text of F.J. Furnivall and J.W. Hales.

weathering, is preserved on the outer wall of what is now the Parish Kirk of Linlithgow, but what was earlier St Michael's Kirk. The workmanship of this has been compared to other figure-carving within Linlithgow Palace and suggests the same hand at work in all three places.[42] In any case St Michael is by far the most likely saint to be a guardian of the King's House in Stirling—commander of the heavenly host, watchful over the guardian angels and intervener for the soul at a moment of sudden death.[43] The old Chapel Royal on the other side of the courtyard at Stirling had been dedicated to St Michael in 1501. The Carver Mass for the coronation of King James V is marked for him at Michaelmas.[44] The Order of St Michael, the most prestigious in Europe, had recently been received by King James V at the hands of his father-in-law Francis I. The defence of the King's House at Stirling with Scotland's enemy in faraway view to the south has been singularly well devised. St Michael—'and all angels', as we shall see.

At the corresponding north-east corner of the building on this same level stands a statue of the King himself, an unmistakeable likeness not with any indication of rank or power but in plain cap and gown. There is proof of identity in an inscription 'I.V.' nearby. On the King's right hand, extending along the east wall towards St Michael, there are four figures, three of them planetary powers. First Jupiter, then a laughing youth looking upwards, then Sol and then Venus. The planet figures have been identified in spite of extensive damage, and loss by weathering of all above the waist of Sol and Jupiter. These have been shown to be modelled on engravings by Hans Burgkmair, for luckily the Burgkmair versions show detail of Jupiter's belt and the amply folded 'eastern' trousers or cloak of Sol, which are both extant in the stone figures.[45] Jupiter and Venus are benignant planets good in themselves and in conjunction with one another confirming that benignant influence. The laughing youth looking up partakes of the happy influence, drawing attention to the powers of the sky. The figure-heads on the corbels below are all laughing, singing or rejoicing. At the level of the large statues, the fourth niche has a figure of Venus—a *Venus pudica*, naked but veiling her body with a long scarf of delicate material. She stands slyly—enacting this role.

On the King's left hand, along the northern front at this level are planetary deities also and figures maybe of allegorical intent. Next to him stands a youth with a large covered cup such as was used in the presentation of gold coin to a

---

[42] This is possibly Thomas French's; see *Works Accounts*, I, xxxiii.
[43] See further, D. McRoberts, 'The Cult of St Michael in Scotland', *Millénaire monastique du Mont Saint-Michel...: Mélanges commemoratifs*, III (Paris, 1971), 471-79 (473-74).
[44] See K. Elliott, 'The Carver Choir-Book', *Music and Letters*, 41.4 (1960), 349-57 (352 and 356-57); J. Purser, *Scotland's Music* (Edinburgh and London, 1992), pp. 88-90, and D. James Ross, *Musick Fyne: Robert Carver and the Art of Music in Sixteenth Century Scotland* (Edinburgh, 1993), pp. 31-33.
[45] See RCAHMS, *Stirlingshire*, I, plate 71, B and C and F.W.H. Hollstein, *German Engravings Etchings and Woodcuts*, V, 94-95 (Bartsch Nos. 41-47).

monarch. This cup-bearer is understood to represent fortune or treasure—not fortune in the sense of the as-yet-unforeseen, but rather as good luck and wealth.

The next in the series is Saturn, known by 'the wallet at his back'. Saturn, a malignant planet, had come to be regarded as a figuring of Time, but his were also the early ages of the world and its first happiness, 'the age of gold'. Beyond him is Venus again, but here she is *Venus armata*, helmed and with a dart in the crook of her left arm. Her right hand holds a large ball—the crystal ball that stands for the fragile bliss of a happy marriage. Beyond her is a young woman lightly clad and in a carefree posture—which brings to an end the series that had begun with her counterpart, the girl throwing the ball-flowers on the wall of the sun.

The King by his simple presence guards his House standing near its entrance. With him in the guardianship are ranged St Michael, astral powers and forces for good. And above these, under the eaves, are ranged cherubim, a close-packed rank of winged cherub-heads extending the whole length of all three sides. (I have not managed to count them exactly but they could number nine times nine.) Both choice and disposition of these figures must have been pondered with the greatest care and a finely articulated sequence is discernible. There were, it seems, at one time scrolls above the main figures which when the building was first erected may well have proclaimed their identity and helped to communicate the overall meaning.[46] These have been lost by weathering. But it has been possible to make some sense of the choice and disposition and it may be possible to get near to a meaning for the whole.

The four quarters of the heavens, of which south, east and north have statuary, had each its different nature: the south solarian and lighthearted but with a sinister streak, the east happy, propitious and welcoming (the main doorway of the palace was on that side). The north, always more sombre. As to any larger overall scheme of the carving on one level with another, so much has been destroyed by weathering, neglect perhaps even malice, that the prospect of interpretation is daunting. But here and there a juxtaposition rouses conjectures.

On the east side of the lower level the corbel-heads are much decayed but enough survives to bear witness to the fact that as we saw they are all laughing or rejoicing; this holds good whether they are 'real' people of the courtly company, or creatures not completely and solely human, for instance with a hint of wings folded behind shoulders or (always a possibility with representational art at that time), a portrait of a known person in a rôle, whether mythological or allegorical person or character from history.[47] Many of the corbel heads have the air of being individual portraits. One such of the merry faces is of an older lady,

---

[46] Ibid., I, 220.
[47] Bentley-Cranch, 'An Early Source for Falkland', also notes this popular fashion (p. 92) and gives French instances of it, note 39, p. 95.

for example, who may be singing, though closer inspection reveals that she was winged. A siren? Or a compliment to a musical member of the society at court in the depiction of her as such? From certain of them a challenging sense of individual identity emerges. One is of a court lady who bears a salamander on her shoulder (it has been claimed that she is suckling it) and the salamander was the personal device of King Francis I of France. Perhaps this sculptured head and shoulders shows one of the ladies from French royal circles who came to Scotland with Princess Madeleine de Valois, King James V's first Queen. On the other hand a woman's bust with a creature at her breast was a known mode of depicting sensuality. Another again of a court lady has been claimed as a portrait-bust of Margaret Tudor, Queen Mother at the court of James V but by then remarried and more than once. The creature-device below her is of two parrots—'love-birds'.

This north front in its corbel heads, though they have suffered much decay, can be seen to sort well with the spirit of the major figures above; riches, rank and honours and a darker aspect of ageing and misfortune. Alas that so many of the heads or figures are so defaced that their outline is all but destroyed. The intriguing thing is that despite the lamentable loss of surface and detail one can perceive the spirit of many of these human faces and one can here and there distinguish a relevance of one carving to another and to what must have been an eloquent whole.

Would that we could discover or establish the horoscope of James V, King of Scots.[48]

A case has been outlined that the King's House in the devising of its unparalleled scheme of exterior figuration shows a responding affinity to the quarters of the heavens and to the working of planetary influence. There could be more to it. The wall of the happy faces and propitious planets is on the King's right hand, as he stands there in stone. On his left is fortune, wealth and a reminder of the distinguished match he made with the princess of France, the happiness it brought, so tragically brief, for along with *Venus armata* is the inauspicious planet Saturn.

Such a disposition of forces to right and to left stirs a memory. Could there be a relevance of Holy Writ as there was in the case of the heraldic ceiling, where shields of the earth were raised up to God? In the Old Testament Book of Proverbs is the famous passage urging the pursuit of wisdom. It is familiar to Scots from childhood. In the favourite paraphrase of wisdom it is said:

---

[48] In England at this time Nicolaus Kratzer was possibly involved in such activities for Henry VIII. See J.D. North, 'Nicolaus Kratzer—The King's Astronomer', *Studia Copernicana*, 16 (1978), 205-34; S. Anglo, *Spectacle, Pageantry and Early Tudor Policy* (Oxford, 1969), pp. 217-19 and W. Hackmann, 'Nicolaus Kratzer: the King's Astronomer and Renaissance Instrument-Maker', *Henry VIII: A European Court in England*, ed. D. Starkey (London, 1991), pp. 70-73, in which mention is made of 'judicial horoscopes' (p. 70).

THE KING IN HIS HOUSE

> In her right hand she holds to view
> a length of happy days.
> Riches with splendid honours bound
> are what the left displays.
>> (3 Proverbs, 16: longitudo dierum in dextera eius in sinistra illius divitiae et gloria.)

The right hand / left hand disposition is closely relevant to the figure of King James standing as he does at the corner of the palace, close by the entrance doorway. But is wisdom and the search for it relevant to a King's palace?

If we read farther in the Book of Proverbs—yes. In the same chapter, 1 Proverbs 20-21, wisdom makes herself known in the streets, outdoors in the principal meeting place:

> Sapientia foris praedicat in plateis dat vocem suam.
> In capite turbarum clamitat in foribus portarum urbis profert verba sua dicens.

In the Jacobean translation:

> Wisdom crieth without; she uttereth her voice in the streets:
> She crieth in the chief place of concourse, in the openings of the gates....

'Chapter and verse' in the Bible, precedent perceived in Holy Writ, was one way of testifying to the oneness of truth—a way of evincing or demonstrating participation in the huge order of the cosmos. It is possible, then, that the disposition of the large carved statues was intended to suggest the presence of a desire for wisdom in the monarch, 'I.V.', who is, in terms of worldly pomp or royal circumstance, otherwise so modestly presented.

The presence of the planetary powers in statuary incorporated in the architecture of an eminent building is a feature unique at the time and very impressive. At Falkland in all probability a social presence as of friends or companions at court had been recorded in the stone carved medallion 'portraits'. We can have no certain idea what were the five great stone images being sculpted for the outside wall of the Chapel Royal for the same palace and about the same time. They were Christian in subject. Biblical, moral—of religious purport, saints or prophets, virtues or acts of mercy? We cannot know, as all traces of them have disappeared, and no other reference to them has been found.

But planets? They were not an obvious or indeed an expected feature of a King's House in the older or indeed in the newer style of architecture on the continent. Planetary powers make their way into secular art, in a domestic context, early on. As themes or presences in more public painting or sculpture they were, as Seznec shows us 'fighting their way up to inclusion on a level with the virtues or the liberal arts', certainly by the opening years of the sixteenth century.[49] At this point the planetary powers began to be depicted prominently in print, delineated by Flemish and German engravers. At a learned and sophisticated level then, and also at a wider level of all those enjoying from pictures in books what Sol or Saturn looked like, the attributes that served to identify them or expound their nature would be becoming largely established and known. But at a much wider and humbler level—the nature of the planets, their habitual guise, who were their 'people' or 'children',[50] and what their influence— these were made known in print with woodcut illustrations in a very popular book quickly disseminated widely in Europe. This was *Le Compost et Kalendrier des Bergers*. It was composed by the theologian and printer Guy Marchand. For 1490 and '92 he issued a calendar for shepherds (understand 'for everyman'), a book of instruction and guidance in matters of religion and science, health care of man and beast, and weather-wisdom. Printed in French, this wonderful *vade mecum* and guidebook to health and self-knowledge (it tabulated the sins and depicted their penalties) was rapidly translated and printed in other tongues. Very early on, in 1503, it was printed in Scots of a kind, for the first time in a language of these islands—printed by Vérard in Paris.[51] This like every other version from 1492 onwards had a good number of pages devoted to planetary lore, with woodcut illustrations. By 1535, then, one can assume, from an availability at a not too expensive level, a spreading printed version in Scotland of visual images and useful facts in this realm of knowledge. (English editions had followed fast on the Franco-Scottish one.)[52] Planetary lore fit for shepherds and needful for their instruction and behaviour comes in the astronomical part of the chapter, between explanation of the zodiac and a discussion of the complexions.

How seriously was planetary lore taken at a sophisticated level of educated belief? Coupled with this question, another: by whom was the devising done of the scheme of figuration for the outer wall surface of the King's House at Stirling? Was it the architect *alias* the skilled mason and stone-cutter of the sculpture in stone? Or was it a council (including both of these) of court officials which would number among them dignitaries of the church? The King himself must have been in their counsels—having in all probability seen Chartres, the only building known that is invested with sculptured figures in stone in an array that is pregnant with meaning and wonderfully 'ordered'. Did he, James V, make the mental leap from an ecclesiastical masterpiece of the French middle ages, Chartres or Nôtre Dame in Paris, to a possible palace prestigious in its new

---

[49] This quotation has not been located. Jean Seznec discusses and illustrates this concept in *The Survival of the Pagan Gods* (1940; English trans. 1953; rpt. Princeton, 1972), pp. 69-83 and 126-47.
[50] See Seznec, *Survival*, pp. 70-76.
[51] *STC* 22407: *The kalendayr of shyppars*.
[52] See *STC* 20480: Ptolemy, Claudius, *Here begynneth the Compost of Ptholomeus* (R. Wyer,) [1530?], which consists of extracts from *The kalendayr*. Further editions appeared in 1540?, 1550?, 1552?, 1562? and 1638?

architectural style and to be to an unprecedented extent, invested in this way by meaningful figuration of sculpture without? There his new building would indeed excel.

There must have been a gifted assembly of intelligence and of artistic skills available to him for consultation after his return from his half-a-year in France. At home there were those in Scotland who had been at work on the Cathedral in the north-east. We know he commissioned the services of several prominent or promising master masons while he was with his father-in-law's court.[53] We know that he appointed as Master of Works for a year Sir James Hamilton of Finnart, bastard son of the Earl of Arran and a lady named Boyd.[54] He had been educated abroad, travelled to the French court as envoy for Scotland in 1517,[55] and for a time was intimate friend to the King, being very much of an age with him.[56] Hamilton had been with him in France.[57] We know that influence from another quarter of Europe—Flanders—was present in Scotland, not only in the region of stone-cutting and engraved pictures used as models but also in tapestries bought or commissioned for the furnishings of the palace walls. (We know George Steill, poet, friend and courtier, was sent for a year to the continent to procure them.)[58] But whose was the creative imagination that devised the concept of this unique House for the King must remain a mystery.

Recently only has it been emphasized that 'architects' of this era in Europe were highly educated in other disciplines of learning also. We have details of the principal architect employed on the Wawel Palace in Cracow, an Italian who was learned in mathematics, science, theology, and *magia naturalis* (understand 'magic' and 'natural sciences'). Like his fellow architects working there on the new palace for King Sigismund and his Queen Bona Sforza, he came from her home region of Milan.[59] An architect of extensive and sophisticated education could certainly be aware of planetary powers as astral influences. Contemporary thinking in Italy by such scholars as Cinthio and Pico della Mirandola considered with the greatest seriousness the nature of natural image and the existence and nature of the 'influences' of the planets on men on earth, of communing between earth and heaven. 'Magia naturalis est maritare coelum'.[60]

---

[53] *Works Accounts*, I, xxxiii-xxxiv; Moses (or Mogin) Martin and Nicolas Roy.
[54] For a documented listing of Hamilton of Finnart's involvement with royal architectural projects, see *Works Accounts*, I, xxv. See also C. McKean, 'Finnart's Platt', *Architectural Heritage*, 2 (1991), 3-17 and idem, 'Hamilton of Finnart', *History Today*, 43 (January, 1993), 42-47, which includes an artist's impression of Finnart's own castle of Craignethan, where heraldic beasts were used as decorative elements at rooftop level (43).
[55] McKean, 'Hamilton of Finnart', 42.
[56] Ibid. Finnart was born c. 1500.
[57] *TA*, VII, 20.
[58] *TA*, VII, 17.
[59] See further, A. Misiąg-Bocheńska, *Głowy Wawelskie* (Cracow, 1953), pp. 5-24.
[60] See Pico della Mirandola, *On the Dignity of Man*, trans. C.G. Wallis (Indianapolis, New York, 1965), p. 28. I am grateful to Dr W. Craven for help with this quotation.

The planets were, through the 'astral demon' present in each, transmitters of God's will and power. (They could 'incline' a man to a state of mind, a course of action, but they could not 'make him sin'.)[61] For some scholars the astral beings of the planets were ranked with angels, as messengers of God. It was moreover, held that their power could be attracted—and held—if an image of their nature were created. A whole huge perspective, then, exists of possible motives instigating the choice of such-and-such figures as 'guardians' of the King's House at Stirling, or declarations of its nature. Why they? Why there? And what did the ordering portend? These are questions we have been right to raise whether or not we have hit on the real, or complete answer.

The King's House at Stirling has one aspect broached earlier but worth discussing further—an absence of 'vainglory' in Kingship. The King as we saw is represented in simple dress, without ornament. There are no symbols of royalty as such and very few heraldic devices among the carved images on the outer walls. But on the very highest points of the palace, where the four roof-sections converge, at the apex of each, not visible from the ground below but there as finial, as significant 'headpiece' for the building, is a lion sejant, within the circlet of an open crown. A reticence of royalty, apt as lookout and guard for the King's House of Scotland.[62]

III

THE KING'S HOUSE AT STIRLING: ITS CARVED ROUNDELS IN WOOD

Unparalleled in Scotland though not unprecedented in Europe is a third artefact in the style King James V, and a very fine one—in the King's House at Stirling, the ceiling of the presence chamber. This lofty room, for whose furnishing magnificent tapestries were purchased, had a flat ceiling of wood—of oak, possibly native. A subsequent history of a palace no longer occupied, of hazard, dismantling and dispersal, destruction and loss, means that we have no direct evidence of the ceiling's appearance when it was first devised. But it seems very likely that its spacious extent was, in a continental style of the day for palatial building, panelled and marked off into squares. Within each square was a carved roundel of foliage wreathed or living forms in array. Within each roundel appeared a carved figure of a human being, for the most part head and shoulders only, in a few cases the figure complete. The number of carved roundels on the ceiling in 1540 is reckoned to have been fifty-six, of which some forty survived. The space on the ceiling reduced because of the large chimneybreast may have

---

[61] See further, D.P. Walker, *Spiritual and Demonic Magic from Ficino to Campanella* (London, 1958), passim.

[62] For further discussion of the heraldic lion see J.H. Stevenson, *Heraldry in Scotland*, 2 vols (Glasgow, 1914), II, 391-92.

been compartmented in smaller units, which could have accommodated the several smaller figures among the carvings extant.

What the presence chamber looked like with its 'coffered' and carved figures in place was imaginatively reconstructed in a drawing made by 1817. In that year efforts to record and rescue the remnants of the ceiling bore fruit in *Lacunar Strevelinense: A Collection of Heads Etched and Engraved after the Carved Work which formerly decorated the Roof of the King's Room in Stirling Castle* (Edinburgh, 1817). In this volume, with text by the publisher and antiquarian, William Blackwood, there are line drawings by Jane Graham of the carved figures then available, which fortunately preserved the appearance of two then extant which later perished by fire. There is also a careful sketch of the presence chamber with heads in place. Though the artist of this general interior drawing, Edward Blore, had never himself seen the presence chamber before the ceiling was dismembered, he apparently had help from local inhabitants who had, and recalled it clearly. A version of this drawing corrected as to the proportions of the room and redrawn is printed on page four of *The Stirling Heads*, a booklet produced for the Royal Commission on the Ancient and Historical Monuments of Scotland, with text by J.G. Dunbar, photographs by G.B. Quick and edited by K.A. Steer (1960; rpt. Edinburgh, 1975).

The admiration the presence chamber had inspired in the beholder is recorded in the comments of several travellers, including J. Macky's:

> In this Palace is one Apartment of Six Rooms of State, the noblest I ever saw in *Europe*, both for Heighth, Length and Breadth: And for the Fineness of the Carv'd Work, in Wainscot and on the Cieling, there's no Apartment in *Windsor* or *Hampton-Court* that comes near it...And in the Roof of the Presence-Chamber, are carv'd the Heads of the Kings and Queens of *Scotland*.[63]

With the interior of the palace also, then—imagine the presence chamber with great tapestries in place on the walls. King James V had aimed to excel and had succeeded.

Nowadays it is possible to view the chamber with most of the surviving 'heads' displayed, though three of them including the one believed to be King James V are in Edinburgh in the National Museum of Antiquities. In Stirling then, some small idea can be gained of the dignity and idiosyncrasy of the King's House interior in the presence chamber of the seventh Stewart King of Scots.

---

[63] J. Macky, *A Journey through Scotland, Being the Third Volume which completes Great Britain* (Edinburgh, 1723), 187-88.

These Stirling carvings, except those few now fragmentary, each had a roundel which consists of a wreath, single or double, one within the other. These are composed of foliage or branches, or in a few cases from other living forms. Inside each of these roundels there appears as in a portrait, a human figure, usually a head-and-shoulders or the body to the waistline or just below. Several show the arms complete, bent at the elbow, hands clasped or grasping the roundel, with the handhold reaching beyond it. The carved figures are in low relief, the relief of the roundels being in some higher, in some lower, than the surround. In a number of them, then, the figure projects towards the observer beyond the surrounding frame. The plant or foliage forms of the roundels do not appear to have any symbolic or heraldic meaning such as might serve as a clue to the family or significance here of the figure they surround. But the several exceptional roundels prove to supply relevant comment on the personality or character within, as we shall see.

The work named above, *The Stirling Heads*, provides photographic illustrations of all the extant carvings made for the presence chamber. These are grouped and a description of the costume is provided, a number being allotted to each carving. In the belief that this booklet is still available, I give the number assigned to each roundel therein, as I refer here to each figure.

Some fifty-six characters or personalities were carved for the King's presence-chamber ceiling. What are they? Who are they? There is a longstanding tradition that they number among them 'the Heads of the Kings and Queens of Scotland'. Whether or not this is so is very difficult to ascertain. We do not know what 'likenesses' in the form of paintings or drawings or what accounts available of their appearance existed in 1540 for the royal forbears of the King. We do not know whether these were likenesses directly taken or concepts of the monarch or his consort made after the event. Nor do we know what force a 'likeness' would exert in the creation in 1540 of a head of an earlier monarch. With the portraits, pictures or carvings now extant we are almost as unsure: we lack information often as to whether what has survived is an original ('a limning, from the presence'), a copy, a copy of a copy, an interpretation where the artist was supplied with oral or written description, or a totally imaginary portrait.

For King James I there is the fresco in the Cathedral Library at Siena, painted by Pinturicchio and his assistants over the years 1502-7—a series of scenes illustrating the life of Pope Pius II who, as Æneas Sylvius Piccolomini, had visited the Scottish monarch in 1435.[64] The commission for this fresco had stipulated that the heads be painted by Pinturicchio himself.[65]

---

[64]See *Early Travellers in Scotland*, ed. P. Hume Brown (1891; rpt. Edinburgh, 1978), pp. 24-29.
[65]Cardinal Francesco Piccolomini (later to be Pius III) commissioned the ten-scene fresco series.

The painter was furnished with a text, presumably Æeneas Sylvius's own *Commentaries* and possibly other accounts now lost. The writer had characterized James at the age of forty-one as 'quadratus et pinguedine grauis' (*Historia*, 46); he had described Scotland as 'a cold country where few things will grow and for the most part has no trees' (*Commentaries* I; *Historia*, 46). But in the fresco a southern landscape provides the background for a lean, grave, and sagacious monarch's meditation on a point just made by the papal nuncio in his oration.[66]

The King is 'a perfect prince', enthroned, gently engaged in learned discussion. He has a long face, very fine features, white hair and a long white beard. A certain resemblance was found by Blackwood in *Lacunar Strevelinense* between the Italian depiction and the Stirling head No. 9.[67] Then there is the painting 'by author unknown', provenance uncertain, which is in the Scottish National Portrait Gallery. This is reproduced as frontispiece to *The Kingis Quair,* edited by Matthew P. McDiarmid (London, 1973). This, as Pinturicchio's, bears some resemblance in feature to No. 9 of the Stirling Heads.

King James II is better documented with some half a dozen 'likenesses' preserved in the Scottish National Portrait Gallery.[68] What is more, 'James of the Fiery Face' had a noticeable birthmark on one cheek,[69] as has No. 10 among the Stirling carvings, but the fifteenth-century warrior in helm (No. 4) also bears such a mark and the physiognomy is not dissimilar. (We should allow however for the grain or knot of the wood being utilized to convey the character of features.)

What James III looked like we can presumably learn from the painting of van der Goes, the altarpiece from Trinity College Chapel, Edinburgh. This shows the King at his devotions, and on the same panel his Queen Margaret of Denmark. Behind King James III appears her son, the next James, as a child, also kneeling. To my mind there is no carved head at Stirling that resembles King James III in this painting.[70]

---

[66]James I of Scotland, *The Kingis Quair*, ed. J. Norton-Smith (Oxford, 1971), pp. v-vi and frontispiece, a black and white detail, showing Pinturicchio's portrait of James I, from the second fresco.
[67]*Lacunar Strevelinense*, p. 17.
[68]For one painted in the sixteenth century, see the booklet produced by the Scottish National Portrait Gallery (text by R.E. Hutchison), *The Royal House of Stewart* (1958; rpt. Edinburgh, 1973), p. 6 and plate 2.
[69]Cf. '[A]ne schort memoriale of ye scottis corniklis for addicioun', NLS MS 16500 (Asloan), fols. 114-114^b): 'king Iames ye secund yat had ye fyre marke in his face ...'. See also C. McGladdery, *James II* (Edinburgh, 1990), pp. 1-2 and the illustration on the book's jacket, taken from Württembergische Landesbibliothek, Stuttgart, Cod. his. 4° 141 (Das Tagebuch von Georg von Ehingen), cover.
[70]Illustration of the Trinity panel depicting James III and, according to Macdougall, his son, is found in N. Macdougall, *James IV* (Edinburgh, 1989), Fig. 3 (adjacent to p. 148).

For King James IV as a monarch there are a number of paintings and one carving of himself and his queen—on the newel posts of a staircase in Holyrood Palace. None of the portraits are originals 'limned in the presence'.[71] The painter may be knowing but the picture was made 'after an earlier portrait'[72]—or the drawing is one of a series made by an archivist to record the painting of his patron.[73]

For Queens of the early Stewart kings, record from which one could 'recognize' a presence among the Stirling carvings is rare or non-existent. If we allow costume or headdress as an indication of identity then for Joan Beaufort, Queen of James I who came from England, the court lady who wears a folded English hood, richly jewelled and prominently featured, is a possibility (No. 28). One hand is raised, index upright, in a gesture of 'Hark!': could this glance towards the poem the King wrote for his love of her?

For Queen Margaret of Denmark, consort of James III, there is the altarpiece of King and Queen at their devotions.[74] Among the noble ladies of the Stirling ceiling, those that survive, I find no striking resemblance to her features as there portrayed, but the carvers may have seen pictures of her later in her life.

Margaret Tudor, long resident in Scotland, at times Regent of the kingdom and Queen Mother in 1540, is highly likely to be included in any 'Kings and Queens of Scotland'. No. 17 of a noble lady of mature years carrying a small dog has been claimed as a portrayal of her because a dog was a Tudor emblem.[75] The pictorial records of Margaret Tudor as royal bride, Stewart Queen or Queen Mother have not, to my knowledge been completely collected and compared. They exist in different media. There is the well known portrait of her as a marriageable girl—by Mytens from an earlier portrait.[76] There is the carving of her on the newel post in Holyrood, previously mentioned. There is a satiric

---

[71] L. Macfarlane, 'The Book of Hours of James IV and Margaret Tudor', *Innes Review*, 11 (1960), 3-21 (10-11), notes the discrepancy between the Book's contemporary portrait in which James has a clean-shaven face, and the known facts. The portrait appears on fol. 24, Österreichische Nationalbibliothek Wien, Codex Lat. 1897.

[72] This is so for the well known portrait of James IV with a peregrine falcon by Mytens (Macdougall, op. cit., fig. 3), painted in the early seventeenth century, but based on an earlier painting. (See C.R. Beard, 'Early Stewart Portraits', *Connoisseur*, 71 (1925), 5-10 and 13-15.)

[73] See for example the sketches in the Recueil d'Arras, MS 266 (Bib. Municipale, Arras), especially that of James IV, fol. 18, wrongly identified as James V. For the identity of the artist, see Beard, op. cit., and L. Campbell, 'The Authorship of the *Recueil d'Arras*', *Journal of the Warburg and Courtauld Institutes*, 40 (1977), 301-13 and plates 23-26.

[74] For colour illustration: A. Cherry, *Princes, Poets and Patrons: The Stuarts and Scotland* (Edinburgh, 1987), verso of unnumbered leaf adjacent to p. 30.

[75] Cf. also the portrait of Margaret Tudor at prayer, c. 1503, fol. 243^v, Österreichische Nationalbibliothek Wien, Codex Lat. 1897 (reproduced in Macfarlane, 'Book of Hours', plate III), in which her dog, an unmistakeable greyhound, sits at the foot of the altar.

[76] It is reproduced in P.H. Buchanan, *Margaret Tudor Queen of Scots* (Edinburgh and London, 1985), unnumbered plate adjacent to p. 40.

sketch in Colville's Account Book (Treasury), which very likely depicts her.[77] (She is portrayed playing the small bagpipes, an uncomplimentary presentation of a Queen figure.) Then it is suggested that she appears as one of the royal ladies complimented in the stained glass at Fairford church by being 'models' for the Maries. (Margaret was there while on a 'holiday' in England in 1516.)[78] All of these are credible representations of the round faced girl depicted as bride for James IV.

What of the other figures on the ceiling? They fall into several groups distinguished by costume or headdress. Some are ladies of a courtly company. They wear contemporary dress, though this may in some cases verge on fantasy, especially as to head gear. These could be 'portraits'—for which certain Scotswomen of birth or ladies in the train of Queen Madeleine, Queen Marie or the Queen Mother had 'sat'. There are one or two gentlemen also, some of them youths. Of particular interest is the witty personality, carved in profile, with laughter lines showing at eye and mouth, No. 14. He is wearing a simple cap and gown, the cap the 'double Scotch bonnet' of the time.[79] These could be younger kinsmen of the King, pages, courtiers or court officials. Four or five by their dress and manner seem to be of humbler status, very possibly members of the royal household. The naively smiling woman, her hair in loose locks, could be the 'female fool' of Queen Marie's circle, No. 27.[80] There is a court jester, a wonderfully lively figure, and two dancing putti, Nos. 36, 37 and 38. These last could credibly be personalities in actual service about the king, while at the same time being 'favourite subjects for the carver'. Then there is a man with a lion on his shoulders, No. 39. Should we see him as winning a place in his own right as keeper of the royal lion resident in Stirling Castle,[81] or should we read him as standing for another embodiment of Hercules—or Samson—or even Androcles? His dress is contemporary of a humbler sort and his relationship with the beast he carries on his shoulders is apparently amiable. There are two men, or two studies of one man whose costume is that of the *landsknecht* or mercenary from the German continent, Nos. 22 and 23.

This problematic question of the mode of representation operating in these creations is not easy to solve. For instance there may have been a group of ancient gods or planetary powers of which one, Apollo who is Sol with a sunburst headdress, has survived, No. 7, with a possible Venus, No. 21, among the smaller figures and a possible Mars, No. 4. On the other hand Sol, as kingly

---

[77] Scottish Record Office E 31/6, covering the period 23 September 1534 to 25 August 1535. Dr M.H.B. Sanderson kindly provided this reference.

[78] See also H. Wayment, 'The stained glass in the Chapel of the Vyne', *National Trust Studies* (1980), pp. 35-47 and its cover illustration, which depicts the panel of Queen Margaret and her name saint at the Vyne chapel.

[79] See H. Bennett, 'The Scots Bonnet', *From the Stone Age to the 'Forty-Five: studies presented to R.B.K. Stevenson*, ed. A. O'Connor and D.V. Clarke (Edinburgh, 1983), pp. 546-66.

[80] *TA*, VII, 102, 151.

[81] See RCAHMS, *Stirlingshire*, I, 192.

planet, may have been the only luminary here included and a young man of the entourage may have been presented in this role.[82]

Two groups can be placed by the manner of their garb and presentation because these are based on the costume-code of engravers such as Burgkmair: potentates or heroes of classical antiquity wear a toga knotted heavily on one shoulder, the shoulders often bare. Of these there is a Hercules, as we shall see. On the other hand among the smaller figures, another Hercules with his club wears indeterminate, but not contemporary, garments, No. 34. Kings of long ago, or rulers of eastern lands wear costume and headdress that is rich but strange, somewhat in the manner of the engravers, again.

How does this repertory of varied figures assort with the idea that a 'ceiling' composed of these should, in terms of artistic concepts of the time, present a perceptible 'cosmos' or order? I tentatively propose one scheme that could accommodate both the variety and the probable number of carvings involved, allowing for some sixteen that are now missing. Certainly an arrangement that was random is not credible. Such an array of carvings must have taken some years to prepare. And the passage of time may explain certain characteristics. There is one motif that has been noted by Dunbar in *The Stirling Heads* but not discussed, whose presence in close association with several of the carved figures suggests the wish to indicate a recent death or one still mourned. This is the cherub's or angel's head with wings, usually looking down or away from the viewer. The most interesting example is No. 26, a young woman who wears a particular kind of small lace cap, pointed at the back and close under her chin. She is the only one in the gathering of ladies to wear this pattern of headdress. In the Seton Armorial (1591) the young Queen Madeleine, in resplendent heraldic skirt, wears just such a cap.[83] (No-one else would wear a replica of what the Queen chose as headdress.) In the Stirling Heads, the winged cherub is prominent at her waist, his face turned away from us and hidden in her dress.

One other lady, of maturer years, No. 20, has a carved winged-cherub's head poised on her bosom. The winged-cherub's head is a known motif, prominent in the Baroque period, which has been variously interpreted. It certainly indicates angelic presence. (We recall the rank of similar winged-cherubs' heads carved in stone under the eaves of the palace—fulfilling there an obviously protective function.) It has been explained as 'the human soul' or (mistakenly, I believe) as 'a resurrection symbol'—and its presence on funerary monuments in Scotland after the Reformation has been noted.[84] (Pre-Reformation tombstones surviving in Scotland are rare indeed.)

---

[82]See further, *Stirling Heads*, p. 28 and note 41.
[83]Seton Armorial, NLS ACC. 9309, fol. 19, reproduced in C. Bingham, *James V, King of Scots, 1512-1542* (London, 1971), frontispiece.
[84]Informally discussed by B. Willsher, 'The Glories of Greyfriars', *Scots Magazine*, 119.5 (1983), 486-92 (487-88 and 491).

An angelic presence such as this can indicate that the human being it is lodged with is dead and mourned. Perhaps the carvings of those ladies was begun during their lifetime and the 'mourning' cherub added after their death, out of sympathy and artistic tact. Two small figures in the Stirling ceiling carvings have the cherub's head depicted. The young man, No. 8, a carving that survives only in part, wears a tunic ornamented in low relief, which is heavily embroidered. This figures a cherub's head, winged, and behind it there appear to be two animals, in combat. Should we look for a young man mourned, close to the king's company as kinsman or friend? One can suggest young Lennox, a dear friend of the young James V who tried to help the King escape from the Douglases in 1526, and was afterwards murdered for it. The most interesting use of the winged-cherub's head is one not noted by Dunbar, in No. 13: a man of middle age bareheaded and his hair in some disorder, wearing a collared cloak and tunic. His expression is distressed and grim. For him the roundel is formed of four winged-angel heads, their faces towards us, their wings outstretched. They have every appearance of being the four guardian angels. There is in this a good reason to think the carving indeed represents King James IV, the King's father, who met his death on Flodden Field and whose body was never found by the Scots, so never by them given formal burial. The angelic presence here could be protective of the soul of one who had died excommunicate. And what is more, this impressive male figure wears around his neck, its lower links under his tunic, a very heavy chain—as did King James IV all his life in penance for implication in his father's death.

The significance of the roundel where it is, exceptionally, *not* composed of foliage, is found also with two figures of the ancient world—No. 5 and No. 30. One is the reverse of the other, possibly by a different artist. Perhaps two versions were needed for the overall pattern of the ceiling to be completed. These figures, costumed in the toga for character of the antique world, each have as roundel two serpents, which suggests that this is Hercules who in his infancy strangled two serpents.

Unparalleled in Scotland, the presence chamber ceiling repays consideration in terms of precedents in Europe. The first is that of 'medallion' figures such as had already appeared on the outer walls of the new building at Falkland. The use of medallion heads on exterior and / or interior walls and ceilings was already popular in France[85] and in certain instances the roundels were sited inside a square carved 'compartment' or coffer. The famous example is the ceiling above the staircase in the castle of Azay-le-Rideau.[86] For an important public chamber in palatial building this compartmenting or marking of the *ceiling* into squares or other shapes was used extensively in the early decades of the sixteenth century— in continental Europe and also at Hampton Court in these islands. (A certain

---

[85]Bentley-Cranch, 'An Early Source for Falkland', pp. 86-87 and 91-92, and Dunbar, 'Some French Parallels', p. 4.
[86]*Stirling Heads*, p. 27.

kinship will be perceived with the panelled heraldic ceiling of 1520 in St Machar's Cathedral.)

The most famous example and the most extensive and varied use of such squaring of the ceiling space are to be found in the farthest eastern kingdom of Europe—in Poland at Cracow—in the rooms of the prestigious new palace built within the old stronghold of the Wawel Castle. The new building had begun by the time the Queen, Bona Sforza, came from Italy to marry King Sigismund I in 1518; interior decoration, however, was in progress during the late 1520s and into the 1530s. Understandably, architects from Italy were brought in for the planning and erection of this palace in Renaissance style.[87] The manner of ceilings devised in rooms of royal use was at this point changing from Gothic vaulting to the flat surface. The Wawel Palace has ceilings with a compartmented surface. They are called 'coffered', or *Kasetonowe*, as each square is outlined in a deeply carved wooden border shelving inwards. The space recessed within may be decorated with a painted motif or a motif carved in relief and painted. And in one case, the ceiling of the Hall of the Ambassadors, each 'coffer' contained the head of a man or a woman, powerfully and delicately carved.[88] The ceiling frames and the heads are of lime wood. The style of the Wawel Palace was of Italian inspiration but the genius carver in wood who is believed to have devised and executed almost all of the 'ceiling of heads', Sebastian Tauerbach, is believed to have come to Cracow from Silesia.[89]

The stimulus of a dynastic royal occasion and a confluence of talent and craftsmanship of the highest order brought from far afield presents a situation in Stirling and in Cracow with some similarities. In both cases, unfortunately, the carved ceiling survives incomplete with so many of the important parts destroyed that authoritative reconstruction is well-nigh impossible. In the palace at Cracow there were one hundred and ninety-four heads of which only some thirty survive, while Stirling has retained some forty out of a calculated fifty-six. Another serious matter is of course that in both cases the order is lost in which the carved figures were disposed—an order that not only conveyed the meaning of the whole but also affected the significance of the individual carving as contributory to that whole. In both cases it can be hazarded that the ceiling of a great hall of the king, whether Hall of Ambassadors or presence chamber, was devised to body forth in some fashion, and to reflect on, a pattern of society, the King and his kin

---

[87]From 1502-16, Franciscus Italus, or Florentinus, was employed at Wawel, his first project the decoration of the late king's tomb, and his chief work, only partly completed at his death in 1516, the new royal residence. (He had worked previously in Hungary, where Sigismund himself had spent some years at his brother's court of Buda before returning to Poland in 1501.) From 1530-37, the Florentine, Bartolommeo Berrecci was employed. See J. Białostocki, *The Art of the Renaissance in Eastern Europe: Hungary, Bohemia, Poland* (Oxford, 1976), pp. 10-11, 18-21 and notes 44 (chapter 1) and 25, 30 and 32 (chapter 2).
[88]Ibid., p. 24 and notes 65 and 66 (chapter 2).
[89]A. Misiąg-Bocheńska, *Głowy Wawelskie*, (Cracow, 1953), pp. 16-20; Białostocki, *Renaissance in Eastern Europe*, p. 25. Both sources note that Tauerbach is assumed to have had the assistance of others, including Hans Schnitzer (Janda Snycerz), a master carver himself from 1532.

and royal forebears, of the host country. While the company at court and the royal household was the probable theme in Stirling, in the Wawel Hall very possibly the company at court was embodying the regions of that far-reaching kingdom of Poland. In both cases an inclusion of heads of a different character lent a farther dimension, linking actual personalities portrayed to faraway and long ago, myth, legend or allegory—as they were ranged in association, parallel or contrast.

In both cases, Stirling and Cracow, the majority of the carved figures are presented in a version of contemporary dress and headgear. In both cases a certain number appear in a guise or headdress of faraway or long ago or of another world. For the Cracow heads of ruler, sage or poet from the eastern world or former ages of antiquity, costume or headgear is often that attributed to such figures in the engravings made in the first decades of the century, for instance those by Burgkmair. Cracow has a 'philosopher' (or prophet?) with loose hair and beard and penetrating glance,[90] and four examples of the ruler wearing the heavy hooked crown that in Burgkmair indicates the potentate of an earlier civilization (including Julius Caesar?)[91] Cracow also has two poets of ancient times— powerful faces, clean shaven and short haired, wearing a laurel wreath—Virgil and Ovid?[92] It also has a poet likewise laurelled, with medieval haircut and dress— perhaps Dante?[93]—while a beautiful woman wears fantasy headdress believed by Polish scholars to render an 'allegorical' figure.[94] One male head has ram's horns.[95] As far as can be ascertained the surviving heads do not there include King or Queen as such though one male head wears a cap described as 'princely' in style.[96] For other ranks of society one or two of the women are plainly capped and dressed (to judge by the neckline of the costume) and could be serving women: one of these has the ignominy of a heavy 'branks' on mouth and shoulder. (She goes by the title of *plotki*—'gossip'.)[97] One of the men wears a helmet headdress associated with a provincial governor.[98]

The heads are now assembled in the centre of the ceiling of the *Sala Poselska* (Hall of the Ambassadors), in ten rows of six, while the rest of the ceiling's 'coffers' are blank. As to the order in which these differing types of personalities were presented, that is irrecoverable. (We recall the complex interrelationships indicated and preserved in the ordering of the shields in the heraldic ceiling in Aberdeen.) With the heads of the ladies, high fashion may border on fantasy. There is always the possibility, pointed out by Joan Evans

---

[90]*Głowy Wawelskie*, plates 16 and 18.
[91]Ibid., plates 4-11.
[92]Ibid., plates 20-23
[93]Ibid., plates 17 and 19.
[94]Ibid., plates 61 and 63.
[95]Ibid., plates 60 and 62.
[96]Ibid., plates 12 and 14.
[97]Ibid., plates 44 and 46.
[98]Ibid., plates 56 and 58.

and brought to notice again by Dana Bentley-Cranch's discussion of medallion heads, that the carved figures may be at one and the same time personal portraits and renderings of a role: it was evidently the vogue to be painted 'as Venus' or depicted 'as Hercules'.[99] (Later, in England, Queen Elizabeth's portraits present her in many costumed rôles such as that of Astraea.)[100] For a parallel from the first half of the century in England, we can look to the stained glass windows at Fairford, previously mentioned, where royal ladies were complimented by being used as models for a rendering of 'the Maries'.

The ceiling in the Wawel really is a 'ceiling of heads'. The Cracow carvings are fixed to their 'base' in their coffer at shoulder level and all the back of their heads. They look out from the carved recesses, and the bend of the neck is in a number of cases very truncated. Most of them are looking down at us or at the company below them in the Hall of the Ambassadors; but one or two of them look sideways as if towards a companion figure. Their expressions vary markedly, from faraway and meditative (the philosopher or poet) to acute surprise and shock in some of the younger and more naive faces. But each of the very different physiognomies is eloquent of a person, an individual. Often the regard of the eyes is veiled, controlled, discreet—especially in the ladies—while the mouth suggests lively consciousness of what is to fore. The lips in every case are chiselled with such precision that the personality—the presence—is articulated so expressively as to be disquieting.

It is not suggested that the ceiling of carved figures at Stirling is directly derived from the 'ceiling of heads' in Cracow. But the idea of a ceiling of heads, original and unprecedented in the Wawel (it is believed) must have occasioned excited and admiring comment by all who saw it achieved.[101] With nearly two hundred carvings it must have been some time in the making. It was new in 1534-35. And those who saw it numbered the envoys from far and wide in Europe and even beyond into Muscovy. The new Renaissance palace in the Wawel, devised by picked architects from Italy, was a trendsetter in several important ways and among the most prestigious innovatory palace-buildings of its time. The idea of a coffered ceiling with figure-carvings of this nature is very likely to have been transmitted to royal circles in France, where palatial building was strongly to the fore, whether by word of admiring architect or a sketch in a portfolio or by an admiring account in words or letter by a visiting envoy. We

---

[99] J. Evans, *Dress in Mediaeval France* (London, 1952), p. 66; D. Bentley-Cranch, 'L'iconographie de Marguerite de Savoie (1523-1574)', *Culture et pouvoir au temps de l'Humanisme et de la Renaissance*, Actes du Congrès Marguerite de Savoi, Annécy, Chambery, Turin (Geneva and Paris, 1978), pp. 243-56 and plates 1-XXIV, esp. VIII. See also H. Smailes and D. Thomson, *The Queen's Image* (Edinburgh, 1987), pp. 13-14.

[100] See J. Pope-Hennessy, *The Portrait in the Renaissance* (Princeton, 1966), pp. 238-56.

[101] See further, T. Gostyński, 'Przypuszczalny prototyp wawelskiego stropu z głowami', *Biuletyn Historii Sztuki*, 12 (1950), 316-21, cited by Białostocki, op. cit., p. 25. Alfonso I's triumphal arch in Castel Nuovo at Naples, where Bona Sforza spent part of her youth, is pointed out as a prototype (built in 1465), but though coffered, it is also vaulted, which the Sala Poselska is not.

THE KING IN HIS HOUSE 95

should ask: could word have come directly from Poland to Scotland? I cannot discover whether Scotland at this time sent any representative, cleric or layman, to the court of King Sigismund I, but we should bear in mind that the kingdom of Poland was present in the European count of kings on the heraldic ceiling of shields of western Christendom at St Machar's Cathedral.[102]

It has been pointed out that these Scottish ceiling carvings are not uniformly masterly in concept or execution. Indeed it has been most plausibly suggested that some show the finish and proportion of a work by a master craftsman while others may well have been made by learners under him. To me the discrepancy appears in skill in rendering a personality or character and, more markedly, in the placing of the half figure within the given space of roundel, in its pose, in the proportion of arms and hands to torso and head, and the contact of the figure with its roundel. In the medallion roundels at Falkland it was noted that the half-figures, in high relief and projected beyond the circular surround, had the air of looking out in friendly fashion, each from a small 'port hole' window onto the company assembled or passing below. Some of them, less aware, look down as from a framed portrait on the wall, though many are badly weathered now; all seem to me to have been masterly carved and in style to resemble the best of the 'portraits' in carved wood executed for the ceiling in the King's House at Stirling. I suggest that these are those, according to *The Stirling Heads,* numbering 13, 16, 17, 18, 20, 23, 24, 26, 27, 28, 36 and several of the smaller ones, or sections now imperfect. Also impressive and finely related to their roundels from which they jut out slightly, are Numbers 1, 2, 3, 4, 9, and 10, potentates of distant lands or times—or with 10 and 12 possibily Stewart monarchs James II and James V himself.

Disproportion of head to arms and hands or to torso is marked in No. 5, a Hercules, and also in the full-figure Hercules with his club, No. 34; in No. 22 (especially when compared with its 'alternative' version, No. 23), in No. 30, No. 34 and unfortunately No. 12, 'the King himself'. Of course, there is always the possibility that the head itself was carved by a master and the rest was left for an 'assistant' (a learner or junior) to complete. With No. 5, No. 30 and No. 22, disproportion of hands and arms to the head is marked and results in an unpleasing impression of deformity.

The figures are all in deep relief and especially the heroes project beyond the level of the surrounding wreath or circular frame. Some give the impression of readiness to emerge from it. But only a few are looking towards us, presented full face or nearly so—the dancing boys, No. 37 and No. 38, the jester, No. 36, the

---

[102]Note also the features of the Sigismund Chapel at Wawel, begun by 1519, where the exterior tower has a *corona clausa* atop it and the interior contains among its decorative elements heraldic shields (of the Polish Kingdom and the Duchy of Lithuania). For illustrations see M. Rożek, *The Royal Cathedral at Wawel* (Warsaw, 1981), pp. 38-53. I am greatly indebted to Mrs B. Rastawicki for her skill in translation and her advice on the Polish references herein.

female fool, No. 27, the man with the lion on his shoulders, No. 39 and Samson / Hercules with his lion, No. 33. With one or two the effect of looking out from their roundel has been given by letting the hands rest on it. Perhaps this contact of hands with roundel evolved in an attempt to make the figures participant, as it were, in the scene below. But none of the figures, save the entertainers perhaps, is engaging our regard. It is in this engaging or not, the regard of the company below that the Stirling figures differ from the Cracow heads, which have also been called 'the watching heads'.

Altogether I hazard a thought that the tradition of portrait-roundels was a starting point that occasioned the masterly-carved and well-proportioned studies of members of the courtly company and perhaps earlier members of the Stewart royal line—but that at some point the idea of the ceiling feature intervened—the walls being given over to tapestry—and the looking or leaning out and so to some extent making a contact with the observer was a further development via the hands of perhaps another master-carver or learner. But at no point did the concept of looking *out and down* come into it. Those who carved the medallion half-figures at Stirling may have been directed to create a 'ceiling of heads' for the presence-chamber but no-one directly concerned may have *seen* the watching heads of the Wawel. For the Cracow ceiling the 'medallion' suggestion is absent, with the absence of a roundel. And the heads are heads only, with or without significant headgear, with perhaps a hint of collar or shoulderline. They are moreover carved in full relief, attached to their background at shoulder level while frequently a bend of the neck enables them to look down of intent—to watch, express immediate reaction to or otherwise betray a consciousness of the company below. A certain interaction of regard between watching head and company below was intended, invited and achieved.

5

EXCHEQUER, COUNCIL AND SESSION, 1513-1542

Athol L. Murray

Recent research has thrown much new light on the development of the council during the fifteenth century and up to the death of James IV.[1] The re-issue of R.K. Hannay's pioneering work on the judicial council[2] and the origins of the College of Justice has highlighted the need for further work on James V's council, for which the sources are fuller and more informative than in his predecessors' reigns. The subject is a wide one, and the present paper has the more modest aim of re-examining a small, but important part of it, the relationship between the judicial role of the council and that of the exchequer.[3]

Though the exchequer may have been one of those Anglo-Norman institutions which were imported into Scotland during the twelfth and thirteenth centuries, by the sixteenth century the Scottish exchequer was very different from its English counterpart. It was not a permanent body with its own premises but simply the annual audit of the accounts of the royal revenue, carried out by a body of lords auditors of exchequer specially appointed by commission under the quarter seal, whose powers expired once the audit was completed. Even the audit of the two principal officers, the comptroller and the treasurer, which usually followed the main exchequer, was carried out by separate bodies of auditors. By James V's reign the exchequer almost invariably sat in Edinburgh, the only two exceptions being adjournments to Stirling in 1528 and to Linlithgow in 1530. In Edinburgh it sat in the Blackfriars, part of which was rented for the occasion, whereas the council normally met in the 'council house' in the tolbooth.[4]

Sheriffs and other officials who rendered accounts in exchequer, known collectively as the 'comptars' (accountants), were summoned by brieve on forty

---

[1] Particular mention should be made of theses by A.R. Borthwick, 'The King, Council and Councillors in Scotland c. 1430-1460', Diss. Edinburgh, 1989, and T.M. Chalmers, 'The King's Council, Patronage and the Governance of Scotland 1460-1513', Diss. Aberdeen, 1982.

[2] *The College of Justice: Essays by R.K. Hannay*, ed. H.L. MacQueen, Stair Society (Edinburgh, 1990), [Hannay, ed. MacQueen]. This contains (pp. 345-48) a bibliography of recent research on the council and administration of justice in Scotland.

[3] An earlier version of this paper, which appeared as 'Exchequer and council in the reign of James V', *Juridical Review*, New Series 5 (1960), 209-25, owed a great deal to the comments and suggestions of Professor W. Croft Dickinson.

[4] A.L. Murray, 'The procedure of the Scottish exchequer in the early sixteenth century', *SHR*, 40.130 (1961), 89-117 (93).

days warning. The brieves ordered a compearance on specific days, according to a predetermined timetable, the 'ordour of table', first mentioned by name in 1532[5] but clearly of much greater antiquity. Those who failed to compear [appear in court] on the appointed day incurred the exchequer unlaw [penalty] of £10. The summons and unlaw denote a body functioning as a court and there can be little doubt that the audit, like that in the English exchequer, was judicial in character. There are indeed references to comptars attesting payments and other matters on oath, though not, as in England, swearing to their account as a whole.[6] The oldest surviving exchequer commission, that of 1543, lists the auditors' powers and responsibilities in very general terms including that of 'punishing officers negligent remiss or disobedient in their offices by ward or otherwise'.[7]

The earliest statement concerning the exchequer's judicial powers is to be found in Balfour's *Practicks*,[8] probably written in the 1570s, but referring to cases from James V's reign:

> All civil actiounis, clames and contraversies concerning the Kingis propertie, quhairof compt is maid in the chekkar, aucht and sould be discussit befoir the Auditouris of the chekkar and befoir na uther Judge within this realme .... As also, the Auditouris of the chekkar, and nane utheris within this realme, ar Jugeis competent in all actiounis and contraversies anent allowance and comptis concerning the Kingis houshald.

We will look at the cases in more detail later, but it is important to note Balfour's reservation:

> Bot the Auditouris of the Kingis chekkar hes na power to judge or decide upon ony summondis or materis in the chekkar, bot allanerlie upoun sic summondis and materis as belangis and pertanis to the chekkar, and to the Kingis comptis to be maid thairin: And gif thay do the contrare in sic caisis quhilk be not chekkar materis, the samin is of nane avail, force nor effect.

Taken at face value these passages seem to state that the auditouris of exchequer had exclusive jurisdiction in cases affecting the king's property and revenue, but none in matters falling outside their remit as auditors. As the cases he cites date from the 1520s and 1530s, the implication is that this was the situation under James V.

---

[5]*ER*, XVI, 551.
[6]*ER*, IX, 343; XII, 223; XV, 443, 681, though Sir John Skene, *De Verborum Significatione* (Edinburgh, 1597), s.v. 'Schirefe' implies that sheriffs made a general declaration.
[7]Scottish Record Office, Register House charters RH.6/1319.
[8]*The Practicks of Sir James Balfour of Pittendreich*, ed. P.G.B. McNeill, Stair Society (Edinburgh, 1962), p. 136.

Before considering James V's exchequer, it is necessary to take a brief look at developments prior to 1513. It is not requisite, however, to go into the origins of the civil jurisdiction of the lords of council nor the relationship between them and the lords auditors of causes and complaints.[9] One of relatively few extant judicial records prior to James III's reign is that of a joint decision by the lords auditors of exchequer and lords of council concerning a claim by the abbot of Dunfermline for the eighth penny of justice ayres of Fife and Fothrif, heard in exchequer at Linlithgow on 18 July 1449.[10] But between 1478, the start of the earliest surviving council register, and the end of James III's reign there is no record of civil causes being heard in exchequer. On the contrary the evidence suggests that the lords of council were the appropriate forum in revenue matters.[11] The auditours seem to have confined themselves to business arising directly from the accounts, for instance calling before them those who had intromitted with the royal revenues and occasionally ordering distraint.[12]

During the first exchequer of James IV's reign, on 26 July 1488, the auditors decreed that Thomas Ross of Auchlossen should fulfill his obligation to relieve a former sheriff of Aberdeen of a sum due to the king. But the lords of council also sat during the exchequer, dealing with other actions until 18 August, when they continued all cases until 7 October 'except acciouns concerning our soverane lord, his chakker and acciouns of strangearis'.[13] In the following year the exchequer began on 15 June and on 23 June the auditors decreed that letters passed on a former decree, apparently of the council, should be put to execution.[14] Here the exchequer may have been acting as a vacation court in dealing with a dispute over the possession of lands, though it should be noted that the lands formed part of the lordship of Kilmarnock, which belonged to the crown, rather than one between the king and a subject.

Whatever the significance of these two cases, several years elapse before we come across any others. However, from 1493 the exchequer rolls do record judgements against persons defrauding the customs or detaining royal revenues.[15] In these the auditors appear to have acted alone but, directing a case to be heard in exchequer in 1497, the lords of council required 'that the lordis of the chekkir certefy the day of the summondis to the lordis of consale that thai may avise

---

[9] For a general survey see A.A.M. Duncan, 'The central courts before 1532', *Introduction to Scottish Legal History*, Stair Society (Edinburgh, 1958), pp. 321-40.

[10] *Registrum de Dunfermelyn*, Bannatyne Club (Edinburgh, 1842), p. 310.

[11] *ER*, IX, 77, 363, 380, 462, 534-35. A council decree of 2 August 1479 that the inhabitants of Dysart should pay custom on salt exported was recorded on the dorse of an exchequer roll (*ER*, VIII, 628).

[12] *ER*, VIII, 65, 236, 554; IX, 343, 406-7, 480.

[13] *Acta Dominorum Concilii 1478-1494* (Edinburgh, 1839) [*ADC*, I], 85-86, 88.

[14] *Parliamentary Records of Scotland* (Edinburgh, 1804, suppressed edition), 355, not printed in *ADC* or *Acta Dominorum Auditorum* (Edinburgh, 1839).

[15] *ER*, X, 381-82, 536-37.

tharewith and syt with thame the sade day'.[16] On 25 November 1500 there was clearly a joint session in which one judge identified as sitting '*pro actibus scaccarii*',[17] that is taking no part in business unrelated to the exchequer. On 31 July 1501 the king with advice of the sadis lords of council continued ordinary actions to 20 October but declared that 'the chekker wil remane and syt still and al accionis dependand thairapoun'. The two cases heard thereafter on 31 July and 5 August were both concerned with revenue matters.[18]

Despite Hannay's judgement that 'James IV never succeeded in putting the administration of civil justice on a satisfactory footing', by the end of his reign the judicial role of the council had been extended.[19] Civil causes were being heard in special terms or 'sessions' and the lords of council included legal experts who could be called upon as 'lords of session'. While the beginning of James V's accession did see a breakdown in organization,[20] the records of both exchequer and council become fuller and more informative. Minutes of proceedings in exchequer, both administrative and judicial, were entered in blank pages in the responde books, at first intermittently, more consistently from 1536 onwards.[21] This might not have been an innovation, as earlier responde books, now missing, may well have contained similar entries. There does not seem to be any clear division between the business recorded in this form and that recorded in the council registers. These, too, changed after 1513 in that they contained a much larger admixture of administrative and political business, reflecting the conciliar form of government made necessary by a royal minority and the regent's frequent absences from the country. Although some aspects of the exchequer's work do become better documented, there seems to have been no change in its administrative relationship with the council.[22]

While the council record becomes much fuller (apart from an unfortunate gap between December 1519 and November 1522), it is not always easy to identify exchequer proceedings. In 1518 a mass of judicial business is recorded during the period of the exchequer but only three sederunts are noted specifically

---

[16]*Acts of the Lords of Council in Civil Causes 1496-1501*, ed. H. Paton and G. Neilson (Edinburgh, 1918), [*ADC*, II], 79.

[17]*ADC*, II, 447.

[18]*Acts of the Lords of Council in Civil Causes 1501-1503*, ed. A.B. Calderwood (Edinburgh 1993), [*ADC*, III], 76.

[19]'On the antecedents of the College of Justice', *Hannay*, ed. MacQueen, p. 200. For a more favourable view see L.J. Macfarlane, *William Elphinstone and The Kingdom of Scotland 1431-1514* (Aberdeen, 1985), pp. 420-23.

[20]*Hannay*, ed. MacQueen, pp. 27-29.

[21]The responde books recorded sums due for feudal casualties for which the sheriffs would answer *(respondere)* in exchequer and are printed as appendices to *ER*, XIV-XXIII. Judicial proceedings appear in 1520 (*ER*, XIV, 608-9) and 1527 (*ER*, XV, 651-52).

[22]For the financial administration see A.L. Murray, 'Financing the royal household: James V and his comptrollers 1513-43', *The Renaissance and Reformation in Scotland*, ed. I.B. Cowan and D. Shaw (Edinburgh, 1983), 41-59.

as '*in scaccario*'.[23] By contrast the sederunts of 1, 2, 4, 5, and 7 March 1524 were '*in scaccario*' or '*in domo scaccarii*'. With only one exception all the lords present on these dates and on 8 March too were auditors of exchequer, but very little of the business was exchequer-related. Though also held '*in scaccario*' the sederunt of 9 March included the Earl of Lennox and Lords Hume amd Sempill, who were not auditors.[24] Faced with these anomalies it is a relief to turn to 1525 where, for once, the exchequer has been given a separate section in the council register, though this is not quite as straightforward as it might seem.

It must be noted, firstly, that the circumstances were unusual, in that the exchequer's sittings overlapped not only with the council's but also with parliament. Having met early in July, parliament followed its normal practice of remitting its business to the lords of the articles, who continued to sit for the rest of the month. Moreover the session of 1525 for ordinary actions before the council was not adjourned until 5 August, parliament having stipulated that the lords 'nemmit and written of before in the counselhous sall proceid apoun the materis of the sessioun'.[25] Meanwhile the exchequer had begun on 30 June. The exchequer rolls show accounts being rendered on most weekdays up to 15 August.[26] The register, however, indicates that lords auditors of exchequer only dealt with judicial business on seven days between 5 and 28 July and a further five between 11 and 18 August. In between these periods two further sederunts, in the morning and afternoon of 9 August, appear to have been of a different nature. From 15 August onwards the exchequer may have been sitting by virtue of a new commission to audit the comptroller's accounts.

Those named to audit the comptroller's accounts were James Beaton, Archbishop of Glasgow (the chancellor), Gavin Dunbar, Bishop of Aberdeen (the clerk register), Colin, Earl of Argyll, George Crichton, Abbot of Holyrood, Alexander Mylne, Abbot of Cambuskenneth, Robert Forman, Dean of Glasgow, James Kincragy, Dean of Aberdeen, John Dingwall, Chancellor of Aberdeen and Archdeacon of Caithness, James Colville of Ochiltree (director of chancery, appointed comptroller on 14 August), Nichol Crawfurd of Oxgangs (justice-clerk) and Sir John White, parson of Pitcox. The auditors for the main exchequer would have included the retiring comptroller, Robert Barton of Over Barnton, and probably also the treasurer, John Campbell of Lundy. All those named, including the treasurer, were appointed to a special commission for setting the crown lands of Fife on 4 July 1525, though the auditors themselves had a general

---

[23] SRO MS Acta Dominorum Concilii, CS.5/31 fols 53-177 (July-August 1518). The convenient modern listing of daily attendances in council, in 'Sederunts in Acta Dominorum Concilii 1501-1553' (2 vols, typescript, SRO RH.2/1/8-9), has been used throughout.
[24] CS.5/34 fols 132-157; RH.2/1/9, p. 155 omits the sederunt of 2 March 1524 (fol. 136^V). There was a further sederunt, *in scaccario*, on 13 April 1524.
[25] *APS*, 293; see also Duncan, 'Central courts', p. 338.
[26] *ER*, XV, x-xiii.

power of filling vacant tenancies.[27] Several cases involving tenancies were heard during the 1525 exchequer.

Of the twelve sederunts (excluding 9 August) which appear in the record between 4 July and 18 August, four are merely headed '*Sederunt domini auditores scaccarii*', without listing those present individually. Those named for all the other eight were the Bishop of Aberdeen, the Deans of Glasgow (Forman) and Aberdeen (Kincragy), and the comptroller, though after 14 August it is not known whether this refers to Barton or Colville. The justice-clerk (Crawfurd), sat on several occasions, the Earl of Argyll on three, the Archdeacon of Caithness (Dingwall) twice and James Colville once (up to 14 August). Those who appear not to have attended at all were the chancellor, the treasurer and the Abbot of Holyrood, who appear in sederunts of the main body of the council, and John White, by then an old man, 'unable to work as he used to' in his office of clerk of chancery.[28] Sederunt lists of the lords of the articles are only recorded on three occasions (27, 30 July, 3 August). Five auditors of exchequer were present on all three (the chancellor, Bishop of Aberdeen, Earl of Argyll, Abbot of Cambuskenneth and the treasurer), two more (Abbot of Holyrood and Crawfurd) on the last two only.[29]

Among those attending the exchequer sittings a further distinction can be made between those paid for performing special duties and those who were not. Of the former, Crawfurd received £15 for 'remaining continually upon the said chekker' and Dingwall £20 for his 'labours'. Though no payment was made to Kincragy in 1525, he normally received a similar fee from both the comptroller and the treasurer.[30] It seems reasonable to assume that these three attended to the routine financial work and that when there was no judicial business in exchequer the Bishop of Aberdeen, Abbot of Cambuskenneth and Dean of Glasgow sat with the main body of the council. They all sat in exchequer on the morning of 7 August and in council in the afternoon, having previously attended seven, six and two sittings of the council respectively between 5 July and 5 August. The comptroller, however, had to be in constant attendance in exchequer, not only because his presence was essential for a quorum, but also because he acted as pursuer in revenue cases, received money from those accounting and attested previous receipts. The sederunts show, therefore, that at every sitting for which

---

[27] *ER*, XV, 194, 559, 576.
[28] *ER*, XV, 206-7. White had been connected with the exchequer since 1484, when he was a writer of the rolls (*ER*, IX, 256). He received a pension from the burgh maills of Wigtown as a royal clerk from 1488, specifically as clerk of chancery from 1497 to 1516 (*ER*, X, 66; XI, 62, XIV; 206), and was director of chancery 1517-22 (*ER*, XIV, 279, 440). Having been an auditor from 1516 to 1526, he was described as 'recently deceased' at the 1527 audit (*ER*, XIV, 214; XV, 282, 386).
[29] *APS*, II, 296-97.
[30] *ER*, XV, 98, 207; *TA*, V, 238, 268, 332. Kincragy was paid 20 merks in 1526 for 'diting the rolls' (*dictando rotulos*), sharing this work with Dingwall in 1527 and with Dingwall and Crawfurd from 1528 (*ER*, XV, 292, 385, 464, 549). The dictator or 'diter' of the roll was responsible for the 'diting' of them, i.e. the act of composition or writing (*DOST*, s.v. 'dyting').

attendance is recorded six or seven auditors were present but (except on 9 August) no one who was not an auditor.

The importance of this last point will become apparent in examining the cases heard, especially in the light of the clerk's use of the terms 'lords of council' and 'auditors of exchequer'. The first, that of David Balfour of Burleigh against William Scott and Elizabeth Muschett, concerned a tack [lease] of the crown lands of Kinloch in the lordship of Fife; it will be remembered that the auditors had been empowered to set all the lands in that lordship. On 5 July the auditors ordered the parties to appear before them on 12 July but, after a further continuation, the 'lords of council' on 24 July ordained the pursuer to have possession according to the tenor of the last rental, without prejudice to the rights of both parties. In the second, Andrew Mowbray craved that William Lauder of Halton be decerned [ordered] to relieve him of an annual payment from his lands, which Lauder and his father had received as sheriffs for twenty-four years. This case had been referred by the lords of session to the lords of exchequer, who continued it to allow the defender to compear [appear in court]. Decree was given for the pursuer in exchequer on 13 July, but by the 'lords of council'.[31]

In the next two cases Robert Barton, the comptroller, appeared as pursuer on behalf of the king. On 8 July the 'lords of council' decerned the alderman and bailies of Cupar, to pay £25 for the rent of a mill 'restand and dependand on thair hedis [= remaining due by them], as the fute of the chalmerlanis compt maid in the last chekker proportis'. However a similar decree of 21 July against Malcolm Drummond and David Murray for rents of lands in Strathearn bears to be given by the 'lords of council and auditors of exchequer'. Again, on 28 July judgement was pronounced in two actions concerning crown lands in the lordship of Stewarton. The 'lords of council and auditors of exchequer' decerned that William Schaw of Sornebeg should pay Elizabeth Elphinstone, lady Dunrod, the violent profits of the lands of Blaklaw so that she could pay the comptroller 'the malis and dewiteis aucht be hir to the kingis grace thairof', but the 'lords of council' assoilzied Margaret Boyd, Lady Rowallan of a claim by Isobel Elphinstone and Robert Maxwell of Calderwood, her husband, for the maills of Ormisheuch.[32]

On 5 August the session was 'continued' (adjourned) until 3 November, despite which some civil cases were heard in the morning and afternoon of 9 August. Although these sederunts are recorded along with those of the exchequer, they clearly relate to the whole council. Not only are the headings '*in scaccario*' and '*sederunt domini auditores scaccarii*' absent, but of the ten lords sitting in the morning only six were auditors and in the afternoon a mere two out of nine. The cases heard involved the parsonage of Kirkmichael, spuilzie [spoliation] at Glenluce abbey and exemption from the sheriff of Fife's jurisdiction; that is

---

[31]CS.5/35 fols 139, 142^V.
[32]CS.5/35 fols 140-43.

litigation between private parties unconnected with the crown's property or revenue.[33] On 11 August we find the auditors themselves dealing with similar matters—protests concerning delivery of the heir of Craigiehall and the house of Strathbogie and by the Abbot of Glenluce of his readiness to answer at the instance of the Bishop of Galloway. The same day Lord Somerville constituted procurators in his action against the Earl of Morton. On 12 August the sederunt was again of '*domini auditores scaccarii*', but it was 'in presens of the lordis of consale' that the provost of Aberdeen 'grauntit him awand' [acknowledged that he owed] to John, Lord Erskine, of £100 for which he had taken allowance in the account of the bailies of Aberdeen, rendered in exchequer the previous day. The 'lords of council' ordained Somerville to deliver the place of Morton to the Earl of Morton and the Abbot of Glenluce repeated his earlier protest.[34] On 14 August we have a good illustration of the limits of the auditors' administrative powers. James Colville, newly appointed comptroller, attempted to resign, alleging that the conditions on which he accepted office had been breached, to which the auditors replied that, as they did not have power to make a comptroller, they had no power to discharge him, referring him to the king and secret council. Two days later the retiring comptroller, Robert Barton, became bound as surety for Malcolm, Lord Fleming, for payment of what appears to have been a private debt.[35]

The last recorded sitting of the auditors, on 18 August, also dealt with mixed business. The 'lords of council' gave judgement in two actions concerned with crown lands, the first brought by Nichol Crawfurd, one of the auditors, as lessee of the Loch-miln at the west end of Linlithgow, and the second by the Earl of Angus concerning the mill of Dulcrufe. An action by Fergus McDowall of Freuch 'tuiching the landis of Sonnenes', previously heard by the council on 26 July, was continued to the third day of the next session. Robert Barton again became bound for Lord Fleming, and Nichol Cairncross protested against his removal from the office of custumar of Edinburgh.[36]

The proceedings of 11-18 August clearly show the exchequer functioning as a vacation court following the continuation of the session. Such continuations normally preceded the exchequer: for instance in 1519 the council continued the session from 20 June to 20 October 'becaus it is understand to the saidis lordis that the chakker is to be haldin in the mene tyme quhilk may nocht gudlie stand with the sessioun', and in 1526 the continuation was 'specialie becaus the halding of the chekker quhilk will continew quhill the feryate tyme of hervist' [harvest time, when courts could not be held].[37] From such general

---

[33]*Acts of the Lords of Council in Public Affairs*, ed. R.K. Hannay (Edinburgh, 1932), [*ADCP*], 226; CS.5/35 fols 144-46.
[34]CS.5/35 fols 147-48.
[35]*ADCP*, 227; CS.5/ 35 fol. 148.
[36]CS.5/35 fols 108, 149. The mill of Dulcrufe was part of Queen Margaret Tudor's jointure lands of the lordship of Methven (*ER*, XV, 557).
[37]*ADCP*, 146, 243.

continuations the privileged actions of the king and 'strangers' were expressly exempt, but it is clear that other litigants sought the same consideration. Such actions could be dealt with by the auditors of exchequer, not as auditors but as lords of council sitting in exchequer. It is more difficult to interpret 'lords of council and auditors of exchequer', assuming that the framers of the record had any distinction in mind. At first it might imply a joint session of council and exchequer, like that of 1497, noted earlier. But examination of the sederunts has shown than in 1525 only auditors of exchequer were sitting. A second possibility is that there were two classes of auditors, those who were also lords of council and might hear any type of action, and others who were confined to specifically exchequer matters, like the comptroller, Robert Colville, in 1500.[38] There was indeed a distinction between those who were continuously employed there, receiving payment for the duties they performed, but the latter included Crawfurd, the justice-clerk, a regular attender in council at other times and one of the lords of the articles.

It seems, therefore, that 'lords of council' and 'auditors of exchequer' could be used as alternative descriptions of those named in the exchequer commission. Like those named 'of the session' or 'of the secret council' they were given special powers and responsibilities without prejudice to those already incumbent on them as lords of council. The same could even apply to the lords of the articles, albeit they were a committee of parliament. On 17 July 1525 a sitting of the lords of the articles was called upon to decide whether one foreign national had lawfully taken another's ship as prize. Their decision was given as 'lords of council'.[39] Thus their sederunt lists normally described the auditors as *domini auditores scaccarii* but in their decrees they are called 'lords of council', that being the capacity in which they gave judgement. So there was no real incongruity when the continuation of a case by the 'lords of council' was followed by a protest by the king's advocate 'albeit the lordis auditouris of the chakker had for certane considerationis moving thaim continewit the said summondis to ane certane day'.[40] It may be possible, however, to make some distinction between cases in which the exchequer was merely acting as a vacation court and those directly concerned with the exchequer accounts and the latter may have been in the clerk's mind when introducing the words 'auditors of exchequer' into their decrees. Thus in 1518 the auditors decerned that Nairn and Kintore had 'tynt thar previlege and fredome of burgh' by failing to pay their burgh maills and that the comptroller should levy customs on certain types of skins exported from Haddington because the bailies and community had failed to produce the charter by which they claimed exemption.[41]

---

[38]*ADC*, II, 447.
[39]*ADCP*, 225; CS.5/35 fol. 96.
[40]CS.5/31 fol. 168.
[41]*ADCP*, 126; CS.5/31 fols 122, 153.

Even if the ambiguous term 'the lords' is taken into account, very few decrees are recorded in the name of the auditors. Any distinction, therefore, was imperfectly made, but decrees of the lords of council in revenue cases are to be found in plenty. Even while the auditors were sitting in exchequer on 5 July 1525, the main council entered a decree against the comptroller, with his consent, for repayment to the Archbishop of St Andrews of £500 disbursed by him 'in the materis concernyng the commone weile of the realm and to the furnising of certane ambassatouris in uthir realmis'.[42] In the exchequer itself decrees of 8 July against the burgh of Cupar and of 21 July against Drummond and Murray both concerned arrears of rent due to the king, but the former purported to be given by the lords of council and the latter by the lords of council and auditors of exchequer. In 1529 the auditors observed that 'the custumaris bukis and the clerk of coquet [the clerk who issued certificates showing that customs dues had been paid] bukis of Perth aggreis nocht' and the following year the custumar was summoned to answer at the instance of the king and comptroller for omission of £23 2s 1d from his last account 'as is clerelie understand to the lordis auditouris of the chakker and verefeit to thame be the coquet bukis and uther wais'. But, although the matter was heard in exchequer, the case was continued by the 'lords of council' to 31 August 1530, when the clerks of cocket were to compear before the lords auditors of exchequer to give their oath upon the 'buke of custume' presented by them.[43]

If the lords auditors decided cases in exchequer by virtue of their judicial powers as lords of council, then it is also evident that the lords of council could deal with revenue cases during the ten or eleven months of each year when the exchequer was not sitting. The cases cited by Balfour are only concerned with conflict of jurisdictions between royal and ecclesiastical courts and were themselves heard in council, not in exchequer. In *The poor tenants of Uchtermukty* v. *Official principal of St Andrews* the lords of council found that the official could not 'curse' (excommunicate) the tenants at the instance of sir Laurence Alexandersoun for payment out of rents of crown lands, 'becaus thai understand that the said mater concernis the kingis propertie and suld be discussit befor the auditouris of chekkir and na uthir wais; and gif the said schir Laurence has ony actioun aganis the said pure tennentis for thair fermis or dewiteis ordanis him to call thame before the lordis auditouris of chekkir for the samin and he sall haf justice ministerit to him with expeditioune'.[44] In *Bertoun* v. *Thomsoun* an action by a chaplain as executor against the comptroller for payment of sums contained in extracts of the royal household books had been heard by the commissaries of the official of St Andrews 'quhilk wes nevir hard of befor that thai suld be jugeis to the kingis comptis'. The lords of council prohibited any further procedure because 'the samyn is ane chekker mater concerning the kingis

---

[42] CS.5/35 fol. 78.
[43] *ER*, XV, 666-67; CS.5/41 fol. 104.
[44] 7 March 1529/30, CS.5/41 fol. 3.

bukis of houshald and suld be decidit befor the auditouris of the chekker'.[45] A very similar case relating to Barton's accounts as treasurer was decided by the lords of council.[46] One may also notice a later ruling that an action by the comptroller against Hamburg merchants for unpaid custom should not be heard before the admiral because it was 'na seyfair mater'.[47]

Balfour's reservations about the exchequer's competence to deal with extraneous cases, not concerned with revenue matters, rests on the authority of a mandate addressed to the auditors on 29 July 1527, in which the king complained that they 'daylie callis summondis now in our chekker and vaikis nocht apoune [do not have time for] the making of our comptis', ordering them to choose certain persons to adjourn to the tolbooth 'for calling of all materis that occurris'.[48] In the following year the auditors and lords of council, 'understanding the gret hynder and delay of expeditioune in the chekker be inopportune solicitatioune and calling of summondis and utheris materis quhilk pertenis nocht tharto', ordered that privileged cases were to be heard in the tolbooth on two days each week, so that in future 'the chekker be nocht stoppit with syk besynes'. A month later even privileged cases were continued 'sa that in the meyntyme the chekker may proceide and be endit without inquietatioun of calling of civile actiounis'.[49] In 1530 the exchequer had to move to Linlithgow, for 'eschewing of the pestelence now regnand in Edinburgh'. On 21 July the king commanded the auditors to call no summonses or letters 'nor deliver na billis tharin bot sa mony as concernis the materis of our said chekkir'. Accordingly they made a further continuation of a case which they had been due to hear on 26 July, because of 'inhibitioun maid to thame be the kingis grace that thai suld nocht proceid bot apoun chekkir matteris', despite a protest by one of the parties. On 17 August, however, they continued a case for five days 'nochtwithstanding the act maid in the chakker that na materis be callit thairintill', because the parties had consented. Any bar to the exchequer's jurisdiction was therefore administrative rather than legal, imposed by the king so that the auditors could concentrate on financial business. Without such a bar it seems that any action might be heard in exchequer if the parties consented.[50]

It is, of course, as difficult in some cases to distinguish between administrative and judicial acts, as it is to decide whether a petitioner is seeking an administrative or judicial remedy. Nevertheless the comparatively late development of judicial proceedings in exchequer should not obscure the lack of any clear demarcation between the work of the council and that of the exchequer.

---

[45] 25 May 1533 (wrongly dated by Balfour 25 March). CS.6/2 fol. 168; *Acta Dominorum Concilii et Sessionis 1532-1533*, ed. I.H. Shearer, Stair Society (Edinburgh, 1956) [*ADC&S*], 5.
[46] *ADC&S*, 3; *ADCP*, 404; CS.6/2 fol. 176. Cited by Balfour, *Practicks*, 135, but wrongly dated 27 July, instead of 27 May 1533.
[47] *ADCP*, 637.
[48] *ADCP*, 262.
[49] *ADCP*, 277, 281.
[50] *ADCP*, 331-32, 338, 442; CS.5/41 fol. 94.

The council's original province was the general administration of the realm, with no real differentiation between its sittings for justice, for finance or for state affairs, except that a special commission was necessary for auditing accounts in exchequer. Although those commissioned united in their persons the dual functions of lords of council and auditors of exchequer, they did not keep those functions separate. Just as the full council could deal with administrative and judicial business affecting the revenue, so the smaller council-in-exchequer could do the work of the whole council if necessary.

Continuation of cases to exchequer was partly a matter of administrative convenience where they involved consultation of the exchequer rolls or where they referred to accounts which were coming up for audit. Again, a hearing in exchequer might be more convenient for litigants who had to be there in any case to present their accounts. In February 1535 an action by the crown against Sir John Campbell of Cawdor and others, concerning rents wrongfully uplifted from royal property, was continued to allow the parties to produce their rights before the auditors of exchequer and for the exchequer rolls to be inspected.[51] If the auditors were unable to give a final decreet, however, the case was to come back to the session in November. Nevertheless the auditors remained under the control and direction of the council, as in 1498 when the lords 'consalis the lordis of the chekkir til remit thir religious men this unlaw that thai fell in'.[52] Similar control was exercised over the admiral when the council claimed the right to sit with him as assessors or to hear admiralty actions themselves.[53] Furthermore, apparent confusion of the records of 'council', 'secret council',[54] 'session' and 'exchequer' in James V's reign reflects their administrative unity and the existence of an undifferentiated body of lords of council, some of whom received special commissions for certain administrative or judicial purposes.[55] In appointing James Colville to the council on 9 March 1529 James V specified that he was to 'have place tharof in oure sessioune, chekkir, generale consale and all uthir tymis as accordis'.[56]

It remains to be seen how far the exchequer was affected by changes in the administration of civil justice in the 1530s, namely the reform of the 'session' in 1532 and the founding of the college of justice. Though these changes did not create a new 'court of session', their effect was to make the lords of session a

---

[51] *ADCP*, 434.
[52] *ADC*, II, 268.
[53] *ADCP*, lxiv, 76; *APS*, II, 449-50.
[54] The secret council is not well documented but clearly had over-riding authority. In 1525 an administrative decision to allow a grain rent from Freuchy (Fife) to be paid in barley instead of corn involved the lords of secret council as well as the auditors of exchequer (*ER*, XV, 120-21). On 6 June 1531, before the lords of secret council, the Earl of Argyll, heritable chamberlain of Kintyre, agreed that the comptroller or his depute should exercise that office for a year and inbring the king's property for his profit (*ADCP*, 356).
[55] For a decree by the lords commissioners for setting crown lands, 7 January 1522, see *ER*, XIV, 505.
[56] *ADCP*, 307.

permanent, paid body of judges, with what soon came to be a universal jurisdiction in all types of civil causes.[57] Administrative continuity was reflected in the continuity of the records, unfortunately obscured by an unwarranted division introduced in the early nineteenth century.[58] Certainly there was a diminution in the amount of administrative business recorded in the 1530s, but this can be attributed to James V having reached an age when he could take full control of the administration. His death and Mary's minority brought a reversion to earlier practice with a large admixture of administrative business until a separate privy council record was started in 1545.

Of those nominated as senators of the new college of justice and lords of session in parliament on 17 May 1532, only three were to serve as auditors in that year's exchequer: Alexander Mylne, Abbot of Cambuskenneth, the president, James Colville (re-appointed comptroller in September 1539), and Nichol Crawfurd, the justice-clerk.[59] A fourth, the recently-appointed clerk register, Sir James Foulis, was added at the inaugural *'sessio dominorum'*, on 27 May, and thereafter all four sat regularly until the end of July.[60] During this period the record uses the words *'sederunt domini sessionis'*, a change from pre-1532 practice, though decrees continued to be in the name of the 'lords of council'. Auditors thus formed a minority of the ordinary lords of session, as lords of session were of the auditors. This fact, and the decision that the session was to continue until Lammas (1 August) may have reflected the problems encountered in the previous year when the auditors had been so 'infestit' with extraneous business by the end of July that 'thai may nocht vaike upoun chekkir materis'.[61]

In the event the exchequer got off to a very slow start. By 7 July the auditors had lost patience, imposing a fine of £100 on sheriffs who failed to appear on the appointed day or left before making 'fynale compt and pament'; other officials escaped with the standard £10 penalty.[62] The lords of session appear to have heard no revenue cases during July. On 10 August nine lords, of whom only two were auditors, dealt with a sum due to Colville, as comptroller, by the Earl of Huntly, as chamberlain of Strathdee and Cromar. On the same day the chancellor *'cum ceteris domini concilii et sessionis'*, empowered those lords of session 'as sall happin to remane in this toun' to 'sitt and minister justice

---

[57]G. Donaldson, *Scotland: James V to James VII* (Edinburgh, 1965), pp. 46-48; *Hannay*, ed. MacQueen, 110; H.L. MacQueen, 'Jurisdiction in heritage and the lords of council and session after 1532', *Miscellany Two*, Stair Society (Edinburgh, 1984), pp. 61-85.

[58]See *ADC*, III, introduction, xiii.

[59]*ER*, XVI, 165 (auditors of comptroller's account). The auditors of the main exchequer would have included the comptroller himself. For a list of lords of session see G. Brunton and D. Haig, *The Senators of the College of Justice* (Edinburgh, 1832), pp. ix-x. One lord of session, John Dingwall, had been an auditor from 1522 to 1527 (*ER*, XIV, 451; XV, 373), but did not serve as such after 1532.

[60]CS.6/1 fols 1-99 passim.

[61]*APS*, II, 336; *ER*, XVI, 539.

[62]*ER*, XVI, 550.

quhen sic materis cumis that requiris hasty acceleratioun and expedition'.[63] Although lords of session did sit during the exchequer, other bodies dealt with judicial business. On 12 August the king charged the chancellor and treasurer to convene the lords of council to deal with Hermitage Castle and the assembled lords also found time to give a decree against Barton, the former comptroller, to pay the bairns of Henry Borthwick, gunner, slain at the siege of Tantallon, the arrears of his wages, for which he had taken allowance in his accounts as in the 'outdrawcht of the rolls'.[64] The only sederunt of named *'domini auditores scacarii'* occurred on 14 August 1532, when the Master of Hailes, sheriff of Haddington, with Lord Maxwell as surety undertook to pay Colville a sum which he had 'tane on his heid in the roll of this instant year of the scherefdome' of Haddington. Lord Maxwell also protested against the refusal of David Beaton, the Abbot of Arbroath, to append the privy seal to a respite signed by the king and treasurer to the inhabitants of Eskdale, Ewesdale and Wauchopedale, which could not have been exchequer business. On 21 August an unnamed body of auditors received a plea by the comptroller for allowance of his 'hors meit' and servants' wages.[65]

In considering the last ten years of James V's reign, we shall be trying to determine whether the auditors of exchequer continued to be a court for cases involving the king's property and revenues and whether the exchequer was also used for other types of cases. But first it is necessary to take a brief look at the personnel involved. Under the 1532 act the lords of session became a restricted body, comprising only a president and fourteen ordinary senators of the college of justice. This can be compared with the thirty-eight lords chosen to sit in the session as recently as December 1531.[66] Henceforward new appointments could only be made as vacancies occurred, though the king did have power to nominate additional 'extraordinary lords'. Auditors continued to be appointed annually, not just for the main exchequer but also, separately, for the comptroller's and treasurer's accounts, but in practice they, too, were drawn from a comparatively limited pool. Though individual commissions varied between ten and seventeen auditors, the total number of persons involved over the ten years 1533-1542 is unlikely to have exceeded thirty-five.[67] Some made only one or two appearances; others recur over a period of years. Alexander Myln, president of the college of justice until his death in 1548, was in every exchequer commission from 1524 onwards.[68] James Kincragy, who died in 1539, had been an auditor

---

[63] CS.6/1 fol. 101; *ADCP*, 380.
[64] *ADCP*, 380-81; CS.6/1 fol. 104; *ADC&S*, 3.
[65] *ADCP*, 381-82.
[66] *ADCP*, 368.
[67] Auditors are listed for the exchequer, *ER*, XVI, 225 (1533), 302 (1534), 402 (1535), 447 (1536); XVII, 1 (1537), 70 (1538), 313 (1540); comptroller's accounts, *ER*, XVI, 286 (1533), 341 (1534); XVII, 155 (1538), 269 (1540); treasurer's accounts, *TA*, VI, 65 (1533), 167 (1534), 269 (1536), 366 (1538); VII, 65 (1539), 232 (1540), 364 (1541); VIII, 1 (1542). Treasury audits of February 1536 and June 1537, which fell outside the normal exchequer sessions, are not included.
[68] *ER*, XV, 84. He had been Abbot of Cambuskenneth since 1517 (*Registrum monasterii S. Marie de Cambuskenneth*, ed. W. Fraser, Grampian Club (Edinburgh, 1872), pp. lxxxviii-xcvi).

since 1516.[69] Two newcomers, Alexander Scott, provost of Corstorphine, and Robert Reid, Abbot of Kinloss, served every year from 1534.[70] The commissions tended to have a large admixture of clergy, up to eight bishops and abbots (1535) and five others (in 1538). Apart from officials, comparatively few laity were involved. The four in 1533 comprised Robert Barton, formerly comptroller, Thomas Scott of Petgormo, an ordinary lord of session who became justice clerk in 1536, William Hamilton of Sanquhar, who was paid for his services from 1531 to 1537,[71] and Lord Erskine, an extraordinary lord of session, the only nobleman to be appointed consistently (1532-35, 1537, 1540-42). The number of officials increased over the period. In 1533 they comprised the comptroller, treasurer, clerk register, and justice-clerk, who were later joined by the advocate (from 1537), the treasurer clerk (1538-41) and secretary (1542). The number of ordinary lords of session who were auditors varied between five (out of 14) and seven (out of 16 or 17); that of extraordinary lords from four or five (1534-37) to none (1538-39).

With the end of the summer session now fixed by statute as 1 August, there seems to have been no scope for judicial sittings of the exchequer in July. That is not to say that revenue cases were not dealt with. In 1533 the comptroller sat with the lords of session for such cases on 18 July but was absent the following day. On 25 August, however, a gift of ward and marriage was decerned to be 'of nane availe' by the 'lordis of counsale and auditouris of chekkir'.[72] The 1533 exchequer proved unusually protracted, not ending until early October. Perhaps for this reason in the following year its start was delayed to 23 July, remaining in mid to late July for the rest of the decade.[73] On 5 September 1534 the auditors, with consent of parties, continued a case relating to the assize herring of the East Sea until 6 October. Their remaining decrees on that day were given as lords of council. Curiously although the record is headed '*sederunt domini auditores ut in die precedenti*', the previous day's sederunt was indubitably of lords of council, two of whom were not auditors.[74]

In 1535 a decreet involving a question of Border law, quite unrelated to the king's property or revenue, was suspended until 10 August, when by consent of

---

[69] *ER*, XIV, 214; D.E.R. Watt, *Fasti Ecclesiae Scoticanae medii aevi ad annum 1638*, SRS (Edinburgh, 1969), 9.

[70] Scott's connection with the exchequer began in 1509 as its chaplain and (by 1516) one of the clerks writing the rolls (*ER*, XIII, 260; XIV, 223). From 1524 his services were rewarded with an annual pension until he obtained the provostry of Corstorphine in 1529 (*ER*, XV, 98, 550). He was diter of the rolls from 1538 to 1543 when he last appears as an auditor, dying in May 1544 (*ER*, XVII, 172; XVIII, 33, 41; *TA*, VIII, 2; Watt, *Fasti*, 348). Reid became Bishop of Orkney in 1541 (Watt, *Fasti*, 254).

[71] *ER*, XVI, 127, 137, 480H; *TA*, VI, 316. He was an auditor again, but unpaid, 1539-46 (*TA*, VII, 65; VIII, 194).

[72] CS.6/3 fols 27^V, 29^V, 62^V; *ADCP*, 407.

[73] *ER*, XVI, 286, 302, 402, 447; XVII, 1, 70, 313. An exact date is not known for 1539, but the earliest account was rendered on 29 July (*ER*, XVII, 187).

[74] CS.6/5 fol. 115. The assize herring was a levy paid to the king on boats taking part in the herring fishery, in this case in the Firth of Forth (*RSS*, I, nos. 286, 2823).

party the matter was to be heard before the lords of exchequer. But the six lords who considered the case on that day and referred it to the warden of the Middle Marches included two who were not auditors, though all were lords of session.[75] In fact, of twelve sederunts recorded in August 1535, none were expressly of lords of exchequer, though five were of lords of council with (unnamed) auditors of exchequer. On 14 and 26 August all the named lords were actually auditors themselves, perhaps indicating some difference in ranking between them and those not named. Nevertheless any decrees were given by the 'lords of council'.[76] On 26 August the lords ordered a report to be made on the state of the common good of Perth, the exchequer having recently acquired statutory responsibility for the oversight of burgh accounts.[77] On 3 September 1535 the sederunt was of 'the lords of session along with the lords auditors of exchequer as before', but none of the business was specifically exchequer-related.[78] In 1536 the exchequer began on 17 July. On 7 August an action by the comptroller and the tacksman of the assize herring of the West Sea against several burgesses of Ayr was settled by an agreement in presence of the lords auditors between the defenders and the tacksman, following which the auditors ordained them to pay in future under pain of being held as 'defraudaris of the kingis grace'.[79] The sederunt of 17 August was of the lords of session '*cum auditoribus scaccarii*' but it was in presence of the 'lordis of consale' that Patrick Hepburn of Wauchton and John Simson, burgess of Edinburgh, agreed to pay a sum assigned by the king to Sir James Hamilton of Finnart.[80] Of five named lords of session sitting with the auditors on 17, 29 and 21 August four were also auditors of exchequer. Although the exchequer continued until the audit of the comptroller's account on 9 September, the council record is not extant after 25 August, from which point there is a gap extending to November 1537, well after the 1537 exchequer.[81]

1538 presents a similar picture of council proceedings being largely in the hands of those who were also auditors of exchequer. On 9 August all nine lords were auditors.[82] On 23 August the eight lords present seem to have drawn a nice distinction between their functions. As auditors of exchequer they ordained that letters should be directed to charge the laird of Anstruther 'to compear befor thame apoun Wednesday nixt to cum to answer apoun sic thingis as salbe schawin to him at his cuming', but they dealt with all the remaining business as lords of council.[83] On 3 September ten named lords, all auditors, sat '*cum ceteris auditoribus scaccarii*'. The identity of 'the rest of the auditors' is not clear. If the

---

[75] *ADCP*, 441-42.
[76] CS.6/6 fols 218^V, 222^V.
[77] *ADCP*, 444-45; *APS* II, 349.
[78] CS.6/6 fol. 227.
[79] CS.6/8 fol. 159. The 'west sea' comprised the whole west coast, sea lochs and tidal part of the Clyde (*RMS*, III, no. 1602).
[80] CS.6/8 fol. 167^V.
[81] *ER*, XVI, 478; *ADCP*, 459.
[82] CS.6/10 fol. 167^V.
[83] CS.6/10 fol. 174.

Bishop of Ross and the treasurer (Kirkcaldy of Grange) had been present they would surely have been named. This leaves only four auditors, all clerics: the veteran James Kincragy, Alexander Scott and two newcomers, John Danielston, parson of Dysart, and John Colden, provost of Methven and clerk of expenses in the king's household. Business included an action by the king against the Bishop of Aberdeen, a former treasurer, for production of an assignation to him by the comptroller of the ward and marriage of Culzean. The following day the ten lords, joined by the secretary but sitting without the other auditors, decerned 'be sentence interlocutour' that they could not 'justlie allow and defeis' [discharge] the bailie of Carrick of the ward and marriage until the assignation had been 'first sene and considerit'.[84] It is not clear why the 'other auditors' should have been involved in the first day's hearing but not in the second.

Some revenue cases were dealt with as part of normal session business between January and March 1539, following which there is another gap in the council record until February 1540.[85] A change in record-keeping means that no names are listed for most of the sederunts in August 1540, though a decree for the comptroller on 18 August, relating to the customs of Linlithgow, was pronounced by the lords of council and auditors.[86] On the other hand on 3 August the lords of council alone decerned Lord Drummond, steward of Strathearn, to make compt and reckoning of all duties and casualties since his entry to office and to pay them to the treasurer 'now in this present chekker'. As Lord Drummond had summoned John Drummond of Innerpeffray before the auditors to relieve him of the sums with which the latter had intromitted during his minority, both were ordered to remain 'in this toun' until they had 'enterit thair compt in this present chekker' and made 'reknyng and payment thairof as accordis'.[87] On 13 August the auditors set a day for the Abbot of Dunfermline to show his right to stop English men coming to the port of Kirkcaldy from paying customs to the king's custumars. On 23 August, however, the case was continued by the lords of council to 31 August, when they, not the auditors, found in his favour. It may be that the matter was considered too important to be settled by the auditors alone, as the lords found that the abbot and convent had right under a charter of Robert I, not just to the great customs of Kirkcaldy but to those of the burghs of Dunfermline, Queensferry and Musselburgh as well.[88] A joint decree of council and auditors on 7 September extinguished the claims of any creditors of the comptroller and treasurer who had failed to produce their evidence and receive payment in response to an earlier charge. The council's involvement here may stem from novelty of the procedure, as this was the first (and indeed the last) time such a decree was pronounced.[89]

---

[84] CS.6/10 fols 177^V, 179-80.
[85] ADCP, 477, 480-82; CS.6/11 fols 199, 206, 217, 228^V, 259^V.
[86] CS.6/13 fol. 196.
[87] CS.6/13 fol. 188.
[88] ADCP, 493-94; CS.6/13 fols 193, 198^V, 201.
[89] ADCP, 494-95.

The 1541 exchequer began in August,[90] about a week after the end of the session. As in 1540 few sederunt lists are recorded and it is difficult to tell which members of the council were acting at any particular sitting and in what capacity. On 18 August the widow of Sir James Hamilton of Finnart appeared before the lords of council and auditors of exchequer and delivered to William Menteith of Kerse signet letters charging him to become bound in the books of council to allow her and her tenants peaceable possession of the lands and barony of Tillicoultry for her lifetime in terms of his agreement with the treasurer on being granted infeftment of them. On 22 August she again appeared, this time before the 'lordis of counsale' alone to ask whether he would obey and the lords 'interponit [interposed] thar decrete' to his consent.[91] On 25 August the auditors dealt with a complaint first raised in the previous February by the burgh of Dundee. They found 'be ane decreit' that the magistrates and community of Dundee paid customs on certain types of skins, assolzied [absolved] the custumar and clerk of cocket from their allegation that they had 'tane mair custume fra thame nor cummys to the kingis profitt' because the goods in question had appeared in their account, but laid down detailed rules for future charging and collection of the duties on skins and cloth.[92] On 30 August, however, a summons by the king and the alderman and bailies of Wigtown against Thomas Kennedy and William Nisbet 'to heir and se thame be decernit be decrete of the lordis auditouris of the chekker' to deliver salt belonging to the king 'be ressoun of eschete' was continued by the lords of council to 2 December.[93] In 2 September an obligation was registered in the books of council but before the lords auditors of exchequer. On 3 September the auditors found that they could not command the treasurer to pay more than was allowed in his account.[94] On 10 September, in presence of the 'lordis auditouris of chekker and counsale' Robert Barton's widow renounced any sums still due for his expenditure while treasurer and comptroller. On 12 September the lords of council discharged officers at arms from distraining for taxation due by the commendator of Culross, Lady Sinclair's procurator appeared in presence of the auditors to require the comptroller to pay the annual sum promised to her by the king for the lands she had in assedation [on lease] in Orkney and Shetland, and an action by the comptroller concerning unpaid customs on English goods brought to Leith was continued for proof on 16 November.[95]

If we compare the 1541 exchequer with that of 1525 the general picture seems, if anything, less clear. Instead of auditors of exchequer sitting *in scaccario* we have a body, sitting at an unspecified location and acting both as auditors and lords of council. The one recorded sederunt list, that of 9 August, contains only

---

[90] Earliest accounts rendered 8 August (*ER*, XVII, 391, 398).
[91] *ADCP*, 506-7.
[92] *ADCP*, 500, 507-8.
[93] CS.6/16 fol. 136^v; *Wigtownshire Charters*, ed. R.C. Reid, SHS (Edinburgh, 1960), 146.
[94] *ADCP*, 508-9; CS.6/16 fols 138, 140-41.
[95] *ADCP*, 509; CS.6/16 fols 142-43.

five names, all of whom were auditors of exchequer. Two of these, Foulis, the clerk register, and Bellenden,[96] Thomas Scott's successor as justice-clerk, were lords of session and royal officials, though not of the first rank; others were the three clerics, John Colden, John Danielston and Alexander Scott, who had been lumped together by the council clerks in 1538 as 'the rest of the auditouris', an indication, perhaps, of inferior status. In their presence as 'lordis auditouris of chekker', a burgess of Wigtown, who had obtained licence to charter a French or Breton ship for catching fish in the Outer Isles, found caution [surety] that he should compear yearly in exchequer to give his oath on 'quhat fische beis tane' and pay the due custom. At the same sitting, however, but as lords of council, they dealt with several civil actions, fixing a diet for proof in one and making an order following on an earlier decreet in another.[97]

As in 1525 the cases heard formed a continuum with those before and after the period of the exchequer. During the exchequer, the lords dealt with a number relating to castlewards, annual payments by crown vassals collected and accounted for by the sheriffs.[98] But similar cases had been heard by the lords of session in July[99] and some of those during the exchequer were continued to dates falling after its conclusion. More significantly when, just before the end of the session on 30 July 1525, an action against the bailies of the barony of Broughton was continued, the clerk register asked instruments that the lords of council 'was content to tak the said mater in the chekker and to do justice thairintill', with the pursuer's consent, 'quhill [until] the nixt sessioun'.[100] On 9 August the five auditors, sitting as lords of council, made an order in a case between two private parties, notwithstanding 'thai ar nocht of sufficient number'.[101] Here we see them acting as the judicial council, even though they did not constitute a quorum. Nevertheless the existence of some sort of limit on the exchequer's competence is implied by another case from 1541. Thomas Weir of Blackwood summoned Archibald Blair and others to compear before the lords of council 'in the chekker' for suspension of letters proceeding upon 'cursing' by the commissary of Douglas. But 'at the calling thairof the saidis [lordis] in the chakker allegeit thai mycht nocht proceid thairintill becaus thai wer nocht ane nowmer and the mater wes ane sessioun mater and that thai wald nocht proceid thairintil quhill the nixt sessioun'.[102]

---

[96] Bellenden was a diter of the rolls with Alexander Scott, 1539-42 (*TA*, VII, 207; VIII, 107; *ER*, XVII, 292).
[97] CS.6/16 fols 125-26; *Wigtownshire Charters*, 146.
[98] CS.6/16 fols 127, 138, 143. For castlewards see *The Sheriff Court Book of Fife*, ed. W.C. Dickinson, SHS (Edinburgh, 1928), 372-75.
[99] CS.6/16 fols 54^V, 74. The lords of session had also dealt with cases involving the customs of Wigtown and Whithorn and the sheriff of Berwick's exchequer account (CS.6/16 fols 21, 70, 83).
[100] CS.6/16 fol. 96.
[101] CS.6/16 fol. 125.
[102] CS.6/17 fol. 83.

In 1542 the start of exchequer reverted to late June,[103] giving a five week overlap with the session, which continued until 31 July. Apart from one sederunt '*in scaccario*' on 9 August, involving six auditors, all lords of session,[104] the record contains nothing of interest for present purposes, though this may in itself be significant. For the impression given by the council record after 1532 is that the lords of session were expanding their judicial role at the expense of other conciliar bodies. Certainly there appears to have been no judicial activity in exchequer during term time, even for cases involving the king's property and revenue. But it also seems that the lords of session could not by themselves provide adequate cover for a vacation court and that business continued to be handled by whatever element of the council happened to be on hand. While the exchequer was sitting it provided a convenient forum, even for cases having no revenue implications, but those hearing such cases would not necessarily be auditors and all would be acting in the capacity of lords of council, though there were still instances where the clerks, for whatever reason, chose to refer specifically to the auditors of exchequer.

While developments after 1542 lie outside the scope of the present study, it is worth noting the emergence of a separate privy council with its own records in the mid-1540s. This marked a split between the adminstrative and judicial councils, with the latter evolving into court of session. The exchequer remained attached to the judicial council and its proceedings must be sought in the increasingly voluminous record of acts and decreets.[105] From the late 1550s, however, it became common practice to enter obligations for appearance of payment in the responde books rather than in the court registers.[106] Overlapping dates of session and exchequer evidently continued to cause trouble. In 1564 the privy council decided that the exchequer should begin in future on 2 August 'to proceid but continewation unto the end of the haill comptis, alsweill of the thesaurare [and] comptrollar as of the utheris inferiour officiaris'.[107] In 1567 parliament ordered that it 'be kepit in the auncient and accustomat tyme of the yeir', that is during the court vacation, otherwise replacements would have to be found for the lords and clerks of session as auditors and clerks of exchequer.[108] This shows the exchequer still dependent upon the court of session, which remained the appropriate forum for cases involving the revenue when the exchequer was not sitting. The privy council had a general oversight of all aspects of administration, including finance.

---

[103] Earliest account rendered 26 June (*ER*, XVII, 465).
[104] SRO Register of acts and decreets, CS.7.1 fols 103A, 118^V (originally continuation of same series as CS.5-6).
[105] See for example *ADCP*, 533, 611, 617-18.
[106] *ER*, XIX, 217-18, 460-1 etc. For decrees by the auditors, March 1570 and February 1575 see *ER*, XX, 397-39, 464-65.
[107] *RPC*, I, 278.
[108] *APS*, III, 43.

It was not until 1584 that the exchequer finally emerged as a separate and permanent court. Its earliest register dates from February 1584, the month in which James VI and his council made provision for the exchequer to deal with problems relating to the revenue.[109] An act of parliament of May 1584 laid down that suspensions and letters conform in matters concerning the revenue should be granted only 'be sic of the numer of our college of justice as ar constitute auditouris of our chekker' and that such matters should be discussed 'befoir our chekker in our chekker hous'. The auditors were to sit on Tuesdays and Thursdays during session and when they pleased in vacation, their decisions and decreets to be 'as vailable and effectuall in all respectis as gif the samyn were gevin and pronunceit be a full and haill numer of the saidis lordis of counsell sittand in the tolbuith of Edinburgh'.[110] It is not clear whether this implies an existing distinction between those auditors who were qualified to sit in a judicial capacity and the rest who were not. With this act, however, a year after Balfour's death and fifty years after the cases to which he referred, his statement about the judicial role of the exchequer at last approximated to the true position.

---

[109] SRO E.4/1; *RPC*, III, 626-27.
[110] *APS*, III, 309, ratified 1593 and 1633 (*APS*, IV, 27; V, 35). A statutory ban on permanent commisions (*APS*, IV, 165) from 1598 to 1633 does not seem to have affected the exchequer's status as a court.

6

MUSIC FOR 'GODDIS GLORE AND THE KINGIS'

Helena M. Shire[1]

King James V of Scotland was born at Linlithgow a year and a half before his father's death on Flodden Field. A year after the battle he was crowned King at Stirling in September 1513 and Scotland entered on a long period of minority in its monarch and regency and warring faction in its rule. What music there was in Scotland during these years 'for Goddis glore and the Kingis', in great abbey, Chapel Royal or royal household we can discover only with difficulty. The several splendid masses that Robert Carver had been composing from 1513 in the twenty-second year of his age are preserved in National Library of Scotland Adv. MS 5.1.15.[2] They are testimony to a vigorous culture in Scotland under King James IV of sacred music that was native in provenance yet European in tradition. But this *fyne musick* of the canon of Scone Abbey was, like the poetry of the age of makars, silenced or diminished after the national disaster of Flodden. No other texts of *musick fyne* survive dated or signed from this era.[3] For music of the court, the official records give the bare outline, and that only for part of the time, for the Accounts of the Lord High Treasurer of Scotland have survived only between 25 June 1515 and September 1518, from June 1522 to April 1524 and from August 1525 to August 1527. Some information, however, can be drawn from the Register of the Great Seal and the Register of the Secret Seal though those, too, are incomplete.

---

[1]This article is an edited version of an unpublished typescript written by Helena Shire in the 1960s. Permission to publish it in this form has been most generously granted by Dr Alisoun Gardner-Medwin. Dr Shire's publications of the 1950s and 60s, including *Song, Dance and Poetry of the Court of Scotland Under King James VI* (Cambridge, 1969) and, with Kenneth Elliott, *Music of Scotland 1500-1700*, Musica Britannica XV (London, 1957 and revised editions), greatly assisted and encouraged research in early Scottish music and poetry in the years that followed. Where possible, the editing of the typescript has taken account of this fact.

Editing and notes within the text and at foot are by Dr J. Hadley Williams; Dr A. Gardner-Medwin and Dr J. Purser kindly commented helpfully upon an early version of the edited typescript.

[2]See further: *MB* XV, 30-57 and 87-102. See also K. Elliott, 'The Carver Choirbook', *Music and Letters*, 41.4 (1960), 349-57; I. Woods, 'The Carvor [sic] Choirbook', 2 vols, Diss. Princeton, 1984; D.J. Ross, *Musick Fyne: Robert Carver and the Art of Music in Sixteenth-Century Scotland* (Edinburgh, 1993). See also the bibliography in Richard Turbet, 'Scotland's Greatest Composer: An Introduction to Robert Carver (1487-1566)', *Bryght Lanternis*, ed. J.D. McClure and M.R.G. Spiller (Aberdeen, 1989), pp. 48-54. Among recorded performances of Carver are those by Cappella Nova: *Scottish Renaissance Polyphony: Robert Carver*, ASV Gaudeamus LP/MC/CD GAU 124, 126 and 127.

[3]For the term '*musick fyne*' see *MB* XV, p. xv and Shire, *Song, Dance and Poetry*, p. 2.

It is hard to describe a court-culture during an era of anarchy—of faction, sudden reversal and changing regency, of struggle for the custody of the young king, with which went power in the land. The personalities who wielded power were, first, the Queen Mother, Margaret Tudor, daughter of King Henry VII of England. She was named Regent in her husband's will, against Scots usage, which takes the next-in-succession for this role. A few months after the battle she gave birth to a posthumous prince. Speedily taking a new husband, Archibald Douglas created Earl of Angus, she proved unacceptable as Queen Regent. In 1515 the Duc d'Aubigny (the Duke of Albany), cousin to the dead King James IV, descended from the exiled younger brother of King James III, and next-in-succession to the throne, was called to Scotland and was made Lord Governor of the realm by parliament. From then until 1524, when he left Scotland for the last time, he is the acting head of the state. After 1524 we have to do with the youthful king himself, in association, variously, with his mother 'Margarete our quene' and—or—her second husband and his family 'the Douglases'.[4] After 1528 the young king escaped 'from cure', and reigns in his 'aistait Royall', alone.

At best over these years of intermittent rule we can assemble the fragmentary evidence for a continuing pattern of culture, of music 'for Goddis glore and the Kingis' for ceremony and for recreation of the court.[5] During the greater part of these periods covered by the surviving records, the Lord Governor was present in Scotland. For the 'music of the royal household' the records yield substantial information as to personnel and some as to function. Extracts are given here from the Lord High Treasurer's Accounts tracing the presence, wages or reward, and—where it is indicated—function of, first the Italian minstrels, a stand of musicians, a permanent feature of the royal establishment from 1502 until 1548; next of Bontans (Bontemps?) the French minstrel, known at court in King James IV's time and traced to March 1517/18 six months before that stretch of the records ends; and finally, other instances of minstrels, musicians and so on, are summarized.[6]

---

[4]For further details of the roles of these figures in the minority years: M.G. Kelley, 'The Douglas Earls of Angus: A Study in the Social and Political Bases of Power of a Scottish Family from 1389 until 1557', Diss. Edinburgh, 1973, esp. Part II, chapters vi-viii; W.K. Emond, 'The Minority of James V, 1513-1528', Diss. St Andrews, 1988. See also P.G.B. McNeill, 'The Scottish Regency', *Juridical Review*, 12, n.s. (1967), 127-48 and R.G. Eaves, *Henry VIII and James V's Regency 1524-28: A Study in Anglo-Scottish Diplomacy* (Lanham, New York, London, 1987).

[5]Evidence of the influence of Margaret Tudor's presence in Scotland is found in 'Alas that same sueit face', the English court-song named a Scottish favourite in Robert Wedderburn, *The Complaynt of Scotland*, ed. A.M. Stewart, STS, Edinburgh 1979), p. 51. See further *MB* XV, No. 34 and H.M. Shire, *The Thrissil, the Rois and the Flour-de-lys* (Cambridge, 1962), pp. 14-17 and 28.

[6]In the early 1500s, £1 sterling was worth £4 Scots; see further, J.M. Gilbert, 'The usual money of Scotland and exchange rates against foreign coin', *Coinage in Medieval Scotland (1100-1600)*, ed. D.M. Metcalfe, British Archaeological Reports, 14 (Oxford, 1977), 131-53. In the present text, li. = libri (pound); s. = shilling(s); d. = pence.

'ITALIAN MINSTRELS':
THE DRUMMONDS WITH GEORGE FOREST

From 1502 onwards a stand of Italian minstrels, originally eight in number, have their place in the records of the royal household and entries recur regularly of their wages, but they are not identifiable as the family group of Drummond before 1512.

> 1512. Item, the x day of November, to Juliane Drummond and his vij complicis, Italiane mentralis and trumpettis [trumpeters], for the monethis of November instant, December, and Januar to cum, to ilkane of thame iiij li. vij s. vj d. be the said tyme...
> Item, to James Dauenecurt, Bontais, and thare complicis menstralis, Franchemen, quhilk ar vj personis in the haile, for thare wagis of the said monethis of November, December and Januar, to ilkane of thame iiij li. vij s. vj d...[7]

> 1513 Item, to the Italiane menstralis for thame and the Franch taberneris [drummers], fidlaris, organeris, trumpettis, extending to the nowmir of xj personis, to every ane of thame iiij li. vij s. vj d. for thare termes wagis of Lammes [Lammas] last bypast... xlviij li. ij s. vj d.[8]

When the records resume two years after Flodden the French minstrels are no longer 'a stand', though one French minstrel, and perhaps other individual French musicians, remained in attendance in Scotland. The history of Bountans will be traced later.

The entries of the Italian minstrels are full. It is patently a family group of musicians, characteristic of the calling, found again in the latter half of the century with the Dows (or Dowies) under Queen Mary and the Hudsons at the marriage of 'Mary and Henry' and, later, with their son King James VI. This Drummond group seems here to entail two generations; at least one or probably two, of the elder generation, 'Vincent' and 'auld Julian'—if they are named in order of precedence (*TA*, V, 53). Certainly 'Anthone'—as far as I can judge this very Anthone Drummond—is still in service after King James V's marriage in 1537; and Julian Drummond, trumpeter—this 'younger Juliane' or a later bearer of the family name, was trumpeter at the battle of Pinkie Cleuch in 1547. The last member of the group enumerated here, 'George Forest, scottisman' (*TA*, V, 53), indicates in all probability a Scotsman born, George by name, who had

---

[7] *TA*, IV, 440.
[8] *TA*, IV, 443-44.

studied in Italy, where he had earned the tee-name of 'forestieri' (one come from abroad) commonly accruing in Italy to the immigrant musician.

> 1515 Item, to the v Italian menstrallis viz. Vincent, auld Julian, ȝoungar Julian, Anthone and Bestian Drummonth, and George Forest, scottisman with thame makand vj personis, takand ilk persone monethly for thair expensis thretty fyve schillingis ansuerand for the saidis vj personis to ten pundis ten schillingis and for ilk quartar ilk persone takand for thair feis four pundis sevin schillingis vj d., makand to thame all ilk quartar twenty six pundis v s., deliverit to thame this day, and at divers tymes befor the samyn in complete paiment of v monethis immediat befor this day, and for thair lammes [Lammas] quartar precedand this day, like as the breviat and thair compt beris in thaim, lvxviii li. xv s.
>
> Item, be my lord governouris command to Bestian Drummonth, ane of the said menstrallis, becaus he past with licence to vesy his frendis in Italie, to help his expensis by his wagis abuff writin. x li.
>
> Item, the secund day of October, deliverit to the saidis menstralis for thame that wes present and for the forsaid Bestian Drummonth becaus he past with licence to returne in haist, for his wagis and feis like as was promyst to him, in complete paiment of thair wagis for the moneth of October, and in complete paiment of all thair feis for the Martymes terme within the tyme of this compt, xxxvj li. xv s.
>
> Item, the penult day of November, and the xviij day of December deliverit to thame be Master George Langmur in complete paiment of the samyn tua monethis of November and December within the tyme of this compt for thair wagis. xxj li.
>
> Item, the forsaid xviij day of December, deliverit to the forsaid vj menstralis for thair ȝule abilȝementis and leverayis in the ȝere of God $1^m v^c$ and xv ȝeris within the tyme of this compt, ilk man vj lycht franche crounis, be compositioun maid with thaim becaus thai war wount to get twyis ilk ȝere, viz., ȝule and Witsunday, ilk tyme, goune, dowblat and hois, or ellis ilk persone six pundis ten schillingis in money for thair leverayis and abilȝementis, like as certane comptis maid befor this day beris in thame at mair lenth and without prejudice of thair dewiteis, haill leverayis and abilȝementis in tymes cumming. summa xxv li. iiii s.[9]

---

[9]TA, V, 53-54.

1516   Item, to the fyve Italian menstralis and George Forrest with thame, makand sex personis, ilk person takand monethlye efter the callander for thair meit and drink effor handis, thrette fyve s. answerand in ilk moneth to ten li. ten s. deliverit to thame in complet payment of the monethis of Januar, Februar, March, and Aprile within the tyme of this compt, xlij li.

Item, the xv day of Aprile, deliverit to thame be my lord governouris command to by thame hors, to wait on my lord governouris service, xx li.

Item, the xix day of September, deliverit to the forsaidis sex menstralis for thair abil3ementis of Vitsonday within the tyme of this comput, ilk persoun sex li. ten s. in complet payment thairof; summa xxxix li.[10]

The musicians of the royal household are here glimpsed 'mobilized' to attend the Lord Governor. In the same year, 1516, we find them in the context of the household of the child king, with his gentlewoman, his eight servitors and his schoolmaster (*TA*, V, 96). The year 1517 has the Whitsunday-term entry for the 'vj Italianis abil3ements' (*TA*, V, 124). When the records resume after June 1522 there is an order of the the Lord Governor delivered on 1 September to the Italian trumpeters to 'furniss thaim to the camp' (*TA*, V, 203). It is beyond doubt that here the same musicians of the household are commanded in their aspect of furnishing music of ceremony in martial array. In October the Lord Governor left Scotland for the second time. There is a large payment to the five Italian minstrels at Yule, 'ij^c libri viij s', the sum for three years' wages and maintenance (*TA*, V, 198). This could be payment in arrears; the break in the records makes it impossible to be sure. It could equally well though not so plausibly be payment in advance: it would stretch to the next entry that has survived, Yule clothes in the year 1525.

The entries in the record have not acquainted us extensively with the function of the Italian minstrels. Tabourners and trumpeters, they would seem to have been the 'lowd musick' of royalty, the music of ceremony of the court of Scotland. Ceremony was for peace as well as for war. Tabourner or trumpeter marked ceremonial movement or gesture at court as he followed to furnish martial array to camp, on raid or into battle. No link between these established musicians of the Scots court and the Lord Governor from France beyond that of official service is suggested by these entries.

---

[10]*TA*, V, 87.

BOUNTANS (BONTEMPS), THE FRENCH MINSTREL

In the last year of the old order under King James IV the court had a stand of six French minstrels: with other musicians they were paid their wages on 6 August, 1513—shortly before the battle of Flodden. Whether, in this entry it is to be understood that the 'French' applies only to the tabernaris [drummers] or also to some or all of the fiddlers, players of the organ and trumpeters, is hard to tell. Luckily the entry (already quoted) for the wages of 1512 makes it clear that the six French minstrels were established members of the King's music: they receive wages as such. The names are given of two, perhaps of three, for 'James', 'Davencourt' and 'Bontais' may be three separate persons. The remaining three are unnamed. James and Davencourt appear elsewhere.

Bontais had been known at court from the beginning of the century, the time of the royal marriage of King James IV and Margaret Tudor. On 29 September 1502, for example, 'Bountas' is paid for playing the 'cornut in the Quenis chalmir' (*TA*, II, 403). In the following month he is paid for a similar reason (*TA*, II, 403). He is paid again that year on October 31 in the records of lavish largesse or a big party—or both—on Hallowe'en (*TA*, II, 404). In 1508 'Bountas' the 'Franch fithelar' received four French crowns (*TA*, IV, 115).

It is difficult to establish whether he was resident in Scotland during the years between these entries, 1503-1508, 1508-1512, or a visitor on occasions of festivity. Unnamed in the records he may yet be present there under an entry such as that of 1506 to 'the four schawmeris and thair iiij childir' (*TA*, III, 189) or he may be included in the New Years' Day largesse in 1507 under 'divers menstrales, schawmeris, trumpetis, taubronaris, fithelaris, lutaris, harparis, clarscharis, piparis, extending to lxix persons... xlj li. xj s.' (*TA*, III, 360).

After Flodden and the two years' gap in the records, Bontanis, his French 'complicis' dispersed or dead, receives wages at the Lord Governor's command on 12 or 13 October 1515 (*TA*, V, 44); wages again in December (*TA*, V, 53), partly in payment of arrears. In February 1515/16 Bonetans—Boynetampus or Boynetans, fiddler or minstrel—to rehearse the variations, is paid directly by the Lord Governor's command or through his secretary 'Maister Galter' on the first day of parliament. Thereafter on 1 March 1516/17 a payment to Boyntamps occurs in circumstances where we must believe his skill was solacing to the Lord Governor sick and miserable in an inhospitable climate against which a Scottish castle offered little protection:

> 1516/17 Item, primo Marche, to Maister Johne Wrycht, to by plastere and burd for my lord governouris chamir quhen he wes sumthing seik iij li. v s.
> Item, to Boynetamps xviij s.

> Item, to James Nesbyt, that samin day for expensis of his self and ij utheris with him, brocht out of Dunbrattan to my lord governouris and had agane xlij s.[11]

He appears later with Anthone [Drummond?] trumpeter by command of the Lord Regent—money delivered to him to hire a horse and for expenses; and to Boyntans that same day (*TA*, V, 156). Then he could be among the French 'talbanaris' and minstralis that 'woik [waked] and playit all that nycht' (*TA*, V, 157)—rewarded with ale. What were they celebrating? Could it have been news of the Battle of Marignano and Francis I's return home? The accounts suggest festivity on a tremendous scale.

The presence of a French minstrel, rewarded then employed in the court of Scotland, is established. He is traced through the later reign of King James IV and through the infancy of King James V, now in the context of the young king's household, now in association with the Lord Governor whose compatriot he was. We know his name, variously spelled by a Scots hand, and we can hazard a guess that it was, in French, Bontemps. Skilled in different instruments, cornut, shawm and fiddle, he played at any rate in a musical group. His service appears also in context of civil ceremony or of martial array. His payment and probably his personal attendance was associated (except for the recorded instance with the child king) with the Duke of Albany until that Regent's second departure from Scotland. Trace of him is then lost in the ensuing gap in the records and his name does not reappear when the Lord Governor made his third stay in Scotland and the records resume. Did he go back with the Duke of Albany to France? I hope that this summary of his sojourn in Scotland may sometime link with study of minstrelsy on the continent, and that we may one day know more of him.

'KING IN TENDIR AIGE': 1512-24

In the years of the 'troubles' and thereafter in the climate of the young king's court, *musick fyne* sacred or secular and *Scottis poesie*—the fruit of meditation and imagination or the voice of ceremony couched in the literary language of Northern Inglis—had to flourish as they could and where they could. The religious houses or the universities, now here, now there, could prove nourishing forces, but it was from the court that interests and advancement flowed, in lands or money in civil life and to a great extent also in the life of the church. What music and poetry were to James V in childhood and as he was growing up—what songs and service of 'Venus quene' were to him in his royal person and in his governance as he came to manhood and personal rule we can read in the poetry of the time, above all in the works of David Lyndsay, the king's close devoted and familiar servitor—from birth his master-usher, his

---

[11]*TA*, V, 113-14.

playmate and music-maker in infancy, deviser and writer of court entertainments, and actor in them, pusuivant then, later, Lyon King of Arms, trusted envoy to European courts.

From the Treasurer's Accounts we can catch glimpses of the household of the child monarch:

> 1516   Item, for xij elne franche russat to be thre gounis to the Kingis gentlewoman, price of the elne xvj s.; summa of the haile ix li. xij s.
> Item, for vj quartaris of blak weluous, for the saidis gounis, price of the elne, 1 s.; summa iij li. xv s.
> Item for abil3ementis to the Kingis viij servitouris viz. Purves, [David] Crechtoun, [David?] Strageiht, Donaldsun, Dillye, [William], Dempstar, Craig, and Bissat...
> Item, for doublattis to the saidis servitouris ilk man haffand x quartaris skarlot, price of the elne xj s.
> Item, for viij pair of hois to the saidis servitouris ilk pair viij s.; summa iij li. iiij s.
> Item, for the sex Italianis abil3ementis, ilk man vj li. and x s.; summa xxxix li.
> Item, to Dowglass be the Kingis maister for his 3oyle clais v li. iij s. vij d. [12]

The six Italians, certainly the stand of musicians, are here in company with the King's gentlewoman and eight servitors. The 'lowd musick' of ceremony was for the fourteen-year-old King, also. Of the servitors, Donaldson is elsewhere named pursuivant and messenger (*TA*, V, 277, 278). Bissat (Bisset) bore messages for the Lord Governor (for example, *TA*, V, 128, 202, 319). William Dalye is 'Auld Wille Dile', mentioned in Lyndsay's *Complaynt*, a figure who grows old in royal service (he first appears: *TA*, III, 352, 1506; last appears: *TA*, V, 383, 1529). Craig is in all likelihood Johnne Crag of the King's household (*TA*, V, 197, 1522), Johne of Craig, groom of the chamber (*TA*, V, 261, 1525). If he is also Johne Creek, menstrale 1526/27, Johnne Craik, menstrale (*TA*, V, 435, 1531), Johne Craik mynstrale (*TA*, VI, 207, 1533/34 at New Year) here is another possible source of musical enjoyment in the King's circle from his early years. On this point we can add to surmise the certain presence in 1516 of other persons named minstrels to the king.

One was James Tabbaner [= tabranar?] 'now the King's minstrale in Striveling [Stirling] at the lordis delivera[n]s, for his goun, dowblat and hois' (*TA*, V, 82-3). I hesitate to equate this James with the 'French' James of the household last of 1512 (taberner to the Queen, James, Jakes, Jacques), for he is

---

[12] *TA*, V, 96.

almost certainly, 'James Grame the kingis menstrale' (*TA*, V, 117, 1517) and 'Grame, the kingis tabornar' (*TA*, V, 128). The interesting possibility remains, however, that they are all the same person, that here we have a Scot-born and foreign-trained minstrel as was the case with George Forest of the Italian group of musicians probably trained in Italy. In 1516/17 there is an entry showing that the royal presence even of a child, drew minstrelsy to it, the payment of ten pence 'to the menstralis of Striveling that followit the King to Lithqw' (*TA*, V, 111).

The 'Kingis maister' who paid Douglas in 1516 is James's 'magister', schoolmaster Gavin Dunbar, for a similarly worded entry for 1517, 28 August, reads: 'to Maister Gawan Dunbar, the Kingis maister, for expensis maid be him in reparaling of the chamir in the quhilk the King leris now in the castell...' (*TA*, V, 129). It is less likely to refer to the master-usher of the King, David Lyndsay himself. He and the lady he married complete our picture of the circle about the child king: 'Jenet Dowglas, spous to David Lindsay maister Ischare to the King' was rewarded at Yule 1522/23 'for sewing of the Kingis lynnyng claithis, de mandato domini gubernatoris xxiiij li.' (*TA*, V, 196).

The springs that in his *Complaynt* Lyndsay remembers playing to the child king on his lute are lost. Were they 'native airs' for dancing? They should have been, from the name he gives them: and such 'folk' dance tunes, seldom thus early thought of in terms of music-on-the-page, have survived in several manuscripts of the early seventeenth century, recorded delicately for this instrument. Of 'Gynkartoun', his favourite, the music may one day come to light; some of its words were in Constable's Cantus, as John Leyden discovered:[13]

> I would go twentie mile, I would go twentie mile,
>   I would go twentie mile on my bair foot,
> Ginkertoune, Ginkertoune, till hear him, Ginkertoune,
>   Play on a lute.

'ANE MUSITIAN HIMSELFF': 1524-27

The place of music in the studies of a child of the house of Stewart is described in the words of Erasmus speaking of Alexander Stewart, bastard son of King James IV, who had been his pupil in 1509 at the age of twelve.

> ...I lived with him once in the town of Siena; he was having lessons from me at the time in rhetoric and Greek.... At the same time he was studying law.... He used to listen to the theory of oratory, and write out a speech and declaim it, thus exercising

---

[13]*Complaynt of Scotland* (Edinburgh, 1801), p. 283.

both tongue and pen. He was learning Greek and every day at a certain time handed back the exercise he had been given. In the afternoon he would study music, playing the monochord, the recorder or the lute. Sometimes he would sing.[14]

This was he, who, when he had fallen in the shield ring round his father at Flodden, was lamented in these words: '...what had you to do with Mars,...you who were consecrated to the Muses, nay, to Christ?'[15]

His younger half-brother, monarch of Scotland, taken 'frome the sculis' at just this age, grew up with small Latin. To judge from his entourage at that time, we should look for social value rather than moral or intellectual discipline in any later teaching he got. Here music had a part to play. It would appear that this subject was congenial and perhaps persisted in when soldier studies were left behind. That he was musically gifted we know from Lyndsay's poetry, his 'capacitie / To lerne to playe so plesandlie, and syng' (*Papyngo*, 283-84), and from the explicit testimony of Thomas Wood, Vicar of St Andrews, in his annotations to his part-books:

> ...David pables first set it [*si quis diligit me*], and presentit the sam to kyng Iamis the fyft (quha wes ane musitian himselff; he had ane singular gud eir and culd sing that he had never seine before, but his voyce wes rawky and harske....[16]

As to how the musical boy came by his musical education we have no direct information. We may guess that he had some teaching in the elements from David Lyndsay in childhood, but in that case Lyndsay would probably have mentioned it! We should look rather for instruction from a professional musician, and for that we have only the staccato evidence of entries in the records available after August 1515. In September or October of that year is an item for lute strings costing 'vi s.' alongside a spear for the King, money given to him to 'play' [at cards or dice] and the cost of tassels for his saddle. In 1526 there appears in the court a 'luter' whose name suggests a French or Flemish origin. 'Franche Orry, menstrale', whose reward at the Easter festival at Stirling is recorded (*TA*, V, 256). He entered the royal service, for a complete livery is ordered for him. (I take this to be the same person.) 'Urre Schennek, lutair...ane

---

[14] M.M. Phillips, *The 'Adages' of Erasmus: A Study with Translations* (Cambridge, 1964), pp. 305-6, and *Opera Omnia*, Lugduni Batavorum, 1703-6, II, 554F.

[15] Ibid., p. 307.

[16] TWC_1, p. 176. See also H. Hutchison, 'The St Andrews Psalter: Transcription and Critical Study of Thomas Wode's Psalter', Diss. (Mus.), Edinburgh, 1957, p. 191. A list of Wood's manuscript part-books, with their standard abbreviations and manuscript locations, is also to be found in *MB* XV, p. 202 and in Shire, *Song, Dance and Poetry*, p. 266; see also K. Elliott, 'Another one of Thomas Wood's Missing Parts', *Innes Review*, 39.2 (1988), 151-55. Subsequent quotations from Wood have been checked against the printed text extracts in *MB* XV or Hutchison, since it has not been practicable to check against the widely-scattered part-books themselves. Neither secondary source gives Wood's page / folio numbers.

franche rede bonet' (*TA*, V, 312-13: combined entries); the red bonnet is the characteristic livery of the musician. Is he Henri Jeannèque—perhaps Jeannequin? or 'Arry (Urry) Senneck, Englishman, trained to be a 'Franche menstrale'? Or had he come from Albany in France? He appears to have resided for a year: the records stop at August 1527. I do not find mention of him after August 1529, from which time onwards records are substantially complete and continuous. Between whiles there had occurred the 'coup' of the king's escape and the reorganization of offices at court that ensued.

I suggest that, besides himself playing and singing, the luter may have taught his skill to the king and to a musical servant. In 1526 a lute was bought for Williame Calbrath [Galbraith] in the King's chamber (*TA*, V, 276). There were two William Galbraiths in the King's household service, one 'yemen' [yeoman] (*TA*, V, 310) and the other 'sangstar' (*ER*, XV, 292). The wording of the entry precludes our taking them for a single person. One Galbraith of the King's chamber was still in his service and, according to the Register of the Great Seal, was rewarded in January 1528/29 '*Rex,—pro bono servitio et pro speciali favore*'.[17] The only other possibility that comes to mind is that the King could have been taught by a musician of his Chapel Royal.

Inborn facility, instruction in instrumental playing of the lute and in singing at sight, and tone of court society described in Lyndsay's *Papyngo*—these add up to the notion of young King James as a gifted cultivated amateur of music. Just at this time there was being formulated in Italy the ideal character of education suited to a courtier, and this should point the way for what was fitting for a King to learn. In treating here of the place of music in education emphasis was moving away from moral or philosophic values or music as recreation from soldier studies to value of music in society. Castiglione, in Book I of his *Book of the Courtier*, captures the concept:

> I shall not be content with the courtier unless he be a musician and besides being able to sing safely at sight can play on various instruments, for if we consider well there is no more honourable and praiseworthy employment of leisure than music as a rest from toil, a medicine for sick souls. And this is still more true of courts where apart from the refreshment that music brings to everybody, many things are done to give pleasure to the ladies, whose tender and gentle souls are easily penetrated by harmony and filled with sweetness.[18]

---

[17]*RMS* [III], 160, No. 739. See further, J. Bannerman, 'The Clàrsach and the Clàrsair', *Scottish Studies*, 30 (1991), 1-17 (7 and note 8), and K. Sanger and A. Kinnaird, *Tree of Strings* (Temple, 1992), pp. 39 and 82-83.

[18]This particular translation has not been located, and is possibly Dr Shire's own, from the Italian *Il Libro Cortegiano*, Venice, 1528. For a 1561 translation of the passage see Baldassare Castiglione, *The Book of the Courtier*, trans. Sir Thomas Hoby, intro. J.H. Whitfield (1928, rpt. London and New York, 1974), p. 75.

The ideal courtier was to be a cultivated amateur, a social gulf maintained between the courtier and professional musician no matter how much the latter might be a favourite figure in the court. Precedence was given to singing well at sight, the solo voice to an instrument or of poetry recited to an instrument. A quartet of bowed instruments is praised but wind instruments do not attain courtly status. This is how opinion was running in Italy.[19]

The small northern court of King James V at Holyrood, Linlithgow, Falkland or Stirling stood remote but not aloof from the culture and civilization of continental Europe. The King was a musical amateur. There was some skill of *musick fyne*, still, in the once-magnificent Chapel Royal. There was lute-playing and singing at court. There was, over long periods, a resident French minstrel: Bountans, succeeded by Franche Orry. The royal household numbered a stand of minstrels, instrumental musicians. Whether they played on bowed instruments other than the 'fithel' is however not shown in the records. They hailed from Italy, but had been established in the Court of Scotland since 1503. Apparently a younger Drummond, if not two Julianes, trumpeter and Anthone tabourner, had grown up there. We know of only one return visit to Italy by one of this family group. The Scots court was a retaining vessel of European musical tradition. This, as much as geographical remoteness may help to explain the time-lag in taste and currency, in Scotland, of cultivated music of Europe. And the wildness of the times must be kept in mind. An eloquent reminder of the use of the King's Music of ceremony is the entry for 1527 (*TA*, V, 318):

> Item, to Juliane [Drummond], trumpet, beand at divers raidis
> with the King and the lordis, for his expensis xx li.

For three years of the King's youth into his sixteenth summer, he was in cure guarded by a group of lords and a hundred gentlemen to wait upon him 'whenever he passed'. These years show jejune fare for the vigorous powers of mind of this spirited youth—'his pringnant fresche ingyne'. Perhaps some recourse still to Maister Gavin Dunbar; schemes to interest him in history; some pleasurable study of music, sovran against boredom; on festival days a 'mumming' or two; and music, reward to minstrels, resident and perhaps some visiting also. And sport and play *ad infinitum*.[20] Small wonder that the King beat his wings and planned escape. How much of 'youth's felloun rage' was youth frustrated?

---

[19]See further, P. Holman, 'Music at the Court of Henry VIII', *Henry VIII: A European Court in England*, ed. D. Starkey (Greenwich, 1991), pp. 104-6 and J. Stevens, *Music and Poetry in the Early Tudor Court* (1961, rpt. with corrections, Cambridge, 1979), esp. Part Three, pp. 265-328.

[20]The Treasurer's Accounts, sparse of details and incomplete, must be used with caution, but on the topic of the king's recreation consider entries covering Easter to midsummer, 1526 (V, 256-57): the king enjoys a feast with ox and venison, has the music of 'Franche Orry', a harper, and Anthon Talboner; he plays cards and 'chachespele'; attends church services, making various offerings; has new clothes made for him; is perhaps involved in a sporting event with 'queyk' [living] herons; celebrates Easter ('eggis...castin efter supper') and buys a horse.

Could we imagine the jostling cosmopolitan court of his father—that vigorous and inquisitive mind, its tourneys advertised the length and breadth of Europe, its magnificent endowment of sacred music, its 'xli' musicians of the household, its roll of 'makars'—imagine that reign extended for twelve more years *in peace*, how different would have been the development of this young Renaissance Prince. But that, in terms of sixteenth century Scotland, is vain imagining indeed.

'IN HIS AISTAIT ROYALL': 1527-37

In the early summer of 1527 King James V, now fifteen years of age, escaped from Falkland Palace and from cure of the Lords. 'The King', as Drummond tells the story,

> resolveth to accomplish by Stratagem, what the Factions of the Nobles could not perform by force.... He suppeth sooner than his custom was, entertaining the Captain of the Guards with more than usual ceremonies and representations of the next morning's sport, withall *inviting him to go to his rest, the Night being short about the Summer solstice*. The Waiters all shifted and the Court husht, shutting his Chamber door, in the apparel of one of his Grooms, unperceiv'd he passed the Guard to the Stable; where with two who attended him, with spair Horses he posted to *Sterlin*...[21]

At Stirling he was received with rejoicing, the great gate barred behind him. The Douglases were forbidden to come within six miles of the person of the king on pain of death (*ER*, XV, lii). King James was his own master. From this time we can speak of him as '...in his aistait Royall,/ Hauand power Imperyall' (*Complaynt*, 115-16)[22] and we can consider him as acting in his own right as patron of music and poetry. How did his hereditary gifts, his education and upbringing bear fruit as he grew to manhood and kingship? How in the life of his court—call it late medieval or early Renaissance—did a King's delight in music manifest itself, inseparable from policy?

Lyndsay speaks at length of the pleasures and duties of kingship in his *Papyngo*. Alongside the manly sports there is high place for music:

> Halkyng, hountyng, armes, and leiffull amour
> Preordinat ar, be God, for thy plesour:

---

[21] W. Drummond of Hawthornden, *The History of Scotland from the year 1423 until the year 1542* (London, [1655]), pp. 193-94 (Wing D2196).
[22] *The Works of Sir David Lindsay*, ed. D. Hamer, 4 vols, STS (Edinburgh and London, 1931-36), [Hamer], I, 40-53.

> Maisteris of Museik, to recreat thy spreit
> With dantit voce and plesande Instrument:
> Thus may thov be of all plesouris repleit,
> So in thyne office thov be deligent.
>   (274-78)[23]

That King James's pleasure in music extended to *musick fyne* of Europe—of Italy and probably of the court of France—there is very pleasing and certain testimony. In December 1529 a letter passed from the King in Edinburgh to Maximilian [Sforza], Duke of Milan:

> Maximilian's man Thomas [de Averencia] came to Scotland recently, and his ability and qualities have induced James to keep him during the winter. The King asks for Maximilian's assent.[24]

In March 1529-30 James writes again, referring to this former letter and his request:

> that Thomas de Averencia of Brescia who visited Scotland and gave James great pleasure owing to his interest in music (*arte musica qua oblectamur nonnichil solatii nobis prebuerit*) should spend the past winter there. Though there was no answer James believes that his excellency consented. Thomas now returns. James requests that he may be allowed to come back as soon as possible, and spend some considerable time in Scotland.[25]

To judge from the terms, 'Maximilian's man', de Averencia would appear to have been well-born musical amateur rather than professional musician—though this latter possibility cannot be ruled out. He brought six servants with him: this status strongly suggests an envoy who may have numbered among his attendants a stand of musicians. De Averencia did not go back empty handed. There is an entry in the Treasurer's Accounts against March 1529/30—for a gift to the Duke of Milan. Let us put this winter guest, who brought the solace of music to the King of Scotland, into the context of history.

There was ample reason why the powers of Europe should wish to be informed at first hand of how things stood in Scotland under the freshly assumed authority of a young King. In January 1527/8 James had written to Albany warning him that if he intended to come to Scotland he the King would be glad if it were 'in ane honest and gud maner' and not to the King's 'hurt and displeasour'; no royal invitation appears to have been extended.[26] Within a few days of this King James wrote to King Francis I of France:

---

[23]Hamer, I, 56-90 (64).
[24]*James V Letters*, p. 163.
[25]Ibid., p. 169.
[26]Ibid., p. 143.

> The faction and ill-will prevailing among the nobles before James assumed control are all too well known. There was no breathing-space which might be used in the interests of peace. Now, however, that James has begun to set justice in motion throughout the realm, things are very much better....Should Albany persist, he [King James] begs Francis to forbid the expedition, or give no help.[27]

By October 1529 the letters show a happier relationship.

> James rejoices at his letters delivered on September 24 by William Stewart, captain of Milan (*arcis Mediolani prefectus*), intimating that Albany showed to Francis letters from James containing secret and weighty matters, and affirming James's inclination to preserve the auld alliance. Albany stated that the feeling was reciprocated, and Girard Bion, Albany's secretary, testified to the sincere friendship and affection of Francis for James.[28]

King James declared his intention of consulting with King Francis in matters of common policy.

De Averencia was subject to the Duke of Milan: he had in December of the year arrived 'recently', which suggests that he may have come in September in company with William Stewart, captain of Milan. This Stewart had been sent to Scotland as envoy to King James before, in the spring of 1526/7. In that case, too, he had come from Albany, bearing gifts 'avec toulx plain de chevalx et aultres beaulx presens'.[29] I suggest that this coming of de Averencia some years later was conceived somewhat in the same spirit: as envoy was chosen a cultured musical amateur apt to catch the favour of the young musical King. (The pattern was to be repeated later when Esmé Stewart, Sieur d'Aubigny arrived in the court of the young King James VI.)

In this year, 1529, lines of policy can be traced from the King of Scotland to France and Milan—and to the court of James's royal uncle, King Henry VIII. Consider the letters written between 1530 and 1532 now among state papers existing in Venice relating to English matters. One speaks of a league between Venice, France and Milan being disapproved by his English majesty. Another, in the same year, is sent to the new Duke of Milan (Maximilian having died in Paris in June 1530) by his envoy in England. The envoy, Scarpinello, discusses as unlikely the rumour that Cardinal Wolsey might escape to France or Scotland,

---

[27]Ibid., pp. 143-44.
[28]Ibid., p. 161.
[29]Ibid., p. 135.

as it was not envisaged that the monarchs of either of those countries would renounce the valuable friendship of the King of England.

King of a country not rich, but providing a coign of vantage and strategy remote but not aloof, James V of Scotland must have been reported on with lively interest by returning envoys—his character, his governance, his talents and tastes (as in music), his parts and his prospects as bridegroom, son-in-law or ally.[30] Whether that winter of musical pleasure bore fruit in policy is for a historian to tell us. As to its influence in the music and poetry of Scotland I shall indulge in surmise. There is a group of Italian pieces—sacred and secular—for four voices in Wood's part-books, side by side with Scottish compositions of just this time by Peebles and Fethy. Did some of this music reach the Scottish court with de Averencia?

In the world of sacred music, '*musick fyne* to Goddis glore', it was to be hoped that the young monarch, beginning to set justice in motion throughout the realm, might also bring better times for the church in the kingdom. Of religious foundation he says, 'better to make amendis than found anew'. The king's letters of 1529 to the Pope or the Cardinal of Ancona show a deep concern for the state of the Chapel Royal, 'nobly built and amply endowed by James IV',[31] for the state of the Abbey of Tongland 'in a ruinous condition and lying waste',[32] and for the see of the Hebrides:

> It is now the seventeenth year since the see became vacant. During that period those born in the more remote isles have not had baptism or other sacrament—not to speak of Christian teaching—and are not likely to have it unless a bishop be appointed.[33]

Had efforts towards a better state of affairs succeeded, a Chapel Royal restored to the grandeur of his father's reign would have entailed a renewed health and splendour in the music of that royal college. Elsewhere also in a freshly flourishing foundation the church's music might flourish anew.

But in the 'timeous remeid' now brought to the church there was no breathing space. Already in the letter to the Pope that speaks of measures to make restitution of the Chapel Royal, 'which is a special monument to the name [of King James IV]', his son gives his reasons. 'James is not so anxious about his father's renown as with the help of God to banish the foul Lutheran sect,

---

[30] Some observations of this kind are also found in entries in *Calendar of State Papers Relating to the Negotiations between England and Spain*, ed. P. de Gayangos, IV, pt. ii (London, 1882), for example, No. 653: Miçer Mai to the Emperor, 10 March 1531, 85-87.
[31] *James V Letters*, James V to Clement VII, 27 October 1529, p. 161.
[32] Ibid., James V to Peter, Cardinal of Ancona, 1 November 1529, p. 162.
[33] Ibid., James V to Clement VII, 1 November 1529, p. 162.

which seeks to destroy churches, abolish monastic institutions, and profane all sacred rites'.[34] The restoration of the Chapel Royal is a move against the new forces, the 'wind from Germany' that was already blowing hard.

In the opening year of the young King's personal reign a black shadow fell on Scotland, with the burning as a heretic of Patrick Hamilton, distinguished young musician and composer. But it fell so early in the year and was—with the act of 1525/6—the working out of a series of events already in train, that the young king may in this sense not be impugned for the martyrdom. Patrick Hamilton (1504-1528), the second son of Sir Patrick Hamilton, was educated at Paris and Louvain. Returning to Scotland he entered the University of St Andrews in 1523 where he appears to have become the precentor cantor. Alexander Alesius tells us that he 'composed a mass for nine voices for the office of the missal which begins, *Benedicant Dominum omnes angeli ejus*, and superintended its execution in the cathedral as precentor of the choir'.[35] In 1527 the Archbishop of St Andrews ordered that Hamilton should be seized and interrogated as a heretic, but he escaped to Germany. Here, he met Luther, Tyndale and Frith, and it was the latter who translated his *loci communes* into English.[36] He returned to Scotland where he was arrested, tried, convicted and burnt at the stake. In the same year, Taverner was seized for heresy at Oxford 'but the Cardinal for his musick excused him, saying that he was but a musician'.[37] Unfortunately for the music of Scotland, Hamilton was deemed more than that.

The young monarch, a musical Stewart, if he had had 'breathing space in the interests of peace' might have given distinguished patronage to sacred music—splendid polyphony of the church. As it is, in everything we know of the Chapel Royal events, musicians or the composition of music there is something of admonition, of violence feared, or threatened or inflected. Robert Johnson 'ane scottis preist borne in dunce [Duns]' in about 1490, fled to England 'lang befoir reformation...for accusation of heresy'. This is Thomas Wood's note against his composition, to which is added: 'thomas hutsons father knew him weill'. 'thomas hutsons fayt[her] now wyth *the* king kend him.' 'thomas hutcheon that is with the king knew him in Ingland. ...and sa the firstand report wes wrang...'. These notes are added against the text of *Domine in virtute tua*.

---

[34]Ibid., James V to Clement VII, 27 October 1529, p. 161.

[35]H.G. Farmer provides this quotation in his *History of Music in Scotland* (London, 1947), p. 113, but he does not give his source.

[36]For Frith's text of *Patrick's Places*, see J. Foxe, *Acts and Monuments*, ed. S.R. Cattley (1843-49; rpt. New York, 1965), IV, 563-78, or *The Works of John Knox*, ed. D. Laing, I (Edinburgh, 1846), 19-35. See also J.T. McNeill, 'Alexander Alesius, Scottish Lutheran (1500-1565)', *Archiv für Reformationsgeschicte*, 55 (1964), 161-91 (164-65) and J. McGoldrick, *Luther's Scottish Connection* (London and Toronto, 1989), pp. 74-100.

[37]*Tudor Church Music*, I (1923), 1.

The 'firstand report' was written into the Quintus Part Book and crossed through. It read: 'qd. ane Inglische mane as I have heard he wes blind quhen he set it'.[38]

We are to take it, I conclude, that Robert Johnson was well known in England by the father of Thomas Hutson [Hudson] now with the King [James VI]. The omission of 'father' in the Treble Book is accidental—or the word may have been destroyed in the binding (it is at the very end of the inside margin).[39] I have found what I believe to be confirmation of this: a possible ground of acquaintance not far apart in time or situation. In the year 1530 a Robert Johnson is recorded as having arrears owed to Cardinal Wolsey.[40] In 1527 there was a William Hudson Chantry priest of Topcliffe who may well be a relative.[41] But, more important, in the same volume is a grant to John Peter and Robert Hudson.[42] Now Robert Hudson was very probably the name of Thomas Hudson's father, who was with King James VI. For the first news we have of the Hudson family group of musicians is of *five* Hudsons who may have played at the wedding of Mary Queen of Scots and Lord Darnley, for shortly afterwards a grant was made to *Robert* Hudson for five liveries.[43] Other music by Robert Johnson (called 'I' of that name to distinguish him from the later Robert Johnson), show that Scotland's loss was Tudor England's gain, to the tune of *fyne musick*: *MB* XV, No. 7 the 'Deus misereatur nostri' (Psalm 67), is one example. Wood notes that it was 'set in Ingland ten or xii yeiris before reformation'.[44]

There is the story told by John Knox of the singer in the Chapel Royal, of R. Carmichael ('sangstar' in the Treasurer's Accounts) who was accused of heresy and had his goods escheated, till he 'burnt his bill', for doing no more than cry out in his sleep, 'The devill tak away the preastis, for thei ar a gready pack'. Who heard him and pursued him to judgement? Someone in the little world of royal musical service: Calderwood says it was Sir George Clappertoun, Sub-Dean of his Chapel Royal, and author of that ugly poem in the Maitland Folio MS, 'In Bowdoun on Blak Monunday'.[45]

Of music known to be given 'in propine' to the King only one piece appears to have survived, from a young musician one generation later than Robert Carver. David Peebles (1510-79), was a canon of St Andrews, according to Thomas Wood 'ane of the principall musitians in all this land in his tyme', who 'set the Antiphon for the Vigil of Pentecost in four parts about the yeir of God

---

[38]Hutchison, 'St Andrews Psalter', pp. 180-81
[39]See further, Shire, *Song, Dance and Poetry*, pp. 71-75.
[40]*L&P Henry VIII*, IV, pt. iii, 3047.
[41]Ibid., IV, pt. ii, 1533.
[42]Ibid., IV, pt. i, 124.
[43]Shire, *Song Dance and Poetry*, p. 72 (Treasurer's Accounts for 1565, fol. 87^v).
[44]Hutchison, 'St Andrews Psalter', p. 183.
[45]*Works of Knox*, ed. Laing, I, 45-6; *M. Folio MS*, I, 243-44.

1530...and presentit the sam to Kyng Iamis the fyft'.[46] 'Si quis diligit me sermonem meum, servabit et pater meus'—'shall serve within my house forever'. The words of the Antiphon, and their timing—just after the death as a heretic of a distinguished young musician, Patrick Hamilton—ask the question: and what of him who chose otherwise? Did King or musician choose the 'letter'?[47]

From this one propine we can judge the beauty and distinction possible in sacred music in the reign of King James V. How much more may not have been lost in the holocaust of church ornament and fabric, vestments and instruments, mass-books and music-books, that was to come. And how long 'before Reformation' did this pursuit of many to judgement chase from the realm other poets and musicians unknown who preferred exile to the imprisonment of Buchanan, accusation of heresy suffered by Carmichael and Johnston, or the stake of Patrick Hamilton? The very royal act that was to give timeous remeid hastened the destruction of the fabric of musical culture—at its heart—the gifted young composers.

The life of the court of King James V as a young monarch as yet unmarried is recorded vividly in the satiric poetry of David Lyndsay. In describing the state of poetry at that court, the prologue to the *Testament and Complaint of the Papyngo* refers to court entertainments, ballats and farces that have not come down to us. When we imagine what these court pieces may have been like, we should not omit to allow for a musical aspect in conception or in performance. The musical personnel, the Italian minstrels, the luter and sangstar Galbraith were to hand—and some voices probably among the 'officials' of the Chapel Royal.

Did David Lyndsay himself ever write song, or words for *fyne musick*? Lyndsay, who could balance the staitly style of Venus queen against satiric flyting, could certainly write 'poetry of Venus observance' in its natural vein. Again he could 'change it for new' into a 'spiritual version'. His *Satyre of the Thrie Estaitis* shows him a virtuoso in metre and in style of language: witness the superb entry of Dame Sensuality into the King's presence (271-78):[48]

> Luifers awalk! behald the fyrie spheir,
> Behauld the naturall dochter of Venus:
> Behauld luifers this lustie Ladie cleir,
> The fresche fonteine of Knichtis amorous,
> Repleit with ioyis dulce and delicious:
> Or quha wald mak to Venus observance
> In my mirthfull chalmer melodious?
> Thair sall thay find all pastyme and pleasance.

---

[46]*MB* XV, No. 8. For Peebles' settings of Psalms 1, 18, 113 and 124: *MB* XV, Nos 15, 18, 21 and 25; for quotations: Hutchison, ibid., p. 191.
[47]See note 60, hereinafter.
[48]Hamer, II, 53.

The first stanza is all staitly, of classical pedigree, Venus and her sphere. The oblique intention is loaded into the word, the '*natural* dochter of Venus', and in the earlier Bannatyne text it is also emphasized by the word '*laitis*', the line there reading: 'Quhat thay desyre in laitis delitius' (275). 'Natural' is too full of meaning, and 'laitis' is a sensual tell-tale: the cult word was 'trane'. For the rest Venus is suitably upheld in style and rhythm with the first line of the next stanza. Sensuality displays her rank—'Behauld my heid'—her headdress, the ornament of the courtesan. The satiric display soars up in height to be all sensuality—and 'pleasouris infinite' (285) in a huge destructive arc, lighting specially 'vnto the Court of Rome' (286).

These stanzas of joyous entry appear to be said not sung. But as always with Venus observance 'solace sall sweetly sing for evirmair':

> I hauld it best now or we farther gang,
> To Dame Venus let vs go sing ane sang.
> (293-94)

Sensualitie, her attendants Hameliness and Danger catching up Fund Jonet to 'beir a bais' (316)—are four voices to sing Venus 'ane sang'. I believe that here the song was 'O Ladie Venus heir complayne' of which I have spoken before.[49] Only the opening line survives of the words, but the music to four voices is preserved. Here is the moment in *poesie* and in life to which such a song belongs. The music is a galliard. It may have existed first and have been chosen here to bear the words of a song newly devised for the dramatic occasion, or it may have been already current in all seriousness as a *galliard chanté* in Venus observance. Whether it was staitly or bawdy or both by virtue of a nice obliquity of tone, we can glimpse it behind the words of the spiritual version. Look at the way the meaning goes—to the selfsame tune, and intending the godly audience to be conscious of the banished words (*MB* XV, No. 42):

> You luvaris all that love would prove
> Come learne to know true love indeed
> First love the Lord your God above
> From whom all goodness doth proceed
>
> Als love thy neighbour heartfully
> Wishing his welfare night and day
> Deal with all men faithfully...
>
> Since that the time is here but short...

---

[49]See *MB* XV, No. 42 (where it appears to the text of Scott's 'Departe, departe'), and note, p. 212, and H.M. Shire, 'What Song did Dame Sensuality Sing?: the ghost of a courtly lyric', *The Scotsman*, 12 September 1959, p. 10. See also Purser, *Scotland's Music*, pp. 94-95, where the reconstruction suggested by Dr Shire is printed.

In the surrounding text of the interlude there is word of haste and of teaching and learning the art of Venus. Lyndsay—dramatist fashion—could be using with telling effect a known song. Or the song that is lost could have been of his writing.

A vast subject stretches out beyond our reach here, in Sir David Lyndsay and the music of his time: music in *Ane Satyre of the Thrie Estaitis*; the role of music and dance-form in the stanzas in Lyndsay's repertory, poetic and dramatic. Only one of many issues is germane to our general argument here: that of Lyndsay's poetry set to music. The matter of his poetry, above all his later *Monarche* [*Ane Dialog*], had very wide appeal. This interest was met by the casting of passages from his works into shape for currency as printed balladry. This reshaping was done *to a known tune*. Lyndsay's version of the story of Adam and Eve (*Monarche*, 685-1122) was recast by Sir Richard Maitland of Lethington, and stands prominent at the outset of Bannatyne's collection: 'Ane ballat of the creatioun of the world man his fall And redemptioun, maid to the tone of the bankis of helecon'.[50] Lyndsay's description of the Siege of Jerusalem (*Monarche*, 3952-4125) was made into a song by John Barker, for circulation as a broadside, to the tune of the 'Queenes Almayne'.[51] These tunes act here as vehicles purveying poetry from the court or serious reader to the wider currency of the ballad sung or sold in the street. Conversely, both of these tunes enter also into the worlds of cultivated music, past writing of the trained musician, even a musician of the church. They belong to *musick fyne*.

No line of verse survives that is certainly from the pen of King James V himself: otherwise we should be tempted to wonder whether his 'singular gude eir' in music and his skill in 'qwik flowand vers of rethorik cullouris'[52] ever combined in writing words for music—in staitly style for *fyne musick* or in satire undress to the tune of, say, 'gynkartoun'. We cannot even tell whether any poetry the King wrote was in the staitly style, that, descended from Chaucer and through the 'Quair' of the first Stewart King James, extended by Henryson and reinvigorated by Dunbar, was lively and present in this court of 1530 in the hands of David Lyndsay and his fellow courtier poets. The only poem we know he wrote was indeed in 'ornat meter', but cannot have been in staitly style. Existing today only as an echo in our minds as we read David Lyndsay's reply to it, *The Answer...maid to the King's Flyting*, the style of the King's poem must have been the invective of the flyting game.

---

[50]*Bann. MS*, II, 26-32 and *MB* XV, No. 49, set to Montgomerie's 'Adeu, O desie of delyt'; music by Andrew Blackhall. See also Elliott, 'Another missing part', 152. For performance: The Baltimore Consort, *On the Banks of Helicon*, Dorian DOR-90139.
[51]See Hamer, IV, lv.
[52]*Livy's history of Rome. The first five books, translated into Scots by John Bellenden, 1533*, ed. W.A. Craigie, 2 vols (1901-3), I, 1.18.

Excellent poems have been attributed to King James V: *Peblis to the Play*[53] and *Christis Kirk on the Grene*,[54] but they are of a different calibre, neither 'staitly' nor 'Chaucerian'. The imagined author is the King James V of popular legend, 'The King of the Commons', 'The Gudeman of Ballengeich'.[55] These poems though 'popular' in subject belong to the main current of Scots poetry that stretches from Douglas's *Eneados* translated to the opposite extreme, the ribald flings in Lyndsay's great moral satire and dramatic 'folie'. There is, too, the ragment—a rig-ma-role of proverbs and pithy sayings—which was called 'King James the fyft his pasquill' by Andrew Melville in 1637.[56]

Instead of discussing these poems as perhaps by the King, I should like briefly to take another bearing on *Peblis to the Play* and *Christis Kirk on the Grene*. They are festival pieces: their substance a recreation of the celebration of a festival day in its secular aspect, the 'fair', the 'play'. Examples survive in Scotland of the festival piece in its sacred aspect, or in its aspect of ritual Christianized yet retaining attitudes from earlier times in modified form, 'All sones of Adam' (*The Christmas Medley*)[57] and 'A heartly service to you, my Lord' (*The Pleugh Song*).[58] These pieces are artefacts, the words in verse set for three voices. A third, 'Trip and goe, hey', may be a secular piece, perhaps for the observance of May-day, though it may celebrate one of the days of Our Lady, 'Our Lady will come here today'—the holy image will be borne in procession. An example from the north of England, the cathedral city of Durham, celebrates the feast of St Cuthbert's day; only one of three parts survive but the incomplete text suggests a content strongly resembling these two Scottish pieces of *the fair*. The issue is: are we right in seeing the emergence in the sixteenth century in these islands of a *genre* of festival piece, an artefact of poetry, characteristically of poetry-and-music, wherein the festival as actually celebrated in real life, is imitated in art, whether in the aspect of fair, market, or of religious holy-day? It may well prove that not only are *Peblis to the Play* and *Christis Kirk on the Green* to be associated with the court festivity and poetry of King James V, but so also are the 'Pleugh Song' and others of its kind, in continuing currency if not in origin.

---

[53] *M. Folio MS*, I, 176-83.
[54] Ibid., I, 149-55.
[55] A. Cherry, in *Princes, Poets and Patrons: The Stuarts in Scotland* (Edinburgh, 1987), pp. 29-32, gathers together these popular legends, which are ripe for detailed study.
[56] It is found on folios 27^r-29^v of Aberdeen MS 28, which was compiled by Andrew Melville and his family. Priscilla Bawcutt most kindly supplied this information. See also P. Bawcutt, 'An Index of Early Scottish Verse', *Studies in Scottish Literature*, 26 (1991), 254-70 (257).
[57] *MB* XV, No. 36. For performance: 'The Later Middle Ages 1250-1550: The King's Music', *A History of Scottish Music I*, Scottish Records LP SRSS1, MC SRCM 111.
[58] *MB* XV, No. 30; H.M. Shire and K. Elliott, 'Pleugh Song and Plough Play', *Saltire Review*, 2.6 (1955), 39-44, and Shire and Elliott, 'La fricassée en Ecosse et son rôle dans les fêtes', *Les Fêtes de la Renaissance*, ed. J. Jacquot, Collection 'Le Chœur des Muses', CNRS (Paris, 1956), pp. 335-45. For performance: Baltimore Consort, *Banks of Helicon*, track 4, 'My hartly service'.

What survives of the poetry of this epoch is focussed directly on the personality of the king. The image of the age is satiric; there was one 'general satire' against many couched in terms of the King's youth or his education, with exhortations to him to mend misgovernance. His faults are 'young counsel'—immature or ill-chosen counsellors—'covatyss and volupte'. The King's third weakness, 'volupte', 'the leesome love of ladies' at court, bred that considerable number of poems of love-service, many good, some dull and repetitive, in the Bannatyne collection—or so I believe from evidence of reading and comparative study. How much of this lyric-writing was linked with music *before* the coming of the French queens, we are able only to surmise; the fragmentary repertoire barely reaches that far back in time. Certainly in the next phase of court-culture, poetry of the 'style King James V' is found matched with *musick fyne*, of the dance-tune and *chanson* of the court of France—songs from the Catholic courtier Steill, before his death in 1540;[59] love-songs, music probably as well as words; from Fethy, though in complete form we have only his later 'Sang of Repentance', in which he recants;[60] 'Only to yow my Ladie'—and perhaps 'O Ladie Venus'; 'For love of one?' and those others unascribed published in *Music of Scotland 1500-1700*. These are all of the court, courtly. But poetry of the reign of James V found its way into wider currency in printed broadside form, and here the common ground is with England and the matter—David Lyndsay's—is nearer reformed religion.

By the same token, in flesh and blood this decade of James V's reign was important for the future. A son of the King, born of his love of these years, Margaret Erskine, later proved his true son as powerful patron of music. Lord James Stewart was created at the age of four—on the eve of his father's marriage to the princess Madeleine—Prior *in commendam* of St Andrews: he was later Earl of Moray and Lord Regent of Scotland, when his royal sister was cast from her throne. He was principal succourer of sacred music in the realm of Scotland after it had shipwrecked on the destructive tide of the Reformation. Himself a power for reform, he preserved and protected and helped to re-establish music and musicians in St Andrews and farther afield. He was Thomas Wood's patron and commissioned David Peebles to write four-part settings of the psalms.[61] All aspects of the King of Love were execrated by the reformers: the royal child-bastards put to powerful places in the church, the revenues into the father's coffers till they came of age; the flattering impious favourites in power at court; both the 'fair semblance' of Venus observance in poetry or ceremony and its bawdy underplay, in filth, vice and disease. Voices Catholic and Protestant cried for reform in Church and State, using the figures of court game in festival play to castigate court evil. There was no breathing space to rebuild the world of music,

---

[59]These include 'Support your servand', *MB* XV, No. 39.

[60]*MB* XV, No. 38, and notes, which quote Wood's comment that this was 'composit be Schir Jhone Futhy bayth letter and not [note]'; see also Hutchison, 'St Andrews Psalter', p. 178. For performance: Coronach, *O Lustie May*, MC CMF003.

[61]See further, Hutchison, ibid., pp. 194-96.

but the little world of court poetry, hedged in by outer hostility—yet having Lyndsay as critic on the hearth—had some twenty years to flourish, up to and beyond the French marriage. For the wedding of King James to a French princess meant consolidation of the Franco-Scottish alliance, new impetus to Catholic power in the land, keener persecution on suspicion of heresy, bringing, as we saw, evil with good to the world of sacred music and its trained musicians. The coming of a Queen meant ordering of music of the household afresh in handsome terms. Whether a proportionate replenishing of the Chapel Royal ensued or not, I cannot ascertain. It seems doubtful. To the world of poetry, however, it meant a new fructifying contact, new rhythms, new music, new breath through France from Italy, new court manners and modes of entertainment. And both the bachelor court and the wider culture that succeeded it were to be faced by one rendering then another of criticism from within, in the performance of Lyndsay's *Satyre of the Thrie Estaitis*.

Let us take farewell of James V not as he was reported to have turned to the wall after the Battle of Solway Moss, 'with a little lauchter', saying, of the sovereignty, 'It cam wi' a lass, and it will gang wi' a lass'; not as he sat on his throne as young King Manheid after hearing Lyndsay's satire, and thereupon set himself to reform his three estates, but not on the terms of his impious uncle King Henry VIII; nor yet in his bachelor Court of Love, with David Lyndsay's pungitive salutation dirling in his ears, but as he goes on shipboard to seek a wife in France, a princess of the blood royal. His 'lowd musick' goes with him, 'iiij trumpetouris, iiij tabernaris, and iij quhistlaris quhilkis passit in the schippis to France, the vij day of May' in doublets of red and yellow satin. He is to be married on New Year's Day in Nôtre Dame to Madeleine, the delicate 'deathbound' daughter of the King of France, and his page, Pierre de Ronsard, comes back to Scotland with the royal pair. Not only is a fresh era of *musick fyne* and *Scottis poesie* opening for the court of Scotland, but a new age of poetry—often linked with fine music—is about to dawn in Western Europe.

7

GREYSTEIL

John Purser

If ever there was a poem which breathed the imaginative fire of mediaeval epic romance, then *Greysteil* is that poem. But it is only half itself on the page, little attention has been given to it, and thus it was that I came to read it through my pursuit of the music, which I could not find published anywhere. The Robert Gordon of Straloch lute book (1627-29), in which it was recorded, is now lost, but the music was transcribed incomplete by George Graham in 1847. Fortunately this still exists, as National Library of Scotland MS 5.2.18. After a brief tussle with the notation in the nineteenth century transcription I had my own edition from it, reproduced below.

It was obvious from the beginning that this was no ordinary tune, but one that carried with it implications of a style of performance which did not match the general run of tunes in this or other Scottish lute manuscripts, full of fascinating oddities and beauties as they are. There was no question in my mind that if this tune was intended to be sung, then it would require epic singing. The wide range, as well as the high tessitura; the hypnotic repetitions; the simple but magnificent formal balance of the phrases; the high declamatory repeated notes; all these were dramatic indicators of some special function and manner. From the musical evidence alone one could reasonably deduce that this extraordinary piece of music was intended for the public performance of an epic.

It was only then that I discovered that the tune had already been 'transcribed' in, of all places, Chambers' *Book of Days*,[1] a two-volume compendium of delightfully useless calendrical information designed for a wide and eclectic readership, with a paragon of an index, and clearly edited by a scholarly maniac whose joy it was to bring together under two sets of commercially successful covers, all the delicious impedimenta of his brain for which no decent home could be found elsewhere. The transcription is somewhat lacking in faith to its original on account of the substitution of the harmonies in Straloch with the editor's own notion of what his readers could stomach. But full marks to his sense of adventure in even mentioning the piece at all, the excuse being an entry for April 17 (see below). William Dauney, in writing to the anonymous author of the

---

[1] R. Chambers, *The Book of Days: a miscellany of popular antiquities in connection with the calendar*, 2 vols (London, 1864-66), I, 523-24.

article (Chambers himself?), thought 'Greysteil' was 'not Scottish in its structure or character', believing it to be more Spanish than English.[2] I can make no real sense of his remarks. The tune is not known from any other source.

The first two phrases employ a powerful contrast of intoning on one note, followed by a leap—first of a sixth, then of a seventh—and a descending phrase. The second descending phrase, however, poises itself for the next section, which consists of a repeated formula based on a descending fourth. The third section is pitched dramatically high but drops to the final section which is an exact repeat of section 2.

The overall structure is A1, B, A2, B. These four sections (unrepeated) accommodate eight lines of text. The internal structures are as follows:

      A1   a1b1a2b2
      B   c1c2c1c2
      A2   a3a3a4b3
      B   c1c2c1c2

The economy of the whole is obvious. What is surprising is that it yields a tune of such extraordinary distinction.

The presence of an harmonic underlay, however simple, for such a piece, is of great importance. Basically our journey into epic singing is via the oral tradition or through much later manuscripts in which the harmonies (where offered) are often suspect. But the Straloch and other Scottish lute manuscripts of the early seventeenth century show a marked tendency to antiquarianism when compared with their continental counterparts; and there is no question but that a number of the pieces included in them are transcriptions from the clarsach repertoire. Others (and amongst them I would include 'Greysteil') are, at the very least, intimately allied to that repertoire in style.

One could argue from the basis of their lack of elaboration that the harmonies given in Straloch could not have undergone any extensive development, unless (as should not be discounted) the development was towards greater simplicity. Suffice it to say that there is nothing in the Straloch 'Greysteil' that strikes this listener's ear as being incompatible with the late fifteenth century, when we know it was performed before James IV:

> Item, that samyn day to twa fithelaris that sang Grey Steil to the King . . . ix s.[3]

---

[2]Ibid., I, 523.
[3]*TA*, I, 330.

The day was 17 April 1498. On 22 January 1508, a payment of 'v s.' was made to 'Gray Steill, lutar'.[4] Either this was a nickname given to the lutar, perhaps because he was a regular performer of the piece, or else because it is an uncharacteristic contraction to express a payment to a lutar who actually performed 'Gray Steill' that day.

The tune established, I then made for the text, in volume II of David Laing's *Early Popular Poetry of Scotland and the Northern Border* (London, 1895), pp. 131-210 (hereinafter 'Laing').[5] Volume II also gives the history of the surviving texts and outlines its popularity through the centuries (pp. 118-31).

That it was known to James V is certain. His own personal servitor, unofficial tutor and playmate, Lyndsay, refers to it twice—in *Squyer Meldrum* and in *Ane Satyre of the Thrie Estaitis*; and it is also mentioned in the *Complaynt of Scotland*, written less than ten years after James's death. Its publication by 1577, evidenced by Thomas Bassandyne's stock list of that year, which included 'iii^c Graysteillis, the pece vi d.',[6] suggests that it was a well known favourite. It may be this publication that is referred to in John Davidson's metrical *Memorial of the Life and Death of Two Worthy Christians, Robert Campbel...and his Wife Elizabeth Campbel*, composed in 1574 and published in 1595, with the lines:

> Euen of Gray-Steill, wha list to luke,
> Their is set foorth a meikle buke....
> [19-20][7]

According to Laing, the next mentions of *Greysteil* are in repeated licences to print it granted to Robert Smyth and his heirs in Edinburgh in 1595 and 1602;[8] and to Thomas Finlayson and his son Walter in 1606 and 1628 respectively. Then in 1627 appears the title of the tune in the Straloch manuscript.[9] In the circumstances it seems likely that such an obviously popular work would be the one referred to by the title.

But how was it performed to James IV, or to his successors? The fact that 'twa fithelaris' undertook it, strongly suggests that they accompanied the poem on their fiddles. But do we know what is meant by 'sang'? Might not the tune

---

[4]*TA*, IV, 96.

[5]This is W. Carew Hazlitt's re-arranged and revised edition of David Laing's two earlier editions, *Early Metrical Tales; Including the History of Sir Egeir, Sir Gryme and Sir Gray-Steill* (London, 1826), and *Select Remains of the Ancient Popular Poetry of Scotland* (London, 1822).

[6]See *The Bannatyne Miscellany*, ed. D. Laing, II (Edinburgh, 1836), 185-296, especially 118-19 and 199.

[7]Printed by Robert Waldegrave in Edinburgh.

[8]See also *Bannatyne Miscellany*, ed. Laing, II, 233-35 (234).

[9]W. Dauney, *Ancient Scotish Melodies* (Edinburgh, 1838), pp. 368-69, lists by title the contents of the original lute book.

noted down over a century later without any text, be purely instrumental? Does the tune itself inform us? The answer, as suggested above, is that it does. The character of the repetition of notes is not an instrumental one. It is the kind of repetition that represents sung syllables. Given that these repeated notes are an integral part of the structure of the tune, it seems likely that this tune was indeed used for the purposes of singing the text referred to in the title. The next question is: which text?

It has been suggested to me that the 'Greysteil' that was sung must really have been a much shorter ballad derived from the epic romance, on the grounds that it was improbable that anyone would be able to perform the full work satisfactorily. This suggestion can be rejected on two grounds. The first is that no shorter text has ever been discovered or alluded to, to my knowledge, and all the evidence points to it as being a major work. The second is that there are solutions to the problem of performing an epic. Sung or intoned, the two and half thousand lines printed in Laing would take two and a half hours to perform. This was the standard length for a concert or recital well into the nineteenth century.[10] One could speak the text a little faster, but at the price of dramatic effect, and probably coherence. But sung, intoned or spoken, the voice would be put under considerable strain if required to continue for that length of time without several breaks. Hence two performers. In fact, might one not reasonably suggest that the fact that 'twa fithelaris' were the performers implies that 'Greysteil' was a long work; and the rare inclusion in the records of the title of what was sung suggests strongly that it was noteworthy on some ground or another, length being an obvious candidate.

But why not 'twa sangstaris'? Here again we have a clue to the manner of performance. It is still common for singers and fiddlers to get together in performing ballads or to unite the two skills in themselves—Martin Carthy and Dave Swarbrick, for example, make a wonderful combination of fiddle and voice in their rendering of *Reynardine* on Topic 12TS 344.

So it seems probable that the two fiddlers supported their own and each other's singing with fiddle accompaniment. The fiddles could also have been used to supply instrumental interludes. As for the payment, it is commensurate with a fair length of performance, though two women received exactly double (eighteen shillings) for singing in 1506.[11] However, we do not know how long they had been in the court and they may have performed a number of works on various

---

[10] See also H.M. Shire's comment, *Song, Dance and Poetry at the Court of Scotland Under King James VI* (Cambridge, 1969), p. 173, that '...music for the long poem matching its stave, such as was performed in Italy in the sixteenth century, is found in Scotland well into the seventeenth—witness the recording in manuscript music-books of items that, to judge by their entitling, must be music for the old-type romances such as "Graysteil" or "Sir Lemuel" or for some rehandling of the knightly adventures going under their names'.

[11] *TA*, III, 331.

occasions. In 1505 two women received fourteen shillings for singing,[12] but again we do not know how long they had been at court. It is also possible that the payments may reflect the King's (or his treasurer's) perception of the quality of the performance. Suffice it to say that for the performance of a single work of this length, nine shillings for the two performers was no insult, and this would imply that five shillings was also reasonable for the single lutar who may have performed part or whole of the work in 1508.

Does the scheme of the poem match the scheme of the tune? The answer is a mixed one. While it requires no more than the normal ingenuity expected of a singer to fit the lines to the phrases of music, the over-all form of the tune as transcribed does not match the over-all form of the poem as it appears in Laing. There are never bits of a phrase left over or short; but sections of the poem, taken in grammatical units, do not marry up with the tune as a whole without repeating a section on one occasion and failing to repeat it on another. This is not in any sense difficult to accomplish, and produces a satisfactory result for both words and music; but does this presuppose a planned, and possibly memorized, layout of the relationship for round about two and a half thousand lines, and is such a plan likely? The evidence from such traditions as that of the Kvaedermen of Iceland would suggest that it is certainly possible. Not only did they memorize thousands of lines, they also memorized and adapted a variety of melodies to different sections of the text. But it may not be necessary to presuppose such a plan, for, judging by the subtlety of variation that is evident in our own oral traditions in dealing with anomalous situations of this kind (whether in Gaelic or Scots), it is fair to say that experienced performers would be able to hear in their mind's ear, any impending anomaly, and adjust the repeats accordingly.

Of course, the harmonies given in Straloch are not consistent with or even clearly suggestive of the harmonies that might have been provided by the fiddlers. The Straloch harmonies are basically a shadowing of the melody line in octaves, with fuller chords at the ends of phrases. This is typical of the Scottish lute repertoire, especially that part of it probably derived from the clarsach repertoire. The recent partial reconstruction recorded for the BBC was therefore for voice and clarsach—Andy Hunter and Rhona Mackay.[13] Rhona played the gut strung clarsach, which is more appropriate for Scots than the wire-strung clarsach which belongs more essentially with the Gaelic tradition. No reconstruction with two voices and two fiddles has yet been attempted, though one with lute is proposed.

At this point it is important to say that audiences of 'Greysteil' so far divide evenly into those for whom it is unutterably tedious, and those for whom

---

[12] *TA*, III, 162.
[13] The reconstruction was broadcast during BBC Radio Scotland's 'Scotland's Music: a radio history', Programme Five, October 27, 1991. The recording, specially made for the radio series, is not commercially available but may be consulted at the Scottish Music Information Centre, 1 Bowmont Gardens, Glasgow G12.

it is a deeply evocative experience. The latter group includes many for whom the words are as incomprehensible as they are for the former. But, and this is a crucial piece of evidence, for Andy Hunter who was the first to record the singing of any part of 'Greysteil', the melody was not only one that held his concentration over many stanzas; it was absolutely in character with the poem. To some, however, the repetition of a repetitious tune for something around three hundred times is not acceptable. An inability to follow the narrative has been the usual source of their difficulty, but others are not interested in the narrative anyway and will never be drawn to such a work.

Greysteil is a great narrative. A thrilling story, full of incident, suggestive encounter, sensuality, violence; but of what use is that to someone unable to follow Scots, or unable to follow words when they are sung, or not interested in them in the first place? Of course the tune alone cannot bear three hundred repetitions. Not even the theme of the 'Ode to Joy' could survive that. But its function is as a bearer of the words. It is the great tumbril upon which the drama is enacted as it moves through the imagination. It is a resource for the singer that can be used to extend the natural emphases, inflections, and passionate responses that a speaking, or even intoning voice cannot match. It is the secure basis through which the variety of the story can find an immediate coherence. The remarkable thing is that at no point does the tune seem to fight the text. Its combinations of rise and fall; of repeated notes, leaps, and conjunct motion; of assertion and yielding; the hexatonic ambiguities of the mode (is it Ionian, Aolian or Lydian?): these seem to be capable of matching or constructively counterpointing every mood—and there are many—in this vast conception. If for no other reasons than these, I would argue that the tune is the right one for the text.

Of the extended commentaries on this great poem, I have read only the typescript of Deanna Delmar Evans's paper given at the 1993 Glasgow Conference on Medieval and Renaissance Scottish Language and Literature, which helpfully reviews previous publications and makes a case for locating the original Greysteil in the Cumberland area, as well as underlining the significance of the theme of Fortune.[14] Evans does not refer to the Caithness tradition (see below) but it is a tradition which may simply have been appropriated from the poem at a much later date because of some matching circumstances between the poem and the history of the area. Since so few people have actually read *Greysteil*, I make no apology for mixing the raw product of my own delight in, and speculation about the poem, with a brief synopsis of the action.

The poem is a mixture of drama, didacticism, supernatural power and human weakness and nobility. Behind it and central to it is a deeply symbolic

---

[14] 'Re-evaluating the Case for a Scottish *Eger and Grime*', forthcoming in the conference proceedings, ed. G. Caie, R. Lyall and K. Simpson.

sexual motivation, on which subject I read the poem as being a remarkable document of good down-to-earth advice set in the midst of a courtly convention which is accepted without destructive criticism, but singularly lacking in enthusiastic recommendation. Nobody behaves especially well in it; and the pivotal encounters which ensure the equivocally happy ending are with a high-class prostitute.

For those who do not know the story, here is a selective synopsis. It is based on the version of Laing in preference to that of Bishop Thomas Percy, because that is closer to the presumed original Scots and because its narrative is much more coherent.

Sir Eger (Eager) is a knight of low degree in love with a scornful lady of high degree. In order to impress her he insists on taking on the uncanny and almost invincible Sir Greysteil, who rules in the land of Doubt, and cuts off the right hands of those whom he defeats. He defeats everyone, including Sir Eger, whom he leaves for dead. But he only cuts off the little finger of Sir Eger's right hand, perhaps because Sir Eger put up a good fight, but was let down by his sword, which broke. This and the mutilation of the right hand are sexually symbolic, as is the name 'Greysteil'—supreme sword.[15]

Sir Eger, his body and manhood broken, is nursed by a lady—Lillias—whose joined eyebrows are described as 'ready tokening' (Laing, 952) and indicate sensuality; and whose bower is surmounted by a weathercock—symbol of Fortune. Lillias tells him that all her efforts are in vain if the woman he loves will not do the same for him as she has done. Sir Eger knows full well that she will not and tries, but fails to conceal from his scornful lady, his humiliating defeat and injury. His only hope is to return and defeat Greysteil, and for this he is too weak from the wounds of love as well as of body. His friend, Sir Graham (Grim) decides to go in Sir Eger's place, wearing his armour. They manage between them to deceive the scornful lady into believing that it is indeed Sir Eger recovered and ready for the fray.

The story now shifts to Sir Graham's adventure. He is of noble birth, he is untrammelled by the coils of love, and he is armed with a sword of particular virtue at whose forging he was present. Once again the symbolic significance of the sword is underlined. But the strange symbolism of this tale requires that he also have Fortune and true love to support him if he is to defeat the uncanny champion of his almost other-world, the land of Doubt.

Sir Graham spends the night before the battle with the lady Lillias, to whom Sir Eger has directed him. She it is who tells him that he must have both Fortune on his side and be able to keep his own true love, whoever she may be,

---

[15]Cf. *DOST*, s.v., *gre*, sense 4, with a probable pun on *gray*, the colour, also intended.

in his mind, for Greysteil will try to make him doubt her. The poem however, tells us that Lillias and Sir Graham have fallen in love (though neither has declared it) and, since Lillias is Dame Fortune, the auguries are good on both counts.

In a magnificent climax, Sir Graham finally defeats Greysteil in a battle that is both gory and awe-inspiring. So Fortune has deserted Greysteil for Sir Graham, who marries his Lillias, and returns in the guise of Sir Eger. Sir Eger rises from his sickbed with Greysteil's right hand in its glove, to prove the victory to the scornful lady. He at first scorns and taunts her, but he is rebuked by the true hero, Sir Graham.

In the end Sir Eger marries his lady, but reveals his secret to her when Sir Graham dies, and she promptly leaves him for a nunnery. Sir Eger then does great deeds in the Crusades and returns to marry Sir Graham's widow, Lillias.

The story has features much older than the Crusades and these last lines read very much like an attempt to Christianize a tale that blends pagan and courtly elements into a remarkably coherent whole.

Apart from the history of the tune and the epic poem and their publication, the tale has left resonances down through the centuries. The name 'Greysteil' was used more than once as a nickname. James V is said to have given it to Archibald Douglas of Kilspindie, and it was also used of William, first earl of Gowrie, and of Alexander, sixth earl of Eglinton, who took to the sword as superior to the law when it came to getting results. David Laing (II, 126-30) discusses the contexts for the application of 'Greysteil' to these men, particularly the latter two. For the former, it would seem that David Hume of Godscroft, in his *History of the Houses of Douglas and Angus* (Edinburgh, 1644, p. 262), was the first to refer to the legend that James V called Douglas of Kilspindie 'Greysteil':

> [James V] when he was young, loved him singularly well for his
> ability of body, and was wont to call him his Gray-Steill.

Archibald Douglas of Kilspindie, provost and custumer of Edinburgh, treasurer and chief custumer of Scotland, auditor of the exchequer, had been part of the boy-king's household during the years 1526-28. Like his nephew, Archibald, earl of Angus, Kilspindie had been summonsed for treason at the time James V had taken personal control of his kingdom, and with Angus, the earl's brother, George Douglas, and Alexander Drummond of Carnock, Kilspindie had been outlawed on 5 September 1528. The idea that Godscroft's story was based on fact is fed by James's documented reaction to Kilspindie's attempt, in 1534, to obtain a royal pardon. Kilspindie could not change the king's mind, but the clemency with which he was treated is notable. As one who had committed treason against the Crown, Kilspindie's re-appearance in Scotland could have meant imprisonment or execution, but he was only ordered to leave the realm.[16] The fact that Greysteil is described in terms such as 'uncannand' = uncanny (Laing, l. 443), suggests that the name may have been used to identify people suspected of dabbling in black arts.

The ruins of a Greysteil's castle are to be found on the shores of Loch Rangag, north of Latheron in Caithness—indeed it is called 'Greysteil's Castle' on Bartholomew's *New Reduced Survey for Tourists and Cyclists*, Sheet 27 (undated). The castle is in ruins and there are mixed opinions as to whether it was a broch or a castle, situated as it is on a spit of land projecting into the loch. In 1725, according to MacFarlane's description of the parish of Lathron in his *Geographical Collections*,[17] it was approached by an avenue 'where the red curran grows and bears fruit'.

Two legends in particular are associated with the ruins.[18] The earlier Caithness legend[19] tells of a fourteenth-century 'Greysteil', thought to have been a Douglas, who was a kind of local Robin Hood. The Robin Hood character is obviously at odds with the epic, but the Douglas association (though geographically unlikely), and the suggested date, imply some kind of remembered link.

The later legend is supposed to refer to a 'Greysteil' who was a freebooter and a man of extraordinary physical strength, and who challenged and slaughtered any who trespassed on his property. The route past Loch Rangag was boggy and hazardous and much of the surrounding land is mountainous, so the approach was never easy. The tale, as told by James T. Calder, in *Sketches from John O'Groats* (Wick, 1842), pp. 77-81, has it that in 1660 Greysteil was finally defeated by a Sinclair, laird of Dunn, avenging Greysteil's murder of his friend, the brother of Sinclair's fiancée. The points of contact between Calder and that of the epic poem go further than the name of the villain, his extraordinary strength and apparent invincibility, and the fact that his was 'the land that was forbidden' (Laing, l. 128). In both the uncanny and unchristian nature of Greysteil is either implied or actually stated. In both renderings of the tale, the use of a magical sword is crucial to the victory, and the additional motivation of love is a major feature. And in both the hero spends the night before the encounter in the company of the woman who is in some way an enabling agent. In Calder, she is the widow and the owner and lender of the sword of Saracen origin (suggesting a

---

[16]*Acts of the Lords of Council in Public Affairs 1501-1554*, ed. R.K. Hannay (Edinburgh, 1932), p. 427. See further, M.G. Kelley, 'The Douglas Earls of Angus: a Study in the Social and Political Bases of Power of a Scottish Family from 1389 until 1587', Diss. Edinburgh, 1973, pp. 423-26. (I am grateful to Dr J. Hadley Williams for providing this information.)

[17]Ed. A. Mitchell and J.T. Clark, SHS, 3 vols (Edinburgh, 1906-08), I, 169.

[18]I am grateful to Mrs T. Mann of Wick Public Library for providing background material for the Caithness legends connected with Greysteil Castle.

[19]See 'Know Your Kaitness III ', *Caithness Courier*, author, date and pagination unknown.

connection with the Crusades), given by a Polish Jew whose life he had saved, to her husband while he was a mercenary for Gustavus Adolphus. The widow is referred to as having a Bible open. In the epic she is younger and wealthier, but also unattached, has magical healing skills and stresses the importance of true love as a weapon against Greysteil. She is also marked out in other ways:

> With brows brent, and thereto small,
> A drawing voice she speaks withall:
> Betwixt her een and eke her neise
> There is the greatness of a piese,
> A spot of red, the lave is white;
> There is none other that is her like:
> And so her brows on a running,—
> There is a gay ready tokening!
> (Laing, ll. 945-52)

Is this mark on her forehead a caste mark? Is her unusual voice a hint of a foreign accent? Does this strange description give us a clue to a deep-lying Indo-European origin for this epic? That it is full of fascinating pointers should be clear enough, and I hope that this brief discussion of it will lead to more detailed research and analysis—perhaps even to publication of a new critical edition of what is, to me, one of our great literary and musical treasures.[20]

---

[20]*Greysteil*, sung by Andy Hunter, accompanied by Robert McKillop (lute), and Bill Taylor (clarsach), will appear in 1996 as a Dorian CD.

8

TRIP AND GOE, HEY

'A TRULY SCOTTISH SONG'

Kenneth Elliott

Trip and goe, hey, a Scottish part-song for three voices dating from about 1530, and one of a set of three medleys, survives only in a fragmentary state. This article summarizes existing references to the subject, indicates the work on it and the other medleys by Helena Shire and myself, and gives an account of how we came to reconstruct it into a complete performing version.

The suggested date of composition, based on the evidence of its musical style, would indicate that it marks the period of James V's early active reign. Considering the music of James's reign as a whole (1513-42), much of the surviving music of Robert Carver, the early works for the Roman rite by Robert Johnson, the Masses from the Douglas-Fischear part-books, a Mass from 'The Art of Music', and motets by David Peebles and anon. in Thomas Wood's part-books all date from this period. A number of songs show a variety of forms and styles. *O God abufe* by John Fethy reflects the motet-like Josquin chanson tradition, and a group of anonymous part-songs (such as *Richt soir opprest*) the newer Claudin forms—mildly polyphonic 'chanson' and harmonic dance-song—brought over from France in the late 1530s in the wake of James's marriages with the French princess, Madeleine and, after her early death, with Marie de Guise-Lorraine. And a few instrumental consorts are recorded in 'The Art of Music' and Duncan Burnett's music-book.[1]

References to musicians, both singers and instrumentalists, at Court and Chapel Royal at this time abound: James himself played the lute and, according to Thomas Wood, writing later in the century, 'had ane singular gud eir and culd sing that he had never seine before, bot his voyce wes rawky and harske'.[2] Other instruments frequently mentioned in contemporary accounts and commentaries are harp, fiddle, viol, cittern, recorder, rebec, organ, shawm and other wind

---

[1] Some of this music may be found in *Music of Scotland, 1500-1700,* ed. K. Elliott, song-texts ed. H.M. Shire, Musica Britannica XV (1957; 3rd rev. edn, London, 1975), [*MB* XV], (Nos. 1, 3-8, 35, 37-41, 74, 84), which also gives description and location of sources and a note of some published work; see also my articles on 'Robert Carver', 'Robert Johnson', 'David Peebles', 'Thomas Wood' and 'Sir John Fethy' in *The New Grove Dictionary of Music and Musicians* (London, 1980).

[2] K. Elliott and F. Rimmer, *A History of Scottish Music* (London, 1973), p. 21, quoting Wood (TWC$_1$, p. 176).

instruments.[3] Music also flourished at the numerous religious foundations, both monastic and secular, and at the university colleges and song-schools.[4]

The earliest reference to *Trip and goe, hey* seems to be by Joseph Ritson in his two-volume *Scotish Song* (London, 1794) where, in a discussion of a group of Scottish folk-songs, he states:

> ...Waly, waly up the bank...is also in a strange but curious, and apparently antique musical medley published in 1666:...[it] may be regarded as having been [a] popular song before the year 1600.

And in a footnote to this correct (though uncharacteristically unsubstantiated) comment: 'The following passages, from others of the like kind in the same performance, seem also scraps of old songs: Ioly under the greenwood tree...[and here he quotes from *Trip and goe, hey* bars 25-46 and 57-111, lines 7-14 and 19-41]'.[5] This material is, of course, taken from the second edition of John Forbes's *Songs and Fancies* (Aberdeen, 1666), which forms the top part of *Trip and goe, hey*. Later, Ritson remarks: 'At the end of the same publication are three singular compositions for as many voices, which are conjectured to have been sung by peasants in the Christmas holidays, before the Reformation; the music is a church chant'. And in a footnote to this:

> They are all very rude, and their antiquity is collected from the following lines: All sones of Adam...[here he quotes the text from *All sons of Adam*, (MB XV, No. 36), bars 1-16 and 24-64]. In the 'Pleugh Song', all 'the hyndis' are named, and all things belonging to the plough enumerated; the ploughman's cries to his oxen are given, and the like; *but it will not bear transcribing*....[6]

Presumably Ritson was referring to transcribing the text as, throughout his Historical Essay, by 'song' he means 'lyric' not always associated with a musical setting, and where one exists he rarely refers to it.

John Leyden, in his edition of *The Complaynt of Scotland* (Edinburgh, 1801), links Forbes with another, more elusive, cantus part-book. In his discussion of the dances, musical instruments and songs mentioned in the text, he comments: '...the following lines occur in a medley in Constable's MS. Cantus:

---

[3] See for example, *TA*, V-VIII (1515-46); R. Wedderburn, *The Complaynt of Scotland*, ed. A.M. Stewart, STS (Edinburgh, 1979), pp. 50-52.

[4] See for example, *Medieval Religious Houses: Scotland*, ed. I.B. Cowan, D.E. Easson and R.N. Hadcock, 2nd edn (London, 1976); *Acta Facultatis Artium Universitatis Sancti Andree 1413-1588*, ed. A.I. Dunlop, 2 vols, SHS (Edinburgh, 1964), I, clix-clx.

[5] Ritson, I, xlix-l. The earliest source of the native air generally associated with 'O waly, waly' is probably W. Thomson's *Orpheus Caledonius*, 1725.

[6] Ibid., I, civ, italics mine.

"Wee be all of Maiden land, / Maidens you may see" [that is, *Trip and goe, hey*, bars 235-6, line 91]'.[7] Later, he observes:

> ...*Thom of Lyn*...occurs in the enumeration of rustic names in the Pleugh Song, a strange medley in Forbes' Aberdeen Cantus. ...The tale of the Young Tamlene, is alluded to in another medley in the same Cantus, where the name is made Thomlin....
> 'The pypers drone was out of tune,
>   Sing *Young Thomlin*,
> Be merry, be merry, and twise so merrie,
>   With the light of the moon.'
> [that is, *Trip and goe, hey*, bars 82-91, lines 31-34].[8]

Later still, Leyden quotes the catalogue of songs and dances in the late fifteenth-century poem, *Colkelby's Sow*,[9] observing that one of these, 'Lutecok', is 'mentioned in Constable's MS. Cantus [also in *Trip and goe, hey*, bar 273, line 109]'. Further, he notes,

> Lindsay mentions, in his Complaynt, the air of '*Ginkerton*,' which he had been accustomed to play on his lute to James V. during the minority of that Prince. A verse of this song occurs in Constable's MS. Cantus. 'I would go twentie mile...on my bair foot... till hear him, Ginkertoune, Play on a lute'. From the medley songs of this curious Cantus, which are probably transcribed from the first [second, in fact] edition of Forbes' Aberdeen Cantus, which contains the Pleugh song, *likewise found in this MS.* [italics mine], I transcribe the following scraps of ancient songs....[10]

Here Leyden makes a list of some twenty-four fragments, then continues: 'Besides these fragments, this curious Cantus contains several others...' and adds five more short extracts to his list.[11] This publication is the first to contain a reference to Constable's Cantus. Leyden was wrong, however, to suggest that Constable's medley was copied from Forbes: only some material is common to both, namely six extracts that correspond to *Trip and goe, hey*, lines 50-51, 54, 65, 100-1, and from the additional extracts, lines 9, 71-2. Elsewhere there are

---

[7] Preliminary Dissertation, p. 245.
[8] Ibid., pp. 273-74. The extract presumably corresponds to bars 68-76 in *MB* XV, No. 30; there the names are different—'Nicol and Colin' rather than Leyden's 'Tarbute and *Tomlin*'—which must indicate yet another printed version of the second edition, of which two are known (see Wing D380 and D381). There is no reason to suppose that this was a gross error of transcription on Leyden's part: his work is accurate in this respect. Also, see below in the paragraph on Helena Shire's work on Forbes.
[9] Ibid., pp. 281-83.
[10] Ibid., pp. 283-85.
[11] Ibid., p. 285.

lines in Constable's medley that are very similar to those in *Trip and goe, hey*. On this evidence, Constable's medley must have been an independent, though perhaps similar, composition.[12]

William Dauney, in his *Ancient Scotish Melodies* (Edinburgh, 1838), uses material from Ritson when discussing the medleys in Forbes's second edition.[13] He quotes titles of songs in 'Wedderburn's *Complaynt of Scotland*, 1548', and adds,

> ...the series of fragments, however slight, which offer themselves in a curious medley, contained in a MS. Cantus, formerly the property of the late Archibald Constable of Edinburgh; because, although the date of that MS. is not older than 1670 or 1680, there are few of the songs to which they belonged likely to have been written in the course of that century....[14]

Later Dauney briefly refers to the content of another Scottish song-book of the seventeenth century, formerly known as John Leyden's Vocal MS, now called the William Stirling Cantus after its compiler and dated 1639.[15] He concludes: 'There is also another MS., called "Constable's Cantus",...the contents of which appear to be nearly the same'.[16] If true, this would mean that Constable's Cantus would contain Scots sixteenth-century polyphonic songs and instrumental pieces, and seventeenth-century continuo songs; one or two French chansons and Italian madrigals, and instrumental pieces; English lute-songs; psalmody.

Meanwhile notice began to be taken of the other voice-parts of the medleys. In the reprint of James Johnson's original six-volume edition of *The Scots Musical Museum* (Edinburgh, 1787-1803) 'with copious notes and illustrations...by the late William Stenhouse [1839], with additional notes and illustrations [by David Laing] (1853)', William Stenhouse, writing in 1820, was the first to note the presence of *Trip and goe, hey* in a Bassus part of Thomas Wood's set, though he imagined it was part of Wood's original document. In his discussion of *O waly waly* and *Tam Lin*,[17] he quoted the text of *Trip and goe, hey*, bars 47-56, lines 15-18 and bars 67-93, lines 24-35 respectively. David Laing more correctly observed that '...some subsequent possessor has inserted the

---

[12]Leyden's substantial and scholarly Dissertation and ensuing edition were nevertheless pioneering, as J.A.H. Murray, a later editor of *The Complaynt of Scotland*, acknowledged (EETS, London, 1872, Introduction, cxvi-cxvii).

[13]Dauney, Preliminary Dissertation, pp. 23-24.

[14]Ibid., p. 55; the list on pp. 56-58 is practically identical to Leyden's, though he conflates the latter's two.

[15]See *MB* XV for present location. Contents listed and discussed in K. Elliott, 'Music of Scotland, 1500-1700', Diss. Cambridge, 1959, pp. 318-26.

[16]Dauney, p. 284.

[17]*Museum*, IV, 147 and 369.

Basses of a number of secular airs...The handwriting is evidently not earlier than 1620...The Christmas Carol, and the Medley which Mr S. quotes, must be considered as inserted in this MS. nearly half a century after Wood's time [referring to the date '1566' that appears in Wood's hand]; and they are also contained in the second edition of "Cantus, Songs, and Fancies", Aberdeen, 1666'.[18]

C.S. Terry, in his 1936 article, 'John Forbes's "Songs and Fancies"',[19] fairly accurately dates the *addenda* to Thomas Wood's set as c. 1600-1620, but comments disparagingly on the three medleys:

> The Pleugh-Song, a monotonous chant, is chiefly of local linguistic interest. Wood alone records it [i.e. out of twelve seventeenth-century Scottish MS sources cited in the article]. The second is a Christmas Carol also recorded by Wood. The third is a lengthy ballad devoid of musical interest [sic!]. Wood again records it.[20]

H.G. Farmer, in his *A History of Music in Scotland* (London, 1947), prefers to quote Sanford Terry's solitary favourable if anodyne comment that the three medleys in 'Forbes' *Cantus*' showed 'distinctively national or local flavor'.[21]

This brings us right up to Dr Helena Shire's work on the subject of the medleys, followed by the fruit of our collaboration, and my own subsequent independent contribution. A joint paper, entitled 'La Fricassée en Écosse et ses rapports avec les Fêtes de la Renaissance', given at the Journées Internationales d'Études, Abbaye de Royaumont, 8-13 July, 1955, was published in *Les Fêtes de la Renaissance*.[22] This must have been the first time that the three medleys were recognized as being related to international musical forms and styles and not just of 'national or local flavor'.[23] A joint article, 'Pleugh Song and Plough Play'[24] was entirely devoted to the first medley and expanded the content of part of the foregoing. My talk, 'A Scottish Christmas Medley', for the BBC Third Programme, 28 December 1955, drew on all this material in a discussion of the

---

[18] Introduction, I, xxviii-ix. Later (IV, 440*), he suggests 'between 1600 and 1620'. But the earliest possible starting point for the extensive *addenda* is more likely c. 1606, as the second item, 'Earth's but a point', is evidently copied from Richard Alison's *An Howres Recreation in Musicke*, published in that year. The reference to the 'Contra-tenor' of the set on I, xxviii must be a mistake for 'Tenor', as the 'Contra-tenor', or 'Altus' (which contains the middle voice-part of *Trip and goe, hey*), now in the British Library, was, according to the inscription on the fly-leaf, 'Purchd. of Mrs H.S. Andrews 14 Nov. 1890.' This is borne out by the entry in the *Catalogue of Additions to the Manuscripts in the British Museum, 1888-93* (London, 1894), p. 129.
[19] *The Musical Quarterly*, 22.4 (October, 1936), 402-19.
[20] Ibid., 417-18.
[21] Farmer, p. 194.
[22] Ed. J. Jacquot, Collection 'Le Chœur des Muses', CNRS (Paris, 1956), pp. 335-45.
[23] See articles in *Grove* on 'Fricassée', 'Medley', 'Ensalada', and especially 'Quodlibet', which has a useful bibliography.
[24] *Saltire Review*, 2.6 (1955), 39-44.

three medleys. For musical illustrations I used specially made recordings by the Saltire Singers: two were complete, but *Trip and goe, hey* had perforce at that time to end rather abruptly at bar 208.

Eventually the two complete medleys, 'My heartly service' (The Pleugh Song) and 'All sons of Adam' (The Christmas Medley) reached print in *MB* XV, in the section devoted to 'Songs' (Nos. 30, 36).[25] Helena had also prepared a paper for the Colóquio de Estudos Etnograficos, in Oporto in June 1958, entitled 'Remains in folk-currency of festival interlude (fricassée) and ritual mime: Scotland and Northern Portugal'.[26] And in her article, 'Court Song in Scotland after 1603: Aberdeenshire III. Andro Melvill's Music Library: Aberdeen, 1637',[27] Helena suggested that 'the pleuch books' there listed would 'presumably be part-books of the long medley in three parts, of which the cantus part was printed in the second edition (1666) of Forbes's *Songs and Fancies* as the fifty-fifth [fifty-sixth, in fact] song, "Pleugh Song"'.[28] I would add here the possibility that the entry could refer to a set of part-books, the top part of which came to be known as 'Constable's Cantus', when that MS surfaced briefly in the nineteenth century. Helena had also prepared notes for a projected bibliographical study of Forbes's *Songs and Fancies* in collaboration with Phyllis Giles.[29]

Recent accounts of the subject by other writers are disappointing. John Purser's references to the three medleys in his *Scotland's Music* (Edinburgh and London, 1992) are poorly presented. The music example (p. 67) for *The Pleugh Song*, for instance, is cropped at the right-hand side, and omits an essential reference to the music of the cantus part printed by Forbes in the second edition of *Songs and Fancies*. And although Purser has transcribed afresh (p. 68) the first part of his music example of *Trip and goe, hey* (lines 1-3), for the last four lines he has quoted exactly part of the music extract published in Shire and Elliott, 'La Fricassée en Écosse', pp. 338-39. This has resulted in an unfortunate discrepancy between those time-signatures and note-values Purser has used at the beginning and those used at the end. The *Christmas Medley* (p. 81) has fared better: Purser's informative commentary, and the music example's layout, *musica ficta* and emendations agree exactly with my own (Elliott, 'Music of Scotland', pp.

---

[25] Accounts (in English) of *The Pleugh Song* and *Trip and goe, hey* may be found in Elliott and Rimmer, *History of Scottish Music*, pp. 13-15, 21, and of all three medleys in Elliott, 'Music of Scotland', pp. 96-108, Here are references to the various sections of *Trip and goe, hey*: invitation to the dance (from bar 1, line 1); medley of songs and dances (47, 15); the *bourde* or bawdy tale (181, 69); the resumption of the dance as the 'virgins' assemble (224, 87); the women's rejection of the married men (240, 94); their choice of lovers of their own (252, 100); the atmospheric *envoi* (274, 110).

[26] This was not published, and a recent search among the Shire papers held by the Department of Special Collections and Archives, Aberdeen University Library, has not traced it.

[27] *Edinburgh Bibliographical Society Transactions*, 4.1 (1960), 3-12.

[28] Ibid., 7.

[29] This remained unpublished, and again is untraced in the Aberdeen University Library's Archives; it is referred to in a statement prepared by Helena for inclusion in Elliott, 'Music of Scotland', p. ix (as is the Oporto paper, p. vi), and in my own correspondence with Helena Shire.

104, 106). D. James Ross, in his *Musick Fyne* ('Notes to the Text', pp. 168-69),[30] while indicating the existence of both our unpublished performance edition and the recorded performance by the King's Singers[31] of *Trip and goe, hey*, does not discuss our previous commentaries, and provides his own versions of two musical examples. He does, however, have some interesting ideas about the social context of *The Pleugh Song* (p. 120).

Turning to our reconstruction of *Trip and goe, hey*, it probably came about as a result of a proposal to extend into a series the 1967 recording of 'Musick Fyne'.[32] I began to consider the possibilities of completing *Trip and goe, hey* for inclusion in the proposed first record in the series.[33] At this time I was in constant touch with Helena Shire about the series, the second edition of *MB* XV, and, of course, the editing of the musical illustrations for her book, *Song, Dance and Poetry of the Court of Scotland under King James VI*.[34] Of the three parts, only the top one (Forbes) is printed complete; the two lower MS ones (TWA$_{[1]}$, TWB$_1$)[35] being mutilated by having the last page (or pages) torn out by some puritanical soul just at the point when the tale of the 'jolly yong Frier' is becoming mildly indecent (bars 206-10). And so, in the surviving material, out of a total of 282 bars, only 205 are complete. The trouble is that the top part often engages in a kind of dialogue with the other two voices (e.g. the opening and bars 80-93, 112-25 etc.), so that it often drops out of the proceedings for one or two bars. This dialogue effect is very prominent towards the end of the piece, and so it would seem to present very great problems indeed in an attempt at a reconstruction of both words and music. In fact, Helena's initial response to my idea was to say that it was impossible!

I persevered and wrote out the surviving text from Forbes, leaving gaps in square brackets between these phrases, roughly corresponding in length to the missing lines, and sent it to Helena. At this point I began to glimpse some possible ways of fleshing out the music. For instance, bars 241ff. seemed to use rhythmic/melodic material in a repetitive pattern of regular two-bar phrases. The material from the end of 252 to 256, and 260 to 274 was especially revealing. The harmonic implications were unmistakeable. Most of the two-bar phrases could be harmonized in the same way, using a repeated ground of the following notes: F | E-flat F C (or B-flat) C | F. And remembering the occurrence of repeated harmonic patterns earlier in the piece (e.g. the opening, 12-20, 120-27,

---

[30] *Musick Fyne: Robert Carver and the Art of Music in Sixteenth Century Scotland* (Edinburgh, 1993), pp. 119-20, 122-23, 125-26.
[31] 'The Later Middle Ages 1250-1550: The King's Music', *A History of Scottish Music I* (Scottish Records, LP SRSS1, and MC SRCM111).
[32] 'Musick Fyne: Songs and Dances of the Scottish Court 1550-1625'. This eventually became the second record in the series, *A History of Scottish Music*, Scottish Records, LP SRSS2.
[33] Nos. 3 and 4 (1972) and No. 1 (1974).
[34] Cambridge, 1969.
[35] Thomas Wood's part-books: TWA$_{[1]}$ = Altus: BM Add. MS 33933; TWB$_1$ = Bassus: Edinburgh University Library MS Laing. III. 483. The top part was probably originally in TWQ, but is now missing. See Elliott, 'Music of Scotland', pp. 210-11.

and especially 185-208, a true four-bar ground involving four notes, A G F F), I suddenly had the outline of a complete bass part from 241 to the end. Rhythms of missing bars began to take shape, mostly as *q. sq q q. sq q* | *q q q c.* (or *c*) | [*c* = crotchet *c.* = dotted crotchet *q* = quaver *q.* = dotted quaver *sq* = semi-quaver | = bar-line]. I sent all this to Helena, assuring her that I still thought it was possible to complete the whole piece. A lengthy correspondence ensued, involving, for example, distribution of long and short syllables of text within the bar, my requests for an extra word here, an extra syllable there, one less elsewhere, and so on. Helena responded admirably to all of these.

On the musical front I began to see other possibilities. At bars 219-20 there is a brief quotation of the well-known ballad tune, *The Woods so Wild*, much set later in the century, for instance by William Byrd as a set of keyboard variations.[36] In fact the whole of this passage (from bars 213 to 224) is heavily indebted to the tune in its melodic constituent and its structure of phrase repetition a tone apart, as it were on F and G (though in the later versions it was a G-major triad rather than the present G-minor). I have adopted Byrd's harmonization—as indeed John Dowland did when he introduced the tune into one of his 'ayres' for four voices and lute, 'Can she excuse', from the *First Booke of Songs* (1597).[37] And at 217, rather than have a strict repetition of musical material, I have borrowed Dowland's trick of using canonic imitation in the middle part. For the rest of my reconstruction of the music of *Trip and goe, hey* I have tried to retain the simple melodic-harmonic style of the original. Helena meantime was providing some marvellous ideas for missing phrases, some derived in style from the list of songs in Constable's Cantus ('Ginkerton' in bar 272 is a direct quotation) but many derived from the context and of her own invention—in her own words: '...phrases based on Dauney's "bits" of Constable and phrases from similar song-sequences in medieval German...'. There were some misgivings about 'And who plays on your pen? Jolly Robert. Your gimpinot plays the tirl, the tirl...'—too much for Edinburgh (the erotic metaphor is tirling on the pin/playing with the door fastening)? No! 'And sa wer done', in the words of Thomas Wood on completion of a substantial piece of editing.

For the first performance, by the King's Singers at the 1972 Edinburgh International Festival,[38] Helena prepared a 'singing version' of the text, simplifying many of its original idiosyncrasies (for example using the slightly anglicized forms and spellings from Forbes). This was also intended for inclusion in the programme note and arranged in one long continuous verse paragraph. Also for that performance I specially arranged the music into passages for two groups of three voices, sometimes separate (thus enhancing the dialogue

---

[36] *William Byrd: Keyboard Music, II*, trans. and ed. A. Brown, Musica Britannica XXVIII (London, 1971), No. 85.

[37] *John Dowland: Ayres for Four Voices*, trans. E.H. Fellowes, ed. T. Dart and N. Fortune, Musica Britannica VI, 2nd edn (1963; rpt. London, 1970), No. 5.

[38] Freemason's Hall, 21 August 1972.

nature of the piece), sometimes doubling. For the present edition I have retained the earlier verbal forms as found in Wood's copies, resorting to Forbes only when Wood might be obscure to a modern reader or singer. This was, after all our policy in preparing final editions of the songs for *MB* XV.[39] I have also tentatively divided up the text into stanzas for the sake of clarity. All important variants are noted or discussed in the Commentary. Similarly for the music any alterations/emendations are duly recorded. We purposely left the precise nature of the extent of the reconstruction vague, so that it could be more systematically dealt with at a later date. I had met the singers for rehearsal beforehand but neither Helena nor myself was present at the performance. It was, however, broadcast, and Helena immediately telephoned: 'That was *a truly Scottish song!*' I saw what she meant: with its simple, direct style, its fresh lyricism as well as frank bawdiness of content, and sheer liveliness and exuberance—brilliantly captured in the performance by the King's Singers—it seemed to epitomize the atmosphere of the licentious court of the young King James V, the 'Guidman of Ballangeich'. Fortunately I was able to employ the good services of the King's Singers again for the recording of the first volume of *A History of Scottish Music*, which appeared in 1974 and included performances of all three medleys. This was first issued under the title 'The Later Middle Ages', but subsequently given the additional and wholly appropriate title of 'The King's Music'.[40]

I had always been aware of the dramatic/pictorial element in all three pieces, but after the Edinburgh Festival performance and the recording wondered if it might be possible actually to perform them in such a way. The opportunity came early in 1981 when my colleague Rod Lyall, then of the Department of Scottish Literature, approached me with a request for presenting something of the sort at the forthcoming Third International Conference on Scottish Language and Literature, to be held at the University of Stirling in July of that year. Together with another colleague, Graham Barlow, of the Department of Drama,[41] we devised a programme to include the three medleys, along with Alexander Montgomerie's *Melancholie, gryt deput of Dispair* in its pavan-galliard musical setting, and William Dunbar's *Thrissill and the Rois*, all conceived as court entertainments variously combining song, declamation, mime and dance. I gave it the title '*Games Joyous* of Early Scotland: Masks and Mummings of the Scottish Court', and we used a small group of singers, instrumentalists, actors and dancers drawn mostly from the students and staff of the Departments of Music and Drama. Graham Barlow produced, and I arranged and directed the music from the harpsichord. A performance was given at a conference of the Royal Musical Association, Northern Chapter, which was held at the University of Glasgow in April 1981, and then repeated at the Stirling Conference in July as a concert in the prestigious surroundings of the Chapel Royal in Stirling Castle. Helena

---

[39]See Editorial Notes, xxi-xxii. My version of the text is based on Helena's provisional one, plus my own more recent thoughts. I hope I have made it clear which is which.
[40]See note 32 above.
[41]Now the Department of Theatre, Film and Television Studies.

attended the latter, and afterwards greeted me with the glad if ironic cry, 'We've made it!'

Future lines of inquiry would include further examination of the rôle of popular elements and grounds in the construction of the medleys and their related European forms, and a study of the development of the fifteenth-century *basse-danse* into a wider medium for song composition. Above all, it would be wonderful to track down Constable's Cantus, which would seem to be a key document in the present enquiry. It seems to me, that having been glimpsed in the last century, the MS is not quite so irretrievably lost as, say, the other part-books of the David Melvill or the Alexander Forbes sets. Is it perhaps languishing unrecognized in the private library of some inheritor of the books of Archibald Constable, the publisher of Sir Walter Scott?

In our Edition of *Trip and goe, hey*, below, additional material is indicated as follows:
MUSIC: by small notes, rests, time-signatures, accidentals etc.
TEXT: everything in italics is derived from another existing part (usually the top), and everything in square brackets is purely editorial.

Trip and goe, hey

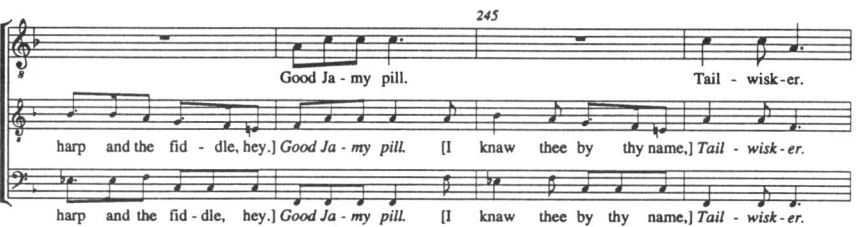

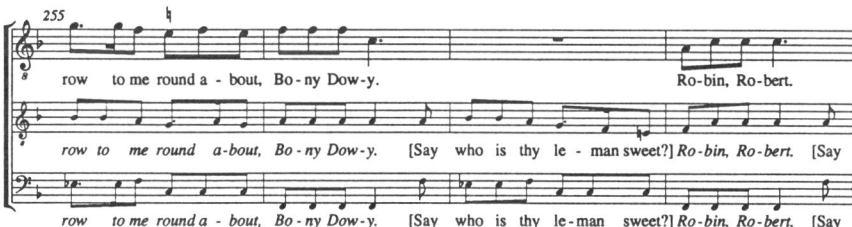

Trip and goe, hey. How sould I goe, hey?
It is the guyse of France, hey.
That ye sould sing and play w*ith* us
To stuffe our jolly dance hey.

5   Nou lett us sing w*ith* Jov*is* leave
Our mirrie song no man to greiv.
Jollie under the grein wood trie,
Jollie under the grein wood trie.

Be soft and sober I you pray:
10   My ladie will come heir away;
Goe graith you in your glancing geir
To meet my ladie pair and pair;
W*ith* harps and lutts and guthorns gay
My ladie will come heir away.

15   Hey trollie lollie, love is jolly
A whyll whyll it is new;
When it is old it grow*is* full cold:
Woe worth the love untrew.

Underneath the grein wood trie
20   Ther thy good love bidis thee,
        Frisca jollie.
Pulland the sloe so does she goe
Singing so mirrily.

I saw three ladies fair,
25   Singing hey and how
        Upon yon layland-a:
I saw three marinells,
Singing rumbelow
        Upon yon seastrand-a.

30   As they beg*a*ne ther notts to toone,
The pypers dronn was out of toone.
Sing Jollie Roben, sing Young Thomlin.
Be mirrie, be mirrie and twice so mirrie
W*ith* the light of the moon, hey.
35   Hey doune *doune* a doune, hey doune *doune* a doune.
Aleluja, nou sing we all,
Be mirrie, be mirrie, the malt's come doune.

Hey trollie, lollie, lollie.
Three bird*is* on a trie,
40 Three and three, and other three,
The boniest bird come doune to me.

Burrie, my boy! What will ye, my joy?
Wher hes thou been? On the grein at the dancing.
What saw thou ther? Gay ladies fair.
45 Saw thou Meggie? Ma*rr*y, man, did I;
I saw Meggie and w*ith* her spak.
Spak she to thee? Ay indeed did she;
Be our sueet ladie I ferly of that.

Hey doune a doune a doune a doune.

50 The ring of the rash of the gowan
In the cool of the night came my leman home, hey.

Cattrein cam attowr the streit
W*ith* prettie pan'tons on her feet,
And yellow hair above her brow:
55 My jolly taill hou comes thou now?

Sir, saw ye so bonyly as she beckit,
So daintely as her hair was deckit?
So lustaly she did allso
Both wink and blink and twinkle too,
60 So fresily she did agoe.

Yea did she so, she ran lyk a roe;
No, no, not so, she tript lyk a doe;
I would have caught her by the toe.
W*ith* that she vanisht and home did goe, hey.

65 Sing Silverwood and thou werr myne,
Sing Jolly love one line, hey.
There sould nothing w*ith*in thee grow
But a hert and a hynd, hey.

Now heir, hey, now heir, how,
70 A jest of a jolly yong Frier, hey.

The Frier had on a cowle of ridd,
He spied the prettie wench ke*a*ming her head;
He winkit, he blinkit, he lurkit, he lourd;

　　　　　To sie as he jinkit, it was a good bourd,
75　　　　　　So privily caught he the prettie wench all alone.

　　　　　The Frier had on a belt with knotts,
　　　　　He spied the prettie wench filling the cups;
　　　　　He winkit, he blinkit, he lurkit, he lourd;
　　　　　To sie as he jinkit, it was a good bourd,
80　　　　　　So privily caught he the prettie wench all alone.

　　　　　Ever alace! for earthly shame,
　　　　　A jolly young Frier hes raised my wame.
　　　　　That ever I did it, ever I did it,
　　　　　Ever I did it, did it, did it.
85　　　　Ever alace! for earthly shame,
　　　　　Betrayed am I uncurtously, alone.

　　　　　Hey how, hey how, hey how.

　　　　　Meet we your maidens all in array,
　　　　　With silver pins and virgin lay.
90　　　　[Are ye maidens of the band? Truly tell to me.]
　　　　　We be all of maiden land, maidens ye may see.

　　　　　Come in our ring, then saith Pleasance:
　　　　　Give us your hands, let us go dance, hey.

　　　　　[Sing dedillum ridil,] sing dedillum Will,
95　　　　[The harp and the fiddle, hey.] Good Jamy pill.
　　　　　[I knaw thee by thy name,] Tailwisker.
　　　　　[Get thee now to thy hame,] to thy supper.

　　　　　[Redi ad conjugem] derecundam.
　　　　　[She will be ready to greet her guidman.]
100　　　Come rake me the rowing [root under the] tree,
　　　　　Come row to me round about, Bony Dowy.

　　　　　[Say who is thy leman sweet?] Robin, Robert.
　　　　　[Say who is my leman sweet?] Joly Janet.
　　　　　And who plays on your pen, Joly Robert.
105　　　Your gimpinot plays the tirl, hey.

　　　　　Sing didil dow, ridil dow, [ridil dow dee.]
　　　　　And like ye not play with me, [I'll play with thee.]
　　　　　And can ye dance on a peat? [Ay, Ginkerton.]
　　　　　Play Lutcock and Light-the-gate, Futtikinton?

110 [The dancing is done;] sisters, adew.
[So hie we now home;] sisters, adew.
The heav'n is full of mirth and jo;
Adew, farewel, now will we go.

CRITICAL COMMENTARY: See *MB* XV, 202-3 for an explanation of the symbols in the following note of variants, emendations etc. / xF2, song 57: 'CANTUS. Three Voices'; TWA[1], f.90v; TWB1, p. 207 [TWA2 has recently been recovered: see K. Elliott, 'Another one of Thomas Wood's Missing Parts', *Innes Review*, 39.2 (1988), 151-55] / Trip and go: see W. Chappell, *Popular Music of the Olden Time* (1859, rpt. 1965), 130 / 1 II: what look like 2 bars' rests om. before first note / 16 III 2-20 III 1 not in original / 22 I 1-2: Christes; III 1-2: *m*; II III 3; live / 27 I 4: B-flat / 37 t-s: ¢3 (I) Ø-over-3 (II, III), note-values divided by four, and so thoughout in such passages; II, 1: *m* in preceding t-s / 42 II 1: F / 46 t-s: ¢ / 53 II 1-2: *c*. grows / 55 III 3: F / 57 II 1-3: *c c. q* / 61 II, III 1-2: brav and; frisca preferred as being both authentic and more colourful / 71 II, III 1: *m c*-rest / 74-5: cf. Ravenscroft's 'We be three poor mariners', Dauney, op. cit., 307, E.H. Fellowes, *English Madrigal Verse*, rev. F.W. Sternfeld and D. Greer (1967), 223 / 76: rumbelow, cf. Fellowes, 206; II, III 1-2: sing row / 80 change of t-s brought forward one bar / 81 III 2-3: begoud / 91: hey doune etc., cf. Fellowes, 203 / 92 II 5: a / 96 III 5: G / 97 II 2: *sq sq*; II, III: maltis, cf. Fellowes, 225 / 99 II 1: *q q*; II, III: maltis / 100 III 1: *s* / 101 III 5: trol- / 103, 105: birds / 111 I 1: C / 117 I 2-118 I 1: *c A m* D / 118 III 3: *c*. / 119 I 1: fair? / 120 II 4: *c*. A / 122 I 3-4: Peggy / 123 I 3: *c q*-rest / 125 I 1-3: by my faith / 127 II, III & 129 II 1-2: mervaill / 131 III 1-2: *c*. / 134 II 1-2: *c m* / 138 II 1-2: ladie / 155 I 1-3: *c*. F *q* E dinckly / 158 II, III 1: theid / 161 II, III 2-4: lustaly / 162 I, III 3-163 I, III, 1: *s* in preceding t-s; 163 II 1: *c*-rest in preceding t-s / 170 I 3-4; c; III 3-4: *c* vinsht / 171 II, III 1: hence / 171 II 5-175 II 2: perhaps a reference to the tune of 'The gowans are gay' (*MB* XV, No. 28) / 174 II, III 4-175 II, III 1: on land / 175 III 1: *c* A / 177 III 2: E / 178: a hert and a hynd, cf. Fellowes, 201; III 4: B-flat / 181 III 1-2: *c. c.* in preceding t-s / 185 III 1: m in preceding t-s / 188 II, III 1-2: *c* / 190 III 1-6: all notes are Cs; I 3-4: prinked / 192 I 4-5: jouked / 195 III 4-197 III 2: *c*. G *c*. F *q* F *c*. F *c*. F *c* F / 200 III 1-2: *c* / 201 II, 1-4: dressing her locks; III, 4: copps / 207 I 1-2: *q q* / 208 I after 5: *c*.-rest om. / 210 I 1-3: shame alone / 250 I: this word does not exist; the 'd' could either be a misreading of an earlier written form of 'v' (which is unlikely) or it could be correct and signify a deliberate distortion of 'verecundam' (modest) for comic effect.

GLOSS: ladie: *May Queen* / graith: *prepare* / frisca jollie: refrain for jovial songs / marinells: *mariners* / ferly: *marvel* / leman: *lover* / attowr: *across* / pan'tons: *slippers* / fresily: *freshly* / and thou: *if thou* / lourd: *leered* / jinkit: *dodged* / bourd: *jest* / pill: *bold young man* / wisker: *caresser* / guidman: *husband* / rake: *deck* / rowing: *rowan* / gimpinot: *jesting song* / Ginkerton, Lutcock, Light-the-gate, Futtikinton: names of games, songs, dances / jo: *joy*.

SCORE: In preparing the music score I used *Calliope* computer software application, developed by Dr William Clocksin of Cambridge.

9

WILLIAM STEWART AND THE COURT POETRY OF THE REIGN OF JAMES V

A.A. MacDonald

The Prologue to Sir David Lyndsay's *The Testament and Complaynt of Our Souerane Lordis Papyngo, Kyng Iames the Fyft* (1530) consists largely of the *topos* of a list of poets. Lyndsay begins with the English trio of Chaucer, Gower and Lydgate, proceeds to mention the Scottish poets of the fifteenth and early sixteenth centuries, and lastly moves on to the contemporary literary scene. This list consequently provides a convenient introduction to the literary court culture of the age of James V:

>And, in the courte, bene present, in thir dayis,
>That ballattis, breuis lustellie and layis,
>Quhilks tyll our Prince daylie thay do present.
>Quho can say more than schir Iames Inglis says,
>In ballatts, farses, and in plesand playis?
>Bot Culrose hes his pen maid Impotent.
>Kyde, in cunnyng and practick rycht prudent;
>And Stewarte, quhilk disyrith one staitly style,
>Full Ornate werkis daylie dois compyle.
>
>Stewart of Lorne wyll carpe rycht curiouslie;
>Galbreith, Kynlouch, quhen thay lyst tham applie
>In to that art, ar craftie of Ingyne
>Bot, now, of lait, is starte vpe, haistelie,
>One cunnyng Clerk, quhilk wrytith craftelie,
>One plant of Poetis, callit Ballentyne,
>Quhose ornat workis my wytt can nocht defyne:
>Gett he in to the courte auctoritie,
>He wyll precell Quintyng and Kennetie.
>   (37-54)[1]

From this passage the reader gains the impression of a group of poets working side by side and possibly competing with each other in a spirit of *camaraderie*. It

---

[1]*The Works of Sir David Lindsay of the Mount 1490-1555*, ed. D. Hamer, 4 vols, STS (Edinburgh and London, 1931-36), [Hamer], I, 57.

is clear, moreover, that in Lyndsay's judgement, this new generation of courtly writers is well able to brook comparison with their illustrious predecessors.

This impression is confirmed by John Rolland's prologue to his version of *The seuin Seages* (written in 1560, although not published until 1578):

> In Court that time was gude Dauid Lyndsay,
> In vulgar toung he bure the bell that day
> To mak meter, richt cunning and expart,
> And Maister Iohne Ballentyne suith to say
> Mak him marrow to Dauid weill we may.
> And for the thrid, Maister Williame Stewart,
> To mak in Scottis, richt weill he knew that Art,
> Bischop Durie, sum tyme of Galloway,
> For his plesure sum tyme wald tak thair part.
>   (19-27)[2]

In this passage Rolland is looking back to the Scottish poets of an earlier generation, from whom he took lessons in the craft, and to whom he submitted his *Court of Venus* for approval (64-77).[3]

Of the poets listed in the stanzas just quoted, Sir David Lyndsay is now the best known. His fame, however, is principally grounded upon the poems composed subsequent to the death of James V, when, in the absence of a real court, Lyndsay understandably began to move away from courtly topics in order to concentrate on such public and national themes as the governance of the kingdom and the controversies of religion. As far as is known, no poems by 'Stewart of Lorne' (see below), Galbraith,[4] Kynlouch,[5] or Durie (see below) have

---

[2] Iohne Rolland, *The seuin Seages*, ed. G. Black, STS (Edinburgh and London, 1932), pp. 1-2. This version should not be confused with the earlier one, preserved in the Asloan MS: *The Buke of the Sevyne Sagis*, ed. C. van Buuren (Leiden, 1982).

[3] Iohne Rolland, *The Court of Venus*, ed. W. Gregor, STS (Edinburgh and London, 1884). This poem was not published until 1575, as far as is known, but it is, on the author's testimony, a product of the age of James V.

[4] It is most likely that this was Robert Galbraith (or Caubraith), the scholastic philosopher and humanist, author of the *Quadrupertitum* (1510), who became professor of law at the Collège de Coqueret in Paris, and who was later treasurer of the Chapel Royal at Stirling 1528-32: J. Durkan, 'The Cultural Background', *Essays on the Scottish Reformation 1513-1625*, ed. D. McRoberts (Glasgow, 1962), pp. 282, 295; A. Broadie, *George Lokert, Late-Scholastic Logician* (Edinburgh, 1983), p. 8 et passim; A. Broadie, *The Circle of John Mair* (Oxford 1985), pp. 4-5 et passim. Carol Edington has called attention to a group of humanistically-minded legal professionals at the court, many of whom can be 'directly related' to Lyndsay, and she names in this context James Foulis, Adam Otterburn, Robert Galbraith and Thomas Erskine of Brechin: *Court and Culture in Renaissance Scotland: Sir David Lindsay of the Mount* (Amherst, 1994), p. 46. Other associates were the evangelical Protestants James Kirkcaldy of Grange, James Learmonth of Dairsie and Henry Balnaves: Edington, *Court and Culture*, p. 49. On the close-knit nature of the contemporary cultural scene in Scotland, see further, below. For more information on Robert Galbraith, and other persons of the same name, see: *Charters of the Abbey of Inchcolm*, ed. D.E. Easson and A. Macdonald, SHS (Edinburgh, 1938), pp. 188-89. It is perhaps worth noting that there was a Mr

survived, and only one poem each by Inglis (if correctly attributed) and Kyd.[6] Durie is a particularly interesting case, in view of a piquant jibe by John Knox:

> This tragedy of Sanct Geill was so terrible to some Papistes, that Dury, sometymes called for his filthines Abbot Stottikin, and then intitulat Bischope of Galloway, left his rymyng wharewith he was accustumed, and departed this lyef, even as that he leved.[7]

Lyndsay's remarks about John Bellenden, remembered nowadays principally for his prose translations of Livy and Hector Boece, are intriguing.[8] Only four poems by Bellenden survive, but of these two were composed c. 1531 to accompany his Boece and another one in 1533 to accompany his Livy, and are thus too late for the *Papyngo*. These three poems cannot, therefore, have contributed to the sudden *éclat* of Bellenden at the court, to which Lyndsay bears witness, and it is natural to conclude that a substantial part of Bellenden's poetic output has been lost.[9] For his part, William Stewart is the author of some dozen

---

Peter Galbraith whose name appears in a record together with that of William Stewart, when both men received payment (1553) 'for their labours': *TA*, X, 214. See also Hamer, III, 77-78.

[5]Not known to Hamer, III, 78. However, a Paul Kinloch appears sporadically in the Treasurer's Accounts, and his name occurs, for example, alongside that of Mr William Stewart as a recipient of livery in 1529: *TA*, V, 383. Paul Kinloch was in 1527 appointed 'court stewart to the kingis grace of his houshold, for his lifetyme', and in the following year he received a grant of land in Freuchie, in Fife. Edington finds him a plausible candidate for Lyndsay's poet: *Court and Culture*, p. 96. Could it be that Paul Kinloch is to be identified with the 'Master Paul' who gave instruction in Latin verse to Pierre de Ronsard, on the latter's visit to Scotland in 1537, in the train of Madeleine de France? C. Binet, *La Vie de P. de Ronsard (1586)*, ed. P. Laumonier (Paris, 1910), pp. 9, 84-86; Durkan in *Essays*, ed. McRoberts, p. 290. There is uncertainty, however, in the early texts of Binet as to whether 'le seigneur Paul' was an 'Escossois' or a 'Piemontois'. See also P. Laumonier, *Ronsard, Poète Lyrique: Etude Historique et Littéraire* (Paris, 1932), pp. 6-7.

[6]'Doverrit with dreme' is attributed to Inglis by Maitland, but to Dunbar (twice) by Bannatyne: *M. Folio MS*, I, 211-13; *Bann. MS.*, I, 79-82, II, 147-50. Baxter declares that there can be 'no certainty' as to the question of authorship, and Kinsley and Blanchot omit the poem: J.W. Baxter, *William Dunbar: A Biographical Study* (Edinburgh and London, 1952), p. 208; *The Poems of William Dunbar*, ed. J. Kinsley (Oxford, 1979), pp. 374-75; J.-J. Blanchot, *William Dunbar (1460?-1520?) Rhétoriqueur Ecossais*, diss. Paris IV-Sorbonne, 2 vols (1987), I, 258. For the poem by Kyd: *Bann. MS*, II, 242-45. On Inglis, Kyd, Durie and Stewart, see further, below. For a review of the circle of poets at the court of James V see Edington, *Court and Culture*, pp. 89-114.

[7]*The Works of John Knox*, ed. D. Laing, 6 vols (Edinburgh, 1846-64), I, 261-62. Knox quotes a satirical jingle as a specimen of Durie's work, but it may be hoped that this is merely a travesty of the bishop's poetical talents. It is likely that Knox's invective is motivated by the fact that Durie was the cousin, and close associate, of one of the reformer's greatest enemies, David Beaton: M.H.B. Sanderson, *Cardinal of Scotland: David Beaton, c. 1494-1546* (Edinburgh, 1986), pp. 26, 117, 225, 288.

[8]*Livy's History of Rome*, trans. John Bellenden, ed. W.A. Craigie, 2 vols, STS (Edinburgh and London, 1901-3); *The Chronicles of Scotland*, trans. John Bellenden, ed. R.W. Chambers, E. C. Batho and W. Husbands, 2 vols, STS (Edinburgh and London, 1938-41).

[9]A.S.G. Edwards has also noted that Bellenden's contemporary reputation was surprisingly high, but he calls attention to a stanza preserved in a Lydgate MS (now in Boston Public Library) owned by the family of the Campbells of Glenorchay: 'Bellenden's *Proheme of the history and croniklis of Scotland*: a note', *The Bibliotheck*, 6 (1971-73), 89-90. See further, P. Bawcutt, 'A First Line Index of Early Scottish Verse', *Studies in Scottish Literature*, 26 (1991), 254-68 (257).

short poems, preserved in the Bannatyne and Maitland Folio manuscripts.[10] He is also generally credited with a lengthy versified translation of the *Chronicles* of Boece, contemporary with the prose rendition of Bellenden.[11] Two poets, however, may be added to those mentioned in the lists given by Lyndsay and Rolland: George Clapperton and George Steill.[12]

On the basis of the poems which have survived it may be conceded that these poets, taken as a whole, do not offer the brilliance and range of either their predecessors or successors—on the one hand, the generation of William Dunbar, Walter Kennedy and Gavin Douglas, on the other, that of Alexander Scott and the young Alexander Montgomerie. The vernacular poets of the age of James V give the impression of a certain loss of artistic confidence; one may suppose that the cause of this had largely to do with the national trauma of Flodden. This was perhaps less true of the poets—such as James Foulis, Florence Wilson and George Buchanan—writing in Latin, who *ipso facto* operated within a more general, European perspective.[13]

Whereas in the main it is no great trouble to determine the corpus with which we have to deal, the poems of William Stewart present an especial problem: this comes from the fact that Stewart is a common name, and that several contemporary William Stewarts are known from the records.[14] Presumably, however, one may leave out of account the poems which Bannatyne attributes to 'Henrye Stewart' and to 'King Hary Stewart': these may be taken to be the work of Henry Stewart, Lord Darnley, second husband of Mary Queen of Scots, or at least to date from that period.[15] Nothing whatever is known about a poet called 'Stewart of Lorne' (*Papyngo*, 46): the best that Lyndsay's editor could do was to make a tentative identification with Alan Stewart (son of John, Lord of

---

[10] With due respect to Maurice Lindsay, who asserts that only one poem has survived: *History of Scottish Literature* (London, 1977), p. 68. This statement may be traced to T.F. Henderson's questionable identification of William Stewart with 'Stewart of Lorne': *Scottish Vernacular Literature: A Succinct History* (London, 1898), p. 236.

[11] William Stewart, *The Buik of the Croniclis of Scotland*, ed. W. B. Turnbull, 3 vols, Rolls Series, (London, 1858). M.P. McDiarmid, however, would attribute this work to William Stewart, bishop of Aberdeen (d. 1545): *The History of Scottish Literature I: Origins to 1660*, ed. R.D.S Jack (Aberdeen, 1988), p. 36.

[12] For Clappertoun's poem, 'In Bowdoun on Blak Monunday': *M. Folio MS*, I, 243-44; for Steill's poem, 'Lanterne of lufe and lady fair of hew': *Bann. MS*, III, 312-13; for a modern edition of both poems: *Ballatis of Luve*, ed. J. MacQueen (Edinburgh, 1970), pp. xxxiii-xxxv, 68-72. In the Bann. MS a second poem, 'Absent I am rycht soir aganis my will', is attributed to Steill (though in a different hand): *Bann. MS*, III, 319; poem and music are printed in *MB* XV, p. 167.

[13] Durkan, 'The Cultural Background', pp. 284-95; J. IJsewijn and D.F.S. Thomson, 'The Latin Poems of Jacobus Follisius or James Foullis of Edinburgh' *Humanistica Lovaniensia*, 24 (1975), 102-52; on Foulis, see the discussion by L.O. Fradenburg, *City, Marriage, Tournament: Arts of Rule in Late Medieval Scotland* (Madison, 1991), pp. 47-64; I.D. McFarlane, *Buchanan* (London, 1981); James Macqueen, 'Scottish Latin Poetry', *History of Scottish Literature*, ed. Jack, pp. 213-25.

[14] J. M. Sanderson, 'Two Stewarts of the Sixteenth Century: Mr William Stewart, Poet, and William Stewart, Elder, Depute Clerk of Edinburgh', *The Stewarts*, 17 (1984), 25-46. As well as the two persons mentioned in the title of Mrs Sanderson's article, one may note, among others, William Stewart, bishop of Aberdeen (d. 1545).

[15] *Bann. MS*, II, 227-28; III, 338-39, respectively.

Lorne, who died in 1463), mentioned as a former captain of the King's Guard.[16] Why this Alan Stewart, assuming that he was a poet (for which, however, there is no evidence), should be mentioned in the middle of a list of writers from the period 1520-40 remains a problem. But in fact it is not certain that Lyndsay is actually distinguishing two separate poets: the Stewart with the 'staitly style' could be the same person as the Stewart who 'of lorne [whatever that may mean, a place or a person] wyll carpe rycht curiouslie'.[17] A further complication lies in the fact that a second William Stewart poet is known: this was Stewart the Ross Herald, appointed Lyon Herald on 20 February 1568, deprived of that office in August, tried for witchcraft and sorcery, and burnt in the following year. This William Stewart was the author of a sonnet 'To the Church of Scotland', published in the *Forme of Prayers and Psalmes* printed by Robert Lekprevik in 1565; he is also said to be 'translator of sic werkes in the Kirk as is necessar for edifying of the people'.[18] It is very possible that William Stewart, the herald, was acquainted with Lyndsay, who was himself Lyon Herald until his death in 1555, and whose later works betray a sympathy for religious reform. It does not, however, seem likely that Stewart the herald was the author of any of the 'Stewart' poems preserved in the Bannatyne or Maitland Folio MSS: Stewart the herald was clearly a modernist in both religion and poetic practice (for example in his use of the sonnet), and this is at variance with the traditional character of the topics and forms of the other Stewart poems. In the light of the foregoing, therefore, it seems reasonable to make the assumption that all scribal attributions in the Bannatyne or Maitland Folio MSS to 'Stewart' (with or without first name (unless Henry, or initial thereof) relate to only one other poet, by the name of William Stewart (but not the herald). A list of the poems which on this basis may be ascribed to William Stewart is given in the Appendix, below. Even so, matters are not altogether settled, since the poem 'Musing allone this hinder nicht' is attributed by Bannatyne to Dunbar and in the Maitland Folio to Stewart.[19] In view, however, of the consensus among Dunbar scholars that the earlier makar is the author, I omit this poem from the list of Stewart's works.[20]

---

[16]Hamer, III, 76-77.

[17]I am very suspicious of the phrase 'of lorne', even though it is certainly the reading of the prints, since it makes for a peculiarly flaccid opening to the stanza. A 'John Stewart in Lorne' is mentioned in 1564, but there is nothing to connect him with poetry: *RPC*, I, 293.

[18]For a convenient text of this sonnet: *The Gude and Godlie Ballatis*, ed. A.F. Mitchell, STS (Edinburgh and London, 1897), p. [clvi]; also *Works of Knox*, ed. Laing, VI, 334. William Stewart is recorded as carrying messages between Mary and Elizabeth in 1562 and 1565, he was sent by the Regent Moray on an embassy to Norway, Denmark and Flanders in September 1567, and he was employed again by Moray in early 1568: *TA*, XI, 102; *CSP Scot.*, II, 250, 255; *TA*, XII, 75, 128, 149. In 1568, Moray seems to have believed that there was a conspiracy against him, and that Stewart was a party thereto; the accusations of sorcery may thus have been made merely to mask a political murder: *CSP Scot.*, II, 665. Stewart is furthermore said to have been the translator of *Ane Breif Gathering of the Halie Signes* [etc], printed by Lekprevik in 1565: R. Dickson and J.P. Edmond, *Annals of Scottish Printing* (Cambridge, 1890; rpt. Amsterdam, 1975), pp. 222-23.

[19]*Bann. MS*, II, 156-57; *M. Folio MS*, I, 191-93, 372-74 (in the first of the two occurrences in the M. Folio MS the poem is without ascription). On this poem see also: P. Bawcutt, *Dunbar the Makar* (Oxford, 1992), pp. 133-40.

[20]An exception is Baxter, but, although he found the idea that Dunbar was the author 'difficult', he was not prepared to go so far as to the delete the poem from the canon: *William Dunbar*, p. 193.

It is perhaps significant, nonetheless, that at least one poem should be variously attributed both to Stewart and to Dunbar, for to a considerable extent the poets of the reign of James V do depend upon their predecessors for inspiration and models. Thus one finds the same gamut of genres: occasional poems; entertainments, including flytings; dream visions; lyrics on the theme of love; religious verse; satires on life at court; poems of moral advice to the king.[21] The similarity may be thought somewhat disappointing, and one critic has been scathing about William Stewart, calling him a 'servile imitator of Dunbar, lacking his genius'.[22] On the other hand, it could also be claimed that the very similarity suggests that the poets of the turn of the century had quickly acquired such prestige that their successors would inevitably fall heirs to a Scottish and Jacobean tradition, as well as to a more familiar English and Chaucerian one.

The year 1513 marks a watershed in the political and cultural life of Scotland. Most obviously, the death of James IV at Flodden removed from the scene the principal patron of the arts, and a decade and a half would elapse before the youthful James V might resume the role. In one of his poems to the king, Stewart traces the present social problems back to their source in that tragic event:

> For all this sort with schame mon be exylit,
> Or than demanit, as I haif deuysit,
> And vþir personis in to þair placis stylit,
> The quhilk sen Flowdoun feild hes bene dispysit
> In this cuntre, and in all vþiris prysit...
> ('This hindir nycht', 57-61)[23]

Nothing is known of Dunbar after 1513, and Gavin Douglas's last poetic work, the *Eneados*, was finished in the same year, a few months before the battle. Nonetheless, there are a few points of connection between the earlier and later generations of poets. When in 1515 John Stewart, Duke of Albany, was summoned from France to be Governor of Scotland, a poem of welcome was composed for him by a Scottish poet; unfortunately only the French translation of this poem survives.[24] In 1517 an anonymous poet (formerly supposed to be Dunbar) composed the verses 'Quhen the Governour past in France', and sometime between 1517 and 1521 the same or another person addressed a poem to Albany, when the latter was still in France.[25] David Lyndsay had been at court

---

[21]This has been noted by Denton Fox:, Bann. MS (facsimile), p. xlii.
[22]J.T.T. Brown, 'The Bannatyne Manuscript', *SHR*, I (1904), 136-58 (146).
[23]Lyndsay says similar things in the *Papyngo*, 507.
[24]For the text of the French poem: *The Thrissil, the Rois and the Flour-de-lys*, ed. H.M. Shire (Cambridge, 1962), pp. 10-11. Shire argues (p. 26) that the Scottish poet could have been Dunbar.
[25]These are most easily consulted in *The Poems of William Dunbar*, ed. W. Mackay Mackenzie, revised B. Dickins (London, 1960), poems 65 and 92 (pp. 139-40; 181-82). Mackenzie's poem 91 ('To the Queen Dowager') is also anonymous, but it is not clear (a) whether it actually refers to a

since at least 1511, when he was granted money for a costume in which to play before the King and Queen at Holyrood; thereafter he appears regularly in the Treasurer's Accounts.[26] On the birth of James (10 April 1512), Lyndsay was appointed usher (chief page) to the young prince, in which function he continued until 1522.[27] Another poet who had contacts with the court of James IV was John Bellenden, who, after studying at St Andrews, went straight into royal service. Bellenden's mother, Marion Douglas, was the nurse, or 'kepar' of the infant prince, and thus herself a colleague of Lyndsay.[28] The Bellendens' family connections and sympathies with the Douglases would make it only natural that there should have been some contact with Gavin Douglas, and indeed on 5 November 1520 John Bellenden witnessed a contract between the bishop of Dunkeld and his (Douglas's) sister-in-law, Elizabeth Auchinleck, on the latter's entry to the convent of Sciennes.[29] In 1528, a John Bellenden, who may be the poet, was secretary to the Earl of Angus.[30] On 2 February 1546 John's elder brother, Thomas Bellenden of Auchnoull, together with his assistant, John Mudy, finished copying what is now the Lambeth MS of Douglas's *Eneados*.[31] Thomas Bellenden, it may be remembered, was, while yet a student in Paris, the dedicatee of a Latin poem by James Foulis, printed in the *Quadrupertitum* (1510) of Robert Galbraith.[32] In sixteenth-century Scotland cultural interests tended very much to run in families.[33]

The Scottish poets active in the 1520s and 1530s are a fairly homogeneous lot, and belong to a nucleus of court servants, churchmen and administrators. Of the latter, one of the most notable, although not himself a poet, was Gavin Dunbar, dean of Moray (1517-25), archbishop of Glasgow (1523-47), and Lord Chancellor of Scotland (1528-43), who, as the 'King's Master' (i.e. tutor), was an associate of Lyndsay.[34] Lyndsay himself was a layman, descended from minor landowners in Fife. From 1511 onwards he is recorded in connection with

---

queen, or (b) if so, to which one it refers. For his part MacQueen connects the poem not with Margaret Tudor but with Mary Stewart: *Ballattis of Luve*, ed. MacQueen, pp. 129-31.

[26]Hamer, IV, 241-76.

[27]Hamer, IV, xi.

[28]For details of the Bellendens I am obliged to the unpublished paper of Mr J. H. Ballantyne: 'Mr Thomas Bellenden of Auchnoull (c.1490-1547)'. See also E.A. Sheppard, 'John Bellenden', in *Chronicles of Scotland*, ed. Chambers and Batho, II, 411-61.

[29]Ballantyne, 'Mr Thomas Bellenden', p. 3; Christian, one of the daughters of Thomas (elder brother of John, the poet), was the last prioress of Sciennes, dying in 1571.

[30]P. Bawcutt, *Gavin Douglas* (Edinburgh, 1976), p. 194; *Chronicles of Scotland*, ed. Chambers and Batho, II, 426.

[31]*Virgil's 'Aeneid' Translated into Scottish Verse*, ed. D.F.C. Coldwell, 4 vols, STS (Edinburgh and London, 1957-64), I, 98-99.

[32]IJsewijn and Thomson, 'The Latin Poems of Jacobus Follisius', 133-34, 150-51.

[33]For a detailed study of some of the literary interests of the Bellenden and Bannatyne families see T. van Heijnsbergen, 'The Interaction between Literature and History in Queen Mary's Edinburgh: the Bannatyne Manuscript and its Prosopographical Context', *The Renaissance in Scotland: Studies in Literature, Religion, History and Culture offered to John Durkan*, ed. A.A. MacDonald, M. Lynch and I.B. Cowan (Leiden, 1994), pp. 183-225.

[34]D.E. Easson, *Gavin Dunbar: Chancellor of Scotland, Archbishop of Glasgow* (Edinburgh and London, 1947).

activities in or around the court; from 1529 he acted in various capacities as a herald, and participated in several Scottish embassies on the Continent; after 1542 he is referred to as a knight, and is known to have held the office of Lyon King of Arms.[35] Lyndsay's wife, it may be noted, was royal seamstress—an honourable position, in which she was succeeded by John Bellenden's sister, Katherine.[36] George Steill (d. 1542) was another layman, and possibly groom of the chamber; his familiarity with the king is emphasized by Knox, who gloats at the sudden death of the 'greattest ennemy to God that was in [the] Court'.[37] George Clapperton was sub-dean of the Chapel Royal (1535-74), 'Maister Elimosinar' to James V (1538-42), and provost of Trinity College, Edinburgh (1540-66).[38] James Inglis was another associate of Lyndsay, and combined his poetic career with that of royal chaplain, secretary to the dowager queen Margaret, and chancellor of the Chapel Royal at Stirling (1515-29).[39] John Bellenden was clerk of the king's expenses (1515-22), archdeacon of Moray (1533-38), precentor of Glasgow (1537-47), and rector of Glasgow University (1542-44).[40] Robert Galbraith was treasurer of the Chapel Royal (1528-32).[41] The Cistercian Andrew Durie, a student of St Andrews, Glasgow, Paris and Montpellier, was appointed treasurer of the Chapel Royal in 1520 (and in that function seems to have coincided with the great John Major).[42] He has been described as 'worldly' and guilty of such 'indolence and absorption in secular affairs' that he was replaced in 1530 as visitor-general in Scotland for his order, by the reforming abbot of Glenluce, Walter Malin.[43] Durie was abbot of Melrose before being appointed bishop of Galloway (1541-58); by virtue of the latter appointment he was also titular bishop of the Chapel Royal, with authority over all the royal palaces in Scotland.[44] Alexander Kyd was succentor of Aberdeen (1553/4-63)—at St Machar's cathedral, which bishop Gavin Dunbar had recently adorned with a magnificent heraldic ceiling (constructed 1519-22).[45] The association of John

---

[35] Hamer, IV, ix-xivff., 288-90.

[36] Katherine Bellenden's third husband was Oliver Sinclair of Pitcairns, the favourite of James V since at least 1535, when he, together with David Lyndsay (and, it has been said, Lyndsay's wife) accompanied the king on his marriage-voyage to France: Sanderson, *Cardinal of Scotland*, p. 63.

[37] *Works of Knox*, ed. Laing, I, 68.

[38] *Fasti Ecclesiae Scoticanae Medii Aevi ad annum 1638*, ed. D.E.R. Watt (St Andrews, 1969), pp. 340, 359; *Works of Knox*, ed. Laing, I, 45. Clapperton, it may be noted, was the godfather of Marioun, younger sister of George Bannatyne: A.A. MacDonald, 'The Bannatyne Manuscript—A Marian Anthology', *Innes Review*, 37 (1986), 43-44.

[39] Hamer, III, 75; *Fasti*, ed. Watt, p. 338. Inglis held the benefice of Southwick within the Chapel Royal: *RSS*, I (1488-1529), No. 2572.

[40] J. Durkan and J. Kirk, *The University of Glasgow 1451-1577* (Glasgow, 1977), pp. 201-16.

[41] *Fasti*, ed. Watt, p. 339.

[42] Durkan and Kirk, *University of Glasgow* pp. 148, 184, 202; *Early Records of the University of St Andrews*, ed. J.M. Anderson, SHS (Edinburgh, 1926), p. 206; Paris, Sorbonne, Archives de l'Université, Registre 91, fols 171, 181.

[43] A. Ross, 'Some Notes on the Religious Orders in Pre-Reformation Scotland', in *Essays*, ed. McRoberts, p. 217.

[44] *Fasti*, ed. Watt, pp. 132, 336, 339.

[45] *Fasti*, ed. Watt, p. 17; W. Duguid Geddes and P. Duguid, *Lacunar Basilicae Sancti Macarii Aberdonensis*, New Spalding Club (Aberdeen, 1888), and D. McRoberts, *The Heraldic Ceiling of St Machar's Cathedral Aberdeen* (Aberdeen, 1981). Kyd founded in the cathedral a service altar for the Lady Mass for the choirboys of the 'sang schwyll' (1537), a mass 'de compassione gloriose

Rolland (c. 1504-c. 1575) with the court poets has been noted above. Originally an Ayrshire man, Rolland practised as a notary in Melrose and Dalkeith, was a supporter of the Douglases, and became parson of Ettletown.[46] In spite of the fact that William Stewart's personal history has been declared to be 'an absolute blank',[47] it can be shown that he fits perfectly with the constellation of literary-minded civil servants just discussed. It is likely that his dates are c. 1476-1548. In his translation of Boece's *Chronicles* he claimed descent from Sir Alexander Stewart, first earl of Buchan (the so-called 'Wolf of Badenoch'), fourth son of king Robert II.[48] He may have been a cousin of Henry Stewart, first Lord Methven and third husband of Margaret Tudor. He seems so have graduated master of arts at St Andrews in 1496, and to have remained there until 1506. After some time, during which he was possibly in the service of Edward Stewart, bishop of Orkney, he entered royal service in 1525/6, as servitor to Margaret Tudor and tutor to James. He may well have been apppointed vicar of Pencaitland (1534), and rector of Quothquan (1538), and even have continued in royal service under Mary of Lorraine.[49]

From the evidence at our disposal several conclusions may be drawn. It is clear that we are dealing with a group of men of culture, royal officals and churchmen, several of whom had a professional interest in the moral and political education of the king. One or two, moreover, had particular connections with Margaret Tudor. The Chapel Royal at Stirling—which, as institution, functioned to bring together courtly activities, religious devotion, and the composition of lyric poetry and music—seems to have been something of a cultural centre for several of these poets: this would also remain true under Mary, with Alexander Scott and Sir John Fethy.[50] It was in Stirling that James had passed his early years,[51] it was to Stirling that James withdrew, on escaping from the control of the Earl of Angus in 1528, and it was on the Palace of Stirling that James was to lavish huge expenses. To some extent James's favouring of Stirling recalls a

---

virginis' (1544), and two lights before the Virgin Mary of Pity on the south side of the lady altar (1553): *Registrum Episcopatus Aberdonensis*, ed. C. Innes, 2 vols (Edinburgh, 1845), I, 413, 424, 459.
[46]*Protocol Book of John Foular*, ed. J. Durkan, SRS (Edinburgh, 1985), p. xix.
[47]T.F. Henderson, *Scottish Vernacular Literature*, p. 234.
[48]Stewart, *Chronicles*, ed. Turnbull, I, vii; III, 442-43.
[49]This biographical sketch is heavily dependent upon Sanderson (see above, note 14); a slightly different version is offered by Hamer, III, 76-77. Note that a William Stewart, who may be the poet, held the prebend of Southwick within the Chapel Royal (before 1508): *RSS*, I, 'Index of Offices'.
[50]*Ballattis of Luve*, ed. MacQueen, passim. See also T. van Heijnsbergen, 'The Scottish Chapel Royal as Cultural Intermediary between Town and Court', *Centres of Learning: Learning and Location in Pre-Modern Europe and the Near East*, ed. J.W. Drijvers and A.A. MacDonald (Leiden, 1995), pp. 299-313.
[51]After the discomfiture of Angus in 1515, Margaret Tudor handed over control of the princes to Albany, at Stirling, before fleeing to England.

pattern of court life known under his father, even if the impetus may have been different.[52]

For the poets of the age the king himself was easily the most important topic of interest, and there are few poems which are not concerned with James, both as individual and as political figurehead. The extreme youth of the king (one year) at the moment of his father's death gave grounds for thinking that the succession was precarious: by contrast, James IV had been fifteen, and James III eight years old, on their respective accessions to the throne. The guardians of the young king thus had to bear a great responsibility. James's mother, by virtue of her marriage (August 1514) to Archibald Douglas, sixth Earl of Angus, had disqualified herself from guardianship, and she only regained a position of influence over the king after the final departure to France of John, Duke of Albany, cousin of James IV, and Governor of Scotland. Margaret, together with the Earl of Arran, had her son 'erected' as king in the same year (1524), and from that moment James, theoretically, ruled in his own name. This was a fiction, of course, and remained so even after the second erection of June 1526, as a result of which James became more or less the prisoner of Angus (since 1517 estranged from Margaret). Not until James's escape in 1528 did he really begin to rule in person, but he was still only sixteen. It is hardly surprising that the works of the court poets are full of advice to the King, as to the double necessity of providing good government in the state and restraining his precocious inclination to sensuality.[53]

Stewart, for example, writing to James 'in so tendir aige', says: 'I the beseik aganis thy lust to stryue' ('Precellend prince', 3), and in another poem he prays: 'Chryst, bring our king to perfyt ege,/ With wit fra ȝowthis fellon rege' ('Rolling in my remembrance', 45-46). This remark clearly reflects a longing for James to emerge from adolescence and assume full authority, but in the meantime he could do worse than indulge in such youthful sports as hawking, hunting, archery, jousting, and playing cards with his mother ('Schir sen of men', 16-25).[54] This touching vignette of happy family life is not entirely convincing, however, and James needed better moral guidance than the sister of Henry VIII

---

[52]For James IV, Stirling was connected with his religious observances: A.A. MacDonald, 'Catholic Devotion into Protestant Lyric: the case of the *Contemplacioun of Synnaris*', *Innes Review*, 35 (1984), 58-87 (70-72).

[53]On the Scottish tradition of literature on this theme see: S. Mapstone, '*The Talis of the Fyue Bestes* and the Advice to Princes Tradition', *Scottish Language and Literature, Medieval and Renaissance*, ed. D. Strauss and H.W. Drescher (Frankfurt, 1984), pp. 239-54. See also: S. Mapstone, 'The Wisdom of Princes', forthcoming.

[54]Stewart's phrase, 'perfyt ege' [age], besides having a legal sense in referring to the age at which the King might begin to rule in his own name, also recalls the medieval interest in the theory of ages in man's life. According to one Scottish treatment of the subject, *Ratis Raving*, even in the third age, from seven to fifteen, 'reason and judgement are still weak and cannot restrain the boy from spending his time in games': J.A. Burrow, *The Ages of Man: A Study in Medieval Writing and Thought* (Oxford, 1986), p. 49, citing *Ratis Raving*, ed. R. Girvan, STS (Edinburgh and London, 1939), pp. 33-36. See also M. Dove, *The Perfect Age of Man's Life* (Cambridge, 1986).

could provide. Stewart urged the king: 'Thairfoir submit the to thy counsale seige,/ And in all wayis wirk as thay devyis' ('Precellend prince', 11-12), and Kyd dropped the following hint:

> Quhen thow ingyne, maner and conditioun
> Off euery man hes tane experiance,
> Than of law the administratioun
> To prudent men committ in gouernance,
> Quhilkis ar kend and knawin of conscience,
> And with budis will nocht corruptit be...
> ('The rich fontane of hailfull sapience', 49-54)[55]

The most extensive treatment of the topic of the king's advisers is found in Stewart's allegorical vision of Dame Verity, who longs for the banishment of 'wilfull wrang', 'hid hatreit', '3ung counsale', 'singular proffeit', 'dissimvlance', 'flattery', 'falsheid' and 'ignorance' ('This hindir nycht', 41-48), and their supplantation by a totally new council, headed by the four cardinal virtues:

> First iustice, prudens, fors and temperans,
> With commounweill and auld experience,
> Concord, correctioun, cunnyng and constans,
> Lufe, lawty, science and obedience,
> Gud conscience, trewth and intelligence,
> Mercy, mesour, fayth, houp and cherite,
> Thir in this[56] court mon mak residence
> Or 3e gett plenty and prosperite.
> ('This hindir nycht', 65-72)

The degree to which this poem anticipates the argument, and even several of the very characters, of Lyndsay's *Ane Satyre of the Thrie Estaitis* is remarkable. This is doubtless a reflection of the close contacts between the court poets of the reign of James V, and also suggests that when Lyndsay composed his *Satyre* during the minority of Mary, he had not forgotten the troubles of the previous generation. With a ruler of impressionable age it was imperative that the members of the king's council be chosen for their virtue and wisdom.

One strategy used in the education of the prince was the appeal to ancestry. This was an issue of great contemporary importance; in the late fourteenth century John of Fordun had, in his *Scotichronicon*, laid the ideological basis for the antiquity of the Stewart line, and this reached its apogee in the *Scotorum Historiae* (1527) of Hector Boece, who 'proceeded not only to name all forty of the hitherto anonymous kings of Dalriada, but also to describe with a wealth of

---

[55] *Bann. MS*, II, 242-45.
[56] An emendation from Bann. MS 'his'; the M. Folio MS reads '3our'.

circumstantial detail both their warlike deeds and the workings of the polity over which they ruled.[57] William Stewart tells the king what to put in his notebook:

> And mark in thy memoriall
> Thy predecessouris parentall,
> Quhais fructous fatis and deidis he
> Makis þair fame perpetuall,
> Throw potent princely maiestie.
>
> Sen throw þe erd, in lenth and breid,
> Thow art þe most illustir leid,
> And most preclair of progenie,
> Think þairvpoun and caus thy deid
> Appreif thy princely maiestie.
> ('Schir, sen of men', 6-15)

In the early 1530s the history of Boece was translated by both Bellenden and Stewart. In the Prologue to Stewart's version (completed 29 September, 1535), the lady who commands the poem[58] indicates what she hopes will be its effect:

> I traist, scho said, fra that his grace hes sene
> Sa nobill kingis befoir his tyme haif bene,
> Will he considder the rycht ay as he reidis,
> Thair nobilnes and als thair douchty deidis;
> Thair sall he find als nobill and als fyne,
> As euir wes ony of the nobill nyne.
> And fra his grace considder weill sic thing
> How that he wes predestinat to ring,
> Siclike as tha, into thair settis suir,
> I traist he suld do diligence and cuir,
> To follow thame with possibilitie,
> So like with poettis for to prysit be.[59]

Not surprisingly, similar thoughts emerge in Bellenden's *Proheme of the History*:

> Schaw furth ylk king quhill thow come to the prince
> That regnis now in gret felicite,
> Quhais anciant blud, be hie preeminence,
> Decorit is in maist excellent gre

---

[57] R.A. Mason, '"Scotching the Brut": the Early History of Britain', *Scotland Revisited*, ed. J. Wormald (London, 1991), pp. 49-60 (54).

[58] Because of the loss of the beginning of the Prologue, it is not clear whether the lady is an allegorical dream-figure, or a real person, though the fact that she has a cousin called 'Discretioun' (12) suggests the former. The editor took her (perhaps needlessly) to stand for Margaret Tudor: *Chronicles*, ed. Turnbull, I, vii.

[59] *Chronicles*, ed. Turnbull, ll. 28-39.

> (Without compare) of hie nobilitie.
> With giftis mo of nature to hym geuyn
> (Gyf nane abusit in his ʒoutheid be)
> Than euir was geuyn to noble vnder heuyn.[60]

In his Prologue to his translation of Livy, John Bellenden rose to even greater heights of patriotic adulation:

> And ʒe, my souerane, be lyne continewall
> Ay cumin of kingis ʒoure progenitouris,
> And writis in ornate stile poeticall
> Qwik flowand vers of rethorik cullouris,
> Sa freschlie springand in ʒoure lusty flouris,
> To þe grete comforte of all trew Scottismen;
> Be now my muse and ledare of my pen.[61]

It is possible that Bellenden was impelled to such flattery in an attempt to compensate for his former Douglas affiliations; but however that may be, his words testify to a cult of royalist sentiment, in which a poet might make a discreet attempt to steer the king's thoughts by evoking an illustrious Stewart tradition.

For all the poets of the age, the foundation of public and political morality was ultimately the law of God. Lyndsay reminds James of this, in his 'Ane Exhortatioun to the Kyngis Grace', after giving him a stiff warning about the dangers of lechery.[62] In Stewart's view, if James should fail to institute justice in the land he 'sall accusit be,/ Afoir the king þat wore the croun of thorne' ('This hindir nycht', 87-88); in 'O man, remember and prent in to thy thocht' he gives an affective picture of that very same king, in the hope of inducing compunction within the man who 'lykis in lust and ryalte to ring' (108).[63] Elsewhere Stewart makes more sharply explicit the contrast between the earthly and heavenly kings:

> Think þat thair is ane king of kingis,
> Our heving, erd and hell þat ringis,
> Quhilk with the twynkling of ane E,
> Ma do and vndo all kyn thingis,
> So mervellus is his maiestie.
>
> ('Schir, sen of men', 41-45)

---

[60]Hector Boece, *The Hystory and Croniklis of Scotland*, trans. John Bellenden (Edinburgh, c. 1535; rpt. Amsterdam, 1977), Fvi^v; also *Bann. MS*, IV, 316.
[61]Bellenden, *Livy's History of Rome*, ed. Craigie, I, 1.
[62]Hamer, I, 35-38.
[63]On this poem as a religious lyric, see the present writer's 'Religious Poetry in Middle Scots', in *History of Scottish Literature*, *I*, ed. Jack, 91-104 (98).

Presumably this is intended to be a timely reminder to the peccant monarch that God is ever likely to depose the potentates from their seats. The lesson is utterly conventional, as is the political theory behind it: originality of thought is not the strongpoint of Stewart and his contemporaries.

Worthy didacticism may be at a discount nowadays, but it was different in the sixteenth century; of all Stewart's productions, it is only the moral poems which have survived in more than one manuscript copy. Another subject of interest to the court, of course, was love, and lyrics on this theme were greatly in demand, to judge by the large quantity preserved by Bannatyne. There is only one love lyric by Stewart in which he speaks putatively in his own voice:

> Maist ameyn roseir, gratious and resplendent,
> Excedand trew, benyng and verteus,
> Fragrant olif, violat rubicumbent,
> To mans sycht is wondir gratious;
> Hir benyng luk, with blenkis amorus,
> Persis my hairt, þat soir I syche oft syis,
> Bot for remeid my wit can nocht devyis.
> ('Maist ameyn roseir', 1-7)

One will probably be more impressed by the smooth expression of such lines, rather than by the content of their message. One suspects that Stewart is using the surface decoration of aureation to compensate for the absence of passion; that may well be the reason why, in the space of seven lines, he has repeated the words 'benyng' and 'gratious'. Nor can one say, alas, that the phrase, 'blenkis amorus', is a curious felicity of the author's, since it had earlier been memorably used (three times) by Robert Henryson.[64] Stewart, however, should not be judged too harshly: William Dunbar—another poet-priest, significantly—likewise fails to rise much above superficial accomplishment, when he attempts erotic verse in the first person singular.[65] Likewise George Steill's lyric, 'Lanterne of lufe and lady fair of hew', smoothly repeats the required formulae.[66] We do not know, unfortunately, how such poems were *used*: whether, for example, they were composed at the demand of someone at the court, for a particular occasion. One must also take into account the derivativeness of some poems: the anonymous lyric, 'Support 3our seruand, peirles paramour', takes as its starting-point a *chanson* by Clément Marot, from c. 1530.[67] In the case of either commissioned or translated work, it is hardly surprising that the tone of the resulting pieces should sound a trifle disengaged.

---

[64] *The Poems of Robert Henryson*, ed. D. Fox (Oxford, 1981): 'Testament', 226; 'Orpheus', 81, 355. Stewart's debt to Middle Scots poets other than Dunbar has not previously been noted.

[65] For example, in 'Swete rois of vertew and of gentilnes', *Poems*, ed. Kinsley, p. 24.

[66] *Ballatis of Luve*, ed. MacQueen, pp. 71-72.

[67] *Bann. MS*, III, 295; *The Thrissil*, ed. Shire, pp. 12-13 (both French and Scots texts). See also H.M. Shire, *Song, Dance and Poetry of the Court of Scotland under King James VI* (Cambridge, 1969), pp. 39-41. The Scots poem is printed, with music, in *MB* XV, pp. 158-59.

Like Dunbar, Stewart is essentially not a poet of love but rather a commentator on love as a social phenomenon. Writing in the positive vein about the fair sex, he resorts to a mere catalogue of virtues:

> Ladeis, þai ar of excelland valour,
> Ladeis ar ding to haif auctoritie,
> Ladeis ar clene of confortand cullour,
> Ladeis ar wyis and full of veritie,
> Ladeis ar chest and full of cheritie,
> Ladeis ar menis parradice erdly,
> Ladeis ar plantit full of puritie,
> Thairfoir all men þair fame suld fortefie.
> ('For to declair', 49-56)

The rhetorical effect would make any reader wonder whether some irony may be lurking behind the over-blatant asseverations, but that does not seem to be the case with the *significatio* of this poem.[68] When Stewart turns to write about love as part of the *comédie humaine*, however, his verse takes on a new vitality. In 'Thir lenterne dayis ar luvely lang' the poet affects to speak as one betrayed, but the conventions of courtly love are comically countervailed by his sturdy realism:

> Allace, þat evir fader me gat,
> Or moder me wend in clais,
> Gif I sowld for ane womans saik
> My lyfe thus leid in lais;
> For 3e saw nevir so fair a caik
> Of meill, þat millar mais,
> Bot 3it ane man wald get the maik:
> As gud luve cumis as gais.
> ('Thir lenterne dayis', 41-48)

One is amused at the protagonist's theology, in another stanza from this poem (17-24), as he charitably wishes success to his lady:

> O lord of luve, how lykis the
> My lemmens laitis vnleill:
> Scho luvis ane vþir bettir than me,
> I haif caus to appeill.
> I pray to him þat deit on tre,
> That for ws all thold baill,
> Mot send my lemmane twa or thre,
> Sen scho can not be leill.

---

[68] Satire upon, and defence of, women frequently co-existed: F.L. Utley, *The Crooked Rib*, (Columbus, Ohio, 1944), p. 26 et passim.

The humour of such a poem looks back to such a piece as Dunbar's 'Rycht airlie on Ask Weddinsday', and forward to the cynical realism of Alexander Scott's 'In June the jem' and 'To luve unluvit it is ane pane', which both use the proverb, 'as gud lufe cumis as gais'.[69] The same sense of humour is seen in Clapperton's 'In Bowdoun on Blak Monunday'[70] with its anti-romantic refrain, 'Way worth maryage for evirmair!', and in Stewart's contribution to the subgenre of lyric which Bannatyne called the 'ballat of vnpossibiliteis'.[71] In 'Furth ouer the mold at morrow as I ment', the poet has a meeting with the authoritative figure of Pandarus, in a manner similar to that in which, in the Prologue to *The Lion and the Mouse*, Henryson had encountered Aesop. To Stewart's 'obscure' question, 'Quhen ladeis to thair luvaris salbe leill?' (28), Pandarus gives an equally obscure answer:

> Quhen firn flurichis and beiris gude frute,
> And gud reid wyne growis on the roddyne treis,
> And on the hadder growis the hassill nvte,
> Hony and walx ar maid but werk of beis...
> ('Furth ouer the mold', 43-46)

In such a poem love is converted (some might say reduced) to an intellectual game, but the poet's sense of enjoyment is evident.

Flyting was an art-form much appreciated in mediaeval Scotland, and the most distinguished examples are those involving William Dunbar and Walter Kennedy, and Alexander Montgomerie and Patrick Hume of Polwarth, at the courts of James IV and James VI respectively.[72] Clearly, Stewart's 'Flytting betuix þe sowtar and the tailʒeour' (the title is Bannatyne's) belongs to the same genre. There are, however, differences, of which the most important is that Stewart places the dispute in the mouths of two artisans (in the other specimens just mentioned the interlocutors are all courtiers, and socially well connected).[73] What Stewart offers is a ridiculous quarrel between two buffoons, in order to elicit a smile from their superiors. Here the affiliation is rather with Dunbar's 'Turnament' between the tailors and sutors, Lyndsay's *The Justing betuix James Watsoun and Jhone Barbour, servitouris to King James the Fyft*, and Alexander Scott's *The Justing and Debait up at the Drum*.[74] The consequence is that, although Stewart's flyting is certainly entertaining, it necessarily lacks the

---

[69]Dunbar, *Poems*, ed. Kinsley, pp. 197-98; *Ballattis of Luve*, ed. MacQueen, pp. 106-7, 104-5). This proverb also appears in Henryson: *Fabillis* (512).
[70]*Ballattis of Luve*, ed. MacQueen, pp. 68-70.
[71]*Bann. MS*, IV, 43.
[72]Dunbar, *Poems*, ed. Kinsley, pp. 23-95; *The Poems of Alexander Montgomerie*, ed. J. Cranstoun, STS (Edinburgh and London, 1887), pp. 59-87. See also P. Bawcutt, 'The Art of Flyting', *Scottish Literary Journal*, 10 (1983), 5-24; P. Bawcutt, 'A Miniature Anglo-Scottish Flyting', *Notes and Queries*, 233 (1988), 441-44.
[73]This would also apply to the flyting that apparently took place between David Lyndsay and James V, of which only Lyndsay's part is preserved: Hamer, I, 102-4.
[74]Dunbar, *Poems*, ed. Kinsley, pp. 154-57; Hamer, I, 114-16; *Longer Scottish Poems I: 1375-1650*, ed. P. Bawcutt and F. Riddy (Edinburgh, 1987), 271-78.

interplay of learned wit and verbal pyrotechnics which makes the reading of the more famous flytings such a rewarding, if linguistically challenging experience.

Not surprisingly, therefore, Stewart is seen at his best, when he can apply his gift of satirical humour to some occasion in the life of the court. This is the case with his New Year's day carol, 'First lerges the king, my cheife', which stands in a Middle Scots tradition of Yuletide poems.[75] The Latin *Strena* (1528) attributed to James Foulis, which addresses the 'erected' James V, is a more learned specimen of the genre.[76] Stewart's poem has traditionally (since Lord Hailes) been taken to date from 1527, for a variety of reasons, of which perhaps the most weighty is the reference, lines 46-50, to Margaret Tudor[77] (in that year Margaret was in eclipse, as a result of the machinations of her husband, Angus):

> Grit God releif Margaret our quene,
> For, and scho war as scho hes bene,
> Scho wald be lerger of lufray
> Than all the laif that I of mene,
> For lerges of this New Yeir day.

Sir David Lyndsay also alluded to the fall of Margaret, in the *Papyngo* (542-48). However, it is possible that the reference to Margaret actually relates to 1 January 1542, thus *after* the death of the Dowager Queen (variously given as October or November 1541). According to this latter reading, Stewart's lines would have been intended as a prayer for Margaret's soul, from a poet who, as has been seen, had been closely associated with his royal mistress, and who may also have been a cousin of Henry Stewart, her third husband.

In support of the later date one may note certain details given in the poem about the abbot of 'Halie Croce' (Holyrood). In 1527 there was an abbot new, namely William Douglas, brother of Archibald, sixth Earl, appointed in June 1526; Douglas, however, was born c. 1495, and was to die in October 1528. He therefore scarcely qualifies as the poet's 'abbot ȝing' (16). A much better candidate is Robert Stewart, bastard son of James V and Euphemia Elphinstone, and later Earl of Orkney. Stewart was born in 1533, obtained a grant *in commendam* of Holyrood in 1539, and in 1542 would well merit the poet's description.[78] A further interesting aspect of the later dating of the poem is that

---

[75]For example: Dunbar, *Poems*, ed. Kinsley, pp. 69, 126-28. See also P. Bawcutt, 'Dunbar's Christmas Carol', *Scottish Language and Literature*, ed. Strauss and Drescher, pp. 381-92.

[76]IJsewijn and Thomson, 'Latin Poems of Jacobus Follisius', 105, 135-38, 151-52.

[77]*Ancient Scottish Poems*, ed. Sir D. Dalrymple, Lord Hailes (Edinburgh, 1770), pp. 151-52, 289-91; Hailes was followed by Sibbald: *Chronicle of Scottish Poetry*, ed. J. Sibbald, 4 vols (Edinburgh 1802), II, 40-3. Hailes and others also attributed the poem to 'Stewart of Lorne' (on whom see above), and this opinion was adopted by the authoritative Thomas Warton: *The History of English Poetry*, 3 vols (London, 1774-81), II, 258.

[78]*The Scots Peerage*, ed. Sir J. Balfour Paul, 9 vols (Edinburgh, 1904-14), I, 188-89; *James V Letters*, pp. 357-58.

the 'bischop new' of Galloway (11) would be none other than Andrew Durie, nominated in July 1541;[79] we have earlier noted John Rolland's association of Stewart and Durie as poets at the court. On the assumption of a date of January 1542, one may proceed to identify the other persons mentioned by the poet: the Lord Chancellor (6) would be Gavin Dunbar, archbishop of Glasgow (and *inter alia* patron of John Bellenden), chancellor of Scotland from June 1528 until September 1543. The Secretary (21) would be Sir Thomas Erskine of Halton and Brechin (like Stewart also a tutor to James), in office from October 1526 until January 1543. The Treasurer (26) would be Sir James Kirkcaldy of Grange, in office from March 1538 until 1543. The Comptroller (26) would be David Wood of Craig, in office from September 1538 until 1543.[80] The Lord Bothwell mentioned in the penultimate stanza[81] (whether in 1527 or 1542) was Patrick Hepburn, third Earl of Bothwell; the latter's mother was Agnes Stewart, illegitimate daughter of James Stewart, Earl of Buchan, and before her marriage to Adam Hepburn, second Earl of Bothwell, she had been a mistress to James IV, and had borne him a child.[82]

The Stewart court was a small world. It is evident that William Stewart's poem is designed to amuse at least some of the officials named; in this respect it resembles certain poems by Dunbar, which transform the art of begging into court entertainment.[83] The 'fair haiknay but hyd or hew' (14), which the poet received from the Bishop of Galloway, is but one of the non-existent presents received.[84] Best of all, perhaps, is the stanza of 'First lerges' (21-25) that demonstrates that the Circumlocution Office is of some antiquity:

> The thesaur and compttrollar,
> Thay bad me cum I wait nocht quhair,
> And thay suld gar I wait nocht quhay
> Gif me I wat nocht quhat full fair,
> For lerges of this new 3eirday.

The only concrete remuneration consists of the paltry two shillings from the King (3), and the 'cursour gray' (43) given by Bothwell. This horse, however, may be another piece of unreality, since the Earl seems to have been banished from court between 1538 and 1542.[85] Not surprisingly, the poet curses the keen

---

[79] *Fasti*, ed. Watt, p. 132. In 1527 there was also a new bishop: Henry Wemyss, provided in January 1526.

[80] It may be noted that both Sir Thomas Erskine of Brechin and David Wood of Craig were Angus men, but that each represented at court one of the two opposing interests of the Angus magnates: F.D. Bardgett, *Scotland Reformed: The Reformation in Angus and the Mearns* (Edinburgh, 1989), p. 13.

[81] Stanzas 1, 5, 9 and 10 are omitted from the M. Folio MS.

[82] *Scots Peerage*, II, 156-57, 266.

[83] Cf. Bawcutt, *Dunbar the Makar*, p. 109.

[84] In this line, W. Tod Ritchie gives the erroneous reading 'kaiknay': *Bann. MS*, II, 254.

[85] Robert Lindsay of Pitscottie, *The Historie and Cronicles of Scotland*, ed. Æ.J.G. Mackay, 3 vols, STS (Edinburgh and London, 1899-1911), I, 353; II, 15.

frost (36) which restrains hands and locks up purses; he clearly believed that he was entitled to better treatment. The ceremony which Stewart recounts in this poem seems curiously flawed, as if he is trying to make the best of a bad job: if the 1542 date is correct, it would be only natural that this should be so, since the death of Margaret in the late autumn (and of James's two sons in the spring) would have overshadowed the customary merrymaking.[86] It is perhaps significant that Bannatyne placed this poem in the second section of his manuscript—not among the comic, but among the moral poems.

The details given in this work impart to it a sense of historical occasion unusual in Stewart's *œuvre*, and the only parallel which suggests itself is Dunbar's 'Ane Dance in the Quenis Chalmer':[87] both poems evoke the indoor, closed world of the social elite at play. With the exception of Lyndsay, only seldom, or *en passant*, do the poets considered here make reference to matters beyond the court. Stewart seems to share the opinion of the Wife of Bath, when it comes to anti-feminist literature:

> Bot titar mak plane proclamatioun,
> To gaddir all sic bybillis besely,
> And in the fyre mak þair locatioun,
> Off famenyne þe fame to fortefie.
> ('For to declair', 13-16)

Is it possible that these lines contain a reflection of the fate of Protestant writings (including Scriptures in the vernacular) under James V?[88] Again, near the end of his *Ane Proheme of the History*, John Bellenden forsakes generalities to comment on the corrupting effect of the wealth of the Church:

> Schaw how of kirkis the superflew rent
> Is ennyme to gud religion,
> And makis preistis more sleuthfull than feruent
> In pietuus werkis and deuotion,
> And not allanerly perdition
> Of commoun weill be bullis sumptuus.
> Bot to euyll prelatis gret occasion,
> To rage in lust and life maist vicius.[89]

---

[86] The alternative date, 1527, was not such an auspicious one either, since James was then still under the control of Angus. The fact that Stewart makes no mention of the latter, and indeed shows the king apparently as a free agent, is perhaps further evidence in favour of the later date.

[87] Dunbar, *Poems*, ed. Kinsley, pp. 100-1.

[88] The word 'libels' is expected, but *bybillis* is confirmed by the reading of the second text of this poem in the Bann. MS. Chaucer's Jankyn, however, draws some of his calumnies upon women from the Bible: *The Riverside Chaucer*, ed. L.D. Benson (Boston, 1987), p. 113 (l. 650).

[89] *The Hystory and Croniklis of Scotland*, Fvi.

These lines betray the influence of the stronger voice of Lyndsay, for whom, ever since *The Dreme*, concern for the Commonweal was a characteristic subject.[90]

A discussion of the poetry of the age of James V must also touch on some of the anonymous works contemporary with the known productions of Stewart and others. At least three poems included at the end of the second section of the Bannatyne Manuscript fall into this category. 'Now is our king in tendir aige',[91] putatively spoken by one Iohne Vponland, makes a fierce denunciation of the social injustices which have grown up during the minority. While the name of the persona recalls post-Langland protest literature,[92] this figure also anticipates Lyndsay's Iohne the Common-weill, hero of the *Satyre*. Indeed certain points of complaint are strikingly similar: the authors of both works point out that while petty crime is punished harshly, larger depredations are tolerated.[93] The other two poems address themselves to the problem of the regency: in 'Suppois I war in court most he' we find a warning to the nobles not to put too great trust in fortune, and in 'Iesu Chryst, þat deit on tre' the poet reviews the lamentable state of the administration of justice and predicts, hopefully, that all will be put to right when the king comes of age.[94] Lyndsay was thus not alone in making his criticisms of society, and he perhaps ought to be situated more in the context of the other poets of the reign, who all shared many common concerns.

Of William Stewart and his contemporaries it can be said that they learned much from the works of their Scottish predecessors, and they form an essential link in the chain of literary tradition that continued into the reign of Mary, and beyond. While the sheer volume and topicality of Lyndsay's achievement has tended to overshadow the minor poets, the latter have their place in any overall assessment of the state of literary culture under James V. A poet who, like William Stewart, is fond of impossibility and modesty *topoi*, runs the risk of being taken at face value by the critics, but it would be wrong to undervalue him. John Bellenden is a different case: the heavily Latinate vocabulary and the classicizing tendency of his poems are signs both of his debt to Gavin Douglas, and of his own ambitious nature. For John Rolland there was no incongruity in mentioning these poets alongside the great Lyndsay; such a collocation, made at the very moment of the triumph of the Protestant party in 1560, may be construed as praise.

---

[90] See 'Complaynt of the Commonweill of Scotland', *The Dreme*, ll. 918-1036: Hamer, I, 32-35.
[91] *Bann. MS*, II, 247-49.
[92] *Jack Upland, Friar Daw's Reply and Upland's Rejoinder*, ed. P.L. Heyworth (Oxford, 1968).
[93] For example, 'Now is our king', ll. 40-46, and Sir David Lyndsay, *Ane Satyre of the Thrie Estaitis*, ed. R. Lyall (Edinburgh, 1989), pp. 96-97 (ll. 2658-73).
[94] *Bann. MS*, II, 233-34, 245-57, respectively.

APPENDIX

The rationale of the attribution of poems to William Stewart is set out above, pp. 147-49. In this list, which is alphabetical by first lines, the Bannatyne and Maitland Folio MSS are designated B and MF respectively, and the page references are those of the STS editions.

(i) THE POEMS OF WILLIAM STEWART

1. First lerges, the king, my cheife[95]
    B, II, 254-57: 'q Stewart to þe kingis Grace'.
    MF, I, 248-49.
2. For to declair þe he magnificens
    B, III, 256-58: 'q stewart'.
    B, IV, 71-73: 'q stewart'.
3. Furth ouer the mold, at morrow as I ment
    B, IV, 40-42: 'q Stewart'.
4. Maist ameyn roseir, gratious and resplendent[96]
    B, III, 265: 'q stewart'.
5. O man remember, and prent in to thy thocht
    B, II, 90-95: 'q Stewart'.
6. Precelland Prince, havand prerogatyue
    B, II 231-32; 'q w [interlined] stewart'.
    MF, I, 396-97: 'Quod stewarte to þe king'.
7. Rolling in my remembrance
    B, II, 249-51.
    MF, I, 370-72: 'Quod Stewarte'.
    CUL MS Ll.v.10 (Reidpeth MS) fols 35-36: 'q Stewart'.
8. Schir, sen of men ar diuers sortis
    B, II, 256-57: 'q Stewart to þe kingis Grace'.
    MF, I, 246-48.
9. Thir lenterne dayis ar luvely lang
    B, IV, 6-8: 'q stewart'.
10. This hindir nycht, neir by the hour of nyne
    B, II, 228-31.
    MF, I, 353-55: 'Quod williame stewart to þe king'.
11. Thow leis, loun, thow leis[97]
    B, III, 22-26: 'Quot stewart'.

---

[95]This is preceded in the MS by the burden: 'Lerges, lerges, lerges ay,/ Lerges of this New 3eir day'.
[96]This is not attributed to the poet by Tod Ritchie in his list of contents: B, III, xii.
[97]This is the first of three linked flyting poems.

(ii) POEMS GENERALLY ACCEPTED AS WILLIAM STEWART'S

12. In Grece sumtyme into Achchaya land[98]
    CUL MS Kk.ii.16.
    (No pre-modern attribution to Stewart)

(iii) POEMS WITH CONTRADICTORY ATTRIBUTION

13. Musing allone this hinder nicht
    B, II, 156-57: 'quod Dumbar'.
    MF, I, 191, 191-93.
    MF, I, 372-74: 'quod Stewarte'.
    (Generally taken to be by Dunbar)

---

[98] This is the opening line of the versified *Croniclis* proper. The Prologue begins: '[...] ris as the ald cok crawis'.

I am much obliged to Mrs Priscilla Bawcutt, Dr John Durkan and Mr Theo van Heijnsbergen for their constructive comments on an earlier draft of this essay.

10

DAVID LYNDSAY AND THE MAKING OF KING JAMES V

Janet Hadley Williams

The prince who was to become James V of Scots was a key figure in Scottish politics from his first breath. Born on 10 April 1512, the fourth child of Queen Margaret and James IV, James alone survived to secure the succession: his elder brothers, James and Arthur, and an unnamed sister born between them, all died in infancy.[1] A younger brother, Alexander, had lived for two years, his early death again emphasizing James's importance.[2] Beyond his own country, James's birth and survival were also of immediate import. In England, the son born to Henry VIII and Queen Katharine at the beginning of 1511, and welcomed with such glad relief, had lived for only seven weeks.[3] As a result, for the brief period (1511-1516) when Henry VIII was without a successor, his sister, Margaret Tudor, was presumed heir to the English throne. The very existence of her son seems likely to have had a part in shaping Henry VIII's attitude towards Scotland. If so, it gave James a role, albeit unwitting, in the events that led up to the disastrous battle of Flodden in 1513. Afterwards, with his father dead, it was the young king's vulnerability that drove Scotland's lords—as fearful of Henry VIII's claim to be 'Protector of Scotland' as they were of his widowed sister's powerful position and divided allegiances—to seek to strengthen ties with France. Before the end of that year, the lords had asked French-born John, Duke of Albany, the heir presumptive, to 'cum hame to þe Realme of Scotland for þe helping of þe said Realme and contrair þair Inemyis of Ingland, to do seruyce to þe ȝung king quene and Realme...'.[4]

An important dynastic symbol, James V was also a demanding infant. He was cared for by six 'rokkaris and nurisis' (*TA*, V, 74), three gentlewomen, eight servitors (*TA*, V, 96) and others of the royal household. One of these was David Lyndsay, in his twenties when at the prince's birth he became his personal

---

[1] James, Prince of Scotland and the Isles, b. 21 February 1507, d. 17? or 27? February 1508; an unnamed girl, b. and d. July 1508; Arthur, b. October 1509, d. June 1510.
[2] Alexander, Duke of Ross, b. 30 April 1514, d. 18 December 1515.
[3] See E. Hall, *Chronicle: containing the history of England during the reign of Henry the Fourth...to the end of the reign of Henry the Eighth...collated with the editions of 1548 and 1550*, ed. H. Ellis (London, 1809), pp. 519, 526.
[4] *James V Letters*, p. 1: Louis XII to Margaret and Council, 4 October 1513; ibid., pp. 2-3: Instructions by Albany to de la Bastie, [October 1513] and *APS*, II, 281-82, 26 November 1513 (in fact, from Acts of General Council; see *ADCP*, p. 6).

servant. Like many others (among them William Dunbar, John Bellenden and William Stewart), Lyndsay's activities at court included the writing of verse and prose. Eight of Lyndsay's poetic compositions dating from the late minority years and into James V's personal reign have survived, as has an Armorial Register, compiled by Lyndsay late in the reign, in the course of his duties as senior herald. The poems are the works of a politically- as well as poetically-knowledgeable 'insider' and they are addressed to the king, sometimes also his courtiers. The Armorial Register, documenting with authority the arms of the sovereign and the great families of his realm, is made the more interesting through its spare prose commentary, which draws attention to related contemporary issues. The nature of this output, taken as a whole, would argue that Lyndsay's was an important influence on James's development and on the ways in which the king was perceived by his realm. The output is examined here in the light of this argument, prefaced by some brief details about Lyndsay himself, of James V's attitude towards him, and of the court context of both men.

'MY SERUYCE DONE ONTO THY CELSITUDE':
LYNDSAY AS JAMES V'S USHER

If he was the 'Lyndesay' described as the stable servant of James's short-lived brother,[5] then the young David was about the court from 1507.[6] By 1512, perhaps as a result of the good impression he made on the king and queen the previous year when he appeared in a play at Holyrood Abbey,[7] David Lyndsay was listed as 'ischar to the Prince' and then, after Flodden, usher to the King.[8] Also serving the king from the early 1520s were other men of good standing such as William Barde, Paul Galbraith, William Galbraith, James Boswell and John Lawson.[9] These men held chamber posts of varying seniority and thus proximity to the royal person,[10] but Lyndsay's position alone, whether described in official record as 'hostiario domini regis' or as on other occasions 'kepar of the Kingis grace' or 'Kingis uschar', was always directly and closely linked to the king

---

[5] *ER*, XIII, 127. Lyndsay's stable post is not unlikely; he looked after the king's horses and saddles during the marriage celebrations in France in 1536 (*TA*, VI, 455 and 456).

[6] The position was not necessarily incompatible with Lyndsay's university study. See W. Barclay, 'The Role of Sir David Lyndsay in the Scottish Reformation', Diss. Wisconsin, 1956, pp. 11-14.

[7] *TA*, IV, 313. Family background also was appropriate; he was a Lyndsay of the Mount, Fife, and kin of the Lyndsays of the Byres. See *The Works of Sir David Lindsay of the Mount*, ed. D. Hamer, 4 vols, STS (Edinburgh and London, 1931-36), [Hamer], IV, ix, App. I, entries 1-22 and App. IV, and C. Edington, *Court and Culture in Renaissance Scotland: Sir David Lindsay of the Mount* (Amherst, 1994), ch. 1 and App. 2. (It should be noted that Lyndsay did not, as Edington states, p. 12, style himself 'the Anscient laird', *Complaynt*, 262. This was Lyndsay's tongue-in-cheek name for George Douglas, the 'uthir [who] slippit in my place' (260), and who therefore could be considered a usurping newcomer.)

[8] *TA*, IV, 441.

[9] *ER*, VI, 260, 310, 380. See also *TA*, V, xxii-xxiv for the king's other personal servants.

[10] See, for example, *TA*, V, 310 (referring to positions in the inner and outer chamber).

himself.¹¹ The singular designation given to Lyndsay possibly related to the modest establishment thought necessary for the king during his first twelve years. Other factors probably contributed: the reduction in crown revenue during the minority,¹² and the considerable if intermittent demands on the treasury by Margaret¹³ and Albany.¹⁴ Yet in these circumstances Lyndsay's position was influential, perhaps somewhat disproportionately, and its specific duties where known worth close examination.¹⁵

The epistle to the king that opens Lyndsay's *Dreme* (c. 1526) and the more informal *Complaynt of Schir Dauid Lindesay* (c. 1529) are exceptionally informative about Lyndsay's service. In the first he reminded the king:

> Quhen thow wes ȝoung, I bure the in myne arme
> Full tenderlie, tyll thow begouth to gang,
> And in thy bed oft happit the full warme,
> With lute in hand, syne sweitlie to the sang:
> Sumtyme, in dansing, feiralie I flang;
> And, sumtyme, playand fairsis on the flure;
> And, sumtyme on myne office takkand cure;
>
> And, sumtyme, lyke ane feind transfegurate;
> And, sumtyme, lyke the greislie gaist of gye;
> In diuers formis, oft tymes, disfigurate;
> And, sumtyme, dissagyist full plesandlye.
> So, sen thy birth, I haue continewalye
> Bene occupyit, and aye to thy plesoure;
> And, sumtyme, seware, Coppare, and Caruoure,
>
> Thy purs maister, and secreit Thesaurare,
> Thy Yschare, aye sen thy Natyuitie,
> And of thy chalmer cheiffe Cubiculare,
> Quhilk, to this houre, hes keipit my lawtie.
> (*Dreme*, 8-25)¹⁶

---

¹¹*ER*, XIV, 8-9, 127-28, 156-57, 220; *TA*, V, 37; *TA*, V, 112.

¹²See *APS*, II, 287. This act of 1524, 'anent þe Inbringing of our soueraue lord[is] p[ro]pirtie', signifies earlier failures to collect Crown revenue. See also *ER*, XV, xv-lxvii and A.L. Murray, 'Financing the Royal Household: James V and his Comptrollers 1513-43', *The Renaissance and Reformation in Scotland*, ed. I.B. Cowan and D. Shaw (Edinburgh, 1983), pp. 41-59 (42-49).

¹³Murray, 'Financing the Royal Household', p. 44.

¹⁴For examples: *ER*, XV, 90, expenses for the Wark expedition (£1297 13s. 9d.), and ibid., 89-90, household expenses (£2343 11s. 4d.).

¹⁵Lyndsay is referred to once as 'Kingis master of houshald' (*TA*, V, 160), but it is difficult to see this as a promotion when later references revert to 'ostiario regis'.

¹⁶Hamer, I, 4-5. Internal evidence supports an earlier date for this poem than that given by Hamer (III, 1-2); see Edington, *Court and Culture*, pp. 24-25. Hamer (III, 9) cites 'Lyndsay's description of himself' in the poem's title as verification for a 1528 date, noting the similar descriptions of Lyndsay in the Exchequer Rolls for 1528/29. This is of limited usefulness: the title, taken from *The Dreme*'s earliest extant edition, which postdates the poet's death, may not be his.

He added more memory-tugging details in *The Complaynt* (76-100):[17]

> I praye thy grace for to considder
> Thow hes maid baith lordis and lairdis,
> And hes gewin mony ryche rewardis
> To thame that was full far to seik,
> Quhen I lay nychtlie be thy cheik.
> I tak the Quenis grace, thy mother,
> My lord Chanclare, and mony vther,
> Thy Nowreis, and thy auld Maistres,
> I tak thame, all, to beir wytnes.
> Auld Wille Dile, wer he on lyue,
> My lyfe full weill he could discryue:
> Quhow, as ane Chapman beris his pak,
> I bure thy grace vpon my bak,
> And, sumtymes, strydlingis on my nek,
> Dansand with mony bend and bek.
> The first sillabis that thow did mute
> Was *pa, Da Lyn*: vpon the lute
> Than playt I twenty spryngis, perqueir,
> Quhilk wos gret piete for to heir.
> Fra play thow leit me neuer rest,
> Bot gynkartoun thow lufit, ay, best.
> And, ay, quhen thow come frome the scule,
> Than I behuffit to play the fule:
> As I at lenth, in to my dreme,
> My sindry seruyce did expreme.

To verify his claims about specific duties performed, Lyndsay called by name or office upon such prominent figures of the court as Margaret Tudor, Queen-mother; Marion Douglas, James's nursery mistress or governess; Elizabeth Douglas, his nurse; and Gavin Dunbar, the king's former tutor, now Lord Chancellor. Only written witness remains for consultation, but neither the Treasurer's Accounts nor the Exchequer Rolls confirm or elaborate upon the many recreational activities Lyndsay described; the incompleteness and insufficient detail of both these sources do not help investigation. Revealed by Lyndsay's diverting poetic exposition of out-of-school songs, disguisings, nursery stories and dances, however, is a programme of indoor recreation that was matched, we know from the Treasurer's Accounts, by the attention to the king's prowess outdoors in the martial arts, to his exercise in hand tennis and in riding, hawking and hunting.[18] Lyndsay told of chamber activities tailored to a

---

[17] Hamer, I, 42.

[18] For further selected details: *TA*, V, 146, 147 (for 'schoyne and removes to the Kingis mvle and hors'), 195-96, 252 (a payment for 'ij speris to the King'), 254, 256, 258 (a reference to the 'mending of the Kingis culvering'), 259 (a record of the gift from Henry VIII of 'blawin hornis,

particular child king—lively, musical, demanding[19]—yet their resemblance to kingly leisure activities in general argues for the likelihood of Lyndsay's claims. This is evident when James's games are compared with the privy chamber recreations of his uncle, Henry VIII. His 1526 Ordinance of Eltham set down formally that in those of the king's hours spent away from business matters, familiar servants were to be concerned for 'the King's quiet, rest, comfort, and preservation of his health'.[20] In practice, his privileged familiars acted as partners or performers in such amusements as chess, cards, tennis, dancing, singing to musical accompaniment, speaking entertainingly, and reading aloud from the chronicles or other literary works.[21] These activities for a mature monarch do not seem so distant from Lyndsay's for the child; Lyndsay, indeed, recalled that the king, having discarded his infant pastimes, had been 'rycht Inquisityue' of 'antique storeis and dedis marciall' (*Dreme*, 30-31), and that he, Lyndsay, had described such tales and chronicles to the king 'at lenth' (*Dreme*, 33).[22]

One specific role of the king's usher was referred to in the Ordinance for the Keeping of King James the Fifth, drawn up in the 1520s. Among its provisions was the direction that the king's schoolmaster, the usher, and the valets were 'to ly in the Kingis chalmer', while outside it were to be his captain of the guard, his lieutenant, and four from a pool of twenty footmen, who 'sall nightlie weche'.[23] Though more prosaic, this appears to be the circumstance to which Lyndsay referred in his reminder that he 'lay nychtlie' by the king's cheek (*Complaynt*, 80). By contrast, the distinct chamber positions that Lyndsay alleged he filled during this same period, including those of sewer, carver, and privy treasurer, do not appear in record, although such multi-skilled service for the king's usher seems likely when the monarch in question was an infant. In the household of an adult lord or king, as Russell's *Boke of Nurture* makes plain, each of these roles

---

leschis, and dog collaris'), 265, 275 (mentioning both the necessity 'to bind the Kingis suorde handis, and to be ane gluve till his sair hand' and a payment 'for ballis in Crummis cachpuyll quhen the Kingis grace playit with the lord Glammis'), 276 (noting the delivery of 'halkis to the Kingis grace'), 277.

[19] In the late sixteenth century Thomas Wood noted that James had possessed 'ane singular gud eir and culd sing that he had never seine before, bot his voyce wes rawky and harske', Cantus partbook, Edinburgh University Library MS Laing III. 483, p. 176. From his early 'teens, James's interest in lute music is recorded (*TA*, V, 252 and 276). On the place of music in the life of a prince: P. Holman, 'Music at the Court of Henry VIII', *Henry VIII: A European Court in England*, ed. D. Starkey (London, 1991), pp. 104-6 and J. Stevens, *Music and Poetry in the Early Tudor Court* (1961, rpt. Cambridge, 1979), esp. pp. 233-328. For comment on some of James's other personality traits: J. H. Williams, 'David Lyndsay's "Antique" and "Plesand" Stories', *A Day Estivall*, ed. A. Gardner-Medwin and J. Hadley Williams (Aberdeen, 1990), pp. 155-66.

[20] Quotations from the Ordinance of Eltham are from R. Green's useful discussion of the camera regis, *Poets and Princepleasers: Literature and the English Court in the Late Middle Ages* (Toronto, 1980), pp. 38-39, 54. For full text : *A Collection of Ordinances and Regulations for the Government of the Royal Household*, ed. M. Lort et al, Society of Antiquaries (London, 1790), 135-207.

[21] Green, *Poets and Princepleasers*, pp. 54-59.

[22] By 1525 James, too, was playing cards, *TA*, V, 252, 254, 255, though not with Lyndsay.

[23] Historical Manuscripts Commission, *Report on the Manuscripts of the Earl of Mar and Kellie* (London, 1904), pp. 11-12. On biographic fact and literary convention: J.A. Burrow, 'Autobiographical Poetry in the Middle Ages: the case of Thomas Hoccleve', *Proceedings of the British Academy*, 68 (1982), 389-412.

was that of an individual privy chamber servant.[24] True to pattern, this was so for James's household from 1526, although initially the increased numbers close to the king were also in the interests of the then-ascendant Douglases, who had given the positions to family and supporters.[25]

'HIS GRACES MYND WAS EUER TO ME TREW AND KYND': JAMES V AS LYNDSAY'S PERSONAL LORD

If in the above extracts from his poems we can learn of Lyndsay's affectionate attitude towards the young king, and the degree and nature of his involvement in the king's well-being, what of James V's own early regard for his chief usher? This may be inferred from the minimal impact Lyndsay's replacement by Douglas kin had upon the payment of his yearly pension. It was continued without interruption until 1527, though Lyndsay was now listed laconically as 'quondam hostiario domini regis' [former usher to the king].[26] When James began his personal rule in 1528, Lyndsay received a double payment to cover the amount in arrears for 1527.[27] By then Lyndsay had become a 'king's familiar', which would suggest that from the time James himself took control, Lyndsay was once more placed in close proximity to him. Three years later, a rare direct statement of James V's trust in Lyndsay is found in a letter to Charles V. James writes that the emperor 'may repose confidence in' Lyndsay, who, as the king's 'chief herald...called Snawdon' was to travel as ambassador to the imperial court in Brussels.[28] This royal commendation was something of an epistolary formula, but its use grouped the herald significantly. Others similarly described ranged from two unnamed bearers of letters abroad, to Thomas Erskine, James V's chief secretary, and to David Beaton, then Abbot of Arbroath and later Archbishop of St Andrews.[29] Since the identity of the first two men is unknown, their importance cannot be assessed,[30] but the power and influence of both Erskine and Beaton is explicit or implicit in many a record of this time.[31]

---

[24]John Russell, *The Boke of Nurture*, in *Early English Meals and Manners*, ed. F.J. Furnivall, EETS (London, 1868), 1-112.

[25]*TA*, V, 307, 308; *ER*, XV, 288.

[26]*ER*, XV, 116, 229.

[27]*ER*, XV, 395.

[28]*James V Letters*, p. 193; *L&P Henry VIII*, V, 254. Hamer (IV, 254) gives a transcription of the Latin text, B.L. Add. MS. 21505, fol. 12.

[29]*James V Letters*, p. 293, letters to Francis I and Sir Nicholas Bilde; pp. 176 and 237, to Charles V and the Queen of Hungary respectively.

[30]One of the unnamed bearers, who travelled to England, could have been Lyndsay; he was there several times in August 1535 (*State Papers, Henry VIII*, V, 30 and *L&P Henry VIII*, IX, 151 and 165), but the possibly helpful Treasury Accounts between 2 October 1534 and 30 July 1535 are wanting.

[31]See James V's warm letter to Erskine in 'Papers from the charter chest at Pittodrie MDXXIV-MDCXXVIII', *Miscellany of the Spalding Club*, ed. J. Stuart, II (Aberdeen, 1842), lxxxii-lxxxiii and 193. For Beaton: M. Sanderson, *Cardinal of Scotland* (Edinburgh, 1986), p. 53.

The position of Lyon King of Arms, in which Lyndsay at first acted,[32] held as required on embassies abroad,[33] then held outright from about 1538 (and certainly from 1542, when he is also first described as 'knight'),[34] was in itself an indication that Lyndsay's special standing with the king continued as the reign advanced.[35] This senior heraldic post retained Lyndsay as James's 'familiar daylie servitor' but gave him, as an officer of state, high judicial, administrative and executive duties.[36] It was Lyon King who granted, recorded and corrected abuses of arms, preserved and certified the royal genealogy, received the king's pronouncements and proclaimed them to the people, carried out diplomatic missions on the king's behalf, and was deviser and recorder of State, royal and public ceremonial.[37] At coronations, royal baptisms and marriages, and at the riding of Parliament, Lyon King officiated in his robes of state, but he carried out judicial duties in his tabard embroidered with the 'beast' of his king.[38] The poet is depicted in this distinctive piece of clothing in the woodcut on the title page of an edition of his works published only three years after his death.[39] Thus used the woodcut is a small but suggestive piece of information about the way in which Lyndsay was commonly regarded by the end of his life and his works read: his official duties for and relationship with Scotland's monarch were judged as paramount, his written work seen as a part of this.

'OR HE BE OF PERFYTE AIGE':
LYNDSAY AND THE COURT OF JAMES V'S EARLY YEARS

> Honor & gloyr mocht beyr in hycht
> Jamys ye fyft in goddis sycht
> Quhilk rengand is in yis regeown
> All grace fra hevyn commys daly down.

---

[32]'Protocol Book of Mr Meldrum 1520-33', SRO B 30 1/1/1, fol. 110^v, 4 January 1529.

[33]He was so called on embassies in France in 1534 (*Catalogue des Actes de François Ier*, VII, 28885), and England in 1535 (*L&P Henry VIII*, IX, 151 and 165). (Prof. R. Lyall kindly provided the first reference.) At this time the host court received and rewarded visiting ambassadors one degree higher than their actual rank as a courtesy to the king and court from which they came; see further, Green, *Poets and Princepleasers*, p. 25.

[34]*TA*, VI, 423; *RSS*, II, 4910. See also Hamer IV, Appendix V. Between 1529 and 1542, Sir Thomas Pettigrew was also called Lyon King in Scotland. He is so described in more than the two records Hamer and Edington note; see J. Balfour Paul, 'Clerical Life in Scotland in the Sixteenth Century', *SHR*, 17.67 (1920), 177-89 (179).

[35]James V's regard for Lyndsay also took the form of substantial financial gifts; see *ADCP*, 488.

[36]*Court of the Lord Lyon; List of His Majesty's Officers of Arms and Other Officials...1318-1945*, ed. F.J. Grant, SRS (Edinburgh, 1945), Introduction, n.p.

[37]See T. Innes of Learney, 'Heraldic Law', *An Introductory Survey of the Sources and Literature of Scots Law*, ed. H. McKechnie, Stair Society (Edinburgh, 1936), 379-95.

[38]Ibid., 'The Style and Title of "Lord Lyon King of Arms"', *Juridical Review*, 44 (1932), 197-220.

[39]*STC* 15673, *Ane Dialog betuix Experience and ane Courteour. Off the Miserabill Estait of the Warld, And Imprentit at the command, and expenses of Maister Samuel Iascuy, In Paris* [Jean Petit? Rouen?], *1558*. It is thought that several of Lyndsay's poems were published soon after their composition, but if so these earlier editions are lost; see Hamer, IV, 15-122.

Thus, one hopeful Scotsman annotated his Dioscorides in the years of James's minority.[40] Later an anonymous celebratory *Strena*, printed by Thomas Davidson, echoed this expectation more formally and with the European courts in mind, since its author wrote in Latin.[41] The opening prophesied: 'Tempora magnanimo que nunc felicia Regni...' [A fruitful time for the magnanimous King...]. Notwithstanding such hopes, uppermost in the minds of those closest to the king, if we may judge from the number of 'advice' poems from intimate sources that have survived, was the unfinished state of the royal education, and what, furthermore, had replaced it—the less fitting accomplishments of gaming, sexual pleasures and misguided open-handedness towards flattering, would-be leaders in both secular and spiritual spheres.

There were works of counsel to hand that could return the young king to the better path. Among those available from the time of James's father were John Ireland's theological treatise, *The Meroure of Wyssdome* (1490)[42] and probably also a version of William of Touris' seven-part devotional meditation for kings, *The Contemplacioun of Synnaris*, a popular work of this time. Both were available in Scots, to which the young king could respond most easily. Ireland's prose *Meroure* gave helpful temporal analogies in the discussion of the sacraments contained in the first six books. The seventh book examined those issues of the moment—elective kingship, for instance—of which James needed to be aware. All the same, these works were not instantly appealing. In style the *Meroure* was sometimes elaborate and complex. The metrical *Contemplacioun*'s moral and spiritual instruction to princes was lightened by skilfully used alliteration and 'figur', but it was nevertheless direct in its didacticism.[43] Moreover, both *The Meroure* and also, it has been argued,[44] *The Contemplacioun*, had been written specifically for a young James IV, whose circumstances and personality were very different from those of his son. The works of Gilbert Hay, including the poetic translation, *The Buik of King Alexander the Conquerour*, and the prose translation of the French *Secreta Secretorum*, *The Buke of the Governaunce of Princis* (1456), also were potentially helpful to the young king. James V may well have known already the first of these, or another from the same tradition, for stories 'Off Alexander'

---

[40] See the entry for Robert Gray, second Medicinar, King's College, Aberdeen, c. 1502 to c. 1507, in J. Durkan and A. Ross, 'Early Scottish Libraries', *Innes Review*, 9.1 (1958), 21 and 105 (where it is noted that Gray's Dioscorides was published in Florence in 1518), and L.J. Macfarlane, *William Elphinstone and the Kingdom of Scotland 1431-1514* (Aberdeen, 1985), pp. 383-84. I am grateful to Mrs Priscilla Bawcutt, who has inspected the volume annotated by Gray. Her reading of line 3, replacing 'us' with 'is', is here preferred for its improvement to sense and syntax.

[41] *STC* 14435, *Ad Serenissimum Scotorum Regem Iacobum Quintum de suscepto Regni Regimine a diis feliciter ominato Strena*, [Edinburgh], [1528].

[42] Johannes de Irlandia, *The Meroure of Wyssdome*, ed. C. MacPherson, F. Quinn, and C. McDonald, 3 vols, STS (Edinburgh and London, 1926-90).

[43] *Asloan Manuscript*, II, 187-241 and *Devotional Pieces in Verse and Prose*, ed. J.A.W. Bennett, STS (Edinburgh and London, 1955), v-vii, xxv-xxxii, xxxv-xxxvi, 64-169.

[44] A.A. MacDonald, 'Catholic Devotion into Protestant Lyric: the case of the *Contemplacioun of Synnaris*', *Innes Review*, 35.2 (1984), 58-87.

were among those Lyndsay says he told him in his youth (*Dreme*, 35).[45] Since both were commissioned works, there is some doubt that they would have been available to James, yet the reference to a now lost work or works by Hay in *The Asloan MS* provides evidence that Hay was known beyond the circle of his two patrons, William Sinclair, Earl of Orkney and chancellor of Scotland, and Lord Erskine.[46]

Remedial works, of a shorter and less openly pious or learned kind than those mentioned above, were soon directed explicitly to James V by royal servants such as Galbraith, Kinlouch,[47] William Stewart and Alexander Kyd. Galbraith the poet was perhaps one of those of that name who served from the early years as privy chamber servants.[48] The more logical choice is William Galbraith, the servant most closely identified with the king's interest in lute playing, a pastime frequently associated with verse composition.[49] If so, he was in a better position to pitch his work to influence the particular personality he knew well from day-to-day meetings than was Stewart, servant of the dowager Queen, Margaret Tudor.[50] Galbraith's writing in Scots, as Kinlouch's, was praised by Lyndsay (*Papyngo*, 47-48), but the works themselves have not survived. Some of Stewart's compositions, by contrast, are extant, written in the style that Lyndsay was later to imply was would-be 'staitly' (*Papyngo*, 44-45). The poems suggest that Stewart was unable to maintain his 'Ornat' dignity and at the same time speak to the king in terms to which the young man could warm. His 'Precelland prince' was tediously orthodox, counselling James to 'Dreid god do counsale off thy leigeis leill /... / ffleme frawd and be defender of Iustyce' (49,

---

[45] Lyndsay certainly knew of Hay's poetic abilities in the vulgar tongue by 1530; Hay is mentioned in *The Testament of the Papyngo*, 19-21.

[46] See Sir Gilbert Hay, *The Buik of King Alexander the Conquerour*, ed. J. Cartwright, 3 vols, STS (Edinburgh, 1986, 1990-); *Gilbert of the Haye's Prose Manuscript*, ed. J.H. Stevenson, 2 vols, STS (Edinburgh and London, 1901-14); *Asloan MS*, I, xiv. See also *Longer Scottish Poems I: 1375-1650*, ed. P. Bawcutt and F. Riddy (Edinburgh, 1987), 85-86. A possible later link between court and patron was Oliver Sinclair of Pitcairns, one of James's great favourites during the mid-1530s. His family was a cadet branch of the Rosslyn Sinclairs, owners of the prose manuscript. See P.D. Anderson, *Robert Stewart Earl of Orkney, Lord of Shetland, 1533-1593* (Edinburgh, 1982), pp. 19 and 26, and Haye, *Prose Manuscript*, ed. Stevenson, I, vii-xxxv.

[47] A Paul Kinloch was appointed 'court stewart to the kingis grace of his houshald, for his lifetyme...', 9 May 1527, *RMS*, I, No. 3757.

[48] Another possible Galbraith was Robert, a rising Edinburgh notary public and procurator in 1522 who by 1528 was Treasurer of the Chapel Royal at Stirling. He is known to have been interested in verse in Latin, not Scots. See W. Menzies, 'Robert Galbraith, 148--1543', *Aberdeen University Library Bulletin*, 7.39 (1929), 205-13.

[49] He bought a lute at the king's command in 1526, *TA*, V, 276; see also *TA*, VI, 18. See Stevens, *Music and Poetry*, pp. 278-81.

[50] If he was the 'Mr William Stewart' of the *Treasurer's Accounts*, Stewart received annual livery and pension from 1526-34, and was named by Margaret as 'oure servitour Maister William Steward', *The Hamilton Papers. Letters and Papers illustrating the Political Relations of England and Scotland in the XVIth Century*, ed. J. Bain (Edinburgh), I, 12, Queen Margaret to Thomas Cromwell, 4 July 1534. A connection is frequently made between Stewart's later metrical translation for the king of Boece's chronicles and Margaret as its patron-commissioner (*The Buik of the Croniclis of Scotland*, ed. W.B. Turnbull, London, 1858, I, vii), but there is no evidence to support it. Nor are there surviving treasury entries describing Stewart as tutor, as is sometimes stated.

52) and emphasizing to James the need 'aganis thy lust to stryue' (3).[51] Stewart came nearest to discarding stiff sermonizing when matters touched his own position most closely, as in his homely appeal for kingly generosity (25-29):

> Bettir is gutt in feit nor cramp in hands
> The falt of feitt with hors yow may Suppoirt
> Bot quhone yi handis ar bundin in to bandis
> Na schyrurgane may cure yame or confoirt
> Bot yow yame oppin patent as a poirt...[52]

Familiarity with the activities of the wilful young monarch made another poem by Stewart, 'S*chir* sen of men',[53] something more than a dutiful exercise in petition and counsel, although the concerned and authoritarian tones suggest that it was not the poet but the king's mother (removed early from her role of *tutrix testamentum* by remarriage), who supplied the information. James was urged to play cards and dice, if he must, not with 'pure men' but with those who are fit companions: '...thy noble lord[is] / Or w*ith* the quene thy mother fre' (27-28). (Here, perhaps, is an early reference to behaviour that earned James a reputation as 'the poor man's king'.) He was rebuked—with a petitioner's severity?—for keeping his winnings when he could 'gif agane' (27), and later criticized, seemingly for the exuberance of youth as much as for his lack of the decorum necessary to kings: 'To ryd or rin our rekleslie / or slyd w*ith* lad[is] vpoun þe yce / Accordis noc*h*t for þair maiestie' (38-40).[54] The use of a refrain with variations looked back to the poems of William Dunbar—'This waverand warldis wretchidnes', for example—but Stewart did not have Dunbar's leavening humour or skill in shifting the refrain's focus: in such variations as 'and mar[is] thy ryall ma[ies]^(tie)'(25), 'And far fra princely ma[ies]^(tie)' (30), there was almost a nagging quality.

The learned canon of the Chapel Royal, Alexander Kyd, tried to find more acceptable ways to instruct the young king in 'vertew'—that moral rectitude symbolized by the valuable cardinal and theological ideals of the Christian king: prudence, justice, courage, temperance; faith, hope, charity. His now sole-surviving work, 'The rich fontane',[55] bore out the prominence Lyndsay gave to the word 'prudent' in his later assessment of Kyd (*Papyngo*, 43): in his poem all that could be said about the virtues and kingship was said, not without rhetorical skill, but with too much repetition for a young man impatient to reign (34-40):

---

[51] *Bann. MS*, II, 231-2 . On advice themes see R.J. Lyall, 'Politics and Poetry in Fifteenth and Sixteenth Century Scotland', *Scottish Literary Journal*, 3.2 (1976), 5-29 and S. Mapstone, 'The Advice to Princes Tradition in Scottish Literature, 1450-1500', Diss. Oxford, 1986.

[52] See B.J. Whiting and H.W. Whiting, *Proverbs, Sentences and Proverbial Phrases from English Writings Mainly before 1500* (Cambridge, Mass., 1968), M127, for a similar phrase. The reading of *M. Folio MS*, I, 396-97 ('patent' = open) is preferred to Bannatyne's 'payntit'. Stewart's entertaining Yule piece, 'First lerges' (Bann. MS II, 254-55), has a similar personal involvement.

[53] *Bann. MS*, II, 256-57.

[54] *Bann. MS*'s plural subject, 'princis', (II, 257), which is maintained in the refrain, is preferred to *M. Folio's* 'Or aventure to go on yce / Accordis nocht to thy maiestie' (I, 247, 39-40).

[55] *Bann. MS*, II, 242-45.

> All morall vertew ar neidfull in to a king
> ffortitud but prudens is verry tirrany
> Prudens but iustice is reput for no thing
> Iustice but temperance is bot crudelite
> Temperans is no*ch*t bot liberalite
> Amang all vertew Iustice is lawreat
> And prince of Iustice The verry Image suld be
> The quhilk but vertew is blind and obsecat.

David Lyndsay was already long-serving among those of his fellows who were part-time poets in the late 1520s: he had seen from close quarters the sociable court, the effective domestic policies, and the expensive, ambitious but less successful foreign policies of James's father. As well, Lyndsay had experienced the sudden extinction of that communal vitality, fragile order and impressive display.[56] His awareness of the loss of what this young monarch had never known—strong yet popular rule (with its religious, moral and social obligations and proprieties, its arts of political caution)—is likely to have been as acute, from his perspective of king's usher, as Margaret Tudor's from hers.[57] In *The Complaynt* Lyndsay is particularly outspoken in his condemnation of 'that garisoun' (233)[58] which, because it 'tuke that ȝoung Prince frome the sculis' (133) from the age of about twelve, deprived him of the chance to learn the 'vertew and science' (134) necessary for good government.[59]

With affection and knowledge, Lyndsay looked for practical solution. James's deficiencies in 'science' (his formal education), could be glossed over or circumvented. Within his own supportive poem, *The Dreme*, Lyndsay included, with a conscious diligence, material that might have been found in any handbook for a perfect prince. In style 'after Macrobius', *The Dreme* also placed Scotland within global and universal contexts. The young king thereby gained a better understanding, both of his realm's location and importance and his own future role as its ruler, as did his court and realm at large.[60] In an increasingly humanist climate, moreover, the probable gaps in James's skill in Latin and French were accommodated, even harnessed advantageously to the interest in the country's own tongue and to the reputation abroad of Scotland's skilled poet-translators: by

---

[56] See further, R.L. Mackie, *King James IV of Scotland* (Edinburgh, 1958) and N. Macdougall, *James IV* (Edinburgh, 1989).

[57] On the education of Margaret and her siblings: D.R. Carlson, 'Royal Tutors in the Reign of Henry VII', *Sixteenth Century Journal*, 22.2 (1991), 253-79 and N. Orme, 'The Education of the Courtier', *English Court Culture in the Later Middle Ages*, ed. V.J. Scattergood and J.W. Sherborne (London, 1983), pp. 63-85.

[58] The parties of the earls of Angus and Arran, and the Duke of Albany were all at various times during the minority struggling for custody of the king and control of the government; see W.K. Emond, 'The Minority of King James V 1513-1528', Diss. St Andrews, 1988.

[59] See further, Edington, *Court and Culture*, 18-20.

[60] See J. Hadley Williams, 'Lyndsay and Europe: Politics, Patronage, Printing', forthcoming in 'The European Sun: Proceedings of the Seventh International Research Conference on Scottish Language and Literature', ed. G. Caie, R. Lyall and K. Simpson.

1530 Lyndsay was able to highlight the talents of these writers in the vernacular within the opening to *The Testament and Complaynt of the Papyngo*.

In his early written approaches to James, Lyndsay took a similar petitionary stance to that of some of his colleagues—*The Dreme* had the familiar respectful address, the request for 'recompence', the chronicling of vivid personal details of faithful service—but the degree and nature of the poet's involvement were not the same. In such lines as those quoted earlier ('Quhen thow wes ȝoung...'), Lyndsay presented a brief narrative of the king's boyhood that gave the petitionary enumeration of his own service a different role. The king-centred 'biography' was highly selective. It showed James the royal child in a secure world, made so through the imaginative and responsible initiative of David Lyndsay, the young adult who was his confidant and companion. With fresh reminder of this, the culmination was striking—Lyndsay's humble assertion that he was now not the leader of their games but a 'wracheit worme' (27), blessed to have been found 'so agreabyll' to 'sic ane Prince' (28). The reversal of roles drew immediate, though not direct or admonitory, attention to the implications of the king's new circumstances. It was James, Lyndsay's deferential compliments made plain, who had become the initiating participant at court, the leading patron and responsible 'Potent Prince'. He was now the man who could provide to his needy realm the security and cheer that earlier had been provided to him.

The remainder of the poem, the king was forewarned, would be 'ane storye of the new' (48). This was a dream-vision with a traditional basis, as Dr Cairns has shown in a perceptive study.[61] It kept the individual James V in mind; within it the poet-dreamer looked to Scotland's past and future, intertwining this concern with the theme of good kingship and what it must entail. King-centred retrospection dominated the earlier stanzas, but the dream's date, the 'Calendis of Ianuarie' (57), denoted the 'double face' of the poem, its concern with both past and future.[62] In accord, the dreamer was presented 'Rememberyng on diuers thyngis gone' (67).[63] His guide was 'Dame Remembrance', the personification of the act of remembering or, indeed, a vivification of the king's 'buke of rememberans' in *The Thre Prestis of Peblis* (350). A less common choice among dream vision figures of authority,[64] her name was appropriate to this

---

[61]'Sir David Lindsay's *Dreme*: Poetry, Propaganda, and Encomium in the Scottish Court', *The Spirit of the Court. Selected Proceedings of the Fourth Congress of the International Courtly Literature Society*, ed. G.S. Burgess and R.A. Taylor (Cambridge, 1985), pp. 110-19.

[62]Dunbar had earlier alluded to an aspect of this when he spoke of Janus as 'god of entree delytable,' *Goldyn Targe*, 120, *The Poems of William Dunbar*, ed. J. Kinsley, 1979.

[63]See further, A.C. Spearing, *Medieval Dream-Poetry* (Cambridge, 1976), esp. ch. 1.

[64]Contrast Bellenden's 'vertew' and 'delyt', *Proheme*, 81 (*Bannatyne MS*, ed. Ritchie, II, 9-20, fols 4a-8b); 'varite' [verity], 'This hindir nycht', 16 (op. cit., II, 228-31, fols 87b-88b); Calliope's 'Nimphe' in Douglas's *Palice of Honour*). Lyndsay possibly knew Lydgate's *Testament* (*The Minor Poems*, ed. H.N. MacCracken, pt. 1, EETS, London, 1911) in which '"remembraunce/Of myspent tyme," in youthes lustynesse' (269-70) appears to the dreamer. 'Remembrraunce' is also the 'chambrelayn' (330-36) to 'Loiaulte', a noblewoman 'of grete astate' (97) in *The Assembly of Ladies*, ed. (with *The Floure and the Leafe*) D. Pearsall (London and Edinburgh, 1962).

vision in several ways. In terms of the dramatic presentation Lyndsay employed, Remembrance recalled and took over the role that Lyndsay himself had had in the boy king's waking hours after school. Like a 'dissagyist' David Lyndsay, Remembrance offered her charge 'pastyme and plesoure' (155), 'companye' (156), and counsel in present dilemma. In this instance, moreover, Remembrance and the dreamer (who in turn had taken on the role of the young James V) actually participated in this new 'storye'. This was an enhancement of the earlier play-acting and disguisings, foreshadowing the king's real-life involvement in the country's government. Remembrance also embodied one of the three intellectual powers (intelligence, reason, and memory) then accepted as essential attributes of all men. These, the act of remembering, most of all, had particular pertinence to *The Dreme*'s images of sovereignty, which culminated in the depiction of 'God, in his holye throne deuyne' (516), as the 'blyssit Trynitie' (533).[65] Douglas's 'similitudes', possibly known to the king, set out this concept (*Eneados*, Prol. X, 66-72):[66]

> Lyke as [th]e sawle of man is ane, we wait,
> Havand thre power[is] distinct and separate,
> Vndirstandyng, rayson and memor;
> Intelligens consideris [th]e thing befor,
> Rayson discernys, memor kepys [th]e consait.
>
> As [th]ai beyn in a substans knyt all thre,
> Thre personys ryngnys in a Deite.

Against this background, Lyndsay's 'Memor'/ Remembrance signalled that the 'consait' [idea, imagining] of the latest story that Lyndsay had told should be 'kept' and meditated upon, and its examples of good and bad kingship in past times referred to in future.

Lyndsay used the device of selective retrospection more extensively in *The Complaynt*, written just after James V had begun to rule personally. Once again ostensibly in the cause of long-service enumerated, Lyndsay reordered and interpreted details of political changes perhaps barely remembered or only partially understood by the young king. Likewise, Lyndsay redefined for the king youthful impressions of his own place within these early events and, in doing so, rehabilitated the idea of the rightful ruler and of James V's role as leader in particular. The past 'reigns' of the court factions were set down in order, with the impact of each ascendancy on the well-being of James noted in the rhetorically balanced phrases of a plain-spoken bystander and loyal servant—'Thus euery man

---

[65]This paradox, of powers demonstrably different yet bound together, was well known: 'Memor' frequently was referred to in sermon, fable, religious or advisory poem. Among others, Hay's personification of 'Memor', as one of God's 'Grete Counsale', may have been known to Lyndsay (*Buik of King Alexander*, ed Cartwright ('Off the Regiment of Princis', II, 9703-758). See also, ibid., 9703-8, where the soul is compared to a king.

[66]*Virgil's 'Aeneid' translated into Scottish Verse by Gavin Douglas*, ed. D.F.C. Coldwell, 4 vols, STS (Edinburgh and London, 1957-64), III, 223-28.

said for hym self,/And did amangis thame part the pelf' (253-54); 'Sum gadderit gold, sum conqueist land' (218). Like Stewart, Lyndsay showed in *The Complaynt* that he was familiar with James V's dubious activities at this earlier period, but unlike his colleague, Lyndsay did not mention them only to condemn. Instead, the exciting incidents and the sense of freedom that the changing circumstances had immediately given to the king were recalled vividly in flexible tetrameter couplets: the reckless horseback rides across the sands to Leith ('For wantones, sum braik thare neckis', 182),[67] the exhilarating but treasury-denuding games of cards and dice, the pleasurable flatteries, the sexual encounters permitted and encouraged were all represented. Lyndsay heightened their immediacy and attractiveness by his use of small colloquial excerpts of conversation apparently overheard at the time (238-44):

>   Bot, schir, I knaw ane maid in fyfe,
>   Ane of the lusteast wantoun lassis,
>   Quhare to, schir, be gods blude scho passis.
>   Hald thy toung, brother, quod ane vther,
>   I knaw ane fairar, be fyftene futher.
>   Schir, quhen 3e pleis to Leithgow pas,
>   Thare sall 3e se ane lusty las.

He referred also to specific games, all pastimes that the physically restless king would remember with pleasure. As described, however, they encouraged a reconsideration. The comment, 'Sum gart him raiffel [play] at the rakcat' (175) implied that the king was not just encouraged, but persuaded or forced into leisure activities. Another, 'To play with him pluke at the crawe' (230), depicted the king not as the laughing instigator of the fun but the fool or the victim of the game. The suggestion that James was an innocent, ill-used participant was strong in the words, 'Sum harld hym to the hurly hakcat' [slippery slope, as in tobogganing] (176), and was further shadowed by the sobering reminder of Fortune's instability it presented. So much more effective than Stewart's admonitions on the same topics, such dramatized scenes and vivid allusions made a significant contribution to the reinterpretation of James's minority. They set up echoes of Lyndsay's own kinder 'fairsis on the flure' and packman rides, only to reveal the difference, and to emphasize obliquely that their continuation in either form would be evidence of immaturity. They stressed the fact that, through inexperience, James had allowed the various 'new rewlaris' of the minority years to neglect the proper government, and exploit the riches, of his realm.

By such indirect yet lively means Lyndsay brought James to question the nature of his kingship. Yet royal self-doubts, though they had a place, were undermining to the realm's confidence in the king; they were not permitted to

---

[67]In the same vein an *ER* entry for 1525 (XV, 206) refers to a horse that the king had drowned in the lake at Linlithgow ('Et pro equo submerso in lacu de Linlithqw per dominum regem').

remain dominant. Lyndsay gave comforting praise in familiar advice-to-princes terms for the king's first reforms, and referred confidently to James's open-armed reception of the 'foure gret verteous Cardinalis' (379), with the problem of continuing church abuses the only issue singled out as an area worth the royal 'Ee' (412). The lighter petitionary thread was re-introduced to put further distance between serious questioning and the king's self-assurance. With the teasing trust of an intimate to a liberal patron known for his card-playing, Lyndsay requested a loan 'Off gold ane thousand pound, or tway' (462), then set down in fashionable mock-prophetic form the terms for its repayment (467-74):

>Quhen the Basse and the Yle of Maye
>Beis sett vpon the mont Senaye;
>Quhen the lowmound besyde Falkland
>Beis lyftit to Northhumberland;
>Quhen kirkmen ȝairnis no dignitie,
>Nor Wyffis no Soueranitie;
>Wynter but frost, snaw, wynd, or rane;
>Than sall I geue thy gold agane.

'THAT THYNE VERTEW THYNE HONOUR MAY AUANCE':
LYNDSAY AND THE COURT OF JAMES V'S MATURITY

From 1530, the year in which he turned eighteen, James V took serious interest in the image of his court in and beyond Scotland and in his own place at its centre. There was some awareness of this abroad. Erasmus, writing from Freiburg to Hector Boece in the same year, praised Scotland's civilizing practice of the liberal arts under James IV, adding of James V: 'I don't doubt that he will follow in his father's footsteps...'.[68] By 1532 Sir Peter de Rosimboz, councillor and chamberlain of Charles V, and John Clanuet, Burgundy herald, had visited Scotland to invest the king with the Order of the Golden Fleece. These men, bringing with them something of the magnificence of the European courts, could in turn have taken back to the Emperor first-hand observations of the changing tenor of Scottish courtly activities.[69]

Within the royal household, there was evidence of change in many forms. Lyndsay's wife, royal seamstress Janet Douglas, responded in her work to the marriageable king's growing attention to his own appearance. She sewed for him in increasing numbers elaborate shirts with 'double hankis of gold', silk and ribbons;[70] by 1536, the year of the king's wedding journey to France, the labour

---

[68] *Opvs Epistolarvm Des. Erasmi Roterodami*, ed. P.S. Allen et al, 12 vols (Oxford, 1906-1958), VIII, 2283, 'To Hector Boece', 15 March 1530.
[69] *James V Letters*, 221-22.
[70] *TA*, V, 408, 417, 418; on this subject see M. Swain, *The Needlework of Mary Queen of Scots* (Carlton, Bedford, 1986), pp. 28 and 31-33.

of her fine needlework had to be shared with Katherine Bellenden, sister of the writer-servitor John.[71] Her brother had been at court during the minority as a clerk of the exchequer.[72] Now, in echo of the patronage of New Learning associated with Francis I and Henry VIII, James V commissioned from Bellenden 'a new kind of courtly prose'—translations of Hector Boece's *Scotorum Historiae* and of Livy's history of Rome, completed in 1531 and 1533 respectively.[73]

David Lyndsay, having sought ways to shape James V's understanding of his past and of his present role, now also began to build the king's reputation as a 'Redoutit Roy'. In his first poem of this decade, *The Testament and Complaynt of the Papyngo*,[74] Lyndsay expounded and celebrated the accomplishments of the Scottish king and his court. With no sign of subservience to the learned courtly circles on the continent, yet clearly in awareness of the humanist ideals they were embracing, the opening to the poem assembled and selectively praised a large contingent of talented poets and poet-translators who had written or were presently writing in native Scots. The recently-dead translator of Virgil's *Æneid*, Gavin Douglas, though formerly identified with the Douglas ascendancy, was given the central honour, both structurally and in poetic assessment; John Bellenden, who also had Douglas connections, was next in prominence.[75] The emphasis on this reign's distinction was continued in the 'First Epystyll' to the king. Through the voice of the king's parrot David Lyndsay set out, with elegance, wit, and personal knowledge, the fruits of James V's 'capacitie / To lerne' (283-84). He noted the king's pleasant 'playe', his singing and riding, prowess with spear, bows and culverin (hand guns).[76] The compliment to James's abilities was undoubted, but it also

---

[71]*TA* VI, 298 and they shared the tasks again in 1537-38: VI, 380. Katherine's advantageous marriages, like that of Janet Douglas herself, helped to give her access to the king's inner circle. Her first husband was Adam Hopper (d. 1529), brother-in law of the former Treasurer, Archibald Douglas. Hopper did not fall with the Douglases, and was customer of Inverness, Ross, Sutherland and Caithness (*ER*, XV, 270, 360-61, 440, 513-14). Her third husband was royal favourite, Oliver Sinclair of Pitcairns. See M.G. Kelley, 'The Douglas Earls of Angus: A study in the social and political bases of power of a Scottish family from 1389 until 1567', Diss. Edinburgh, 1973, p. 383; Anderson, *Robert Stewart*, 33-34

[72]E.A. Sheppard, 'John Bellenden', *The Chronicles of Scotland*, trans. J. Bellenden, ed. R.W. Chambers, E.C. Batho and W. Husbands, 2 vols, STS (Edinburgh and London, 1938-41), Appendix, II, 411-61 (424-25).

[73]See R.J. Lyall, 'Vernacular Prose before the Reformation', *The History of Scottish Literature I: Origins to 1603*, ed. R.D.S. Jack (Aberdeen, 1988), 163-82 (173); R.A. Mason, 'Kingship and Commonweal: Political Thought and Ideology in Reformation Scotland', Diss. Edinburgh, 1983, pp. 78-90; L.J. Macfarlane, 'Hector Boece and Early Scottish Humanism', *Deeside Field*, 18 (1984), pp. 65-69 and J. MacQueen, 'Aspects of Humanism in Sixteenth- and Seventeenth-Century Literature', *Humanism in Renaissance Scotland*, ed. J. MacQueen (Edinburgh, 1990), pp. 10-31 (esp. 11-19); for James V as patron: Sheppard, 'Bellenden', 436-38; *TA* VI, 97 also refers to 'ane new cornikle' by Bellenden. On the French court: R.J. Knecht, 'Francis I: Prince and Patron of the northern Renaissance', *The Courts of Europe: Politics, Patronage and Royalty: 1400-1800*, ed. A.G. Dickens (London, 1977), pp. 98-119 (100-1, 107-14).

[74]Hamer, I, 86-90.

[75]Sheppard, 'Bellenden', 424-25 and R.W. Chambers and W. Seton, 'Bellenden's Translation of the History of Hector Boece', *SHR*, 17 (1919), 5-15 (9-10).

[76]See note 18 above.

became the means through which Lyndsay could append a cleverly-timed comment: 'Amang the rest, schir, lerne to be ane kyng' (287). The clear-eyed advice that followed was traditional, yet it also recognized the king's individual weaknesses—less-than perfect bachelor behaviour (295-96), unwillingness to seek advice (301), and lack of interest in sustained study (306-7, 311). Even so, James's strengths remained set out for admiration. Similarly, in the papyngo's 'Secunde Epistyl', addressed to her 'brether of court', the 'hie and tryumphand' reigns (423), and 'the gret renoun' (437) of the illustrious Stewart monarchs who had preceded James V were recalled as fulsomely as were those features and events that had brought about the downfalls and deaths of every one of them.

'Brether' of James V's court also featured in another poem of this period, the *Complaynt and Publict Confessioun of Bagsche*.[77] This 'beast fable' was richly entertaining in its use of the gruff, insistent and not altogether repentant canine narrative voice; for its in-group references to members of the court by name, and in its jocular allusions to Dunbar's petitions and Henryson's *Fables* of the tod.[78] Like *The Iusting betuix Watsoun and Barbour* and the lighthearted berating, *Ane Supplicatioun in Contemptioun of Syde Taillis*, *Bagsche* gives the impression that it is a privy chamber performance-piece, in its case perhaps founded upon a real chain of events—either in the royal kennels or among the past and present activities of the courtmen themselves, or both combined. Yet even in this context, the guiding presence of the king was felt throughout, his stern administration of justice mixed with mercy frequently noted (61-67):

> Bot quhen he knew my crueltie,
> My falset and my plane oppressioun,
> He gaue command that I suld be
> Hangit without confessioun.
> And ȝit because that I was auld,
> His grace thocht petie for to hang me,
> Bot leit me wander quhare I wald....

Later in the 1530s, in what seems to have been an actual interchange with the king, Lyndsay celebrated the accomplishments of James V and his court again. His message here was also a mixed one. *The Answer quhilk schir Dauid Lindesay maid to the Kingis Flyting* responded to the king's taunting allegations, now lost, of the poet's inadequacies in 'Uenus werkis' (30) and hence of his unfitness for James's bachelor court. Lyndsay ostentatiously backed away from the challenge. He described his sufferings at the hands of 'Lustie Ladyis' who had read the king's 'ragment', and conceded the king's literary superiority: 'Quharefor, *Cor mundum crea in me*, I cry, / Proclamand ȝow the Prince of Poetry' (20-21). The comment, with its concession to a more talented antagonist

---

[77] Hamer, I, 92-99.
[78] See J.H. Williams, 'The Lyon and the Hound: Sir David Lyndsay's *Complaint and Confessioun of Bagsche*', *Parergon*, 31 (1981), 3-11.

where an attack was expected, established Lyndsay's poem as something of a mock flyting; in other works of the type the well-known '*Cor mundum*' formula was used in the humbling of the opponent.[79] In the same inverted manner, Lyndsay described the king's prowess in both the courtly and the not-so-chivalrous games of love. His description was implicitly complimentary, if also pungently insulting in the alliterative flyting fashion. The half-offensive, half-admiring jests indeed carried a sting, for Lyndsay used them to expose the king's unmeasured behaviour, and to offer his monarch some serious warning and firm counsel. If Lyndsay made it clear that his *Answer* was never intended to succeed as a flyting, his work successfully offered a piece of pointed advice in a form answering the style of the challenge. Furthermore, it is arguable that in doing so, Lyndsay was upholding the literary reputation of James V's court after all, for the structure and tone of the *Answer* seem to glance with assurance towards the diverting and outspoken epistles that were a current pre-occupation at the French court.[80]

'IN HEUIN AND ERTH THY GRACE SALBE COMMENDIT':
LYNDSAY AND JAMES V'S ROLE IN RELIGIOUS REFORM

As he impressed upon the king the meaning of sovereignty and its responsibilities, Lyndsay did not confine himself to the world of the court. On the contrary, in the *Testament of the Papyngo*, for example, the interplay between the parrot and her 'Holye Executouris', the preying priests of various orders, took up the longest section of the poem (over 77 stanzas). This section drew the king's attention, through the entertaining 'closed' avian world, to the unhappy nature of relations between secular government and the Church. In this and his earlier references, Lyndsay was in part following literary tradition: much of what he said of church abuses in the poems written during James V's lifetime was familiar from works of the previous century.[81] Such features of church life as, for instance, the dereliction of their preaching duties by some prelates and priests mentioned in *The Complaynt*, or the unkept but financially rewarding promises to the dying made by unscrupulous confessors, satirized in *The Testament of the Papyngo*, were longstanding and widespread. These issues, and others that Lyndsay drew to James V's notice for repair, must be considered as part of a much larger picture—well known to Lyndsay and to his contemporaries—in which the church was continuing to make a beneficial

---

[79] See further, P. Bawcutt, *Dunbar the Makar* (Oxford, 1992), pp. 127-28 and 224.

[80] See J. Hadley Williams, '"Thus euery man said for hym self": the voices of Sir David Lyndsay's Poems', *Bryght Lanternis*, ed. J.D. McClure and M.R.G. Spiller (Aberdeen, 1989), pp. 258-72 (263-66); H. H. Kalwies, 'The *Responce* genre in early French Renaissance poetry', *Bibliothèque d'Humanisme et Renaissance*, 45.1 (1983), 77-86 and, as example, Clement Marot's 'Epistre à son amy Lyon' (Epitre X), composed 1526, published 1534: *Clément Marot, Les Epîtres*, ed. C.A. Mayer (London, 1958), 127-31.

[81] See V.J. Scattergood, *Politics and Poetry in the Fifteenth Century* (London, 1971), pp. 218-63.

contribution to many aspects of society.[82] Equally, Lyndsay's close and sometimes sustained satiric attention to abuses demonstrated that he saw, as increasingly critical, the need for the king to realize that it was his kingly duty to intervene, or else to support those who wished to make improvements within the Church. Without question it was James V whom Lyndsay saw as the vital player in the accomplishment of religious change, hence it was the king whom he addressed on the subject of the wayward spirituality, from early in the reign:

>   Cause thame mak ministratioun
>   Conforme to thare vocatioun,
>   To Preche with vnfenӡeit intentis,
>   And trewly vse the Sacramentis,
>   Efter Christis Institutionis,
>   Leuyng thare vaine traditiounis
>   ...
>   As superstitious pylgramagis,
>   Prayand to grawin Ymagis,
>   Expres aganis the Lordis command.
>   (*Complaynt*, 413-18; 421-23)

Speaking from the official Catholic viewpoint that was James V's, his familiar servitor illustrated persuasively to the king how he might act in dealing with Church corruption, and why it was necessary to do so. In the process he ignored issues as much moral as political, such as James's exploitation of the Pope's need to retain him as an ally.[83] Rather, for example, Lyndsay emphasized the central place of the scriptures in providing precedent for James V's own behaviour as king (*Complaynt*, 446), though he did not yet, as others were doing, speak of their translation into the vernacular. Via the clerical raven's 'replycacioun', he appealed more broadly to 'Prencis' to dispose of benefices with more thought for those under 'spirituall cure' (*Papyngo*, 1004-25) and, in the interests of better future preachers and teachers, to make the sons of the Lords 'seik science and famous sculis' (1030). Revealingly, the 'replycacioun', one of Lyndsay's more outspoken appeals, was placed in the mouth of a churchman. The raven, by his own admission less than perfect in his words and deeds (*Papyngo*, 997-99), shared the blame for the present state of the Church between 'Our Spirituall Fatheris' (1000) and the 'Prencis' (1004), and looked very pointedly to the present king for help (1018-31).

---

[82] See I.B. Cowan, 'Church and society', *Scottish Society in the Fifteenth Century.* ed. J.M. Brown (London, 1977), 112-35.

[83] C. Burns, 'Rome and Scotland, 1513-1625', *Essays on the Scottish Reformation 1513-1625*, ed. D. McRoberts (Glasgow), pp. 463-83 (pp. 463-72); *The College of Justice. Essays by R.K. Hannay*, ed. H.L. MacQueen, Stair Society (Edinburgh, 1990), pp. 27-78, and M. Mahoney, 'The Scottish Hierarchy', *Essays on the Scottish Reformation*, ed. McRoberts, pp. 39-84 (pp. 39-51).

In making these comments on the king's role in Church-State relations, however, Lyndsay was also reacting on the king's behalf to new factors that had been added only recently to the traditional grounds for complaint. Of these, the spreading influence of Martin Luther's activities and writings was perhaps the most important. 'Luther and his discipillis' were the subject of legislation in Scotland from the time James V was thirteen, with the unnamed 'heretik' and 'heresie' the topics of other acts.[84] That James V and his court were alive to the debate is not to be doubted. During the 1530s, James had referred to the subject (or had the subject mentioned to him) in communications to or from the Pope, King Ferdinand, Alexander Alesius, Cochlaeus, and Erasmus.[85] By 1539 the king's own confessor, Alexander Seton, Dominican prior of St Andrews, had been persuaded to join his fellow friars who had earlier fled south.[86] By 1540 James's courtier, John Borthwick, who (with Lyndsay and two others) had been appointed early in the year to accompany the visiting English ambassador, Ralph Sadler, was by May forced to leave Scotland because of his heretical views.[87] Lyndsay showed that he understood the difficulties that were besetting Scotland's king, as they were Catholic monarchs elsewhere, by the comments in his brief report to the Scottish government on his diplomatic mission to Brussels in 1531.[88] Therein he had noted as newsworthy his talk with the new regent, Mary of Hungary, whose interest in reform was likely to have been known to those in Scotland.[89] Lyndsay had also marked the fact that Charles V 'purposis to depart at the fyn of yis moneth and passis wp In alman3e for the reformation of ye luteriens', clear sign to those at home that the Emperor himself had recognized the political impact the religous upheaval was having.

The Scottish king's own 'mynde' on religious reform was discussed in the letter by William Eure to Thomas Cromwell.[90] This had accompanied a report of a now-lost dramatic interlude, thought to be Lyndsay's, which had been performed at the court at Epiphany 1540.)[91] Eure reported that Thomas Bellenden, whom he called 'inclyned to the soorte vsed in our souerains Realme of England' and one of the 'councellours' to James V, had told him that '...the King of scotts hym self with all his temporall Counsaile was gretely geuen to the reformacion of the mysdemeanours of Busshops Religious persones and preists within the

---

[84]*APS*, II, 295, 341-42; 370, 371.

[85]*James V Letters*, 130, 134; *Opvs Epistolarvm Des. Erasmi Roterodami*, ed. Allen, X, 2886; J.T. McNeill, 'Alexander Alesius, Scottish Lutheran (1500-1565)', *Archiv für Reformationsgeschichte*, 55 (1964), 161-91 (170-73).

[86]J. Durkan, 'The Cultural Background in Sixteenth-Century Scotland', *Innes Review*, 10.2 (1959), 382-439 (414-20), and idem, 'Scottish "Evangelicals" in the Patronage of Thomas Cromwell', *Records of the Scottish Church History Society*, 21.2 (1982), 127-56 (141-42).

[87]Ibid., 132-3, and J. Hadley Williams, 'Shady Publishing in Sixteenth-Century Scotland: the Case of David Lyndsay's Poems', *Bibliographical Society of Australia and New Zealand Bulletin*, 16.3 (1992), 97-105 (101).

[88]B.L. Cotton Caligula B. I. fol. 313

[89]See futher, J. Hadley Williams, '"Writtin with my hand at handwarp": David Lyndsay's diplomatic letter of 1531', forthcoming in 'Middle Scots at the Millennium', ed. R. Greentree.

[90]B.L. MS Reg. 7. c. xvi., fol. 138^r; Hamer, II, 4-6.

[91]B.L. MS Reg. 7. c. xvi., fols. 137^r-139^r; Hamer, II, 2-4.

Realme...'. Eure presented his information to Cromwell as evidence that James V wished to follow his uncle's lead and oppose the authority of Rome, but Bellenden's reported words would equally well indicate a concerned conservatism. The interlude itself, from the report chiefly an exposure of church abuses, appears to have expressed this reformist view. It was already evident, however, in Acts of Parliament passed earlier in the year, 'For the honour of þe haly sacrame[n]tis', 'For worschip to be had to þe Virgin mary', 'That na ma[n] Argvn þe papis auctorite', For reformi[in]g of kirkis and kirkme[n]',[92] as it was in those poems certain known to be Lyndsay's, in James's own letters to Clement VII and Paul III, and his Catholic marriages. Yet the ambiguity emphasized the external difficulties—the complex political setting—that beset those who wished to make Church reforms. Matters were deeply affected by Henry VIII's schismatic acts and by each change in the alliances and counter-alliances of Francis I, Charles V or the Pope.[93] Armed from 1537 with his gifts of the blessed Sword and Hat, and with them the hopes of further financial assistance from the Pope, James V was unlikely to adopt a policy that would jeopardize his position as 'Defender of the Christian Faith'.[94] And in this shifting context, the king's known encouragement of the pedagogue and Latin poet, George Buchanan, to write the satire against the monks, *Franciscanus*, or his toleration of debate among his courtiers if they did not speak out publicly, were not at odds with his summary punishment of 'heretics' on other occasions.[95]

'WITH HIS MOST HARDIE NOBLIS OF SCOTLAND':
LYNDSAY AND THE INTERNATIONAL IMAGE OF JAMES V

Just as Lyndsay's literary works gave him the chance to portray and interpret James V's reign, so did Lyndsay's heraldic duties within Scotland offer him the opportunity to use formal visual symbol to create a recognizably 'James V' royal image. Lyndsay's diplomatic journeys abroad perforce extended his appreciation; they showed him how the larger and wealthier courts of Europe created, by allegory and spectacle, powerful yet personal statements of monarchy.[96] Heraldry, like literary comment, could separate James V's reign from what had preceded it or selectively link it with past Stewart renown. It could display, as perhaps it did at James's chivalric wedding tournament in Paris

---

[92] *APS*, II, 370-71.
[93] See further J.H. Burns, 'The Political Background of the Scottish Reformation, 1513-1625', *Essays on the Scottish Reformation*, ed. McRoberts, 1-36.
[94] See J. Durkan, '*The Trompet of Honour* (Edinburgh? 1537)', *The Bibliotheck*, 11.1 (1982), 1-2 and C. Burns, 'Papal Gifts to Scottish Monarchs', *Innes Review*, 20.2 (1969), 150-94.
[95] I.D. McFarlane, *Buchanan* (London, 1981), pp. 48-54; witness John Borthwick's experience, summarized by Durkan, 'Scottish "Evangelicals"', 132. See further, J. Kirk, 'The "Privy Kirks" and their antecedents: the hidden face of Scottish Protestantism', *Voluntary Religion*, ed. W.J. Shiels and D. Wood, Ecclesiastical History Society (Worcester, 1986), pp. 155-70.
[96] See Hadley Williams, '"Writtin with my hand"', op. cit., and R. Strong, *Splendour at Court: Renaissance Spectacle and Illusion* (London, 1973).

in 1537,[97] the ancient and honourable nature of Scotland's noble houses. Or it could provide, as in the impalement of James's arms with the French princess Madeleine's, or in the carvings of his knightly orders that the king placed above his palace entrance at Linlithgow, instant and accurate communication of Scotland's growing importance in European politics. In *The Papyngo* Lyndsay had called the king's attention to the meaning of the physical symbols of kingly office: 'thy sceptour, swerd, & croun' (310), but these could also be emphasized by heraldic means. Indeed, it seems probable that Lyndsay was closely involved in revisions to the design of the royal arms itself, including additions that produced a crest displaying together for the first time all of these symbols of sovereignty.[98]

After the death of the French princess Madeleine, the royal accounts recorded the part that heralds and heraldry played in the funeral ceremonies that Lyndsay almost certainly oversaw.[99] Taffeta banners were made for the king's trumpeters; herald painters produced 'iiij^c armyis'; the 'grete armys', the 'small armys', 'tua crocis' and hangings in the palace chapel were sewn.[100] To those who saw them, these visual symbols of sorrow expressed the country's grief, but words were required to portray and convey furth of Scotland the sorrow of James V and his kindgom. Lyndsay's *Deploratioun on the Deith of Quene Magdalene*[101] provided this formal diplomatic communication. It was highly orthodox, like Dunbar's earlier poem on Bernard Stewart, in its references to James V and his French queen in classical terms, 'Discending both of blude Imperiall' (41), Leander to Hero, Penelope to Ulysses. It differed from the earlier poem, however, in addressing the delicate political circumstances by way of heraldic as well as poetic resources. This, too, was far from unprecedented—there was, for example, Dunbar's more complex achievement in the celebratory and counselling *Thrissill and the Rois*—yet it seems likely that preparations for the civic pageantry of Madeleine's reception, much of it heraldic in form, influenced Lyndsay's approach. Thus the depth of James V's sorrow was measured in terms of the described magnificence of Scotland's planned reception. And thus the final stanza of the poem was not the expected prayer. A last address to Death drew away from

---

[97]*L&P Henry VIII*, XI, 1315, Bishop of Faenza to Mons. Ambrogio, 15 December 1536.

[98]C.J. Burnett, 'The Development of the Royal Arms to 1603', *The Double Tressure*, 1 (1977/78), 7-19. One can only speculate on Lyndsay's role in the changes made to James V's coinage, on which see herein, p. 296. The use of a fine portrait of James V on the gold ducats of 1539 and 1540 shows an awareness of the 'prestige element' in these changes, such coins being considered appropriate royal gifts to ambassadors: J.E.L. Murray, 'The Organisation and Work of the Scottish Mint (1100-1603)', *Coinage in Medieval Scotland (1100-1600)*, ed. D.M. Metcalf, British Archaeological Reports 45 (Oxford, 1977), 155-69 (163).

[99]He appears to have devised the formal welcome, returning from France ahead of the wedding party (*TA*, VII, 16); see Hadley Williams, 'Lyndsay and Europe', forthcoming.

[100]*TA*, VI, 327, 334 and 352.

[101]*The Deploratioun* is believed to have been printed first by Davidson, but the earliest extant text is that printed in France in 1558. The poem's French title ('Deploratioun'), although diplomatically appropriate, is not conclusively Lyndsay's own.

individuals. Royal heraldic symbols emphasized a link between realms that 'outlived' death; 'Impit' (grafted) admitted here the sense 'impaled' (197-203):

> Thocht thou [Death] hes slane the heuinly flour of France,
> Quhilk Impit was in to the Thrissill kene,
> Quharein all Scotland saw thair hail plesance,
> And maid the Lyoun reioysit frome the splene:
> Thocht rute be pullit frome the leuis grene,
> The smell of it sall, in dispyte of the,
> Keip ay twa Realmes, in Peice and Amite.

By 1538, in the Armorial Register that he had begun to compile,[102] there was substantial evidence of Lyndsay's efforts to give James V's Scotland a heraldically documented place among the major powers, be they mythical, classical or contemporary princes. This volume was more than a herald's personal notes,[103] for the illustrations, especially those of the foreign and Scottish kings and queens (and from among them those of James V and his two queens in particular), were designed for show as well as information; they were careful and splendidly decorative depictions. Interspersed were brief but informative captions, short genealogical notes, and a few longer explanations. In the nineteenth century, these were considered to be 'in the hand-writing of the Author'.[104] This is questionable,[105] yet Lyndsay called himself the 'autor of this present buke' on the final folio of the manuscript.[106] It therefore is probable that he was closely involved with the volume's compilation and this in turn is strong support for the argument that the occasional comments in it are his own. Thus though the record book's style and tone are impersonal, its emphases and selection principles, even in simple matters, are worth examining.

---

[102] NLS MS 31.4.3; *Facsimile of an Ancient Heraldic Manuscript Emblazoned by Sir David Lyndsay of the Mount Lyon King of Arms 1542*, ed. D. Laing, Edinburgh, 1822.

[103] On 9 December 1630 it was recognized by Lord Lyon Sir James Balfour as an official record; see J.H. Stevenson, *Heraldry in Scotland*, 2 vols (Edinburgh, 1914), I, 61-62. There were, however, personal aspects. For example, among the leaves representing the arms of principal families of Scotland, fol. 100^v is devoted to men either known to Lyndsay or with whom he had worked closely, 'Foulis of Colintoune', 'Bellendene of Auchnoule', 'Otterburn of Reidhall' and 'Balnavis of Hawhill' (on whom see *Extracts from the Records of the Burgh of Edinburgh*, ed. J.D. Marwick, 5 vols, Scottish Burgh Records Society (Edinburgh, 1869-92), II, 88-91; note 88, above; 'The Treatise by Balnavis on Justification by Faith, as Revised by Knox', *The Works of John Knox*, ed. D. Laing, Bannatyne Club (Edinburgh, 1854), III, 405-542 (405-30); J. Durkan, 'The Beginnings of Humanism in Scotland', *Innes Review*, 4.1 (1953), 5-24 (7-9) and J. IJsewijn and D.F.S. Thomson, 'The Latin Poems of Jacobus Follisius or James Foullis of Edinburgh', *Humanistica Lovaniensia*, 24 (1975), 102-60.) On fol. 133^r Lyndsay notes among others the origins of his own family.

[104] Laing edition, p. iv.

[105] Dr G. Simpson, letter to the author, 27 July 1994. Dr Simpson sees no 'basic identity' between this secretary hand and that of Lyndsay's holograph letter from Antwerp, B.L. Cotton Caligula B. I. fol. 313.

[106] Laing edition, fol. 132^r. This edition does not follow the foliation of the original, on which see H.A.B. Lawson, 'The Armorial Register of Sir David Lindsay of the Mount', *The Scottish Genealogist*, 4.1 (1957), 12-19 and J. Balfour Paul, *Heraldry in Relation to Scottish History and Art*, (Edinburgh, 1900), pp. 189-91.

As befitted the task, Lyndsay glorified the royal house, referring more than once, for example, to 'the nobyll suirname of the Stewartis', or merely 'the noble Stewartis'.[107] For edifying contrast, he portrayed in heraldry and commentary those who, notwithstanding their nobility, had committed various offences against the crown of Scotland. For instance, John Balliol, though nicknamed 'Toom Tabard', was not passed over by the herald.[108] He was represented in the manuscript by the arms he bore 'or [before] he was crownit king of Scotland':

> Quha for his homage making to Eduard Langschankis king of Ingland contrair the aviss of the counsale off Scotland and resinging of the croune in his handis was deprivit of the croun and thair efter past in france quhair he miserabilly decessit blynd[.][109]

Lyndsay's interpretation of events made of the written portrait a *speculum principis* in miniature. By omitting to mention the destabilizing divisions within Scotland over the rights of succession of Robert Bruce senior, John Balliol, and others, that led to Balliol's oath of fealty to the English king, Lyndsay focused on and preserved the honour of Scotland as separate from the actions of the man who was then its fallible king.[110] Lyndsay added to this by touching upon the limits to the rights of kings, a topic of some importance during the fifteenth and sixteenth centuries.[111] The interpretation of Balliol's behaviour also provided an interesting parallel-in-potential to the decision to follow England that some were urging on James V during the 1530s, especially in matters of religion.[112] Given the setting, it is less likely that this was a conscious admonition to James V to beware the blandishments of Henry VIII than that it expressed the attitude of the king himself.

To an extent the register's many short decriptions of royalty followed a set form—the noble parentage of each royal spouse was listed, for example—but some descriptions also varied in the treatment and inclusion of further information. For instance, in the case of Mary of Gueldres, wife of James II, the fact that she 'fundit the trinite college of edinburgh'[113] was set down even before the names and marriages of the children she bore. The reason for this would seem again to lie in contemporary matters. Trinity collegiate church was also favoured by Mary's great grandson, James V, who in March 1531-32 petitioned the Pope

---

[107]Laing edition, fols 21ᵛ (twice) and 23ᵛ.

[108]See G. Simpson, 'Why was John Balliol called "Toom Tabard"?', *SHR*, 47.2 (1968), 196-99.

[109]Ibid., fol. 17ᵛ. Laing's use of 'y' to represent the thorn is silently emended to 'th'.

[110]On Balliol see W. Bower, *Scotichronicon*, ed. D.E.R. Watt, (Aberdeen, 1991), VI, Book XI, chapters 1-27 and notes, 191-234.

[111]See R. Mason, 'Kingship, Tyranny and the Right to Resist in Fifteenth Century Scotland', *SHR*, 66 (1987), 125-51 and J.K. Cameron, 'John Major: A Disputation on the Authority of a Council: Is the Pope Subject to Brotherly Correction by a General Council? (1529)', *Advocates of Reform from Wyclif to Erasmus*, ed. M. Spinka (Philadelphia, 1953), pp. 175-84 (180).

[112]*Hamilton Papers*, ed. Bain, I, 22, 'Instruction to Barlow and Holcrofte', 3 October 1535, and 30, 'Queen Margaret to Cromwell', 8 March 1535-6.

[113]Laing edition, fol. 27ᵛ.

to grant indulgences to those 'who shall visit the college on the feast of Holy Trinity and during the Octaves, for the purpose of devotion, being truly penitent, contrite, and making confession, and who shall put forth helping hands to the building of the same...'.[114] Moreover, in listing Mary's children, Lyndsay gave an additional detail of some interest to a contemporary reader. Going beyond the names of sons and daughters to a third generation, he noted that Mary's second son, Alexander, was the father of John, Duke of Albany, who 'wes gouernour of Scotland eftir the decess of James the ferd'.[115]

A longer passage of commentary referred to the inclusion of the arms of 'thame quhilkis been forfaltit and banisit for crymes of lesemaieste and vtheris enormiteis' beside those of them 'q^{lk} hes bene euir haill and trew till the crowne and comonn-weill':

> It is to be vnderstand that the samyn is done for thre causis the first causs is to the grit hon^r and lowing of thair nobill p[re]decessors quhilk, be thair val3ea[n]t and honerabill dedis and gude service done to prencis wer begynnaris and co[n]quereo[ris] of thaire nobil houss the Secund causs is to the gryt schame ande dyshon[our] of tham quhilkis be thair tresonabill dedis wer forefaltit and condamnit be the Law and tynt all that thair nobill p[re]decessor[is] hed wyne of befoir The thyrd causs is that nobill mene beholdand the armis of tham quhilk ar fourfaltit may inquire and considder the causis and tak exempill to eschew in tyme cu[m]yng sic exorbitant transgressionis agains thair princis in auetuir thai incur siclyk punischement to thair p[er]petuell scham and distructioun of thair nobill housis[.][116]

The relevance of this passage to the forfeiture in 1528 of Archibald Douglas, earl of Angus, which was still enforced at the time Lyndsay was compiling his armorial, is obvious. His classification of such matters in terms of the ancient chivalric court of law legitimately perpetuated the dishonour of the earl, the earl's brother, George, his uncle, Archibald Douglas of Kilspindie, and Alexander Drummond of Carnock. In doing this it would seem very likely that Lyndsay was expressing the attitude of the king himself; part of Angus's formal protest against

---

[114]*James V Letters*, p. 217, and for the text in Latin and English: *Charters and Documents relating to the Collegiate Church...of the Holy Trinity*, ed. J.D. Marwick (Edinburgh, 1871), pp. 54-55. See Royal Commission on the Ancient and Historical Monuments of Scotland, *An Inventory of the Ancient and Historical Monuments of the City of Edinburgh* (Edinburgh, 1951), pp. 36-40, which states that 'in 1531, [building] operations were broken off, never to be resumed' (p. 36), but see also D. Wilson, *Memorials of Edinburgh in Olden Time*, 2nd ed. (Edinburgh and London, 1891), II, 248 and *The History of the Collegiate Church and Hospital of the Holy Trinity and the Trinity Hospital*, ed. J.D. Marwick (Edinburgh, 1911), pp. 26-28, which provide information to the contrary. (I am grateful to Dr T. van Heijnsbergen for his help with the latter two references.)
[115]Laing edition, fol. 27^v.
[116]Ibid., fol. 66.

his treason charge, it must be remembered, had been concerned with a technicality that challenged the unlimited sovereignty of the king.[117]

'MYNE HOLE INTENT ONTYLL THYNE EXCELLENCE'

Lyndsay alleged that James V spoke his first infant syllables to 'Da Lyn', his personal servitor (*Complaynt*, 91-92). Later, as the poetry written before 1542 attests, it was Lyndsay who addressed James V. Those poems offered the king traditional advice on the arts of rule, but they also enhanced his reputation as perfect prince and enlightened patron, and that of his court as a revitalized centre. The poems supported the king's attention to internal law and order, expressed the appropriateness of the king's involvement in church reform urgently needed, and undertook on behalf of king and realm the challenges of public diplomacy between nations. These were the tasks of many a royal servant; in the case of James V and Lyndsay there was clearly something more between them. Servant and playmate of the king's early years, Lyndsay was in a strong position, possessed the information and trust necessary to shape for James V his own image as the seventh of the Stewart kings of Scots, but it was the later heraldic component of the relationship that proved crucial to the making of the king. Because of it, Lyndsay's words in ceremonial settings were truly those of James V,[118] and Lyndsay's own words in poetry and prose gained by the association. His Armorial gave James V's Scotland unique configuration, 'speaking' in visual as well as verbal terms. Even after the death of James V it was Lyndsay, Lyon King, who oversaw very closely not only the banners, effigy, targe and small arms of funeral arrangements, but also the embellishing of the royal tomb at Holyrood Abbey.[119] Thereon were heraldic symbols, of 'the fygour of ane lyoun set abone the croun', but once again these were accompanied by plain-spoken words, an engraved 'superscriptioun...in Romane lettres':[120]

ILLVSTRIS. SCOTORUM. REX. JACOBUS.
EJUS. NO[MIN]IS. 5. ETATIS. SUE. ANNO. 31. REGNI.
VERO. 30. MORTEM. OBJIT. IN. PALACIO. DE.
FALKLAND. 14. DECEMBRIS. ANNO. D[OMI]NI. 1542.
CUJAS. CORPUS. HIC. TRADITV[M]. EST SEPULTURÆ.[121]

---

[117] See Kelley, 'The Douglas Earls', pp. 398-532; Edington, *Court and Culture*, pp. 38-39.

[118] T. Innes of Learney, 'The Scottish Parliament; its Symbolism and its Ceremonial', *Juridical Review*, 44 (1932), 87-124 (114).

[119] See *TA*, VIII, 142-43, where various accounts are reported to be 'subscrivit witht Lyoun herauldis hand'.

[120] Ibid., 143.

[121] A.H. Dunbar, *Scottish Kings: A Revised Chronology of Scottish History 1005-1625*, 2nd edn (Edinburgh, 1906), p. 240, quoting NLS Adv. MS 33.3.26 (Sibbaldi Caledonia) into which the inscription had been copied in 1683.

I am most grateful to Mrs P. Bawcutt for her helpful comments on an earlier form of this article.

11

THE FINAL FOLIOS OF ADAM ABELL'S 'ROIT OR QUHEILL OF TYME':

AN OBSERVANTINE FRIAR'S REFLECTIONS ON THE 1520S AND 30S

Alasdair M. Stewart

The unpublished sixteenth-century Scots vernacular manuscript, National Library of Scotland MS. 1746,[1] contains internal evidence about its author and composition. Adam Abell was born in Prestonpans,[2] probably between 1475 and 1485. As a child he was boarded out with a canon of Holyrood.[3] The abbot of Holyrood was a kinsman, Robert Bellenden. Abell's grandfather's brother married Bellenden's sister.[4] Thus Abell would be able to claim distant relationship

---

[1] I am indebted to Dr I.A. Olson for permission to use my material from *Aberdeen University Review*; to Prof. A.J. Aitken; to the late Dr T.I. Rae; also to the Manuscript Department and to the Trustees of the National Library of Scotland for permission to reproduce material from MS. 1746.

[2] 'in saut prestone quhar i wes born' (fol. 113ᵃ).

[3] 'i wes at burd in barnhage (childhood) wi*th* a cha*n*non of *th*e forsaid abbay' (of 'halie rudhouss') (fol. 113ᵃ).

[4] '1500...*Th*e abbot of halie rudhouss callit robert bellentyne left his office & dignite & entrit in *th*e ordur of charto'ris monk*is* for heill of his saule & lufe of god *th*oc*h*t (= though) he wes myrro*ur* before till o*dir* abbat*is* of Scotland in pece & exemplair life. He wes born in saut preston quhare i wes born and his sist*ir* mareit my gudschir*is* brod*ir*. I shall schaw noc*h*t of inordinad effectioun to him bot werite at i knaw. Quhen I wes at burd in barnhage wi*th*t a cha*n*non of *th*e forsaid abbay he gaif ilk friday to *th*e pure (= poor) folk*is* in almwss four(e) boll*is* of quheit in bakin breid & gife *th*at steddit noc*h*t *th*e multitude at come he gart gife silu*er* almwis to *th*e laif. He biggit *th*e brig of leith *th*e quhit kirk of lowdian & mony o*dir* brigg*is* in *th*e west land He biggit *th*e stepill in *th*e kirk zard & brocht hame *th*e bell*is* of it and cust ane o*dir* gret bell in *th*e todir stepill hingand. He feft *th*e almwshouss of sanct leonard*is* He thekit *th*e kirk all wi*th*t leid. He broc*h*t hame *th*e funt of brass & pillar*is* of brass about *th*e altar*is*. He brocht hame all *th*e cap*is* of ony priss mony stand*is* of claith of gold and finalie a sort of kap*is* all of quit silk for all *th*e cha*n*non*is* to wss in *th*e fest*is* of o*ur* lady He gart mak *th*e gret & precius eucharist & ferttur in silu*er* & gold mony croc*is* and othir sanct*is* relik*is*. Mony od*ir* notabill turn*is* he did eftir and befor at I wes it *th*at place In his exemplair life abbat*is* now ma tak document*is* He come dailie to lady mess pryme mess quhen he held cheptur & hie mess and eynsang quhen he wes noc*h*t stoppit (folio 113ᵇ) be his erand*is* In principall fest*is* he did *th*e office in *th*e queire & oft tyme come to maten*is*. He lauborit all wa*is* to causs obse*ru*ance to be kepit bot maist*ir*full subdi(ti)s ay resistit to him and wexit him. He zeid ay in *th*e place owd*ir* in caip ond*ir* kirktill or fut ma*n*till w*ith* abbot huid. In his hall wes noc*h*t admittit bard*is* na fenzeit fuli*s* bot ane certane of pure (= poor) barn*is* callit his saul*is* & ane of *th*ame wes his play fule He wes newir fund ydill bot ay in honest exercition He wes ane cu*n*nying ma*n* and a gret poeyn. Of him in sport yronice spak ye lord lile to *th*e king sayand schir *th*is abbat bellentyne of haly rudhouss is noc*h*t for wss courteowr*is* He biggis brigg*is* rep(er)al*is* halie kirk*is* reknand hes is before said etc. Than said he co*n*cludent put down *th*is abbet and get ane at will play ane hundret (mark*is*) at a*n* cast of *th*e diss. *Th*at is ane ma*n* for wss Sic abbat*is* hes robert bellentyne ar now far to seik...'

perhaps with Bellenden the translator of Boece. Abell next went to Inchaffray,[5] the Augustinian 'Insula Missarum', where he 'professed the rule' in 1495. From Inchaffray Abell moved to the more rigorous discipline of the Observantines[6] at

---

Abell then goes on to condemn the appointment of secular abbots (who remain dressed 'in seculair habit'), questioning the Pope's right to go against natural law, scripture, civil and canon law, the very foundations of society, in sanctioning such abuses, finally saying (fol. 114[b]) 'the paip ma do all thing the ke of power nocht excedent and the ke of science nocht errand'. Abell also condemns James III and James IV for appointing secular heads of religious establishments (fol. 115[a]) and appeals to James V to remedy the situation. Abell's description of his kinsman (fol. 113[a]) quoted above, tallies with the slightly shorter one by John Bellenden the translator of Boece. See *The History and Chronicles of Scotland written in Latin by Hector Boece Translated by John Bellenden*, 2 vols (Edinburgh, 1821), Bk. XII, Ch. 16, pp. 298-99. This description is omitted in the STS text based on the Pierpont Morgan MS though the editors quote the passage (II, 422) in a note. In the *Liber Cartarum Sancte Crucis: Munimenta Ecclesie Sancte Crucis de Edwinesburg*, Bannatyne Club (Edinburgh, 1840), p. xxxii (Dipl. 285) we have the statement that Bellentyne was abbot the 18 July 1493 and still abbot 13 September 1498. He was abbot for sixteen years and it would appear that he was abbot from 1484 to 1500.

[5] Abell left Holyrood before his uncle as we have seen above. '1495. This zere I professit the reull of sanct.aug in inchauffra' (fol. 113[a]). Inchaffray or Insula Missarum is indeed signposted on the Perth-Crieff road but there is not even a plaque at the historic site. Abell links the story in the *Scotichronicon* (XII, 21) of Abbot Maurice of Inchaffray at Bannockburn and the detail found in Boece (XIV, fol. 314) that Maurice carried the sacred relic of the arm of St Fillan. Abell adds the information that 'mariche abat of inchafray' was later bishop of Dunblane and 'He liys in inchafray in the north side of the hie altair ondir the repositur of the blist body of christ witht inscription in the stane'. This may be a reference to the coffin lid which in a footnote to Whyte's article (p. 142) is thought to be now a tombstone in Madderty. J.F. Whyte, 'The Abbey of Inchaffray', *Transactions of the Scottish Ecclesiological Society*, 10.2 (1932), 134-42. See *Charters Bulls and Other Documents relating to the Abbey of Inchaffray (1190-1609)*, ed. W.A. Lindsay, J. Dowden, J.M. Thomson, SHS (Edinburgh, 1908); *Liber Insule Missarum*, Bannatyne Club (Edinburgh, 1847); on Maurice see too G.W.S. Barrow, *Robert Bruce* (London, 1965), esp. p. 226 and n.

[6] Abell adds an aside, in folio 82[b]; 'scone and inchaffra quhar in wmquhill I professit that reow (= rule) or (= before) I wes a brothir of sanct francis obseruance'. Here and again at folios 86[a] and 113[a/b] Abell identifies himself (by implication by his approval) with men who move to stricter orders. As we have seen (note 4 above), Robert Bellenden 'left his office & dignite' as Abbot of Holyrood 'and entrit in the ordur of charto'ris monkis for heill of his saule & lufe of god'. Similarly (fol. 82[b]) Abell mentions under 1153 the death of King David and adds: 'In the auld cornikill (= chronicle) it is red at he marit sanct walteynis wife quhilk wes erll of northumbirland and martirit He had a sone callit Walteyn to at left the warld & wes a channon regulair in sanct oswaldis eftirwert priour of kirkhaym quhare he maid a collegion of the obseruance of regulair of channonis in a buke quhilk in wlgair zit in Scotland it is callit the ordur buke at the leist to thame at come out of oswaldis hes scone & Inchaffra quhar in wmquhill I professit that reow (= rule) or (= ere) I wes a brothir of sanct francis obseruance. Efterwert this halie man sanct walteyn thinkand at he wald leif a strater life for cristis saik he come to the ordour of sisterche in the abbay of melros quhar eftirwert for his halie life he wes chosin abbat And eftirwert lauchfullie he wes chosin bischep of sanct andros bot be wald nocht accep it'. D.E. Easson, *Medieval Religious Houses: Scotland* (London, 1957), p. viii, p. 11, states that St Waldef or Waltheof, the king's stepson was canon of Nostell, prior of Kirkham, monk at Wardon and Rievaulx before becoming abbot of Melrose from 1148 to his death in 1159. Cf. *Chronica de Mailros*, ed. J. Stevenson, Bannatyne Club (Edinburgh, 1835) pp. 73, 76 ('Walteuus', Waldeuus); cf. Fordun, II, 222-23, 'Waldeof'.

Abell also refers (folio 86[a]) to another cleric in the year 1206: 'That sam zere the bischep of gallowa gaif o'r his dignate and wes ane channoun in halie rudhouss'. Abell also refers to 'wilzem' abbot of Holyrood who in 1207 wanted to go and live as a hermit on Inchkeith but was too old and feeble. Thomas, prior of St Andrews, gave up his office and became a novice in 'Cowper in Angus'. Abell follows this with a scriptural and Canon Law-based discussion on promotion and ambition.

the Franciscan Friary at Jedburgh.[7] This move was presumably after 1513. It was at Jedburgh that Abell wrote his chronicle, the *Wheel of Time*.

The title is given in the superscription of the prologue: 'The roit or quheill of tyme heir begynnis in nayme of *the* blissit trinite our lady and sanct francis'. The title is then explained as a reference to the cyclical precession of the equinoxes,[8] a commonplace of historiography and cosmography at that time. The 'rote', 'roit' or 'rute' as Abell variously spells it, is abridged from Abell's Latin version, presumably entitled 'Rota Temporum'. This translation 'in yngligis' has been undertaken 'to *the* hono'r of god *the* wirgin mary and o'r halie fad*ir* sanct francis my merit and alswa plesour to my lord setone'.[9] The first 120 folios were concluded, as Abell writes, 'the zere of god 1533 inw*ith the* oct of the natiuite of our lady the mothir of god quene of hewin' (fol. 120^b), and the continuation is from 1534 till 1537.[10] The text ends with reference to the fate of Lady Glamis[11] and to a suspended divorce of the royal widow and Hary Stewart.[12]

---

[7] The Friars were possibly in Jedburgh earlier but the Friary of Jedburgh seems to have been founded after Flodden. See G. Watson, 'The Franciscan Friary of Jedburgh with some account of Adam Bell Its Historian', *Berwickshire Naturalists Club*, 20 (1906-8), 82-88. See also W. Moir Bryce, *The Scottish Grey Friars*, 2 vols (Edinburgh, 1909), 69-70, 378-79. Papal sanction was given by Adrian VI on 31 January 1521-22 for the erection of the friary. See Easson, *Medieval Religious Houses: Scotland*, p. 112.

[8] *the precession of equinoxes*. On the Mundane Year, see, e.g. *Cicero: De Natura Deorum*, ed. A.S. Pease, 2 vols (Camb. Mass., 1955-58), II, 668-69. For survivals of the concept see 'magnus annus' in the indexes to L. Thorndike, *A History of Magic and Experimental Science*, 8 vols (New York, 1923-58). Abell also refers to other 'topoi' of historiography, such as the 'translatio imperii', the 'scourge', the 'tempus gratiae', but he shows none of the classical learning, of, say, Robert Wedderburn in the *Complaynt of Scotland* who comprehends the astronomical precession of equinoxes.

[9] Lord Seton, the Fourth Lord George Seton died on 17 July 1549 in Culross and was buried there because of the English invasion of East Lothian and Haddington. His wife and friends later carted the body 'in ane kist' to the college kirk of Seton. See Sir R. Maitland of Lethington, *The History of the House of Seyton to the year MDLIX*, Bannatyne Club (Edinburgh, Glasgow, 1829), p. 42. Abell also comments, at fol. 101^b, on the notable and continuous loyalty of the House of Seton: 'This hous of seton wes ewir fund traist and trew to *the* crown and I traist to god e*uir* salbe. It detestit ewir prodition and falsat for tratury is *the* maist wile wice at ma ring in a nobill'.

[10] 'The forsaid brothir adam abell continuand his proces of the forsaid rote heir he begy*n*nis quhair he lewit in *the* zere of god 1534 zeris and sa procedand for his schort tyme...'.

[11] Lady Glamis: see A.H. Dunbar, *Scottish Kings*, 2nd ed. (Edinburgh, 1906), p. 235, and n. 46: 'Jane, Lady Glammis, sister of Archibald Douglas, 6th Earl of Angus, widow of John Lyon, 6th Lord Glammis then wife of Archibald Campbell of Skipnish, tried and convicted of conspiracy to poison King James V, was burned on the Castle Hill, Edinburgh on the 17th of July, 1537'. Buchanan refers to 'Gilespicus Cambellus' (*Rer. Scot.*, Bk. 14): cf. G. Buchanan, *History*, ed. Aikman, II, 316-17.

[12] See further, 'Adam Abell's "Roit or Quheill of Tyme"', *Aberdeen University Review*, 44.148 (1972), 386-93. As early as 1846 attention had been drawn to MS. 1746. David Laing repeated the notice in 1877. See *PSAS*, 12 (1876-78), 72-75. See also George Watson's article mentioned in n. 7. The manuscript was deposited in the National Library of Scotland in 1935 by Lt.-Col. W.W. Cunninghame of Caprington.

We know that the chronicle, a translation from a Latin original, was written for Lord Seton, and was thus in Seton's possession at least initially, we may assume, possibly from its conclusion about 1537 till his death in 1549. (See n. 9 above.)

Our manuscript contains a number of names and dates. On folio 1^a we have: D Sinclair of roisling. On folio 2^a there is: W Santclar of roislin knecht. On folio 126^b we have: W Santclair of Roislin...1555. On folio 1*b we have: W Santclair of Roislin...this time with the date '-lxv'. This

It reveals a lack of sympathy with Abell's aims to condemn the work as being 'of small historical value'.[13] It is an anachronism to demand 'originality'; and dates and accuracy of facts are almost of secondary importance. What is important for Abell is the interpretation, the providential pattern revealed by historiography, the implicit moral guidance of the 'exempla' and the explicit moral guidance which Abell includes for lay readers. Abell gives his very strong views on various matters and supports them with references to natural law, scripture, canon law and civil law, the foundations of society. What is important for us is less the historical accuracy than how Abell borrows, what he selects as important, and perhaps how he formulates it. Originality is expressed mainly in the Franciscan emphasis in the selection, since the sources are mainly scriptural and patristic. Most frequent reference is made to scripture, canon and civil law and to St Augustine, as Abell's education would lead us to expect. Abell also refers to a score of other sources,[14] and uses commonplace topics and

---

date is presumably 1565 and we can assume that the Sir William Sinclair who signed in 1565 is the Lord-Justice General whose antiquarian efforts saved many Scots manuscripts from destruction. See Father R.A. Hay, Prior of Pierrement, *Genealogie of the Saintclaires of Rosslyn*, ed. J. Maidment (Edinburgh, 1835), p. 135. An example of the sort of manuscript he rescued is printed in the Abbotsford Club volume *Extracta e Variis Cronicis Scocie* (Edinburgh, 1842), as the editor W.B.D.D. Turnbull mentions in his introduction (pp. xii-xiii). As Hay states, Sir William Sinclair was Lord-Justice General from 1559, 'sided with the Queen att Langside in 1568, for which fact he obtained a remission in 1574. He was confirmed in his office of Justiciarie in 1570. He gathered a great many manuscripts which had been taken by the rabble out of our monasteries in the time of the Reformation, whereupon we find as yet his name written thus, Sir William Sinclar of Roslin, Knight; he delivered once ane Egyptian from the gibbet in the Burrow Moore, ready to be strangled, returning from Edinburgh to Roslin, upon which accompt the whole body of gypsies were, of old, accustomed to gather in the stanks of Roslin every year, where they acted severall plays during the moneth of May and June. There are two towers which were allowed them for their residence, the one called Robin Hood, the other Little John.'

Other names occur: Walter Ker (fol. 1*b); Mark Ker (fol. 14*a) and James Tullo (fol. xix a), who signs again later, adding, 'mussellbrugh the 19 of May 1629' (fol. 14*a). Less legible is the name which looks like John Calderwood, dated 'musleburgh the 30 of May 1624' and John Cadie dated '291' [sic] (fol. xix a) which is evidently a playful reference to one of the other various ways of calculating the year. On folio xix-a there is 'Walterus Scotus' and on folio xvi-a there is 'Mr James Scot'. Our manuscript seems to have been in the Musselburgh area in the years 1624-29.

Our manuscript is again mentioned in 1700. Father Augustine Hay, writing in that year, says he lost the manuscript, when a 'rabble' attacked 'Rosslyn' 'the eleventh of December 1688, about 10 of the clock at night'. The manuscript in 1688 was on loan to Father Hay from Sir George Mackenzie of Rosehaugh, Viscount Tarbet. It would appear to have been only briefly lost. Possibly Sir George issued a threat—return my manuscript or else—at any rate Viscount Tarbet was created Earl of Cromarty in January 1703; and died 17 August 1714, in his 84th year; and when his library was sold in 1746 there occurs in the sale catalogue the title of 'apparently the MS in question', as David Laing indicates. Thus our manuscript appears to have remained in the Roslin and Musselburgh areas at least till the mid-eighteenth century. David Laing speculated that a copy might be in the Earl of Pembroke's library, but the Earl of Pembroke kindly took the trouble to check and, even if the 1731 reference mentioned by Laing was accurate, 'there is no trace of any such manuscript at Wilton, nor is there any information regarding its disposal' (letter to the author, 20 December 1971). Whatever the whereabouts of the manuscript in the intervening years, it has lain since 1935 in the National Library, deposited there by Lt.-Col. W.W. Cunninghame of Caprington.

[13]Moir Bryce, *Franciscan Friary of Jedburgh*, I, 379.

[14]Abell refers to the Franciscan Alexander of Hales, 'doctor irrefragabil of our ordur'; St Thomas Aquinas; Hector Boece; Boethius; John Chrysostom; Petrus Comestor; Cornelius Nepos; Eusebius; John Gerson; St Gregory; Isidore; Jerome; Josephus; Livy; Petrus Lombardus; Lucan;

'exempla',[15] but he reveals his specific interest in St Augustine, St Francis and the Franciscan order. His selective interest in specific themes, persons and things, reveals firstly what he considered worth handing on from his sources but secondly his strongminded individuality. Abell's strong views on moral issues are of this second kind. He gives his views on free will, adultery, covetousness, theft (especially as practised by the Border reivers), clerical pluralism, absenteeism, and especially secular control of religious establishments. Abell even says that the Pope is exceeding his powers by allowing lay men to be appointed to lead religious establishments. Abell criticizes James III and James IV for this and appeals to James V to right the wrong. Abell praises strict adherence to the 'rules' of religious orders. He lauds the ascetic example given by St Francis. He also praises the lead given in renunciation of power and ambition in favour of stricter adherence to a 'rule' threatened by lax 'consuetude' by a number of Scottish clergy. Abell gives thumbnail sketches of these religious men who are minor figures in any political history but major figures in any account of exemplary living.

Abell singles out for example Robert Bellenden, St Walteyn (Waldeof, Abbot of Melrose) and Thomas, Prior of St Andrews, who 'for his zeill of obseruance and disciplyne he saw part of his subditis mowit aganis him', gave up his office and became a novice at Cupar Angus (see n. 6). This reference to the difficulty encountered by an individual attempting to adhere to a religious rule, and the opposition from others within the same establishment who refer to 'consuetude' in defence of their laxity, sounds autobiographical. It is evident, too, that there was just as much criticism of abuses by reformers within the church, such as Abell and Richardinus,[16] as criticism from without. Abell condemns reformers from outside like Craw and Hus and Luther and the 'turkis of ingland'.

Abell attacks not only moral evil but social ills such as taxes, 'maill ferme and gersum harich and carich'[17] and the indolence that is rife among the

---

John Major; Orosius; Sallust; Seneca; Valerius; Vincent of Beauvais. He only once refers to Cicero, quoting *De Off.*, II, 24. Abell refers readers to other chronicles by 'Antonyne, Wincent, Martyne, Augustin', but the sources named by Abell, whether genuine sources or name-dropping, show greater patristic bias than classical interest. There are of course the odd few who might try to label even this chronicle as a document of the Scottish Renaissance, if only on the grounds that translation is a Renaissance exercise.

[15] A number of 'exempla' and references are found for example in Lyndsay, Boece, Major; and all of the following references occur also in Robert Wedderburn's *Complaynt of Scotland* (Paris, c. 1550): references to Sardinapallus (fol. 9^a); Phalayr (10^b, 11^a); Darys dochtir Loxam (= Roxana) (14^a); Hermes trimegistes (15^a); 3 bollis of goldin ringis (16^a); Attell, the tyrant as scourge of God (41^a); hengist and ors (42^b); Merlin (referring to the account by 'maistir hector' (i.e. Boece) (43^a); arthur (46^b); Holofernes 'tane' with drink, Iudith 'straik his heid fra him' (78^b); robert brus (94^b, 97^b); William Wallace (95^b); Harlaw (107^a).

[16] See *The Commentary on the Rule of St Augustine by Robertus Richardinus (1530)*, ed. G.G. Coulton, SHS (Edinburgh, 1935); see too *Statutes of the Scottish Church 1225-1559*, ed. D. Patrick, SHS (Edinburgh, 1907), as in the 1549 Statutes, pp. 84-134.

[17] 'maill ferme and gersum harich and carich': this refers to the evil of short leases and soaring rents. *The Complaynt of Scotland*, written about 1548-49, similarly mentions these specific evils. The 'labourer' complains (fol. 97): 'the malis and fermis of the grond that i laubyr is hychtit to sic

'curtiouris in gret mennis howsis of Scotland'. 'Quhen *th*ai haif fillit *the* wame at nwne with meit and drink at *the* pure lauborar swetis fulsaire fore' ('full sorely for') they then go off to their cards and dice till supper and thereafter '*th*ai pas to hwirdwme and harlatre'.

If the 'Roit' were full of moralization only it would make dull reading but in fact there are many anecdotes. Though much of the material is of course derivative this is no condemnation, since standard 'exempla' indicate a mode of thought. What is worth repeating and becomes commonplace forms the background of assumptions and ideas. A single keyword can then unlock a whole storehouse of associations and ideas. Historical fiction becomes propaganda and a mainspring to action.

Abell, still before Shakespeare, repeats the story of King Lear and his daughters, and the story of Macbeth with reflections on witchcraft, both extracts worth reprinting. Abell repeats the story of the Stone of Destiny ('the fataill marmour') quoting the inscription (as in the Mar Lodge Translation of Boece). Abell mentions Hay of Luncarty, a forerunner of Hal o' the Wynd, and many other small fragments of the legendary history of Scotland which has had so powerful a hold on the imagination of Scots throughout the centuries. When Abell is writing about contemporary events he is even more personal. Abell includes what must be one of the earliest extant foreign mission reports in Scots.

Abell relates that 'mathi wincent' the 'commissar generall' had visited Scotland in 1530, then later he continues, under the year 1532, 'Heir come word witht our ministir fra *the* generall cheptur of *the* new spanze or hirketan at we call *the* new fund yle in gret ynd in afrik. Brodir martin of walence wrait to mathi wincent commissar generall. This martin wes custos custodium sancti ewangelii in *th*is forsaid land and he send and said...' and then follows the report. Martin of Valence is Juan Martino de Boil of Valencia in Spain who in 1523 was sent to Mexico with twelve Franciscans. He established the Custody of the Holy Spirit of which he was elected 'custos'. He died in Mexico in 1534. The Twelve were sent by 'maist reuerent fadir francis of angellis *th*an ministir generall now cardinall of *the* halie cruss', that is, Franciscus Qui(g)nonius, Cardinalis S. Crucis in Hierusalem. Abell also mentions an account sent by the 'bischep of tymistitan of our ordur and *the* bredir wi*th*t him in *th*at sam forsaid land', namely, New Spain where the Franciscans evangelized to the North and North East of Mexico City and in Yucatan. In this account Abell then mentions 'petir of gante', who is Pedro de Gante or Petrus a Gandavo, a Flemish Franciscan

---

ane price that it is fors to me and vyf and bayrns to drynk vattir': he also complains (97^V) of 'arrage carage, taxationis, violent spulze'; and he says (98^V) 'i am maid ane slaue of my body to ryn and rashe in arage and carraige'. The development of a money economy and the practice of feu-ferme tenure changed the situation eventually. The 'gersum' or premium for each lease, was an intolerable burden while the leases were very short. 'Arage' and 'carriage' referred to the feudal obligation to supply carts and horses to plough the laird's land, fetch fuel and carry in the harvest.

described by Abell as 'principall paranymph'. Abell then continues, 'This sam zere wes martirit wenerable fadir brodir andro of spoleit of our ordur fra prechin of *th*e faith of christ in affrik in *th*e cete of fey the 9 day of Ianuar *th*e zere of god 1532...'. Abell thus links three reports to the General Chapter at Toulouse in 1532. The suggestion is that 'mathi wincent' sent on these reports but it seems likely that Abell's source may have been the book in French whose title alone indicates most of the above contents.[18] We have fascinating parallel confirmation of the impact of this report about New Spain (which is still not identified as the New World). In Trier Municipal Library there is a copy of a letter from Nicholas Herborn, Franciscan provincial of the Cologne Province, who was elected commissary general at Toulouse.[19] (Herborn is noted for a work on missiology (*Epitome convertendi gentes Indiarum ad fidem Christi*) based on the accounts from South America of a Flemish friar—presumably Abell's 'petir of gante'.)

Abell thus reveals the interest in the international work of the Franciscans. In another incident Abell reveals the popular interest in bloodthirsty scandal. This is the account of the madness and suicide of Sir James Sinclair of Orkney.[20]

> This sam zere about *th*e feist of natiuite of sanct Iohne *th*are hapnit ane horrible caiss in orknay. Iames synclair at i kennit weill quhen ye king schort quhile before had maid knycht *thoch*t (though) he forseruit erar (sooner) to haif bene hangit for his wikkit life he was haldin court wi*th*t gret gloriatioun & arrogance.

---

[18] *Hystoire et lettres du glorieux et bienheureux frere Andre de Spolete de lordre des freres Mineurs de la reguliere obseruance. Lequel a souffert martyre en la cite de Fez en affricque. Lan. MD xxxij. et le ix Januier. Comme a enuoye par expres message le hault et trespuissant roy de Portugal et algarbe, au chapitre general desd freres mineurs clebre en la illustre et magnifique cite de Tholose en lan que dessus, en la solennite de la penthecoste. Est contenu aussi la teneur de aultres certaines lettres de la miraculeuss conuersion and augmentation de la foy catholicq*ue au pays de Huketan aultrement dict terre neufeu, ou bien neufeu Hespaigne. [In fine:] 'Imprimee...a la request du marchant Jehan Barril...a Tholose Mil cinq cens xxxij'. See R. Streit, J. Dindinger, *Bibliotheca Missionum*, XV (Freiburg, 1951), 298-301 (African Mission Literature, 1053-1599, item 942).

[19] See A. Tibesar, *Franciscan Beginnings in Colonial Peru* (Washington, 1953), pp. 7 and n. 16 and 98-104. See too R. Ricard, *The Spiritual Conquest of Mexico* (Berkeley and Los Angeles, 1966): cf. my more detailed version of Abell's account, and notes, in *The Bulletin of Scottish Institute of Missionary Studies*, 11 (1972), 4-10.

[20] See Jo. Ben's 'Description of the Orkney Islands, 1529' in *Walter Macfarlane's Geographical Collections*, ed. A. Mitchell and J.T. Clark, 3 vols, SHS (Edinburgh, 1906-08), III, 302-13 and translation 313-24, especially pp. 308-9, 318-20: 'The second parish is called St Andrews. The parish is large and fertile is corn. There is nothing memorable here unless what happened to a very noble person named James Sinclair who dwelt there and when a war began with the Caithness men (of which it will be spoken in its proper place) that noble leader was taken captive, madness seized him, and he precipitated himself into the sea, where he ended his life, which indeed was lamentable...' ('captus est, demens evasit, et seipsum in mare precipitavit, ubi vitam finit, quod quidem lamentabile fuit...'). The battle with the men of Caithness is the battle of Summerdale described in the account of the parish of Stenhouse by Ben. See *Records of the Earldom of Orkney*, ed. J.S. Clouston, SHS (Edinburgh, 1914), pp. xlvii-xlix and 57-61 for discussion of Summerdale and Sinclair.

> In *th*is mentyme *th*e king send Wt (= writ, Royal letter of four forms) to him anens (= anent) ane herand of his desire quhilk ekit his want & wantones. Behald heir *th*e fals smyling of deme fortoune (Dame Fortune) & how p*er*olus it is to *th*ame at sche smylis on. This miserabill man lang rynnand in his wykkit will heir be permissioun of god he wes heltrit be *th*e fend (= fiend) his maistir & led in repreuable wit he raiss wp fra *th*e court as it wes schawin & beguth (= began) to dance & cast gamwntis (throw his legs about in leaping dance movements) him alane na he my*ch*t no*ch*t be stanchit. At ewin he zeid to his bed wi*th*t his wife barbara hare stewartis (fol. 125ᵃ) sistir. Bot he mycht nocht sleip. He rais sone eftir day and put *th*e forsaid writ witht his ring ondir his wiffis side quhen sche wes slepand and passit furth before his houss quhare *th*are wes ane peit stak and nocht fer fra yin ane fowll deip dub. Now he zeid dansing and castand gamwndis about *th*e stak takand petis out of it and castand agane at it, now he wad leip fra yin and douk him in *th*e dub and sin hes before rin to *th*e stak. And eftir *th*at he had done *th*is ane lang tyme at *th*e last he cust his clathis and bonet fra him and tuk ane rent at ane heich craig & lap in *th*e see and drownit him self. Othir sais at *th*e ewill spret led him be *th*e hokster in *th*e se & drownit him   This miserable man lewand ane lang tyme in tirannide warldlie prosperite folloit him. *Th*e warld kissit him but finalie put him in *th*e hands of his enemy. He or be (= by) him wes slane *th*e erll of caitnes the laird of beridaill & mony othir gentill men *th*am at fled to kirkis²¹ he ruggit *th*ame furth nakit & slew *th*ame. Ten in *th*e kirtown of kirkway at he resauit ondir souerance bot he and his bred*ir* cruellie slew *th*ame Before he slew captane Walless ondir trowis and segit *th*e kingis houss in kirkwa & gret in*iu*ri*s* to *th*e lady sinclair for hir awne richt.

The battle of Summerdale and the subsequent knighting of one of the villains is an example possibly of the international politics game in Orkney. As Clouston says[22] the king was possibly afraid that Sinclair might throw in his lot with the ancient suzerain Denmark, and, to avoid this, knighted Sinclair and granted him Sanday and Stronsay.

'Derivative' though Abell's chronicle is, then, it is not just yet another chronicle. It is of interest for the facts and anecdotes selected, the manner how sources are used, and for vernacular formulation even down to such details as the

---

[21] Abell is aware of the importance of the right of 'girth' or sanctuary from Holyrood. See the Canon Law references mentioned in *Statutes of the Scottish Church*, ed. Patrick, p. 204 (Book III, title xlix—in chapters from Papal Decretals).

[22] *Records of the Earldom of Orkney*, p. xlix.

translation of epigrams and proverbs.[23] The particular slant is of interest also. Abell, an Augustinian by training and a Franciscan by choice, views Scots and international events from Jedburgh, from a non-Court, non-University vantage point, a different, perhaps more objective 'grass-roots' perspective. He reveals, as he promises, a moral didactic intention but never forgets that he is writing for 'plesour to my lord setoune' also, and selects anecdotes, historical fiction, legends and gossip worth relating. We see the world as seen by the Franciscan Adam Abell of Jedburgh.

NLS MS 1746[24]

folio 116ʳ

1513 ... SCOTTIS king 106 wes Iames at [that] now is ringand [reigning] quhem god conserf. He is sone to forsaid Iames qhem christ assolze. He wes skant thre zere quhen he wes crownit. Than wes wersit the word of the wisman: We terre vbi puer est rex. Wa [woe] is the kinrik quhare the king is ane barne for than nowdir pece nor iustice rang. That sam zere his modir [Margaret Tudor] mareit

1514 the erll of angus to his gret desolatioun eftirwert hes now is sene. / PAIP leo 10 sat 3 zeris. He confermit all our priuilege before grantit and gaif mony ma. He confermit the ordur of the salutacyon maid be brothir gabriel of owr ordur. That sam zere the lordis of Scotland send to france for Iohne stewart duke of albane [Albany] to be gubernatur of the kinrik and thotht he resistit in the begynnyng at the last he condescendit and come to dunbertane quhilk wes eftirwert deliuerit to him. Soyn eftir ane certane lordis rebellit aganis him bot thai prewalit nocht. He wes sa prudent in his doingis. He exilit the erll of angus & the lord hwym [Hume]. The lord huym wes eftirwert resaifit in grace bot for causis eftirwert occurrand he and maistir wilzem wes iustifeit [tried; put to death] in edinburgh. About this tyme the duke with a gret host passit to carlill and mycht haif had the cete with litill laubour bot the inglis men subtile promist a gret sovm of gold to the gubernatur & sa thai ewadit. Bot quhen the message come for it thai tauld it down to him bot thai lut

1520 him nocht haif ane penny awa. / The duke with leif of the lordis passit to his lady in france and left delabaute [De la Bastie] ane nobill knytht behind him quhilk wes eftirwert slane be the lard [laird] of

---

[23]For example (fol. 37ᵃ), 'The Sentence of Salusty is parue res concordia crescunt discordia delabuntur maxime Litill geir growis in concord gretest riches failzes in discord': (fol. 51ᵇ), 'Honores mutant mores. Thai that had before sueit maneris in honoris thai change in crudelite', (fol. 1ᵃ), 'Felix quem faciunt aliena pericula cautum. He is happy that the fate of wthir men makw wis or were'.

[24]I have, throughout the following transcript, expressed 'ye' as 'the' and have expanded most of the abbreviations, except where the sign may be a scribal flourish, in which case the apostrophe is used. Gloss and explanatory comments in square brackets are by Dr J. Hadley Williams.

weddirburn and his bredir. ROMAYN Impriour wes and is charlis 4 [i.e. 5] sone of duke philip forsaid archeduke & king of castell [Castile] Tha at wes religait in ingland come hame in Scotland and syne with the sowthland men com to edinburgh and tuke down the lord hymenis [Hume's] heid of the heicht of the towbuth [tolbooth]. Before the hwmenis heid put delabawtis heid on weddirburn at now is cassin [cast]

folio 116ᵛ

Anno X
1522

downe be the inglis men. Secundlie the duk returnit fra france and sone eftir he institut with consall of the lordis 4 keparis of the king be zerlie quarteris viz: the erll marchell lord erskin lord borthik and the lord rothuen. Bot in the tyme of his cuming fra france the erll of surre with the erme [army] of ingland cust down our howsis of fenss [defence] on the bordour abone the nowmer of 30 and birnt the towne of iedburgh and gret othir skaith had thai done & thai had nocht hard of the cuming of the gubernatour quhem gretumlie thai drede & zit dredis. PAIP hedrian [Adrian] sat a zere. He wes chosin in his absence beand in spanze [Spain]. He wes ane werra iust man and proponit to reforme halie kirk and mak pece in all stait bot god tuik him haistelie awa at malice suld nocht change his thocht. Clement sat 12 zeris. That sam zere the duik segit the castell of Work [Wark] quhare the franche men excellandlie thai facht and quhen the houss wes narrest [all but] wan ane lard of tewidaill [Teviotdale] desirand the spulze of the houss and saw he cuth nocht get it exhortit the inglis men to perseweire in thare defence and sa thai did. On the todir part the haill power of ingland wes gathirit quharfore the duik dredand falset and dissait of scottis men he lowsit the sege and

1523

returnit hame. The zere folloand the duik considderand the falset of Scotland he returnit in france. His men of weir passit before him. Thare come with him vii thousand men of weire. Than the erll of anguss at wes exilit to france without leif he come hame in Scotland and soyn be consall of ewill awisit kynnismen (at considerit nocht perrell eftirwert to cum) he tuik haill cuyre of the king and gidit the kinrik be archbald his eym [uncle] and george his brodir. And sa the laif [rest] of the lordis deput to him be the duik passit fra him. The kingis modir remanit in the castell of striwiling [Stirling] for before the erll of angus with his complices had segit the castell of ediburgh quhare wes the king and eftir it wes gewin owr he kepit the king as said is before. He maid archbald his fathir brodir [i.e. Archibald Douglas of Kilspindie] thesaurar and his pridfull wife dik opparis douchtir [Dick Hopper's daughter] of edinburgh wes callit my lady thesaurer and it is said sche wes ane compositour in the iustice aire. And the comon woce is that had nocht bene hir heichness the noble erll of angus had bene peceablie now in Scotland. The king thotht

he wes zoung he dissimilit and falloit thare directioun thotht his hart
wes far fra thame. Diuerss tymes he prewit [tried] subtile to pass

folio 117ʳ

1525
fra thame bot he mycht nocht. First quietlie he inducit his brodir the
erll of moraif [Moray] and the lord hammiltone to cum with thare
power bot thai prewalit nocht. Secundlie the lard of baulouch

1526
[Buccleuch] and he come thare to beside melross. The king wald haif
passit to him hes thai schew me at stude beside. The erll said na &
sa thai struke the feild of melross quharin wes slane the lard of
cesfurd [Cessford]. Thridlie be the erll of lennox. His eym

1527
confiderit with the erll of anguss met him be west lithquow and gaif
him feld quhare in he wes slane and the lard of hustone [Houston] &
othire diuerss. At the last quhen he grew to maire age first he wes
aperandlie commowit aganis hare stewart [Harry Stewart] at maret
his modir. Eftir diuerss betuix the forsaid erll and hir and be his
moderis request eftir he wes forgewin sche deliuerand the castell of
striwiling. Than quhen he had that howss to duell in with consall of
lordis and his modir he expellit the forsaid erll fra him. He held ane
parliament and callit the forsaid erll & maid thare his accusatioun and
forfautit [confiscated his estates] him and exilit him out of his ring.
In the sam parliament he maid hare stewart lord of methquhen
[Methven]. Eftirwert this forsaid erll tribulatioun gewand him
ondirstanding he forthocht at he had him sa he be the forsaid consall
and oft tymes with meik profferis he hes askit forgifance at the king
be owr bredir bot he hes nocht optenit it zit. Heir all man and
principallie lordis may tak documentis. Ane is at ane lord or ony
noble at leiffis at hes in his awne lordschip or bowndis he is nocht
wiss to ingire [push in] him to the kingis court and maist of all to
reull the court. For ane king natralie hes desire to reull and nocht be
rewlit. Tharfore sais lucayn li i: Nulla fides regni sociis omnisque
potestas impaciens consortis erit. Na faucht is in falloschip of
renging. All in dignate is impatient of ane marro [partner]. Rome
mycht nocht thoil tua brethir king in it. It cummis of pride to
contemp the thing at thow ma nocht beir furth. Of siclik it is said
Iere. [Jeremiah] 44: Quia plus fecit quam potuit id circo periit.
Becauss (sais he) he hes done maire na he mycht beir furth he hes
perich [died]. A man he wald reull king answer bot finalie he put
him to deid hester 3 et 7. Ionathas sun callit miphebosath dauid
king callit to his court bot be relatioun of his awn

folio 117ᵛ

serwand fals siba he wes innocentlie depriuat of his heretage 2
Regum 19. Considir to that the warldlie honour in the court is bot
schort and it is falss. It is bot schort. O quhow mony haif I sen in
my tyme gidderis of the court and consularis to 3 kingis bot haistelie
thai wer tane awa sum be suddand deid and sum be the swerd. Sa

sais sanct augustin to the place or sepultur of deid men thare ar the banis bot the man is deid bot his causs is reseruit to the day of iugement. He wes wmquhill lefand hes thow in wanite of the warld. He conquest land he gatherit gold and siluer and wes blyth in his abundance and lu all is passit awa fra him has ane dreym. Quare ar all at follouit him at the bak. Quhare ar thai that flatterit and flechit with him. Quare ar the delicait coursis the gentill wemen at he put his plesure in. All ar passit awa fra his sicht and soyn rememorance of him is tint [lost] and the maire plesance heir he takkis the maire pane to him remanis. Apoc. 14: Quantum glorificauit et in deliciis fuit tantum date ei tormentum et luctum. Secundlie the warldlie plesure is falss. Sanct Ieron [Jerome] sais and the warld wer cuttit in tua with the knyf of werite na thing suld appeire in it bot falset. For all at is in the warld odir it is preter [past] tyme and now it is nocht or the futuyr at it is wncertane or the present that is wnstabill vnde eccle^{ci} 3: Cuncta subiacent vanitati. De terra facta sunt omnia et in terram pariter reuertuntur. Ane othir document we haif here in this noble lord at we follo nocht the consall of carnall frendis bot gife thai be parfit in life for oft tymes thai consall aganis the saule heill it at is to temporall honour or dignate. Our saluitour wes nocht exempit fra sik consulouris for it is writing Ioha 7 at his kynnismen bad and consulit him to schaw him to the warld saand vade in Iudeam et manifesta te mundo. Cresost [Chrysostom] schawis the causs in a sermon of sanct Iames. He said at carnall mothir or frendis desiris thare barnis to haif warldlie honour in this life bot thai cvir nocht quhat thai sall thoill in ane nodir warld. And thai se thame leif the warld & pass to the seruice of christ thai mwrn & makis caire. Bot & thai se thame sin thai cvir nocht and sa thai schaw thame sib to thare body and nocht to thare saule. Tharfore eftir the consall of toby [Tobit] 4 c: Consilium a sapiente semper inquere. Ask consall fra ane sapient man at luffis thi saull bettir

folio 118^r

than thi body.

[*Margin*] Wmchow als the consel of flechuris [flatterers] fro tha consel nocht for thyn profit bot for thar profit is sayis sant aug. For tha ar the piparis of sathan plaand to the and puttand a cod ondir this heid to sleip in sin. Sant gregor says 26 di c. Sunt nonnulli quisquis male agentibus adulatour pulvinar sub capite eius ponit. And it is said ii 43 Nemo pitore. It is bettir to thole [suffer] pan for the verite na get benifice for falsite.

The king of france wes tane in feild be duik wrbane [Charles, Duke of Bourbon] chiftane of the impriouris host and led in spanze in the quhilk feild wes slane mungo stewart brodir to the erll of lennox. ROYM wes tane be the impriouris host kirkis spulzet and the paip wes put in castell angell [Castel Sant' Angelo] quhill owre minister generall callit francis angelori passit to the impriour in spanze and be him the paip wes deliuerit. The impriour declarit als at it wes nocht his will na his wittin the forsaid inwasion of rome and the paip bot it wes done by the luthirianis of ducheland....

[*Margin folio 116^r*] Abwt this tyme the apostat & heresyarche martyn lutheir left his haly relegyon & beguth his herise sa that he & his wikkit discipulis hes infekkit a gret part of euroyp viz: anno X 1520

folio 118^r contd

1530   Our commissar generall brodir mathy vincent come in Scotland & did gret gude anenss our halie obseruance quhair of his memoris beris witnes. Mony lutharianis wes summwnd to edinburgh and wes thare conwikkit & abiurit thare herese & birnt thare opinionis promisand thare self sa to be birnt & thai fell agane. This zere charlis 4 [i.e. 5] impriour with help of god he had singulare wictorie of saltan salaman [Suleiman] the gret turk enemy to god and distroiyr of the christin pepill. He passit out of reuchbrig [Regensburg] in ducheland to wngare with authorite of the paip and mony gude kirk men with him for by thare consall he dois na thing. Als with him wes paull graif the duke of gillire the duke saxon and all the laif of the 12 duchesperis and mony othir lord and knytht born in almane [Germany] & in spanze. The duke of gillire askit the first feild desirand to de for christ and promist to thare to win the turkis artailze and sa he did. He had with him xii thousand hagbuche & culwery and thotht he kepit his promiss he wes as relacyon schow slane & all at wes with him. Eftir him come the duke of saxon & with him 30 thousand gude christin men of evirbandis. Of thame xx thousand gunnis less & maire and x thowsand albertis and thai wer all on fut. Eftir thir tua forsaid dukis had wan the artailze come paule graif & with him mony nobillis of almane on bardit [armoured] hors x thowsand and 30 thousand on gret horss weill gerit and brak taxton matalebe his array quhilk lay nixt the gret turkus artailzery & slew of the turkis 90 thousand and nane of thame chapit. Eftir come the impriour in

folio 118^v

propir persone on the morne with x thousand gret bardit horss and 60 thousandis and 50 nobillis of almane and spanze rund about him on fut. x thousand of thame had culwerenis xx thousand had halbertis and rund about him behind 8 thousand ianettis [small horses] of spanze and gret horss of turke with lycht gerit men to hald the herme [damage] in. Soyn thare eftir the sam day com his brodir fermond [Ferdinand] king of wngare & Albert king of poill [Poland] and frederik lord of the cruciaris [crusaders] with the duke of pomeire the duke als of carion and xx bischeppis of thare kinrikis 68 abbatis wdir spirituall lordis with xl thousand horss men fifty thousand fut men with 80 pece of artailzere for ane feild and come on the northest part of the gret turk and slew rycht mony. Thair wes neuir christin pepil sa few at be manlie way did bettir. Thai put the gret turkis folkis abak the space of 12 mylis. Than the impriour and the tua kingis met to giddir with all the laif of the christin pepill and skatterit the turkis sua at thai come neuir to gidder. Thai slew the first da & on the morn 220 thousand turkis of the christin pepill 60 thousandis of the quhilk nowmir wes the duik of giller & his xii thousand the duke of pomeiris brodir 9 bischeppis 30 abbatis and xx thousand of othir kirk men. This feild wes strikin the xxvii day of september and endit on mychaelmes day at ewin & sa it lestit 3 dais the zere of christ 1532. Before this feild the impriour his consaill & lordis fastit 3 dais & 3 nychtis wattir and breid & zeid baire fut & bair heid implorand the help of god. Alsua the impriour & his companye gat all the turkis artailzere & all his Iowellis & spulzet the feild & gat sa mekill riches quhilk wes neuir gottin in christindome at anis. Alsua the papis galionis & the impriouris met to giddir 8 dais before the feild & set on the 2 turkis gret galionis & wauchtaris & tuke thame full of artailzere & trasour & monye and mannit thir galionis with the turkis awne artailzere & set on the turkis awn schippis in nwmyr 48 schippis ladin all with witalis to the turkis and sa the

folio 119^r

turkis mycht nocht bide for want of wittalis. Thai that ewadit fled to constantinople. On thame follouit fermond king of Wngary & the king of poill with the duik of pomeir & liys still and hes recowerit all thare landis and mekill maire agane. The impriouris galionis & the papis liys still with thame. The dewot & wictoriouss impriour with lowin of god in blythnes returnit in duchland with his nobill company quhem almythty god conserf in halie perseuerance and to him grant ane gude end Amen. This zere our king and the lordis lauborit for pece of ingland be commissionaris bot the inglis men subtile delayit and gaif thame sum beleif of pece quhill thai come wnwernestlie & birnt coldyngame dowglass and mony odir townis and gat haill the stoire and spulze and sa returnit. Capitanis to thame wes the erll northumbirland and the erll of angus sworn inglis man hes it said becaus he cowth nocht get grace at the king. Than follouit forro on forro & birnyng of corn.

1532 Heir come word with our ministir fra the generall chepture of the new spanze or hirketan [Yucatan] at we call the newfund yle in gret ynd [India] in afrik. Brodir martin of walence [Valencia] wrait to mathi vincent commisser generall. This martin wes custos custodium sancti ewangelii in this forsaid land & he send & said: We at ar in the extreme part of the warld in gret ynd in gret asy [Asia] quhare be our bredir minoris of obseruance zour subditis first the halie ewangell is prechit and the seid of it wes sawin quhilk hes accressit and multipleit I sa to zour fadir hede that be our bredir in ynd ar baptis [baptised] ma na x hundreth thousand of forsaid ynd.

Ilk ane of the xii bredir at wes send with me be maist reuerent fadir francis of angellis (than ministir generall now cardinall of the halie cruss) ma than a hundir thousand hes baptist. And thai all bot I hes lerit the ledis [languages] of the land diuerss and prechis to tham & instrukkis the multitude of pepill. And amang thame ar mony barnis nobilis sonnis at gewis to ws gret hoip of profectioun [progress]. Thai ar instrukkit be our bredir in life and gude maneris & ar nwrist spirituallie in our placis quhilkis places ar big-

folio 119^v

git to the nowmir of 20 and ma ar multiplian dalie bigand be the yndis. And herd beside ilk place is ane odir hous biggit [built] for instruktioun of the forsaid barnis with librell dortur fratur and chapell. Thir barnis ar werra meik and obtemperand [compliant] to the bredir and lufis the bredir bettir na thare carnall fadir. Thai ar chest & faithfull to the bredir. Thai ar ingenios in pictur. Thai preche to thare fadir and modir quhen thai ar weill instrukkit in christin doctrin and als to odir in pulput. In ilk place of owris in hous before said ar 500 of the forsaid barnis in sum place ma. Thai rise in the nycht hes the bredir dois & singis our lady matenis and howris be thare self and thai sing mes solempnitlie to a brodir in the alter. Thai ar werra agill of ingin & gude of rememorance. Thai ar werra pecefull amang thare self & na strife is amang thame. Thei speik with sobire and suet woce and depressit eyn without ewagatioun. / MULIERUM COMMENDATIO. Wemen thare schenis [shine] with ontrowable honeste & wemenlie scham. Confessionis thare & principale of wemen all full of purite without palliatioun [concealment]. The body of christ with abundance of teris thai dewotlie resawis. Religios men principalie bredir minoris thai had in gret rewerence becaus thai spirituallie first generit thame to god. Thai obey to tham and takis pennance thankfullie and all doctrin concernand the faith. All this zere bigane the bischep of tymistitan of our ordur & the bredir with him in that sam forsaid land send a pistill to the generall cheptur haldin in tholos [Toulouse] the zere of christ 1532 schawand mekill before said and ekand at 500 tempillis of fals goddis thare ar distrosit and ma than 20 thousand figures of ewill spretis at thai anornyt ar brokin & birnt & in thare placis kirkis & ymage of the crus ar put wp & ar honorit be yndis men and wemen. Als it at is horrible to heire before in the said cete of tymistitan thare wes offerit to thare fals goddis ilk zere ma than 20 thousand hartis of thare slave barnis and zoung wirginis in sacrifice. Bot now thai hartis nocht to ydolis bot to almythty god ar offerit in honour and dewocion nocht deid bot in lewand lufe and glore to god be doctrin & halie exempill of our bredir minoris. This dewot pepill multipleis in fastin disciplin & orison with teris & sichin. Many of thare

folio 120ʳ

barnis can weill reid and writ sing and puynt [mark up a musical text (with points) for chanting]. Oft thai confes thaim and with maist dewotion resaifis the body of christ. Speciall dewocion thai haif to the glorius wirgin. Ydolis of thare fatheris & mothiris at ar nocht perfitlie conuertit thir barnis sekis quietlie and bringis faithfullie to our bredir and thotht sum of thame for that ar slane be thare fatheris thai leif with god lawreat in the hewin. Thare is ane lawd brodir amang the laif callit petir of gante. He is werra perfit in the leid of the land. He hes cuire of 600 & ma of thir barnis with gret diligence. He is principall paranymph [advocate] gewand on halie dais with gret solempnite cristin madynis weill instrukkit in mariage to the forsaid barnis. And for the instruction of the forsaid madenis the imprice [Empress] send 6 honorabill wemen werra cunnyng and commandit be writ at thare suld be ane houss biggit sa gret at thai dewot ladeis ondir the bischeppis fauor mycht teche and instruk 1000 madenis honestlie lewand. Heir we haif diuers documentis. Ane is at barnis suld soyn begin to serf god exempill of thire forsaid barnis of infidelis. It is said parali. [Paralipomenon] 34: Iosias cum adhuc puer esset cepit querere dominum deum suum. Iosias king quhen he wes bot ane barne he beguth to seik his lord god. Secundlie christin wemen heire hes document to follo thire forsaid wemen & thare awne naturall conditioun that oft tymis schenit in gude wemen. Wemen folloit our saluatour to his passioun mwrnand for him quhen his discipulis fled fra him luc. 23. Thai stude beside the crus murnand. Thai come to his sepultur settand nocht by dreid of the knythtis. Ioh. 20. Thare chestite is patent in susan that chesit [chose] erer the deid na excers lichorie by hir husband. Dani. 13 [Vulg. Susanna]. Thair pete in martha at wes herbriour of our saluitour. luc. 10. Thar mercy in follouing of our saluitour prechand and makand ministracyon to him of thare substance. luc. 8. Quharfor sais sanct paul cor. [*Ad Corinth*. I, viii, 14] 8: Sanctificatus est vir infidelis per mulierum fidelem. Tharfore gret is the nwmyr of wemen in the hewin at sall ioy with christ in paradis. / This sam zere wes martirit wenerable fadir brodir andro of spoleit [Spoleto] of our ordur fra prechin of the faith of christ in affrik in the

folio 120ᵛ

cete of fey [Fez] the 9 day of Ianuar [in fact, February] the zere of god 1532 the quhilk passion and the miraculis of the sam send Ione⸱ [John III] king of portingaill to the forsaid cheptur of tholois. Our king herand the skaith done on the borduris be the inglis men of the borduris & the quhit cotis [white coats] he callit his consall for remeid and it wes decretit at the kinrik devidit in four quartaris the lordis and gentilmen of ilk quartar suld remane thare ane moneth abowt on the bordur to defend it and sa thai did faithfullie. Als thare

1533

wes ane certane of wagiouris at remanit in kelso quhilkis kepit it.
The lordis remanit in iedwart [Jedburgh] and for thare fidelite and
obedience christ be thare reward. Amen.

Soli a deo honor et gloria

Heir endis the rute or quheill of tyme
Be ane pure brothir of the brethir minoris
of obseruance in our place of Jedwart
the zere of god 1533 inwith the oct of the
natiuite of our lady the mothir of god
quene of hewin.

Mensalis lectio verba B p uri francisci
Magna promisimus maiora promissa sunt nobis
Servemus hoc aspiramus ad illa. Brevis volup
tas perpetua pena. Modica passio gloria inifinita
Tu autem domine miserere nobis.

[CONTINUATION OF ABELL'S CHRONICLE]
folio 120^v

The forsaid brothir adam abell continuand his
proces of the forsaid rote heir he begy
nnis quhare he lewit in the zere of god 1534
zeris and sa procedand for his schort tyme.

1534 King henry wranguslie expellit fra him be wrangus diuors haly quene katherin [Katharine of Aragon] aganis the determinatioun of the halie kirk and marit Annas bulan [Anne Boleyn] and beguth to rebell aganis the kirk of rome &

folio 120 (bis)^r

slaid in herise with his pepill of martin. And that sam zere he wes declarit nocht allanerlie ane cesmatik [schismatic] bot als an heritik and becaus our brethir of obseruance prechit aganis this error tua of thame he martirit with tua monkis and ane nwn & ane preist. Alsua eftir that he gart be his corruppit consall gathir all oure brethir of obseruance in the cete of luve the nowmir of 180 and gart propone thir folloand articulis. First at thai suld preche aganis the wsurpatife power of the bischep of rome and at he had na mair power na ony othir bischep in ony othir prowince. Item at thai suld preche and hald king hary heide of the kirk of ingland. Item at thai suld allanerlie obey and apply to king hary and his successouris and his statutis of his parliament and renunce the law decretis and canonis maid be the papis and consallis as thai wer aganis the law of god & halie writ. Alsua in thare preching thai suld first commend the king hes [as] heid of halie kirk syne anne his quene be lachtfull [lawful] mariage. Syne the bischep of cantirberre with othir kirk men bot na word of the paip. Alsua at thai suld obey to tua wisituris maid be the king that is for to say George brown prowinciall of the augustin freris & Iohn lilpen prowinciall of the blak freris quhilkis suld schaw all the fawtis and secretis of ws and othir religios men & all precious iowellis in religios placis to the king and at thai suld sweire to this and gife thare comon seill tharwpone and mony othir erroris. Amang all this forsaid nowmir of our brethir thar wes newir ane at consentit to thir forsaid erroris bot offerit thame to the deid for defens of halie kirk & the trew faith quharfore be command of the king thai wer all put in presone. Bot part of thame be menis of dewot folkis wes deliuerit and fled in Scotland & graciuslie eftir the rewll wes resaifit be our bredir & als be the seculair stait. Heir we ma draw furth diuers documentis. First how this noble king wes blindit be carnall plesur of the flesche for ane hure his lauchfull wife quhilk failzeat neuir to him quharfor his falt wes to

folio 120 (bis)^v

aggrege [the graver]. For it is said 32 q 6 c indignat that man committand adultrie ar hewier to be punist than wemen. For he suld haif maire ws [use] of resone. Nocht with standing thotht thare quhilis cumis mair skaith be adultre of the women hes wrangus haris & wrang barnis part of gudis. Bot the argument at he & his fals consall mowit is becaus at arthur his brodir mareit hir before him allegent it at is writ in leuitici 18: Turpitudinem uxoris fratris tui non reuelabis quia turpitudo fratris tui est. Quia vir et uxor sunt una caro. Tamen excipitur casus videlicet quum frater moretur sine liberis tunc eius frater viuens. Than the brodir lewand nocht allanerlie [not only] he mycht mary his brodiris wife bot he wes oblist tharto to get succession as it is patent. Deut° 25. Quhy that bot becaus the resone of the law heire waris the law of natur and of god standand still with thare resone or caus ar indisponable. Bot we ma noit heire that thai ar sum thingis of the law of nature as begynnyngis knawin be thare self or thare termis. Exempill finall gude is desirable. Ewill at turnis fra this gude is wmchouabill that is deidlie syn heir ma nocht be dispensatioun. Othir thingis ar of the law of natur as conclusionis neidfullie follouand of the forsaid begynnyngis. Exemple god is to be lufit and our nychtbur and sa heir fallis na dispensation as it is patent di. 6 para i. The resone is becaus the resone of the law is inseuerabill fra it. Alsua thare ar othir thingis of the law of natur nochthe(le)s the knawin begynnyngis na hes neidfull conclusionis deducit fra thame thotht thai be werray consonant tharto as the preceppis of the sicund table and all the morall preceppis in the law of moeses & the ewangell. And in thir remanend the caus & resone of thare institutioun thare fallis nocht dispensatioun bot weill follois dispensation in obseruation of the caus of thame. Quharfore quhen thare concurris a caus particulare in the quhilk failzes or is absent the resone or caus of that law

folio 121^r

be speciall causis occurrand and impedient [obstructive] obseruance of thame than the paip ma dispence in siklik casis for as richard sais 4 di 38: and he mycht nocht it apperit at christ wer nocht ane gude maister of howset [household] bot gife he left his hird on his flok at mycht occur and help all nedis at occurrit in it and that at is said of the preceptis in the sicund table sa the sam of the morall preceppis of the auld and new law. To approbation of the ilk archi flore in his soym sais at he knew be sewir relatioun that paip Martin 5 of that name dispensit be determinatioun of gret iurist and theologie with ane at tuik his awne sister to his wife and the mariage stude for wmchouyn of gret skaith and sclandir that othir wais had occurrit and sa is till ondirstand of siklik. To that is argument appartatife 2q i c multi in fi quhar sanct aug. sais: Iuge nocht thi nychtbur haistely of thi temerat will bot iuge be law of god eftir ordur & diffinitioun of halie kirk. This dispensatioun forsaid of king henry & his quene katherin wes prewit lauchfull be halie kirk nocht allanerlie be resone at wes in the law of moeses bot als for propheit baith of the kinrik of spanze & ingland and wnchewin of strife of the sam. Ze as I hard be relatioun of inglis bredir sche had neuir carnall daill of his brodir. Bot thotht sche had the dispensatioun wes werra & wndutabill. Secundlie ze ma considdir heir how peralus it is to rebell aganis the heid of halie kirk & christis wicair & wald anull his power gewin be christ to sanct petir and his successouris. It is werra herise determit in the law 22 di c omnis & 99 di. c nulli. Bot the herritik sais quhare will ze get at the 4 auld doctouris or thai at wes before thame apprewis that the kirk of rome or the paip is heid of halie kirk. To appreif that first I introduce sanct ambros 2 q 7 c beati quhare he sais petir and paull tholit martirdom in rome quhilk wes heid of all nationis than at quhaire the heid wes first of superstitioun thare the heid suld rest of haliness and quhare the prince remanit of gentilis sa thare suld duell the prince of halie kirk. Als this sam doctour

folio 121^v

sais 22 di c omnes: I profes sais he and will follo in all thyngis our maistrace the kirk of rome. Idem doctor 24 q i c non turbetur. He sais quhow ma the schep be perturbit quhare petir is skipper quam christ put the fundament of halie kirk Aug. q 2 q 7 c puto: Quha misknawis sanct petir principat of the apostilis to be preferrit to all othir bischeprik. Et ea tam & q c hoc est sanct Ieron to paip damass says This is the faith maist blist paip quhilk we in the kirk catholik we hes lerit and ay hes haldin. Quharin gif we haif failzet we desir to be correckit be ye at haldis the faith and the sait of sanct petir et c. Item sanct ciril doctour contemporand to sanct Ieron sais li thesaurorum: Hes christ resaifit be his fadir ceptur and dukre [dukedom] of the kirk of gentilis passand furth of israel abwfe all principat & power at till him all knee sall bow sa to petir and his successouris he hes grantit maist haill power and to na othir. Idem eod li he sais at the apostilis in the ewangelis & epistolis affermit and in all doctrin at petir held the place of christ and the gidin of halie kirk and at thai gaif place and rewerens to him in all synogoig in chesing & confirmatioun. Alsua christost [John Chrysostom] in homaly of sanct Iohne sais at christ determit sanct Iames prelat in a place bot petir he ardanit maister and doctour of all the warld. Lu thow heritik gife thow will nocht resaif the halie papis at sched thare blude for christ and kithit gret myraculis for witnessing of papaill power thow ma nocht deny the testificatioun of thir auld halie doctouris. Alsua tak heir ane document of trew & fals religios men. For hes I schew before the sentence of sanct augustin quhare he sais I fand neuir sa perfit hes religios men quhare thai stude na wnperfit quhare thai failzeit in religioun. / This zere the chiftanis of the borduris in the est partis of Scotland quhilkis ar mers [Merse] & tevidaill [Teviotdale] wes tane be the king and put in ward for tresone principalie at the chais of zatwm [Yetholm] eftir the inglis men. Thair my lord Setone with his gude fadir lord Zester [Yester] folloit formast on the chais. Bot his banerman [banner-bearer] quhem god now deit assol-

folio 122ʳ

-ze wes stoppit be thame to ga forward and mony othir thingis wes schawin aganis thame. The sam zere auestell the town of mussilburgh wes biggit ane oritur in honour of the wirgin mare of lawret [Loretto] quhare mony miraculis wes kithit in confusioun of herittikis at than beguth to multiple. Quharfor that sam zere abowt the feist of the eucharist wes solempnit examination of ane certane heritikis in the kirk of halryrudhous king Iames fift beand present quhar two heritikis wes birnt wiz: maister normand gurlaw and dauid straton. Othir tua fled and apperit nocht for thai wer abiurit before viz.: the schirref of lithquhow and maister wilzem Iohnstone. Amang the laif of thare erroris condempnit be halie kirk wes ane at the man had nocht fre will quhilk error is aganis halie writ baith new and auld testment and docturis of the sam. Sum creaturis ar at hes na will nothir fre na coakkit [coerced] hes thai at knawis nathing hes stayn at naturalie discendis. Fir naturalie ascendis and huiusmodi. Thare is othir corporall creatur at hes will bot nocht fre bot coakkit eftir the bir [force] of natur without resone hes brutall best at naturalie dredis inwasion as the mows dredis the cat the scheip the tod et c. Bot to the man hes he gewin will and iugement for thotht he iuge ane thing gude or prophetable to him self zit he iugis that it is skaithabill till his nychtbur. Tharfore he dois it nocht. Exempill of grace. Ane man desiris ane thing plesable as halk or hund. Lu thare is arbitratioun or wil. Bot he will nocht tak that fra his nychtbur for it wer aganis god and his conscience. Than his will is fre and nocht strenzet. Tharfore to the man alanerlie now is imput merit gife he dois gude & demerit gif he dois ewill of his fre will. To that we haif sufficient auctorite of haly writ eccle^{ci} 15: Deus ab initio constituit hominem et reliquit eum in manu consilii sui. Gloria in libertate arbitrii sequitur. Adiecit mandata et precepta sua si volueris mandata consuerare consueruabunt te. Apposuit tibi ignem et aquam ad quod volueris porrige manum tuam. God sais he fra the begynnyng hes maid the man

folio 122^v

and hes left him in the hand of his awne consall. The gloiss [gloss] sais of his awne fre will. He hes gewin to him commandis and preceppis. Will thow keip his commandis thai sall keip the. He hes put befoyr the fire and wattir to put thi hand to any of thame thow will. This fre will all the angellis baith gude and ewill had be god in thare first creatioun as the maister and othir docturis concludis in the sicund buik of the sentens the 5 distinctioun quhar be the ta part turnit to god and gat confirmatioun of beatitude and the todir part turnit thame fra god be pride and wes expellit out of the hewin impir and now is confirmit in ewill. Bot the man in this present life is indifferent haifand fre will to cheis ewill or gude. Sanct aug. de peni di 2 c: Vt cognouerunt para liberi circa fi: Fre will sais he is faculte of resoun and will in the quhilk gude is chosin grace assistant or ewill grace desistent and is callit fre in sa fer hes will ma be bowit to baith the partis. It is callit chesing anens rasone of it at it is faculte of it. Item chrisost apone sanct math. sais: Owr fre will thotht it be potent be the self to ewill it is nocht potent to gude without the grace of our redemer adiutrice [helper]. Item sanct aug. li de li arb. sais: Wictore quhare with sin is wincust is nathing bot the gift of god helpand the fre will of man in this batell of temptatioun. Item Iero contra Ione manum et ponitur de peni di 2 c prealle para et paulo part: Sic liberi arbitrii nos condidit deus nos ut nec ad virtutem nec ad vicia necessitate trahimur. Sa sais he god hes maid ws with fre will that nodir to wice nor vertu of neid ar we drawin. PAIP paull 3 of that name sat [ ] zeris. He wes hes it wes schawin to ws confirmit be his predicessor clement or he deit quhilk I red nocht afore at I rememor. He wes ane stark post before with the impriour aganis the infidelis quhen he wes cardinall in the first wictorious expeditioun. Mony bredir of obseruance of our religioun fled the

1534   persecutioun of the said king hare fra ingland and come in Scotland

folio 123^r

resauit be our brethir as we wer oblist baith be the rewll and law of natur. Part of thame wes deliuerit out of presone be dewot & noble inglis men & sa come in Scotland fra the ewill and peruersit religious men (allanerlie of name) quhaire thai mycht nocht keip thare obseruance. For in all ingland thare wes na mendicantis at apponit [opposed] thame for the faith bot our bredir. Of possidens [possession] principalie stude the charturis [Charterhouse] monkis with the maistir of brigittais ordur hes sone eftir is patent. The laif sum for corporall dreid sum for tynyng of possessionis othir appliyt to the kingis error or lurkit in lay and held thare tung. Bot nane of thir wos excusit fra sin for perfit faith standis in thre thingis. First in hart without hesitatioun. For it is said extra de per. c dubius: Dowtsum in the faith is infideill Iaco. 1: In fide nihil hesitans In the faith sais he haif na hesitatioun. Nocht withstanding to be tempit in the faith without consent thare is mekill merit to win. Iaco i: Beatus vir qui suffert temp. quem cum probatus fuerit. Blissit be the man at sufferis temptatioun for quhen he prewit constant he sall resaif the crowne of glore. Secundlie to sufficient faith is requirit confession in word and a man be requirit of it be infidelis as the apostil sais ad rhomanos 10: Corde creditur ad iusticiam ore autem confessio fit ad salutem. To trow the faith in thi hart it is to thi iustice bot to get eternall heill it is requirit at thow confess it in thi mowth and thow be requirit and thotht thow be nocht requirit and thow be prelait or prechour thow suld reprwfe herice and conferme the faith. For it is said math. 10: He at confessis me before men I sall confess him before my fadir and sa he at denyis me I sall deny him. And sa the lordis of ingland at oblist thame to stand at thare herittik kingis statutis thai incure the cryme of faueris of herice & ar cursit and mony wais suld be punist. Thridlie sufficient faith requiris gude werkis in life. Isidorus sais Blissit is he at trowis weill and trowand leifis weill and at he be sa constant at or he leif his faith he suld erer leif his life luc. 12: Dico vobis amicis meis et c. I sa to zow my frendis dreid nocht thame at

folio 123ᵛ

may slay zour body and syne ma do na maire to zow. Bot dreid him that eftir the deid he ma put zow in the hell. For sanct aug. sais: Gife pane giffis terror glore bidis the. All the lordis of ingland infekkit with the forsaid herice thai haif tint thare landis temporall gudis and thare haris ma nocht succeid to thame as it is patent extra de heri c vergentis.

1535 Our king this zere had gret laubour in compessing [repressing] of thewis and reweris [thieves and reivers] baith in the south and north part of Scotland. Item amangis the laif at wes martirit in ingland for the faith wes the bischep of rogester [Rochester] nobill and halie baith in life & doctrin with lord thomas more maist excelland in charge & schort tyme before chanslaire of ingland. The first that is the bischep eftir the paip paul had maid him cardinall the king herand that and considerand that he wes on turnabill to his ewill wais he gart strik his heid fra him with ane dewot chaplane. Rychtsua lord Thomas mycht nocht be brocht to his wikkit intent nothir be persuasioun na buddis [bribes] quhar richtsua he gart heid him. Bot eftir thare martirdome he excersit crudelite unhard before in 6 charturis monkis and the rector of sanct brigittais abay. First he gart draw them throw the cete of lundon confusionablie. Secundlie he gart hing thame bot nocht to the deid. Eftirwert thai wer nakit bandin to stakis & thare secret membris cuttit fra thame. Syne thai wer slittit wp fra place of thare secret partis to the slot of thare breist. Thai zit lefand thai turmentoris raif out thare bowellis cust in the fire thare maid. And last of all thai powit out thare hartis and cust in the sam fyre & syne thai dewidit thare bodeis deid and send to diuers townis. Bot in all thir turmentis the maistir of brigittis abbay prechit quhill his hart wes rewin furth. That sam zere this tirand send ane herittik that wes before wes a post of our ordur & syne passit to herice to be promowit with the wikkit king to subuert our king quhilk wes his sistir sone and at suld tak his part aganis the impriour quhilk he dreid and send agane to ingland our forsaid bredir at fled his persecutoun to keip thare obserwans amang ws. Our

folio 124ʳ

king constantlie denyit & detestit thare errour saand at he suld constantlie defend the faith of halie kirk gif he cowth nocht be disputatioun at the leist he suld be his swerd. And sa this herittik with his company passit hame confusitlie. Swin eftir paip paull send ane breif to our king inducent him to constance in the faith & defens of halie kirk & nocht to inclin to the herice of his eym. In the quhilk breif he preferrit the martirdome of the bischep of rochestre to the martirdome of sanct thomas of cantirbery becaus sanct thomas wes slane be the kingis curtiouris he wes slane be turmatouris sanct thomas wes exilit he wes presond sanct thomas for his awne singular kirk bot he for wniuersall kirk. This zere wes send to france for mariage the erll of moraif the kingis naturall brodir with the bischep of moraif and the lard erskin.

1536 / Quene katherin the werra quene of ingland passit to god paand the det of deid quhilk in werite ma be contit in numyr & merit of the forsaid martiris for pacientlie sche sufferit mony kind of iniuris done to hir for goddis saik. Bot this sam zere god almythtie beguth to punis hirris [whores] & the forsaid martiris iniuris in the moneth of Iwn. First the forsaid hure anne bulen wes comprehendit and conwikkit in hurdome with diuers by king henry thotht sche denyit quharfor sche wes hedit & thai wer be diuers turmentis put to deid et c. Heir gentill wemen ma tak document in this halie quene katherin to haif pacience thoth thare husband ly by thame be adultre & lichlie [slight, insult] thame. Sche did nocht as mony wikkit women dois.

For & thare husband ga to folie thai do siklik & ekis ewill apone ewill. Bot sche leifit in chestite in religios place & gaf hir caus to christ & halie kirk excersand hir in prayng fasting & almws deid folloand ay consall of our bredir & othir conyng men. It mycht weill be said in his commendatioun it at is writin eccle^{ci} c 26: Gratia super gratiam mulier sancta et pudorata. Grace is ekit to grace to ane wemen at is halie and chest. The tane concernis the saull the todir the body. Now sche is

folio 124^v

deliuerit and hir enymes punist ar for god sais as it is writin deut° 32: Mihi vindictam et ego retribuam. Refer thi caus and iniuris to me & I sall punis quhilk is aganis impacient & endlent [jealous] wemen quhilkis quhilis without caus thai will wex thare husband & caus him quhilumis to do it at before he wes clene of. Of thame it is said eccl^{ci} 26: Dolor cordis et luctus mulier zelotipa. Flagellum linguae omnibus communicans. He sais: Ane endlen women is dolor of hart & murnyng to hir husband & scurge of hir tung is comon to all. Nochtwithstanding men suld wmschew occasioun of endling in thare wife & do nathing to odir wemen at ma gyf occasyon of handlyn quhilk is aganis miserable men at nocht allanerlie thai brak thare band of mariage be adultre bot als thai rus thame of sic miserite. Ane dewot man of tewidaill within this 4 zeris shew to me at ane capitane of the borduris quhilk I knew said to him: Quhow mony women said he haif ze had be zour wife sen ze wer marit. He answert & said: Lowit be god I had neuir women by my marit wife. He answert: Fy apone zow man ze ar na worth. Quhat follouit on him. Lang before he expellit his lady of heretage quham be he wes maid wp & lay in adultre mony zeris. Bot within thir iiii zeris he wes tane with the king for prodicion [treason] & put in ward quhare in he is...& his lady is restorit to hir awn. Of this mater I haif spokin sum thing before fol 50. / This sam zere about the feist of natiuite of sanct Iohne thare hapnit ane horrible cais in orknay. Iames synclaire at I kennit weill quhen the king schort quhile before had maid knytht thotht he forseruit erar to haif bene hangit for his wikkit life he wes haldin a court with gret gloriatioun & arrogance. In this mentyme the king send wit to him anens ane herand of his desire quhilk ekit his want & wantones. Behald heire the fals smyling of deme fortoune & how perolus it is to thame at sche smylis on. This miserabill man lang rynnand in his wykkit will heire be permissioun of god he wes heltrit be the fend his maistir & led in repreuable wit he rais wp fra the court is it wes schawin & beguth to dance & cast gamwntis him alane na he mycht nocht be stanchit. At ewin he zeid to his bed with his wife barbara hare stew-

folio 125^r

-artis sistir. Bot he mycht nocht sleip. He rais sone eftir day and put the forsaid writ with his ring ondir his wiffis side quhen sche wes slepand and passit furth before his hous quhare thare wes ane peit stak and nocht fer fra thir ane fowll deip dub. Now he zeid dansing and casting gamwndis about the stak takand petis out of it and castand agane at it. Now he wald leip fra yin and douk him in the dub and sin hes before rin to the stak. And eftir that he had done this ane lang tyme at the last he cust his clathis and bonet fra him and tuk ane renk at ane heich craig & lap in the see and drownit him self. Othir sais at the ewill spret led him be the hokster [armpit] in the see & drownit him. This miserable man lewand ane lang tyme in tirannide warldlie prosperite follouit him. The warld kissit him but finalie put him in the handis of his enemy. He or be him wes slane the erll of caitness the laird of beridaill & mony othir gentill men. Tham at fled to kirkis he ruggit thame furth nakit and slew thame. Ten in the kirtown of kirkway [Kirkwall] at he resauit ondir sowerance bot he and his bredir cruellie slew thame. Before he slew captane walles ondir trowis and segit the kingis hous in kirkwa & gret iniuris did to the lady sinclaire for hir awne richt. Heir ze ma tak a nobill document to considdir quhow peralus is temporall prosperite of the warld in dignite and riches principalie in wikkit personis of life for sanct aug. sais 23 q li c paratus in fine Nihil infelicius na the prosperite of ewill men for in it is nurist penall impunite & wikkit will as inwert enemy is maid stark and the warld sais to sathan at Iudas said to the Iowis math. 26: Quemcunque osculatus fuero ipse est tenete eum. Quhem euir I kiss be temporall prosperite hald him fast. For sanct augustin sais: We suld fle the peralus of the warld as the wemen of the fend quhilk nocht allanerlie infekis the body bot als it slais the saull and mairatour it is mixt with soro for the halie doctour callit prosper sais: Temporall geire in dignite or riches tint to ane iust man is exercitioun of wertu bot to ewill men it is torment & pane for a guid mannis desire is festnit in hewinlie thingis. He giffis litill cuire

folio 125ᵛ

of temporall thingis bot ane ewill man partis nocht without soro fra it at he inordinatlie lufit. Ane carnall man quhen he desiris temporall plesur he hes haivit with the burdin of his desire. It is hewy labour in seking of warldlie glore and dreid is in the keping of it bot it sall nocht lest lang with him for deid finalie sall sewir him fra it. Iab. 27: Diues cum dormierit nihil secum auffert aperiet oculos et nihil inveniet. A riche man sais he slepit in this present life he sall haif nathing with him. He sall oppin his eyn eftir this life and all salbe awa at he here weild. Sanct bernard [Bernardino] sais: This warld hes maid ane scheip porter callit deid quhilk of all the riches at ane man brwkit heir it lattis nocht haif furth with him ane penny Iob. i: Nudis egressus et c. I passit sais he nakit and baire fra my mothiris wame and nakit sall I pas out of the warld. Alsua on mary maddalenis day oure king without consent of the lordis with ane gret thesaur salit to france. There wes principall with him than Schir Iames hammiltone bot tempest rais on the west see quhen thai wer neire france and sa be inductioun of his fallowis he mysknawand the marinaris returnit in Scotland. Bot eftirwert about the natiuitie of our lady he salit agane in france with the erll of arran argile rothtes the lord flemeng the lard of lochinwer drumlanrik and diuers othiris and come to france. And in ane dissimilit westment he com to the duik of wandair [Vendôme] fathir of the lady at he suld haif mareit. He wes knawin thare be his picture bot I wait nocht quhat causs he had. He proponit to return agane haistelie in Scotland bot this beand knawin to the king of france he send haistelie for him and resaifit him with gret triwmph & blythnes saand: Blissit be god for thotht he haif tane ane son fra me that wes the dalphin [dauphin] he hes send to me ane othire sone agane. And at his petitioun he gaif his douchtir to him in band of mariage be word of present tyme and that on the sonday eftir sanct katherinis day bot the solempnizatioun wes maid eftirwert on new zere day. This zere about sanct francis day the comwnis of ingland kinlit with the zeill of god thai rais aganis thare wikkit king on this wis. He distroyit (320) of abais and the iowellis and landis appliyt to his temporall ws and prophet. That mycht nocht suffice him

folio 126ʳ

in the south parteis bot he send his lymmaris [brigands] to do the sam in the north to the abbais. Bot ane abbay with his assistans repugnit thame & chasit thame awa. Bot ane of thir herittik lymmaris come to ane kirk and quhen the mes wes done he reft challis and brak it. Fra yin he reft the depositur fra the body of christ with the sacrament in it. The preist said to him: Frend put furth the body of christ and then do as ye pleis. This considerand ane dewot seculaire man he said to othir nychtburis thar present: Is thare ony heire that of gude zeill will tak our lord Ihesus part. Thai answert and said: We haif all the zeill of god to defend the faith. Incontinent this forsaid dewot man with the laif distroeit the herittik and restorit the challis and eucharist to the forsaid preist. The comonis than chesit ane chiftane at thai namit powerte and sa conglobait [assembled] aganis thare heritik king thai rais bot quhow thai haif don zit thare haill proces is nocht patent. Thare is word cummyng that he offerit to thame mendis and tuik with thame trewis bot ondir thir trewis he hes slane dissaitfullie x or xii of the chiftanis to the comonis be frawd and falset of the duik of norfolk and mony eftirwert he crowelly martirt.

1537 On new zere day in france wes spousit our king and the king of francis douchtir in the cete of paris with gret triwmphe & blythnes quhare thare wes thre kingis vii cardinalis and mony bischeppis. That sam zere in the town of kelso as it wes said ane women wes deliuerit of ane monstur. Alsua about the feist of sanct barnardin [Bernardino] returnit our king fra france with his spous in Scotland and wes resaifit with gret blithnes...[Illegible sentence due to manuscript damage]

Son eftir folloit grit calamite & tribulacyon eftir the sentens of...extreme gaudii luctus ocupat the hand of warldly plesur...soro & cayr. Abowt the natiuitie of sant iohn lurkand perdycyon aganys the king wes propalit quhow the lady (of glamys [Glamis]) & hir complycis ordand to distroy the king (be pusen [poison]). And son eftir his quheyn magdaleyn payt the det of deid with grit skatht to scotland mornyng & cayr to al gud scottis men bot abuyn al othiris to the kyng for luf at he hed to hir. Quhat sche hed in thezaur wes left to hym be legace quhilk wes grit & marwalus to tel. Son eftir...

folio 126^v

wes condempnit to deid the foirsaid lady glamys with hir gud son maistir of....[Forbes] for the sam cryme quhilk befoir trasonably & ondir trowys murdyrist the gentil lard of meldrum and diwers othiris gentil men of the leslies cruellie wes hedit & quartyrit quhilkis wes put in diuers placis. Sche wes byrnt. Hir son wes condempnit to deid bot zit he bydis the kyngis wil. Hir husband archbald cambel put in ward passand owr the castel wal of hedynbrouch [Edinburgh] he fel & deid suddanly. This sam zeir the kyngis...procurit a diwos [divorce] betuix hir & hare stouert [Stewart] bot the sentens is zit suspendit.

       W Santclair of roislin
       knecht anno domini mv c lv
       fra the begyneng of the varld 5527
       eftir the gret flud iii^m viii^c lxxi

12

THE SCOTS-GAELIC SCRIBES
OF LATE MEDIEVAL PERTHSHIRE:

AN OVERVIEW OF THE ORTHOGRAPHY AND CONTENTS OF
THE BOOK OF THE DEAN OF LISMORE[1]

Donald E. Meek

The Book of the Dean of Lismore is one of the best-known manuscripts in Scotland.[2] Like some other key manuscripts, it assumes great importance because it is a particularly fortunate survivor from the medieval past. It may be that, because of its special place as a unique manuscript, it assumes rather too much importance, but its contents and the nature of its orthography would suggest that it deserves to hold the centre-stage in the field of medieval Gaelic literature, at least for the immediate future. Over the last few years, there has been something of a revival of interest in this manuscript, after a 'closed season' of some forty years.[3] Such a revival of interest is to be welcomed, since there is still much to be learned about the Book and its scribes. Indeed, it is apparent that, as its mysteries are uncovered, the Book of the Dean of Lismore provides an ever-broadening perspective in which to view eastern Perthshire in the Middle Ages. This is the region in which the manuscript was compiled, and it is a part of Scotland which has received comparatively little attention as an area of literary activity in the medieval period.

The reference in the title of this chapter to the 'Scots-Gaelic' scribes of late medieval Perthshire has been chosen with care. It will be noted that the defining phrase is not 'Gaelic' or 'Scottish Gaelic'. The point is that to define its scribes in strictly Gaelic terms would be to overlook a most important dimension of the Book of the Dean of Lismore, namely the Lowland Scots dimension. The

---

[1]This chapter was presented at the Fifth International Conference on Scottish Language and Literature, Medieval and Renaissance, Aberdeen, 1987, and first published in the conference proceedings: *Bryght Lanternis*, ed. J.D. McClure and M.R.G. Spiller (Aberdeen, 1989). Professor Meek, the editors of *Bryght Lanternis* and Mr C.B. Kirkwood, Managing Director, Aberdeen University Press, have most kindly granted permission for its reproduction in this volume. Small modifications to the original text have been made by Professor Meek.

[2]The manuscript is owned by the National Library of Scotland, Edinburgh, shelf-mark 72.1.37.

[3]Three important works on the manuscript were published in the late 1930s: *Scottish Verse from the Book of the Dean of Lismore*, ed. W.J. Watson, Scottish Gaelic Texts Society (Edinburgh, 1937); *Poems from the Book of the Dean of Lismore*, ed. E.C. Quiggin (Cambridge, 1937); and *Heroic Poetry from the Book of the Dean of Lismore*, ed. N. Ross, Scottish Gaelic Texts Society (Edinburgh, 1939). A new wave of editing began in the 1970s.

manuscript intermingles Gaelic culture and Scots culture in a manner which may appear remarkable, if not bizarre, to us today. When our Scots-Gaelic scribes were active, however, it may have seemed entirely natural to fuse the cultures in this way. Such fusion may well have been wholly in keeping with the conventions of their time and place.

It will be useful if we remind ourselves, at the outset, of the distinctive features of that time and place. The Book of the Dean of Lismore was compiled, it would seem, in the first half of the sixteenth century, and its compilation falls within a period which was bounded by historical events of considerable significance. In 1493 the Lordship of the Isles was forfeited by the Crown, although attempts were made thereafter to restore it by force. The forfeiture marked the end of the MacDonalds as the major political family in the Gaelic west.[4] As the power of the MacDonalds declined, that of the Campbells grew. The MacGregor scribes who were involved in the compilation of the Book of the Dean were vassals of the Campbells of Glenorchy. Like the MacGregor scribes, the Campbells generally had an interest in Gaelic culture and Scots culture, and they owed much of their prestige to the manner in which they could operate in both the Lowlands and Highlands. The Campbells were ready to absorb new impulses from the Lowland south, and this is underlined by the espousal of reforming principles by their leaders some time before the Reformation Parliament of 1560.[5] The Reformation is the second historical event of relevance to the compilation of the Book of the Dean of Lismore. While its scribes do not show any nascent sympathy for Protestantism, certain aspects of the compilation of the manuscript may suggest that the influence of Renaissance humanism could have been percolating through to eastern Perthshire. As I hope to show, the Book of the Dean of Lismore is a manuscript which owes its format to a number of strong impulses, some from within the Highlands, and others from the far side of the Highland line.

In assessing the Book of the Dean of Lismore, it is important to realise that we see 'through a glass darkly'. We have to hazard an intuitive guess where hard evidence seems to fail, and we have to struggle with an orthographic system to which we, in large measure, have lost the key (a key which we are in the process of rediscovering). The struggle to interpret the manuscript, in its broader and narrower aspects, can be frustrating, and we cannot but sympathize with those who have given vent to their feelings by condemning the Book and its scribes. The Gaelic scholar, faced with its peculiar orthography and appearance, may regard it as deviant and grotesque in terms of the native Gaelic scribal tradition; the Scots scholar will appreciate the format more readily, but will soon find that, while the application of Middle Scots orthography to Gaelic may facilitate

---

[4]K. Steer and J.W.M. Bannerman, *Late Medieval Monumental Sculpture in the West Highlands* (Edinburgh, 1977), pp. 211-12.

[5]D.E. Meek and J. Kirk, 'John Carswell, Superintendent of Argyll: A Reassessment', *Records of the Scottish Church History Society*, 19 (1975), 1-22 (4-5).

pronunciation of the language, it will provide no easy bridge to the contents of the manuscript. There are, in fact, some very basic questions about the manuscript which are not likely to be resolved easily. We do not know how many other manuscripts of this kind were compiled, and we do not know whether the Book of the Dean is complete as it stands. Wherever we look, there are puzzles and problems, but these add to the fascination of the manuscript as a whole.

SCRIBES AND THE PERIOD OF COMPILATION

The Book of the Dean of Lismore would appear to be the work of a group of scribes, although it is extremely difficult to define the size of the group or the contributions of its individual members. The manuscript itself takes its name from one of the three scribes who identify themselves clearly in its pages. This is sir James MacGregor, titular Dean of Lismore, who records his name and refers to the manuscript as his 'liber'. At his death in 1551, James MacGregor held the benefice of Fortingall in Perthshire, his native district, as well as the office of Dean of Lismore, of which he had possession from at least 1514.[6] If the Dean received a university education, he evidently did not progress beyond the level of bachelor, since he uses the title *dominus* ('sir') rather than *maister* ('master'), the latter signifying, in this period and later, a graduate who had gone through the full Arts curriculum of a Scottish university.[7] His brother Duncan was also involved in the compilation of the manuscript, which contains a number of his poems.[8] The manuscript may attest the signature of the father of the MacGregor brothers, Dubhghall mac Eoin Riabhaich, but his contribution to the manuscript is difficult to determine. In one poem in the manuscript, Dubhghall is portrayed as a man of literary taste, capable of compiling a *duanaire* ('poem-book'). The poet asks him to compile a poem-book without delay, and informs him that MacCailein, the Campbell chief, knows a good poem when it is taken to him to be read. It has been suggested that the poem-book in question was, in fact, the Book of the Dean, and that Dubhghall may have delegated the work to his sons.[9] This identification is arguable, since the poem does not occupy a prominent place in the manuscript itself, but it does show that the compilation of poem-books was by no means unknown in Perthshire. In addition to his apparent literary interests, Dubhghall acted as a notary public, and both he and his son James are on record in this capacity in 1511.[10]

The evidence thus indicates that the Book of the Dean had a fairly specific connection with the family of James MacGregor, Dean of Lismore. That it may

---

[6] *Scottish Verse*, ed. Watson, pp. xiv-xv.
[7] It is not unusual to find references in this period to clerics who apparently did not obtain the level of Master in the Arts curriculum.
[8] *Scottish Verse*, ed. Watson, pp. 212-17.
[9] Ibid., pp. 2-5.
[10] Ibid., pp. xiv-xv.

occasionally have gone beyond the family circle is suggested by the signature of a certain William Drummond, curate in Fortingall, who writes a brief note in Latin at the top of a page containing the opening of a well-known Gaelic ballad, 'Laoidh Fhraoich' ('The Lay of Fraoch').[11] Drummond's note and signature need not imply that he had any significant part in the compilation of the manuscript, if indeed he added anything other than his signature. Presumably such manuscripts could have travelled among different scribes and readers who would have enjoyed their contents and would have been wholly familiar with the Scots-based othography which now seems so strange to us.

The Book of the Dean contains a number of dates by which its period of compilation can be determined fairly accurately. The earliest of these is 1512, and the latest is 1542.[12] The dates recorded between those years suggest that the scribes worked on the manuscript fairly consistently throughout this period of thirty years. The compilation of the manuscript was obviously not a hasty business; it reflects the gradual compilation and recording of relevant material over a generation.

SCRIPT AND APPEARANCE OF THE MANUSCRIPT

In writing their material, the scribes of the Book of the Dean of Lismore employed what is known as secretary hand. This form of handwriting was employed by literati in England and Scotland from the late fifteenth century, and by the mid-sixteenth century it functioned as the normal business hand of both countries. In Lowland Scotland, its range of uses—legal, ecclesiastical, personal and literary—is attested by a wealth of material, much of it written in Scots and Latin.[13]

The use of this hand connects the Book of the Dean of Lismore with the wider literary world of Lowland Scotland and England, and sets it apart from Gaelic convention, both in Scotland and Ireland. In the Gaelic west, scribes generally used the script known as *corr-litir* (literally 'peaked letter'), a development of medieval insular book-hand. The Gaelic hand was highly ornate, and could be richly elaborated by means of decorated initials and such devices as rubrication.[14] Compared with medieval Gaelic manuscripts in conventional Gaelic script, the Book of the Dean looks dull and even amateurish; but it is similar in style to Lowland Scots compilations, such as the Asloan

---

[11] MS, p. 301. I am grateful to Mr. Ronald Black for allowing me to consult a draft of his forthcoming catalogue of the Book of the Dean, in which this identification is made.
[12] MS, pp. 35, 82, 144.
[13] L.C. Hector, *The Handwriting of English Documents* (London, 1958), pp. 60-61; G.G. Simpson, *Scottish Handwriting 1150-1650* (Edinburgh, 1973; rpt. Aberdeen, 1986), pp. 14-16, and plates 11-20.
[14] For an introduction to the early form of this script, see W.M. Lindsay, *Early Irish Minuscule Script* (Oxford, 1910).

Manuscript.[15] Only occasionally do its scribes attempt to provide a decorated initial, and such decoration is decidedly plain. It corresponds to the type of decoration sometimes found on contemporary notarial instruments.[16] This is what one would expect, since the scribes were schooled in the tradition of the Lowland Scots notary public. It is difficult to know whether they had any practice in the writing of the Gaelic script, although it is highly probable that they could read manuscripts written in that script.

The scribes of the Book of the Dean were capable of using different forms of secretary hand. For their poems, they employed a 'set' form of the hand, in which letters stand unconnected. For occasional jottings they often use a 'free' form of the hand with a more prominent cursive element.[17]

ORTHOGRAPHY: THE SOCIAL AND CULTURAL BACKGROUND

The greatest difference between the Book of the Dean and most other manuscripts containing Gaelic material lies in its orthography. Not only have the scribes used a form of hand quite different from Gaelic script, they have also employed a spelling system largely unrelated to the standard orthography of Classical Common Gaelic, which was taught in the bardic schools, and which can be seen in John Carswell's translation of *The Book of Common Order* of 1567.[18] The scribes were evidently not ignorant of normal Gaelic orthography, since characteristics of that othography are fossilized in certain of their spellings, and entire words occasionally appear in Gaelic form, where it would have been possible for the scribes to produce alternative spellings more in line with the basic patterns of their own method. This might suggest that their decision to reject conventional Gaelic orthography was deliberate, but that this orthography continued to exert some influence, particularly where non-Gaelic orthography was incapable of conveying the desired sounds, or could do so only clumsily.[19]

The basis of the orthography in the Book of the Dean has long been recognized to be that of Middle Scots, the term usually applied to the stage in the development of Scots—the vernacular language of the Lowlands—which had been

---

[15] *Asloan MS*, II, plates facing pp. xii and 141.

[16] An example occurs on p. 301 in the MS; cf. Simpson, *Handwriting*, p. 25.

[17] For examples, see ibid., plates 11-14. The style of the Book of the Dean of Lismore most closely resembles that of plate 12.

[18] K. Jackson, 'Common Gaelic', *Proceedings of the British Academy*, 38 (1951), 71-97; B. Ó Cúiv, 'The Linguistic Training of the Medieval Irish Poet', *Celtica*, 10 (1973), 114-40; *Foirm na n-Urrnuidheadh*, ed. R.L. Thomson, Scottish Gaelic Texts Society (Edinburgh, 1970). See also J. Bannerman's important discussion of 'Literacy in the Highlands', *The Renaissance and Reformation in Scotland: Essays in Honour of Gordon Donaldson*, ed. I.B. Cowan and D. Shaw (Edinburgh, 1983), pp. 214-35.

[19] On the orthography, see further D.E. Meek, 'Gàidhlig is Gaylick anns na Meadhon Aoisean', *Gaelic and Scotland*, ed. W. Gillies (Edinburgh, 1989), pp. 131-45; abstract in English, pp. 233-35.

attained by c. 1400, and which persisted until c. 1560.[20] The extension of Middle Scots orthography to Gaelic is a step of much greater significance than the adoption of an alien script, especially when it is maintained consistently throughout the Gaelic items in the manuscript, and with only occasional evidence of conventional Gaelic orthography. The degree of scribal commitment to the Scots-based system is all the more striking when one considers that the manuscript is probably the work of more than one scribe, that it was compiled over a long period, and that James MacGregor, whose name it bears, must have encountered practitioners of 'traditional' Gaelic orthography. The question of why the scribes utilized this orthography must be asked, since it is integral to our understanding of the manuscript.

Hitherto, it has been customary to relate the nature of the orthography to the widely-held view that the verse was recorded from oral transmission.[21] Such an opinion implies that the orthography constitutes some form of shorthand, better suited to rapid writing than conventional Gaelic orthography. Quite apart from the fact that it is by no means certain that the verse in the Book of the Dean was transcribed from oral transmission, it is apparent that words written in the orthography of the manuscript make markedly less use of scribal abbreviations than material in normal Gaelic orthography. While the orthography of the Book of the Dean does indeed allow for the removal of certain syllables which were evidently not pronounced in the scribes' dialect, it also insists upon writing in full certain other syllables which would have been abbreviated in standard Gaelic scribal practice. In the Middle Ages, speed in writing was more a matter of script than orthography, and it was this which led in large measure to the emergence of secretary hand, which the scribes use. Oral transmission of the material might be a partial explanation of the use of secretary hand in the manuscript, were such an explanation needed, but it does not account for a radical orthographic change, such as is found in the Book of the Dean. Equally unsatisfactory is the view that the scribes may have been trying to bridge the seeming gulf between the literary language of the time and the vernacular by adopting an orthography which would have given greater prominence to Scottish Gaelic and its dialects. The orthography of the manuscript preserves a great deal of the classical language alongside the vernacular; and, in any event, conventional Gaelic orthography could have been modified to incorporate vernacular features where desired, as the appearance of modernisms in contemporary (and earlier) Gaelic manuscripts amply demonstrates. At the other end of the scale, it seems unwise to attribute obscurantist motives to the scribes, since this violates the principles of manuscript compilation in the Middle Ages.[22]

---

[20]Bannerman, 'Literacy', pp. 220-21; D. Murison, *The Guid Scots Tongue* (Edinburgh, 1977), pp. 4-5.
[21]Cf. B. Ó Cúiv, *The Irish Bardic Duanaire or 'Poem-Book'*, The R.I. Best Memorial Lecture (Dublin, 1973), pp. 14-15.
[22]Most of the views considered in this paragraph have been encountered in discussion.

More cogent reasons for employing the type of orthography found in the Book of the Dean are suggested by a consideration of the linguistic situation in Scotland and the relative status of the country's two main languages in the period in which the manuscript was compiled. While Scottish Gaelic was still spoken by the bulk of the population in Galloway and Carrick until at least the time of the Reformation,[23] the language had begun its regression from the Lowlands by the second half of the fourteenth century.[24] By c. 1400, the southern boundary of Gaelic speech probably coincided with the geographical line distinguishing Highlands from Lowlands, with the exception of the areas already defined. Yet even by 1500 it would be the language of much of the Lennox, Menteith and Strathearn.[25] In the east and the north-east, few Gaelic speakers would be found on the coastal plain. Here, as in the Lowlands, the inhabitants spoke 'Inglis', that form of the Northern dialect of Anglo-Saxon which, by 1494, had come to be known by the more familiar name of 'Scottis'.[26] This change of nomenclature acknowledged the status of Scots as the national language of Scotland. At the same time, Scottish Gaelic, which had once been known in official documents as 'lingua Scotica', had come to be called 'lingua Hibernica', or 'Erse', in Scots.[27] From a Lowland viewpoint, therefore, Scottish Gaelic was to be identified with Ireland rather than with Scotland in the fifteenth century. It is probably significant that the first comic Highlander who appears in Lowland Scots verse, and who is described in 'The Buke of the Howlat' of c. 1450, is said to be 'a bard owt of Irland'.[28] Indeed, Lowland commentators who included 'Erse' in their descriptions of Scotland did so only to emphasize the deep cultural gulf separating the so-called Wild Scots from the 'domesticated' 'house-holding' Scots. Thus, in 1521, John Major could write:

> One-half of Scotland speaks Irish, and all these as well as Islanders we reckon to belong to the Wild Scots. In dress, in the manner of their outward life, and in good morals, for example, these come behind the householding Scots.

Major made it clear that the language of the latter was English.[29] In developing his theme of contrasting cultures, Major has nothing to say about the possibility of Scots/Gaelic bilingualism of the kind so obviously attested by the Book of the Dean of Lismore.

---

[23] J. MacQueen, 'Gaelic Speakers of Galloway and Carrick', *Scottish Studies*, 17 (1973), 17-33.
[24] W.F.H. Nicolaisen, *Scottish Place Names* (London, 1979), pp. 121f.
[25] R. Nicholson, *Scotland: The Later Middle Ages* (Edinburgh, 1978), Map A.
[26] J. Templeton, 'Scots: An Outline History', *Lowland Scots*, ed. A.J. Aitken, Association for Scottish Literary Studies, Occasional Papers 2 (Edinburgh, 1978), 4-19 (6).
[27] Murison, *Scots Tongue*, p. 5; D. Murison, 'The Historical Background', *Languages of Scotland*, ed. A.J. Aitken and T. MacArthur (Edinburgh, 1979), pp. 2-13 (8).
[28] M.A. Mackay, 'The Scots of the Makars', *Lowland Scots*, ed. Aitken, pp. 20-37 (27).
[29] *Scottish Historical Documents*, ed. G. Donaldson (Edinburgh, 1974), p. 101. The reference is presumably to 'Inglis', the earlier name for Scots.

The importance of Scots, at least in the Lowlands, had not come about overnight. As far back as 1398, the Scottish parliament had endorsed the status of 'Inglis' by authorizing its use as an alternative to Latin when recording Parliamentary business.[30] Such innovation served to increase the prestige of Scots in the higher domains of commerce and law. During the fifteenth century, also, the literary range of the language was being extended considerably by the Makars, whose works have come to represent the high-water mark of the Middle Scots period.[31] By the beginning of the sixteenth century, therefore, Scots had become a powerful, all-purpose language. There is evidence that it had already begun to cross the Highland Line, probably well before 1500.

In promoting the use of Scots within the Gaelic-speaking Highland area, no influence was more potent than that of Lowland central government. During the last quarter of the fifteenth century, the Scottish Crown continued its attempts to bring the Wild Scots of the north and west under its direct control.[32] This policy struck most noticeably at the Lordship of the Isles, which was finally forfeited in 1493. It also furthered the interests of clans known to be sympathetic towards central government.[33] The increasing prestige of such clans was underpinned by documentation, principally charters and bonds of manrent. The Campbells, in particular, were careful to consolidate their position in this way, and their expansion eastwards into Perthshire is witnessed by a substantial body of bonds, dating back to 1488 and continuing well into the sixteenth century. These bonds were drawn up in Scots, and they are now preserved in the Black Book of Taymouth.[34]

It is of great importance that these bonds contain evidence of the application to Gaelic of a system of spelling which is similar to that in the Book of the Dean. This system is applied primarily to place-names, personal names and surnames, but it also includes Gaelic epithets. The practice is maintained throughout this corpus, and it would appear to represent a deliberate policy by the notaries who drew up the documents. In some respects the system found in the Black Book bonds resembles the orthographic treatment given to the effusions of the 'bard owt of Irland' in 'The Buke of the Howlat'. In the case of the latter, however, the composer desires a comic effect, and he was not himself a Gaelic speaker. The Black Book bonds, on the other hand, show the application of Scots orthography to Gaelic in official documents, and the notaries may have included men who were themselves Gaelic-speaking.[35]

---

[30]Murison, *Scots Tongue*, p. 4.
[31]Mackay, 'Scots of the Makars'.
[32]R. Nicholson, 'Domesticated Scots and Wild Scots: The Relationship between Lowlanders and Highlanders in Medieval Scotland', *Scottish Colloquium Proceedings* (Guelph), I (1968), 1-16.
[33]Steer and Bannerman, *Monumental Sculpture*, pp. 207, 210-11.
[34]*The Black Book of Taymouth*, ed. C.N. Innes, Bannatyne Club (Edinburgh, 1855), pp. 177f.
[35]See further, Meek, 'Gàidhlig is Gaylick'.

Equally impressive evidence for the pervasiveness of Scots orthography in a Gaelic context in this period is furnished by West Highland monumental sculpture.[36] Here too, Gaelic personal names and surnames have often been 'Scotticized' with the occasional appearance of epithets in similar form.[37] Chronologically, the monuments suggest that the method was much in vogue after 1500, but that its beginnings may be traced well into the fifteenth century, if not the fourteenth.[38] While the Black Book bonds are pre-eminently concerned with Perthshire, stone monuments bearing 'Scotticized' forms of Gaelic names occur in the Hebrides and mainland Argyll.[39] Indeed, the inscriptions most heavily influenced by the conventions of Scots orthography are found at Kilmichael Glassary in Mid Argyll.[40] It is suggested that this may reflect the fact that:

> ...of all the districts lying within the area in which late medieval West Highland carving is found, Glassary had been most open to Lowland influences for the longest period of time. Thus, since c. 1374 the leading family in Glassary was that of Scrymgeour, whose main centre of activities was Dundee, of which they were constables.[41]

The settlement of families of Lowland origins in the Gaelic-speaking area may well have been another important factor in encouraging the extension of Scots orthography to Gaelic. In mainland Argyll, such settlement is not surprising, given the strong Lowland affiliations of the dominant clan, the Campbells.[42]

The use of 'Scotticized' forms of Gaelic names on monumental sculpture is a significant indication of the status of this orthographic trend. Clearly, such a convention was acceptable to the nobility who commissioned the monuments. Equally clearly, there existed men of letters who could supply inscriptions of this kind, and who were familiar with the basic principles of the type of orthography found in the Book of the Dean. This, together with the evidence of the Black Book bonds, is sufficient to suggest that the orthography of the Book of the Dean was not devised by its scribes. While they may have helped to develop this orthographic style, it is hard to believe that they invented it.[43]

---

[36] Steer and Bannerman, *Monumental Sculpture*, pp. 91-92.
[37] Ibid., p. 142, no. 71.
[38] Ibid., p. 146, no. 76.
[39] Ibid., pp. 97, no. 2 and 99, no. 5.
[40] Ibid., p. 143, no. 71.
[41] Ibid.
[42] Ibid., pp. 210-11; cf. W.D.H. Sellar, 'The Earliest Campbells—Norman, Briton, or Gael?' *Scottish Studies*, 17 (1973), 108-25.
[43] For the view that the Dean of Lismore may have been regarded by his Argyllshire contemporaries 'with disfavour as a Scotticized Perthshire innovator' see D.S. Thomson, 'Gaelic Learned Orders and Literati in Medieval Scotland', *Proceedings of the Third International Congress of Celtic Studies*, ed. W.F.H. Nicolaisen (Edinburgh, 1968), pp. 57-78 (68).

While the orthography of the Book of the Dean is closely related in form to the examples found in the Black Book bonds and on monumental sculpture, the scale on which it is employed in the manuscript is obviously much greater. Apart from the Book of the Dean itself, we lack evidence which might indicate at what precise time such orthography began to be used extensively in Gaelic writing, or what stimulated such a departure. The apparent fluency of the scribes of the Book of the Dean, and the small number of blunders which can be ascribed to othographic uncertainty on their part, would suggest that they were working with what was already a relatively stable tradition. Indeed, it has been argued recently that certain errors in the manuscript text are to be explained in terms of miscopying from an exemplar written in the same orthography.[44] Given the misfortunes which have so severely reduced the number of Gaelic manuscripts surviving from the Middle Ages, it would be foolish to emphasize the uniqueness of the Book of the Dean, since other compilations of a similar nature may once have existed.

In stimulating the emergence of a developed othography based on Scots, such as one finds in the Book of the Dean, it seems likely that the question of linguistic status would have been important, the more so in the unsettled period which preceded, and followed from, the forfeiture of the Lordship of the Isles.[45] It may have been envisaged by certain bilingual Scots/Gaelic scribes that the advance of Lowland bureaucracy in to the Highlands, at the hands of a Scots civil service, would alter the existing orthographic base of Gaelic. Indeed, scribes like James MacGregor, who operated as notaries public on the frontier of Scots and Gaelic, would have been particularly prone to think in these terms. Whatever the precise reason for the development of its orthography, the Book of the Dean certainly bears witness to a strong Lowland consciousness on the part of its scribes, and the evidence of monumental sculpture in particular suggests that they were not alone.

With hindsight, it is possible to conclude that the Book of the Dean of Lismore coterie had over-estimated the potential effect of Scots linguistic dominance on Gaelic orthography. Clearly, native Gaelic scribal tradition employing conventional orthography continued well beyond 1500, and the orthography of present-day Scottish Gaelic is based ultimately on that of Classical Common Gaelic. In guaranteeing the survival of the tradition, we may owe more than has hitherto been conceded to John Carswell's translation of Knox's *Book of Common Order*. Appearing as *Foirm na nUrrnuidheadh* in 1567, Carswell's translation employed the orthography of Classical Common Gaelic, and it had the vital distinction of being the first printed book to be published in

---

[44] W. Gillies, 'The Gaelic Poems of Sir Duncan Campbell of Glenorchy (I)', *Scottish Gaelic Studies*, 13.1 (1978), 18-45 (24). Parts II-III of this series are to be found ibid., 13.2 (1981), 263-88 and 14.1 (1983), 59-82.
[45] Steer and Bannerman, *Monumental Sculpture*, pp. 209-10.

Irish or Gaelic.[46] As a work of major liturgical significance, it would have exerted an influence over the writing habits of literate Gaelic ministers even if it had remained in manuscript.

The importance of such liturgical documents in directing the orthographic development of a language is paralleled, though not precisely, in the instance of Manx. Bishop Phillips's translation of the English Prayer Book into Manx, which was completed c. 1610, adopted an orthography based on that of English. Although this translation was not, in fact, available in print until the nineteenth century, it evidently set a trend, since the first Manx printed book, a bilingual version of Bishop Wilson's *Principles and Duties of Christianity*, published in 1707, also adopted an orthography based on English. While the orthography employed in the translation of Wilson's *Principles* differed from that of Phillips, and from that of subsequent Manx works, the distinctive nature of Manx orthography was thereby confirmed.[47] If the first specimen of printed Scottish Gaelic had employed a spelling system similar to that of the Book of the Dean, the orthography of the language might well have assumed a form very different from what we know today.

PRINCIPAL CONTENTS

The Book of the Dean of Lismore bears eloquent testimony to the cultural ferment of the southern Highlands (and particularly of Perthshire) in the late Middle Ages. The manuscript intertwines no less than three different cultures: Gaelic culture, in both its Irish and Scottish dimensions, which supplies the bulk of its material; Scots culture, which provides its orthography and script; and the medieval Latin culture of the pre-Reformation church.

Although the Book of the Dean is devoted primarily to verse, it does contain some prose items, mainly in Latin and Scots. The longest of these would appear to be a Latin canonical text, written on the former vellum covers of the manuscript (and therefore indicating that the Book of the Dean as we now know it consists of at least two different manuscripts). There is a substantial amount of historical material, consisting chiefly of king lists, chronicles and pedigrees;[48] and there is a wide variety of notes and jottings, relating to domestic, personal, scientific and business matters, some of these being in Gaelic.[49] The relative scarcity of Gaelic prose material in the manuscript is interesting, and suggests that the scribes were aware of a distinction between the roles of the

---

[46]Meek and Kirk, 'John Carswell'.
[47]R.L. Thomson, 'The Study of Manx Gaelic', *Proceedings of the British Academy*, 55 (1969), 177-210 (178-84).
[48]MS, pp. 27, 44, 78, 83, 141, 144, 171, 186, 242, 243.
[49]MS, pp. 48, 59b, 74, 92d, 250.

languages at their disposal. The manuscript clearly indicates language-switching (Gaelic/Scots/Latin) and probable diglossia (Gaelic/Scots).[50]

If Gaelic prose items do not figure prominently in the Book of the Dean, Gaelic verse accounts for the largest part of its contents. Extracts from the Scots poets Dunbar and Henryson, and the English poet Lydgate, do of course appear, and these are an important indication of the compilers' contact with the literary world of the Lowlands and beyond;[51] but they are overshadowed by the large collection of Gaelic poetry found in the manuscript. This collection consists wholly of *dán* or syllabic verse, in varying degrees of strictness. Such verse was the primary literary product of the classical Gaelic world.[52]

Apart from individual quatrains, which are often very difficult to classify in broad terms, the Book of the Dean contains three main types of *dán*. These intermingle throughout the manuscript, although sequences of related items occur from time to time. The most conspicuous category is bardic verse, which includes elegy, eulogy, satire and religious poetry. Irish and Scottish authors are represented, the latter outnumbering the former by about 44 to 21.[53] Much, but not all, of this type of verse has been edited.[54] Heroic verse or 'ballads' forms the second largest category of poetry in the manuscript.[55] The third category of *dán* in the Book of the Dean is courtly and satiric verse, ascribed to Irish and Scottish authors. This has received much less attention than the other two types, but it is currently being studied in considerable detail, notably by Professor William Gillies, who has produced very important editions of the poetry of Sir Duncan Campbell of Glenorchy.[56]

PROVENANCE OF BARDIC VERSE
IN THE BOOK OF THE DEAN OF LISMORE

Although the compilers of the Book of the Dean operated in the Perthshire area, the contents of the manuscript indicate that they were drawing on the resources of the classical Gaelic world, embracing Ireland and Gaelic Scotland. The bardic verse in the manuscript is of particular value in demonstrating the

---

[50] Items such as shopping-lists tend to be in Scots rather than Gaelic.
[51] MS, pp. 48, 77, 92b, 144, 184.
[52] For a general introduction with numerous references to the Book of the Dean, see E.C. Quiggin, *Prolegomena to the Study of the Later Irish Bards 1200-1500*, American Committee for Irish Studies (reprinted from *Proceedings of the British Academy*, 5 (1911-12), 89-143).
[53] T.F. O'Rahilly, 'Indexes to the Book of the Dean of Lismore', *Scottish Gaelic Studies*, 4 (1934), 31-56.
[54] *Scottish Verse*, ed. Watson, contains only a selection.
[55] D.E. Meek, 'The Corpus of Heroic Verse in the Book of the Dean of Lismore', Diss. University of Glasgow, 1982.
[56] W. Gillies, 'Courtly and Satiric Poetry from the Book of the Dean of Lismore', *Scottish Studies*, 21 (1977), 35-53; see also note 44.

specific parts of Ireland and Scotland in which they were interested, and to which they had ready access.

The Irish material in the Book of the Dean represents the following areas and families:

Tyrone	Ó Néill (1 poem), MacGillmurray of Clandeboy (1 poem)[57]
Brefny	Ó Ruairc (2 poems)[58]
Connacht	Ó Conchobhair (?6 poems), MacDiarmaid (3 poems), de Burca (2 poems), Ó Ceallaigh (1 poem)[59]
Fermanagh	Mág Uidhir (2 poems)[60]
Westmeath	Mág Eochagáin (1 poem)[61]
Thomond	Ó Briain (2 poems)[62]
Munster	Ó Caoimh (1 poem)[63]

Such evidence would seem to show that the scribes of the Book of the Dean were interested in the north and west of Ireland, but that they were pre-eminently concerned with Connacht (and specifically the district to the east and south of Sligo).

The territorial bias of Scottish bardic verse in the Book of the Dean has been recognized for some time. The following Scottish families are represented: MacGregor, MacDonald, Campbell of Argyll, MacDougall of Dunollie, MacLeod of Lewis, MacLeod of Harris and Dunvegan, Stewart of Rannoch, MacNeill of Gigha and MacSween of Knapdale.[64] Dr John Bannerman has recently argued that this distribution pattern, beginning at Fortingall and proceeding westwards to the islands of Lewis and Gigha, 'would be an extraordinary one seen in any light other than that of the Lordship of the Isles'.[65] The manuscript seems indeed to confirm on other evidence that the scribes were in touch with poets who had enjoyed the patronage of the Lordship in the concluding years of its *de iure* existence. Giolla Coluim mac an Ollaimh, for example, is represented by four poems in the Book of the Dean, two of which deal with matters relating to the Lordship—the one a lament on the death of Angus, son of John of the Isles, and the other lamenting the demise of the Lordship itself.[66] It seems possible that Giolla Coluim was a member of the most prominent bardic family within the Lordship, the MacMhuirichs.[67]

---

[57] MS, pp. 75, 122.
[58] MS, pp. 8, 54.
[59] MS, pp. 16, 20, 41, 97, 101?, 106, 153, 244, 246, 269?, 286, 287.
[60] MS, pp. 177, 244.
[61] MS, p. 177.
[62] MS, pp. 124, 310.
[63] MS, p. 226.
[64] *Scottish Verse*, ed. Watson, pp. xvii-xviii.
[65] Steer and Bannerman, *Monumental Sculpture*, p. 206.
[66] *Scottish Verse*, ed. Watson, pp. 66-95.
[67] D.S. Thomson, 'The MacMhuirich Bardic Family', *Transactions of the Gaelic Society of Inverness*, 43 (1960-63), 276-304.

The territorial and cultural interests of the Lordship of the Isles were not restricted to Gaelic Scotland. Ireland came firmly within its orbit, and the links between the Lordship and the north of Ireland were especially strong from the late fourteenth century, when John Mór acquired possession of the Glens of Antrim through his marriage to the Bisset heiress.[68] Such marriages served to strengthen the wider political framework, within which there existed a web of interconnections, linking Scottish professional families—clerics, poets, craftsmen, doctors, musicians—with their Irish blood relations.[69] The MacMhuirichs provide a fine example of a Scottish family of poets descended from an Irish ancestor, Muireadhach Ó Dálaigh. At the time of his flight to Scotland in 1213, Muireadhach resided at Lissadil, near Sligo—a geographical point of interest which may bear on the regional pattern of Irish bardic verse in the Book of the Dean.[70] It is certainly evident that the scribes of the Book of the Dean afford considerable prominence to Ó Dálaigh poets.[71]

It would be incorrect to suggest, however, that the Irish material in the Book of the Dean was acquired solely through the MacMhuirichs, or that kin connections were indispensable. Professional men moved between Ireland and Scotland in pursuit of patronage from willing employers. Two Scottish poets represented in the Book of the Dean—Fionnlagh Ruadh and Giolla Críost Brúilingeach (the latter possibly a Galbraith from Gigha)—evidently attended the court of the MacDiarmaids of Loch Cé in Connacht in the mid-fifteenth century. Gioll Críost was also familiar with the court of Mág Uidhir of Fermanagh.[72] Both courts lie in the part of Ireland of greatest interest to the scribes of the Book of the Dean.

While the Lordship of the Isles provided outstanding opportunities for cultural links between Scotland and Ireland, these links did not cease with the collapse of the Lordship. The Campbells, it must be remembered, had strong Gaelic interests, with Irish dimensions. Their own poets, the MacEwans, were probably a branch of the Irish bardic family of Ó hEóghusa (O'Hosey).[73] Irish poets also came to the Campbell court, as when Mac Cailein received, sometime around 1555, a chief-poet on an errand from an O'Donnell chief.[74] A consciousness of Ireland is evident too in the work of John Carswell, himself a protégé of the Argyll house with a classical bardic training.[75]

---

[68] Steer and Bannerman, *Monumental Sculpture*, pp. 162-63.
[69] See, in general, J. Bannerman, 'The Lordship of the Isles', in *Scottish Society in the Fifteenth Century*, ed. J. Brown (London, 1977), pp. 209-40, and Thomson, 'Gaelic Learned Orders'.
[70] Thomson, 'MacMhuirich Bardic Family', 277-78.
[71] Thomson, 'Gaelic Learned Orders', p. 74.
[72] Ibid., p. 69; *Scottish Verse*, ed. Watson, pp. 32-59, 148-57.
[73] Bannerman, 'Lordship', p. 234.
[74] W. Gillies, 'Some Aspects of Campbell History', *Transactions of the Gaelic Society of Inverness*, 50 (1976-8), 256-95 (260).
[75] Thomson, *Foirm na n-Urrnuidheadh*, p. 10.

While the Book of the Dean may be retrospective in its choice of material, and much indebted to the heritage of the Lordship of the Isles, it must equally be emphasized that it has close connections with the Campbells. Its scribes were vassals of the Campbells of Glenorchy, it contains verse dedicated to or even composed by members of the Campbell aristocracy, and the whole manuscript was compiled in territory under Campbell sway.[76] Such circumstances suggest continuity of traditional Gaelic values among a clan usually portrayed as enemies of the old Gaelic world.

THE NATURE OF THE SCRIBES' SOURCES: ORAL OR LITERARY?

The question of whether the scribes of the Book of the Dean used oral or literary sources, particularly in the compilation of their Gaelic verse material, has not yet been investigated with reference to the entire manuscript. Opinions expressed hitherto have applied to specific genres within the manuscript, or even to individual items of verse. The dangers of generalization, or mere assumption, must therefore be emphasized in view of our knowledge to date and the intrinsic complexity of the manuscript. However, we may review the conclusions reached by scholars since 1803.

Early investigators do not appear to have been troubled by this matter. The Highland Society's *Inquiry into the Authenticity of the Poems of Ossian*—more concerned with the existence of Ossianic verse than with its transmission—did not pronounce on the possible sources of the Book of the Dean's ballad texts. Their Report draws attention to the correspondence between the items in the Book of the Dean and versions in later collections from oral tradition.[77] This could indicate that the Book of the Dean was regarded as drawing on what was available orally. Nevertheless, the Report also notes that the pedigree on page 144 of the manuscript was derived from 'the books of the history of the kings'.[78]

One suspects that the heroic ballad material in the Book of the Dean was of considerable importance in determining scholarly attitudes to the compilation of the manuscript, especially since numerous collections of heroic verse had indeed been made from oral transmission in the Highlands in the eighteenth and nineteenth centuries. This, in part, may well have influenced Professor Donald MacKinnon to conclude that 'the greater part, if not the whole, of the Gaelic verse must have been written to dictation or from memory'.[79] This general conclusion was inscribed in a preface to the manuscript which was added (presumably by Professor MacKinnon) when it was rebound in 1911.

---

[76]Gillies, 'Campbell History', 258-59.
[77]H. Mackenzie, *Report of the Committee of the Highland Society of Scotland appointed to Inquire into the Nature and Authenticity of the Poems of Ossian* (Edinburgh, 1805), p. 301.
[78]Ibid., p. 300.
[79]D. MacKinnon, *A Descriptive Catalogue of Gaelic Manuscripts* (Edinburgh, 1912), p. 229.

MacKinnon was, however, prepared to admit that 'the writers may have sometimes transcribed from manuscripts', and he too noted the significance of the scribal note on the source of the pedigree on page 144 of the manuscript.[80] It would seem, therefore, that he made a distinction between Gaelic verse items in the manuscript and other material.

Support for the view that the Book of the Dean drew on oral sources was also derived from certain features of the manuscript itself. Neil Ross argued in 1939 that 'the reproduction of the spoken dialect, and the nature of the corrections, tend to show that the ballads were not transcribed from a written source'.[81] More recently, the unusual orthography of the manuscript has been adduced as evidence of transcription from dictation or recitation.[82]

This approach to the compilation of the Book of the Dean has not received unqualified acceptance, nonetheless. In 1931, Professor Christiansen noted the close correspondence between certain of the ballad texts of the Book of the Dean and versions in Irish manuscripts. He concluded from a detailed scrutiny of one particular text that it was 'legitimate' to think that 'the Dean copied this from some songbook, and did not write it down from what he heard recited'.[83] In 1937, Professor Watson, with specific reference to the bardic verse in the manuscript, wrote: 'Whether the writers consulted manuscripts or depended mainly on oral sources is a difficult question'.[84] This non-committal statement is at least interesting in that it does not endorse fully the prevalent oral theory.

The latest textual research on sections of the Book of the Dean, undertaken by Professor William Gillies, has similarly raised the possibility that the scribes had access to manuscripts, at least in certain cases. Gillies has also suggested that, on occasion, they may have used exemplars in an orthography similar to that of the Book of the Dean itself. Yet, in the case of one poem, the same editor concludes:

> ...there seems at least a possibility that...[it] was at some stage written down from recitation or dictation by someone who did not recognise or comprehend all he heard.[85]

The evidence of the body of heroic ballads in the manuscript suggests that most of these items were probably transcribed from manuscripts, and not recorded from oral transmission as has generally been maintained. Such a conclusion is by no

---

[80] Ibid.
[81] Ross, *Heroic Poetry*, p. xiv; cf. MacKinnon, *Catalogue*, p. 229.
[82] Ó Cuív, *Irish Bardic Duanaire*, p. 14.
[83] R. Th. Christiansen, *The Vikings and the Viking Wars in Irish and Gaelic Tradition* (Oslo, 1931), pp. 40-46 and especially p. 42, note 7.
[84] *Scottish Verse*, ed. Watson, p. xviii.
[85] Gillies, 'Duncan Campbell (I)', 24, 31, 35, 41; W. Gillies, 'A Religious Poem Ascribed to Muireadhach Ó Dálaigh', *Studia Celtica*, 14-15 (1979-80), 81-86 (83-84).

means inconsistent with the methods of transmitting ballad verse, or with the nature of the medieval Gaelic world, which supported a vigorous scribal tradition alongside a flourishing oral culture. At the same time, it does not deny the possibility that such verse could have been transmitted orally before it was placed in the exemplars which may have been used by the scribes of the Book of the Dean.

SCRIBAL ALTERATION OF TEXTS

The question of whether the scribes of the Book of the Dean of Lismore had access to oral or written sources is raised by the manner in which they present some of their texts. In a number of texts, especially among the ballad items, the scribes have obviously been at work emending their first drafts, and their emendations are generally represented by the cancellation of words, phrases and occasionally whole lines. When the scribes cancel their first readings, they write their 'new' readings in superscript, immediately above their cancellations. When the superscript readings are checked, it can be seen that they derive from alternative versions of the texts. In some instances further quatrains are added to the text, usually in the bottom margins of pages. Such emendation is to be distinguished carefully from scribal attempts to correct spelling or to rewrite 'difficult' words employing a more satisfactory 'set' of letters from the options available within their orthographic system. Elsewhere I have given a fairly detailed account of these emendations as they affect the ballad texts in the manuscript, and I have discussed their significance for the likely development of the texts themselves.[86] On this occasion I wish merely to draw attention to the wider implications of these emendations for the compilation of the manuscript; and I wish to conclude the chapter with a speculative touch, since the Book of the Dean of Lismore sometimes invites speculation.

It needs to be noted that the Perthshire scribes' practice of visible emendation within the manuscript is, as far as I am aware, unique within the Gaelic and Scots tradition in the Middle Ages. Gaelic manuscripts, compiled in the traditional manner in Ireland or in Scotland, do not show emendation of this kind. The same family of scribes could record different versions of the same poem, but this is normally done in separate manuscripts. I know of no other Gaelic manuscript before 1600 which shows signs that a scribe was comparing one version of a poem with another, and making alterations as he went along. Evidence for this sort of 'editing' is, however, found after 1600, chiefly in the manuscript collection of the Rev. James McLagan, which includes many ballad texts collected in the Highlands after 1750.[87] On the Scots side, I am informed that there is no equivalent to the practice of the scribes of the Book of the Dean.

---

[86]D.E. Meek, 'Development and Degeneration in Gaelic Ballad Texts', *The Heroic Process: Form, Function and Fantasy in Folk Epic*, ed. Bo Almqvist et al. (Dublin, 1987), pp. 131-60.

[87]See, for example, the text of the 'Lay of Fraoch' in McLagan MS 245. (The McLagan MSS are housed in Glasgow University Library.)

We may be permitted to draw one or two conclusions from the evidence of the Book of the Dean of Lismore with regard to the attitudes of the scribes to the texts available to them. The first conclusion is that they were poring over different versions of their texts, and looking out for textual divergence. When they found divergences, they attempted to produce a single text of an eclectic type, perhaps believing that there ought somehow to be a single, reliable text of a poem. The second conclusion which, I think, is warranted, is that the scribes were probably using manuscript versions of at least some of their poems. It is very difficult for me to conceive of their 'editing' in terms of memorization and subsequent comparison of orally-derived versions, especially in instances where the poems are extremely long.[88]

The real difficulty, however, is to find a suitable context for such activity, and to know why the scribes should have operated in this matter. It is at this point, therefore, that I propose to become speculative, and to advance what can be no more than a theory. My guess is that we are seeing here some degree of humanist influence, and I suspect that our scribes, although tucked away in their corner of eastern Perthshire, are responding to a characteristic urge of the European scholars of the Renaissance, namely the desire to gather, compare and 'edit' manuscripts.[89] The humanists were primarily concerned with classical texts, and sought to edit influential Greek and Latin works; but it is not impossible that some turned to the vernacular tradition, since an interest in vernacular languages was developing in this period.[90] We are, of course, entirely in the dark as to how the Perthshire scribes may have absorbed such principles. It would be intriguing to know who taught them to write, and whether they even paid the occasional visit to that centre of humanism in the north, namely King's College, Old Aberdeen.[91]

CONCLUSION

The Book of the Dean of Lismore can be viewed in many different ways, depending on which strand of its complex make-up one is prepared to emphasize. It owes much to the cultural riches of the defunct Lordship of the Isles; its catchment area extends as far north as Lewis and as far south as Co. Clare in Ireland, through a network of family loyalties and cultural relationships; it was compiled in an area under the jurisdiction of the Campbells of Glenorchy; and its

---

[88]The poem which shows the greatest amount of emendation is 72 quatrains in length; see Meek, 'Development and Degeneration', 141-43, 147-51.

[89]Studies in this field include J.R. Hale, *Renaissance Europe* (London, 1980), especially Chapter 8; and R.H. Bainton, *Erasmus of Christendom* (London, 1972), especially Chapter 6. For Scotland, see the succinct discussion of 'Humanism' by A. Ross, in *A Companion to Scottish Culture*, ed. D. Daiches (London, 1981), pp. 173-74.

[90]It is important to bear in mind that the Book of the Dean contains an extensive selection of the 'classical' Gaelic verse of the Middle Ages.

[91]Ross, 'Humanism'.

scribes employ an orthography which is unashamedly derived from that of Middle Scots. Yet, if we persist in seeing the manuscript in terms of individual strands, we do it less than justice. It is more satisfying, if at times more perplexing, to take the broadest possible view, and to see this 'fortunate survivor' as part of a larger European cultural tapestry which was being woven in the first half of the sixteenth century.

13

ICONOGRAPHY AND LITERATURE IN THE SERVICE OF DIPLOMACY:

THE FRANCO-SCOTTISH ALLIANCE, JAMES V AND SCOTLAND'S TWO FRENCH QUEENS, MADELEINE OF FRANCE AND MARY OF GUISE

Dana Bentley-Cranch & Rosalind K. Marshall

On the 22 December 1536 the President of the Parliament of Paris rode out to Fontainebleau to complain to King Francis I that it was not customary for his members to wear their red robes to honour a foreign Prince entering their city. The French King replied firmly that the red robes were obligatory on this occasion; that for the marriage of his daughter Madeleine to the King of Scots, the same honour given to Francis himself must be bestowed upon James V, his 'très cher et très amé frère et filz', who had come in person to ask for Madeleine's hand.[1] The importance accorded by the French to the Scottish marriage and their anxious desire to make the ceremony a solemn and noteworthy one is encapsulated in this little incident.

In the Auld Alliance that had linked it to France since 1295, Scotland was generally considered to be the 'junior partner'. How had it thus come about that, by 1536, Scotland had achieved, to say the least, an equal role?

To determine the answer one has to go back to the events of 1525. The crushing defeat of France's army in February of that year at the Battle of Pavia left her King Francis I a prisoner in the hands of the Emperor Charles V and the country in disarray. The King's mother, the Regent Louise of Savoy, and her chief minister, Florimond Robertet,[2] quickly set in motion a number of diplomatic moves designed to marshall France's allies and avert the threatened

---

[1] See *Papiers d'etat, pièces et documents inédits ou peu connus relatifs à l'histoire de l'Écosse au XVI*^{e} *siècle*, ed. A. Teulet, 3 vols, Bannatyne Club (Paris, 1852-60), I, 122-23, and *L&P Henry VIII*, XI, no. 1352.

[2] On Florimond Robertet see C.A. Mayer and D. Bentley-Cranch, *Florimond Robertet (?-1527): Homme d'état français* (Paris, 1994); C.A. Mayer and D. Bentley-Cranch, 'Florimond Robertet: Italianisme et Renaissance française', *Mélanges à la mémoire de Franco Simone*, (Geneva, 1983), IV, 135-49, rpt. in *C.A. Mayer, Clément Marot et autres études sur la littérature française de la Renaissance en l'honneur du 75*^{e} *anniversaire de C.A. Mayer*, ed. T. Peach and P.M. Smith (Paris, 1993), pp. 339-53, and R. Scheurer and A. Lapeyre, *Les Notaires et Secrétaires d'Etat du Roi sous les règnes de Louis XI, Charles VIII et Louis XII (1461-1515)*, 2 vols (Paris, 1978), I, no. 589.

English invasion of that stricken country. One of these moves was to invoke the Treaty of Rouen signed with Scotland in 1517. That Treaty,[3] sealed by the Duke of Albany for the then five-year-old James V, and by the Duke of Alençon for his brother-in-law King Francis, followed the conventional lines of requiring the two countries to render mutual assistance if attacked. A supplementary clause, however, although couched in vague terms, inaugurated the notion of a Franco-Scottish marriage, by promising to James V 'a daughter of the French King already living or yet to be born'.[4] At the time of the Treaty in 1517, Francis's first daughter Louise had just died; the only living French Princess was the 'puisnée' Charlotte, aged one year. By 1525 she too was dead, but the 'yet to be born' condition was fulfilled by the appearance of two further daughters, Madeleine, born on 10 August 1520, and Marguerite, born in 1523. In June 1525 a long Memorandum of Instructions was prepared by Louise and Robertet for the French envoy to Scotland, Monseigneur de Sagnes.[5] Sagnes was instructed to emphasize the necessity of maintaining the Auld Alliance, to point out the dangers for Scotland in uniting with England, to offer James V's mother, Margaret Tudor, acting at that time as his Regent, a pension and, if necessary, a refuge in France, to arrange pensions for various friendly 'seigneurs d'Escosse' and, finally and most important, to prevent the possible English marriage alliance between James V and Henry VIII's daughter Mary, by stressing the advantages of the French alliance proposed in the Treaty of Rouen.[6]

Was it at this interesting moment that the French conceived the notion of bringing iconography into the service of diplomacy by commissioning from the Court painter Jean Clouet a picture of the 'available' little French Princess Madeleine? Clouet's drawing [Fig. 1][7] portrays a pretty, plump, healthy-looking—and potentially marriageable—five-year-old girl. Politically motivated, and perhaps originally intended mainly as a preliminary sketch for the little oil painting (now unfortunately lost[8]) of the Princess, this drawing not only

---

[3] See *Papiers d'état*, ed. Teulet, I, 39-43.

[4] Ibid., I, 42: 'Outre plus, pour la grande amour et très cordialle affection que ont les dicts Seigneurs Roys l'un à l'autre, et pour corroboracion de l'alliance et confédéracion faicte entre eulx, avons accordé que, si la promesse par le dict Seigneur faicte de sa fille puisnée au Roy Catholique ou à son frère n'a lieu, au dict cas, et elle parvenue en l'aage de povoir contracter mariage, procurera le dict Seigneur envers elle de prendre et avoir pour mary et espoux le dict seigneur Roy d'Escosse; et si la promesse faicte par le dict Seigneur de sa fille au dict Roy Catholique ou à son frère a lieu, et il plaise à Dieu lui donner une autre fille, quand sera venue d'aage parfaict à contracter mariage, procurera le dict Seigneur envers elle de prandre pour mary et espoux son dict frère et cousin, et le tout si nostre Mère Saincte Église s'i accorde'.

[5] Ibid., I, 59-66: 'Instructions à Monsr. de Sagnes, conseiller en sa court de Parlement à Toulouse [envoyé] devers le Roy, Royne, Seigneurs, Conseil et Estatz d'Escosse'.

[6] Ibid., I, 66: 'D'autre part, par le traicté de Rouen, ledict Roy d'Escosse doit avoir une fille de France qui est telle alliance et affinité que chacun congnoist'.

[7] Musée Condé, Château de Chantilly. See R. de Broglie, *Les Clouet de Chantilly, Catalogue illustré, extrait de la 'Gazette des Beaux-Arts'* (Paris, 1971), no. 349; inscribed 'La Royne Madellaine descoce', black and red chalk, 27.6 x 19.8 cm, large damp stain at lower right.

[8] P. Mellen, *Jean Clouet, Complete Edition of the Drawings, Miniatures and Paintings* (London, 1971), catalogue no. 137 and plate 39; oil on panel, c. 16.2 x 12.7 cm. This portrait was in the collection of Baron Edouard de Rothschild in Paris in 1933, when it was described by L. Dimier in

demonstrates the artist's unusually sensitive approach to a child sitter, but achieved widespread popularity in its own right—Clouet copied it himself at least once,[9] and it appeared in six contemporary albums.[10]

Eleven years later France was still embroiled with the Emperor and her need of Scotland as an ally had not diminished. In July 1536, although war had not been declared, the Emperor invaded Provence in the south of France while his ally Henry of Nassau attacked in the north. On the advice of his generals Francis directed the campaigns against both these invasions from the vicinity of Lyons. His Grand Master, Anne de Montmorency, compelled the Emperor to retreat, and Nassau eventually had to retire into Flanders. But before the news of the French successes reached Scotland, James V, according to a contemporary chronicle, had already set sail to offer help to the French King.[11] Landing at Dieppe and hearing that Francis and the Emperor were about to engage in battle, he had travelled post-haste towards Lyons and was received by Francis with open arms.

At the age of twenty-four James had rejected several prospective brides, including the daughter of the Duke of Vendôme,[12] and was still unmarried. When

---

'Un nouveau portrait de Jean Clouet', *Gazette des Beaux-Arts*, 2 (1933), 100-3. It disappeared during the 1939-45 War, and is known now only from a photograph. Madeleine is shown exactly as in the drawing, with the addition of her two hands holding a toy decorated with bells.
[9]Musée Condé, Château de Chantilly. See de Broglie, *Catalogue illustré*, no. 350; inscribed: 'AN. ÆT. SUÆ 4'.
[10]Drawings by the Clouets were often copied by unknown or amateur artists, and the copies copied in their turn and bound into albums, some of which have survived to the present day. The drawings in these 'home-made' albums are often crude and of little artistic merit, but they provide evidence of what was obviously a popular practice. Copies of Clouet's 'Madeleine' are in the Uffizi, Hermitage, Aix, Medici, Walpole and Bibliothèque Nationale, Paris, Albums. See Mellen, *Jean Clouet*, p. 217.
[11]*Mémoires de Martin et Guillaume Du Bellay*, ed. V.-L. Bourrilly and F. Vindry, 4 vols (Paris, 1908-19), III, 338-39: 'Octobre 1536. Le Roy [Francis] des lors qu'il eut donné ordre à Lion pour toutes les frontieres de son royaume, deslogea de Lion, et sur le chemin au hault de la montagne de Tarare, entre ledit lieu de Tarare et de S. Saphorin, où il y a un lieu qui s'appelle La Chapelle, auquel lieu estant là au disner, le vint trouver le Roy d'Escosse, lequel ainsi comme j'ay dict en autre endroit, ayant eu nouvelles de la descente de l'Empereur ès pais du Roy, avait fait faire en ses pais discretion de seize mille hommes pour venir au secours dudit seigneur, et ce sans requeste ny sceu d'iceluy; et jà s'estoit ledit Roy d'Escosse embarqué par deux fois, mais avoit esté repoussé par vent contraire, finablement et sans difficulté, arriva jusques en Normandie avecques aucuns de ses navires et print terre au havre de Dieppe. Là il oit nouvelles que l'Empereur et le roy estoient sur le point de se donner la bataille, et à ceste cause pour n'y faillir il print la poste, mais sur le chemin il eut nouvelles de la retraite de l'Empereur, qui fut occasion qu'il modera la diligence de ses postes, pour surattendre son train qui venoit apres luy; mais le Roy envoya au devant de luy pour le haster et qu'il laissait venir son train apres, et trouva ledit Roy d'Escosse ainsi que j'ay dict cy devant à ladite Chapelle, auquel lieu il fut grandement recueilly du Roy et apres plusieurs autres propos lui demanda l'une de ses filles en mariage'.
[12]In 1534 Francis had offered James Marie de Vendôme as a bride. James had agreed, somewhat reluctantly, and Francis had subsequently taken Marie under his protection as the future Queen of Scots; the marriage contract was signed on 6 March 1536. According to some sources, James, after landing at Dieppe in October 1536, travelled first, incognito, to St Quentin to see Marie for himself and finding her very plain, resolved not to continue with the marriage. This incident may have taken place, although it should be noted that St Quentin is far from being on a direct route from Dieppe to Lyons. The Du Bellay chronicle does not mention this detail; it points out, however,

he asked Francis for the hand of his daughter Madeleine, the French King now gladly accorded it to his ally who was presumably fulfilling the terms of the Treaty of Rouen by coming personally to his assistance in a moment of danger.[13]

When the French Court was still in the vicinity of Lyons, the English ambassador was writing home anxiously: '[t]he King [James V] is made much of and treated as the Dolfynne was, with the Dolfynne's servants to wait on him'.[14] The Papal Nuncio was reporting similarly: '...he stands on the most familiar footing [and]...it is considered certain that they will give him Madame Madalena'.[15] It was at this moment, October 1536, that iconography took a part in the events, when the young couple were probably painted by one of the leading French Renaissance portrait-painters, Corneille de Lyon. Corneille, highly praised by his contemporaries for his ability to catch a likeness, lived and worked in Lyons where his *atelier* responded to the overwhelming demand for portraits of notables by producing multiple copies of his works. The portrait believed to be of James, [Fig. 2][16] shows him as handsome and elegant,[17] with possibly a

---

the double difficulty in which Francis found himself in giving offence to both England and to the Duke of Vendôme.

[13]*Mémoires*, ed. Bourrilly and Vindry, III, 339: 'Le Roy [Francis] encores qu'il sceust très bien combien il seroit difficile de le faire trouver bon au Roy d'Angleterre, aussi qu'il luy sembloit aucunement faire tort à la fille de Vendosme qu'il avoit desjà comme future royne d'Escosse adoptée en fille, n'osa purement esconduire ledict Roy, considerant la franche volonté dont il avoit usé envers luy considerant aussi l'ancienne alliance des deux royaumes de France et d'Escosse et que le pere dudit Roy estoit mort en bataille pour le parti du feu Roy Lois douziesme [a reference to the death of King James IV at the Battle of Flodden Field when fighting England to help his ally France]...remist la chose en deliberation d'entre eux deux...'.

[14]*L&P Henry VIII*, XI, no. 916: John Penven to [Sir George] Douglas, 29 October 1536.

[15]Ibid., no. 848: Ridolfo Pio, Bishop of Faenza, Papal Nuncio in France, to Mons. Girolamo Dandino, 23 October 1536.

[16]In the Collection of the National Trust at Polesden Lacey, oil on panel, 15 x 12.5 cm with a bright green background which was one of the hall-marks of Corneille's style. The King wears a black court bonnet with a white plume, a black doublet decorated all over with gold bugles and fastened on the right shoulder with four red jewels or buttons. His shirt has an elaborately frilled and embroidered collar; its ties, or bandstrings, hang down at the front. He wears the medallion of an Order, possibly that of the French Order of St Michael, bestowed on him by King Francis early in 1536. An inscription in an old hand on the back of the panel reads: 'Le Roi âgé 25'. Another version of this portrait has recently come to light in the London salerooms and a third was sold in Paris in 1921, but its present whereabouts are unknown. There remains at the time of writing some debate as to whether the sitter is James, since it has been pointed out that in the extant portraits of the King his nose is longer and more aquiline than in the Polesden Lacey images. On the other hand, no alternative candidate for 'Le Roi âgé 25' exists; James was in Lyons at the right time; the costume he wears is appropriate to him and the presumed date; and the existence of multiple copies of a Corneille portrait signifies a sitter of prime importance. Again, the features of Mary of Guise in the double portrait at Blair Castle do not bear much resemblance to those seen in the later drawing of her in the British Museum.

[17]The principal evidence for James V's appearance is iconographic, but a few verbal references do exist. On 15 November 1524 the English envoys to Sotland, Magnus and Ratcliff, reported to Cardinal Wolsey that 'in person, face and manner he [James V, aged 12] resembles Henry VIII', *L&P Henry VIII*, IV, pt. i, 372. John Leslie's *The Historie of Scotland*, published in 1596, has one relevant passage. The Scottish Text Society version of 1895, edited by J. Dalrymple, records (II, 260) that James was 'of midway stature; of a notable forme; a cumlie countenance...his face sa sueite; humane wes his speiche and gentle, his eye verie modest, bot quick and scharpe', while the Bannatyne Club version of 1830, ed. T. Thomson, reads (p. 166), 'his eyes graye and

glimpse of the deeper and introspective nature of this intelligent and highly-strung young monarch. There can be no doubt that Madeleine's portrait, showing her as a sweet-faced young girl of sixteen, was popular and fulfilled its political purpose; of the many copies which were probably produced, two examples have survived to the present day [Fig. 3].[18] And Corneille's charming representation was reproduced, either by the master himself or by an unknown artist, in a Book of Hours belonging to Francis in a tiny picture portraying the ladies of the King's family [Fig. 4].[19] It also served as the official image of the young Queen of Scots in Guillaume Roville's genealogical picture-book [Fig. 5].[20]

Francis, accompanied by Madeleine, James V, the Dauphin, the French Court and the ambassadors, set off towards Fontainebleau, despatching on the way a stream of orders and instructions for the wedding arrangements. These revealed that the 'Scottish marriage', in spite of the anticipated objections from England, was viewed as a diplomatic triumph for France, for the preparations set in train for the ceremony were elaborate. The marriage contract was signed at Blois in the presence of leading French notables, 'presentibus illustrissimis Principibus et Dominis, Delphino Franciae, Rege Navarrae, Cardinalibus de Lotharingia, Le Veneur et de Bellay, Cancellario Franciae, Domino de Montmorency magno magistro et Mareschallo Franciae...'.[21] The event was duly reported by the Papal Nuncio: 'Yesterday evening the king of Scots and Madame

---

scharp of sicht, that quhomsoevir he did ones see and marke, he wald perfytly knawe in all tymes thairefter'. See also R. K. Marshall, '"To be the Kingis Grace ane Dowblett": The Costume of James V, King of Scots', *Costume*, 28 (1994), 14-21, R.K. Marshall, *Mary of Guise* (London, 1977), p. 41 and R.K. Marshall, *Queen of Scots* (Edinburgh, 1986), p. 21.

[18]One example (reproduced here) is in the Château of Blois, to which it was donated in 1854, oil on panel, 14 x 10 cm, bright green background. Madeleine's dress is black with a square collar edged with jewels, ermine sleeves and a necklace of pearls and jewels attached to the shoulders. This picture was exhibited in 1907 in Paris, *Exposition de Portraits peints et dessinés du XIIIe au XVIe siècle*, no. 403; in 1932 at the Royal Academy, London, *Exhibition of French Art*; in 1937 in Paris, *Chefs d'œuvre de l'art français*, no. 47; in 1949 in Geneva and in 1965 in Paris, *Le XVIe siècle Européen*, no. 81. The second example is in the Château of Versailles; it is in a bad state of preservation, the background is dark and discoloured, and the size of the portrait has been enlarged by the addition of a strip of panel, at an unknown date, to measure 21 x 15 cm. It bears on the back the seal of Colbert de Torcy, nephew of the minister Colbert, who organized the sale in 1717 of the famous art collection of Roger de Gaignières (1644-1715) bequeathed to the Crown.

[19]This Book of Hours is in the Bibliothèque Nationale, Département des Manuscrits, *Nouvelles Acquisitions Latines*, 82. Usually known as the 'Livre d'Heures de Catherine de Medicis', it was originally made for Francis I. The six ladies in the picture are the two wives, three daughters and sister-in-law of Francis. On this Book of Hours see D. Bentley-Cranch, 'L'iconographie de Marguerite de Savoie (1523-1574)', *Culture et pouvoir au temps de l'Humanisme et de la Renaissance: Actes du Congrès Marguerite de Savoie, Annecy, Chambéry, Turin, 29 avril-4 mai, 1974* (Geneva and Paris, 1978), pp. 243-56 with plates I-XXIV, and idem, 'Quelques additions à l'œuvre de Nicholas Hilliard', *Gazette des Beaux-Arts*, 102 (1983), 129-33.

[20]Guillaume Roville [Rouillé], *Prima pars Promptuarii Iconum Insigniorum a seculo hominum, subiectis eorum vitis, per compendium ex probatissimis autoribus desumptus* (Lugduni [Lyons], 1553), *Promptuarii Iconum pars secunda incipit a Christo nato, perpetuam ducens seriem ad vsque Christianissimum Francorum Regum Henricum hoc nomine secundum, hodie feliciter regnantem* (N.p., n.d.), pt. ii, 243.

[21]B.L. Harley MS 1244, fols 159^r-163^v; Add. MS 30666, fols 204^r-207^v. 'Contract de mariage du Roy d'Escosse avec Madame Magdaleine de France du 26e jour de Novembre Mil cinq cens trente six, fait à Blois'.

Madalena were betrothed *per verba de futuro*. The marriage will be completed at Paris'. The Nuncio, summing up the diplomatic consequences of the marriage, added: '...and now that by means of Scotland much can be done, no time shall be lost, and the Grandmaster [Anne de Montmorency] will take an active part'.[22] From Fontainebleau more detailed instructions were sent by the King to the Paris authorities: on 11 December for the erection of a wooden gallery along the cloister of Nôtre Dame Cathedral and of a stage, on which the marriage would be solemnized, with steps into the church:

> ...ordonné faire faire une gallerie à garde-folz de largeur de huit à neuf piedz, à prandre depuis le logis episcopal dudict Sr. Cardinal Du Bellay, continuant le long de la nef de l'eglise Nostre-Dame de Paris, jusques devant la grand porte de ladicte eglise; ouquel lieu seroit faict ung theatre de cinq ou six toises en tous sens...avec ung escalier pour descendre dudict theatre en ladicte eglise, pour sur icelluy theatre solempniser le mariage dudict Roy d'Escosse et de madicte dame Magdaleine de France...[23]

On 18 December came orders for the erection of scaffolding and other necessities with an injunction to use the utmost diligence in order to be ready in time.[24] On 22 December, as has been noted, the matter of the 'red robes' was settled, and on the following day the Grand Master, Anne de Montmorency, sent urgent instructions concerning the supper which Paris was to offer to James and his train after his ceremonial Entry on the eve of his wedding.[25] All these complicated arrangements would appear to have been completed in time. On the last day of December James made his Entry into a Paris crowded with visitors[26] through streets decorated and hung with tapestries, accompanied by the Dauphin and the Court, and preceded by a huge array of Parisian dignitaries, notables and Churchmen.[27] After offering up prayers in Nôtre Dame Cathedral, James and his party went to supper and were then lodged for the night in Cluny.

---

[22]*L&P Henry VIII*, XI, no. 1183: Bishop of Faenza to Mons. Ambrogio, 27 November 1536.

[23]See *Registres des Délibérations du Bureau de la Ville de Paris*, ed. F. Bonnardot, A. Tuetey, and P. Guérin, (Paris, 1833-90), XV, pt. ii, 310.

[24]Ibid., XV, pt. ii, 311: '...que vous faictes faire, avec la plus grande diligence que faire pourrez, les eschafaulx et autres choses requises, tant pour l'entrée de nostre trés cher et trés amé filz le Roy d'Escosse que pour la solemnité de ses nopces, de sorte que tout puisse estre assez à temps...'.

[25]See ibid., XV, pt. ii, 313: '...que Messieurs les Prevost des Marchans et Eschevins...receussent le Roy d'Escosse à son entrée à Paris, comme luy mesmes, et qu'ilz le conduisissent jusqu'à Nostre-Dame de Paris et de la jusques en l'hostel d'Hercules (situé l'angle de la rue et du quai des Augustins) ouquel lieu ou autre commandé ledict Sr. voulloit que lesdictz Prevost des Marchans et Eschevins defraiassent ledict Roy d'Escosse avec les princes et seigneurs et autres de leurs compagnes, ledict jour à soupper aux despens de la ville...'.

[26]F. Michel, *Les Ecossais en France*, 2 vols (London, 1862), I, 404: '...et de tous les points de la France la noblesse s'était donné, pour ainsi dire, rendez-vous dans la capitale pour faire fête à un roi sur le compte duquel la renommée n'avait pas été muette...'.

[27]*La Cronique du Roy François Ier*, ed. G. Guiffrey (Paris, 1860), pp. 201-2: 'Pour lui faire honneur Messieurs de Paris allerent au devant en grant triumphe, sçavoir est: Messieurs de la Cour, les quatre présidans et conseillers avec les huissiers, les gens des comptes, Messieurs de la

Next day, 1 January 1537, the marriage was solemnized. On her father's arm, Madeleine mounted the wooden stage, now hung with cloth of gold, distributed largesse in the form of gold and silver coins to the assembled crowds and descended the steps into the Cathedral to hear Mass. A magnificent dinner and supper served on gold and silver plates and lavish entertainment of music and dancing concluded the day's ceremonies.[28] Two weeks of jousting, in which James took part, were then held in specially built and decorated lists in the courtyard of the Louvre, to be followed by an important political ceremony, at which James was present as France's ally, when Francis, in the presence of all the notables of his Court and Government, solemnly summonsed the Emperor for his confiscation of Flanders.[29]

In these obviously strenuous efforts of the French to make the 'Scottish marriage' a memorable event, the help of French poets was enlisted. The leading Court poet, Clément Marot, contributed an epithalamium, 'Chant nuptial du Roy d'Escoce & de Madame Magdelene Premiere Fille de France',[30] in which he praised James's 'beaulté blonde' (2):

> De beaulté d'homme avoit plus grande part
> Que le Troyen qui fut espris d'Helene;
> Si qu'au sortir sa beaulté souveraine
> Les regardans resjouist tout ainsi
> Que le Soleil, quand à l'Aulbe seraine
> Sort d'Orient pour se monstrer icy.
> (19-24)

And described his rich clothing:

> Tandis les Mains des Nobles gracieuses
> De pied en cap richement l'ont vestu,

Chancellerie, le Prevoust de Paris avec ses gens, les notaires et commaissaires du Chastelet, Monsieur le Chancellier avec les Maistres des requestes, le Prevoust des marchans accompaigné des Eschevins de ladicte ville...et les archers de ladicte ville...et plusieurs notables personnaiges gens d'Eglise, evesques, archevesques et cardinaulx en grand nombre...'.

[28] Ibid., pp. 202-4.

[29] Ibid., pp. 205-6: '...et alla ledict seigneur [Francis] à Nostre Dame et à son retour s'en vint au Palais, à pied, accompaigné de messieurs le Roy d'Escosse, du Daulphin, le duc d'Orléans, de Vendosme, de Saint Paul, le grant maistre, l'admiral et aultres grans et notaibles personnaiges, les chevaliers de l'ordre en escharpe, des cent gentilzhommes de sa maison, ses Suisses et archers. Et illec arrivé entra en la chambre du plaidoye, ou illec, en la presence des dessus dictz, Monsieur son advocat Cappel fist ung plaidoye tandant affin ad ce qu'il fust permis par Messieurs de la Court de decerner commission pour adjourner l'Empereur à la plus prochaine ville du Royaulme de France et de la conté de Flandres pour veoir declarer l'Empereur avoir commis et confisqué ladicte conté de Flandres. Ce qui fut octroyé audict procureur, et, pour ce faire, fut envoyé le premier huissier de ladicte Court qui feit ledict adjornement selon sa commission'.

[30] *Clément Marot, Oeuvres complètes*, ed. C.A. Mayer, 6 vols (London, Paris, Geneva, 1958-80), III, *Oeuvres lyriques*, no. LXXXVI, 314-18, and C.A. Mayer, *Clément Marot* (Paris, 1972), pp. 378-79; ed. cit. for all subsequent quotations.

> Son Corps luisoit de Pierres precieuses,
>
> ...
>
> De Musq d'eslite avec Ambre batu
> Parfumé ont son vestement propice....
>   (9-11; 13-14)

Marot extolled the everlasting ties of friendship between France and Scotland,

> Immortel neud d'amytié indicible
> Entre le Sceptre Escossois florissant
> Et le Françoys, par aultres invincible
>   (46-48)

and anticipated children of the union: 'Enfans auras, Enfans.../ Qui porteront & Sceptres & Couronnes' (95-96).

Jean Leblond, seigneur de Branville, produced his *Nuptiaulx Virelayz* in *plaquette* form to be sold on the streets on the wedding-day [Fig. 6].[31] Therein he lauded Madeleine as 'Une princesse à tout bien disposée / Fille de roy la plus belle du monde' (11-12) and James as 'ung beau roy preferé' (Ballade, 24). He referred admiringly to the wedding tournaments:

> Chascun de vous sur la cuisse la lance
> Vienne courir au tournoy d'excellence
> Faict pour ce roy; que chascun doncques s'arme
> Venez jouster, monstrez vostre vaillance
> Rompez le boys, faictes tours de plaisance
> Pour le plaisir de la belle qu'il ayme.
>   (70-75)

Above all, he underlined the political aspect of the alliance by praising the loyal assistance which Scotland had always extended to 'treshonorable' (34) France:

> ...tu veulx guerdonner
> Ung peuple amy, loyal et secourable
> Aux fleurs du lys de tout temps favorable
> Qu'on ne veist onc en fortune ployer
> Mais pour ton nom sa puissance employer
> Si tu veulx donc comme il est bien decent

---

[31][Jean Leblond, seigneur de Branville], *Nuptiaulx Virelayz du mariage du roy Descoce: et de madame Magdaleine premiere fille de France ensemble une ballade de lapparition des troys deesses avec le blason de la cosse en laquelle a tousiours germine la belle fleur de Lys faict par Branuille, Cum privilegio. On les vend au palays au premier piller en la boutique de Arnoul et Charles langelier,* dated, on the verso of fol. 1, 'le premier jour de janvier mil cinq cens XXXVI' [Old Style: 1 January 1537]. (B.L. 11475.a.58).

>   Le contenter du merité loyer
>   Et envers luy ton amour desployer
>   Le droit le veulx et raison s'i content.
>   (36-44)

And on the morning after the ceremony, wedding-poems by anonymous poets were presented to James[32] and to Madeleine.[33] The unknown writer of the latter poem to the French princess calls James: 'Ton blond Phebus, ton mignon coinct & doulx' (28), warning Madeleine that Venus herself might fall in love with his beauty and grace, preferring him to Adonis (49-62). The poet therefore advises her to guard him from the goddesses by clinging to him lovingly (64-73). The nautical deities are summoned to prepare a safe crossing to Scotland for the bridal pair (125; 139-42):

>   Desja Thetis & Ocean t'attendent
>   ...
>   Ja Neptunus avec grant equipage
>   Se tient tout prest au long du beau rivaige
>   Du traict marin, bien pacifique & calme
>   Pour recepvoir des Escoçoys la dame.

A few months later the poets were again called upon when joy turned to mourning. James and Madeleine arrived in Scotland in May 1537; preparations were in hand for the young Queen's triumphal Entry into Edinburgh when she fell ill. Writing to her father on 8 June Madeleine declared herself 'much recovered'.[34] By July, however, she was dead, dying in James's arms, as the poet Ronsard, who apparently witnessed the scene, wrote: 'Elle mourut sans peine ès bras de son mary, / Et parmy ses baisers...' (91-92).[35] An official poem of mourning, *The Deploratioun of the Deith of Quene Magdalene*, was composed by David Lyndsay, Scotland's chief herald, who had been in France for the elaborate wedding ceremonies and celebrations. His poem's emphasis on the equally notable reception preparations in Scotland, now sadly halted, is dignified but carefully calculated diplomacy. The political as well as the family relationship

---

[32]*Epithalame ou vers nuptiaulx pour les nopces du serenissime roy d'Escosse et Madame Magdeleine de France fille aisnee du Roy son espouse. Fait et presente audict seigneur le lendemain de ces nopces: par le dipsosophe prothonotaire de Monseigneur le reverendissime Cardinal de Bourbon*. See *Clément Marot, Oeuvres complètes*, ed. Mayer, III, 314. Bibliothèque Soissons, MS 202, fol. 224ʳ.

[33]*Elegie nuptiale presentee a Madame Magdaleine, premiere fille de France, le lendemain de ces nopces et mariage celebre avec le Roy d'Escoce*, (n.p., n.d. [1537]), Bibliothèque Nationale, Ye Réserve 3955.

[34]*L&P Henry VIII*, XII, pt. ii, no. 61: 'Since the king of Scotland sent for Maître Francisque, the physician, she has much recovered, but if he come he will assist to her complete cure. M. de Limoges, who has taken the greatest care of her in the journey to Scotland, can give the news': Madeleine, Queen of Scotland [sic], to Francis I, 8 June 1537, from Islebourg.

[35]*Ronsard, Oeuvres complètes*, ed. G. Cohen (Paris, 1950), II, 480-91, 'Le Tombeau de Marguerite de France, Duchesse de Savoye'.

between the two countries was emphasized, and with it the suggestion that Madeleine's unlooked-for death could only strengthen Franco-Scottish ties in both contexts.[36]

In France, the poetic outburst commemorating this sad event included epitaphs in Latin from Etienne Dolet,[37] Nicolas Desfrenes,[38] Jean Visagier, who produced three poems,[39] and an anonymous poet.[40] There were also funerary verses in French from Giles Corrozet.[41] Diplomatically motivated though the marriage undoubtedly was, the grief of the King of Scots, and of his people, would appear to have been sincere. Ronsard's image of James in his grief wanting to kill himself is probably a figment of poetic imagination,

> ...luy, tristement marry,
> Ayant l'ame du dueil et de regret frappée,
> Voulut cent fois percer son corps de son espée.
> La raison le retint, et tout ce fait je vey,
> Qui jeune l'avois page en sa terre suivy,
> Trop plus que mon merite, honoré d'un tel Prince,
> Sa bonté m'arrestant deux ans en sa province.
>   (92-98)[42]

Yet the Portuguese ambassador's remark: 'The King makes great mourning, and all the land'[43] may reflect more accurate reporting, and James's own letter to his father-in-law (who was too ill to be told immediately of his daughter's death) movingly describes his sorrow at the loss of his 'very dear companion':

> Mons\[r\], combien qu'il n'y ait chose au monde dont pouvez estre plus desplaisant, que l'occasion que j'ay de vous escripre présentement, qui est le trespas de votre fille, ma très chère compaigne, lequel a esté cejourd'huy après longue maladye, pourtant je n'ay point voulu estre negligent de vous en advertir; si n'estoit le grand confort et fiance que j'ay en vous que voullez tousjours demourer mon bon pere comme ne fauldray jamais à

---

[36]*The Works of Sir David Lindsay*, ed. D. Hamer, 4 vols, STS (Edinburgh, 1931-36), I, 101-12.

[37]E. Dolet, *Carminum libri quatuor* (Lyons, 1538), p. 160: 'Magdalenas Valesiae. Francisci Valesii Regie Galli filiae, et Regis Scotiae coniugis Epitavium' (Carmen X), ('Vere est vicissitudo rerum & mala bonis').

[38]'Quae nil perpetuum toto sperarat in orbe', in Jean Desmontiers, *La sommaire des antiquitez et merveilles d'Escosse* (Paris, 1538), called erroneously fol. xxxvi [correctly fol. xxiv\[v\]].

[39]J. Vulteius [Jean Visagier], *Inscriptionum libri duo* (Paris, 1538): fol. 12: 'Epitaph. Magd. R. Scotiae' (beginning: 'Post matris, fratrisque mei mortemque sororum'); fol. 12: 'Ad F. Regem de morte Magd. filiae Reginae Scotiae' ('Istud es expertus, quod scilicet omnium in ore est'), fols 12-12\[v\]: 'Aliud' ('Dulce decus patris, decus et perdulce mariti').

[40]'Et fratres Helenae et poli nitentes', in Desmontiers, *La sommaire des antiquitez*, fol. xxx.

[41]*Vers funebres sur la mort de tres noble dame madame Magdalaine de France, Royne d'Escosse*, 'Force d'amour et perte regretee', in *La Cronique du Roy*, ed. Guiffrey, pp. 217-20.

[42]*Ronsard*, ed. Cohen, 'Le Tombeau de Marguerite de France, Duchesse de Savoye'.

[43]*L&P Henry VIII*, XII, pt. ii, no. 539: Ruy Fernandez to John III of Portugal, 18 August 1537.

demourer votre bon et humble fils, je seroys en beaucoup plus grande peine que ne suys....[44]

Madeleine's death did not loosen the ties of friendship between the two Kings, nor was Francis's need of Scotland as an ally diminished. Accordingly, he offered James a second French Queen of Scots. James had been on the point of sending his principal adviser, David Beaton, Abbot of Arbroath, on a diplomatic mission to Henry VIII in London, and he now told him to travel to France to give Madeleine's father a detailed account of her death. The significance of his choice of emissary was not lost upon the English. It was Beaton who had negotiated James's previous French marriage contracts and they rightly suspected that the King of Scots was already seeking another French bride.[45]

Beaton's instructions were indeed that, having assured Francis that James desired nothing so much as the continuance of the Franco-Scottish alliance, he should request as tactfully as possible 'quelque honneste et vertueuse princesse de son royaume'.[46] By 22 August Beaton was on his way to Fontainebleau where, he said, 'I am in seur beleif to bring ye materis at 30^r grace directit me apoune, to gud and haisty effect'.[47] Events did not move so swiftly, however. Francis was in good health once more, it was true, but he was preoccupied with military preparations for yet another campaign against the Emperor, and the very day after Beaton's arrival, he left for Eastern France.[48] This was irritating, but Beaton was a man of energy and determination, and he was personally committed to the continuance of the Auld Alliance. He set off after Francis and eventually managed to have several private conversations with him, reporting:

> I schew the king 30ur gracis fader at gret lenth diuerse tymes 30ur gud and constant mynd towart him, quhilk he findis and knawis veray weill; and I assure 30^r grace [he is] als fer affectit towart 30ur grace, as he schewis planelie, as he is to ony of his sons'.[49]

Francis may have had fears that James would turn to England in the aftermath of his bereavement and so he was delighted to have confirmation of his

---

[44]Bibliothèque Nationale, Fonds Clairambault, MS 48, fol. 5971.
[45]*L&P Henry VIII*, XII, pt. ii, no. 370: Sir William Eure to [the Duke of Norfolk], 30 July 1537: '...the king of Scots has sent into France a secretary of the late queen [Jean de Langeac, Bishop of Limoges] and a Scotch gentleman to know the French king's pleasure. If they agree, then James will take the advice of the French king for his marriage, &c.: if not, then that of the King our master. The French men, ladies, and gentlewomen remain in Scotland till they hear from France'.
[46]E. Bapst, *Les Mariages de Jacques V* (Paris, 1889), p. 313.
[47]B.M. Add. MS 19401, fol. 34: David Beaton to James V, 22 August 1537.
[48]Ibid., fol. 35: David Beaton to James V, 13 September 1537: 'Schir. It will pleis 3our grace to onderstand that I haue euer differit to writ to 3our Grace sene my cummyne to yis court...because ye king 3our gracis fader wes euir removand, and I culd neuir gett him and his counsal togiddir' and, ibid., fol. 37: Beaton to James V, 22 October 1537: 'Ye king tuk his voyage of fontaneblew ye morne eftir my cummyne...and na thing heire ado bot assambleing of men of weire'.
[49]Ibid., fol. 35: Beaton to James V, 13 September 1537.

son-in-law's devotion. Beaton no doubt hinted that his master would be happy to accept Madeleine's sister, Marguerite, but Francis had no intention of losing another daughter to Scotland. Instead, he offered a different lady: Marie de Guise, Duchess de Longueville.

Marie seemed suitable in every way. She might not be the King's daughter but she was of impeccable lineage. Her mother, Antoinette de Bourbon, was descended from St Louis, and her father, Claud, Duke of Guise, was one of France's leading generals.[50] Unlike the fragile Madeleine, Marie was healthy, handsome, nearly six feet tall and already, at nineteen years old, the mother of sons. Her first husband, Louis, Duke of Longueville, Grand Chamberlain of France, had died a month before Madeleine, on 9 June 1537, leaving her with a son of almost two and a baby expected later that summer. Her second son, Louis, had been born on 4 August. Here was incontrovertible proof of her childbearing capacity.

Her uncle, the Cardinal of Lorraine, was high in Francis's favour. It was he who had kept Madeleine's death from Francis when he was ill,[51] no doubt it was he who eventually broke the news to him and it was probably he who drew Francis's attention to Marie. At the beginning of October, Beaton told James of the French King's offer, and James accepted with alacrity. He had no fears about this lady's appearance, for he had already met her during his visit to France the previous year: the Duke and Duchess of Longueville had attended his wedding.[52] He gave Beaton instructions to negotiate the marriage contract at once.

Eager to accomplish his mission, the Abbot pursued the French court to Lyons. There were the usual delays, of course, but at last he managed to see the King and gave him James's response. Well satisfied, Francis sent at once for Marie's father to come to Lyons to conclude the negotiations with Beaton, while he himself set off for Grenoble on his military affairs.[53]

---

[50]René de Bouillé, *Histoire des Ducs de Guise* (Paris, 1849), I, 44-50; H. Fornéron, *Les Ducs de Guise et Leur Epoque* (Paris, 1877), I, passim; Gabriel de Pimodan, *La Mère des Guises: Antoinette de Bourbon 1494-1583* (Paris, 1925), pp. 59-60; *Le Journal d'un Bourgeois de Paris sous le règne de François Ier (1515-1536)*, ed. V.-L. Bourrilly (Paris, 1910), p. 357.

[51]Bibliothèque Nationale, Fonds Clairambault, CCCXXXVI, fol. 5969, Villandry to Montmorency: 'A ce soir est arrivé ung personage dépesché par le roy d'Escosse d'Hédimbourg le VII ce moys, lequel a apporte lectres dudict Seigneur au Roy.... Le Cardinal de Lorraine n'a point esté d'advis que l'on en deust encores advertir le Roy, veu l'estat et disposition ou il est, qui est toutesfois beaucoup mieulx que je ne le veis il y a plus de quinze jours'.

[52]Stefan Zweig, *The Queen of Scots*, trans. C. and E. Paul (London, 1935), pp. 1-2, prints a letter purportedly written at this time by James V to Marie de Guise. The modern flavour of its phraseology may be the result of translation from French into German and then into English, but doubts remain about the letter's authenticity. The text is printed in full in Marshall, *Mary of Guise*, pp. 51-52 and is discussed on pp. 268-69.

[53]B.M. Add. MS 19401, fols. 39-40: Beaton to James V, 22 October 1537, reporting that he had told Francis: '...howbeit 3our grace had na mynd nor haiste desire of mariage considering ye recent decese of 3our quene, no^t ye less 3our grace wald ever conforme you to his [Francis I's] gud counsal and mynd, and to that effect 3our grace had condescendit to madame de Longueveil,

Beaton was anxious to finalize arrangements: other suitors had appeared upon the scene. According to a seventeenth-century writer, the Dauphin Henri had fallen in love with Marie and was speaking of sending his own barren wife Catherine de Medici back to Italy so that he could marry Marie instead.[54] Even if there was any truth in that rumour, it was unlikely to have worried Beaton too much: the Dauphin had been in Lyons but he and the Grand Master had set off 'our ye hillis to ye veris [wars]' almost immediately after Beaton's arrival in the city.[55]

Much more dangerous was a threat from a completely unexpected quarter. News of James's marriage plans had reached England by the beginning of October,[56] and by the end of the month Henry VIII had sent word to Francis that he was interested in taking a French bride. His third wife, Jane Seymour, was dead and his council, he said, was pressing him to marry again. He was willing to consider two candidates, the Princess Marguerite or the Duchess of Longueville.

The wait in Lyons seemed interminable to the impatient Abbot, but at last, after two weeks, the Duke of Guise finally arrived, and he seemed exceptionally well-disposed towards the Scots. Showing himself to be 'mervellouss desirouse of ye expeditioun...of ye mater', he had already gained the consent of the head of his family, the Duke of Lorraine, and of the bride herself. She was still with her mother at Châteaudun, where she had been living in retirement since her husband's death, but Beaton had high hopes of returning home very soon with her despite the winter season, for he knew that she was 'stark and weill complexionit and may indure travel'.[57]

Francis I's response to Henry's enquiries was equally reassuring. He laughed greatly at the language used by the English representatives, saying that it would seem that they meant to do with women in England as they did with their geldings: 'collect a number and trot them out to take which goes best'. He had no intention of putting his daughter in a row with the others.[58] In his instructions of 11 December to his own ambassador in England, he declared himself happy to provide Henry with any French lady he chose, apart from

---

and how ye had send me power and commission to end throuch conforme to his mynd and counsel...'.

[54]Hilarion de Coste, *Les Eloges et les Vies des Reynes* (Paris, 1647), II, 538: The Dauphin 'en estant passionnement amoureux pour sa vertu et sa beauté, la desire pour femme...'.

[55]B.M. Add. MS 19401, fols 39-40, Beaton to James V, 22 October, 1537.

[56]*L&P Henry VIII*, XII, pt. ii, no. 829, Sir Thomas Wharton to Thomas Cromwell, 4 October 1537: 'Bearer can declare news of the queen of Scotland [Margaret Tudor], our King's sister, and of the new Queen, as concluded by the abbot of Arbroath in France, widow [sic] of the duke of Guise and daughter [sic] of the duke of Longawell. She brings the King 30,000 francs a year, is 20 years of age, is lusty and fair, and has had one child by her husband. There is talk of bringing her home through this realm'.

[57]B.M. Add. MS 19401, fols 39-40, Beaton to James V, 22 October 1537.

[58]*L&P Henry VIII*, XII, pt. ii, no. 1125, Bochetel to Castillon, 25 November 1537.

Madame de Longueville, 'whose marriage with the King of Scots has been arranged'.[59]

Henry's determination to snatch Marie de Guise from his nephew was redoubled by this rebuff. When he announced that he did not believe that the lady had given her consent to the match, the French ambassador Castillon was driven to remonstrate, 'Would you marry another man's wife?' Why was he so set on her, he asked. Henry declared that he had heard her so much praised that no one could be better. Moreover, he understood that she was large, and he was big in person and had need of a big wife. Francis's own daughter he thought too young, and as for Marie de Vendôme, he was not prepared to take the Scottish King's leavings, as he put it.[60] Eager to promote Henry's interests, Lord William Howard tried to find evidence that Marie had not personally consented to the marriage, but his efforts were in vain and by 31 December the French were laughing openly at Henry and plannning to lead him on in a 'pretty comedy' of his own making.[61]

Marie's personal reaction to all this has gone largely unrecorded. When told of Henry's approving remarks about her large stature, she commented (it has been said), that although her figure was big, her neck was small.[62] Hilarion de Coste in the seventeenth century claimed that, as a widow, Marie's only ambition was to remain on her small son's estates, looking after his inheritance, and this may well have been true.[63] The death of her younger child in December[64] must have made his brother doubly precious, and at the end of the year both she and her mother were deeply concerned that the boy's interests were not being protected by the new marriage contract.

On 1 January their envoy Gilbert de Beaucaire, Seigneur de Puiguillon was writing to Marie to describe his perturbation. Having promised that he would give her a large dowry of 150,000 francs, as though she were his own daughter, Francis I was now saying that he would provide only 30,000 francs. The remainder would have to be met from the jointure lands provided by her first marriage contract and that would prejudice not only her rights but those of her

---

[59]Ibid., XII, pt. ii, no. 1201, Francis I to Castillon, 11 December 1537.
[60]Ibid., XII, pt. ii, no. 1285, Castillon to Francis I, 30 December 1537.
[61]Ibid., XII, pt. ii, no. 1293, Castillon to the Grand Master, 31 December 1537.
[62]Antonia Fraser, *Mary Queen of Scots* (London, 1969), p. 7.
[63]Coste, *Les Eloges*, II, 537: '...garda une telle conduite en sa viduité qu'elle ne voulut jamais partir de sa maison de Chasteaudun, ou de ses autres terres, qu'en la compagnie de la Duchesse de Guyse sa mère. Puis n'ayant rien moins en sa pensée que de se remarier, elle s'esloigna de la Cour et se retira à cet effet dans ses maisons champestres avec son fils unique, François, Duc de Longueville, pour y passer le reste de son aage', and when James and Henry sought her hand, she 's'excusa plusieurs fois, persistant de demeurer en veufvage, jusques à ce que le Roy François I luy ordonnast par commandement exprès d'entendre à l'un des deux partis, à quoy cette Princesse consentit'.
[64]Pimodan, *La Mère des Guises*, p. 65.

son, since on her eventual death the property settled upon her by her first husband was supposed to revert to the Longueville estates.⁶⁵

The Duke of Guise spoke urgently to the French King about the problem, and Francis promised that no more would be done without the bride's consent. Both she and Antoinette continued to suspect that the contract would go ahead regardless of their wishes, but they consoled themselves with the thought that they had many friends who could intervene. Marguerite de Navarre, the King's sister, had already promised to use her influence with him.⁶⁶ Their combined efforts, however, apparently had the desired effect. By the end of March, Puiguillon was able to report that the clauses would be in accordance with Marie's wishes and a few days after that her father signed the contract in Lyons, at a formal ceremony, before the entire court.⁶⁷

The well-known portrait of Marie in mourning must date from this period of her life, and it may have played some part in the marriage negotiations of 1537-8. It shows her clad in a widow's black-draped cap and black gown, her only ornament a fine gold chain disappearing beneath the neckline of the gown. Her hair is auburn, her eyes blue and her expression one of slight, quizzical amusement. Three copies of the little picture exist. One, in the Scottish National Portrait Gallery [Fig. 7],⁶⁸ one at Versailles,⁶⁹ and a third in Indianapolis.⁷⁰ Was the prime image painted to send to James as a reminder of his future bride's appearance? Might a replica have been made to send to Henry

---

⁶⁵*L&P Henry VIII*, XIII, pt. ii, App., no. 1, Puiguillon to Madame [Mary of Guise], 1 January 1538.
⁶⁶Teulet, *Papiers d'état*, I, 131-32, *Foreign Correspondence with Marie de Lorraine, Queen of Scotland, from the Originals in the Balcarres Collection*, ed. M. Wood, 2 vols, SHS (Edinburgh, 1923-25), I (1537-48), 3-5.
⁶⁷*L&P Henry VIII*, XIII, pt. ii, App., no. 13, Puiguillon to Madame [Mary of Guise], 30 March 1538.
⁶⁸This picture is on a panel which originally measured 15.2 x 12.7 cm; later additions have increased its dimensions to approx. 22.86 x 13.54 cm, but have not altered the image. It was presented to the Scottish National Portrait Gallery in 1950, by Mr E. Peter Jones of Chester, who had acquired it as an 'unknown lady' and had proved its identity by comparison with the drawing of Marie in the British Museum and the double portrait at Hardwick Hall. The previous owner, a Major Harrington of Retford, had gone abroad, and so nothing was known of the provenance, but on the back is the seal from the Colbert de Torcy Sale (see above, note 18). Similar seals have been found on the backs of paintings in Chantilly and Versailles and these had been in the Gaignières sale. The seal on the back of the Scottish National Portrait Gallery picture has been put across the added part of the panel, showing conclusively that the additions made to the picture existed before 1717 and that an inscription on the back, at the base, reading: 'Marie de Lorraine, Reine d'Ecosse' must had been extant in his day. A portrait of Gabrielle de Rochechouart, also from the Gaignières collection, has similar additions round the original panel.
⁶⁹The Versailles picture, also on panel, measuring 16 x 13 cm, is catalogued as 'Femme inconnue'. It is in poor condition and likewise has no known provenance.
⁷⁰The third version, also on panel, measuring 13.97 x 10.46 cm, was in Hamilton Palace in the nineteenth century, and was sold in the Palace Sale of 1882, Lot 1653. Exhibited by J. Seligman et fils, Paris, in 1937 as 'Portrait de Femme' and wrongly identified by C. Sterling at the time as Diane de Poitiers, it was taken to the Seligman Galleries in New York and bought by Dr G.H.A. Clowes, Indianapolis. Since 1947 it has been in the possession of the Clowes Fund Incorporated and appears, from its photographs, to be in excellent condition.

VIII, or could the little portraits have been commissioned by Marie herself as mementoes for her family when she left for her new home?

The difficulty with any of these interpretations is that the paintings can confidently be attributed to Corneille de Lyon. It is known that during the 1530s Corneille worked exclusively in that city which is now attached to his name, and that Marie seems to have remained in seclusion at Châteaudun from the time of her husband's death until her own departure for Scotland.[71] Another possibility therefore suggests itself. She was with the French court in the autumn and winter of 1537 when Francis I spent an unusually long time in Lyons after the death of his eldest son. Princess Madeleine, many French courtiers, and to judge from the evidence so far assembled, the visiting James V, sat to Corneille during that period. It is possible that Marie did too, wearing mourning for the recently dead Dauphin. The replicas might have been made later, in the context of her marriage.

This is mere speculation, of course. What is certain, is that the plans for the marriage went rapidly ahead. James sent to the Pope for a dispensation of consanguinity, for he and Marie were third cousins, and on 22 April she wrote impatiently to a court official asking when the 'noble guard' promised by Francis I for her wedding would arrive at Châteaudun.[72] James was not going to attend the ceremony in person: he was sending Robert, Lord Maxwell, to act as his proxy. Lord Maxwell took with him a large company which included David Beaton, and he carried a diamond spousing ring for which James had paid 300 crowns; the diamond in Madeleine's ring had cost almost four times as much. The wedding took place on 9 May, and afterwards the proxy bridegroom distributed forty crowns among the officials and the minstrels who were in attendance. No epithalamia have been found: perhaps none were written, for the bride had still been in mourning, for her first husband.[73]

On 10 June 1538, Marie and her retinue embarked at Le Havre. The same three royal galleys which had taken James and Madeleine to Scotland conveyed her there, and she landed near St Andrews on Trinity Sunday amidst great rejoicing. The Treaty of Rouen had been fulfilled once more.[74]

---

[71] See D. Bentley-Cranch, 'A portrait of Clément Marot by Corneille de Lyon', *Bibliothèque d'Humanisme et Renaissance*, 25 (1963), 174-77.
[72] *Inventaire chronologique des documents relatifs à l'histoire d'Ecosse conservés aux archives du royaume à Paris*, ed. A. Teulet, Abbotsford Club (Edinburgh, 1839), p. 88.
[73] *TA*, VII, xxv-xxvi.
[74] Pimodan, *La Mère des Guises*, p. 66; R. Lindesay of Pitscottie, *The Historie and Cronicles of Scotland*, ed. Æ.J.G. Mackay, 3 vols, STS (Edinburgh, 1909-11), I, 378-80.

The authors wish to thank Professors C.A. Mayer and I.D. Macfarlane for their valuable assistance, and the owners of the illustrations for permitting their reproduction here.

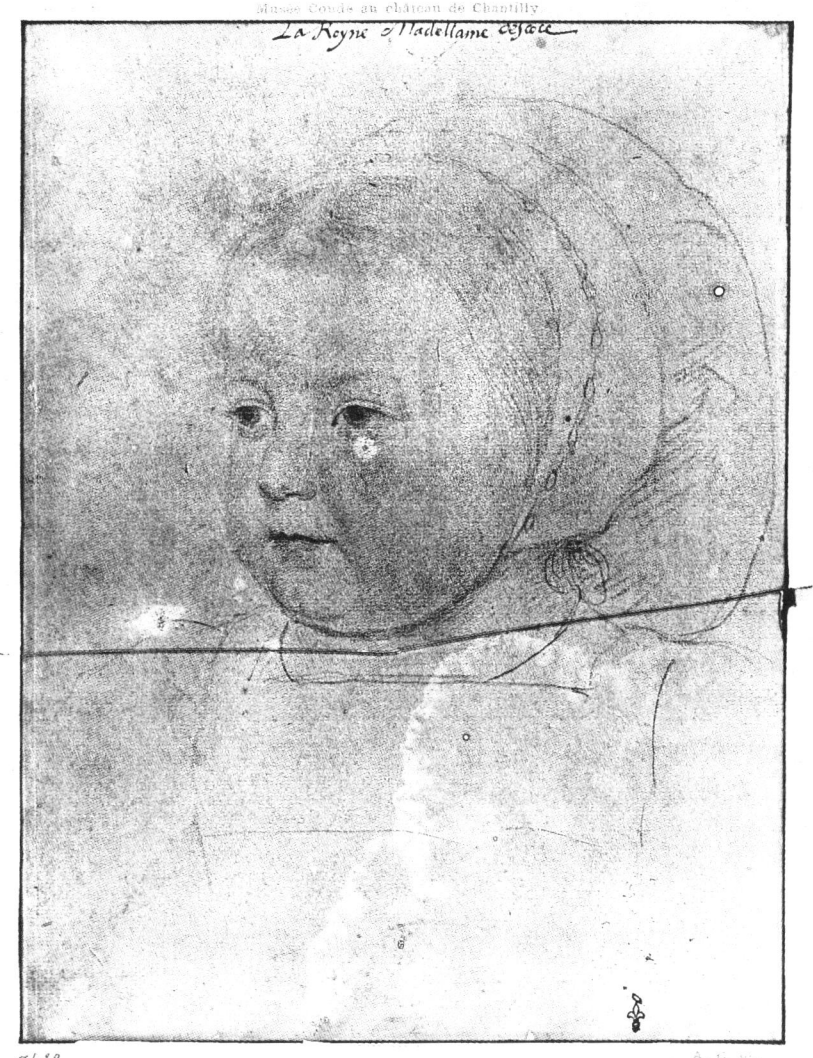

Figure 1. Jean Clouet, *Madeleine as a child*, Musée Condé, Château of Chantilly (*Photo Giraudon*)

Figure 2. Corneille de Lyon, *Portrait of a Gentleman reputed to be James V of Scots*, Polesden Lacey, The McEwan Collection. (*The National Trust*)

Figure 3. Corneille de Lyon, *Madeleine aged 16*, Château of Blois. (*Courtesy of the Director of the Château et Musée de Blois*)

Figure 4. *Madeleine* in Francis I's *Book of Hours* (top row, far right), Bibliothèque Nationale, ms N.A. Latines 82, fol. 100ʳ. (*Photo Bibliothèque Nationale de France, Paris.*)

Figure 5. *Madeleine* in G. Roville, *Promptuarii Iconum*, II, 243, British Library 7755C20. (*By permission of the British Library*)

Figure 6. Woodcut illustrating the wedding ceremony of James V and Madeleine, in Jean Leblond, *Nuptiaulx Virelayz*, Paris, 1537 [Old Style], British Library 11475.a.58. (*By permission of the British Library*)

Figure 7. Corneille de Lyon, *Mary of Guise*. (*Scottish National Portrait Gallery*)

14

OUTWARD SIGNS OF MAJESTY, 1535-1540

Charles J. Burnett
Ross Herald of Arms

During a five year period towards the end of the reign of James V, when his friendship was being sought by more powerful European rulers, the visible prestige of the Scottish sovereign was enhanced by various symbolic and heraldic artefacts that were designed or redesigned at this time. It is my purpose here to highlight them: studied thus they reveal themselves to be a distinguishing feature of the reign.

Towards the mid sixteenth century the King of Scots had an established Court composed of officials who were the instruments of royal authority and dignity. One specialist group involved in the ceremonial and diplomatic activity around the King were the Officers of Arms.[1] They consisted of a principal officer, the King of Arms, six Heralds and six Pursuivants. The Officers granted armorial ensigns in the name of the King to his subjects, and kept records of such grants. They attended the ceremonial attached to ambassadorial visits, and at the creation of peers and knights. They were employed on diplomatic missions to other countries[2] and made proclamations throughout Scotland by the mercat cross of royal burghs. The Officers served writs, particularly those for treason, transported cash from revenue collection points to Edinburgh, and provided a rudimentary postal service between the Crown and administrative local magnates.[3]

While on official duty the Officers wore tabards bearing the King's Arms, so that the royal ensigns formed a colourful and mobile background to the ceremonial dignity surrounding the sovereign.[4] One such occasion occurred in February 1535 at the Palace of Holyroodhouse. On the twentieth of the previous month, James V was nominated as a Knight of the Order of the Garter by King

---

[1] See Appendix 1 for a list of the known Officers of Arms and their titles.
[2] *James V Letters*, pp. 191, James V to Charles V, 25 May 1531; 193-94, James V to Charles V, 30 June 1531; 430-31, James V to John III of Portugal, 26 July 1541.
[3] C.J. Burnett, 'The Officers of Arms and Heraldic Art under King James Sixth and First 1567-1625', Diss. (M. Litt.), Edinburgh, 1992.
[4] See J.H. Stevenson, *Heraldry in Scotland*, 2 vols (Glasgow, 1914), 1, 53-57, T. Innes of Learney, 'The Style and Title of "Lord Lyon King of Arms"', *Juridical Review*, 44 (1932), 197-220 (199-200) and also 'The Scottish Parliament: its symbolism and its ceremonial', ibid., 87-124.

Henry VIII of England.[5] Henry's ambassadors invested James with the insignia of the Order in Holyroodhouse during February, at a ceremony involving his Court and Officers of Arms. The ambassadors stated that there were obligations in accepting such an honour.[6] This was a reference to negotiations between James and the Emperor Charles V regarding a marriage alliance which the English King did not wish to take place. The King of Scots was also presented with a copy of the Garter Statutes, with an armorial title page bearing his Arms within a Garter [Fig. 1]. The rules were written in French, then the official language of the Order. Later the same year, John, Lord Erskine, was sent to England as the King's proxy and was installed, on 22 August, as a Knight of the Garter within St George's Chapel, Windsor Castle.[7]

This was not the first foreign Order of Chivalry granted to James. Four years earlier, the Emperor had nominated Scotland's King as a Knight of the Order of the Golden Fleece at the twentieth Chapter of the Order held at Tournai in December 1531.[8] James was invested with the Collar of the Order on 9 May 1532, at Holyroodhouse, by the Emperor's chamberlain, Sir Peter de Rosimboz.[9]

While James was being favoured by the English sovereign in 1535, diplomatic negotiations were taking place between Scotland and France regarding the possibility of marriage between James and a French lady. Apart from an appropriate dowry, an additional incentive had been offered as early as December 1534, namely the French Order of St Michael.[10] In May 1536 the French Order was sent to Scotland by the hand of Monsieur d'Izernay, valet de chambre of King Francis I. D'Izernay had to deliver the insignia to James, Earl of Moray, himself a Knight of St Michael. Moray was instructed to invest his sovereign with due ceremony,[11] probably again in the presence of the Scottish Heralds and Pursuivants.

Receipt of these international Orders of Chivalry apparently encouraged James to take more interest in the collar of thistles associated with the Royal Arms of Scotland since at least c. 1502.[12] A painted example c. 1535 can be seen on the opening page of the Cartulary of Cambuskenneth Abbey [Fig. 2]. A crowned shield of the Arms is surrounded by a circular border carrying five thistle heads interlinked by leaves. Hanging from the collar is a plaque decorated with

---

[5]G. Holmes, *The Order of the Garter: its Knights and Stall Plates 1348 to 1984* (Windsor, 1984), p. 74.
[6]*James V Letters*, p. 285, James V to Odulph, Lord of Vere, 22 February [1534-5].
[7]Ibid., p. 297, James V to Henry VIII, 31 July 1535.
[8]C. Van Renynghe de Voxrie, *List of Knights of the Golden Fleece*, Exhibition Catalogue, La Toison d'Or (Bruges, 1962), p. 39.
[9]*James V Letters*, pp. 221-22, James V to Charles V.
[10]Ibid., pp. 280-81: Instructions to Nicolas Canyvet for James V, [c. December 1534].
[11]Ibid., p. 318, Francis I to James, Earl of Moray, 29 April 1536.
[12]The collar of thistles with a pendant St Andrew badge is featured in the Vienna Book of Hours, Österreichische Nationalbibliothek, Vienna, Codex Lat. 1897, fol. 14^v. The book is thought to have been a wedding gift from James IV to his bride Margaret Tudor.

the figure of St Andrew holding his cross. Shield and collar are supported by a couchant unicorn associated with a riband bearing the shortened version of the royal motto. (This is the earliest example of the unicorn supporting the Arms in this way.) The display is set on a floral background. It is tempting to consider that the unknown illuminator may have been influenced by the botanical decoration which Sir Thomas Galbraith employed three decades earlier on the marriage contract of James IV.[13]

No documentary evidence survives to confirm if James V instituted an Order of the Thistle with its own statutes and insignia.[14] Nevertheless, the number of surviving illustrations dating from this time indicates that the collar was an important element of the King's public majesty. Carvings of the foreign Collars, including the collar of thistles, were erected on the outer entry to the Palace of Linlithgow soon after James was presented with the Order of St Michael.[15] All visitors therefore shared the King's obvious pride in possessing these tokens as they entered the precincts of the Palace. In 1539, the Mint struck a new gold coin, the 'Bonnet Piece', bearing a portrait of James wearing a collar of thistles [Fig. 3]. In the double portrait now at Blair Castle, of James with his second wife, Mary of Guise-Lorraine, a collar of thistles is again prominent around his shoulders.[16] Having received the three most important European Orders of Chivalry, the King, it would seem, was determined that Scotland should not lag behind in chivalric insignia. However, it appears the King never possessed an actual gold and enamel collar consisting of thistle heads linked by leaves. An Inventory of the King's Jewels made in 1539 lists his collars of the Golden Fleece, Garter, and St Michael,[17] but makes no mention of a collar of thistles. A later Inventory of November 1542[18] notes the Golden Fleece and St Michael but again no collar of thistles is listed.

Apart from the favours of fellow sovereigns, the role of the King in Scottish ecclesiastical affairs was recognized by the Holy See. Pope Paul III blessed a Sword and Hat in Rome on Christmas Eve 1536. These were despatched to James who was in France for his marriage to the daughter of the

---

[13] The contract, dated 17 December 1502, is held in the Public Record Office, London, E/39/81. For Galbraith's role, see *TA*, II, 350. For his other activities, see M.R. Apted and S. Hannabuss, *Painters in Scotland 1301-1700*, SRS (Edinburgh, 1978), pp. 40-41.

[14] The Most Ancient and Most Noble Order of the Thistle, Scotland's premier Order of Chivalry, was founded on 29 May 1687 by King James VII and II. See further, R.J. Malloch, 'The Order of the Thistle', *The Double Tressure*, 1 (1977), 35-46, and C.J. Burnett, *The Green Mantle* (Edinburgh, 1987).

[15] *TA*, VII, 60, 91, 302, 401, 463, details sums spent on building work at Linlithgow but unfortunately do not specify the exact nature of the works. In 1534-5, *Works Accts*, I, 128, notes payment to 'John Ros payntour for the paynttyne of ane Lyon thua unicornis that suld stand upone the foirentres [of Linlithgow]...'.

[16] A reproduction of this is found in R.K. Marshall, *Queen of Scots* (Edinburgh, 1986), p. 8.

[17] *A Collection of Inventories and Other Records of the Royal Wardrobe and Jewelhouse; And of the Artillery and Munitioun in Some of the Royal Castles 1488-1606*, ed. T. Thomson (Edinburgh,1815), p. 49.

[18] Ibid., p. 76.

King of France. James married Madeleine in Nôtre Dame Cathedral, Paris, on 1 January 1537. On 19 February the blessed Sword and Hat were presented at a solemn ceremony in Compiègne. Along with the papal gifts was a letter giving the reasons for this singular mark of favour and explaining the symbolism associated with the Sword and Hat.[19] These gifts no longer survive and we are denied the opportunity to compare the Sword with that given to James V's father by Pope Julius II in 1507. This Julian Sword, however, forms part of the sovereign regalia inherited by James.

James IV also received the Sceptre as an earlier papal gift in 1494.[20] When presented, the Sceptre consisted of a handle attached to a hexagonal rod with an elaborate finial. The finial incorporated three small statuettes and a ball of rock crystal. The total length of the Sceptre was approximately fifty-three centimetres. In 1536 the Edinburgh goldsmith Adam Leys was commissioned to remodel the Sceptre. Leys appears to have taken moulds from the Italian-made finial, which incorporated repoussé elements, and to have cast the work anew in solid silver. He attached another section to the hexagonal shaft which instantly made the appearance of the Sceptre more impressive. The length became approximately eighty-six centimetres.[21] James may have ordered this enriching alteration preparatory to his first marriage in order to impress his bride, Madeleine, daughter of a much wealthier fellow sovereign.

Whether this was so is not substantiated by record, and as it happened, the new French queen had little time to appreciate the alterations; she lived only seven weeks after her arrival in Scotland. Nevertheless, there is a surviving heraldic reminder of her short reign. Her Arms, impaled with those of James, appear on a manuscript possibly executed between January and July 1537—a copy of Bellenden's translation of the *Chronicles of Scotland* by Hector Boece. The armorial detail is contained within a square panel on the title page. Two humorous-looking unicorns support the shield which has Madeleine's Arms in the dexter, or principal, side. This is an unusual arrangement [Fig. 4], particularly as the shield is surmounted by a closed helm. If the lady is being honoured then no helm should appear and in the Queen's case a crown would have been appropriate. Above the helm is the royal crest of Scotland. It is possible the manuscript is the translation commissioned by King James and apparently the shield originally bore the King's Arms. These were overpainted with the Arms of Madeleine.[22] This explains the unusual combination of male and female elements. The alteration may have been ordered by the King so that he could

---

[19] *James V Letters*, p. 328, Paul III to James V.
[20] This is the traditionally accepted date. See C. Burns, *Golden Rose and Blessed Sword* (Glasgow, 1970), p. 23.
[21] For a full description of the Sceptre see J.J. Reid, 'The Scottish Regalia, Anciently Styled the Honours of Scotland', *PSAS*, 24 (1889-90), 18-48 and A.J. Brook, 'Technical Description of the Regalia of Scotland', ibid., 49-141.
[22] Pierpont Morgan Library, New York, MS 527. I am indebted to Mr Alastair Cherry of the National Library of Scotland for this information.

present the manuscript to his Queen as a gift. Floral decoration is a feature of the manuscript's title page. This accords with contemporary illuminated decoration throughout Europe, but the hand is similar to that seen in the Cambuskenneth Cartulary, and suggests that the manuscript could have been compiled in Scotland. An active heraldic painter at the time was Sir John Kilgour or Gilgour [see Appendix 2] and although no payments are recorded for illumination, his clerical status suggests he was not unfamiliar with this art form.[23]

Three years after altering the Sceptre, James decided his Crown required improvement. The decision was taken in light of the forthcoming coronation of his second wife, Mary of Guise-Lorraine, for after Madeleine's sudden death the King had quickly found a new French bride. He married Mary in 1538 but waited until she had produced possible heirs before arranging her coronation. John Mosman, an Edinburgh goldsmith, was commissioned in 1539 to fashion a Crown for the Queen, and at the same time the King ordered changes to his own Crown. An Inventory of March 1539 revealed that one fleur-de-lis from the Crown had broken off and was lost. Instead of a simple repair James sought a major new look for his most significant symbol of kingship.

While it is clear that the Crown incorporated fleurs-de-lis in 1539, we can only speculate on its overall appearance. The Vienna Book of Hours provides an illustration that could have been based on reality: James IV is shown at prayer wearing an imperial crown consisting of a circlet bearing eight large fleurs-de-lis with alternate smaller fleurs-de-lis or crosses.[24] Attached to the circlet are four arches, each decorated with four applied ornaments, surmounted by a small orb and cross. The Crown appears to be set with precious stones and pearls. The general appearance is delicate, suggesting that the Crown was quite light. This could explain why repairs were necessary in 1503, 1532, and 1533,[25] and the reason why it was broken in 1539. The damaged Crown was given to Mosman who also received from the Mint forty-one ounces of gold, which had been mined at Crawford Moor in Upper Clydesdale. He was also paid for twenty-three precious stones to add to the twenty gemstones and sixty-eight pearls on the broken crown.[26] Mosman had to incorporate a new orb and cross, which James may have purchased in France during his second visit in 1538. With the extra gold, new stones and finial, John Mosman set about remodelling the Crown.

Because the remodelling process produced the Crown as it is today we are left with valuable evidence of James's attitude to sovereignty and how it might best be represented. The preservation also allows us to follow the refashioning sequence itself. Mosman began by dismantling the four arches from the broken

---

[23] Apted and Hannabuss, *Painters in Scotland*, p. 1, draw attention to the lack of descriptive classification of the various types of professional painters working at this time.
[24] Vienna Book of Hours, fol. 24^v.
[25] *TA*, II, 207; VI, 73, 179.
[26] *A Collection of Inventories*, ed. Thomson, p. 48.

Crown and removing the existing stones and pearls. After melting down the remaining circlet he added the extra forty-one ounces of Scottish gold. Mosman then cast ten fleurs-de-lis and ten crosses fleury before making a broad flat band edged top and bottom with a moulding. The band was then formed into an oval and soldered together to make a basic circlet. He next attached an undulating strip of forty gold half circles to the top edge of the circlet. This strip carried the ten alternate fleurs-de-lis and crosses fleury, each separated by a pearl. The crosses fleury were enriched by four pearls surrounding a central white gemstone. The twenty precious stones from the broken Crown, either circular, square, triangular, or lozenge-shape, were set below the fleurs-de-lis and crosses. The twenty-two new stones were of varied shape and size but Mosman placed them in individual claw settings. These were each contained within ovoid rectangular frames with leaf-shaped sides and enamelled top and bottom sections. The frames were made singly and attached to the circlet. Between these settings were twenty-two large oriental pearls.

The circlet and its decoration were all new work by John Mosman. To the circlet he then fixed the four arches from the broken Crown. This can be surmised from the fact that they are made from gold of a different colour and quality to the circlet. At the point where the arches meet there was an ornament of four chased gold leaves which formed the base for the new orb and cross. This carried the cipher, 'J R 5', and the only addition by Mosman was a large amethyst, one of the new stones he had acquired [Fig. 5].

To complete the Crown, James ordered a purple velvet bonnet lined with purple satin. The broken Crown had a bonnet from at least 1503 which was renewed in 1532.[27] The new bonnet was tailored by Thomas Arthur of Edinburgh who charged five shillings for manufacture and £3 12s 6d for the materials.[28] Mosman drilled four pairs of small holes on the lower moulding of the circlet to enable the bonnet to be stitched to the Crown. The final touch of richness was given by four delicate ornaments adorned with an oriental pearl set on a pierced oblong of gold, enamelled in red, blue, green, and white. These were attached to the bonnet between the four arches. And when the refashioned Crown of Scotland was ready, Mosman arranged for John Paterson to make a box to hold it.[29] On 13 February 1540 the new Crown was delivered to the King at the Palace of Holyroodhouse. He wore it for the first time at his consort's coronation nine days later in the Abbey Church.

During these five remarkable years, the most public of the King's ensigns—his Royal Arms—also came under scrutiny and were changed in detail. Since first adopted by Alexander II, King of Scots c. 1244, the royal shield of Arms, 'a ruddy lion ramping in his field of tressured gold', had received various

---

[27] *TA*, II, 225; VI, 25.
[28] *TA*, III, 285.
[29] *TA*, III, 285.

additaments. A crowned lion holding a sword appears as a crest over the shield before 1371; unicorn supporters, collared and chained, were acquired during the reign of James I. Soon after 1471 the thistle became the royal plant badge and began to be shown immediately below the shield. A motto was chosen c. 1477 by James III: 'IN MY DEFENS GOD US DEFEND'. By 1503 the crest lion had become sejant and held a saltire banner to balance the sword in the dexter paw. At the same time a collar of thistles was introduced around the shield.[30]

The Arms had reached this stage in their development during the lifetime of James IV, but they apparently did not satisfy his son, James V. Sometime before 1536 the unicorn supporters were given additional burdens to carry, a flagstaff with the saltire banner of Scotland. This new form of Arms was recorded by David Lyndsay of the Mount in his personal Armorial, or record book,[31] to which we shall be returning.

Soon after the Sceptre was lengthened (1536), a decision was made, possibly by the King and his Lyon King of Arms Thomas Pettigrew of Magdalensyde, to alter the royal crest. The saltire banner carried by the lion was replaced by a sceptre. This meant that the crest lion, already crowned, now held a sword and a sceptre so that the Honours of Scotland were represented as part of the Royal Arms. The saltire banners held by the unicorn supporters were also subject to change. That held by the dexter unicorn was replaced by a banner of the Royal Arms. The earliest example of this new version appears c. 1536-37 as a woodcut on the title page of Bellenden's translation of Boece [Fig. 6]. Its publisher was the Edinburgh burgess, Thomas Davidson, who was afterwards king's printer.[32] The same woodcut was employed for *The New Actis and Constitutions of Parliament maid be the Rycht Excellent Prince James the Fift, Kyng of Scottis 1540*, also published by Davidson in Edinburgh after that year's meeting of Parliament. The version carries two scrolls above the head of the unicorns with the words 'JACOBUS / REX 5'. During the reign of his daughter, Mary Queen of Scots, the same woodcut was employed for her own printed Acts of Parliament, with her father's name removed and 'MARIA / REGINA' substituted with cast metal type.

The Royal Arms were reproduced in other media at this time though it is not known if the new version was used. The Accounts of the Masters of Works note that at Holyroodhouse a large version was carved in stone to the design of Sir John Kilgour and mounted on the facade of the Palace in 1536.[33] A version of the Queen's Arms was carved in lead by Adam Leys and placed beneath 'the

---

[30] For a more detailed survey of the Royal Arms in Scotland see C.J. Burnett, 'The Development of the Royal Arms to 1603', *Journal of the Heraldry Society of Scotland*, 1 (1977), 9-19. See also P. Bawcutt, 'Dunbar's Use of the Symbolic Lion and Thistle', *Kingship*, ed. E. Lyle, *Cosmos*, 2 (1986), 83-97.
[31] National Library of Scotland Adv. MS 31.4.3.
[32] R. Dickson and J. Ph. Edmond, *Annals of Scottish Printing* (Cambridge, 1890), pp. 104-35.
[33] *Works Accts*, I, 138, 144, and 270.

gret armis of Sanct Androw' located near the Queen's Entrance at Holyroodhouse.[34] Inside the Palace the Chapel had a wooden carving of the royal Arms which was gilded in 1535 by Thomas Angus,[35] and the Accounts detail payments for painted armorial glass in some of the Palace windows.[36]

In 1538 the heraldic vocabulary available to the King's craftsmen was extended by the introduction of two new symbols—the regal thistle and the regal saltire. They first appeared in that year on a small-denomination coin, the bawbee, struck by the Mint [Fig. 3]. One can speculate that the thistle, adopted as a royal plant badge, had become so popular as a symbol for Scotland that the King, or his advisers, decided that when used in royal circumstances it should be surmounted by an imperial crown. In a similar way the saltire was made royal by the addition of an encircling open crown at the intersection of the cross arms. Both devices, brought to prominence during this reign, remain to this day as the Royal Badges of Scotland. James V's regal saltire can be seen on a contemporary carved panel now built into the wall adjacent to the present main gate of the Palace of Holyrood house [Fig. 7]. A unicorn sejant supports a shield of the Royal Arms and a banner bearing the regal saltire, amidst flowing thistles. Beneath is the cipher, 'I R 5'. The panel was fixed at one time above the now-demolished vaulted gateway to the Palace, and gives an indication of the quality of carved heraldic stonework produced under the patronage of this King.

The Royal Arms are incorporated in two pieces of ecclesiastical stone carving, executed c. 1538-40, which are to be found outwith Edinburgh. The first adorned the gatehouse of the Bishop's Castle once adjacent to Glasgow Cathedral.[37] The stone panel is now in the crypt of the Cathedral but has suffered some loss of detail [Fig. 8]. The Arms of the King occupy the top third and are identified in an unusual way. The pendant St Andrew plaque on the collar of thistles is replaced by the cipher, 'I 5' below the shield. The unicorn supporters do not carry banners. The lower two thirds of the panel bear the Arms of Archbishop Gavin Dunbar, incumbent from 1524 until 1547, with an archiepiscopal cross behind the shield and a salmon with a ring in the mouth below. This is the usual supporter to the archiepiscopal Arms of Glasgow. Dunbar's Arms are placed above those of Subdean James Houston who held office from 1526 until 1550. Both shields have accompanying blank scrolls which had been painted originally with the names of the two individuals. The Arms are flanked by columns carved in a derivative native Renaissance style. The hierarchic composition of the panel predates lay custom found, towards the end of the sixteenth century, at many tower houses, where heraldry is ranged in the same

---

[34] Ibid., 224.
[35] Ibid., 190.
[36] Ibid., 94.
[37] E. Williamson, A. Riches, and M. Higgs, *Glasgow*, The Buildings of Scotland (London, 1990), p. 131.

upward progression above the main entrance. The apogee of such an arrangement is the great heraldic table of Huntly Castle carved in 1602.

The second example of the Royal Arms in an ecclesiastical setting is found on a heraldic font in Newbattle Abbey, Lothian [Fig. 9]. The font had been moved from the Abbey, possibly at the end of the sixteenth century, and was dug up in the grounds of nearby Mavisbank House in 1873.[38] The hexagonal bowl, decorated with six shields, now rests on a nineteenth century stem. There are four royal shields surmounted by crowns, the arms of James V, flanked by an impaled shield of the Arms of James and his first wife Madeleine, and a shield bearing the Arms of James impaling those of his second wife, Mary of Guise-Lorraine. The fourth shield carries the impaled Arms of the King's parents, James IV and Margaret Tudor. The remaining two shields have the eagle displayed of Ramsay of Dalhousie and the Arms of James Haswell, Abbot of Newbattle from 1529 till after 1551.[39] There are at least eight surviving fonts bearing heraldry, but that at Newbattle must have been one of the last to be carved before the Reformation.

An Armorial containing three folios devoted to forty-one Scottish coats of arms was produced in the Low Countries as early as 1370-88. This was compiled by Gelre Herald to the Duke of Gueldres and is named the Armorial of Gelre.[40] The earliest native Armorial, however, was being compiled during the five years we have been considering. This was David Lyndsay of the Mount's fine heraldic record book mentioned earlier. It was probably begun when Lyndsay became an Officer of Arms in 1531 (or in 1528 when he was appointed Lyon Depute), and updated by addition throughout his eventual reign as Lyon King of Arms from 1542 until 1554. Later entries were made by succeeding Kings of Arms and in 1630 the Armorial was recognized by The Privy Council as an official record of Scottish Arms.[41]

The Armorial shows the vitality of heraldic art during the reign of James V, with careful recording of royal, peerage, and other armorial ensigns, and a considered ordering of contents. The first Arms shown are those of the King of Scots; thereafter it is divided into sections beginning with a series of attributed Arms devised for Prester John and the Three Wise Men. Next appear the Nine Worthies.[42] These are followed by European sovereigns and then John Balliol

---

[38] C. McWilliam, *Lothian*, The Buildings of Scotland (London, 1978), p. 347.

[39] This is not the most spectacular heraldic font in Scotland. The finest is to be found in the parish church of Inverkeithing, Fife, dating from the end of the fourteenth century. It bears six shields, held by angels, which are separated by castellated pillars. See J. Gifford, *Fife*, The Buildings of Scotland (London, 1988), p. 249.

[40] It is now in the Bibliothèque Royale Albert Ier, Brussels.

[41] At the end of the Armorial is a signed note by Sir James Balfour, Lyon, and Thomas Drysdale, Islay Herald, stating that the Privy Council approved the manuscript at a meeting held in the Palace of Holyroodhouse on 9 November 1630.

[42] Collective term for nine heroes, first listed in the early fourteenth century in a manuscript on chivalry, *Les Voeux du Paon*, by Jean de Longuyon, comprising three classical heroes: Hector of

who has a page to himself, his Arms surmounted by a symbolic broken crown. The attributed Arms of Saint Margaret, Queen of Scotland, are also shown on a single page.

The most attractive section follows. The Arms of the Queens of Scotland, impaled with the Royal Arms, are all displayed on lozenge-shape shields, the heraldic method to denote the Arms of a lady. Madeleine and Mary of Guise-Lorraine terminate the series [Fig. 10] and unlike the open crowns used for earlier Queens, their Arms are surmounted by an arched imperial crown. Each Queen is identified with her husband on a decorative panel above the Arms. Crown and shield are suspended from the panel by ribbons with flowing ends. These provide visual movement around crown and shield. The composition terminates with a smaller framed panel attached to the individual name of the Queen. This hierarchy of suspension—a three-dimensional effect placed on a flat page—is a delightful solution by the unknown heraldic artist. The other folios are treated in a much less imaginative manner.

Next are fifty Arms of the nobility of Scotland with dukes and earls having pre-Carolean coronets above the shield in the form of jewelled circlets. Cardinal Beaton, Archbishop of St Andrews, receives a full page for his Arms which precede sixty-four nobiliary coats of arms. The concluding sixty-five leaves, some painted on both sides, are devoted to the Arms of ordinary armigers. There are four shields to a page, between which later additions are set. There are also two groups of later Arms at the end of the Armorial dating from c. 1580-84 and 1587-91. The last coat of arms featured is the full achievement of Lyon Sir David Lyndsay of the Mount, surmounted by an inscription stating he is the author of the book, with the date 1542.

The evidence discussed in this chapter demonstrates the considerable importance of the years 1535-40 to Scottish heraldry in general, and to the assessment of James V's reign in particular. With regard to the reign, it is clear that this period shows a King desirous to enhance his royal prestige through the symbolism available in both sovereign regalia and ensigns armorial. Others, such as churchmen, were also prepared to display the Royal Arms, as indication of their dependence on the sovereign for royal authority and patronage, and recognition that symbolism was just as potent a force in this last Stewart reign before the Reformation as it had been in the Middle Ages. Although James V was in many ways a sovereign of the Renaissance, the ethos of his reign continued the traditions of former times. He was fully conscious that outward signs were of first importance in creating for his small and impoverished kingdom an image that allowed it to take a place beside the wealthier or more powerful kingdoms of Western Europe.

Troy, Alexander the Great, Julius Caesar; three biblical: King David, Joshua, Judas Maccabeus, and three Christian: King Arthur, Charlemagne, and Godfrey de Bouillon.

APPENDIX 1

THE OFFICERS OF ARMS 1513-1542

LYON KING OF ARMS

1512-1519 SIR WILLIAM CUMMING OF INVERALLOCHY
Marchmont Herald 1494, Lyon Depute 1508.
1522-1538 THOMAS PETTIGREW OF MAGDALENSYDE
Angus Herald Extraordinary 1492, Unicorn Pursuivant 1507.
1542-1554 SIR DAVID LYNDSAY OF THE MOUNT
Lyon Depute 1528, Snowdoun Herald 1531.

ALBANY HERALD

1516-1540 WILLIAM BROWN OF BALMANGAN
March Pursuivant Extraordinary 1515. Sent to France on a diplomatic mission with the Abbot of Glenluce in 1522.

MARCHMONT HERALD

1515-1562 JOHN MELDRUM
Possibly based in Aberdeen, Meldrum owned a book, *Croniques et Mirouer Hystorial de France*, Paris, 1518, which was subsequently in the library of William Forbes of Tolquhon who died in 1596.[43]

SNOWDOUN HERALD

1511-1513 JOHN SCRIMGEOUR OF GLASSARY
Ormonde Pursuivant 1501. Present at the Battle of Flodden on official duty and conferred with the English Heralds before action commenced.
1513-1531 Office vacant.
1531-1542 DAVID LYNDSAY OF THE MOUNT
Undertook several diplomatic missions for James V including journeys to England, the Low Countries, France, and Portugal.[44]

---

[43] See W.D. Simpson, 'Tolquhon Castle and its Builder', *PSAS*, 72 (1937-8), 248-72 (255, 256).
[44] In the instance of the latter visit, noted in *James V Letters* (pp. 430, 431 and 437), Snowdoun Herald is not directly identified as David Lyndsay, but there is no reason to doubt that it was he who took a letter dated 26 July 1541 from James V to John III of Portugal, and whose arrival was mentioned by John III, Lisbon, 6 April 1542.

ROSS HERALD

1517-1540   JOHN DICKSON
1540-1546   ROBERT FORMAN, *LATER* OF LUTHRIE
              Undertook diplomatic journeys to England in 1544. Succeeded Sir David Lyndsay of the Mount as Lyon King of Arms.

ROTHESAY HERALD

1507-1533   ---? BANELEE
              Had been Bluemantle Pursuivant in England. Came to Scotland in the suite of Margaret Tudor, wife of James IV.
1533-1543   ROBERT HART
              Ross Herald in 1546.

ISLAY HERALD

1505-1525   ---? HAY
              Accompanied John Scrimgeour, Snowdoun Herald, on the pre-battle discussions at Flodden in 1513.
1525-1534   PETER THOMSON
1534-1548   GILBERT LINDSAY OF TRAKWAN

CARRICK PURSUIVANT

1526-1531   JAMES ANDERSON OF STERHEUCH
1531-1537   JAMES WALLACE
1537-1543   JOHN PATERSON
              Succeeded David Lyndsay of the Mount as Snowdoun Herald.

UNICORN PURSUIVANT

? -1507   THOMAS PETTIGREW
              Lyon King of Arms, 1522.
1528-1542   JOHN BALFOUR
              Promoted to Albany Herald 1542.

DINGWALL PURSUIVANT

1531-1545   DAVID BLYTH
              In the company of Somerset Herald and Berwick Pursuivant of England on 25 November 1542 when attacked by English refugees.[45]

---

[45] The Royal College of Arms, *Sixteenth Monograph of the London Survey Committee* (London, 1963), p. 154.

BUTE PURSUIVANT

1527-1533 ROBERT HART
    Promoted to Rothesay Herald in 1533.

KINTYRE PUSUIVANT

1536-1548 SIR JOHN PETTIGREW
    Possibly related to Lyon Thomas Pettigrew but no documentary evidence has been found so far to determine the precise relationship. However, there is ample evidence to show that officers of Arms often came from specific family groups, for example, the Lyndsays from Fife and the Guthries from Aberdeen.

ORMONDE PURSUIVANT

1511-1557 Office vacant

EXTRAORDINARY PURSUIVANTS

1528-1532 ALEXANDER GUTHRIE
    Resident in Aberdeen, was appointed Falkland Pursuivant Extraordinary in 1532.
1538-1539 Name unknown
    Expenses given to Stirling Pursuivant to enable him to travel to the Isles and Ardchattan, *Works Accts*, I, 240.

Information based on F.J. Grant, *Court of the Lord Lyon 1328-1945*, SRS (Edinburgh, 1945), in which some further sources are given, but Grant's work is not completely accurate, nor definitive.

APPENDIX 2

HERALDIC PAINTERS AND CRAFTSMEN

❖ fl. 1527-1541   SIR JOHN KILGOUR [GILGOUR], Chaplain
    Engaged in architectural painting, designed the great Arms for the Palace of Holyroodhouse, undertook heraldic painting on a new ship including the flags and sails, produced trumpet banners bearing the Royal Arms in 1541.
❖ fl. 1535-1536   JOHN ROSS
    Painted a lion and two unicorns and paid for general house painting at Linlithgow Palace.

STEWART STYLE, 1513-1542

❖ fl. 1538   ANDREW BARRY
In 1538 was paid for cleaning and painting the great Arms at the Palace of Holyroodhouse.

❖ fl. 1538   SIR THOMAS CRAGY
Executed shields of Arms for the commemorative mass to Queen Madeleine and gilded the great Arms at Holyroodhouse prior to the arrival of Mary of Guise.

❖ fl.1539-1560   ANDREW WATSON
Assisted Sir John Kilgour with paintwork on the new ship and the trumpet banners. Provided heraldic items for Queen Madeleine's commemorative mass in 1541 and 1542. Painted a very large number of heraldic items for James V's funeral.

❖ fl. 1539   ROBERT GALBRAITH
Assisted Kilgour and Watson with heraldic painting for the new ship.

❖ fl. 1539-1546   ARCHIBALD ROULE
Craftsman painter mainly engaged on general duties but was another paid for work on the new ship.

❖ fl. 1506-1532   ALEXANDER CHALMER
The bulk of work for the royal household undertaken by Chalmer was during the King's minority but he did assist Kilgour at Holyroodhouse in 1532.

❖ fl. 1531-1532   THOMAS PEEBLES
Glazier who supplied painted heraldic glass for the Palace of Holyroodhouse.

❖ fl. 1535-1536   THOMAS ANGUS
Painter who gilded the carved woodwork in the Chapel at Holyroodhouse and gilded the two large stone Royal Arms in the fore-entry of the Palace.

❖ fl. 1535-1538   ADAM LEYS
Goldsmith employed to create three coats of arms in lead, including the Royal Arms, and an image of St Andrew. These four lead carvings were on a large scale and decorated the 'new tour' at Holyroodhouse, that is, the present tower on the north-west corner of the Palace facade. One year later Leys was paid for carving the Queen's Arms which were placed beneath the image of St Andrew.

❖ fl. 1538-1547   ROBERT BINNING
Assisted Sir Thomas Cragy with gilding the great Arms in 1538.

Information drawn from M.R. Apted and S. Hannabuss, *Painters in Scotland 1301-1700*, SRS (Edinburgh, 1978), and *Accounts of the Masters of Works, Volume I: 1529-1615*, ed. H.M. Paton (Edinburgh, 1957).

Figure 1. The Arms of James V surrounded by the Garter of England, Statutes of the Order of the Garter, 1535, NLS MS 7143, fol. 11. (*Courtesy of the Trustees of the National Library of Scotland.*)

Figure 2. The Royal Arms of Scotland surrounded by a collar of thistles, Cartulary of Cambuskenneth Abbey, c. 1535, NLS Adv. MS 34.1.2, fol. 1. (*Courtesy of the Trustees of the National Library of Scotland.*)

Figure 3. Gold and Billon coins of James V. Above: Gold Bonnet Piece of 1539 with profile portrait of the King. Below: Bawbee of 1538 with regal thistle on the obverse and regal saltire on the reverse. (*Courtesy of the Trustees of the National Museums of Scotland.*)

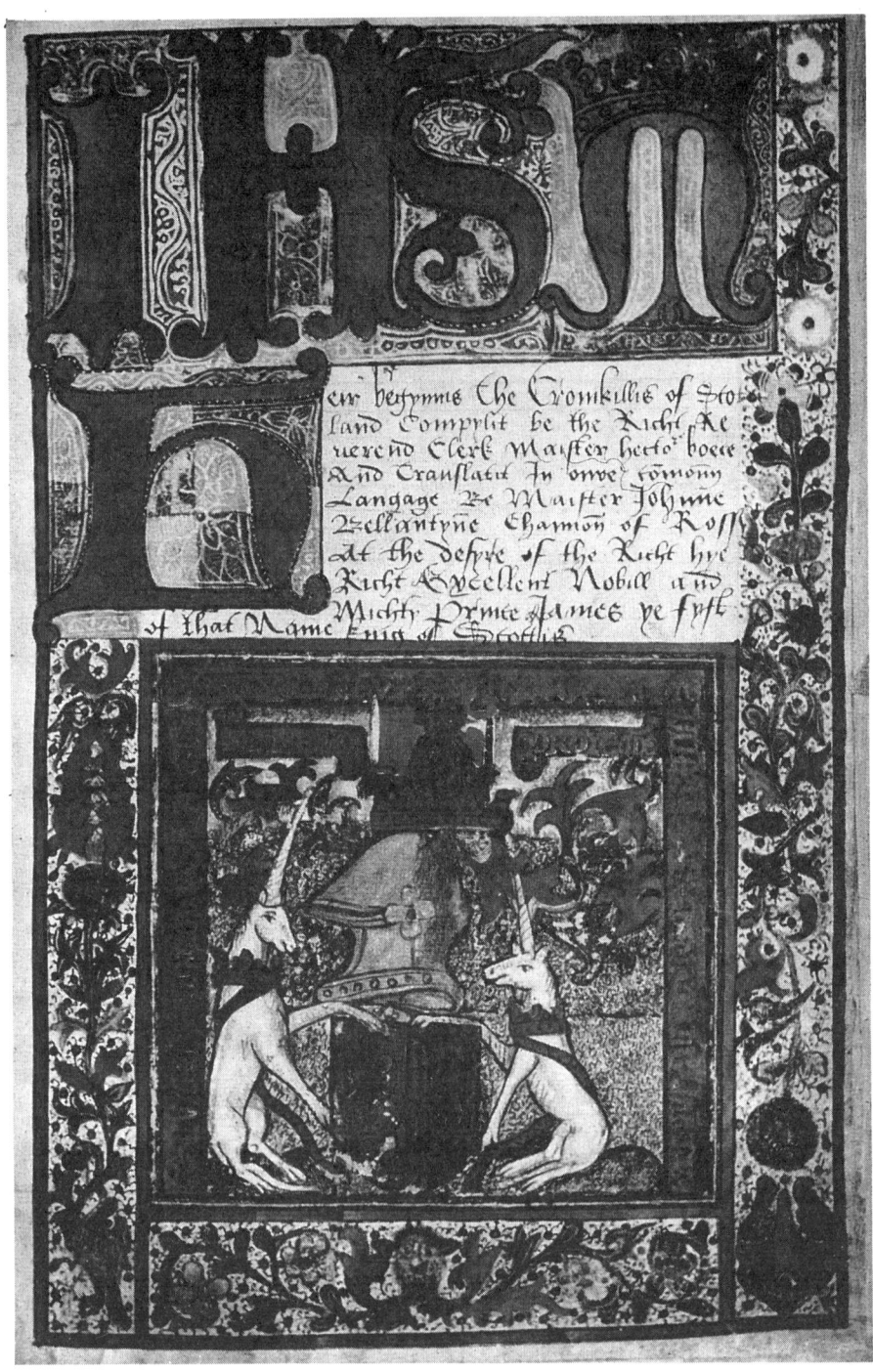

Figure 4. The Arms of Madeleine impaled with those of James V, title-page of Pierpont Morgan Library MS 527, Bellenden's translation of Boece's *Chronicles of Scotland*, c. 1537. (*Courtesy of the Pierpont Morgan Library*)

Figure 5. The Crown of Scotland, 1540. (*Courtesy of Historic Scotland.*)

Figure 6. The Royal Arms of Scotland, showing the new version of the Arms adopted by James V, c. 1536-37, title page of Bellenden's *[H]ystory and croniklis of Scotland*, NLS H.33.b.7. (*Courtesy of the Trustees of the National Library of Scotland.*)

Figure 7. Carved stone panel, c. 1540, main gate, Palace of Holyroodhouse, showing a regal saltire on the banner held by the unicorn. (*Courtesy of Historic Scotland.*)

Figure 8. Panel from the Bishop's Castle, Glasgow, c. 1540, showing the Royal Arms surmounting those of Archbishop Dunbar and Subdean Houston. (*Courtesy of Historic Scotland.*)

Figure 9. Heraldic font, Newbattle Abbey, c. 1540. Four royal shields, one ecclesiastical shield and one lay shield are used for decorative display on the bowl. (*Courtesy of the Society of Antiquaries of Scotland.*)

Figure 10. **The Arms** of James V's two Queens, showing arched imperial crowns, David Lyndsay's Armorial, c. 1538-42, NLS Adv. MS 31.4.3, fol. 22. (*Courtesy of the Trustees of the National Library of Scotland.*)

INDEX

Abbeville, 54
Abell, Adam, 227-29, 230-35; *see also* 'Roit or Quheill of Tyme'
Aberdeen, 104, 301; bps of, *see* Dunbar, Gavin; Elphinstone, William; burgh of barony (Old Aberdeen), 62, 66, 67; St Machar's Cathedral, 62-72, 83, 92, 95, 186; *see also* King's College
Accoltis, Peter de, card. of Ancona, 133
Adagia (Erasmus), 10
Adrian VI, pope (1522-23), 236
Aesop, 36, 38, 194
Aitken, A.J., 31, 49
Albany, Duke of, *see* Stewart, John
Albert, king of Poland, 239
Aldus Manutius, *see* Printers
Alençon, Charles, Duke of, 274
Alesius, Alexander, 134, 220
Alexander, 33, 208, see also *Buik of King Alexander the Conquerour*
Alexander II, king of Scots (1198-1249), 294
Alexandersoun, Sir Laurence, 106
Alliteration, 29, 37, 44, 45, 46, 218
Alnwick Castle, 75
Amours, F.J., 46
Ancient Scotish Melodies (Dauney), 156, 160
Ancona, card. of, *see* Accoltis, Peter de
Anderson, Alexander, 4
Anderson, James, of Sterheuch, 300
Andrew of Spoleto (Andrea della Rosa), 233, 242
Angelori, Francis, 238, 241
Angus, Earls of, *see* Douglas
Angus, Thomas, 296
Answer quhilk schir Dauid Lindesay maid to the Kingis Flyting, see Lyndsay, David
Anti-feminist literature, 27, 29, 193-94
Apothegmata (Erasmus), 1
Apted, M.R., 302

d'Arces, Antoine, Sieur de la Bastie, 235-36
Architecture and architectural carving, *see* James V: and architecture
Ardchattan, 301
Argyll, 262
Argyll, Earls of, *see* Campbell
Argyll, bp of, *see* Hamilton, David
Aristotle, 9, 33
Arnot, David, bp of Galloway (1509-26), 66, 104
Arran, Earl of, *see* Hamilton, James
'Art of Music collectit out of all ancient doctouris' (anon.), 153
Arthur, Thomas, tailor, 294
Asloan, John, 15-18, 19; burgess of Edinburgh, 17; motives for compilation of MS, 18, 30, 49, 51; notary public, Edinburgh, 15; procurator for Herris family, 17; and *Scottish Troy Book* fragments, 15; and Thomas Ewen, 15, 16; and Wyntoun's *Cronykil*, 15
Asloan MS (NLS MS 16500), 15-51, 257-58; and Alexander Boswell, 17, 19; compilation method, 19-20, 29, 39, 49-51; and John Asloan, 15, 16, 36-37; and Thomas Ewen, 15, 16, 27; and M.G. Myll, 16, 27-28; selection criteria, MS texts, 30; table of contents, Asloan's, 16, 17, 18, 31
Contents:
Addicioun of scottis corniklis and deidis, Ane (Ane schort memoriale), 19, 25-26; *Ballat of all officeris, Ane*, 20, 47; *Ballat of disputacoun betuix the body & saull, A*, 19, 34-35; *Ballat of luf, Ane*, 18, 39, see also *Maying & disport of chaucere*; *Ballat of making of, Ane*, 20, 47; *Ballat of our lady, Ane*, 'closter of crist' (Kennedy), 20; *Ballat of our lady, Ane*, 'Hale sterne...' (Dunbar), *see* Dunbar; *Ballat of our lady, Ane*, 'O hie empryss...', 20, 42-43; *Ballat of our lady, Ane*, 'Ross mary...', 20, 44;

INDEX

Ballat of our lady of pete, A, 19, 34; *Ballat of pacience, Ane*, 20, 47; *Ballat of recompence, A*, 19, 34; *Ballat of steidfastness, A*, 19, 34; *Ballat of the abbot of tungland, A (Fenȝeit Freir)*, see Dunbar; *Ballat of the devillis Inquest, A*, see Dunbar; *Ballat of the Incarnacioun, A*, 19, 34; *Ballat of the passioun, Ane (Passioun of Christ)*, see Dunbar; *Ballat of warldlie plesance*, 20, 48; *Buke callit the spektakle of luf, The*, 16, 19, 26-28; *Buke of colkelby, The*, 19, 35-36; *Buke of curtasy and nortur, The*, 19, 32; *Buke of phisnomy, The*, 19, 33; *Buke of schir gologruss & schir gawane*, see *Golagros and Gawane*; *Buke of schir orpheus & erudices, The*, see Henryson; *Buke of the chess, The*, 17, 19, 22-23, 49; *Buke of the contemplacioun of synnaris, The*, 20, 41-42, 43, 208; *Buke of the howlat, The*, 17, 20, 37-38, 46, 49, 51, see also Holland; *Buke of the otter and the ele, The*, 19, 36; *Buke of the Porteus of nobilness, The*, 19, 23-24; *Buke of the sevyne sagis, The*, 15, 19, 27, 28-29, 49; *By a palace as I couth pass*, 20, 37; *Disputacoun betuix the merle & the nyᵗtingale, The*, see Dunbar; *Document of schir Gilbert Hay, The*, 19, 32-33; *Dreme on fut by forth* (Henryson), 19, 30, 31; *Dunbarris Derige (The Dregy)*, see Dunbar; *Flyting betuix kennyde & dunbar*, see Dunbar; *...goldin targe*, see Dunbar; *Iustis betuix the talȝeour & the sowtar, The (Fasternis Evin)*, see Dunbar; *Lyoun and the mouss, The*, see Henryson; *Maner of the crying of a play, The*, 20, 39; *Maying & disport of chaucer, The*, 18, 20, 34, 39, 43-44, 49; *Of chanticlere and the fox (The Cock and the Fox)*, see Henryson; *Paddock and the mouss, The*, see Henryson; *Parliament of bestis, The, (Trial of the Fox)*, see Henryson; *Preching of the swallow, The*, see Henryson; *Regiment of Kingis with the buke of phisnomy, The*, 19, 33-34; *Sawis of the angell*, 19, 31-32; *Scottis cronikle, The (Ane tract of the kingis)*, 19, 26; *Scottis originale, The*, 19, 24-25; *Talis of the fyue bestis, The*, 20, 35, 38, 48; *Testament of Cresseid, The*, 17, 19, 30; *Thre prestis of peblis, The Talis of the*, 20, 40-41, 49, 51, 212; *Tod and the wolf, The*, see Henryson; *Tractact of certane kyngis of yngland, Ane (The Ynglis Cronikle)*, 19, 25; *Uplandis mouss & borowstovnis, The (The Two Mice)*, see Henryson
Auchinleck Chronicle, 26
Auchinleck, Elizabeth, 185
Auchinleck MS, 34
Auchinleck Press, 22
Auld Alliance, 17, 55, 273-74, 280
Averencia, Thomas de, of Brescia, 131-32, 133
Avignon, 6
Awntyrs of Arthure, 46
Ayr, 112
Azay-le-Rideau, Indre-et-Loire, 91

❖

'Balade de bon Conseyl' (*A Ballat of treuth*), see Asloan MS
Balfour, David, of Burleigh, 103
Balfour, Sir James, of Pittendreich, 106, 107, 117, *Practicks*, 98
Balfour, John, 300
Ballat, 34; complaint, 47; impossibilities, 194, 198, 215; love, 18, 20, 30, 39, 192-94; Marian, 17, 19, 20, 34, 42, 44-45, 49; moral, 19, 20, 34-35, 37, 48; Passion, 42, 48; petitionary, 195-98, 209-215
Ballentyne, *see*, Bellenden
Balliol, John, 224, 297-98
Banelee, 300
Bannatyne MS (NLS MS 1.1.6), 29, 30, 31-32, 34, 35, 36, 37, 39, 40, 41-42, 46, 47, 50, 57, 137, 138, 140, 183, 194, 197, 198
Bannerman, John, 266
Barde, William, 202
Barker, John, 138
Barlow, Graham, 161
Barry, Andrew, 302
Barton, Robert, of Over Barnton, 101, 102, 103, 104, 107, 111, 114
Bassandyne, Thomas, *see* Printers
Bawcutt, P., 29, 30, 35, 36, 38, 39, 45, 46, 48
Baxter, J.W., 35, 36
Beal, Peter, 53

INDEX

Beaton, David, cardinal and abp of St Andrews (1539-46), 59, 60, 110, 206, 283-85, 288, 298
Beaton, James, abp of Glasgow (1508-32), and of St Andrews (1523-39), 66, 101, 106, 134
Beattie, William, 23, 43
Beaucaire, Gilbert de, Seigneur de Puiguillon, 286, 287
Beaufort, Joan, queen of James I, 88
Bellenden, John, 115, 179, 180, 181, 185, 186, 191, 196, 198, 202, 216, 227-28; 'Armipotent Lady Bellona', 181, 191; *Benner of peetie*, 'Quhen goldin phebus', 181; *Hystory and cronikils of Scotland*, 181, 182, 190, 216, 232, 292, 295; *Livy's History of Rome*, 181, 191, 216; *Proheme of the Cosmographie* ('Quhen siluer Diane'), 181; *Proheme of the history* ('Thow marcyall buke'), 181, 190, 197
Bellenden, Katherine, 186, 216
Bellenden, Robert, abbot of Holyrood, 227, 231
Bellenden, Thomas, of Auchnoull, 185, 220
Bentley-Cranch, Dana, 94
Berridale, laird of, 251
Berry, John, 56
Bible, 10-11, 28, 65, 77, 80, 81, 235-53
Bibliopegus, Johannes, 3
Bibliotheca Universalis (Gesner), 2
Binning, Robert, 302
Bion, Girard, Albany's secretary, 132
Bishop's Castle, Glasgow, *see* Glasgow
Bissat (Bisset), James, 125
Bitterling, Klaus, 36
Black Book of Taymouth, 261-62, 263
Blackwood, William, *see* Printers
Blair, Archibald, 115
Blair Castle, 291
Blind Harry, 39
Blois, 277
Blore, Edward, 85
Blyth, David, 300
Blythburgh, Holy Trinity Church, 68
Boece, Hector, 1, 2, 14, 71; and Erasmus, 2-3, 4; and humanism, 2-3, 4; and Ogilvie, 1; *Murthlacensium et Aberdonensium Episcoporum Vitae*, 71; *Scotorum Historiae*, 181, 189-90, 216, 292, 295

Bohemia, 67, *see also* Louis I
'Boke of Curtasye' (BL MS Sloane 1986), 32, 47
Boke of Nurture (Russell), 32, 205
Boleyn, Anne, queen of Henry VIII, 243-44, 249
Bona Sforza, queen of Sigismund I, 83, 92
Bontemps, minstrel, 119, 120-24, 129
Bonvisi, Antonio, 4, 5, 6, 8
Book of Common Order, The (Carswell), 258, 263
Book of Days (Chambers), 142
Book of the Dean of Lismore (NLS 72.1.37), 254-72; and Asloan MS, 257-58; contents, 264-65; as 'duanaire', 256; handwriting, *see* Handwriting; and oral transmission, 259, 268-70; orthography of, 255-56, 257, 258-60, 261-62, 263, 269, 271; and Perthshire, 254, 255, 256-57; provenance of contents, 265-68; as Scots-Gaelic compilation, 254-56, 259, 260, 261, 269-70, 272; scribes: Drummond, William, 257; Mac Eoin Riabhaich, Dubhghall, 256; MacGregor, Duncan, 256; MacGregor, Sir James, Dean of Lismore, 256, 259; scribal alterations to, 270-71
Borders, 110, 112, 246, 248
Borthwick, Henry, gunner, 110
Borthwick, Sir John, 8, 220
Borthwick, William, 3rd Lord, 236
Boswell, Alexander, Lord Auchinleck, son of James Boswell of Auchinleck, 17, 18, 19, 22
Boswell, James, servitor, 202
Bothwell, Earls of, *see* Hepburn
Bountans, *see* Bontemps
Bourbon, Antoine de, duc de Vendôme (1537-62), king of Navarre (1555-62), 252, *see also* Marie de Bourbon
Bourbon, Antoinette de, 284-85, 287
Bourbon, Charles, duc de (1490-1527), 66, 67, 238
Bourbon, Marie, de, *see* Marie de Bourbon
Bovillus, Carolus, 4
Bower, Walter, see *Scotichronicon*
Boyd, Margaret, Lady Rowallan, 103
Brechin, bps of, *see* Hepburn, John
Brefny, 266

Bréviaire des Nobles, Le (Chartier), 23
Brigettais (St Brigid's) Order, 248-49
Broughton, barony of, 115
Brown, George, 244
Brown, James, dean, 71
Brown, William, of Balmangan, 299
Bruce, Robert (1210-95), 224
Bruce, The (Barbour), 51
Brussels, 69, 206, 220
Brutus, 25
Bryan, Sir Francis, 5
Buccleuch, *see* Scott, Walter
Buchan, Earl of, *see* Stewart, James
Buchanan, George, 5, 136, 182, 221; and Florens Wilson, 5; *Franciscanus*, 221
Budé, Guillaume, 12, 13
Buik of King Alexander the Conquerour, see Hay, Gilbert
Buke of curtasy and nortur, The, see Asloan MS
Buke of Knychthede, The, see Hay, Gilbert
Buke of phisnomy, The, see Asloan MS
Buke of the chess, The, see Asloan MS
Buke of the Governaunce of Princis, The, see Hay, Gilbert
Buke of the Howlat, The (Holland), 260, 261, *see also* Asloan MS
Buke of the Law of Armys, The, see Hay, Gilbert
Buke of the otter and the ele, The, see Asloan MS
Burgkmair, Hans, 78, 90, 93
Burnett, Duncan, Music Book, c. 1610, 153
By a palace as I couth pass, see Asloan MS
Byrd, William, 160

❖

Cadiou, Andrew, notary, 23-24
Cadoen, Andreas, *see* Cadiou, Andrew
Caerlaverock Castle, 77
Cairns, Sandra, 212
Caithness, bp of, *see* Stewart, Andrew
Caithness, John, Earl of, 251
Calder, J. T., *Sketches from John O'Groats*, 151
Calderwood, David, 135
Calvin, John, 5, 7; and *De Transitu Hellenism ad Christianismum* (Budé), 12; and Florens Wilson, 11; *Institutes*, 11

Cambuskenneth Abbey, Cartulary of, 290, 293
Campbell, family of, 255, 261, 262, 266, 267; of Glenorchy, 255, 268, 271; Mac Cailein, chief, 256, 267; *see also* Book of the Dean
Campbell, Archibald, of Skipnish, 253
Campbell, Colin, Earl of Argyll (1513-33), 66, 101, 102, 252
Campbell, Duncan, of Glenorchy, 265
Campbell, John, of Lundy, 101, 110
Canterbury, abp of, *see* Cranmer
Caravalla, Demetrio, 9
Carlisle, 235
Carmichael, R(ichard), 135, 136
Carpentras, 6
Carrick, 113, 260
Carswell, John, *The Book of Common Order (Foirm na nUrrnuidheadh)*, 258, 263-64, 267
Carthy, Martin, 146
Cartwright, John, 33
Carver, Robert, canon of Scone Abbey, 118, 135, 153; 'Carver Chroirbook' (NLS Adv. MS 5.1.15), 118; *Dum sacrum mysterium*, 78
Castellio, Sebastian, 8
Castiglione, Baldassare, 128-29
Castile, king of, *see* Philip I
Castillon, Louis de Perreau, Sieur de, 285, 286
Catherine de' Medici, 285
Caxton, William, *see* Printers
Cessford, Earls of, *see* Kerr
Cessolis, Jacobus de, 22
Chalmer, Alexander, 302
Chambers, Robert, 142-43
Champier, Symphorien, 4
Chanticlere and the fox, Of (The Cock and the Fox), see Henryson
Chapel Royal of Scotland, 128, 129, 133-36, 141, 153, 186; *see also* Stirling
Chaplains, 16
Chappell, W., *Popular Music of the Olden Time*, 178
Charlemagne, 26, 45, 239
Charles V, Emperor (1519-55), king of Spain (1516-56, as Carlos I), *also* king of Aragon, and of Sicily, 66, 67, 70, 206, 220, 236, 238-39, 240, 273, 275, 279, 290

Charlotte, daughter of Francis I, 274
Charterhouse, Carthusian monastery, 248
Chartier, Alain, 23, 48
Chartres cathedral, 73, 74, 82
Châteaudun, 285, 288
Chaucer, Geoffrey, 18, 20, 34, 37, 39, 43-44, 48, 138, 179, 197; *Lak of Stedfastness*, 34; Chaucerian tradition, 139, 184
Chepman and Myllar prints, 23, 30, 34, 36, 39-40, 43-44
Chisholm, James, bp of Dunblane, 66
Christian II, king of Denmark (1513-23), 66, 67
Christiansen, R. Th., 269
Christis Kirk on the Grene, 139
Christmas Medley, The, 'All sones of Adam', 139, 154, 157, 158
Chrysostom, John, 238, 246, 247
Church: confession, table of, 21
  leaders, religious, 65-67, 231; Marian devotion, 34, 42, 44-45, 139, 229, 241, 242, 243, 246; Passion, instruments of the, 68; and reform, 5, 7, 197, 218-21, 231, 244; sacraments, 20, 21, 219, 252; scriptures, place of, in, 219; Trinity, 213, 229
Cicero, 4
Cinthio, 83
Clanuet, John, Burgundy Herald, 215
Clappertoun (Clapperton), George, 135, 182, 186; *In Bowdoun on Blak Monunday*, 135, 194
Classical background: characters of, in literature and art, 76, 89, 90, 93, 94, 95-96, 222, 279, 281; languages, attitudes to, 15th and 16th c., 2, 3-4, 5, 8, 126-27, 211-12, 271
Claudin (de Sermisy), composer, 153
Claudius, Roman emperor, 26
Clement VII, pope (1523-34), 53, 133, 219, 220, 221, 231, 236, 238, 240, 247, 292
Clichetove, Josse, 4
Clouet, Jean, 274-75
Cluny, 278
Cobham, Dame Eleanor, 25
Cochlaeus, Johannes, 220
Cockburn, Robert, bp of Ross (1507-21), *later* bp of Dunkeld, 53, 54, 66

Coinage of James V, *see* James V, coinage
Coissac, J.B., 4
Colden, John, provost of Methven, 113, 115
Coldingham, 240
Coldwell, D.F.C., 53
Colkelbie Sow (The buke of colkelby), 155, *see also* Asloan MS
Collège de la Trinité, Lyons, 8
College of Justice (Court of Session), 97, 108-09, 110, 117, *see also* Exchequer; Parliament, Scottish
Collège Royal, France, 5
Colonna, Vittoria, 7
Coluim, Giolla, mac an Ollaimh, 266-67
Colville, James, of Ochiltree, 89, 101, 102, 104, 108, 109, 110
Colville, Robert, of Ochiltree, 105
Commentarii in epistolas Pauli (Lefèvre), 4
Commentatio Quaedam Theologica, *see* Wilson, Florens
Commonplace Book (Maxwell), *see* Maxwell, John
Common-weill, Iohne the, 198
Compiègne, 292
Complaint and Publict Confessioun of Bagsche, The (Lyndsay), *see* Lyndsay, David
Complaynt of a Loveres Lyfe, A, *see* Asloan MS, *Maying and disport of chaucer, The*
Complaynt of Scotland, The (Wedderburn), 31, 46, 145, 156; Leyden's edition, 154-55
Complaint of the Black Knight, *see* Asloan MS, *Maying and disport of chaucer, The*
Compost et Kalendrier des Bergers, Le (Marchand), 82
Connacht, 266, 267
Constable's MS Cantus, 126, 154-56, 158, 160, 162
Contarini, Gasparo, cardinal, 13
Contemplacioun of synnaris, The (William of Touris), 208, *see also* Asloan MS; Franciscans, Observant
Contra Haereses, *see* Erasmus
Contrafactum, 137-38
Corneille de Lyon, 276-77, 288
'Corr-litir', *see* Handwriting

Corrozet, Giles, 282
Coste, Hilarion de, 286
Costume, 15th and 16th c., 76, 88, 90-91, 93-94, 176-77, 207, 273, 278-80, 287, 288, 289, 291
Cotton Collection, BL, 52, 54-55
Councils, 5, *see also* Trent, Council of
County Clare, 271
Cracow, 64, 92, 93, 94, 96
Cragy, Sir Thomas, 302
Craig (Crag, ?Creek, ?Craik), John, 125
Craigie, Sir William, 18, 19, 20, 23, 25, 26, 27, 28, 29, 31, 41, 42-43, 44, 45
Cranmer, Thomas, abp of Canterbury, 243, 249
Craw, Paul, 231
Crawford Moor, 293
Crawfurd, Nichol, of Oxgangs, 101, 102, 104, 105, 109
Creichton, James, 53
Crichton, George, abbot of Holyrood, 101, 102
Críost Brúilingeach, Giolla, 267
Cromwell, Thomas, 2, 4, 5, 7, 8, 220-21
Cruden, Stewart, 73
Culross, 114, 179
Cumming, Sir William, 70-71, 299
Cunningham, I.C., 44
Cupar, 103, 106
Cyaneus, L., *see* Printers

❖

Dacre (Dacres), William, Lord, 54, 56, 57
Dalriada, kings of, 189-90
Dalrymple, Sir David, Lord Hailes, 195
'Dán', Gaelic syllabic verse, 265
Dance in the Quenis Chalmer, Ane, *see* Dunbar, Schir John Sinclair
Danielston, John, parson of Dysart, 113, 115
Dante (Alighieri), 93
Darnley, *see* Stewart, Henry
Dauney, William, 142, 144, 178; *Ancient Scotish Melodies*, 156, 160
Dauphin, *see* Francis; Henri, duc d'Orléans
Davencourt (Dauenecurt), James, 120, 123
Davidson, John, *Memorial of the Life and Death of Robert Campbel...*, 145
Davidson, Thomas, *see* Printers
De Animi Tranquillitate, *see* Wilson, Florens

De Burca, family of, 266
De Clementia (ed. Calvin), 5
De immortalitate animorum (Paleario), 9
De quadruplici vita (Champier), 4
'De Regimine Principum' (*Liber Pluscardensis*), 33-34
De Transitu Hellenismi ad Christianismum (Budé), 12
De Unitate (Pole), 7
De Worde, Wynkyn, *see* Printers
Dean of Lismore's Book, *see* Book of the Dean
Debate of the Body and Soul, 34-35
Delabaute, *see* d'Arces
Democritus, 10, 12
Desfrenes, Nicolas, 282
Dickson, John, 300
Dictionarium Hebraicum (Münster), 5
Dieppe, 275
Dile (Dalye, Dillye), William, 125, 204
Dingwall, John, 101, 102
Dioscorides (*Materia Medica*), 208
Diplomacy in the 16th c: language used, 59; missions, 55, 220
Document of...Hay, The, *see* Asloan MS
Dolet, Etienne, 282
Don, river, 63
Douglas, Earldom of, 66; family of, 61, 91, 187, 206, *see also* James V: and Douglas family
Douglas, Archibald, 6th Earl of Angus (1514-1556), 50, 52, 56, 58, 66, 67, 104, 119, 150, 185, 187, 188, 195, 216, 225-26, 235, 236, 237, 240
Douglas, Archibald, 3rd son of 7th Earl of, see *Buke of the Howlat, The*
Douglas, Archibald, of Kilspindie, 150-51, 225, 236
Douglas, Elizabeth, 204
Douglas, Gavin, bp of Dunkeld (1515-22), 52-61, 66, 182, 185, 198; *Colkelbie Sow*, ref. to, 35; correspondence, 52-61; 'Memorial', attrib. to, 53; *Rauf Coilȝear*, ref. to, 45; *Eneados*, 52, 55, 60, 139, 184, 185, 213, 216; *Palice of Honour*, 46
Douglas, Sir George, 150, 225, 236
Douglas, James, 3rd Earl of Morton, 104

INDEX 309

Douglas, James, of Drumlanrig, 252
Douglas, Janet, Lady Glamis, 229, 253
Douglas, Janet, 126, 186, 215-16
Douglas, Marion, 185, 204
Douglas, William, abbot of Holyrood (1526-28), 195
Douglas-Fischear part-books, 153
Dow (Dowie) family, musicians, 120
Dowland, John, *First Booke of Songs*, 160
Dramatic interlude, 31, 39, 220
Dream visions, 10, 29, 30, 35, 212-13, see also *De Animi Tranquillitate*
Dregy, The (Dunbarris Derige), see Asloan MS
Dreme on fut by forth, master Robert hendersonnis, see Asloan MS
Droichis pairt of the play, Ane littil Interlude of (The maner of the crying), see Asloan MS
Drumlanrig, see Douglas, James
Drummond, family of, 52; musical family of, (Anthone, Bestian, 'auld' Julian, 'ʒoungar' Julian, Vincent), see James V, court of: music, Italian minstrels
Drummond, Alexander, of Carnock, 150, 225
Drummond, John, Lord, 113
Drummond, John, of Innerpeffray, 113
Drummond, Malcolm, 103
Drummond, William, of Hawthornden, 130
Du Bellay, Guillaume, 5
Du Bellay, Jean, cardinal, 6, 277-78
'Duanaire', see Book of the Dean
Duguid, Peter, 64, 65, 68
Dunbar, Elizabeth, countess of Moray, see *Buke of the Howlat, The*
Dunbar, Gavin, bp of Aberdeen (1518-32), 65, 66, 68, 70, 72, 101, 102, 113, 185, 196, 204, 296; schoolmaster to James V, 126, 129, 204, 205
Dunbar, J.G., 85, 90
Dunbar, William, 17, 47, 48, 50, 138, 182, 184, 192, 196, 202, 210, 217, 265; *Colkelbie Sow*, ref. to, 35; *Musing allone this hinder nicht*, attrib. to, 183-84; *Rauf Coilʒear*, ref. to, 45; *Maner of the crying of ane playe, The*, attrib. to, 39; *Ballat of our lady, Ane* ('Hale sterne...'), 20, 45; *Devillis Inquest* ('This nycht in my sleip'), 19, 35; *Dregy, The*, 17, 20, 46-47; *Fasternis Evin in Hell (The Iustis)*, 19, 29, 50, 194; *Fenʒeit Freir, Ane Ballat of*, 17, 19, 29-30; *Flyting*, 19, 36, 194; *Goldyn Targe*, 17, 19, 30-31, 34; *Illuster Lodovick, of France (Elegy on Bernard Stewart)*, 222; *Merle and the Nychtingall, The, (The disputacoun betuix...)*, 17, 19, 20, 30, 46; *Off lentren in the first mornyng*, 48; *Passion of Christ, The*, 20, 42; *Rycht airlie on Ask Weddinsday*, 194; *Sir Jhon Sinclair begowthe to dance (Ane Dance in the Quenis Chalmer)*, 197; *Schir, ʒe have mony servitouris*, 47; *Thrissill and the Rois*, 161, 222; *Turnament*, see *Fasternis Evin*
Dunbarton, 235
Dunblane, see Chisholm, James
Duncanson, John, 56
Dundee, 114, 262
Dunfermline, 113
Dunfermline, George, abbot of, 113
Dunkeld, see of, 53, 55, 56, 57, 59; bps of, see Cockburn, Robert, Douglas, Gavin
Dunlop, A.I., 59
Durie, Andrew, bp of Galloway, 180-81, 186, 196

❖

Early Popular Poetry of Scotland (ed. Laing), 143, 145, 149-52
Edinburgh, 97, 107; Castle, 253; Holyrood Abbey, 101, 102, 202, 226, 227, 246, 294, 296; Holyrood, Palace of, 72, 88, 129, 289-90, 294-96, 296, 301, 302; St Giles church, 16; Sciennes convent, 185; Tolbooth, 97, 107, 117; Trinity College and Chapel, 87, 224-25
Edward I, king of England (1239-1307), 26, 224
Edzell Castle, 74
Eger and Grime (Sir Eger, Sir Gryme and Sir Gray Steill), 149-52
Eglinton, Earl of, see Montgomerie, Alexander
Elegantiae (Valla), 2
Elgin, 1, 2, 10
Elizabeth I, queen of England (1558-1603), 94
Elliott, K., 157, 158, 160-61, 178
Ellis, Sir Henry, 52-53

Elphinstone, Elizabeth, Lady Dunrod, 103
Elphinstone, Isobel, 103
Elphinstone, William, bp of Aberdeen (1483-1514), 2, 63-64, 68, 70, 72
Emmanuel, king of Portugal (1495-1521), 66
Enchiridion, see Erasmus
English Madrigal Verse (Fellowes), 178
Erasmus, Desiderius, 1, 8, 9; and Boece, 2-3, 4, 215; and 'Erasmianism', 3; estimate of Wilson, 3; and James V, 220; and King's College, 2-3, 4; tutor to Alexander Stewart, 2, 126-27; *Adagia*, 10; *Apothegmata*, 1; *Contra Haereses*, 4; *Enchiridion*, 2, 3; *Paraphrases*, 3, 4
Erse, *see* Gaelic, Scottish
Erskine, John, Lord, 104, 111, 209, 236, 249, 290
Erskine, Margaret, 140
Erskine, Sir Thomas, of Halton and Brechin, 196, 206
Eure, Sir William, 220-21
Evans, Deanna Delmar, 148
Evans, Joan, 93
Ewan, Sir Thomas, 15, 16, 27
Exchequer, 15th and 16th c. Scottish, 97, 99, 117; auditors, 97, 98, 99, 101, 102-4, 105, 106, 109-117; compearance at, 98, 109, 112, 115; comptars, 97-98; comptrollar, 97, 101, 102, 103, 104, 105-6, 107, 110, 111, 113, 114; custumar, 104, 106, 113, 114; decrees, 99, 103, 104, 105, 106, 108, 110, 111-13, 114, 115; and James V, 97, 98, 99, 107, 108, 109; location, 97, 107, 117; and lords of council, 97, 99-101, 102-6, 107-8, 109, 111-15; and lords of session, 108-10, 111, 112, 114, 115, 116; powers, 98, 99, 100, 103-5, 107, 110, 111-15, 117; and privy council, 105, 108, 116; proceedings, *in scaccario*, 100-1, 102, 103-4, 106, 114, 116; sederunts, 100, 102-5, 108, 110, 112, 114-16; treasurer, 97, 102, 107, 110, 111, 114; vaction court, as, 99, 104, 105, 116, 117; *see also* College of Justice; Parliament, Scottish

❖

Fables: in Asloan MS, 17, 19, 30, 38-39, 49, 51; of Henryson, *see* Henryson, Robert; of Lyndsay, *see* Lyndsay, David, *Bagsche*
Falkland: Chapel, 74, 81; Palace of, 72, 74, 75, 81, 129, 130; Roundels, 95
Farmer, H.G., *A History of Music in Scotland*, 157
Fellowes, E.H., *English Madrigal Verse*, 178
Fenȝeit Fals Frere of Tungland, The (Ane ballat of the abbot of tungland), see Asloan MS
Ferdinand II, king of Aragon (1479-1516), 220
Ferdinand of Austria, king of Hungary; emperor (1526/7-64), 239, 240
Feremond, *see* Ferdinand
Fergusson's Scottish Proverbs, see Proverbs
Fermanagh, 266
Fernandez, Ruy, ambassador, 282
Fêtes de la Renaissance, Les (Jacquot), 157, 158
Fethy, John, priest, poet and musician, 133, 140, 187; *For love of one?* 140; *O God abufe*, 153; *O Ladie Venus*, 140; *Only to yow my Ladie*, 140; *Sang of Repentance*, 140
Fez, 233, 242
Ficino, Marsilio, Platonist, 4, 10
Fidlaris, *see*, James V, court of: music
Fife, 99, 101, 103, 214
First Booke of Songs (Dowland), 160
Fisher, John, bp of Rochester, 2, 5, 6, 12, 248, 249
Fleming, Malcolm, 3rd Lord, 104, 252
Flemisman, Peter, stone carver, 72
Flodden, battle of (1513), 26, 52, 91, 118, 120, 123, 127, 182, 201, 202, 229, 299
Flyting, literary, 36, 61, 195, 217-18
Flyting Betwixt Montgomerie and Polwart, see Flyting; Hume, Patrick; Montgomerie, Alexander
Flyting of Dunbar and Kennedie, The, see Asloan MS; Dunbar, William; Kennedy, Walter
Foirm na nUrrnuidheadh, see Carswell, John
Fontainebleau, 273, 277, 278, 283
Forbes, John, Master of, 253
Forbes, John, *Songs and Fancies*, 154, 155, 156, 157, 158, 159, 160, 161

INDEX

Forbes, Alexander, of Tolquhon, 162
Forbes, William, of Tolquhon, 299
Fordun, John of, 26, 48, 189
Forman, Andrew, bp of Moray, *later* abp of St Andrews (1514-21), 57, 65, 66
Forman, Robert, dean of Glasgow, 101, 102
Forman, Robert, *later* of Luthrie, 300
Forme of Prayers and Psalmes (1565), 183
Forrest, George, *see* James V, court of: music, Italian minstrels
Forrest, William, priest and poet, 44
Fortingall parish, 256, 257, 266
Foulis, Sir James, 109, 115, 182, 185; and *Quadrupertitum* (Galbraith), 185; *Strena*, attrib. to, 195, 208
Fouvières, 1, 9
Fox, Denton, 30, 36, 40, 41, 44, 51
Fox, Richard, bp of Exeter, 2
Francis I, king of France (1514-47), 6, 66, 67, 71, 73, 78, 80, 83, 124, 131-32, 216, 238, 252, 273, 274-76, 277-79, 283, 285, 286-88, 292; court of, 83, 218, 274, 278, 284, 288, 290
Francis, Dauphin (1518-36), 252, 276, 277-78, 288
Franciscans, Observant, 41-42, 46, 228-29, 230, 231, 235, 240-41, 243, 247-48, 249; William of Touris, 41-42; see also *Contemplacioun of Synnaris*
Franciscanus, *see* Buchanan, George
Fraser, Sir William, 53
Frith, John, 134; *loci communes*, *see* Hamilton, Patrick
Furnivall, F.J., 47

❖

Gaelic, Scottish (language), 261-64
Galbraith (Galbreith), 179, 180, 209
Galbraith, Paul, 202
Galbraith, Robert, 186; *Quadrupertitum*, 185
Galbraith, Robert, herald painter, 302
Galbraith, Sir Thomas, 291
Galbraith, William, 128, 136, 202, 209
Galloway, 260
Galloway, Alexander, 4, 70
Galloway, bp of Galloway, *see* Arnot, David; Durie, Andrew

'Galter, Maister', *see* Malevile, Gaultier
Gante, Pedro de, 232-23, 242
Garde, Pierre de la, Sieur de Sagnes, 274
Gardiner, Germain, 8
Gardiner, Stephen, bp of Winchester, 5, 6, 8
Garter, chivalric order of, 289-91
Geddes, Sir William Duguid, 64, 65, 68
Gelre ('gillire' = Gilderland, Gueldres), 239-40; Herald (Armorial of Gelre), 297
Geographical Collections (MacFarlane), 151
Gesner, Conrad, 2
Gigha, 266, 267
Giles, Phyllis, 158
Gillies, William, 265, 269
Gillire, *see* Gelre
'Ginkertoun', *see* 'Gynkartoun'
Glamis, Lady, *see* Douglas, Janet
Glasgow: Bishop's Castle, 296; Cathedral, 186; University, 51, 186
Glassary, 262
Glenluce, abbot of, *see* Malin, Walter
Glens of Antrim, 267
Golagros and Gawane, 20, 46
Golden Fleece, chivalric order of, 215, 290-91
Goldyn Targe, *see* Dunbar, William
Gordon, Adam, Earl of Sutherland, 66
Gordon, Alexander, 3rd Earl of Huntly, 66
Gordon, George, 4th Earl of Huntly (c. 1510-62), 109
Gordon, Robert, of Straloch, see *Greysteil*
Gourlaw (Gourlay), Norman, 246
Gower, John, 179
Gowrie, Earl of, *see* Ruthven, William
Graham, George, 'see *Greysteil*
Graham, Jane, 85
Grame, James, minstrel, 126
Grant, F.J., *Court of the Lord Lyon*, 301
Gray, Douglas, 38, 40
Greysteil: and Graham's incomplete music transcription (NLS MS 5.2.18), 142; Greysteil's Castle, Loch Rangag, 151; and James IV, 144-45, 147; and James V, 145, 150; 'lutar', the, 145; melody, 143, 148; and oral traditions, 147, 148, 152; *Sir Eger, Sir Gryme and Sir Gray Steill*, 145, 148-50, 152;

and Straloch lute book, 142, 144, 145, 147; structure, musical, 144, 146-48; style, musical, 142, 144, 146-48
Gryphius, Sebastian, *see* Printers
Grenoble, 284
Greyhound, as Tudor device, 88
Gueldres, Charles, duke of, 66, 67
Guild, William, 68
Guise, family of, 284, *see also* Longueville
Guise, Claud, duc de, 284, 285, 287
Guise, Jean de, card. of Lorraine, 5, 6, 277, 284
Guise, Mary of, *see* Marie de Guise
Guthrie, Alexander, 301
'Gynkartoun', 126, 138, 155, 160, 177, 204

❖

Hadrian, pope, *see* Adrian, pope
Hailes, Lord, *see* Dalrymple
Hailes, Patrick, Master of, 110
Hallowe'en, 123
Hamilton, family of, 83
Hamilton, David, bp of Argyll (1497-1532), 66
Hamilton, James, 2nd Earl of Arran, 83, 188, 237, 252
Hamilton, James, of Finnart, 83, 112, 114, 252
Hamilton, Patrick, precentor cantor, St Andrews, 134, 136; and *loci communes (Patrick's Places)*, 134; *Benedicant Dominum omnes angeli ejus*, 134
Hampton Court, 58, 85, 91
Handwriting: and Book of the Dean, 257-59; 'corr-litir' (minuscule half- or quarter-uncial), 257, 258; rubrication, 257-58; secretary, 223, 257, 258, 259
Hannabuss, S., 302
Hannay, R.K., 97, 100
Harvey, Gabriel, 5
Hart, Robert, 300, 301
Haswell, James, abbot of Newbattle, 297
Hay, ?, Islay Herald, 300
Hay, Sir Gilbert, 19, 32-34, 48, 208-9; *Buke of the Gouernaunce of Princes, The*, 32, 33, 208-9; *Buke of the Law of Armys, The*, 32, 33; *Buik of King Alexander the Conquerour, The*, 33, 208-9; *Buke of the Ordre of Knychthede, The*, 32, 33

Hay, John, Lord of Yester, 246
Hay, William, 6th Earl of Errol, 66
Hay, William, vice-principal, King's College, Aberdeen, 4
Hay, of Luncarty, 232
Hazlitt, W.C., 39
Hebrides, 262
Heidelberger Schloss, 74
Henri II d'Albret, king of Navarre (1516-1555), 66, 277
Henri, duc d'Orleans, Dauphin, *ltr* Henri II, 285
Henry II, king of England (1154-89), 25
Henry VII, king of England (1457-1509), 119
Henry VIII, king of England (1509-1547), 5, 6, 66, 67, 132-33, 141, 201, 205, 216, 224, 243, 244, 247, 248, 249, 252, 274, 283, 285-86, 287-88, 290
Henry Frederick, prince of Wales, 73
Henryson, Robert, 48, 138, 217, 265; and William Stewart, 192, 194; *Thre Prestis of Peblis*, attrib. to, 41; *Cock and the Fox, The*, 19, 36-37; *Dreme on fut by Forth*, 19, 30, 31; *Fox and the Wolf, The (The Tod and the Wolf)*, 20, 36-37; *Lion and the Mouse, The*, 194; *Orpheus and Eurydice*, 20, 30, 39-40, 48, 194; *Paddock and the Mouse, The*, 19, 36; *Preaching of the Swallow, The*, 19, 36; *Testament of Cresseid*, 17, 19, 30; *Trial of the Fox (Parliament of bestis)*, 20, 36-37; *Two Mice, The (The wplandis mouss and borowstounis)*, 20, 30, 38-39, 49
Hepburn, Adam, 2nd Earl of Bothwell, 196
Hepburn, James, bp of Moray (1514-24), 66, 249
Hepburn, John, bp of Brechin (1517-58), 66
Hepburn, John, prior, St Andrews, 66
Hepburn, Patrick, 3rd Earl of Bothwell (1513-33), 66, 196
Hepburn, Patrick, of Wauchton, 112
Heraldry, 15th and 16th c. Scottish, 62, 65, 67, 68, 78, 80, 84, 88, 93, 215, 221-23, 226, 289-302; Fleur-de-lis, royal device, 293-94; Lion, royal device, 84, 89, 207, 223, 226, 301; Royal Arms, 222, 292, 294-97, 298, 301, 302; Royal motto, 295; Saltire, royal badge, 295-

96; Thistle, chivalric order, 290-91; Thistle, royal badge, 290, 291, 296; Unicorn, royal supporter, 291, 292, 295, 296, 301; *see also* Gelre Herald; Officers of Arms
Herborn, Nicholas, 233
Hermitage Castle, 110
Herris family, 17
Higden, Ranulf, 23, 48, 49
Highlands, 255, 260, 261, 262, 263; scuplture, monumental, in, 262-63
Historiography, 229, 230, 232, 234-35
History of Music in Scotland, A (Farmer), 157
History of the Houses of Douglas and Angus (Hume of Godscroft), 150
Holland, Richard, 20, 37-38, 48
Holyrood, Palace of, *see* Edinburgh
Home, Alexander (Wedderburn), 3rd Lord, 56, 58, 235-36
Home, Alexander, 5th Lord, 101
Homer, quoted, 9
Hopper, Isobel, 236
Horace, 1, 12
Houston, James, 296
Houston, laird of, 237
Houwen, L.A.J.R., 28
Howard, Thomas, Earl of Surrey, 3rd Duke of Norfolk, 236, 252
Howard, Lord William, 286
Howlat, Buke of the, *see Buke of the Howlat, The*; *see also* Holland, Richard
Hudson, musical family of, 120, 134-35
Humanism, 6; and Boece, 2-3; and Calvin, 5; emergence in Scotland, 2, 211-12, 216, 271; and Erasmus, 2-3; 'evangelical', 2, 6, 7, 8, 9, 11; international, 1, 208, 216; and King's College, Aberdeen, 2-3, 6; and Wilson, 1-4, 9
Hume, David, of Godscroft, 150; *History of the Houses of Douglas and Angus*, 150
Hume, Patrick, of Polwarth, *Flyting Betwixt Montgomerie and Polwart, The*, 194
Hume, *see also* Home
Hungary, queen of, *see* Mary of Hungary
Hunter, Andy, musician, 147-48
Huntly Castle, 297
Huntly, Earls of, *see* Gordon

Hus, John, Bohemian reformer, 231

❖

Impossibilities, poems of, *see* Ballat
In Bowdoun on Blak Monunday (Clappertoun), *see* Clappertoun
In psalmum 50 enarratio, *see* Wilson, Florens
Inchaffray Abbey, 228
Inglis (language), 260-61
Inglis, James, 179, 181, 186
Inglis, Nin3ean, 56
Institutes, *see* Calvin, John
'Insular Missarum', *see* Inchaffray Abbey
Ireland, John, 19, 20-22, 48, 49
Irenicism, 6, 13
Isidore, of Seville (c. 570-636AD), 248
Isles, 301; lordship of, 255, 261, 263, 266-67, 268, 271
Italy, 121, 126
Iusting betuix Watsoun and Barbour, The (Lyndsay), *see* Lyndsay, David
Iustis betuix the tal3eour and the sowtar, The (Fasternis Evin), *see* Dunbar
Izernay, Monsieur d', 290

❖

James I, king of Scots (1394-1437), 295; portraits, 86-87; *Kingis Quair*, 87, 138
James II, king of Scots (1430-60), 25, 26, 37, 224; portraits, 87
James III, king of Scots (1460-88), 17, 69, 99, 119, 188, 231; portraits, 87
James IV, king of Scots (1488-1513), 17, 26, 46, 52, 89, 97, 99, 100, 119, 123, 124, 126, 188, 196, 201, 208, 225, 231, 297; and civil justice, 100; court of, 118, 120, 130, 133, 144-45, 185, 194, 202, 211; and Observant Franciscans, 41-42; portraits, 88, 91, 293
James V, king of Scots (1513-42), 17, 59, 60, 61, 66, 67, 71, 80, 81, 82, 85, 100, 107, 118, 119, 124, 133, 136, 139, 188-89, 201, 240, 246, 298; ancestry, 189-91, 207, 224, 226, 297; and architecture and archit. carving, 63-96, 187, 296; Arms, 222, 295-97, 301; and Auld Alliance, *see* Auld Alliance; in Asloan MS, 25, 46, 50; and church reform, 197, 215, 218-21, 224, 231, 239, 246, 249; and Chapel

Royal, *see* Chapel Royal; children of: legitimate, 71, 197; illegitimate, 140, 195; cipher, 294-296; and civil justice, 97-117, 212, 226, 248; coinage, 291, 296; coronation, 78, 118; crown, 293-94, 296, 298; and Douglas family, 52, 56, 61, 150-51, 191, 225-26, 237; death, 226, 240, 253; education, 122, 126-27, 140, 185, 188-91, 208-9, 210-15; entry into Paris, 278; erection, 188, 195; finances, 98, 106-7, 196, 203, *see also* Exchequer; French marriages, 73, 80, 120, 140-41, 153, 215-16, 221-22, 252-53, 273-88, 290-93; funeral, 226, 302; and Lutheranism, *see* Luther; Lutheranism; and Lyndsay, *see* Lyndsay, David; minority, 50, 52, 56, 58, 100, 118-26, 127, 129, 187, 188, 198, 203-6, 208, 210-12, 213, 214, 216, 226, 235, 236-37; and music, 122, 124-25, 126-31, 153, 161; nobility of, 202, 222, 298; orders of chivalry, 78, 215, 222, *see also* Heraldry; patron, *see* Patronage, royal; personal reign, 153, 188, 206, 217; poet, 138-39, 191, 217-18; and popular legend, 76, 139, 161, 210; portraits, 276-77, 288, 291; recreations, 125-28, 130-31, 136-37, 138-40, 203-5, 209, 210, 214, 216; regalia (Honours), 222, 292-95; siblings, 2, 126-27; 'style King James V', 63, 84, 140; tomb, 226

James V, court of: entertainments, 125, 179, 185, 197, 202, 217; image of, 215-18, 221-26, 289, 298; literature, 126, 136-41, 145, 188-200, 209-18; music: and Carver, *see* Carver, Robert; dance tunes, 126, 137, 138, 140; French influence, 119-20, 123-24, 127-28, 129, 140-41, 153, 175; Italian minstrels, 119-22, 124-26, 129; *musick fyne*, 118, 124, 129, 131, 133, 135, 136, 137, 140-41; song, sacred, 133-36, 139; song, secular, 124, 126, 131, 136-38, 139, 140, 153-78; servitors at, 115, 120-26, 127-28, 129-30, 131-32, 135, 141, 179-87, 189, 195-96, 201-2, 205, 206, 209, 215-17, 220; herald painters and craftsmen, 301-2; performers, musical, 119, 120-29, 141, 145, 153; *see also* Bontemps; Fethy, John; *Greysteil*, Hamilton, Patrick; Johnson, Robert; Officers of Arms; Peebles, David; Chapel Royal; Schennek; *Trip and goe, hey*

James VI and I, king of Scots (1566-1625), 117, 120, 132, 135, 194

James Carmichael Collection of Proverbs in Scots (ed. Anderson), *see* Proverbs

Jedburgh, 229, 235, 236, 243

Jeffery, C.D., 36

John III, king of Portugal (1521-1557), 242

Johnson, James, *The Scots Musical Museum*, 156

Johnson, Robert, composer, 134-35, 153

Johnston, William, Maister, 246

Josquin (Desprez), 153

Julian Sword, *see* James V, regalia

Julis II, pope (1503-1513), 292

Julius Caesar, 26, 93

❖

Katharine of Aragon, queen of Henry VIII, 201, 243, 244, 245, 249

Keith, William, 3rd Earl Marischal, 66, 236

Kelso, 253

Kennedy, Thomas, 114

Kennedy, Walter, 36, 45, 179, 182, 194

Kennetie, *see* Kennedy, Walter

Kerr, Andrew, of Cessford, 237

Kilgour, Sir John, herald painter, 293, 295, 301-2

Kilmichael Glassary, *see* Glassary

Kincragy, James, 101, 102, 110-11, 113

Kingis Quair, see James I

King's College, Aberdeen, 2, 3, 4, 14, 51, 63, 66, 70, 71; and Bibliopegus, 3; and Elphinstone, bishop, 2, 63; and humanism, 2, 4, 6, 8, 271; religious style, 2; *see also* Aberdeen

Kingship, 87; advice tradition, in literature, 22, 24, 29, 33, 34, 38, 40-41, 140, 188-92, 208, 209-11, 212-13, 214-18, 219, 224, 226, 235, 237; and crowns, design of, 69-70, 222, 293-94, 296, 298; and portraiture, 84, 86-89, 90, 91, 95, 226

King's Singers, 161

Kinloss (Cistercian house), 4

Kinlouch, *see* Kynlouch

Kinsley, James, 29, 30, 35, 36, 39, 42, 45, 46, 47, 48

Kintore, 105

INDEX

Kirkcaldy, Sir James, of Grange, 113, 196
Kirkcaldy, town, 113
Kirkwall, 234, 251
Kittredge, G.L., 35
Knox, John, 50, 135, 181, 186, 263
Kratzmann, G.C., 35, 38
Kvaedermen, Icelandic, 147
Kyde (Kyd), Alexander, 179, 181, 186, 209, 210-11; *The rich fontane*, 189, 210
Kynlouch, ?Paul, 179, 180, 209

❖

Lacizi, Paolo, 9
Lacunar Strevelinense (Blackwood), 85, 87
Laing, David, 39, 45, 143, 145, 149; *Early Popular Poetry of Scotland*, 145, 146, 149-52; *Scots Musical Museum*, 1835 edn, 156-57
'Lak of Stedfastness', *see* Chaucer
Langland, John, 198
Langmur, George, Master, 121
'Laoidh Fhraoich' ('The Lay of Fraoch'), 257
Lauder, William, of Halton, 103
Lawson, George, 2, 4, 5
Lawson, George, the younger, 4, 5
Lawson, John, 202
Le Havre, 288
Lear, king, 232
Leblond, Jean, Seigneur de Branville, *Nuptiaux Virelayz* 280-81
Lefèvre d'Etaples, Jacques, 3, 4, 5
Lekpreuik, Robert, *see* Printers
Lennox, 260
Lennox, Earls of, *see* Stewart
Leo X, pope (1475-1521), Giovanni di Lorenzo de' Medici, 65, 235
Leslie, family of, 253
Leslie, George, Earl of Rothes, 252
Letter-writing, 15th and 16th c.: and diplomacy, 206, 220, 276, 282, 283, 285; of Gavin Douglas, 52-61; examples quoted, 3, 4, 13, 57-59, 206, 215, 220, 276, 282, 283; idioms, 61; Latin, 3; othography, 61; proverbs in, 61; royal, 59, 131-32, 133, 206, 282-83, 285; style and language, 59-60; *see also* Handwriting
Lewis, 266, 271

Leyden, John, 126, 154-56; 'Vocal MS', *see* William Stirling Cantus
Leys, Adam, 292, 295, 302
Liber Pluscardensis (ed. Skene), 34
Lilpen, John, 244
Lindsay, David, Earl of Crawford, 66
Lindsay, Gilbert, of Trakwan, 300
Linlithgow, 17, 97, 107, 113, 118, 214, 237, 291; Palace, 72, 75, 78, 129, 301; sheriff of, 246
Lion and the Mouse, The, see Henryson
Lochinver, laird of, 252
London, 54-55, 249
Longueville, dukes of, *see* d'Orléans
Longueville, Louis de, first son of Marie de Guise, 284, 286
Longueville, Marie de Lorraine, duchess of, *see* Marie de Guise
Lorraine, Antony, duke; head, family of, 285
Lorraine, cardinal of, *see* Guise, Jean de
Lossie, river, 1, 4, 10
Louis I, Bohemia; II, Hungary (1516-26), 66
Louis XII, king of France (1498-151), 56
Louise of Savoy, mother of Francis I, 273-74
Louvain, university, 134
Lowlands, 254-55, 257-58, 260, 261, 262, 263
Lucan, 237
Lupset, Thomas, 5
Ludus Scaccorum (Cessolis), 22
Luther, Martin, 7, 12, 134, 220, 231, 239
Lutheranism, 7, 11, 50, 133, 220, 239, 243
Lyall, R., 31, 36, 47, 59, 161
Lydgate, John, 15, 43-44, 48, 49, 179, 265; *Troy Book*, 15
Lyndsay, family of, 74
Lyndsay, Sir David, of the Mount: and court colleagues, 179, 180-81, 185-87, 189, 191, 194, 195, 197-98, 201-2, 209-10, 216-20; court poet, 141, 179-81, 184-85, 197, 202-5, 211-15; dramatic interlude, 1540, attrib. to, 220; herald and Lyon King, 55, 186, 202, 206, 207, 221-26, 281, 295, 297-98, 299-300; and James V, 124-25, 126-27, 138, 145, 155, 185, 201-26, 295; and music, 126, 136-38, 155; pension, 206; and reform, 140, 183, 198, 218-21; spouse of, *see* Douglas, Janet; and

William Stewart, herald, 183; usher to James V, 124, 126, 202-3, 205, 211; *Answer...to the Kingis Flyting*, 138, 217-18; Armorial Register (NLS Adv. MS 31.4.3), 202, 223-26, 295, 297-98; *Complaynt*, 125, 126, 130, 203-4, 205, 211, 213-15, 218, 220, 226; *Complaynt ...of Bagsche*, 217; *Deploratioun on the Deith of Quene Magda-lene*, 222, 281-82; *Dialog, Ane (The Monarche)*, 138; *Dreme, The*, 191, 198, 203, 205, 209, 211, 212-13; *Historie of Squyer Meldrum*, 145; *Iusting betuix Watsoun and Barbour*, 194, 217; *Satyre of the Thrie Estaitis, Ane*, 136-38, 141, 145, 189, 198; *Supplicatioun in Contemptioun of Syde Taillis, Ane*, 217; *Testament...of the Papyngo*, 127, 128, 130-31, 136, 179-80, 182, 195, 209-10, 212, 216, 218, 219, 222, *see also* Lindsay
Lyons, 1-3, 6, 8, 9, 275, 276, 284, 285, 287, 288

❖

Mac Cailein, *see* Campbell
Mac Eoin Riabhaich, Dubhghall, 256
Macbeth, king of Scots (1005-57), 26, 232
MacCracken, H.N., 44
MacDiarmaid, family of, 266, 267
McDiarmid, Matthew P., 87
MacDonald, family of, 255, 266
MacDonald, A.A., 41
MacDougall of Dunollie, family of, 266
Macdougall, Norman, 26
McDowall, Fergus, of Fraich, 104
MacEwans, bardic family of, 267
Macfarlane, Walter, of Arrochar, *Geographical Collections*, 151
MacGillmurray of Clandeboy, family of, 266
McGladdery, Christine, *James II*, 26
MacGregor, family of, 255, 266
MacGregor, Duncan, *see* Book of the Dean
MacGregor, Sir James, *see* Book of the Dean
Mackay, Mackenzie, W., 29, 35, 39
Mackay, Rhona, musician, 147
MacKinnon, Donald, 268-69
Macky, J., 85
McLagan MSS, 270
MacLeod, of Harris and Dunvegan, family of, 266

MacLeod, of Lewis, family of, 266
MacMhuirich, bardic family of, 266-67
MacNeill of Gigha, family of, 266
MacQueen, John, 40
McRoberts, David, Mgr, 64
Macrobius, 211
MacSween of Knapdale, 266
Madeleine de Valois, queen of James V, 73, 80, 89, 90, 140-41, 153, 222-23, 252, 253, 273-74, 276, 277-83, 284, 288, 292-93, 297, 298, 302
Mág Eochagáin, family of, 266
Mág Uidhir, family of, 266
Mair, John, *see* Major
Maitland Folio MS (Cambridge, Pepysian Library, 2553), 29, 30, 31-32, 34, 35, 36, 42, 46, 48, 50, 135, 183
Maitland, Sir Richard, of Lethington, 138
Major, John, theologian, 5, 186, 260
Maleville, Gaultier, Albany's secretary, 58, 123
Malin, Walter, abbot of Glenluce, 104, 186
Maner of the crying, The, see Asloan MS
Manx (language), 264
Mapstone, Sally, 21, 22, 49, 51
Mar, Earldom of, 66
Marchand, Guy, *see* Printers
Margaret of Denmark, queen of James III, 87-88
Margaret of Scotland, queen of Malcolm III, *later* Saint, 66, 67, 298
Margaret Tudor, queen of James IV, 50, 58, 67, 80, 88-89, 119, 123, 125, 185, 186, 187, 188, 195, 201, 203, 204, 209, 210, 211, 235, 236, 237, 253, 274, 297
Marginalia (Harvey), 5
Marguerite de France, daughter of Francis I, 274, 284, 285
Marguerite de Navarre, 287
Marie de Bourbon, daughter of the duc de Vendôme, 252, 275, 286
Marie de Guise, duchesse de Longueville, *later* 2nd queen of James V, 59, 71, 89, 153, 187, 223, 284-85, 286-88, 291, 293, 294, 297, 298, 302; *see also* Longueville
Marignano, battle of (1515), 124

INDEX 317

Marischal, Earl, *see* Keith, William
Marot, Clément, 192, 279-80
Martin, brother, *see* Martino, Juan
Martino, Juan, de Boil, of Valencia, 232, 240
Mary of Gueldres, queen of James II, 224-25
Mary, daughter of Henry VIII, 274
Mary, queen of Scots (1542-66), 109, 120, 135, 140, 182, 198, 295
Mary of Hungary, queen, and regent of the Netherlands, 220
Maxwell, family of, 77
Maxwell, John, 48
Maxwell, Robert, Lord, 110, 288
Maxwell, Robert, of Calderwood, 103
Maying & disport of chaucer, The (Lydgate), *see* Asloan MS
'Melancholie, gryt deput of Dispair', *see* Montgomerie, Alexander
Meldrum, John, 299
Meldrum, laird of, *see* Seton, Alexander
Melrose, 237
Melvill (Melville), Andro, 139, 158
Melvill, David, brother of Andro, 162
Memorial of...Robert Campbel (Davidson), 145
Menteith, 260
Menteith, William, of Kerse, 114
Mercy, seven deeds of, 21
Merle and the Nychtingall, The (The disputacoun), *see* Dunbar
Meroure of Wyssdome, *see* Ireland, John
Merse, 246
Mexico City, 232
Michele, Francesco, 9, 11, 12, 13
Mill, A.J., 31
Montgomerie, Alexander, 6th Earl of Eglinton, 150
Montgomerie, Alexander, 182, 194; *Flyting Betuixt Montgomerie and Polwart, The*, 194; *Melancholie, gryt deput of Dispair*, 161
Montmorency, Anne de, grand master, *later* constable of France, 275, 277, 278, 285
Montpellier, 186
Mór, John, 267
Moray, Earl of, *see,* Stewart, James

Moray, bps of, *see* Forman, Andrew; Hepburn, James
More, Sir Thomas, 5, 6, 248-49
Morton, Earls of, *see* Douglas, James
Mosman, John, goldsmith, 293-94
Mowbray, Andrew, 103
Mudy, John, 185
Munster, 266
Münster, Sebastian, 5
Murray, David, 103
Muschett, Elizabeth, 103
Music of Scotland, 1500-1700 (ed. Elliott and Shire), 158, 159, 161, 178
Musick Fyne (Ross), 159
Musselburgh, 113, 246
Myll, M.G., 16, 27-28, 48
Mylne, Alexander, 101, 102, 109, 110
Mytens, Daniel, painter, 88

❖

Nairn, 105
Nassau, Henry, count of, 275
Navarre, king of, *see* Henri II d'Albret
Nesbyt, James, 124
New Spain ('hirketan', Yucatan), 232, 233, 240
Newbattle Abbey, Lothian, 297
Nine Worthies, attrib. arms of, 297
Nisbet, William, 114
Norfolk, Duke of, *see* Howard, Thomas
Northumberland, Earl of, *see* Percy, Henry
Norton-Smith, J., 43-44
Notaries, 15, 16, 17, 18, 23, 47, 50, 187, 256, 258, 261, 263; Protocol books of, 18, 258
Nôtre Dame Cathedral, *see* Paris
'Now is our king in tendir age', 198
Nuptiaulx Virelayz (Leblond), *see* Leblond, Jean

❖

Ó Briain, family of, 266
Ó Caoimh, family of, 266
Ó Ceallaigh, family of, 266
Ó Conchobhair, family of, 266
Ó Dálaigh, Muireadhach, 267
O'Donnell, family of, 267
Ó hEóghusa (O'Hosey), bardic family of, 267
Ó Néill, family of, 266
Ó Ruairc, family of, 266

Ochino, Bernardino, 9
'Ode to Joy' (Schiller/Beethoven), 148
Officers of Arms, 16th c. Scottish, 70-71, 183-86, 202, 206-7, 221-26, 281, 289-90, 295, 297, 299-301
Ogilvie, John, 1, 4, 10
Ollaimh, Giolla Coluim, mac an, 266
Opuscula (Petrarch), 4
Ordinance for the Keeping of King James Fifth, 205
Ordinance of Eltham, 205
Orem, W., 70
Organeris, *see* James V, court of: music
Orkney, 114
Orkney, bps of, *see* Reid, Robert; Stewart, Edward
Orkney, Earl of, *see* Stewart, Robert
D'Orléans, Louis, duc de Longueville, 284, 286
Orpheus and Eurydice (The buke of schir orpheus & erudices), *see* Henryson
Orygynale Cronykil of Scotland (Wyntoun), 15
Ovid, 93
Ossianic verse, 268

❖

Paddock and the mouss, The, *see* Henryson
Paleario, Aonio, *De immortalitate animorum*, 9
Palice of Honour (Douglas), *see* Douglas, Gavin
Panmure MS (c. 1460), 24
Papal Nuncio, *see* Pio, Ridolfo
Paraphrases (Erasmus), 3, 4
Paris, 82, 211, 134, 186, 273, 278; entries, civic, 273, 278; Nôtre Dame Cathedral, 73-74, 82, 141, 278-79, 292; Parliament of, 273; tournament, at James V's marriage, 221-22, 279
Parliament, Scottish, 101, 105, 109, 207, 261; Acts, 116, 117, 221, 237
Paterson, John, Snowdon Herald, 300
Paterson, John, craftsman, 294
Patronage, royal and noble, of the arts, 51, 71, 73, 83, 127-30, 131-32, 133, 134-36, 139, 140, 145, 184-85, 208-9, 215-16, 226, 229, 256, 266-67, 276-77, 279-80, 287-88, 296
Paul III, pope (1534-50), 221, 247, 248, 249, 291
'Paul graif', 239

Pavia, battle of (1525), 273
Peblis to the Play, 139
Peebles, David, musician, 127, 135-36, 140, 153; 'Si quis diliget me', 127, 136
Peebles, Thomas, 302
Percy, Henry, Earl of Northumberland, 240
Percy, Thomas, of Dromore, 149
Perth, 54, 106
Perthshire, late medieval, 261-62, 264, 265, 270
Pettigrew, Sir John, 301
Pettigrew, Thomas, of Magdalensyde, 295, 299-301
Petrarch, 4
Philip I, Duke of Burgundy, king of Castile, 236
Phillips, John, bp of Sodor and Man, 264
Pico della Mirandola, 83
Pinkie Cleuch, battle of (1547), 120
Pinturicchio, Aeneas Sylvius, *later* Pius II, 86; *Commentaries*, 87; *Historia*, 87
Pio, Ridolfo, bp of Faenza, 276, 278
Planetary gods, 74, 76-77, 78-79, 80, 81-84, 89-90, 94, 127
Pleugh Song, The, 'My heartly service', 139, 154, 157, 158, 159
Plotinus, 9
Poland, 64, 67, 92, *see also* Albert; Sigismund I
Pole, Reginald, cardinal, 6, 7
Pomeir, *see* Pomerania
Pomerania, dukes of (Barnim and Philip), 239, 240
Polychronicon (Higden), 23, 25, 48, 49
Porteus of nobilnes, The buke of the, see Asloan MS
Portraiture, royal, 79-80, 85-91, 93-94, 95, 226, 252, 274-75, 276-77, 287-88, 291
Poyet, Guillaume, chancellor of France, 277
Practicks, see Balfour, Sir James
Preaching of the Swallow, The, see Henryson
Prester John, attrib. arms of, 297
Prestonpans, 227
Principles and Duties of Christianity (Wilson), *see* Wilson, Bishop
Printers and publishers: Aldus Manutius, 8; Bassandyne, Thomas, 295; Blackwood, William, 85, 87; Caxton, William, 60;

INDEX

Chepman and Myllar, *see* Chepman and Myllar prints; Cyaneus, L., 5, Davidson, Thomas, 208, 295; De Worde, Wynkyn, 43-44; Finlayson, Thomas, 145; Finlayson, Walter, 145; Gryphius, Sebastian, 1, 8, 9, 12; Lekpreuik, Robert, 45, 182; Marchand, Guy, 82; Ruddiman, Thomas, 52; Smyth, R., 145

Promptuarii Iconum Insignorum (Roville), *see* Roville, Guillaume

Prose, late medieval and Renaissance: Gaelic, 264-65; Latin, 1-14, 264; Scots, 20-22, 23-28, 49, 52-61, 202, 208-9, 216, 220-21, 223-26, 227-53, 265

Protocol Books, *see* Notaries

Provence, 275

Proverbs: *Fergusson's Scottish Proverbs*, 32; *James Carmichael Collection in Scots*, 32; and proverbial sayings, 31, 32, 61, 194, 235, 237, 238; Proverbs (Biblical), 80, 81

Psalmi quintidecimi enarratio, *see* Wilson, Florens

Puiguillon, *see* Beaucaire, Gilbert de

Purser, J., 143; *Scotland's Music*, 158

❖

Queensferry, 113

'Quhen the Governour past in France', 184

Qui[g]nones, Francis, cardinal, 232

Quintyng, 179

❖

Raby Castle, 75

Ralf Coilȝear, 20, 45-46

Ralph Roister Doister (Udall), 31

Ramsay of Dalhousie, 297

Reformation, 13, 260; and Book of the Dean, 255; and Borthwick, John, 8, 220; and Budé, Guillaume, 12; 'heretics', Scottish, 13, 134-36, 141, 220, 221, 239, 246; and James V, *see* James V: church reform; and Luther, *see* Luther, Martin; material destruction at, 68-69, 136; Protestant writings, 197; and Stewart, Lord James, 140; and Wilson, Florens, 11, 13; and Zurich, 9; and Lyndsay, *see* Lyndsay, David; *see also* Alesius, Alexander; Church; Gourlaw, Norman; Straton, David

Regiment of kingis with the buke of phisnomy, *see* Asloan MS

Regensburg ('reuchbrig'), 239; Diet of (1541), 6, 12

Reid, Robert, abbot of Kinloss (1529-50), bp of Orkney (1541-58), 4, 111

Renoir, Alan, 43-44

Reuchbrig, *see* Regensburg

Reynardine (ballad), 146

Riach, D., 36

Richard II, king of England (1377-99), 34

Richardinus, Robertus, 231

Richt soir opprest, 153

Riddy, F., 31, 38, 46

Ridley, F., 39

Ritson, Joseph, *Scotish Song*, 154

Robert I, king of Scots (1306-29), 113

Robertet, Florimond, 273-74

Robinson, F.N., 37

Rochester, bp of, *see* Fisher, John

'Roit or Quheill of Tyme', NLS MS 1746 (Abell), 227-53

Rolland, John, 28, 180, 186-87, 196, 198; *Court of Venus*, 180; *Seuin Seages*, 180

Ronsard, Pierre de, 141, 281-82

Rosimboz, Sir Peter de, 215, 290

Ross, bps of, *see* Cockburn, Robert; Sinclair, Henry

Ross, D. James, *Musick Fyne*, 159

Ross, John, 301

Ross, Neil, 269

Ross, Thomas, of Auchlossen, 99

Rothes, Earl of, *see* Leslie, George

Rouen, Treaty of (1517), 274, 276, 288

Roule, Archibald, 302

Roussel, Gerard, chaplain, 5

Roville, Guillaume, *Promptuarii Iconum Insignorum*, 277

Ruadh, Fionnlagh, poet, 267

Ruddiman, Thomas, *see* Printers

Rule of St Augustine, 228, 231, 235

Russell, John, *Boke of Nurture*, 32, 47, 205

Ruthven, William, 1st Lord, 236

Ruthven, William, 1st Earl of Gowrie, 150

❖

INDEX

Sadler, Sir Ralph, 220
Sadoleto, Jacopo, bp of Carpentras, 2, 6, 8, 9, 13, 14
Sagnes, Sieur de, *see* Garde, Pierre de la
St Ambrose, 245
St Andrew, 291, 296, 302
St Andrews, 288; bps and abps of, *see*, Beaton, David; Beaton, James; Forman, Robert, Stewart, Alexander; metropolitan see of, 18, 27, 67, 140, 288; prior of, *see* Hepburn, John; university, 51, 134, 185, 186, 187
St Augustine, 230-31, 238, 245-48, 251
St Bernardino of Siena, 251, 253
St Brigid, 248-49
St Columba, 63
St Cuthbert, feast of, 139
St Cyril, 245-46
St Francis, 229, 230-31, 252
St Frediano, 9
St George, chapel of, Windsor Castle, 290
St Giles, 181, *see also* Edinburgh
St Gregory, 238
St James, 238
St Jerome, 238, 245
St John, 242, 246, 250, 253
St Katherine, 252
St Machar, 63; Cathedral of, *see* Aberdeen
St Margaret, *see* Margaret, qn of Malcolm III
St Matthew, 247
St Michael, 77-78, 79; chivalric order of, 290-91
St Paul, 10, 12, 242
St Peter, 245
St Thomas of Canterbury, *see* Cranmer, Thomas
St Walteyn (Waldeof), abbot of Melrose, 231
Saltire Singers, 158
Sawis of the angell, *see* Asloan MS
Saxon (Saxony), duke of, 239
Scarpinello, Augustine, 132
Schaw, William, of Sornebeg, 103
Schennek (Senneck), Orry ('Arry, Urry), 127-28, 129
Schipper, J., 39, 45
Scholia in Scipionis Somnium (Wilson), 5
Schort Memoriale, Ane (Ane addicioun of scottis corniklis), *see* Asloan MS

Sciennes, convent of, *see* Edinburgh
Scotichronicon (Bower), 51
Scotish Song (Ritson), 154
Scotland: and Auld Alliance, *see* Auld Alliance; and England, 9, 13, 17, 25, 26, 34, 67, 201, 220-21, 236, 243-44, 246-50, 285-86; and Poland, 67, 95; origin myths, 24, 26
Scotland's Music (Purser), 158
Scotorum Historiae, *see* Boece, Hector
Scots Musical Museum, The (Johnson), 156
Scott, Alexander, poet, 182, 187; 'In June the jem', 194; *Justing and Debait up at the Drum*, 194; 'To luve unluvit it is ane pane', 194
Scott, Alexander, 111, 113, 115
Scott, Thomas, of Petgormo, 111
Scott, Tom, 35
Scott, Sir Walter, 162
Scott, Walter, of Buccleuch, 237
Scott, William, 103
Scottis (language), 216, 260
Scrimgeour of Glassary, 299
Scrymgeour, family of, 262, *see also* Scrimgeour
Secreta Secretorum, 33, 208
Secretary hand, *see* Handwriting
Sempill, Robert, 3rd Lord, 101
Septem Sapientum, Historia, see *Sevyne Sagis*
Seton, Alexander, priest, 220
Seton, Alexander, of Meldrum, 253
Seton, George, 4th Lord, 229, 246
Seton Armorial (NLS Acc. 9309), 90
Sevyne Sagis, The Buke of the, *see* Asloan MS
Sex Werkdayis and Agis, The, *see* Asloan MS
Seymour, Jane, 3rd queen of Henry VIII, 285
Seznec, Jean, 82
Sforza, Maximilian, duke of Milan, 131-32
Shakespeare, William, 77, 232
Shetland, 114
Shire, Helena M., 153, 157, 159-60, 161-62, *Song, Dance and Poetry...Under King James VI*, 159
Siena, 126
Sigismund I, king of Poland (1506-48), 66, 83, 92, 95
Simson, John, burgess, 112
Sinclair, Henry, bp of Ross, 113

INDEX

Sinclair, Sir James, of Orkney, 233, 250-51
Sinclair, Lady Margaret, 114
Sinclair, William, Earl of Orkney, 209
Sinclair, Sir William, of Roslin, 253
Sins, Seven Deadly, 21
Skeat, W.W., 43
Sketches from John O'Groats (Calder), 151
Slezer, John, see *Theatrum Scotiae*
Small, John, 53, 57
Smith, G.G., 39
Solway Moss, battle of (1542), 5, 9, 141
Somerville, Hugh, Lord, 56, 104
Songs and Fancies (Forbes), 154, 155, 156, 157, 158, 159, 160, 161
Spain, 236, 238
Speed, D., 46
Spektakle of lufe, The buke callit, see Asloan MS
Speldhurst, 6
Spurgeon, C.F.E., 44
Starkey, Thomas, 4, 6, 7-8, 11
Steill, George, 83, 140, 182, 186; 'Lanterne of lufe', 192
Stenhouse, William, 156-57
Stewart, of Rannoch, family of, 266
Stewart, Agnes, 196
Stewart, Alan, 182-83
Stewart, Alexander, 'Wolf of Badenoch', 187
Stewart, Alexander, duke of Albany (c. 1454-85), 225
Stewart, Alexander, abp of St Andrews (1504-13), 2, 126-27
Stewart, Andrew, bp of Caithness (1518-42), 66
Stewart, Barbara, 234, 250-51
Stewart, Bernard, *see* Dunbar, William
Stewart, Edward, bp of Orkney (1513-26), 66, 187
Stewart, Esmé, Sieur d'Aubigny, 132
Stewart, Henry, Lord Darnley (1546-67), 135, 182-83
Stewart, Henry, 1st Lord Methven, 187, 195, 229, 237, 253
Stewart, James, Earl of Buchan, 196
Stewart, James, Earl of Moray (1501-44), 66, 140, 237, 249, 290

Stewart, John, duke of Albany (c.1485-1536), Governor of Scotland (1515-24), 53, 55-58, 68, 119, 121-22, 123, 125, 128, 131-32, 184, 188, 201, 203, 225, 235, 236, 274
Stewart, John, 3rd Earl of Lennox, 91, 237
Stewart, Marion, 40
Stewart, Matthew, 4th Earl of Lennox, 101
Stewart, Mungo, 238
Stewart, 'of Lorne', 179, 180, 182-83
Stewart, Robert, Earl of Orkney, 195
Stewart, William, captain of Milan, 132
Stewart, William, Lyon King, 183
Stewart, William ('Stewart'), 179, 180, 181-84, 187, 188-200, 202, 209, 214; and *Croniclis of Scotland* (metrical), 182, 187; 'Flytting betuix þe sowtar and the tailʒeour', 194; 'For to declair', 193, 197, 199; 'Maist ameyn roseir', 192, 199; 'Musing allone this hinder nicht', attrib. to, 183-84, 200; 'Precelland prince', 188-89, 199, 209-10; 'Rolling in my remembrance', 188, 199; 'Schir sen of men', 188, 190, 191, 199, 210; 'Thir lenterne dayis', 193, 199; 'This hindir nycht', 184, 189, 191, 199; 'In Grece sumtyme' (*Croniclis*), 200; 'First lerges the king', 195-98, 199; 'Furth ouer the mold', 194, 199; 'O man remember', 191, 199; 'Thou leis, loun, thow leis', 199
Stirling, 97, 118, 187; Castle, 73, 89, 236, 237; Chapel Royal at, 73, 78, 118, 133-34, 135, 161, 186, 187; minstrels at, 125-26; Palace, 63, 72-96, 130; Parliament House, 73; Prince's Garden, 73; Roundels, 84-96; St Michael's Kirk, 78
'Stirling Heads', *see* Stirling, Roundels
Stone of Destiny, 232
Strachan, William, minister, 68
Straloch Lute Book, see *Greysteil*
Strathearn, 260
Straton (Stratoun), David, 246
Strena (attrib. Foulis), 195, 208
Suleiman I, sultan of Turkey (1520-66), 239
Summerdale, battle of (1529), 234
Supplicatioun in Contemptioun of Syde Taillis, Ane, *see* Lyndsay, Sir David
'Suppois I war in court most he' (anon.), 198

'Support ȝour seruand' (anon.), 192
Surrey, Earl of, *see* Howard, Thomas
Swarbrick, Dave, musician, 146
Sword and Hat, Blessed, 221, 291-92

❖

Tabbaner, James, minstrel, 125
Tabernaris (drummers), *see* James V, court of: music
Talis of the fyue bestis, The, *see* Asloan MS
'Tam Lin', see *Trip and goe, hey*
Tantallon, siege of (1528), 110
Tauerbach, Sebastian, architect, 92
Taverner, John, composer, 134
'Taxton matalebe', 239
Tay, river, 1
Ten Commandments, 21
Terry, C.S., 157
Testament of Cresseid (Henryson), *see* Henryson
Teviotdale, 236, 246
Theatrum Scotiae (Slezer), 75
Theologia Platonica (Ficino), 4
This nycht in my sleip I wes agast (A Ballat of the Devillis Inquest), *see* Dunbar
Thistle, *see* Heraldry
Thomas, prior of St Andrews, 231
Thomond, 266
Thomson, Peter, 300
Thre Prestis of Peblis, The, 212, *see also* Asloan MS
Three Wise Men, attrib. arms of, 297
Thrissill and the Rois, The, *see* Dunbar
'To the Church of Scotland' (Stewart), 183
Tod and the wolf, The (The Fox and the Wolf), *see* Henryson
Tongland Abbey, 133
Toulouse, 233, 241, 242
Tournai, 290
Tractact callit the cart, Ane (The cart of the warld), *see* Asloan MS
Tractact callit the Scottish originale (The Scottish orginale), *see* Asloan MS
Tract of the kingis of Scotland begynnand in the thrid age, Ane (The scottis cronikle), *see* Asloan MS

Translation, 5, 9, 12, 22, 23-24, 27, 32-33, 41, 82, 190-91, 211-12, 216, 219, 229, 263-64
Trent, Council of, 7, 13
Trevisa, 23, 48, 49
Trinity College, Edinburgh, *see* Edinburgh
Triolet, French, 46
Trip and goe, hey, 153-78; and 'Can she excuse' (Dowland), 160; and Forbes' *Songs and Fancies*, 154, 155, 156, 157, 158, 159; and 'Gynkartoun', 155, 177, 204; and 'Ioly under the greenwood tree', 154, 175; and 'Lutecok', 155, 177; May-day observance, as, 139; and medleys, 154-58, 162; performance, 160-61; recent musical versions discussed, 158-62; reconstructed musical version, inc. song-text, 163-78; recordings, 158, 159, 161; and Stenhouse, 156-57; style, musical, 153, 159-60; and 'Waly, waly up the bank', 154, 156; and 'Wee be all of Maiden land', 155, 177; and *The Woods so Wild*, 160; and 'Young Thomlin' ('Tam Lin'), 155, 156, 175
Troy Book, *see* Lydgate, John
Trumpettis (trumpeters), *see* James V, court of: music
Truth, twelve articles of, 21
Turnbull, Alexander, 56, 61
Turretini, Francesco, 8, 9
Turretini, Regolo, 9
Tymistitan, 241
Tyndale, William, 134
Tyrone, 266

❖

Udall, Nicolas, 31
Unicorn, *see* Heraldry
Uplandis mouss & borowstovnis, The (The Two Mice), *see* Henryson

❖

Valencia, 232
Valla, Lorenzo, humanist, 2
Van der Goes, Hugo, Trinity Altarpiece, 87
Vaus, John, grammarian, 2
Vegius, Maphaeus, 52
Vendôme, *see* Bourbon
Venice, 132

Vermigli, Peter Martyr, 9
Verse-epistles, 55, 138, 189, 190-92, 203-4, 209-10, 212-14, 216-19
Vienna Bk of Hours (Österreichische Nationalbibliothek Wien, Cod. Lat. 1897), 293
Vincent (Weynssen) Matthew, 232-33, 239, 240
Virgil, 52, 93, 216
Virgil's Aeneis Translated (Ruddiman), 52
Virtues: Cardinal, 189, 215; of nobleness, 24; seven, 21
Visagier, Jean (Vulteius), 282
Volusenus, *see* Wilson, Florence
Vponland, Iohine, 198
Vulteius, J. *see* Visagier

❖

Wallace, The, see Blind Harry
Wallace, James, 300
Walsh, E., 46
Waltham Cross, 54
Wark Castle, 236
Watson, Andrew, 302
Watson, William J., 269
Wawel Palace, Cracow, 64, 83, 92-96
Wedderburn, Lord Alexander, *see* Home
Wedderburn, Robert, see *Complaynt of Scotland*
Weir, Thomas, of Blackwood, 115
Westmeath, 266
White, Sir John, parson of Pitcox, 101, 102
Whiting B.J., 32, 61
Whiting, H.W., 61
Wife of Bath, 197
Wigtown, 114, 115
William of Touris, see *Contemplacioun of synnaris, The*
William Stirling Cantus (John Leyden's Vocal MS), 156
Williamson, Adam, 54, 56, 57, 60, 61

Wilson, Florens (Volusenus), 1-14, 182; and du Bellay (Guillaume), 5; and Bonvisi, 5; and Budé, 12; and Caravalla, 9; and Castellio, 8; English contacts, 4, 5-7; and Fisher, 5, 6, 12; as Florentinus, 9-10, 12, 13; French contacts, 5; Hebrew, studies in, 5; and humanism, 2, 4; and justification, 13; and King's College, 2, 4, 6; and Michele, 9, 11-13; as proof-reader for Aldus, 8; and Sadoleto, 2, 6, 8, 13, 14; and scholasticism, 4, 6-7; and Starkey, 4, 6; and Turretini, 8, 9, 13; and Vermigli, 9; *Commentatio Quaedam Theologica*, 8, 9; *De Animi Tranquillitate*, 1, 3, 5, 6, 9-12; *In Psalmum 50 enarratio*, 5
Wilson, Thomas, bp of Man, *Principles...of Christianity*, 264
Windsor Castle, 85
Winter, James, 70
Winter, Thomas, Wolsey's son, 2, 5
Wolsey, Thomas, cardinal, 2, 5, 53, 54-55, 57-59, 60, 132, 134, 135
Wood, David, of Craig, 196
Wood, Thomas, vicar of St Andrews, 127, 133, 134-36, 140, 153, 156, 157, 160, 161, 178
Wrycht, John, Maister, 123
Wyatt, Sir Thomas, 9
Wyntoun, Andrew, 15, 51

❖

Yester, Lord of, *see* Hay, John
Yetholm, 246
Ynglis Cronikle, The (Ane tractact of certane kyngis of yngland), *see* Asloan MS
Yucatan, *see* New Spain
Yule, 122, 123, 126; clothing, 121, 122, 125; literary offerings at, 195-98

❖

Zurich, 9